THIRD EDITION

Languages and Children— Making the Match

New Languages for Young Learners

Helena Curtain

University of Wisconsin–Milwaukee

Carol Ann Dahlberg

Concordia College

PEARSON

Boston ∎ New York ∎ San Francisco
Mexico City ∎ Montreal ∎ Toronto ∎ London ∎ Madrid ∎ Munich ∎ Paris
Hong Kong ∎ Singapore ∎ Tokyo ∎ Cape Town ∎ Sydney

Series Editor: *Aurora Martínez Ramos*
Editorial Assistant: *Katie Freddoso*
Senior Marketing Manager: *Elizabeth Fogarty*
Editorial-Production Administrator: *Annette Joseph*
Editorial-Production Service and Electronic Composition: *Stratford Publishing Services*
Composition Buyer: *Linda Cox*
Manufacturing Buyer: *Andrew Turso*
Cover Designer: *Joel Gendron*

For related titles and support materials, visit our online catalog at www.ablongman.com.

Between the time Website information is gathered and then published, it is not unusual for some sites to have closed. Also, the transcription of URLs can result in typographical errors. The publisher would appreciate notification where these errors occur so that they may be corrected in subsequent editions.

Library of Congress Cataloging-in-Publication Data

Curtain, Helena Anderson.
    Languages and children—making the match : new languages for young learners / Helena Curtain, Carol Ann Dahlberg.—3rd ed.
        p.   cm.
    ISBN 0-205-36675-9
    Includes bibliographical references and index.
        1. Languages, Modern—Study and teaching (Elementary)—United States.   I. Dahlberg, Carol Ann.
    II. Title.

LB1578.C86 2004
372.65—dc21   2003054707

Printed in the United States of America

10   9   8   7   6   5   4   3   HAM   08   07   06   05

Permission Acknowledgments:

Standards from *Standards for Foreign Language Learning* reprinted by permission of ACTFL.

Page 4: List from Teacher Partnership at National K–12 Foreign Language Resource Center reprinted by permission from Foreign Language Resource Center, Iowa State University, Ames, IA.

Pages 371: Reprinted with permission from National Education Technology Standards for Students, copyright © 2002, ISTE (International Society for Technology in Education), 800-336-5191 (US & Canada) or 541/302-3777 (Int'l), iste@iste.org, www.iste.org. All rights reserved. Permission does not constitute an endorsement by ISTE. For more information about the NETS Project, contact Lajeane Thomas, Director, NETS Project, 318-257-3923, lthomas@latech.edu.

Continued on page 512, which constitutes a continuation of the copyright page.

CONTENTS

ACKNOWLEDGMENTS

This book is a testimonial to friendship—first of all, to the friendship between the authors that has grown ever stronger through three editions of this book and numerous other projects. It is also an expression of the personal and professional friendships that have supported our work and enriched our understanding. We are deeply grateful, and we hope the book is worthy of you.

Our husbands, Tony Curtain and Duane Dahlberg, have supported us in countless ways, and without them this third edition would simply not have been possible.

Many friends have helped us by giving us feedback and suggestions, but two in particular have spent many hours helping us to make this book as good as possible. We want to thank Nancy Foss and Alisha Dawn Samples for sharing so much of their time, their insight, and their experience.

Many early language teachers have contributed ideas and activities to this book, a number of them through the Early Language Listserv, Ñandu. We have tried to credit all the good ideas that have been shared with us, but several individuals are referred to again and again. We will list their names and affiliations here, and refer to them only by name throughout the book.

> Jo Ellen Hague, Douglas County, Georgia
> Patty Ryerson Hans, The Wellington School, Columbus, Ohio
> Jessica Haxhi, Maloney Magnet School, Waterbury, Connecticut
> Hildegard Merkle, Bethesda, Maryland (formerly Holy Childhood School, St. Paul, Minnesota)
> Alisha Dawn Samples, South Carolina Educational Television, Columbia, South Carolina
> Kathleen Siddons, Goodwin School, Storrs, Connecticut

This book has been written in the spirit of sharing, which is such a marked characteristic of early language teachers when they get together. Many of the teaching ideas presented here have been shared with us in classes and workshops, and we continue to learn daily from our colleagues and from our students.

We would like to thank the reviewers of this third edition: Ruta Couet, South Carolina Department of Education; Mary Lynn Redmond, Wake Forest University; and Marcia H. Rosenbusch, Iowa State University.

Finally, we celebrate especially the network of early language teachers whose dedication, professionalism, and sharing bring the precious gift of new languages to young learners.

PREFACE

Languages and Children—Making the Match is designed both as a methods text and as a practical guide for school districts and teachers. It is intended for those preparing to teach languages at the elementary and middle school level (grades K–8); for practitioners already involved with languages for children; and for teachers, parents, and administrators engaged in the planning or in the evaluation process.

The book has been written by practitioners primarily for practitioners. We have included the historical and theoretical elements that have been important to us in our own classroom practice and that we regularly share with our students and in workshop and in-service sessions. While we do not claim to have placed the teaching of elementary school foreign languages in a comprehensive theoretical or historical framework, we believe strongly that classroom practice must be built on a basic understanding of theoretical and historical issues. An understanding of theoretical issues can help teachers to know why certain strategies are successful; it can empower them to be effective planners of curricula and interpreters of the program and its methodology to fellow teachers, administrators, parents, and the public.

Student Population

The primary concern of this book is with the acquisition of a new language by *majority-language speakers* who are not living in an environment in which their new language is commonly spoken. Students in bilingual and ESOL (English for Speakers of Other Languages) programs, by contrast, are minority-language speakers in the process of learning the majority language, and they have complex needs in their adjustment to a different society—needs that we have not attempted to address. We believe, however, that the principles and strategies for language teaching offered in this book are also applicable or adaptable for teachers working with English language learners (ELL).

Focus on Beginning-Level Classes

Many of the specific teaching suggestions presented here will be of special value to teachers who work in the first years of elementary school programs that provide foreign language instruction for less than half of the school day. Since so many programs across the country are new and are staffed with teachers who are relatively inexperienced at the elementary school level, and because many teachers find it especially difficult to develop activities for meaningful communication in the early stages of second language acquisition, we believe that this emphasis will be the most helpful to the majority of readers. All of the activities can be extended and adapted to higher levels of language complexity and development and to other program models, and most of the ideas apply to the middle school level as well as the elementary school level.

Standards for Foreign Language Learning in the 21st Century

The appearance of the Standards in 1996, and the expanded 1999 edition with supporting standards for nine languages, refocused the vision and the conversation about language teaching and learning. This book makes frequent references to the Standards document, but does not attempt to teach readers about the Standards themselves. We recommend that readers should use this book side by side with the *Standards for Foreign Language Learning in the 21st Century,* available in many libraries. If they are not yet a part of your own professional library, we encourage you to order them from the Web site for ACTFL (American Council on the Teaching of Foreign Languages), *www.actfl.org* (under Special Projects). For quick reference, a brief summary of the goals and standards is found on page xvi.

We believe that the content of the Standards and the teaching philosophy they represent will be useful in any context, even for those who do not teach in a U.S. school setting.

Terminology

The term *early language* is used in this book to mean all types of non-native language programs for children. FLES, which in the past has sometimes had a broader interpretation, is used here to indicate a particular program, as described in Chapter 18. The authors have spent many hours discussing the issue. We considered such terms as *child L2, elementary foreign languages, elementary second languages, world languages,* and use of the word *languages* alone.

No alternative is without its problems or potential for confusion. The term *foreign language,* while still widely used, has negative connotations for some parts of the community. *Second language* is used in some discussions to mean acquisition of the majority language by minority-language speakers. The term *second language* is often inappropriate in any case, because a number of students in these programs may actually be acquiring a third or even a fourth language. The term *language,* when used alone, is easily confused with English language arts.

A number of states have chosen to use the term *world languages,* and still others are using the term *Languages Other than English (LOTE),* a term used in Australia. The National Board of Professional Teaching Standards chose *World Languages Other than English,* abbreviated to *world languages.* In this book we have used primarily the terms *world language* and *foreign language,* occasionally *second language,* and frequently the terms *early language* and *target language*. We make no distinction among the terms—since we don't feel there is a consensus around any one term, we decided to use them all!

New to This Edition

- A much-expanded and updated **assessment chapter** (Chapter 8) incorporates current assessment models and ACTFL Performance Guidelines for K–12 Learners, encouraging current and learner-friendly assessment procedures.
- A **new chapter on classroom management** (Chapter 9) provides clear guidelines for classroom management specific to the early language classroom, helping teachers develop appropriate management procedures, whether they travel from one classroom to another or have their own classroom.
- A **new chapter on technology** (Chapter 15) addresses technology implementation for teachers and students in early language programs, guiding teachers in the use of a variety of resources and strategies in technology.
- **Standards for foreign language learning** have been integrated throughout the book to help teachers plan and implement standards-based instruction.
- Increased emphasis on **early second language literacy** throughout the book includes rich strategies for developing early language literacy.
- **Descriptions of the characteristics of young learners** from the perspective of child development specialists and early language teachers will help teachers plan developmentally appropriate instruction.
- **Background on rationale and advocacy** will help teachers to advocate for early language programs and maintain public support.
- **New examples** directly from classroom practice in the words of classroom teachers have been included throughout the book to help readers apply the principles presented in the book.
- **A new website** with additional materials for students can be found at **www.ablongman.com/curtain**

We hope that this third edition of *Languages and Children—Making the Match* will serve as a useful resource for teachers, supervisors, and planners, and that it will make a contribution to the number and quality of early language programs for children.

INTRODUCTION

This book is about the many ways in which learning a new language with skilled teachers can enrich the world of the learner. There are keys, old and new, to unlock the magic that second languages hold for children.

With this book the authors offer keys that we have found as we imagine what second languages for children might mean, and the potential it can have for all learners in our schools. These keys may be used by teachers already working with children, by those preparing to teach, and by administrators, parents, and others engaged in the planning that brings successful language programs to life and keeps them vital.

Some keys are found in the experiences of the 1960s, when elementary school language programs were popular and numerous. There were serious mistakes made during that boom time for languages, such as inadequate planning, poor preparation of teachers, and unrealistic goals. By acknowledging and analyzing these mistakes we can avoid their repetition. The 1960s left us with success stories, as well, and from those experiences come examples that can guide our planning for the future.

Research in second language acquisition and in related fields, much of it undertaken since 1970, offers other keys. Not all can be translated directly into classroom practice, but the insights provided by research can help us to evaluate programs, materials, and methodology more effectively and consistently. Perhaps the most significant key to the early language learning experience is a dramatic shift in emphasis from grammar to communication in the language teaching profession. The emphasis on communication as the governing idea in curriculum and classroom practice is reinforced both by research and by the experiences of successful language teachers.

The *Standards for Foreign Language Learning in the 21st Century* (1999) have established a new K–12 vision for language education and supported it with challenging goals and standards for curriculum content. *ACTFL Performance Guidelines for K–12 Learners* (Swender and Duncan, 1998) translate those standards into student performances that can guide both curriculum development and student assessment. These key documents are shared by the entire profession and will help us to communicate effectively with one another and with our students, parents, and community.

Communication is the essential element, the fundamental principle of this book. It unifies the guidelines offered and the methods and materials described. Communication has long been a stated goal of the language teaching profession, but it has traditionally been cast in a secondary role to grammar as an organizing principle. The experienced teacher and the beginner alike face the challenge of adapting the methods of the past to a standards-based, communicative emphasis and of developing new strategies to encourage comprehension and communication. There is no age level at which the focus on communication is more appropriate than in the elementary and middle school, and teachers who make the adjustment can expect exciting results. This book suggests guidelines and examples to assist the teacher in creating a standards-based classroom in which communication has the highest priority.

The principles upon which this book is based are summarized in the Key Concepts for Elementary and Middle School Foreign Languages, found in the next section, and on the *Standards for Foreign Language Learning,* which are summarized on page xxi. The Key Concepts have been shaped by the collective experience of many classroom teachers and they offer a classroom application of what many researchers have learned about languages and children. These are the keys, some new and many familiar. The door of opportunity—the magic of language acquisition—awaits their use.

Key Concepts for Success: Elementary and Middle School Foreign Languages

Foreign language programs must take into account the distinctive characteristics and needs found at each level of cognitive, social, psychomotor, and educational development, as well as the insights of second language acquisition research and the *Standards for Foreign Language Learning*. Specific applications for the K–8 learner are identified below.

Children learn new languages best when . . .
1. Teachers consistently conduct instruction in the target language with minimal use of the native language. The target language and the native language are kept distinctly separate.
2. Teachers recognize learners as active constructors of meaning rather than passive receivers of vocabulary and information. They scaffold instruction so that learners become increasingly independent in their use of the written and spoken target language.
3. Learning occurs in meaningful, communicative contexts that carry significance for the student. For the young learner these contexts include social and cultural situations, subject content instruction, and experiences with activities such as art, crafts, sports, and hobbies.
4. Instruction is affectively engaging, made meaningful and memorable through the use of story form and activities such as storytelling, music, games, rituals, drama, and celebrations.
5. Learning is organized in terms of concrete experiences; visuals, props, realia, and hands-on activities are integral components of instruction.
6. Learners are surrounded with meaningful language, both oral and written, from beginning through advanced stages of language acquisition. Expectations for language production, very limited for beginners, increase as learners move from early to intermediate and more advanced stages.
7. Reading and writing are used as communicative tools, as appropriate to the age and interests of the learners, even in early stages of language development.
8. Assessment of learning is frequent, regular, and ongoing in a manner that is consistent with targeted standards, program goals, and teaching strategies.
9. Culture is learned through experiences with cultural materials and practices. Elements from the target language culture are essential components of all planning and teaching.
10. Planning is organized around a thematic center and aligned with content and performance standards. There is a balance among the basic goals of culture, subject content, and language in use.

11. Curriculum and instruction are organized according to a communicative syllabus rather than a grammatical syllabus. Grammar is presented through and for usage rather than analysis; grammar for its own sake is not the object of instruction.
12. Activities are geared to the young learner's interests, cognitive level, motor skills level, and experiential background. They are designed to appeal to a variety of learning styles, to address multiple intelligences, and to incorporate frequent opportunities for physical activity.
13. The foreign language program draws from and reinforces the goals of the general curriculum, including across-the-curriculum goals such as cognitive skills development and global education.
14. Learners have the opportunity to use the new language in meaningful ways beyond the classroom.
15. Learners use their growing awareness of language and language learning strategies to gain increasing independence and self-direction as learners.

Standards for Foreign Language Learning

Communication

Communicate in Languages Other than English

Standard 1.1: Students engage in conversations, provide and obtain information, express feelings and emotions, and exchange opinions.

Standard 1.2: Students understand and interpret written and spoken language on a variety of topics.

Standard 1.3: Students present information, concepts, and ideas to an audience of listeners or readers on a variety of topics.

Cultures

Gain Knowledge and Understanding of Other Cultures

Standard 2.1: Students demonstrate an understanding of the relationship between the practices and perspectives of the culture studied.

Standard 2.2: Students demonstrate an understanding of the relationship between the products and perspectives of the culture studied.

Connections

Connect with Other Disciplines and Acquire Information

Standard 3.1: Students reinforce and further their knowledge of other disciplines through the foreign language.

Standard 3.2: Students acquire information and recognize the distinctive viewpoints that are only available through the foreign language and its cultures.

Comparisons

Develop Insight into the Nature of Language and Culture

Standard 4.1: Students demonstrate understanding of the nature of language through comparisons of the language studied and their own.

Standard 4.2: Students demonstrate understanding of the concept of culture through comparisons of the cultures studied and their own.

Communities

Participate in Multilingual Communities at Home and around the World

Standard 5.1: Students use the language both within and beyond the school setting.

Standard 5.2: Students show evidence of becoming lifelong learners by using the language for personal enjoyment and enrichment.

Source: From *Standards for Foreign Language Learning.* Reprinted by permission of ACTFL.

1 Characteristics of Young Learners

Children have a reputation for being natural language learners, for very good reason. Almost without exception, they have learned their native language with apparent ease, and by the time they are six years old they have brought it to a level of fluency that is the envy of non-native speakers. Parents who bring their children into a second language setting and immerse them in a new situation—for example, an elementary school taught in the foreign language—often experience a kind of miracle. After around six months their child begins to function successfully in the new setting and at a linguistic level to which the parents cannot hope to aspire, even when they have been studying the language seriously for a similar period of time.

These examples of children's natural language learning ability might seem to suggest that the best thing to do to help a child learn a language is simply to place the child in the target language setting and then stay out of the way to let the miracle happen. Unfortunately, this is not an approach that will make it possible to bring languages to every child. There is, however, both linguistic and psychological theory to help explain children's seemingly effortless second-language acquisition and to provide insights that can make the classroom a better place for such language acquisition to take place. An understanding of this theory, consideration of learner differences, and understanding of the principles of child development and of the characteristics of children at different stages of development, will help prepare the teacher to create curriculum and activities that bring languages and children together effectively.

Second-Language Acquisition

Second-language acquisition theory may help to explain the puzzling situation of children who acquire languages more quickly and apparently with much less effort than do their parents when placed in a local school in the second-language environment. The children are in a setting in which they are surrounded by language that is made meaningful because of the context and because of the way teachers speak to them. They are given time to sort out the language that they hear and understand, until they are ready to begin to use it for their own expressive purposes. Their parents, on the other hand, are usually busy learning vocabulary and grammar rules, and they attempt to apply them later to a setting in which they have something to say. For Stephen Krashen, a linguist who has synthesized much of recent second-language acquisition research in his writing, the children would be *acquiring* language, while the parents would be *learning* it.

Krashen has popularized the idea of *comprehensible input,* the amount or level of language that the student can fully understand, plus just a little more: $i + 1$. According to Krashen's *input hypothesis,* the most important factor in the amount of language acquired by a learner is the amount of comprehensible input to which that learner is exposed.

The input hypothesis provides a powerful reason for the exclusive use of the target language for all classroom purposes. However, simply deciding to use the target language is not enough. It must be used in such a way that the message is understood by the student at all times, even though every word of the message may not be familiar. This is accomplished through the use of gestures, examples, illustrations, experiences, and caretaker speech, as described below. When teachers complain that students do not understand them when they use the target language, it may well be because they are using the target language at a level that is too far beyond the child's current ability to understand—actually $i + 10$ or perhaps $i + 50$. Learners who are presented with language too far beyond their current level may well conclude that they are not good language learners and/or that this language is simply too hard to be learned. An important part of the teacher's planning time for a classroom based on the principles of second-language acquisition will be devoted to strategies for making the target language comprehensible to the students.

Paying attention to input focuses on the importance of listening skills and on the potential benefits that can come from increased listening opportunities for all students, especially those at the beginning level. An extended listening period gives learners the opportunity to gather meanings and associate them with language. They can give their full attention to understanding the messages that are being communicated, without the pressure to imitate or respond immediately.

Use of Language—Caretaker Speech

In a classroom designed to encourage second-language acquisition, there is an emphasis on communication. The teacher provides students with an environment in which they are surrounded by messages in the target language that communicate interesting, relevant information in language they are able to understand—language that is comprehensible to them. The teacher uses natural language, not contrived language intended to incorporate all the most recently learned grammar points. It differs from the language used with peers. Part of creating comprehensible input for language acquirers consists of using strategies for making the message understood, variously known as "motherese," "caretaker speech," "teacherese," or "foreigner talk." Some of the characteristics of this speech, as it occurs naturally, will be observed when a grandparent is talking with a young grandchild—or when a skilled teacher is introducing a new language.

1. A somewhat slower rate of speech (still with the normal rate of speech for that speaker, but at the lower end of the range).

2. More distinct pronunciation (not a distorted pronunciation, however, which actually changes the sounds of the language). For example, most American speakers of English pronounce the *tt* in the word *letter* as if it were spelled *dd*. When asked to pronounce clearly, they often change their pronunciation of the sound to "tt," thus distorting the language through an attempt to pronounce it "accurately." Such distortions are not in the long-range best interests of the learner.
3. Shorter, less complex sentences.
4. More rephrasing and repetition.
5. More frequent meaning checks with the hearer to make sure that he or she is understanding.
6. Use of gesture and visual reinforcement.
7. Greater use of concrete referents.
8. Scaffolding. The teacher surrounds the learner with language, allowing them to be actual participants in dialogue. In early stages of language acquisition, the teacher actually provides both verbal parts of a conversation. Later, the teacher might embellish one- and two-word responses by the learner into complete utterances in a natural, conversational manner, at the same time modeling extended discourse and providing meaningful listening experiences. Later students are capable of taking over increasing responsibility as participants in the conversation.

Conditions Necessary for Second-Language Acquisition in the Classroom

According to Krashen and other researchers, language acquisition takes place most effectively when the input is meaningful and interesting to the learner, when it is comprehensible ($i + 1$), and when it is not grammatically sequenced. These ideas contrast sharply with some practices that have been common in language teaching. Language acquisition theory suggests that the language to which learners are exposed should be as natural as possible—that the past tense, for example, should not be postponed until students are able to analyze the past tense themselves. The key factor in the usefulness of input is whether or not it is comprehended. In general, the grammatical details of a message do not have as much impact on comprehensibility as does the context surrounding the verbal message and the vocabulary with which the message is communicated, especially in the early stages of language acquisition. Meaningfulness and interest for the learner may well be the most significant factors of all.

Michael Long (1983) and others suggest that acquisition takes place best in a setting in which meaning is negotiated through interaction, so that the student has influence on the message being communicated. Of course, the greater the language skills of the listener, the more effectively the interaction can influence the message. This suggests to the teacher that there must be early attention to providing students with the ability to communicate messages such as these: "I don't understand." "Could you please repeat that?" "Did you mean. . . ?" "Could you please speak more slowly?" and so forth.

Comprehensible Output

Merrill Swain (1985) has taken Krashen's idea one step further with her suggestion that students acquire language most meaningfully when they also have the opportunity for comprehensible "output." That is, they need to have a setting in which their attempts at communication are valued and shaped to make them acceptable and understandable, through communicative rather than grammatical means of correction. There is mounting evidence to suggest that direct error correction has little or no influence on the accuracy of messages (Dulay, Burt, Krashen 1982). Correction that responds to the *meaning* of a message, however, has a much greater likelihood of making a difference for the speaker. Frequently correcting grammatical errors and interrupting to prod for accuracy tends to shift students' attention away from the message being communicated and to inhibit their willingness to speak.

Essential Concepts of Second Language Acquisition

Awareness of how languages are learned is a part of the essential background of any language teacher, and this is especially the case at the K–8 level. A group of K–6 foreign language teachers and teacher trainers developed the following list of essential concepts of second-language (L2) acquisition for early language teachers. They were part of a Teacher Partnership Institute at the National K–12 Foreign Language Resource Center at Iowa State University. The following list grew out of their experiences and discussion:

- L2 acquisition proceeds according to predictable stages
- degree of acquisition is correlated with the time available for instruction
- children acquire language best in a low-anxiety environment
- culture is closely related to language and is an essential component of instruction
- meaning can be communicated in L2 without the use of English (or L1)
- children acquire language through a focus on meaning rather than on grammar
- children involve many senses in the acquisition process
- meaning in L2 is established, in a school setting, through thematic, integrative approaches incorporating the content of the general curriculum
- meaning is established through visual cues
- children acquire language through extended listening experiences and negotiation of meaning
- a relevant, meaningful context is necessary for effective language acquisition
- the teacher can use a variety of techniques to make the language understandable to children (comprehensible input)
- children acquire language through the tasks appropriate to their developmental level:
  - more manipulation is necessary for younger students
  - language analysis begins later (philosophic layer/late adolescence)
  - older students often demand more translations
- rate and degree of L2 acquisition are affected by differing student learning styles
- learner-centered instruction facilitates second-language acquisition

This is a concise summary of our current understanding of effective foreign language pedagogy for children.

Factors Affecting Second-Language Acquisition

Many factors are at work in the early language classroom. There is variation among the characteristics of the input to which students are or have been exposed, as well as factors relating to individual students.

Some of the most important of these issues are summarized in Figure 1.1, adapted from H. D. Brown (1991). The input factors in this diagram work together to create an environment and a learning career for the student that can lead to eventual fluency in the target language.

How long has the child been learning the language? The amount of language to which the students have already been exposed is a critical element in their current and future levels of language acquisition. Time is the great ally in development of language proficiency.

Does the program offer language every day for at least thirty to forty minutes, for optimal learning in a FLES program, or is there less time available? Met and Rhodes (1990) identified time spent in language instruction and the intensity of that instruction as the two most critical factors in rate and amount of language acquisition. The ACTFL Young Learner Task Force (Swender and Duncan 1998) established thirty to forty minutes per day, three to five days per week, as a minimum time allocation for achievement of the performance goals outlined for K–12 learners (482).

Within the amount of time that is allocated to language in the school day, how much of that time is actually spent on language instruction? How often is the class canceled because of school programs or field trips? How much time is spent moving the students to

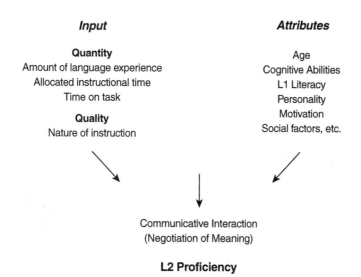

FIGURE 1.1   Input and Attributes in L2 Acquisition

Source: Adapted from H. D. Brown (1991).

the language classroom, or taking out and putting away materials, or on disciplining? All of these factors cut into allocated time, so that time on task is the real measure of the input available during a class period.

In addition to how much time is spent, we also have to look at the quality of that time. What kind of instruction is taking place? Is there intensity of instruction: that is, use of the target language 98 to 100 percent of the time in cognitively engaging, developmentally appropriate activities?

On the other side of the chart are the attributes that the student brings to the language learning process. These are the factors within the student and the student's social setting.

First, how old is the learner? Age is strongly related to learning another language. Children are more likely to develop native-like proficiency before age ten, and they are also at a maximum of openness to other cultures. How literate are the learners in their first language? These skills will influence the ability of the learner to benefit from written forms of input.

In the model (Figure 1.1) there is interaction between the two sides. The best input can also fail a student if it does not take into account the attributes of the individual learner. Every learner also brings significant cognitive abilities. These are related to the student's capacity for analogy and intellectualization. Each learner has a unique array of abilities and capacities, of intelligences, and of learning styles and strategies. All of these dimensions affect the types of experiences that will best facilitate language acquisition for a specific learner, no matter what their age.

What factors in a learner's personality will affect her or his ability to profit from target language input? Is the student a risk taker or an extrovert? Is the learner inhibited? What other personality factors might support or hinder language learning?

How strong is the student's motivation to learn the language? Highly motivated students seek out input and benefit from every opportunity to experience the new language.

What is the child's social environment? Is language learning valued at home and among peers? What is the learner's attitude about speakers of the new language?

Once the input and attributes have been taken into account, the next step is interaction.

The learner must have the opportunity to use the language, to engage with the language, and to construct meaning with the language in order to learn it! With enough opportunities for communicative interaction, the final stage is, of course, proficiency in the new language.

Cognitive Characteristics of the Learner

Just as second-language acquisition research has helped us to better understand the language development of the students in our classrooms, cognitive psychologists have given us information about learning in general. Information about the brain can help us to find better ways to reach our students, and to make our time with them more effective. Multiple intelligences and learning styles models have been developed by psychologists and educators in order to assist the teacher in planning for a whole classroom of learners whose learning preferences and strengths may be different from those of the teacher—and they are certainly not identical with those of each other!

Information from Brain Research

The study of the brain and intensive work in cognitive psychology have resulted in a significant shift in orientation away from the behaviorist principles that once dominated educational thought and practice. Rote learning, habit formation, and observable outcomes are being replaced by an emphasis on meaningfulness, metacognition, and process. For the behavioral psychologist, the student is considered to be a relatively passive subject, to be manipulated through reinforcement techniques and drill. The cognitive psychologist, by contrast, sees students as active participants in the learning situation, controlling and shaping their own learning processes. In the behaviorist classroom the students respond to stimuli and reinforcement, while in the classroom based on cognitive psychology the students' own internal motivation drives the learning process. One of the most important principles of cognitive psychology for the early language teacher is that information is best learned and retained if it is made meaningful to students.

Caine and Caine (1997), in their Brain/Mind Learning Principles (104–108) point out that the search for meaning is innate. Meaningful and meaningless information are stored separately, and meaningless, or relatively unrelated information requires far more conscious effort to learn. Meaningful information is stored in a "spatial/autobiographical" memory that does not require rehearsal and can be recalled as a complete experience.

Patterning. One of the most important points about the brain and learning is the fact that the brain's search for meaning occurs through *patterning*. The brain looks for patterns as it organizes information according to schematic maps and categories. As the young learners in language classes search for meaning in the experiences we provide for them, we must be sure to create complex, meaningful experiences from which they construct their own patterns of understanding.

What we now know about the brain suggests that it resists having meaninglessness imposed upon it; facts and skills that are presented in isolation need more practice and rehearsal to be stored. For example, if we were to ask students to memorize a random series of letters such as *f z g i h r c t u w d h,* students would be able to do this task, but it would require great effort since the series of letters is presented in isolation and is meaningless.

If we were to ask students to memorize a series of letters that are put together into words such as *yet, paper, snow, drive, boat, when, through,* the task would be somewhat easier, since the brain can attach some meaning to the words even though the words themselves are not connected in any way.

If, on the other hand, the teacher uses a meaningful sentence such as "The boy is going to Disneyland when school is over for the summer," the brain has much more of an opportunity to attach meaning and make connections. This last series of letters combined together into a sentence expresses a complete thought.

A child presented with this sentence may think of his or her favorite Disney character, or may think about some of the pictures she/he has seen of the exciting events at this place. This sentence has a much better chance of being remembered, since it connects to an experience that is already in the child's brain and it activates the child's prior knowledge. If the sentence is actually the climax of an engaging and emotion-filled story, it is likely that the whole experience will be stored in memory quite easily.

Although it may seem to teachers that they are making things easier for learners by reducing learning to isolated "simple" words and sounds, such as letters of the alphabet or the names of various vocabulary items, it requires more work for the brain to remember these things, since it has no meaningful experience to which to attach the learning. In the example of asking the student to learn a series of isolated letters or words, the task is actually made more difficult because the student has to rely on rote memory rather than on the context and the connections that make the learning meaningful.

The brain processes parts and wholes simultaneously. While it is sometimes necessary to focus on individual pieces or discrete skills, these individual pieces or discrete skills should be presented within a rich context. Any focus on discrete items, such as individual vocabulary or writing details, for example, must be made for a clear purpose, so that the parts become building blocks for holistic learning.

Emotions.   Another important factor in the child's construction of meaning is the role of emotions in the learning process. Emotions and thoughts cannot be separated, and thus emotions have a great effect on all learning. One of Caine and Caine's (1997) guiding principles states that emotions are critical to the brain's patterning (105). If an event is related to positive emotions, there is more of a chance for successful patterning to take place. Jensen (1998) puts it even more forcefully: "Emotions drive attention, create meaning, and have their own memory pathways" (72).

The role of emotions applies both to the types of experiences we provide for the students and to the classroom atmosphere we create. Many of our student activities have positive emotions associated with them, such as games, songs, rhymes, and lessons involving movement and physical activity. Creating a warm emotional climate in which children feel self-confident, free, and highly motivated is equally as important as providing activities that have emotional connections. Periodic celebrations of learning, of target culture festivals, or of individual achievements can contribute to the positive classroom atmosphere we hope to create. Mascots for the classroom can contribute to the positive environment as well, such as a frog puppet "class member" or a "target language only" bear that goes home with the children on a rotating basis.

Eric Jensen (2000) points out that for many content areas a moderate level of stress optimizes learning. However, for subjects with high complexity and novelty, such as language and mathematics, students learn better with the lower stress environment just described (78).

Stephen Krashen (1981), in his discussion of the "affective filter," highlights the importance of emotions in the language learning process and the fact that children are known to resist learning when learning is unpleasant, painful, or being attempted in a punitive environment. Students' ability to learn more readily those things they *want* to learn is well recognized. Krashen relates these experiences to language acquisition by describing a filter that the brain erects to block out second language input, no matter how carefully designed that input may be. The filter goes up in the presence of anxiety or low self-confidence, or in the absence of motivation. The filter goes down, and the language input can come through, when motivation is high, when a student is self-confident, and when the learning takes place in a relatively anxiety-free environment.

Social Dimension.   Construction of meaning also has a social dimension, especially in a world language classroom. As Frank Smith put it, "Language is not a genetic gift. It is a social gift" (1994). Meaning can be constructed much more readily if social interaction is an important part of the learning. Games, role plays, and partner and small group activities motivate learners at the same time as they enhance learning.

The social dimension of games and classroom rituals provides another way in which the brain can attach meaning. Once the students have learned a concept, they can practice it in partners and small groups. The social relationships of partner and small group activities add to the richness of meaning-based experiences for the brain. Following are some examples of simple social activities that can be done in the classroom.

- At the beginning of class the whole class can greet the teacher in the target language, but then they can also greet several of their classmates in a very short, motivating, social partner activity.
- Students can practice classroom dialogues with partners, or "read" to each other a memorized story that they have written either individually or as a class activity.
- Students can do a partner weather report. After a class member has looked out the window and reported on the weather, the other students can tell their partners about the weather outside.
- Students can turn to their partners to practice or process a new phrase or a new concept. Chapter 6, on partner and group work, will provide many other examples.

Learning Styles

The individual learners in our foreign language classes differ in many ways, at every level of instruction. Writers and researchers about learning styles have given us a plethora of ways to analyze and describe learner differences, and all are useful. Learners can be characterized as visual, auditory, and kinesthetic learners; they can be classified as holistic or linear learners. Some researchers place learners on a continuum from concrete to abstract or from sequential to random. The most important insight, perhaps, from this information, is the realization that almost all of the students in our classes are different from us, their teachers, and from each other, in a large variety of ways. This section describes a few of them.

We know that some learners thrive in a highly social and interactive environment; others feel more comfortable and may do better when they can think and learn alone. Some learners are motivated and empowered by carefully structured, linear tasks and unvarying routines; they may find it annoying and distracting when bulletin boards or visuals are not carefully aligned and the classroom isn't neat and orderly. Other students feel suffocated by so much structure and long for the freedom to problem-solve and create. These same students enjoy classes in which the teacher keeps them guessing and sometimes makes random leaps from one topic to another. These students don't usually mind a little clutter—it makes them feel at home!

Many of our students need a supportive emotional climate in which to learn, and regular assurance that they are valued as people, regardless of their performance. A few of our students, on the other hand, just want to be left alone to learn—on their own!

Some of our students need to touch, or move, in order to learn. (That's probably true of almost every primary school child.) Some students benefit most from our visuals and our gestures when they are learning or reviewing language; others won't feel confident of the information until they see it written out; still others, with poor vision or a brain that processes visual input poorly, don't benefit from either.

Some children learn very well just from listening attentively to what is taking place—they may remember well without ever writing things down. Still others need to take notes and rework the information several times before it is firmly anchored.

These examples just begin to describe the ways in which students differ from one another—and from their teacher!

There are many other differences, too. Does a student learn best in a busy environment, perhaps with a music background, or in a quiet setting? Some students learn best when they can volunteer and try things out; others need to feel very secure before trying anything new.

Nancy Foss (1994), who has done considerable work with the Gregorc learning style inventory, points out that when students are asked to learn in a way that makes them uncomfortable, they experience stress. In a classroom where the student's learning style is never included, that student is constantly operating under stress, and learning is likely to be seriously affected. She recommends that teachers should be aware of when an activity or an assignment will cause stress for one or more groups of students, and try to find ways to make the activity more comfortable. For example, some students who prefer very linear, clearly defined tasks will be under stress when assigned to create a skit with a group. Providing clear written directions and a template for the skit, as well as a written component as part of the skit preparation, will help to make these students more comfortable and help them to learn more effectively.

Multiple Intelligences

As we look at our classes closely we can make an important discovery. Each class is brimming with intelligence—but as with learning styles, each student's profile is different. The work of Howard Gardner (1983, 1993, 1999) and applications by Thomas Armstrong (1993, 1994) make us aware of eight distinct forms of intelligence that exist in our students, identified in Table 1.1. Each of the forms of intelligence is valuable and necessary in society, although our schools have tended to support and nurture only the first two: linguistic and logical-mathematical intelligence. This practice has tended to leave other forms of intelligence with far less recognition in the school setting. Armstrong points out that despite the emphasis on the first two intelligences, our students are not excelling in these areas (1996), and questions whether it might not be the case that children learn best when "their entire range of capability is addressed and when multiple connections are encouraged in a balanced way?" (Web, 2002, 2)

Table 1.1 is adapted primarily from the work of Gardner and Armstrong.

As language teachers in a system that has long valued linguistic and logical-mathematical intelligence above all, we are in a good position to support other kinds of intelligence, as well. Some teachers, as they plan their units and lessons, lay out all the intelligences on a grid and systematically include some activity for each intelligence. Such

TABLE 1.1   Multiple Intelligences and Their Applications to the Language Classroom

Intelligence	Excels at	Language Application
Linguistic	Reading, writing, telling stories, playing word games, etc.	Almost everything we do in class!
Logical-Mathematical	Experimenting, questioning, figuring out logical puzzles, calculating, etc.	Surveys, making charts and graphs
Spatial	Designing, drawing, visualizing, doodling, etc.	Illustrating a Gouin series; creating a picture of an object by writing the word for the object over and over
Bodily-Kinesthetic	Dancing, running, jumping, building, touching, gesturing, etc.	Total Physical Response (TPR) activities, adding motions to songs and chants
Musical	Singing, whistling, humming, tapping feet and hands, listening, etc.	Using songs, rhythmic chants Creating melodies for favorite rhymes
Interpersonal	Leading, organizing, relating, manipulating, mediating, partying, etc.	Small group and partner work
Intrapersonal	Setting goals, meditating, dreaming, being quiet, planning	Journaling, portfolio building
Naturalist	Understanding, categorizing, explaining things in the world of nature	Photography, field trips, classifying

an approach respects the value of all the intelligences and encourages students to do their best work at all times.

In a thirty-minute class period, touching on every intelligence might be quite a challenge, but we certainly can try to keep a balance among all of them over a week, or throughout a unit. Many of the activities and examples in this book show how we can touch on a number of different intelligences in our classes.

One of the important lessons that we can take from the research on learning styles and multiple intelligences is this: What interests and appeals to us as learners and as teachers is an important consideration as we plan, to be sure. However, it is a very unreliable guide to meeting the needs and interests of all the students in our classes. In every class we teach, there are bound to be more students who are unlike us than there are those who are like us. It is our job to build bridges to all learning styles, helping students to learn, as much of the time as possible, in a way that is natural and comfortable to them. Our goal as language teachers is to support the learning of every student, appealing to a variety of learning styles, and to nurture all of the forms of intelligence represented in each of our classes. Our goal is for every learner to experience success—on his or her own terms as well as on ours.

A second lesson, every bit as important as the first, has to do with the use of the information on learning styles and multiple intelligences. Each student in our classes is an individual of remarkable complexity. No single category or set of categories is adequate to describe or explain that individual student, although at times the categories can be useful in finding a way to reach an individual student. If we begin to think in terms of "that concrete sequential in the second row," or "that naturalist right in front of me," however, we have missed the point and also missed the precious individuality of each student in our classes. The categories are useful in helping us to plan our classes and to diversify our teaching, but they should never be used to sort our students into "boxes" that limit our understanding of the whole person. Howard Gardner (1999) identified this danger very clearly: "People so labeled may then be seen as capable of working or learning only in certain ways, a characterization that is almost never true. Even if it has a certain rough-and-ready validity, such labeling can impede efforts to provide the best educational interventions for success with a wide range of children" (91).

Thematic Teaching and Construction of Meaning

Thematic instruction is an integral part of early language learning and provides an ideal environment for constructing meaning. In thematic teaching the curriculum is organized around a thematic center, which can originate in the classroom, the school, the environment, or the target culture. Language concepts and concepts from the regular curriculum and the target culture are interrelated and presented as a whole, within a thematic framework. Language is tailored to the developmental level of the students; activities address a variety of learning styles and call forth a range of multiple intelligences. Students have many opportunities for identifying patterns and connections, experiencing engaging activities with emotional content, and interacting with their peers. It is the goal of the thematic instruction described in this book to reach every child with meaningful language and culture experiences.

Developmental Characteristics of the Learner

The most important factor in teaching and learning in any setting is the learner. Learners of any age differ from one another in significant ways: Individuals may learn best through listening or reading, they may learn more easily alone or within a small group, they may require heavy visual reinforcement or learn better through verbal explanations, or they may respond better to a sequential or to a random organization of materials or experiences. Each learner's experiences differ from those of class peers in a variety of ways. Children and young adolescents, however, differ from older learners in certain patterned and predictable ways as they progress through stages of development. An understanding of these general developmental characteristics is essential for the elementary and middle school language teacher.

Piaget and Stages of Cognitive Development

The teaching of children has been profoundly affected by the work of Jean Piaget, who identified four stages of cognitive and affective development in childhood and adolescence.

The child develops cognitively through active involvement with the environment, and each new step in development builds on and becomes integrated with previous steps. Because two of the four shifts in developmental stage normally occur during the elementary school years, it is important for language teachers working with children to keep the characteristics of each cognitive stage in mind (Piaget 1963). They are as follows:

1. *The stage of sensory-motor intelligence (zero to two years).* During this stage, behavior is primarily motor. The child does not yet internally represent events and "think" conceptually, though "cognitive" development is seen as schemata are constructed.

2. *The stage of preoperational thought (two to seven years).* This stage is characterized by the development of language and other forms of representation and rapid conceptual development. Reasoning during this stage is pre-logical or semi-logical, and children tend to be very egocentric. Children often focus on a single feature of a situation at a time—for example, they may be able to sort by size or by color but not by both characteristics at once.

3. *The stage of concrete operations (seven to eleven years).* During these years, the child develops the ability to apply logical thought to concrete problems. Hands-on, concrete experiences help children to understand new concepts and ideas. Using language to exchange information becomes much more important than in earlier stages, as children become more social and less egocentric.

4. *The stage of formal operations (eleven to fifteen years or older).* During this stage, the child's cognitive structures reach their highest level of development. The child becomes able to apply logical reasoning to all classes of problems, including abstract problems either not coming from the child's direct experience or having no concrete referents.

The thinking skills of most children in elementary school are at the concrete operations stage, and experience plays a major role in all learning. Piaget points out that children are not simply miniature adults who have less experience and thus less knowledge to work with as they approach problems and new situations. They do not think like adults because their minds are not like adult minds. It is the privilege of the elementary school teacher to share their world and learn to work with it. Characteristics of children as learners at different ages and implications for language teaching are described below.

Egan and Layers of Educational Development

The work of the Canadian educator Kieran Egan (1979, 1986, 1992) provides insights about educational development that are especially applicable to the elementary and middle school language program. Egan describes development in terms of the characteristics that determine how the learner gains access to the world. He thinks of educational development as a process of accumulating and exercising layers of capacity for engaging with the world. As individuals develop, they add new layers of sophistication without shedding the qualities characteristic of earlier layers. As he puts it (1979, 86), "Each stage contributes something vital and necessary to the mature adult's ability to make sense of the world and human experience." The final stage, the *ironic layer,* is made up of essential contributions from all the earlier stages, governed by the ironic orientation to the world. The characteristics of each of Egan's four layers are as follows:

The Mythic Layer: Ages Four to Five through Nine to Ten Years

- Emotional categories have primary importance: children want to know how to *feel* about whatever they are learning.
- Fundamental moral and emotional categories are used to make sense of experience: *good* versus *bad, love* versus *hate, happy* versus *sad.*
- Simple binary (polar) opposites provide the easiest access to a subject; they can then be elaborated on by filling in between the poles. Understanding of *hot* and *cold* precedes the concept of *warm.*
- The child often perceives the world as feeling and thinking like the child; the child's meaning for the world is derived from within.
- Children in this layer interpret the world in terms of absolute categories.
- The *story form* is the most powerful vehicle for instruction; in fact, young children require it. It incorporates the categories and processes used by the child in understanding and interpreting the world: *a beginning, a middle, and an end; binary oppositions; absolute meaning; emotional and moral categories.*

The primary task for children in the mythic layer is to begin to understand the world in terms of their own vivid mental categories. At this level those categories are emotional and moral, rather than rational and logical. This means that "access to the world must be provided in terms of emotion and morality, or knowledge will be simply meaningless" (Egan 1979, 15).

The Romantic Layer: Ages Eight to Nine through Fourteen to Fifteen Years

- Children develop initial concepts of "otherness," of an outside world distinct and separate from the world within.
- The separate world is perceived as potentially threatening and alien.
- Children confront the task of developing a sense of their distinct identity.
- Students at this layer learn best when new information embodies qualities that transcend the challenges posed by daily living in the real world, such as courage, nobility, genius, energy, or creativity.
- The romantic learner seeks out the *limits* of the real world, looking for the binary opposites within which reality exists. Thus, the learner is fascinated with *extremes.*
- Romantic learners are fascinated with realistic detail, the more different from their own experience the better.
- Preferred stories and story form incorporate realistic detail and heroes and heroines with whom the learner can identify, who embody the qualities necessary to succeed in a threatening world.
- Students experience overwhelming sentimentality, and defend themselves against it through extreme outward conformity.
- Learning can be successfully organized by starting with something far from the students' experience but connected to them by some transcendent quality with which they can associate.

The key to the romantic layer is in the search for the transcendent within reality, the need to develop a sense of romance, of wonder and awe. The romantic layer learner is in search of answers to the general question, "What are the limits and dimensions of the real and the possible?" (Egan 1979, 125).

The Philosophic Layer: Ages Fourteen to Fifteen through Nineteen to Twenty Years

- Students begin to understand the world as a *unit,* of which they are a part.
- Focus in this layer is on the *general laws* by which the world works.
- Meaning of individual pieces of information is derived primarily from their place within the general scheme.
- Students like to develop hierarchies, as a means of gaining control over the threat of diversity.
- Students at this layer become (over)confident that they know the meaning of everything.
- The general schemes developed at the philosophic layer give control and order to the encyclopedic accumulation of fact and detail of the romantic layer.
- The teacher guides students in the process of acquiring knowledge to feed the development of their general schemes, and then elaborating their schemes to best organize their particular knowledge.

The key task at the philosophic layer is developing the capacity to generate "general schemes," the ability to generalize and organize information.

The Ironic Layer: Ages Nineteen to Twenty through Adulthood

- The learner recognizes that the general schemes of the philosophic layer are not in themselves true, but are necessary tools for imposing meaning on particulars. If the scheme does not serve adequately, it is discarded and another is used instead. At the ironic layer, particular knowledge is dominant rather than the general scheme.
- The ironic layer is made up of contributions from all previous layers, under control of this key ironic perception. The ironic learner is the mature adult learner.

Classroom Considerations for Elementary and Middle School Learners

Several experienced elementary and middle school teachers have added their observations about students in the grade levels below, from the point of view of the language teacher. They are:

Hal Groce, St. Paul, Minnesota
Alan Hans, Columbus, Ohio
Patty Ryerson Hans, Columbus, Ohio
Jessica Haxhi, Waterbury, Connecticut
Hildegard Merkle, Bethesda, Maryland
Joel Swanson, St. Paul, Minnesota

Preschool Students (Ages Two to Four)

These students are in a sensitive period for language development. They absorb languages effortlessly and are adept imitators of speech sounds. Because they are very self-centered, they do not work well in groups, and they respond best to activities and learning situations relating to their own interests and experiences. Although they have a short attention span, they have great patience for repetition of the same activity or game. Preschoolers respond well to concrete experiences and to large-motor involvement in language learning.

> PATTY: Pre-kindergarten and kindergarten students need to know that there will be daily opportunities for moving, wiggling, manipulating objects, and using songs and/or rhythm. They love to share their favorites (favorite color, animal, fruit . . .). They love to use every available sense and to experience "magic" (using colored water, magic boxes, the appearance of unusual things in the classroom . . .). It is crucial for them to "have a turn." When playing games, they are most comfortable when they can see the system for assuring that everyone will have a turn (cards or Popsicle sticks with each child's name).

Primary Students (Ages Five to Seven): Kindergarten and Grades One and Two

Most of these children are still pre-operational, and they learn best with concrete experiences and immediate goals. New concepts and vocabulary are more meaningful when presented as pairs of binary opposites. Children like to name objects, define words, and learn about things in their own world; they also have a vivid imagination and respond well to stories of fantasy. They need to know how to *feel* about something in order to learn it well. Primary-age children learn through oral language; they are capable of developing good oral skills, pronunciation, and intonation when they have a good model. They learn well, especially beginning in first grade, through dramatic play, role play, and use of story form with a strong *beginning, middle,* and *end.* Because of their short attention spans, they need to have a great variety of activities, but the teacher must keep in mind that children of this age tire easily. They require large-muscle activity, and they are still rather unskilled with small-muscle tasks. Teachers of primary students must give very structured and specific directions and build regular routines and patterns into the daily lesson plan.

Kindergarten

> HILDEGARD: I often "forgot" that my kindergarten students were not German, they followed my commands and instructions with such ease. They need to feel accepted, liked, part of the group, and to be noticed and smiled at by the teacher. Feeling uncomfortable in class makes them physically sick (tummy ache). They like to move constantly, manipulate three-dimensional things, put things together and take apart, be enchanted by stories.

> JESSICA: Kindergartners are capable of much higher levels of conversation than we ordinarily assume. They enjoy short dialogues (name, likes, etc.) performed with puppets—especially talking about themselves! They also like being able to com-

ment at every stage of the class, using expressions such as "I'm done!" "Look at this!" and "I did it!"

JOEL: These kids are a lot of fun. They will tell you what they are thinking and will not hold back. If you've gone too long someone will ask when the class is over. If they need to move, they will. When I am planning for kindergarten, I shoot for nine to ten activities in thirty-five minutes. Of course the "new" activity might just be a slight variation. You can throw in a twist on your song, or start making mistakes in a poem, but you have to plan ahead to keep them where you want them.

Grade One

PATTY: First graders still crave structure and routine, but also like more surprises within that routine. Using chairs to help define each child's space is more helpful by this age. A system for turn taking is also still important. My first grade students enjoy creating and playing games that reinforce whatever language elements we are working on. Games that involve closing eyes and hiding objects are especially successful. I generally have one bulletin board dedicated to whatever the first grade students are learning about and they love seeing mysterious changes on the board and trying to figure out what caused them (i.e., what animal broke the branch off our apple tree?). They enjoy songs with big motions and the opportunity to add a silly twist to a song or game. Pretending is still very well received as well.

HILDEGARD: They need to feel successful. They like to take things home, tell endlessly about themselves, move, make things (crafts), draw and label. They are interested in almost everything, holiday celebrations, fairy tales, themselves. Play, play, play! It is a good age to introduce and practice partner work and cooperative learning. Have a take-home folder for the parents to see.

JESSICA: Our first graders have enjoyed cultural activities that they can participate in physically, such as a summer festival dance, tea ceremony, or pretend "flower viewing" picnic. As fifth graders, they often remember these early cultural experiences.

JOEL: They are learning to read and write and love it when they can do those things in the target language. I take advantage of that every time that I can. They love to be read to and are amazed that they can read some things in the target language. Don't forget the short attention span. You will still need to plan a lot of activities for a thirty- to thirty-five-minute class.

Grade Two

JESSICA: The energy of second graders must be cherished! They are most willing to participate in story-form pretending, physical acting out of adventures [TPR], and even repetitive dialogues.

HILDEGARD: They need to feel that they are learning something valuable, and that they can say something in German. They want to learn through language (content). They need to be taken seriously.

JOEL: Every day they remind me that they may be bigger than the kindergartners, but developmentally they have a lot in common. They can do a lot in the target language, but watch out for expecting too much. They still aren't to the point where they can deal in abstracts. They also have difficulties with too many instructions at once. Don't forget to break complicated instructions down into easy chunks.

PATTY: Second graders enjoy silly, surprise endings and having the opportunity to pretend that they are in a variety of situations. They also like to get specific when learning about various animals and enjoy a scientific twist to a lesson whenever possible.

Intermediate Students (Ages Eight to Ten): Grades Three, Four, and Five

Children at this age are at a maximum of openness to people and situations different from their own experience. For these students, a global emphasis is extremely important, because it gives them an opportunity to work with information about countries in all parts of the world. As intermediates develop the cognitive characteristics of the concrete operations level, they begin to understand cause and effect. Students in intermediate grades can work well in groups. They can begin a more systematic approach to language learning, but they continue to need firsthand, concrete experiences as a starting point and to benefit from learning that is embedded in context. The phenomenon of "boy germs" and "girl germs" begins to develop during these years, and children may resist partner situations with children of the opposite sex. They continue to benefit from experiences with imagination and fantasy, emphasis on binary opposites, and strong emotional connection to what is learned, as well as story form with distinctive beginning, middle, and end. In addition, they will benefit from themes based on real-life heroes and heroines who display transcendent qualities in overcoming the challenges of life.

Grade Three

PATTY: My third grade students enjoy legends, geographic facts and details, drama, and dressing up. By this age they appreciate the addition of gross details from time to time (as with the hole in the skull of St. Aubert in the legend of Mont St. Michel). They still need structured dialogues and writing tasks (like postcards) but crave an increased amount of choice within that structure. Math tasks incorporated into our lessons are also well received at this age. For example, during our study of the Loire Valley the students prepare floor plans on graph paper of a dream château. We then spend some time finding and comparing the area and perimeter of each student's château and the various rooms.

JOEL: Most of the kids can read and write in their first language. Working on the same skills in the target language (TL) is a lot easier at this point as well. They love fairy tales and I have yet to meet the third grader who doesn't enjoy trying to make up their own in the TL. They are also at a point where they can help with younger kids because they have such strong language skills. I like to combine classes and have the third graders read to the kindergartners.

JESSICA: Our third graders always seem more settled down and academic than the previous year. They enjoy more complicated story-based themes, but still love pretending. They can also handle more independent activities, such as making charts and illustrative pictures for presentations, surveying others, and working in pairs or groups.

HILDEGARD: They like to collect (the water museum, where students collected all kinds of water and labeled it, was very successful), create with language, write their own texts with the help of word banks, work with a partner (help each other, "proofread" and correct for each other, create together). Competitive games! They love humor, riddles, jokes. They are interested in everything about the country [of] the language they are learning—geography, foods, and climate.

Grade Four

JOEL: You have a new kind of learner in fourth grade. They are getting into a new developmental level. Abstract thought is coming into play. So are hormones and a new kind of peer pressure. In many schools there is pressure to start "dating." Try to push yourself to see what the kids are really capable of. They will surprise you.

HILDEGARD: They need to feel like little scientists, discover, cook, make models, write creatively, perform and memorize plays. I used a "Let's Eat!" and "Let's Be Healthy!" unit with great success. We cooked and baked with each different food group, put on three different plays for the younger students and the parents, planned a healthy meal that everybody liked, cooked it, and served it to the community. After the meal we danced to traditional (live!) German music. The music, physical education, and art teachers were involved, as well as the classroom teacher.

PATTY: My fourth graders enjoy a bit more friendly competition within games than my younger students do. They are fascinated with history, facts, and legends. They are more eager to do written tasks and actually appreciate the responsibility of a little homework as long as it is a clear part of the routine (I give homework every Wednesday that is due every Friday. The parents and homeroom teachers are aware of this from the beginning of the year). Students this age seem to enjoy putting themselves in other people's shoes, so we create imaginary families as we visit French-speaking countries across the world. In this way they choose a new name and must share their likes and dislikes based upon research they have done about the country in which they now "live." We do more activities in the computer lab at this stage. We don't do free Internet searches (not allowed in most elementary schools), but with bookmarked sites the students can do guided research as we explore various topics.

Grade Five

JESSICA: Fifth grade is a challenge! The "newness" of learning another language has worn off long ago, and the language students can use is becoming more difficult. Some students may have decided that they don't like learning the language. The key is to provide experiences that re-ignite students' interest in the language and culture while building on their language ability. They enjoy Internet-based activities, dialogues that they can manipulate to be funny and interesting, assignments with multiple intelligences–based choices (a song, a drawing, a written piece, etc.), and learning about teens in the target culture.

HILDEGARD: They like to sit in their chairs (surprise!), memorize lists and poems and plays, write extensively, create books and projects, and perform. They like to work seriously and be seen as "adults." They used the Internet to research about Germany. They are interested in German peers and their social life; they like to display posters with writing and art. Successful strategies: Give clear expectations at [the] beginning of [a] unit; make students responsible for their own learning. Allow time before or after school (or by e-mail) for extra help and questions. Give directions in written form, in the target language, of course. Students had German pen pals, and many kept them till graduation.

Early Adolescent (Transescent) Students (Ages Eleven to Fourteen): Grades Six, Seven, and Eight

During the middle school and junior high school years students are undergoing more dramatic developmental changes than experienced at any other time in life, and on widely differing timetables. The transescent must learn to deal with a variety of experiences: emerging sexuality in a changing and often unpredictable body; reaching a cognitive plateau for a time, and then finding new, adult intellectual tools; multiplying and rapidly shifting interests; a fluid and flexible self-concept; a need to rework interpersonal relationships with adults; turbulent emotions; extreme idealism; a need to assert independence; and a powerful peer group. A major goal of all schooling for children of this age is the encouragement of positive relationships and positive self-image. Transescent children need the opportunity for broad exploration, as well as an introduction to the demands of academic disciplines.

Because exploring the limits of the real world is very important at this age, students will respond well to opportunities to learn in exhaustive detail about subjects that interest them. Heroic figures with qualities that transcend threats are especially good choices for emphasis, and middle-school-aged children need learning experiences with a strong affective component. Students show high interest in the unusual and the extremes in the real world.

Grade Six

ALAN: What motivates a sixth grader? Extremes, things that are really outrageous or gross. Hearing real stories about real life and problems. Personal tales of challenge and triumph, especially from the teacher's own life. The safety of working and presenting with others. Integrating elements from television, pop culture, and general teen *angst* (remember what it was like to be eleven?) into the curriculum in some way. Don't assume they are adults when giving directions and tasks, but remembering they love to be treated as if they are grown up. They need and want someone to lead, to look up to, even if they don't act that way at times. The love and care of animals and pets is important to them, and it can be a way to connect with those students who are frequently disengaged.

I give them lots of structure—they need it. We often assume they can do more than they are able to, and we tend to get frustrated when they don't understand things with which we should provide them more guidance. Yet within this structure, they have the freedom to create, to share their funny, creative, outrageous, and unpredictable sides. They'll typically share experiences of a painful injury, a "disgusting" thing they did, or sometimes will show a part of themselves which reveals wisdom and reflection beyond their years. These unpredictable behaviors, their ups and downs of everyday living and their outward expression of these feelings makes teaching young people of this age eternally fresh and interesting.

HAL: Sixth graders want to know the "weirdities" in their own culture, as well as in others. They love to compare and contrast. Venn diagrams work extremely well, and prove to be beneficial at proving similarities. They love to research other cultures and find the "strange" points of interest. They also like to determine what would be "strange" to others about American cultures.

Activities must change about every ten to fifteen minutes. Transition is very important. It's hard to keep kids on task when they can't use what they've just learned in the next activity. They like partner work, but still want to work with same-sex groups. They don't seem to mind when partners switch every two to three minutes, such as with interviews, however. Activities are *always* timed so they can't completely "complete" an activity. I give them less time than what it would really take, to keep them on task. It becomes more of a challenge for them to complete an activity. If they're working and on task, I extend their time.

The teacher is a "monitor." The students must be given information to *use*. Once they have enough, they need the opportunity to be creative with it and explore *their* world. They don't want "peer" teachers—teachers who act like they do. They do want teachers who can relate to them and understand their vocabulary and interests. The adult role is extremely important.

Children at this age level love to create new things and show them off. They especially like making menus and doing projects that can be displayed. They love supplemental language that doesn't appear in books and that "only they" know.

Grade Seven

HILDEGARD: They like to go outside the classroom to conduct interviews, and help with and teach the younger grades. They learn (and even study hard!) when it is for a reason.

They like to read authentic texts and discuss them. Nobody liked our textbook. The best-liked unit was "Besuch im Zoo," where groups of students created posters and prepared presentations for the rest of the school and the public, and then talked about their animal at the German Day at the Zoo. It was a good opportunity to use correct spelling and grammar and to work on precision.

HAL: This age is more concerned with getting their point across than correctness of language, although accuracy is starting to develop. They are interested in what kids their own ages are doing in the target culture, and the vocabulary they use in everyday speech. They're more willing to work in mixed partner activities, depending on the time of year. The teacher is more "instructor." Information is still given for immediate use. Students are more intimidated to use it creatively, though. They prefer age-appropriate activities, such as telephone conversation dialogues, or shopping or TV prompts. This age student is a bit more self-absorbed.

Grade Eight

HAL: The "real" world starts rearing its head in the eighth grade. Students are interested in technology and how to communicate with others. A continuation of seventh grade, they need more realistic situations to use language in, such as giving and taking direction, asking and denying information. This age still likes to explore, but a little more outside their "safe" world. This is where technology makes teaching profitable. They're curious about what they don't understand, but are hesitant (at times) to pursue it without guidance. An abundance of vocabulary, especially slang, is a must.

This age student wants more direct answers. They also want to learn things and share with their peers in an "informal" setting. Since seventh and eighth grade culture focuses so much on school and peers, much time should be devoted to this study in the target culture as well. The emphasis should be on similarities rather than on differences. Partner work is much easier at this age level (in comparison to sixth grade). Activities must change about every twenty minutes, depending on interest level. Students begin writing notes and postcards to others at this level as well.

Eighth grade is a good time to "reintroduce" fairy tales and other things kids learned while growing up. They like to be teachers and teach others (younger students or brothers and/or sisters).

HILDEGARD: They need to feel grown up and almost equal to the teacher, respected—their opinion has to count. They like to do their own things their own way. They become self-motivated (some). They are interested in justice, global awareness, world peace, religion(s), and they are out to better the world. The teacher needs to tell students what needs to be done, give them strategies to accomplish the task, and then give them time to do it independently. Give clear descriptors of expectations and grading procedures; rubrics worked best for me. Unfortunately, many students come to our classes with loads of problems, so be gentle with their feelings.

Summary

Teachers of languages for elementary and middle school children can draw on a plethora of resources as they seek to gain greater insight into their task. Second-language acquisition theory, learning styles, multiple intelligences, brain research, cognitive psychology, and information about cognitive and educational development all contribute to a greater understanding of languages and learners. Information in these areas is always evolving and is subject to new questions and interpretations as our understanding of human development and the mind continues to change and grow. The brief overview in this chapter can serve as a starting point for further reading and deeper understanding. Thematic teaching is an approach to curriculum development and classroom planning that can help the teacher to capitalize on the information we have about learners and their wonderful diversity. Each teacher will find individualized ways to use the insights from this chapter to enhance language learning for the students in each of their classrooms.

FOR STUDY AND DISCUSSION

1. Choose a topic or a lesson (such as animals, foods, geography) that could be of interest to children at several age levels and explain how you would approach it differently at each of three different levels:
   a. kindergarten
   b. grade three
   c. grade six or grade seven

2. Examine a lesson you have designed, taught, or found in a book of lesson plans. What learning styles and intelligences are supported in this plan? Are any left out? How could you adjust the lesson to be more inclusive?

3. Choose the grade level with which you are the most familiar, and reread all the descriptions of

students at this grade level found in the chapter. How well do they reflect your own experiences? What descriptors would you add or change?

4. Read additional information about learning styles and multiple intelligences, using references at the end of this chapter or others. Then create a profile of yourself as a learner, in terms of both learning styles and multiple intelligences. Which students in your classroom will you need to pay particular attention to, because of your differences in style and intelligences? What types of activities will you need to include in the class if you are going to meet their needs?

FOR FURTHER READING

The following sources are recommended for additional information about material covered in this chapter. Chapter citations are documented in Works Cited at the end of the volume.

Armstrong, Thomas. *Multiple Intelligences in the Classroom*. Alexandria, VA: Association for Supervision and Curriculum Development, 1994.

Armstrong, Thomas. "Utopian Schools." *Mothering* (winter 1996). Available on-line at: www.thomasarmstrong.com/articles/utopian_schools.htm

Caine, Renate Nummela, and Geoffrey Caine. *Education on the Edge of Possibility*. Alexandria, VA: Association for Supervision and Curriculum Development, 1997.

Bredekamp, Sue, and Carol Copple, eds. *Developmentally Appropriate Practice in Early Childhood Programs Serving Children from Birth through*

Age 8. Rev. ed. Washington, DC: National Association for the Education of Young Children, 2000. Some portions available on-line at www.naeyc.org.

Gardner, Howard. *Intelligence Reframed: Multiple Intelligences for the 21st Century*. New York: Basic Books, 1999.

Jensen, Eric. "Brain-Based Learning: A Reality Check." *Educational Leadership* 57, no. 5 (April 2000): 76–79.

Jensen, Eric. *Teaching with the Brain in Mind*. Alexandria, VA: Association for Supervision and Curriculum Development, 1998.

WEB SITES OF INTEREST

Center for Teaching and Learning (Learning Styles):
   www.indstate.edu/ctil/styles/ls1.html
Foreign Language Study and the Brain:
   http://ivc.vidaho.edu/flbrain/
Lazear, David G. New Dimensions of Learning site: Exploring Multiple Intelligences:
   www.multi-intel.com

Learning Styles Resource Page:
   www.oswego.edu/~shindler/lstyle.htm
Enhance Learning with Technology: Learning Styles:
   http://members.shaw.ca/priscillatheroux/styles.html

2 Creating an Environment for Communication

We are exploring pedagogical means for "real-life" communication in the classroom. We are trying to get our learners to develop fluency, not just the accuracy that has so consumed our historical journey. We are equipping our students with tools for generating unrehearsed language performance "out there" when they leave the womb of our classrooms. We are concerned with how to facilitate lifelong language learning among our students, not just with the immediate classroom task. We are looking at learners as partners in a cooperative venture. And our methods seek to draw on whatever intrinsically sparks learners to explore and to create.

—Brown 1991, pp. 255–256

There is a compelling thrust in language teaching toward a new organizing principle for language instruction: meaningful communication in the context of a holistic approach to learning. The first goal of the *Standards for Foreign Language Learning in the 21st Century* (1999) is communication: communicate in languages other than English. The other four goals—cultures, connections, comparisons, and communities—all flow from and are dependent on the ability to communicate. As the introduction to the *Standards* points out, "to relate in a meaningful way to another human being, one must be able to *communicate*" (11).

The new focus on communication has developed, in part, from the insights of second-language acquisition research, from the communicative competence movement, from brain research, from experience with immersion programs, from cognitive psychology, and—of course—from the *Standards for Foreign Language Learning in the 21st Century*. The principle of meaningful communication replaces the grammatical focus that has been so common in secondary and post-secondary language programs, as well as the emphasis on memorization and recitation that has frequently characterized language instruction for young learners. Grammar has taken on a secondary role, that of supporting communication. The orientation toward communication places language learning in a living laboratory, in which *process* is the primary focus of planning and instruction.

As communication takes on a central position, it is important to understand what it is and how it can be encouraged. Rivers (1986, 2) explains that "students . . . achieve facility in using a language when their attention is focused on conveying and receiving authentic messages—messages that contain information of interest to speaker and listener in a situation of importance to both—that is, through interaction . . . *interaction between people who have something to share.*" Krashen and Terrell (1983, 55) refer to the "Great Paradox of Language Teaching: Language is best taught when it is being used to transmit messages, not when it is explicitly taught for conscious learning." Savignon (1997, xi) reports that "the development of the learners' communicative abilities is seen to depend not so much on the time they spend rehearsing grammatical patterns as on the opportunities they are given to interpret, to express, and to negotiate meaning in real-life situations." The *Standards for Foreign Language Learning in the 21st Century* (1999) define successful communication as "knowing how, when, and why, to say what to whom (11)."

Canale and Swain (1979) contribute the idea that communicative competence is actually the combination of competence in four areas: (1) grammatical competence, the ability to apply the rules of grammar to produce or interpret a message correctly; (2) discourse competence, the ability to connect several ideas together appropriately and to maintain an extended exchange of messages; (3) sociolinguistic competence, the ability to choose language usage according to the social situation; and (4) strategic competence, the ability to understand a basic meaning or to be understood, even when adequate vocabulary and structures are lacking.

Meaningfulness as a Priority for Classroom Activity

The key element in all of these communicative developments and approaches is *meaning*—that is, a primary focus on meaning rather than a focus on form. The brain research that has contributed so much to our understanding of the classroom highlights the crucial role of meaning in learning and teaching. This research offers several insights to guide us in this direction. The brain is always searching for meaning and for patterns in the information and experiences that we encounter. Both attention and memory are focused on what is meaningful (Wolfe 2001, Sprenger 1999, Sylwester 1995, Caine and Caine 1997). The overriding factor in both attention to and retention of new information is emotion—the conscious or unconscious decision that some element of an experience or of new information is emotionally significant and worth remembering (Goleman 1995, Sylwester 1995). We can facilitate the development of communication skills as we provide students with classroom experiences that have both a meaningful context and emotional content.

Meaningfulness—and real communication—always occurs within a context. Fred Genesee, from McGill University, points out that "instruction for beginning language learners, in particular, should take into account their need for context-rich, meaningful environments" (2000). Clear, meaningful, and interesting contexts provide settings in which new language is understandable, and familiar language becomes more memorable and useful. In fact, context creates an environment that allows the brain to do what it does best:

- Identify patterns and make connections;
- Link new information to existing knowledge for effective storage and recall.

When Is "Communicative" Not Communicative?

A common danger for every innovation is that it will be trivialized into a slogan and robbed of its power for genuine change. Not every text, drill, or activity bearing the label "communicative" is an example of communication; not every textbook or unit labeled "standards based" is actually designed to reflect the philosophy of the *Standards for Foreign Language Learning in the 21st Century.* Many attempts to "personalize" activities in a language classroom are actually thinly disguised drills that provide no opportunities for actual sharing of information. For example, the question, "What is your name?" has no communicative value when the name of every student in the class is already known to every other student. The notorious question, "Are you a boy or a girl?" would be considered both ridiculous and insulting to a student of any age if it were asked in the native language instead of the target language. If, on the other hand, one student is blindfolded and trying to guess the identity of another student in a game setting, both the questions "Are you a boy or a girl?" and "What is your name?" could be genuine requests for information; the questions and the answers would have a communicative purpose.

The gap described by the Center for Applied Linguistics (Campbell et al. 1985) between the results of immersion and those of FLES (or "Core" programs, as they are called in Canada) may have been aggravated by the non-communicative ways in which instruction has frequently been organized in these more limited programs. FLES programs have historically had many of the following characteristics:

1. An emphasis on recitation:
   - lists
   - labels
   - memorized patterns and dialogues, usually cued by a teacher question
   - songs, many of which are not integrated into the rest of the language curriculum
   - games, used as a change of pace or for grammar practice
   - rhymes and poems chosen at random
   - reading for recitation; reading aloud
2. Pervasive use of English during the class:
   - for discipline
   - for giving directions
   - for clarifying the target language
   - for checking comprehension
   - for teaching culture

In content-based classroom settings, such as immersion, the context within which communication takes place is well established. The context is the regular day and the regular curriculum of the school with all of its givens. The language becomes a tool of instruction and information exchange is assured. In most FLES and exploratory classrooms, however, in order to avoid the emphasis on recitation, a context for communication must be created, and the teacher must be the one to create it. (See program definitions in Chapter 18.)

A parallel can be drawn between early language programs and music programs with regard to creating a communicative setting. In a music program, the goal of every music teacher is to provide students with the skills necessary to perform music written for aesthetic purposes, both for the sake of their own enjoyment and to communicate a musical experience to others. This process takes a long time and many years of practice, even for very talented students. However, students in a successful music program are not limited to practicing skills, drills, and scales for all those years without any actual musical experiences. In the absence of music originally written at a level that enables children to perform it, sensitive teachers have prepared music at the ability level of the students—music that students can perform with enjoyment and with an authentic musical message for the listeners. These selections are planned and chosen carefully, taking into account the skills of the musician and the limitations of the school setting. Young people in programs like these gain both pleasure and confidence from their experiences with performance and with the communication of musical ideas.

There is a marked analogy between the music setting described above and the foreign-language classroom. While the young learner in the early language program has neither the skills nor the opportunity to use the target language in a natural communicative setting, the teacher can create settings within the classroom that will satisfy the learner because there is a genuine exchange of information taking place. These experiences also prepare the learner for the day when the opportunity for natural communication will be available. The language teacher who thinks only in terms of drilling and mastering a body of grammatical forms, of a series of pronunciation tasks, and of memorizing lists of basic vocabulary is not giving the students the opportunity to exchange authentic messages and not providing inherently motivating tasks.

Developing Contexts for Tasks and Activities

Revision of Traditional Activities

Because the shift to communication as an organizing principle is relatively recent, materials available from commercial sources or through exchanges among school districts frequently provide little help in developing communicative tasks for young learners. The teacher who has made a commitment to communication as an organizing principle must do extensive adaptation of materials in order to provide opportunities for communication. The teacher might choose to revise these, as in the following example.

> A suggested game from the teacher handbook for a textbook series calls for identification and guessing. As one student leaves the room, the others choose a classmate to lie down on a piece of butcher paper, and they then outline the child with a felt pen. The child who is "it" returns to the room, looks at the picture, and asks, "Is it the teacher?" "Is it Mary? John? Is it Miss Jones?" until the child has guessed the identity of the outlined figure. The child then goes on to ask questions like, "Is it a teacher or student? Is it a boy or a girl? Does the person have red hair or green hair?" and so on.

In its present form, about half of the game is non-communicative, because once the name of the person is known, the other information is clearly known to all participants as well. If the questioning had started by identifying first the role, then the sex, and then other information such as hair color, color of clothing, and so forth, the entire task might have been communicative.

Of course, there is a place in a communication-based classroom for practice and drill; the difference is in the motivation and the context for the practice and drill. In a communication-based classroom, the practice and drill take place not for their own sake but in order for a student to participate in a specific communicative setting: to talk about classroom material, to discuss information related to specific interests, or to contribute in some other way to an information exchange that is meaningful to all the participants.

As another example, the teacher may wish to have students practice the phrase "My name is" (for example, in German, *"Ich heisse"*). This phrase will enable them to introduce themselves, perhaps to a visitor in the class, to members of a partner school on a videotape, or in some other natural communication setting. The children in most cases already know each other's names, so to go around the class and have each child say, *"Ich heisse Fritz,"* *"Ich heisse Maria,"* carries no communication value. The teacher may choose to create a context within which *"Ich heisse Maria"* is used in a more meaningful way. One possibility would be for the teacher to put on the nametag of one of the students in the class and claim to be that student. The teacher persists until the child responds with her or his own name. This can be done, as a kind of game, until everyone in the class has had a chance to practice. Another possibility, after the phrase is well established but still needs practice, would be to blindfold the students one at a time and create a game in which they must identify speakers by voice who claim to be the teacher, a favorite fairy tale character, or a famous person.

Surrounding Experiences with Language

An important strategy for creating context falls into the general category of surrounding concrete experiences with language. Many content-related activities lend themselves to this technique. The teacher plans a group lesson in which students are involved with a concrete, hands-on activity. For example, in a French classroom the lesson might be centered around the French food crepes. Together the teacher and the children work through the steps in making crepes, if possible by actually preparing the crepes in small groups, or through pantomime as the teacher gives a demonstration in front of the class. The teacher surrounds the activity of the crepes preparation with descriptions and explanations in the target language, using far more language and repetition than would normally be called for with the same activity in the native language. Some part of this language use might involve invitations for students to imitate phrases, to respond to questions, or even to initiate comments in the language as they participate in the activity.

Now let's make the batter.
I take a bowl. Look how big the bowl is. It's a big, shiny bowl.
I set the bowl down.
I take an egg. Let's see. . . shall I take a white egg or a brown egg?

(Students respond.)
The egg is white and round. (And so forth.)

Later, in recall of the entire experience, the language is reentered and reactivated. Language used to recall the experience provides the basis for discussions, for demonstrations, for a videotape or a slide series, for scrapbook activities, for class group story books, and for a variety of other possibilities. Within the context of this experience, the teacher can embed functions or purposes that are transferable to future settings. The link between language and action enhances the impact of the language itself and encourages its retention in long-term memory.

Games

Games are a familiar method by which elementary and middle school teachers create a setting for second-language acquisition. In addition to context, games also provide an emotional connection and a sense of play that brain research and teacher experience indicate can enhance both learning and memory. Teachers interested in communication often choose or invent games for introducing and practicing the language students will need in natural contexts for communicative purposes. Egan (1986) points out that games share with stories the characteristic of a strong *beginning, middle,* and *end,* an important factor in making learning meaningful for elementary and middle school students. These games should be communicative themselves, whenever possible, rather than heavily drill oriented. Often just a simple twist, as in the examples described earlier, can change a mechanical practice or drill enough to provide a game-like character that makes it consistent with communicative goals for the classroom.

Games can also provide a structured setting for the practice of common social and conversation-starting formulas for which there is not sufficient authentic opportunity in the everyday classroom. A good example of this is one of the "New Games" (Fluegelman 1976), which is easily adaptable to any target language:

> Children stand in a circle, facing the center with hands joined. A child who is IT walks around the outside of the circle, touches another child on the shoulder, and begins to run in the same direction around the circle. The child who has been tapped runs in the opposite direction around the circle. At whatever point the children meet, the two must shake hands, greet one another in the target language, perhaps even adding "How are you? I'm fine" and then race to see who can be the first back at the empty place left in the circle.

There are a number of "New Games" that build on everyday social language and can easily be adapted to the foreign-language setting. These can be very useful as a way of providing context for the practice of language that will later be used in a genuine communicative situation. More examples of games, songs, and rhymes are provided in Chapter 14.

Songs, Rhymes, and Finger Plays

Other powerful vehicles for linking language with action include songs, rhymes, and finger plays that involve large- and small-motor physical actions. Many songs and rhymes for young children are designed to incorporate actions, and the finger play is a rhyme built entirely around the use of the hand and the fingers to enter into the performance of a rhyme. The power of these language resources is clear when one considers how many adults, at least within the authors' Midwestern boundaries, can respond without thinking to the following:

Here's the church,
Here's the steeple
Open the doors and
See all the people

Where is thumbkin?
Where is thumbkin?
Here I am.
Here I am. . . .

Teddy bear teddy bear
Turn around.
Teddy bear teddy bear
Touch the ground.
Teddy bear teddy bear
Show your shoes.
Teddy bear teddy bear
Read the news.

These rhymes are just a few examples of the shared language experiences that unite many adult speakers in the United States. Songs, rhymes, and finger plays from the target culture can be located to bring concepts and common expressions to life for children and to add a cultural dimension to the lesson. In some cases, songs and rhymes may also be adapted from their English counterparts. In an early language classroom, action-oriented songs and rhymes, especially those with humorous actions, become favorites of the children, who want to recite or sing them again and again.

What distinguishes the use of songs and rhymes in a standards-based, communicative approach is their careful integration with the thematic context of instruction. Further ideas for using games, rhymes, and finger plays are found in Chapter 14.

Props, Materials, and Hands-On Experiences

Another important factor in creating context for communication is the use of props and concrete materials. Children throughout the elementary school years continue to learn best from concrete situations; the more frequently the manipulation of actual objects can accompany language use, especially objects representing the cultures being taught, the greater the impact of the language itself. Hands-on activities with these props and materials can range from manipulating puppets to performing science experiments, and they are engaging for students at every grade level. Other possibilities include experiences with art, crafts, and sports activities. Examples of props and materials are found in Chapter 13, together with suggestions for their use.

Content-Related Instruction

The content of the curriculum is a natural context for foreign languages in the school setting. The integration of the language program with the rest of the school day brings interest and relevance to language instruction. Content-related instruction is further developed in Chapter 11.

Stories

Telling and reading stories is one of the most beloved contexts for young children, and students of all ages can become engrossed in a good story. The familiar structure of a story helps to make the meaning comprehensible, especially when it is richly supported with visuals, gestures, and student participation. Many teachers have also found that stories make a good unit focus.

Dialogues

Another set of strategies for creating context to motivate communication is the development of simulations, dialogues, and role plays. Dialogues, the hallmark of the audiolingual method, have value for young learners because they provide a structure for a series of expressions that combine to develop a situation, an idea, or an experience. When they are carefully constructed and chosen, dialogues can provide an outlet for children's natural love of dramatization and role play. A dialogue can prepare students for conversations and situations that will later be part of a story or a fairy tale in the curriculum. The dialogue can also develop as a means of recreating a story that the children loved when the teacher read it or when they saw it in a filmstrip or a movie.

Patty Ryerson, PreK–4 French teacher, uses dialogues that include options for student creativity, beginning in grade two. Here is an example of one of her dialogues. The italicized portions are decided upon by the students, using words they have been learning in class. Patty notes that the students love to make the dialogues silly!

A. Hi!

B. Hi!

A. Where are you going?

B. I'm going into the desert.

A. How?

B. *By bicycle.*

A. Me too.

B. Great! Let's go!

A. Look! *A snake!*

B. Oh! *It's slithering.*

A. Look! *A kangaroo rat.*

B. Oh! *It's jumping.*

A. Look! *A butterfly.*

B. It's attacking! Let's get out of here!

The following guidelines will assist teachers in the choice or creation of a dialogue:

1. It should be short, including short utterances for the children to say.
2. It should feature natural use of language that is not restricted by artificially imposed grammatical limitations.
3. It should be open to many variations so that it can be recast to serve as the basis for future dialogues in other settings.
4. It should be flexible so that children can shape it according to their own creativity and sense of humor.
5. It should incorporate a large proportion of previously learned vocabulary and functions so that children are not overwhelmed by the quantity of new language to be learned.

Role Play

Role play moves a step beyond the dialogue and places students in a situation in which they are called upon to cope with the unexpected or with a new setting, using the material they have memorized through dialogues and other classroom activities. For example, after working with a dialogue drawn from a shopping situation, students of Spanish might be called on to develop a role play in which they go into a Peruvian market to buy an item that represents new vocabulary or a new challenge. Perhaps they look for their favorite American brand of breakfast cereal at the food store, or the clerk has only sizes that are too large or too small in the clothing store. They then work together in a group to develop an unscripted conversation around the new situation.

In most cases role play is beyond the resources of the beginning language learner, who can mainly be expected to provide short, memorized utterances in new situations. It can, however, be a very valuable strategy beyond the beginning level.

Partner and Small-Group Work

Another very powerful context for communication in the classroom involves the use of small group and partner activities within the framework of cooperative learning. Pair and small group work incorporates the benefits of cooperative learning, an excellent vehicle to help students communicate in the new language. When students work cooperatively in pairs or small groups their opportunities for language use are multiplied many times over. Often, while learners are engaged in pair work, meaningful communication stems from "information gap" activities in which one partner or member of the group has information that the other partner does not have. Language has to be used to "bridge the gap" and solve the problem or otherwise achieve some goal.

Cooperative learning (see Johnson and Johnson 1987 and Kagan 1990) offers an approach to small group work and student-student interaction that has natural applications for a foreign language program in which communication plays a key role. Goals of social development can be reinforced through cooperative group work in the foreign-language class, as students are placed in a position where they have need and motivation to communicate with one another.

Nancy Foss, who has researched the connection between language proficiency and learning styles, notes that pair work seems to be comfortable for all learning styles. Learners who prefer to work alone can tolerate working with a partner; learners who like to work in groups will be happy when working with another person (personal communication, 2002).

Specific guidelines for conducting partner and small group work are provided in Chapter 6, together with a variety of sample activities.

Teaching in the Target Language: Context for Communication

One of the most valuable elements of the context for communication is the target language itself. We know from research in second-language acquisition that learners need to be surrounded with comprehensible language—or input—in order to facilitate the acquisition of the new language. This input should be both meaningful and of interest to the learner. Otherwise the brain is not likely to engage with either the language or the information it carries.

We must provide this input consistently, from the very first day and throughout every class period. Some successful early language teachers make it a point to speak exclusively in the target language; others recommend use of the new language 95 to 100 percent of the time. It is especially important that the teacher use the new language for regular classroom tasks, such as giving directions, organizing activities, and managing behavior. It is these regular classroom tasks that demonstrate that the new language "works"—that it can be used for all the important business of the classroom (and by natural extension—of life).

Language is the key or the "ticket" to the culture. We give our students this "ticket" as we give them the language with which they can enter the culture and participate in it. Even though not all teachers are native speakers, all teachers are the culture bearers, the representatives of the culture in the classroom. When students have the feeling of being surrounded by the language, they also have the feeling of what it might be like to actually be in a place where this language is spoken on an everyday basis. We are preparing them for the time when they will actually be in the culture of the new language. In the meantime, the time they spend in our classrooms is the only time they have to experience the new language. If we spend much of this time in English, we are actually denying them access to the language and the culture.

Of course, as we use the new language, we must make sure that our students understand what we are saying and that we use techniques that will make what we say concrete and comprehensible.

We also need to give our students both opportunities and tools so they can use the new language themselves, for meaningful purposes. Early language learners, like young children, will learn most quickly the language that makes things happen. Asking for permission, telling others what to do, claiming a toy or a place to sit—these situations and many more can motivate meaningful language use when the language has been modeled and made available to the learner.

How Do We Keep the Classroom in the Target Language?

Use the target language consistently. Show that this language is important to you and to the students.

Show that the target language is important to the students because it will get them what they need and want: attention, a pencil, help, approval, and permission to leave the classroom.

Surround Students with the New Language
- Talk to them as if they understand and use visuals and gestures to make sure they do.
- Use a "think-aloud" approach to your own activity in the classroom. As you move to the front of the room, for example, you might say (in the target language), "I'm going to my desk now to get the paper and pencils we will need for the next activity. Where did I leave those pencils? Oh, here they are—under my grade book," and so on.
- Help students to understand with the help of predictable activities and verbal routines that you use over and over.
- Use caretaker speech, the kind of speech that parents use with their children. (Caretaker Speech was discussed in detail in Chapter 1.)

Monitor and Assess Target Language Use.   Make sure that the students understand that using the new language is important to you! One way of doing this is to keep track of their language use and to build it into student assessment. This may involve circulating around the classroom during partner or group work to gather information and as a reminder that students are expected to use the target language. Jessica Haxhi, a Japanese teacher in Waterbury, Connecticut, circulates with her clipboard while wearing her Japanese "police hat," on which "Speak Japanese" is written in bold Japanese characters.

Another strategy is to reward student target language use with some visible token—perhaps a reward strip in a pocket chart or a piece of imitation currency from the target culture. This kind of token reward is effective only on a short-term basis, since it cannot replace intrinsic motivation for language use. Language use must become a part of the management of the classroom and an integral part of the classroom culture.

Separate the Native Language from the Target Language.   Evidence from bilingual education shows that students in classes in which the languages are kept separate end up with much greater language proficiency than those in classes that do not maintain such careful separation. Mixing languages, and translating from one language to the other, can cause confusion and tends to be counterproductive for early language learners.

There are two main reasons why language mixing and translation are inefficient. First, if the students know that the teacher is going to use both languages, they will not engage with the target language and will patiently wait for the English "version" to appear. Second, the teacher who knows she or he will be clarifying or repeating in English will not expend as much effort to make the target language comprehensible. It takes considerable effort and many visuals and other materials to maintain a target-language environment. The English "shortcut" robs students of the opportunity to construct meanings and experience the situations that will make the new language meaningful and move it into long-term memory. Our goal is for students to experience concepts through the new language, and not through English!

Using a sign to indicate which language is being spoken has proven to be a very helpful tool for teachers, because it is a tangible reminder for them and for the students that they should stay in the target language. Some teachers make a ritual out of the transition into the target language at the beginning of class and back to English at the end. Rita Gullickson, for example, beats a tambourine as she and the students turn slowly around and count to three, in English at the beginning of class and in Spanish at the end. After a few days of leading the routine, Rita lets the children take turns as the leader. The tambourine, as an instrument used in both Spain and Latin America, adds a nice cultural touch to the activity.

Beginning students cannot always conduct themselves entirely in the new language, of course. When they ask a question or give a response in English instead of in the target language, we can respond to them in the target language by rephrasing what they said and then responding to their question or their comment. This strategy will often provide interested students with new vocabulary or phrases that meet a need or an interest.

Role of English. There certainly are times when it may be necessary and even advisable to use English. There may be an emergency in which the welfare of the children is at stake. Under some circumstances, especially in times of emotional upsets, individual children may need a private conversation in English. There may be extremely important concepts in a teachable moment that absolutely won't be communicated in the target language.

If English is used, it should be intentional, and it should be for a purpose. The use of English should be a conscious decision, not just something the teacher slides into without thinking. The following process can be helpful in making a decision to use English instead of the target language.

The teacher should first ask the following questions:

- Can I find a way to communicate the idea in the target language?
- Can I simplify the concept or the information?
- Can I add concrete materials, visuals, or experiences to enrich the context and to make the concept or the information comprehensible in the new language?

If the answer to these questions is "no," there is another series of questions to consider:

- Can I substitute a different concept?
- Can I delay this topic until the students are ready to do it in the target language?
- Can I ask the classroom teacher to follow up?
- Could this be part of the lessons I leave for an English-speaking substitute teacher on the days I am absent?

If the answer is "no" to all of these questions, there is one more question to consider:

- Is this really important enough to sacrifice valuable time in the target language in order to speak English?

Of course, if after all these deliberations, the teacher finally makes the decision to use English for a specified purpose, it will still be important to stay within the guidelines of target language use 95 to 100 percent of the time.

Some teachers think that they need to discipline in English, just to make sure that the students understand. Yet the very reason we need to discipline in the target language is that it is too important to do in English! When the target language is used for all the important business of a classroom, the message to students is clear: This language is important to me, and worth learning.

Make the Language Comprehensible.   The most important technique for keeping the classroom in the target language is, of course, to make the language as comprehensible as possible. We may attempt to use the target language consistently and constantly, but it will not result in student learning if we fail to use a variety of means to make the language understandable for the students.

There are four key teaching tools that help to make the new language comprehensible. The first of these is caretaker speech, which was discussed at greater length in Chapter 1. That is, the teacher presents the information in simple, direct language and chooses vocabulary and structures that incorporate considerable material that is familiar to the learners.

Second, the teacher breaks down directions and new information into small, incremental steps. The younger the learner, the smaller these steps need to be.

Third, the teacher makes lavish use of concrete materials, visuals, gestures, facial expressions, and bodily movement, on the part of both the teacher and the students.

Finally, the teacher models every step of the process or the directions being presented. This modeling often takes place with exaggerated gestures or materials. After presentation, the teacher might go through the directions again and have the students pantomime the actions required.

Maintain a Physical Classroom and School Environment to Support the Target Language.   Make the classroom and the school an environment where it is obvious that the target language is spoken. For example, the teacher might label the classroom, classroom objects, and the school in the target language. It is very effective to post the class schedule, class objectives, helper charts, and rules for classroom management in the target language. Hallway displays and bulletin boards in the school corridors are effective reminders of the fact that the target language is important in this environment. These displays are especially effective when they incorporate student work in the target language.

In addition to making the language comprehensible and maintaining a language-rich environment, we must make sure that through all of this we are checking that the students are understanding.

Monitor Comprehension.   How can we check for comprehension? Shall we ask the students to tell us in English what we have just said in the target language? *Never!* We want the students to experience the language *through* the language, not to learn it in reference to English. We need to find other ways to have the students show us what they know.

We can ask the students to use signals to indicate their response to a comprehension check. They can hold their thumbs up for "yes," hold their thumbs down for "no," and wiggle their thumbs for "I'm not sure."

If the answer to a question is a number, they can hold up the correct number of fingers for the teacher to see, write the number on a piece of paper, or hold up the correct numerals from an envelope full of numbers that they keep at their desks or in their language folders.

They can draw pictures to signal their comprehension or they can write on small whiteboards, or chalkboards. They can act out the behavior or imitate the performance that the teacher has demonstrated.

Teachers—or students—can ask yes-no, either-or, or who, what, where, when, why questions. Students can complete open-ended sentences or supply missing information. They can supply the next step in a set of directions or the retelling of a story. Students can correct the teacher's (intentional) errors, or contribute to the cognitive mapping of a concept.

When students are working together or alone on the completion of a task, the teacher can circulate and observe student performance, as a measure of understanding.

Teach Functional Chunks of Language (Prefabricated Language). Our last strategy for keeping the classroom in the target language is teaching our students *functional chunks* of language. Young children first learn to interact with others in their native language by using these functional chunks, absorbed from what they hear over and over. "Sit down," "bye-bye," and "thank you," all start out as imitated chunks and are repeated because they can make something happen. In the classroom, these unanalyzed chunks of functional language make it possible for children to make their needs known, to contribute to the conversation, and to understand more of what their teacher and others say to them. Phrases such as, "Please, may I have . . ." or "I don't understand" or "I really like . . ." can give students a head start on language acquisition and communicative competence. More information on functional chunks will be provided in Chapter 3.

Summary

Communication, the first goal of the *Standards for Foreign Language Learning in the 21st Century,* has become a significant organizing principle for world language teaching at every level of instruction. The central task for the elementary or middle school language teacher is to create a communicative climate focused on meaning, within which language acquisition can take place naturally. Meaningful, age-appropriate contexts for language use provide the best support for language development. Some of the best contexts for these age levels are games, songs, rhymes, hands-on activities, dialogues, role plays, arts, crafts, sports, stories, content-related instruction, and partner or small-group work.

One of the keys to teaching for communication is keeping the classroom in the target language. When learners are surrounded with their new language 95 to 100 percent of the class time, and when teachers use the language for all classroom purposes, language use has a purpose and there is motivation to learn. Teachers use many strategies to support this target language environment: they use language to accompany every activity in the classroom; they make a clear separation between the use of English and use of the target language;

they use caretaker speech to ensure that students understand them; they make heavy use of visuals, concrete objects, gestures, and physical actions; they create a target-language presence in the classroom and the school; they monitor for comprehension and language use; they teach functional chunks of language.

FOR STUDY AND DISCUSSION

1. Why is it often so difficult for teachers to make the change from a grammatical to a communicative orientation to language teaching? What kinds of assistance can help them make the transition?

2. Choose a drill-oriented activity that you have observed or used in an elementary school language classroom or have located in a language teacher's manual. Re-design it so that the same goal is being met in a communicative way.

3. Another teacher tells you, in the teacher's lounge, that she has tried teaching in the target language but gave it up. The children, she reports, just got too confused, especially the kindergarten and first grade students. She might be willing to try again, if someone could tell her how to go about it. What could you suggest to her for her next effort?

FOR FURTHER READING

The following sources are recommended for additional information about material covered in this chapter. Chapter citations are documented in Works Cited at the end of the volume.

General Resources: Providing Contexts for Communication

Asher, James J. *Learning Another Language through Actions: The Complete Teacher's Guidebook.* 6th ed. Los Gatos, CA: Sky Oaks Publications, 2000.

Curtain, Helena. "Methods in Elementary School Foreign Language Teaching." *Foreign Language Annals* 24, no. 4 (1991): 323–329.

Hadfield, Jill. *Elementary Communication Games. A Collection of Games and Activities for Elementary Students of English.* Walton-on-Thames, Surrey, UK: Nelson, 1984. (Available in the United States from Delta Systems.)

Krashen, Stephen D., and Tracy Terrell. *The Natural Approach. Language Acquisition in the Classroom.* Rev. ed. Englewood Cliffs, NJ: Prentice-Hall, 1996. (see p. 60)

Savignon, Sandra J. *Communicative Competence: Theory and Classroom Practice: Texts and Contexts in Second Language Learning.* 2nd ed. New York: McGraw-Hill, 1997.

Sprenger, Marilee. *Learning and Memory. The Brain in Action.* Alexandria, VA: Association for Supervision and Curriculum Development, 1999.

Terrell, Tracy. "The Natural Approach to Language Teaching: An Update." *Canadian Modern Language Review* 41, no. 3 (1985): 461–479.

Terrell, Tracy David. "The Role of Grammar Instruction in a Communicative Approach." *The Modern Language Journal* 75, no. *i* (1991): 52–63.

3 Person-to-Person Communication

The Interpersonal Standard (1.1)

The *Standards for Foreign Language Learning in the 21st Century* have helped us to think more clearly about how we use language. Our thoughts often go first to *interpersonal,* or two-way language use—Standard 1.1. This mode includes both written and oral communication in which speakers or writers *"engage in conversations, provide and obtain information, express feelings and emotions, and exchange opinions."* Communication here can be negotiated—that is, either partner can ask for clarification or explanation of the message.

The other two communication standards involve non-negotiable, one-way communication. We listen, read, or view without being able to ask for repetition or rephrasing. This is interpretive communication—Standard 1.2. When we prepare written or oral presentations, they must be clear so that our listeners or readers can understand them, because they will not be able to ask us to repeat or to clarify. This is presentational communication—Standard 1.3.

We know from research in second-language acquisition that extended listening is a crucial first step in developing skills in a new language, and at early stages this listening is highly interactive—or interpersonal—even though students do not have much language at their disposal. Students respond to directions, imitate teacher movements, or otherwise indicate that they have—or have not—understood the message. Yet even during these early stages, students want—and often try—to respond with language; they want to communicate, and vocabulary is the key.

Standard 1.1: Students engage in conversations, provide and obtain information, express feelings and emotions, and exchange opinions.

Vocabulary

Vocabulary is the essential foundation for communication in the second language. The primary task of the novice learner is the development of a strong and useful vocabulary. Early language learners understand what they hear and read largely in terms of the vocabulary they recognize, and their ability to express meaning is limited by the vocabulary they have internalized. One of the first tasks of the teacher, then, is to help students develop a useful working vocabulary.

Most of us, when we hear the word "vocabulary," think about individual words, often in categories. Sometimes when we talk about what our students have learned, we list things like colors, numbers, family members, farm animals, and so on.

Single words are certainly one element of vocabulary development. They are the first clues to meaning for the beginning learner, and the first building blocks for expressing meaning. With each new theme we can present essential vocabulary in a variety of ways and in rich contexts.

Storytelling and story reading provide especially valuable contexts for new vocabulary. Teachers can highlight important or interesting vocabulary and perhaps comment on how it makes them feel, all in the target language, or they may involve students in a physical or emotional reaction to the word. For example, in a spooky story about a haunted house, the teacher might pause at the word *ghost,* shiver and repeat *ghost,* and make a comment such as, "a ghost is scary—ooo! A ghost! A gho-o-o-st!" The teacher might encourage students to repeat the word and pantomime the scary ghost. As part of the process, the teacher might also write the word on the chalkboard, perhaps creating a ghost-like outline around the word. A sequence like this engages both the kinesthetic and the emotional paths to memory.

Graphic or cognitive organizers can show how new words relate to one another and to a theme. The Venn diagram in Figure 3.1, for example, shows relationships among vocabulary used to describe a wolf and a dog.

There are many other ways to encourage vocabulary development with individual words, and most teachers have a repertoire already—listing all the foods you would buy if you were shopping for dinner instead of your mother, naming all the animals you can think of that begin with a certain letter, building a word chain in which the first letter of each word is the same as the last letter of the word before it, playing the "suitcase" game, in which students list all the items packed in the suitcase by the players ahead of them and then add their own.

As students work with new vocabulary in a variety of ways, that vocabulary becomes more securely connected in long-term memory and more available for future use. Students might sort foods according to whether they like or dislike them; the teacher might organize activities in which students provide opposites for new vocabulary, or rhyming words; students might rank order activities from most to least favorite, and so on. The greater the personal connection to the vocabulary, the more likely it is to be moved into long-term memory.

Total Physical Response (TPR)

TPR, or Total Physical Response, uses movement to help establish meaning and set a purpose for language use. This systematized approach to the use of commands was developed by the psychologist James Asher in the late 1960s (see Asher 2000). TPR has become a common and effective means of introducing children and adults to a new language through

FIGURE 3.1 Renate Grant and her students developed a Venn diagram comparing dogs and wolves.

listening and physical involvement, especially in early stages of instruction. Many teachers find it to be an especially engaging and effective way of introducing new vocabulary and making it meaningful.

In TPR, teachers interact with students by delivering commands, and students demonstrate comprehension through physical response. The following sequencing is recommended by Berty Segal (n.d.); examples have been added by the authors.

1. *Commands involving the entire body, large-motor skills*
   - Point to your ear.
   - Put your left hand on your head and turn around three times.
   - Walk backwards to the front of the class and shake the teacher's hand.
   - Clap your hands for Mary. She did a good job.
2. *Commands involving interaction with concrete materials and manipulatives, beginning with classroom objects*
   - Take the red circle and place it in the wastebasket.
   - Pick up your green crayon and lay it under your chair.
   - Walk to the chalkboard, take a piece of yellow chalk, and draw a picture of the sun.
3. *Commands relating to pictures, maps, numbers, and other indirect materials*
   - Go to the map and trace the outline of Paraguay.
   - Go to the picture of the bathroom and (pretend to) brush your teeth.
   - Go to the wall chart and point to a food from the fruit and vegetables group.

When giving a command for the first time, the teacher models the desired behavior, removing the model after several repetitions of the same command. After students respond confidently to a number of single commands, the teacher begins to combine commands in original and unexpected ways, so that students discover that they can understand and respond to language expressed in ways that they have never heard before.

Students are not expected to respond orally until they feel ready, and early oral responses involve role reversal (a student takes on the role of the teacher and gives commands to others in the class), and some yes-no and one-word replies to the teacher's questions. This strategy involves little or no pressure to speak in the early stages.

Some very important aspects of the strategy include the creation of novel commands, which encourages careful and creative listening, and the combination of commands so that students perform several actions in sequence. The sequence of commands must never become predictable, and students must be confident that the teacher will never embarrass them.

In its simplest terms, TPR seeks to teach new concepts through the body, as shown in Table 3.1. Students discover that they can make the connection themselves between new language and its meaning, without translation into English or explanation by the teacher.

The Natural Approach

The Natural Approach (Krashen and Terrell, 1983) is an effort to apply the insights of second-language acquisition, and especially Krashen's five hypotheses, in the beginning

TABLE 3.1   Useful Vocabulary for Beginning TPR

Verbs	Adjectives/Adverbs	Nouns
stand up	fast	
sit down	slow	body parts
lift/raise (hand, etc.)	____ times	
lower	(to the)	classroom objects
point to	left	
lay/place	right	parts of the room
take	front	
jump	back	colors
turn around	high	
clap	low	numbers
open	backwards	
shut	forwards	
wave	sideways	
draw	above/over	
write	below/under	
	in	
	on	
	next to	

TABLE 3.2   Basic Principles of Natural Approach (Tracy Terrell)

Student stage 1: Comprehension (pre-production)
    a. TPR
    b. Descriptions of pictures and persons
          Information is associated with class members
          Students respond with names

Student stage 2: Early speech production
    a. Yes-no questions
    b. Either-or questions
    c. Single/two-word answers
    d. Open-ended sentences
    e. Open dialogues
    f. Interviews

Student stage 3: Speech emerges
    a. Games and recreational activities
    b. Content activities
    c. Humanistic-affective activities
    d. Information-problem-solving activities

---

language classroom. Curriculum and activities are designed to be compatible with the stages of language acquisition as outlined in Table 3.2.

In this approach the teacher seeks to help students "bind" new language by providing experiences and associations with vocabulary in a meaningful context, thus making the language both more meaningful and more memorable. Extended listening experiences are provided during stage one of language acquisition, drawing on TPR, use of vivid pictures to illustrate concepts, and active involvement of the students through physical contact with the pictures and objects being discussed.

In stage two students are drawn into oral participation by means of yes-no questions, choice making, and open-ended statements. The Natural Approach outlines a useful sequencing of teacher questions to help move students from a listening mode to a speaking mode:

    Step 1:   *Students respond with a name*
                Who has the cheese?
                Who forgot his pencil?
    Step 2:   *Yes-no question*
                Does Helena have the cheese?
                Did Duane forget his pencil?
    Step 3:   *Either-or question, using nouns, verbs, adjectives, adverbs*
                (The student answer is contained in the question)
                Does Helena have the cheese or the bread?
                Is the cheese Swiss or cheddar?
                Did Duane forget his ruler or his pencil?
                Is the cheese on the bread or on the floor?

> *Step 4:*   *What, when, where, who questions*
>   (Students answer with a single word, moving toward a phrase answer)
>   What does Helena have?
>   What kind of cheese is this?
>   Where is the cheese?
>   What did Duane forget?
> *Step 5:*   *Students answer with the entire sentence or action.*
>   What did Duane do this time? Or Tell us about what Duane did.

Many teachers have found it useful to plan their questioning of students according to the Natural Approach sequence above, from easiest to more difficult: If students are unable to respond to questions at one level, the teacher can move back to an easier level, still giving students a chance to succeed. There are a number of teachers who have posted this sequence, in the target language, at the back of their classroom, as a reminder of the levels of difficulty of the questions they are using with their students.

Through the use of context and personalization, the listening and speaking practice of Natural Approach stage one and stage two are made meaningful rather than mechanical. Only at stage three does communication really begin to take place, after language and meanings have been acquired and nurtured over some time.

TPR Storytelling (TPRS)

Total Physical Response Storytelling (TPRS) is another classroom strategy that provides a meaningful context for vocabulary development. Based on TPR and the Natural Approach, TPRS embeds new vocabulary and structures in a story line and provides extensive listening practice before students are expected to speak. Many engaging, sometimes (intentionally) rather silly stories are available through materials published by Blaine Ray, the creator of TPRS, and other practitioners. Teachers can also devise their own stories and illustrations based on the model provided by the published materials. Although teachers experienced with this strategy stress that the only effective way to understand TPRS is to attend a workshop and see it in action, the following description will provide a brief introduction.

Step one in the process is to identify the key vocabulary in the story, draw or find pictures, and assign a motion and/or a prop for each item. For a folk tale or fairy tale, it is best to break the story into short segments and present them one at a time. Then teach a few items from the first segment using variations of TPR. For example, a German teacher might wish to teach the German fairy tale *Hans im Glück* (Lucky Hans), in which a naive young man trades away a heavy lump of gold for a horse, then a horse for a cow, and so on, always trading down, until at he is left with a heavy knife-sharpening stone. At last he happily throws the stone away and travels home with nothing, glad to be unburdened.

The key vocabulary for the first segment of the story might be as follows, shown in Table 3.3 and Figure 3.2.

At first students just listen as a new word is presented. Then they practice the motions with the teacher. Next they respond as the teacher combines the vocabulary words in a variety of ways, creating a variety of sentences or questions, such as, "Hans is tired. Are you

TABLE 3.3   **Key Vocabulary for TPRS Story "Lucky Hans"**

Segment 1	Hans, a young man (pantomime thumbs in suspenders)
	Gold (pantomime holding big mass, rays coming off of it)
	Heavy (pantomime holding heavy object in both hands, being pulled down)
	Tired (yawn)
	Walks (fingers "walk" on back of hand)
Segment 2	Soldier (salute)
	Horse (brush hair "mane")
	Rides (hold reins in hand, bounce up and down)
Segment 3	Sees (shade eyes with hand, lean forward)
	Gives. . . (giving motion)
	Happy (big grin, trace smile with fingers)

tired? Who is tired? The gold is heavy. Hans is heavy." And so on. One of the means of checking understanding is to have students do the motions with their eyes closed.

In *step two,* students work in pairs to say or read the vocabulary words to each other and see whether or not they can do the actions. Then the process can be reversed, and the students do the actions for each other to prompt the words.

Steps one and two can be repeated until all the key vocabulary has been introduced with actions and with many opportunities to practice various combinations of words.

Step three is to use the vocabulary in a story. The teacher can use pictures, puppets, or student actors to tell a ministory using the key vocabulary words. A ministory for this set of vocabulary follows:

There is a young man named Hans. Hans is walking. He has a lump of gold. The gold is heavy. Hans is tired. There is a soldier. The soldier is riding a horse. The soldier sees the gold. Hans sees the horse. Hans gives the soldier the gold. The soldier gives Hans the horse. The soldier is walking. Hans is riding the horse. The soldier is happy. Hans is happy.

The teacher retells the story several times, embellishing it in different ways each time, but the basic story stays the same. Each telling should provide an opportunity for students to participate and for the teacher to check for understanding: the students provide gestures; the teacher leaves pauses for students to fill in words; the teacher makes mistakes and the students correct them; the teacher uses yes-no and either-or questions as the story progresses; that is, is Hans carrying gold or a horse?

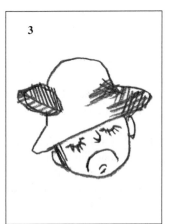

FIGURE 3.2A   Visuals for the TPRS story "Lucky Hans."

FIGURE 3.2B   Visuals for the TPRS story "Lucky Hans."

Step four, after many retellings by the teacher, is for students to practice retelling the story to each other in partner practice. At this point the teacher may want to elicit student volunteers to tell the story, or a variation of it, to the class. Other students may act out the story in front of the class as their peers narrate it. In some classes the teacher may wish to have students write out the story, perhaps first as a copying exercise.

In *step five,* the ministory is revised. The teacher may want to cover up the last frame of the story and ask the students to come up with their own new ending, or have students retell the story, adding new characters and/or new vocabulary. Other possibilities are for the teacher to present a revised story as a model, or for teacher and students together to experiment with revisions. The young man could be carrying something else that's heavy, perhaps—a vocabulary word from another unit. The soldier might be riding a different animal, or the rider might be a grandmother! Anything is possible. The teacher might also help students to revise the story so that it is told in the first person: I am walking. I have a lump of gold, and so on. Students then work in pairs to create their own revisions, which are then presented to the class or written and illustrated for a portfolio or a class book.

For the story of *Hans im Glück,* additional segments would be taught as separate stories, creating a kind of soap opera effect. As a culminating activity, the entire fairy tale could be presented and dramatized, an example of presentational communication.

TPR Storytelling clearly moves students from the interpersonal mode of communication into a limited experience with presentational communication. Students build both vocabulary and structure resources that are readily available for future use. Teachers who use TPRS describe great student success with the strategy, and many ideas are shared on list servs and at conferences. For additional information, consult the resources section at the end of this chapter.

What all of these strategies have in common is the fact that they take place in a context and any vocabulary listing is done for a purpose. They do not incorporate translation to or from English. Whatever variety of approaches we use, it is helpful to keep in mind the guidance offered by Fred Genesee (2000), based on cognitive research: "Students' vocabulary acquisition can be enhanced when it is embedded in real-world complex contexts that are familiar to them" (1). With this advice in mind, teaching vocabulary as lists or in translation would miss the mark. Instead, complex, language-rich environments and contexts provide the most fertile ground for vocabulary growth. Each child will acquire the vocabulary that has meaning and purpose to her or him.

Functional Chunks

The students' working vocabulary consists not only of single words and their meanings, but also—perhaps even more importantly—of "functional chunks"—memorized and unanalyzed phrases of high frequency. There are many terms for these chunks, including *lexical phrases, pre-assembled chunks, prefabricated language.* The phrase "How're you doing?" is one example of such a chunk in English. Other examples include "by the way," "count on it," and "give me a break." Most of the polite formulas in any language are learned first as functional chunks—they are learned as a unit long before the individual words are understood in themselves. Functional chunks can be any length, and for the novice learner, all learned language is a chunk.

Much of the early language that toddlers amaze us with is really *functional chunks,* used because they can always get a reaction. Phrases like, "That's not the point!" or "I've told you a thousand times!" reflect what parents or caregivers have repeated many times, and they are often used in inappropriate—though logical—contexts.

These functional chunks are an especially important part of language development for two reasons. First, they allow students to participate more fully in interpersonal communication even at very early stages. Functional chunks can communicate complete ideas in an efficient and clearly understood way. Functional chunks can "make things happen" in a way that single words never can manage—but they are stored in the brain just as if they were a single word. Functional chunks are a very important part of the young learner's working vocabulary.

Second, functional chunks are a first step toward later grammar acquisition. As vocabulary expands and students become more sophisticated language users, the functional chunks they have stored become the basis for discovery—and for grammar. In fact, these memorized chunks of language are among the best building blocks of grammar.

When one of the authors was a little girl, her mother, who had had two years of high school German, would often finish an explanation or a set of directions by saying (what the little girl heard to be), "Seetsu?" The girl knew what was meant—her mother was checking for understanding—and the girl may even have used the phrase when talking to her mother. But it wasn't until she was studying German herself, as a freshman in college, that she really understood what her mother had said.

As the author was trying to learn the conjugation of the verb *sehen,* to see, she suddenly realized that for all those years her mother had been saying *"Siehst du?"* in perfect German. The author already knew that conjugation, and had for a long, long time, because she had stored it as a functional chunk and it was available for her to analyze when she was ready.

Teachers have many ways to help students learn and practice these useful chunks of language. One of the most effective of these is the use of passwords and language ladders.

Passwords and Language Ladders

These selected phrases give students the language they need to deal with recurring situations in the classroom. Their use has often been demonstrated in workshops by Dr. Constance Knop of the University of Wisconsin–Madison. The phrases usually embed patterns that can later be used for a variety of purposes, but initially they are learned as memorized chunks.

Passwords are phrases such as, "Please, may I sharpen my pencil?" which are taught directly and then posted on the wall with some identifying visual to assist students in recalling the meaning connection. Passwords are frequently taught one each day or each week, and students are then required to produce the password before leaving the class for some desired activity such as lunch, recess, passing to another class, or going home for the day. When a learner struggles to express an idea contained in a password that has already been learned, the teacher can simply refer the student to the password posted on the wall and thus assist the student in recalling the information that has already been learned. These are examples of sample passwords:

> May I go to the bathroom (office, drinking fountain, etc.)?
> How do you say that?
> Can you help me?
> I can't find my eraser (paper, book, homework, lunch ticket, etc.).
> Please give me the _____.
> It's my turn.
> Please leave me alone.
> I have a stomachache (headache, sore throat, etc.).
> I am almost finished.
> May I get my coat (book, pencil, band instrument, etc.)?
> I need paper.
> I'll help you.
> This is very nice of you.
> Hello. How are you?
> Close the door (window, desk, locker), please.
> Please pull down the shade.
> May I borrow that?
> That's mine. (That belongs to me.)
> Don't look at my paper.
> I'll share that with you.
> My bus was late.
> Sit down next to me.
> He was sitting in my place.
> What are we having to eat?
> I was absent yesterday.
> _____ is absent today.
> I don't know how to say that.
> I can't say that.
> What time is it?
> Please may I have a tissue?

One good strategy for choosing passwords to teach is to listen to student conversations and note which expressions they use frequently, but always in English. Passwords will be most effective if they are learned because of a real need to communicate the information involved.

Language ladders are similar to passwords in that they are also phrases taught one per day or per week. They usually represent a series of different ways in which to express a similar idea or a similar need, often in different registers, degrees of politeness, or social context. For example, a language ladder might include levels of reaction to a homework assignment, or different ways of giving a compliment or encouragement to fellow group members in a cooperative learning situation. Language ladders, like those shown in Figure 3.3, are

FIGURE 3.3 The language ladder helps students to recall language they can use in managing their lives in the target language.

posted on the wall with accompanying visual cues, and they are usually sequenced or clustered to show their relationship and to assist the student in remembering their meaning.

Gouin Series

The Gouin series is a great activity for moving students from listening to speaking, and it also provides a good context for embedding functional chunks of language. The steps in this strategy are as follows:

Content of the Gouin Series:
- introduction to set the scene and motivate the action
- six to eight statements (can also use commands)
- seven-syllable limit for most statements
- logical sequence of actions
- single, specific, clear context
- action verbs
- one tense (not necessarily present)
- one person (not necessarily first-person singular)
- simple props or visuals to dramatize the action

Sequence for Teaching:

1. Teacher presents series orally, accompanying words with pantomime and props.
2. Teacher repeats series orally and class joins in with pantomime, not with words.
3. Class pantomimes series as teacher repeats orally but does not model actions.
4. Individuals pantomime the series as teacher repeats orally.
5. Class imitates series orally as well as physically, first together and then as individual volunteers.

Here are some examples:

Making Fondue

I take the fondue pot.
I plug it in.
I pour the chocolate.
I put in some cream.
I stir it.
I smell it.
I taste it.
I say: "Yum, yum, it's good!"

Going to Class

I look for my materials.
I go to the class.
I take off my hat.
I take out my gum.
I greet the teacher.
I sit down.
I hear the bell.
I take out my homework.

In her workshops for teachers, Constance K. Knop from the University of Wisconsin–Madison has identified the following values of the Gouin series in language instruction:

1. It links language to action and visuals, leading to improved comprehension.
2. It teaches appropriate verbal and physical behavior, making it especially useful for teaching cultural behaviors, as well as for shaping classroom behavior.
3. It is easy to recall because it has multiple meaning reinforcers:
   - physical actions
   - visuals and props
   - logical sequence
   - appeal to several senses
   - beginning, middle, end

The cultural potential of a Gouin series is illustrated by Figure 3.4A, intended for a German classroom, and by Figure 3.4B, a Gouin series about Columbus.

Eating a Sandwich the German Way

Oh, I'm really hungry!	Ich habe großen Hunger.
1. I lay my hands on the table.	Ich lege die Hände auf den Tisch.
2. I take my fork in the left hand.	Ich nehme die Gabel in die linke Hand.
3. I take my knife in the right hand.	Ich nehme das Messer in die rechte Hand.
4. I stick my fork into the cheese sandwich.	Ich stecke die Gabel in das Käsebrot.
5. I cut (a piece of) the cheese sandwich.	Icht schneide das Käsebrot.
6. I eat the cheese sandwich.	Ich esse das Käsebrot.
7. I say, "That tastes good!"	Ich sage, "Das schmeckt!"

FIGURE 3.4A This Gouin series illustrates culturally appropriate table manners in Germany.

FIGURE 3.4B Example of how a Gouin series can be extended into reading and writing.

Games

Games are an ideal setting for practicing useful phrases and making them habitual. The challenge for the teacher is to devise games that elicit chunks of language, rather than just one-word responses. In the hot-cold game, for example, one student goes out of the room and the class decides where to hide an object "in plain sight." When the child returns, the children chant the name of the object, louder or softer depending on whether the child is moving nearer to the object or farther away. The same game could practice a whole chunk of language if the class were to chant "I'm missing my ___," or another appropriate phrase, rather than the name alone.

Twenty questions, or other question games, give students the chance to practice phrases, or functional chunks. Many of the activities and games listed in Chapter 14 provide excellent opportunities to practice these chunks of language and to move into genuine interpersonal communication.

Rhymes, Chants, and Songs

Nothing makes a phrase "stick" like a catchy rhyme or a rhythmic chant. Nursery rhymes or finger plays from the target culture make the link with children in other countries; jump rope rhymes and counting-out rhymes can move from the classroom to the playground. All can be chosen for their potential to give children practice with the functional chunks that form the bridge to later fluency.

Any phrase the teacher wants to imprint on children's memory can become a chant with which to play. Brigitte Jonen-Dittmar, an early language specialist from Germany, enjoys using a magic wand to create a chorus of chanters, who repeat a rhythmic phrase over and over. The teacher directs them as if they are an orchestra, calling for the chant to become louder, softer, faster, slower, and finally ending with a grand climax. Other techniques for practicing the same (or another) phrase include:

- Marching single file around the room while chanting, like a train.
- Repeating the phrase as if each student were a baby, a big elephant, a tiny mouse, or a hissing snake.
- Repeating the phrase with varied emotions—as if the students are sad, angry, happy, afraid, or proud.
- Turning to a partner and repeating the phrase as fast as possible, then as slowly as possible.
- Taking turns with a partner saying the phrase as directed by the teacher. For example, one partner might be angry, another might be sad.

Many of these activities appeal to several different learning styles, and they also connect the phrase and the experiences to emotions, a powerful motivator and memory aid.

Songs add the dimension of melody to the power of rhymes and rhythms. Songs with refrains or motions in particular make the learning and repetition of vocabulary and functional chunks effective and meaningful.

Children Playing Teacher

Students draw extensively on their repertoire of functional chunks when they are given the opportunity to take the role of the teacher! After considerable experience with the opening class routines, for example, children can become the leaders. In Total Physical Response activities, one of the goals is to have the learners begin to issue the commands. Some teachers begin every class period with a question-answer session, and children enjoy taking over this responsibility as well. All of these possibilities, and many more, move children toward being full participants in interpersonal communication.

Controlled Personalized Responses

A memorized chunk becomes more meaningful when students have an opportunity to use it to express something about themselves. In a unit on professions, for example, they can use the phase "I would like to be . . ." to express real intentions. The memorized chunk "Please may I have" can become part of regular classroom routines and exchanges. Students become fluent users of the phrase "I'd like to" if they have many opportunities in class to express preferences, or choose among options. Once a chunk has been introduced, the teacher should provide many contexts within which their students can use the expression for genuinely communicative purposes.

Invitations for Students to Speak

One of the challenges that early language teachers face is moving students from the comfortable role of listener to the "riskier" role of language user. The strategies described so far in this chapter, and others developed within the same philosophy, function as invitations to the student to be a participant in the action and the interaction of the language classroom. Our students will learn to communicate by talking about familiar topics of interest to them, using the vocabulary that the teachers have systematically helped them to acquire.

Partner and Small-Group Activities

Carefully designed partner and small-group activities provide the ideal context for developing interpersonal language skills. At their most basic, they give students the opportunity to use functional chunks of language in meaningful, often communicative ways. As student language skills develop, these activities can become more sophisticated and allow for thoughtful exchange of information, feelings, and opinions. Student-to-student interaction gives every member of the class an opportunity to use language more frequently and (often) more meaningfully than is possible with teacher-fronted activities.

Chapter 6 will provide more information about partner and small-group activities, as well as examples and guidelines for a range of interest and ability levels.

Direct Teaching of Speaking

Although most aspects of the audiolingual methodology of the 1960s are a poor fit in today's communicative climate, audiolingualism did lead to the development of several useful strategies to assist with the direct teaching of oral skills. While most student speaking should occur naturally, in communicative settings, teachers may choose direct teaching to introduce activities such as passwords, or phrases in a song or a dialogue. The following suggestions will help them to do so in an effective manner.

1. *Teacher Repetition.* During activities calling for a group or whole-class response, the teacher should never repeat a response with the students. It is very tempting for teachers to try to model a quick, clear, vigorous response by playing the role of cheerleader. However, students quickly become dependent on the teacher's leadership. Moreover, teachers who speak with the students are not in a position to evaluate the quality of the student response and the degree to which students may actually have mastered the material.

2. *Modeling.* Teachers should always model the language with natural speed and intonation, especially in practice settings when they might otherwise tend to emphasize the components of the message that they expect to cause the students problems. When students seem to be having difficulty with a sentence, it is a better strategy to repeat the message several more times, using natural speed and intonation, than to distort the language by slowing it down or giving difficult segments inappropriate emphasis.

3. *Backward Buildup.* Most language in songs, passwords, rhymes, and dialogues should be simple and direct enough for children to understand and learn it in complete utterances. When an utterance is longer than about seven syllables, however, it is often necessary to teach the utterance part by part instead of in a single stream. Under these circumstances it can be helpful to segment the utterance into meaning units so that, for example, prepositions and their objects are not separated into different practice segments. It is also useful to begin teaching the utterance with the segment closest to the end. In the sentence, "I wasn't able to get my homework done yesterday," the teacher might proceed as follows:

> . . . yesterday.
> . . . done yesterday.
> . . . my homework done yesterday.
> . . . to get my homework done yesterday.
> . . . able to get my homework done yesterday,
> . . . I wasn't able to get my homework done yesterday.

Backward buildup should be used only in very specific situations, with language that is understood by the children and highly motivating, such as a very important password, a song that is integral to the rest of the lesson, or the language necessary for a game or for expressing a message of considerable importance to the children.

4. *Answer Precedes Question.* When dealing with question-answer exchanges, it is useful to teach the answer first, followed by the question. For example, one might teach, "It's three o'clock." "Today is Wednesday." "My name is Mary." "I feel terrible." All of these are statements that can stand alone and that clearly communicate information that might have value to the hearer. Once the answer has been learned the statement can be cued with the question, and the question becomes a form of input: "What time is it?" "It is three o'clock." As a final step the question is learned, and the question and the answer can then be used together in natural settings. This is a much more natural approach than teaching the question first, since questions really cannot stand alone without an answer. When the answer is taught first the question is always practiced in combination with an answer, thus creating much more meaningful, realistic practice settings. These experiences lead naturally to awareness of typical adjacency pairs in the target language, typical questions and answers that always occur together.

Teaching Pronunciation

While direct teaching of spoken language may have its place, and while there are useful techniques for accomplishing it, there is probably far less justification for the direct teaching of pronunciation, at least in early stages of language acquisition. As Berty Segal (n.d.) has pointed out, focusing instruction and correction on pronunciation increases the potential for creating problems and for communicating some inappropriate messages. Segal describes three problems that may arise when pronunciation is taught and drilled directly:

1. Students often do not know which sounds to say. They sometimes cannot separate the teacher's command from the word or phrase to be repeated. They frequently cannot determine which part of the phrase is causing difficulty, so they do not know where to focus their attention.
2. If a sound does not exist in the native language, over forty hearings are required before the students even recognize the sound they are trying to imitate. Drilling with a single student who is not able to hear the sound in question is frustrating for both teacher and student.
3. The frustration inherent in premature individual drill work in pronunciation leads to student anxiety and a loss of self-confidence in all areas of the language acquisition process.

In addition to the above issues, and perhaps most important of all, the direct teaching of pronunciation at early stages of language acquisition encourages students to focus attention on the surface features of language rather than on the meaning. It is a way of inviting children to listen for speaking rather than to listen for meaning, of encouraging them to parrot language rather than truly developing language competence.

Avoiding a focus on pronunciation does not mean that pronunciation should be ignored. Teachers need to be sure that they provide an effective language model, both in terms of pronunciation and language structure. An accurate teacher model is a key to accurate student pronunciation. Teachers should also anticipate potential pronunciation problems and plan strategies to give students additional exposure to these sounds. Teachers can playfully emphasize a specific problem sound in a song, a game, or a chant, for example, and students will imitate enthusiastically. As is the case with other errors, early pronunciation problems can effectively be dealt with when teachers restate student messages correctly as a form of reflective listening, rather than in a correction mode. Most children tend to be good imitators, so there is no serious danger of reinforcing poor pronunciation habits.

When students have gained confidence and comfort with the new language, and once the emphasis on communication has been established, attention to pronunciation becomes more appropriate. Teachers can assist experienced students in communicating more effectively and more precisely by guiding improvement in pronunciation as well as in grammar, structure, and vocabulary usage. When correction takes place in the interest of improved communication of meanings and ideas, it is more compatible with how the brain works and thus more effective.

Writing and the Interpersonal Mode

Students need experience with writing for interpersonal communication in the target language, so that they can begin to use the written word as well as oral language for communication. This kind of writing involves students focusing on expressing and exchanging personal messages, not engaging in mechanical drill exercises. For example, they might write notes to each other and put them in the classroom mail or message box. They can write messages (perhaps on self-stick notes) to be placed on a message board. In a game-like setting they might exchange written TPR commands with one another, or develop components of a reading action chain (see Chapter 14). Pen pals or "key pals" provide other rich opportunities for communication in the interpersonal mode.

Dialogue Journals

A dialogue journal is a written conversation in which a student and teacher communicate regularly (Peyton 1993). Students write about topics of their choice, and the teacher writes back with responses, advice, comments, and observations, acting as a participant in an ongoing written conversation, rather than as an evaluator who simply corrects or comments on the writing. Because dialogue journal writing involves exchanging genuine messages for real purposes to a known and interested audience, it provides a valuable context for language and writing development. Dialogue journals can be used with students at beginning or advanced stages of learning a second or foreign language. At very beginning stages, students can write or copy the few words they have learned and combine them with pictures. At more advanced stages, they can engage in discussions of cultural issues or other course content, as well as more personal feelings and opinions.

Borich (2001) reports the value of using dialogue journals as an assessment of a second-grade thematic unit on the Yucatan. She concludes, "The data suggest that student dialogue journals provide documentation of student learning from a cultural unit taught in Spanish" (16).

The success of dialogue journal writing depends in part on the prompt return of the journals by the teacher. With large numbers of students to deal with, teachers can find a dialogue project to be a practical impossibility. Another appealing possibility for effective use of this strategy is journaling with advanced high school or college students, especially students in methods for early language programs. With older learners, journaling might be facilitated by the use of e-mail.

Summary

The communication standard incorporates three dimensions, or modes: interpersonal communication (1.1), interpretive communication (1.2), and presentational communication (1.3). Initial language learning experiences for beginners depend heavily on interaction between teacher and students, and early student responses are primarily nonverbal. Beginning TPR sessions are good examples of this kind of interaction. As students gain experience, vocabulary, and confidence, they take part in interaction with the teacher and with one another and begin to function verbally in the interpersonal mode. These experiences build toward the greater independence demanded by the interpretive and the presentational modes.

Before students can participate fully in the interactions of the classroom (interpersonal mode), and in the interpretive and presentational modes of communication, they must build a meaningful and usable vocabulary consisting of both individual words and functional chunks of language. This chapter has provided tools and strategies for this early focus on vocabulary building: methods of introducing, elaborating, and practicing vocabulary and functional chunks of language.

Approaches such as Total Physical Response, Natural Approach, and TPRS move students from interacting primarily through physical responses to using language in a genuinely interpersonal way. Functional chunks, introduced and reinforced through a variety of different activities, provide a bridge from single words to complete utterances, and they are essential building blocks for communication. All of these approaches involve meaningful language use and continuous invitations for learners to interact using both oral and written language.

From the earliest stages of language learning, these factors help students develop the ability to *engage in conversations, provide and obtain information, express feelings and emotions, and exchange opinions* (Standard 1.1).

FOR STUDY AND DISCUSSION

1. Novice learners in a communication- and standards-based classroom have a greater need of experiences with vocabulary and functional chunks than they have for systematic grammar instruction. Yet grammar is the element that allows learners to create with language, and then create their own communication. What is an appropriate role for grammar in the early language classroom?

2. Choose a phrase that students will need in order to function in the target language in your classroom. Design a sequence of several activities to teach that phrase, and try them out on your students, colleagues, or classmates. Were you able to address several learning styles? Were you able to play with the language?

3. Choose a topic that has value either for helping children deal with their classroom environment in the target language or for teaching appropriate cultural behavior. Use it as the basis for a Gouin series of six to eight sentences; try it in your classroom and demonstrate it to your colleagues.

4. Under what circumstances is the direct teaching of speaking skills necessary or desirable?

5. Create a list of potential writing activities in the interpersonal mode. Identify the level of language development for which each would be appropriate.

FOR FURTHER READING

The following sources are recommended for additional information about material covered in this chapter. Chapter citations are documented in Works Cited at the end of the volume.

Asher, James J. *Learning Another Language through Actions: The Complete Teacher's Guidebook.* 6th ed. Los Gatos, CA: Sky Oaks Publications, 2000.

Caine, Renate Nummela, and Geoffrey Caine. *Education on the Edge of Possibility.* Alexandria, VA: Association for Supervision and Curriculum Development, 1997.

Krashen, Stephen D., and Tracy Terrell. *The Natural Approach. Language Acquisition in the Classroom.* Rev. ed. Englewood Cliffs, NJ: Prentice-Hall, 1996.

Peyton, Joy Kreeft. "Dialogue Journals: Interactive Writing to Develop Language and Literacy." *ERIC Digest* (April 1993). Available on-line at www.cal. org/ericcll/digest/peyton01.html

Porto, Melina. "Lexical Phrases and Language Teaching." *Forum* 36, no. 3 (July–September 1998): 22–25.

Ray, Blaine, and Contee Seeley. *Fluency through TPR storytelling: Achieving Real Language Acquisition in School.* 2nd ed. Berkeley, CA: Command Performance Language Institute, 1998.

Terrell, Tracy. "The Natural Approach to Language Teaching: An Update." *Canadian Modern Language Review* 41, no. 3 (1985): 461–479.

WEB SITE OF INTEREST

TPR Storytelling Web site:
www.tprstorytelling.com

CHAPTER

4

One-Way Communication

The Interpretive and the Presentational Modes (1.2, 1.3)

The *Standards for Foreign Language Learning in the 21st Century* provide us with a new vocabulary for discussing communication. The first communication standard addresses the interpersonal mode: that is, two-way communication in which each participant in an exchange of ideas, information, or opinion can influence the communication in a variety of ways. In the interpersonal mode there is opportunity for negotiation of meaning: asking for repetition or rephrasing, checking for understanding, requesting an example, among many other possibilities. Contexts and building blocks for interpersonal communication are addressed in Chapter 3 and Chapter 6.

This chapter focuses on one-way communication: Standard 1.2, the interpretive mode, and Standard 1.3, the presentational mode. When functioning in the interpretive mode, the listener, reader, or viewer is separated from the creator of the message by distance, time, or the logistics of the situation, and thus cannot request clarification, repetition, or rephrasing. In the presentational mode, the writer or speaker cannot check for understanding and alter the message accordingly. Inadequacies in the areas of language competence or cultural awareness will hamper the flow of communication for either the interpreter or the presenter of the message.

This textbook is a good example of these two types of communication. For the reader, this is interpretive communication—1.2. For the authors, as writers, this is presentational communication—1.3. As readers, you need to understand the vocabulary of pedagogy for early language learning and something about the culture of the classroom and the profession. As writers, we need to make sure that we choose our language and our examples carefully, to help you understand our message clearly. We must always be aware of our audience.

It is important to emphasize here that communication is a holistic concept. The three modes do not occur in isolation during instruction; rather, they flow from one to the other. The interpersonal mode is often used to introduce, reinforce, and connect work with the other modes of communication in the classroom, in addition to being an instructional focus in its own right.

Standard 1.2: Communication in the Interpretive Mode
Students understand and interpret written and spoken language on a variety of topics.

This standard involves listening, viewing, or reading situations in which the message essentially cannot be altered or influenced by the learner. That is, the learner is the audience and has little or no interaction with the source of the message.

Listening

Listening is considered by many teachers and researchers to be the cornerstone of language development. In beginning classrooms, listening is the main channel by which the student makes initial contact with the target language and its culture. The challenge with listening in the interpretive mode is to provide students with opportunities for extended, purposeful listening and viewing in addition to the listening that takes place as a part of conversation.

One simple activity that helps learners to move in this direction is the game "I see something that you don't see." The teacher describes a student or an object in the classroom at some length, and students try to guess who or what is being described. Later a student volunteer may do the describing, after student speaking skills have developed and as the students become familiar with the language of description.

Storytelling and Story Reading

Few listening experiences can compare with a good story, told or read by the teacher. In early stages of language development, the story may be heavily supported with visuals or actions. Using visuals and actions to support the listening experience helps learners to draw on all the resources they have available to understand the message—background knowledge, tone of voice and gestures, pictures or visuals, and motions. This experience helps to prepare them for more independent listening activities in the future.

In the story many values come together: Egan (1986, 1997) identifies the story form as one of the most effective tools for communicating new information to young learners, and Bruner (1990) makes the even stronger claim that our perception of the world is shaped by the stories to which we are exposed and which we have internalized. Certainly the myths, folk tales, fairy tales, and legends of a culture constitute a direct and pleasurable means of communicating cultural ideas and values, and in the language classroom these stories can give children a cultural experience in common with children living in the target culture.

Storytelling.   Storytelling has special pedagogical values for the foreign language classroom. Wajnryb (1986, 17–18) identifies the following reasons for telling stories in the early language classroom:

1. The purpose of telling a story is genuinely communicative.
2. Storytelling is linguistically honest. (It is oral language, meant to be heard.)
3. Storytelling is real! (People do it all the time.)
4. Storytelling is sensual.
5. Storytelling appeals to the affective domain.
6. Storytelling caters for the individual while forging a community in the classroom.
7. Storytelling provides listening experiences with reduced anxiety.
8. Storytelling is pedagogically sound.

Wajnryb suggests several steps in the storytelling process that will help beginners to prepare successfully. After choosing a suitable story, the teller can "skeletalize" it—write out the major features and characters of the story in the order of the action, but in words and phrases. As an alternative, the teacher might devise a story map, described later in this chapter. This information serves as a reminder of the story line, yet allows the teller to narrate in a natural oral style, adapting to the responses and the understanding of the learners. At this point the teacher can also plan for specific vocabulary or linguistic features to be emphasized through repetition, in order to intensify the opportunities for acquisition of useful language. The next step is to develop some form of advance organizer, perhaps presenting or recalling key vocabulary using visuals, physical actions, or other devices, and then setting the stage for the action to follow. Then the storyteller begins the tale, using visuals and dramatic expression, and involving learners through actions and prediction whenever possible. Once the story has been told, many follow-up activities are possible, depending on the story itself and the aspects to which students have responded most enthusiastically.

Storytelling can provide experience with the interpretive mode for children, at even very early stages of language acquisition, when the stories meet the following criteria:

1. The story is highly predictable, or familiar to the children from their native culture, with a large proportion of previously learned vocabulary. In early stages it is especially helpful to choose stories that include vocabulary representing the home and school environments of the children.
2. The story is repetitive, making use of formulas and patterns that occur regularly and predictably. In the best story choices, these repeated elements provide language that children can later use for their own expressive purposes. Pattern stories like *Brown Bear, Brown Bear* (1983) by Bill Martin Jr., or cumulative stories like "The House that Jack Built," are good examples of this type of story. Stories written for children in the target culture, if they have a story structure like those listed above, can be successfully presented in the target language from very early stages of language development.
3. The story line lends itself to dramatization and pantomime.
4. The story lends itself to heavy use of visuals and realia to illustrate its content and progress.

Stories that meet these criteria can be presented without use of English, relying entirely on visuals, pantomime, and the children's existing knowledge of the story or the situation to make meaning clear. "The Three Bears" is an example of a story containing all of the above features. The teacher may check comprehension during or after the telling by using physical responses (point to the big bear, hold up the little bowl), yes-no questions, and other levels of the Natural Approach sequence described in Chapter 3.

After the story has been told several times, children may pantomime the story as the teacher tells it again. This "physical storytelling" can be carried even further, as the teacher recombines previously learned TPR commands with familiar story material to create a new story that the children act out as the teacher tells it.

Many teachers draw stuffed animals, puppets, or other concrete objects representing story vocabulary from a magic box, a mystery bag, or another special hiding place. As the teacher introduces or reviews the vocabulary for the items, one item at a time, they distribute the objects among class members. These objects can be the focus of a game before the storytelling begins, to reinforce the vocabulary, or students can hold up the objects as they occur in the story, perhaps using them to help dramatize the action.

One of the special benefits of storytelling in the early language classroom is that the teacher can tailor the story to the interests and background knowledge of the class. Joe Pennington, a Spanish teacher in Douglas County, Georgia, created a magical listening experience for his second graders to explain the exaggerated limp that he appeared to have from the time the class began. He told his wide-eyed students about his encounter with a dinosaur in the local discount store, at the end of which he saved a little girl from the dinosaur's jaws. Joe's body language, familiar context, and choice of vocabulary empowered his students to gain meaning from context, an essential element of the interpretive mode.

Story Reading.   Reading stories aloud has the additional benefit of connecting narrative with the printed page. The teacher can successfully read very familiar stories aloud at an early stage of language acquisition, especially if the book is heavily illustrated. While reading aloud, it is helpful to point to the words or lines as they are read, to emphasize the connection of oral language to print, even before learners are actually reading. Most primary school teachers follow a pattern of introducing the book by title and identifying the author and the illustrator, and then reading dedications aloud, so that children think of books as communication created by real authors and artists, often with a specific audience in mind. During the reading the teacher may pause frequently to comment on the illustrations or the action, to involve students in reactions or predictions, or to clarify some aspect of the story.

Story Mapping

Story mapping is a strategy to identify and visually organize the central structure and main components of simple stories. It can be used before, during, and/or after reading. Some students do this kind of organization intuitively, but less able students sometimes have difficulty following a story line. Since story mapping simplifies and graphically organizes the story, it helps the foreign language student to sort out the more important information from the less important information in the story, and thus to comprehend the story better. It is also a helpful tool for teachers to use in their planning as they prepare stories to tell or read to their students. The process for story mapping is shown in Figure 4.1.

The teacher decides how and at what point in the lesson to use the story-mapping strategy. The map framework can be the basis for asking appropriate comprehension questions. It can also be used at the beginning of the story as a pre-reading organizer to help the students understand what they are going to read or hear, or it can be filled in by teachers and students together as the story is being read. Students can use the story map to write a summary of the story, or to rewrite the story by changing one or more elements; for example, they can change the setting or invent a new hero. Students, individually or in groups, can develop a story map and then use it to write an original story.

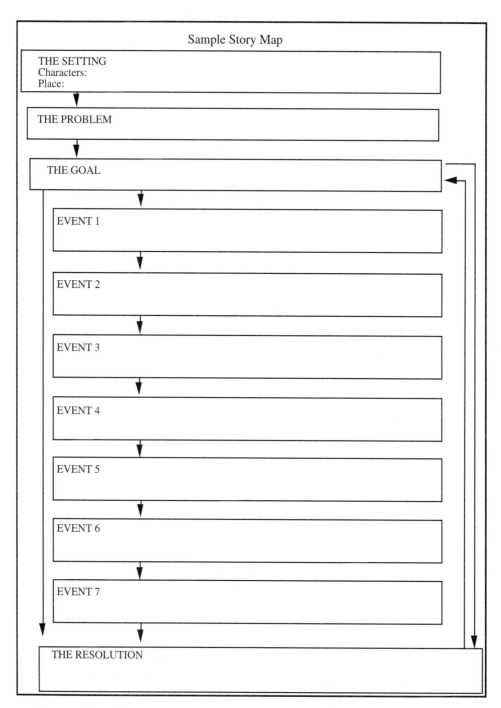

FIGURE 4.1 The teacher reads the story and constructs a story map such as the one found here, to identify central components. The design of the map is based on the components of the story and the language ability of the students.

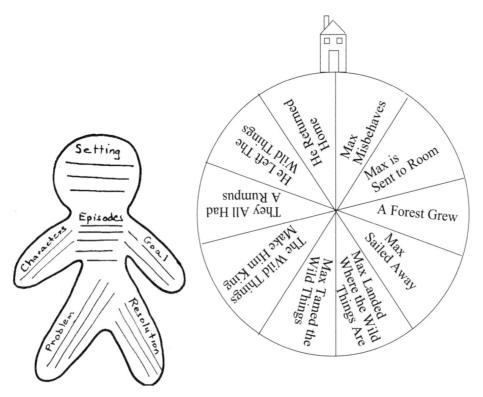

FIGURE 4.2   Story maps for *The Gingerbread Man* and *Where the Wild Things Are*.

Typical questions to ask when putting together a story map include the following:

What is the setting?
Who is the main character?
What did the main character want (goals)?
What was the problem?
What did the main character do to solve the problem?
What happened next?
How was the goal met and the problem solved in the end? Or not solved?
How did the main character feel in the end?

Story maps can take many shapes and forms (see Figure 4.2).

Listening and Reading for a Purpose

Listening, reading, or viewing can all be enhanced when they take place for a purpose. Of course, the purpose in the "I see something" game mentioned earlier is solving the puzzle. The purpose of story reading and telling may simply be the pleasure of following an interesting narrative.

FIGURE 4.3 A worksheet to guide listening or viewing experience with a weather report.

Date: _____ Name: _____

High Temperature _____ ° C.	Low Temperature _____ ° C.	Precipitation light/heavy rain • snow • sleet • hail • mist • thunderstorm	Wind Conditions windy • light breeze • still	Sky Conditions sunny • cloudy • partly sunny • partly cloudy	Humidity
High Temperature feels: freezing • cold • cool • warm • hot • very hot	Low Temperature feels: freezing • cold • cool • warm • hot • very hot				

Sometimes a purpose for listening can be established through use of a worksheet, such as the format shown in Figure 4.3, used for filling in the information from a tape-recorded or videotaped weather forecast in the target language.

The purpose of this kind of activity could be made more meaningful if the learner had to decide which clothes to wear for an imaginary outing, based on the weather forecast, or if they needed to tell a family member how to pack for their coming trip to the city or country in question.

As with any formal listening activity, the teacher would prepare students by activating their existing knowledge of weather vocabulary and expressions, perhaps by brainstorming what they could expect to hear in the weather forecast and creating a word bank or a web of vocabulary. Thus prepared, the students would be much more likely to succeed in the listening experience.

Students need to be carefully prepared for any formal listening or viewing experience. For example, before viewing a videotape about the celebration of Karneval in Germany, students could talk about celebrations they enjoy in this country—in German, of course. The teacher might lead them to share ideas about costume parties, costumes, parades, festive foods, and music—while the teacher or a student writes these ideas on the board. Their purpose in viewing the videotape might be to identify characteristics of this celebration that are the same or different from those they are familiar with at home.

There are many ideas for activities that will give students practice with listening and viewing in the interpretive mode:

- Students might view television advertising in the target language, or listen to radio commercials, in order to choose among several options for the same product on the basis of pre-established criteria. Using the same materials, they might compare the most important criteria (adjectives) listed in the target language with those that would be stressed in an American commercial for a similar product and develop a Venn diagram, creating a good opportunity for addressing the comparisons standard.

- Directions for a task or a project can be an opportunity for extended listening practice. An audiotape or videotape might be set up at a learning center, for example, with directions for completing a puzzle, coloring a picture or chart, or for doing a paper-folding activity.
- Some teachers have recorded a story or a set of directions—perhaps for a homework assignment—on a telephone answering machine. Students call the number and listen to the message in order to complete a task or solve a problem. This is a natural type of listening activity for the telephone-addicted middle school student!
- Sometimes background information about a new unit or project can be presented in modified "lecture" format—another opportunity for practice with interpretive communication.

Many activities that begin as an opportunity for extended listening flow naturally into reading, speaking, or writing—in fact, these competencies are closely interconnected. The Gouin series (see Chapter 3) is a good example of this flow. It begins as a listening activity, heavily supported with actions and sometimes visuals. The series can become a reading activity, as students place written statements from the series in order; or it can develop into a speaking activity, in which students recite the series and perhaps make variations on it.

Reading

Reading is another dimension of one-way, interpretive communication, Standard 1.2. As with listening, reading activities are most successful when they take place for a purpose. Many reading activities will parallel those designed for listening—only the medium for the message has changed. As with listening, the challenge of reading in the interpretive mode is to provide students with opportunities to use reading as a tool, for a purpose, within a familiar and meaningful context.

Reading activities that address the interpretive standard will build on and use the literacy skills discussed in Chapter 6. The interpretive standard is primarily concerned with reading to learn, rather than with learning to read. The goal of these activities will usually not be simple one-word or one-sentence-at-a-time reading. Instead, students will work with longer, connected texts, including authentic materials.

The process of understanding written language involves drawing on experiences and information already stored in memory. Frank Smith (1997) explains, "Reading depends more on what is behind the eyes—on *nonvisual information* than on the *visual information* in front of them" (34). Preparing students for new reading experiences involves activating this nonvisual information. If students do not already have a conceptual framework for what they are about to read, it will be impossible for them to have a successful reading experience. These structures for organization of meaning are called *schemata*. Reading can be understood, then, as a complex process of meaning construction by the learner, who takes information from the printed page and constructs meanings based on schemata already held in memory. The following activities all draw on existing visual and nonvisual information that learners already possess.

Sample Reading Activities in the Interpretive Mode

Students can use selected target language ads or Web sites, for example, to gain information about products that they might want to buy on an imaginary trip to the country in which the language is spoken. There are numerous Web sites available for children who speak the target language, and many of these contain games or information appropriate for American target language learners. They all involve reading the target language for a purpose!

For example, fifth grade German students might read letters from German children describing their household pets, in preparation for writing a description of their own pets. These letters are available on the Blinde Kuh Web site for German children (www. blindekuh.de). The students might later write their own letters to be submitted for inclusion on the same Web site.

Middle school students might read brochures from a variety of cities in the target culture, scanning for several pre-determined characteristics, and then make recommendations as to which city the class should choose for an imaginary trip to the country.

There is clearly a very close connection between reading and writing. Some of the best reading materials for early language learners are those written by themselves or by their classmates. Some very meaningful writing experiences flow from what students have read. Because both the language and the context are familiar, students can read one another's written work for interest and enjoyment.

The Language Experience Approach, described in detail in Chapter 5, is an excellent starting point for this type of reading. The teacher and the class together write a brief story about some shared experience, such as a cooking activity, a field trip, or a story they have enjoyed. Students then read the new story aloud, copy it, perhaps illustrate it, and then take it home to read to others.

The little "puzzles" shown in Figures 4.4a and 4.4b, written by students, provide reading experiences for their classmates—with the purpose of solving the puzzle.

The puzzle frame in Figure 4.5 provides opportunity first for student writing at the single word level, filling in the blanks of a self-description. The self-descriptions can then be posted on a "puzzle board," and students will experience reading for a purpose as they try to guess who is being described.

Many of the examples of student writing presented later in this chapter can be used to provide reading opportunities for other members of the class. Poetry of various types, silly descriptions, new versions of familiar stories, and theme and picture books can all serve as effective reading materials in the early language classroom.

Reading aloud to others is an interesting mix of interpretive and presentational communication. Students can read class-developed books to family—or even to children in other classes.

One of the important elements of the interpretive mode is the ability to recognize and interpret the cultural information embedded in a written, oral, or visual text or product. In order to help students progress toward meeting this standard, we need to provide them with many authentic listening, viewing, and reading experiences. Unfortunately, much of the reading material designed for native speakers of the same age as our students is far too sophisticated linguistically to be appropriate for novice readers.

Materials designed specifically for language learners can serve as a bridge to later independent reading of authentic texts. We need to be careful, as we choose these texts, that the reading material is interesting, communicates needed and important information, and is at the appropriate linguistic level for our students. Some teachers have created their own texts, based on the interests of their students and on the themes presented in their teaching

FIGURE 4.4   Students fold down the flap on these puzzles to see if they have the correct answer.
Source: Reprinted by permission of Patty Hans.

FIGURE 4.5   These self-descriptions can be posted for reading practice.

Wer bin ich?	**Who am I?**
Meine Augen sind _____	My eyes are _____ (color) _____
Meine Haare sind _____	My hair is _____ (color) _____
Meine Lieblingsfarbe ist _____	My favorite color is _____ (color) _____
Ich habe im _____ Geburtstag	My birthday is in _____ (month) _____

units. Some teachers have even made such materials available on their Web sites, for their own students and for other teachers and students, as well. One good example is Lori Langer's Web site, www.miscositas.com, on which she provides beautifully illustrated retellings of authentic stories from Spanish-language and French-language cultures.

Before early language learners attempt to read longer passages or stories independently, it is essential that considerable pre-teaching and preparation take place. Phillips (1984) suggests the following:

Pre-teaching:
1. Brainstorming to generate ideas (and maybe vocabulary) that are likely to occur in the text. These might be written on the chalkboard and later used as a word bank.
2. Looking at visuals, headlines, titles, charts, or other clues that are provided with the text.
3. Predicting or hypothesizing on the basis of the title, first line, or other clues what might happen in the text.

Of course, there are many different elements of reading that our students need to develop, some of which are natural components of the elementary and middle school curriculum. They can read a weather forecast to determine what clothes to pack for an imaginary trip to Hamburg; they can read clues to help them decide where to find a hidden treasure. Reading for specific information can become part of any unit or theme. We need to give our students practice with the skills that will help them to become effective readers.

Among other things, Phillips suggests these activities:

1. Getting the gist of short readings, paragraphs;
2. Identifying topic sentences and main ideas;
3. Selecting the best paraphrase from multiple-choice options of the main idea of a text or of the conclusion;
4. Matching subtitles with paragraphs;
5. Filling in charts or forms with key concepts;
6. Creating titles or headlines for passages;
7. Reacting in some global fashion to a reading passage.

Students can learn to skim a passage to determine in general what it is all about. Then they can scan the passage to locate a few of the main ideas related to its general meaning. Finally, the students can read more carefully in order to achieve their intended purpose. These activities, like the activities in the Phillips list, need to take place within a meaningful context, in which reading is done to accomplish purposes that are important to the student and not just to the teacher.

The goal of all these activities is to move students toward ever-greater independence as readers, whether their purpose is reading for information or for personal enjoyment. This is an important step in moving their learning beyond the classroom into the community (Standard 5.1) and into their personal world (Standard 5.2).

Standard 1.3: Communication in the Presentational Mode
Students present information, concepts, and ideas to an audience of listeners or readers on a variety of topics.

This standard involves oral or written presentation of information, concepts, and ideas to an audience with which there is little or no interaction. In most cases it involves one-way communication in which the audience cannot modify the message or interact with the writer or speaker for purposes of clarification.

In presentational communication, oral or written language is used to accomplish a meaningful purpose. Because there is an important audience, or an important purpose, the learner is more likely to recognize the value of clarity and accuracy in communication. For this reason grammatical accuracy and cultural appropriateness take on greater importance, and careful editing and practice become shared goals for the students and the teacher.

The presentational mode builds on and may go beyond the single words, memorized chunks, and shorter utterances that are characteristic of interpersonal communication for novice learners. In early language classrooms, presentational communication will rely heavily on memorized language, of course, and will need to be heavily scaffolded—that is, it will require a considerable amount of instructional support.

Speaking

One of the best ways to encourage the development of speaking competencies in the presentational mode is through the performance of skits and dramatic songs. Children love to act out stories, songs, and skits for each other and for other classes. Of course, these presentations also serve as interpretive listening experiences for their audience.

Many of the songs presented to students in primary school involve physical actions, accompany dances, or tell a story. All of these types of songs can be presented dramatically to an audience of parents, other students, or community members.

Presentations and performances are popular culminating activities for a unit, and they lend themselves well to sharing with a wider audience. Some types of performances include the following:

Plays in which every student takes a role.

Performances of authentic songs, accompanied by culturally appropriate instruments, such as recorders or rhythm instruments.

Small group presentations of scenes from an authentic story that accompanies a thematic unit.

Student-created skits that tie together the language and information from a thematic unit.

Puppet plays, written by the students and presented before an audience.

PowerPoint or other types of media presentations to share the information gained through research into a topic drawn from the thematic unit.

Short speeches advertising the attractions of a city or a famous landmark in one of the countries in which the language is spoken.

Videotapes or audiotapes of commercials for real or imaginary products that are useful or practical in the target culture.

Videotape production of "how-to" shows, such as how to prepare a recipe or the steps in a craft project—taken from the target culture, of course.

Production of a video essay about the students' school and school life to send to a partner class or partner school in a country where the target language is spoken.

Presentations can be excellent culminating activities for a unit or a series of lessons. In TPR Storytelling, for example, one of the goals is to bring students to the point where they can write and act out their own variations of the stories originally presented by the teacher. Many other classroom activities lend themselves to polishing up and presenting for an audience.

Opportunities for making presentations abound. Parent-teacher organization meetings are always looking for willing program participants. Students can perform for other classes, as part of school assemblies, and for special "classroom programs" to which family members are invited. Some teachers record student performances on videotape or audiotape and students can borrow copies to take home to show their families.

The important element in all of these activities is the audience. Preparing for an audience motivates concern for accuracy and effectiveness. In the case of presentations for an audience of native speakers, attention to cultural expectations also becomes important.

It is evident from many of the examples we have identified that there is a close relationship between oral and written communication for presentation. Students usually write their skits and edit them before presenting them orally. Written revisions of a story can be read aloud to an audience.

Writing

The writing dimension of presentational communication has much in common with speaking. The emphasis here is on developing a product for an audience, and for a purpose. Unlike worksheets, or comprehension questions at the end of another language exercise, writing in the presentational mode has a purpose that goes beyond fulfilling an assignment just to satisfy the teacher. In planning activities that help students work toward this standard, teachers might ask themselves, "When and why would they do this activity in the real world?"

Carolyn Andrade and Julie Benthouse Banner (1993) clearly summarized the potential and the focus of writing in a Central States Conference presentation. Most of their summary is especially applicable to the presentational mode:

Writing
- expresses meaning
- allows for practice (this would be an exercise, or a building block—see Chapter 6)
- provides opportunities to combine learned elements
- results in a product that is a measure of proficiency, and is viewed as an accomplishment by both the author and the teacher

- lends itself to sharing of a social event in the school with classmates or across grade levels, at home, or in other settings
- lends itself to collection
- reflects the creativity and individuality of the author
- involves complex operations that are different from those required for speech.

Successful writing activities provide
- a framework of linguistic structure
- outlets that allow for self expression and creativity, so that the student's writing can extend beyond the model
- realistic, reliable, appropriate, and understandable products.

Written Products Using Individual Words.   Students can use single words to make a creative representation of a vocabulary item or a concept. Sometimes classified as concrete poetry, these products are enjoyable for both the creator and the audience. One strategy is to use the repetition of a single word to develop a picture that represents the meaning of that word. More frequently, several words are used, each outlining a different part of the picture. Figure 4.6 shows two pictures developed in this way, one of a house and another of a head, both using German vocabulary words.

There are many possibilities for using the repeated-word strategy for creating written products for an audience. Teachers must be careful, however, that whatever the student is writing so many times is being written correctly, since practice tends to lead to permanence.

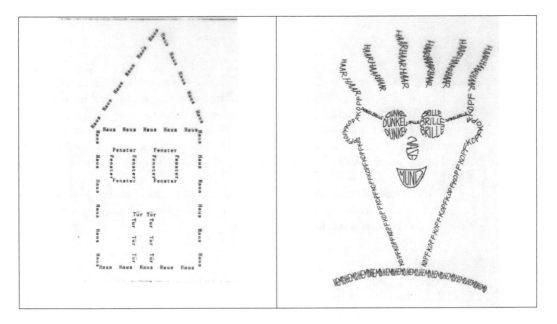

FIGURE 4.6   Repeated words are shaped to form a picture. This strategy requires accuracy and creativity.
Source: Reprinted by permission of Melanie Engel Unger.

FIGURE 4.7   These word pictures reflect the meaning of the words themselves.

Another single-word strategy is presenting a single word, often a new vocabulary word, in such a manner that the way in which the word is written or drawn portrays the meaning of the word. Figure 4.7 shows two examples, both from Spanish. The first depicts the meaning of the word for eye; the second portrays the meaning of the word for clock.

The examples in Figure 4.8 use a word as the basis for a picture of the object.

A more sophisticated use of shape or concrete poetry at the one-word level would be to have the students draw a shape such as a heart, but instead of using the word "heart" over and over, they might use the word "love."

FIGURE 4.8   These drawings were created by students of Rita Gullickson, Whitmall (WI) Middle School.

Scaffolds.   Writing in the presentational mode needs to be heavily scaffolded at early stages of language learning. That is, the writing is based on a clear and well-established pattern, and students succeed by contributing their own content to the pre-existing pattern.

This poem frame, found in a regular second grade classroom, would be an excellent starting point for creative writing with beginning language students. The frame, of course, would be provided in the target language, not in English.

Snow

Snow is as _____

as _____.

Snow is as _____

as _____.

Snow is as _____

as _____.

Snow is as _____

as _____.

by _____

A similar activity, conducted in the target language, would begin with brainstorming of some of the words associated with snow, listed on the board as a word bank. Then the class would brainstorm some things that are similar to snow in some way, listing these words in a separate word bank. The class might then create a group poem as a model, and then each student would create her or his own poem. The poems might be posted in the classroom, or gathered into a class book.

Table 4.2 is another example of a poem built on a similar type of frame—an ode to the color white—in Spanish!

TABLE 4.2   A Pattern Poem Based on the Color White

Blanco	White
Blanco es el color de la nieve.	White is the color of the snow.
Blanco es el color de las nubes.	White is the color of the clouds.
Blanco es el color del invierno.	White is the color of winter.
Blanco es el color al opuesto de negro.	White is the color opposite of black.
Blanco es el color de un oso blanco.	White is the color of a white bear.
Blanco es el color de mi papel.	White is the color of my paper.
Blanco es el color de un cisne.	White is the color of a swan.
Blanco es el color mío cuando estoy miedoso.	White is the color that I am when I am afraid.

The fantastic pictures in Figure 4.9 were the product of another type of writing template or frame. Each middle school student created her or his own fantasy animal by combining the characteristics of three different animals. They then named the animal and described it, using a grammatical framework provided by their teacher, Rita Gullickson:

Here is the writing frame:

My animal is a _____
It has the _____ of a _____
It has the _____ of a _____
And the _____ of a _____
It is _____ and _____ (characteristics)
(It is also) _____ and _____.

One of the beauties of this type of writing activity is that the products can be used in so many different ways. Each student's writing serves as interesting reading material for other students in the class—and it is almost guaranteed to be at an appropriate reading level.

Mi animal es un ofanteafa. Tiene la cabeza como el elefante y las piernas como la jirafa. el es lento, grande, feroz y pesado.

Caridad Falkowski

Mi animal es un jirafpingüpaj. Tiene la cabeza como la jirafa. Tiene el estómago como el pingüino y las piernas como el pájaro. El es tímido y lento. También es alto y grande.

Linda Zoltak

FIGURE 4.9 Student writers in middle school classes create fantasy animals.
Source: These drawings were created by students of Rita Gullickson, Whitmal (WI) Middle School.

The descriptions could be separated from the pictures and placed on notecards. Each student could be given a different notecard and see whether they can match the description with one of the animals posted around the room (interpretive communication).

The teacher or a student could read a description aloud and class members could try to draw a picture of the fantasy animal. They could then compare their animals with the originals (interpretive communication).

Finally, the pictures and their descriptions could be used in partner activities, in which one partner reads a description and the other partner tries to draw the animal. The partner doing the drawing can request clarification along the way. After the activity they can check to see how close their pictures came to those of the original artists (interpersonal communication).

Janet Glass, who teaches at Dwight-Englewood School, Englewood, New Jersey, follows up a similar activity with a reading experience at an "art gallery":

> We have come across about twenty-five or thirty animals in the stories, songs, and games we've done so far this year. I elicited the words and wrote them on the board. I asked them to draw a new animal (a composite) from three different ones and write on the back what they were. As an example, I drew an *oveja-elefante-pajaro* on the board. I told them not to copy from anyone and to keep it a surprise.
>
> The next day I had prepared an Art Gallery with all their pictures hanging around the room. Each one had a number. I gave out a sheet that listed them but not in order. The students had to walk around the room and find which one matched, for example, *vaca-mariposa-gallina*. They then wrote down the number of what they thought matched. Of course they talked about it (all in Spanish) while they were doing it and they read it. They all used their imaginations, too, which made it great fun.

A favorite idea among drawings and descriptions of this type is the monster activity in Figure 4.10! A careful look at the description reveals the supportive framework in place that helps to ensure student success! This would be a natural follow-up to an experience with the book *Go Away! Big Green Monster* by Ed Emberley (1992). This student used many different adjectives, some of which might not have been in the shared vocabulary of the class. An early step in preparing any work for an audience is considering what the audience will be able to understand, as it relates to language structure, vocabulary, and cultural context.

Pattern Poems.   The pattern poem has many possibilities for harnessing the creativity of young learners and focusing it through writing. One example is the acrostic poem, in which a word is spelled vertically, and words or sentences are arranged around the central word to describe it or express its meaning in some way. This kind of poem can also be used as a self-description, or to elaborate any key word related to the theme.

The example in Figure 4.11 is by a middle school student in Spanish II. He also enhanced his poem, "Gracias" (Thanks), with computer images.

Early creative writing experiences might include simple forms of poetry like *concrete poetry, haiku, diamante,* or *cinquain.*

A *diamante* poem might first be constructed by students and teacher in a whole-class setting, and then individual students or pairs working together might construct their own. It's called a *diamante* because the shape of the poem, when it is finished, is like that of a diamond. The directions for a *diamante* and an example in English follow:

Me llamo Norte.
Soy una persona.
Tengo dos narices y dos cabezas.
Tengo cuatro manos y cuatro orejas.
Tengo tres bocas y tres pies.
Tengo viente dientes y quince dedos en los pies.
Mi pelo *es* corto.

Vivo en el océano ártico.
Soy agresivo y áspero.
Soy liviano y timido.
Soy rayado y chulo.

My name is Norte.
I am a person
I have two noses and two heads,
I have four hands and four ears.
I have three mouths and three feet.
I have twenty teeth and fifteen toes on my feet.

I live in the Arctic ocean.
I am aggressive and rough.
I am lightweight and timid.
I am striped and _____?

FIGURE 4.10 Creating and describing a monster is an engaging activity for learners. *Source:* Created by students of Rita Gullickson, Whitmal (WI) Middle School.

ONE WORD: noun	Cats
TWO WORDS: adjective describing noun	soft, warm
THREE WORDS: participles (or verbs)	play, leap, purr
FOUR WORDS: nouns related to subject	tails, tongues, paws, whiskers
THREE WORDS: participles (or verbs)	bite, lick, tease
TWO WORDS: adjectives	elegant, rough
ONE WORD: synonym for first word	Siamese

FIGURE 4.11 An acrostic poem using "Graçias."

Gracias por	Thank you for
Ropa	Comfortable clothes
Mi c**A**sa linda	A beautiful house
Comida deliciosa	Delicious food
Mis am**I**gos	My friends
El tiempo **A**gradable en octubre y noviembre	Nice weather in October and November
Dia de Gracia**S**	Thanksgiving

FIGURE 4.12   A cinquain has five lines.

1. Choose a subject; identify it in one word.	Winter
2. Describe the subject in 2 words (noun + adjective, adjective + adjective).	white snow
3. Describe an action associated with subject 3 words (often 3 verbs).	skiing, skating, sliding
4. Express an emotion associated with the word, using 2 words.	excitement, joy
5. One word to sum up, express the essence.	Wonderland

Some teachers also use a shorter version of this pattern, with three words in the center of the poem instead of four.

The *cinquain,* shown in Figure 4.12, is similar to the diamante, and follows this pattern:

These formats have the advantage of requiring only single words, a natural task for the novice learner, but when they are placed together in a poem they are both interesting and expressive. The format also helps students to recognize words according to their grammatical category—subtly, of course!

Haiku is a more complex format in that it involves whole sentences rather than just single words. It is a kind of Japanese poetry that paints a picture of nature with words in a very controlled pattern of three lines containing seventeen syllables, as shown in Figure 4.13.

The most important quality of this format, as with others already presented, is the fact that it provides interesting reading for other children and adults because it is personally expressive.

Other Writing Activities.   Writing is one of the best ways to reinforce learning and bring it into focus. Of course, it is most effective when it has a clear purpose for the writer—and a ready audience.

The examples in Figure 4.14 from Patty Hans's third grade French classroom at the Wellington School in Columbus, Ohio, are from the culmination of a unit on the French voyageur in Canada. Each of the students describes herself or himself in comparison with a typical voyageur. The products can be posted as reading material for others, or they can be compiled into a class book and shared in many ways.

The culminating activity for an imaginary trip to France is a postcard home, giving important information about the trip. With this type of activity, students can learn to work

FIGURE 4.13   A simple haiku poem.

Line 1: Five syllables	Summer sun is hot
Line 2: Seven syllables	Making grass and gardens brown.
Line 3: Five syllables	Hurry, bring water!

FIGURE 4.14 Third-grade students in Ohio compare themselves to voyageur.
Source: Reprinted by permission of Patty Hans.

with the cultural conventions for writing in the target language. Postcards provide a good context for early experiences with writing in the presentational mode, because the message is short and highly structured, but the context and the purpose are very realistic.

There are many possibilities for meaningful and purposeful products for early language writers. The outcome of a research project on a country or a city, for example, might be a brochure encouraging visits from class members. A successful project of this type will require clear guidelines, models of what a quality brochure might look like, and careful development of the language and structures necessary to communicate the ideas.

Advertising brochures work for other types of units, too. As a culminating activity to a solar system unit, fifth grade French students developed advertising brochures for their favorite planets. How about a visit to Saturn, with its twenty-three moons? Or if you love the heat, maybe a visit to Mercury is for you!

After reading a heavily patterned book like *Brown Bear, Brown Bear* (1983) by Bill Martin Jr., or *The Very Hungry Caterpillar* (1983) by Eric Carle, students might work in pairs or individually to create their own version of the book, written, illustrated, and made available for other students to read and enjoy.

Diane Harris described this writing project on the Ñandu list serv for K–8 foreign language teachers in June 2002:

> A book project that I completed with fourth grade classes (in their third year of Spanish) was to have students produce a class book about the year, *"El libro del año,"* which incorporated vocabulary for months, seasons, activities, and expressions for weather and preferences (*"me gusta/no me gusta"*).
>
> In pairs, students produced several pages about their specific month. This included writing short sentences (in several short paragraphs) with illustrations and graphics as they chose. I then added a title page (ideas for same provided by class), compiled and spiral bound the book for display.
>
> The students enjoyed this project very much and were very proud (and quite surprised) with the finished product and their ability to "write" in Spanish!

For students who have studied the same language for many years, more extensive writing is an appropriate option. The inspiration for a short story or another writing project can come from anywhere. A piece of art or a cartoon could inspire a story—what happened before, what will happen next? A headline from a newspaper in the target language could be used to create the story behind it, perhaps for inclusion in a class newspaper. The slogan and the picture from a magazine advertisement for a culturally significant product, such as a small car from Germany, could lead to a whole advertising campaign for the product, using different methods of presentation.

More advanced learners can create wonderful reading and listening experiences for younger learners. Middle school students can create picture books for primary school learners and then read them to the children, touching on both writing and speaking in the presentational mode. Of course, this also addresses the communities standard 5.1. Depending on the program, older elementary students would be able to create reading materials for younger students, as well.

As projects become somewhat more complex, they will benefit from the "quality control" that is an important component of process writing. That is, because of the importance of the message and of the audience, there is a concern for clarity, accuracy, and cultural appropriateness that goes beyond the need to please the teacher. When students work together to help each other write as well as they are able, the products—and the students' language—are bound to get better and better.

The process approach to writing incorporates the following steps:

1. prewriting—often in large group, directed by the teacher
2. drafting—alone or with a partner
3. sharing and responding to writing—done with partners or in small groups
4. revision—alone or with a partner
5. editing—with partners or in small groups
6. publishing—final draft!

This process can be introduced and developed from the earliest stages of writing in the presentational mode.

As students become more and more proficient in their language ability, teachers will be guiding their second-language writing and looking to improve it based on the same characteristics that they would use to improve their first-language writing. They would make sure that their writing is appropriate according the primary, or six traits, of writing, listed below.

Primary Traits of Writing/Six Traits of Writing
- Main ideas and content
- Organization
  - chronological
  - spatial
  - logical
  - order of importance
  - compare/contrast
  - clarification

- Voice
- Word choice and usage
- Sentence sense and variety
- Correct spelling, punctuation, capitalization

As we have seen, students can use even very limited language to write information, ideas, and personal expression for an audience. While this chapter has emphasized activities for early stages of language development, the principles of writing in the presentational mode remain the same at every level. As learners become more sophisticated language users, they can take over an increasing proportion of the responsibility for structuring and monitoring their own work. To paraphrase a famous Vygotsky (1986) observation, what learners can do with the assistance of the teacher today, or with the assistance of peers, they will be able to do by themselves tomorrow.

In all the communication modes—interpersonal, interpretive, and presentational, the key element is purpose. As learners discover that they can use their new language to achieve purposes that they feel are personally important, their motivation—and their language competencies—will continue to grow.

Summary

In the balanced approach to communication described in the *Standards for Foreign Language Learning in the 21st Century,* students take on many roles in the language classroom. They are conversation partners in oral and written language, they are audience, and they are presenters. The teacher needs to plan a variety of activities to help students develop the competencies necessary for each of these roles.

The listening, reading, and viewing activities suggested in this chapter are intended as idea starters, not as an exhaustive list. Many of them are drawn from resources available through the target culture, because cultural awareness is a key factor in the interpretive mode. Stories, videos, magazines, and other texts with cultural relevance will help students become more sensitive to the cultural messages embedded within the text.

Similarly, the ideas for the presentational mode in this chapter are just the beginning. As teachers provide students with a wide range of opportunities for presenting oral, written, or visual information to an important audience, students will become increasingly aware of the relevance of linguistic accuracy and cultural sensitivity.

Learners of every age and at every linguistic level will benefit from the opportunity to experience and develop the roles described in the communication standard: 1.1 Interpersonal; 1.2 Interpretive; and 1.3 Presentational.

FOR STUDY AND DISCUSSION

1. Communication is a holistic concept, and the three modes of communication are closely interrelated in "real life." What value is there for the teacher in the early language classroom to consider and plan for them separately?

2. How do listening, reading, and viewing in the interpretive mode differ from listening and reading in the interpersonal mode?

3. How does the factor of audience influence the speaking or writing task in the presentational mode?

4. Choose a story that meets the criteria for successful storytelling as detailed in this chapter. Develop a story skeleton or story map and plan an advance organizer for use in telling the story; plan the visuals and activities you will use to accompany the story, and tell the story to a group of peers or of children.

5. Teacher guides for language arts and other sources can be used to develop a collection of simple forms of poetry for early stages of foreign language instruction. Create sample poems in your language, based on models from this chapter or from other sources, and plan a lesson in which you guide students in the development of their own poem.

6. Add at least three possible writing activities to the list in this chapter. What characteristics do they have that qualify them as activities in the presentational mode? For what grade level and language proficiency level would they be appropriate?

FOR FURTHER READING

The following sources are recommended for additional information about material covered in this chapter. Chapter citations are documented in *Works Cited* at the end of the volume.

Redmond, Mary Lynn, ed. *Teacher to Teacher. Model Lessons for K–8 Foreign Language Educators.* Lincolnwood, IL: National Textbook Company, 1999.

Sandrock, Paul. *Planning Curriculum for Learning World Languages.* Madison, WI: Wisconsin Department of Public Instruction, 2002.

5 Literacy in the Early Language Classroom

This chapter will explore the building blocks of literacy in a second language and answer some basic questions about second-language literacy. In order for students to be able to function in both the interpretive and presentational modes, they must develop the tools to communicate effectively using reading and writing skills in the new language.

In Chapter 3 we discussed the interpersonal mode and showed how functional chunks of oral language—memorized phrases of high frequency—serve as building blocks and preparation for later communication. These memorized phrases, such as "How are you doing?" are learned as a unit long before the individual words are understood by themselves.

In this chapter we will look at the kinds of activities that are building blocks in preparing students at early levels of language acquisition to integrate literacy skills into their language learning experiences. We begin by examining some frequently raised issues about literacy in a new language: the connection between oral and written language, when reading should begin, and the transfer of skills from the native language to the new language.

Connection between Oral and Written Language

From both first- and second-language acquisition theory, we know that oral language is acquired in real-life, natural settings through interactions with others. Oral language provides the basis for both first- and second-language reading. Meaningful reading experiences in both first- and second-language classrooms are dependent on the student's oral language comprehension and also on the student's existing background knowledge and experience. As students develop their listening comprehension, they begin to make connections between oral language and the print that represents this oral language. Some students make this connection much faster than others, and some students find great security and support in having written language available. This is more likely to be the case in grades two, three, and higher.

When Should Reading Begin?

In the classrooms and in the methods texts of the 1960s, reading and writing were considered a potential obstacle to the development of speaking because of interference from native language sound-symbol association. Some methods texts of the time recommended that children in early language programs should not be exposed to the written form of the language for up to three years. We have come to realize that this view was counterproductive, since it does not allow students access to visual stimulus, an important means of conveying meaning.

If reading experiences are related to what they have been exposed to during other classroom activities, students can experience success with reading in the new language even at very early stages. Delaying reading in the new language may be very frustrating to students whose learning styles are more visually oriented. Reading delay may also cause some students to develop their own covert writing system.

Here is an example from a fourth grader in a summer school French class. On her nametag on her desk she had written the following: "un du twa kat sank sees set weet nerf dees" (for *un, deux, trois, quatre, cinq, six, sept, huit, neuf, dix*, or one to ten). This student needed to see the written word and its visual reinforcement. She was trying to remember the numbers in French, and since she did not have access to the written version, she made up her own way to write them.

The best answer to the question of when reading should begin is: As soon as possible! This does not mean that we hand out texts to first graders, or that we focus on reading as the primary way to deliver instruction in the new language. It means that we do not leave literacy out even in the early grades and that in the later grades we refer to and reinforce the reading skills that the students have already acquired. We focus on literacy as a tool for communication.

Transfer of Skills from the Native Language to the New Language

Second-language reading differs from first-language reading in that most of the students (except for those in immersion programs) have already made the connection between meaning and written symbols in their first language. They transfer the skills they have acquired in one language to their new language. Cloud, Genesee, and Hamayan (2000) have described and organized some of these skills.

Decoding Skills: Figuring out words
- sounding out the word
- recognizing a sight word
- using context

Text Processing
- directionality of text (not always left to right, as in English)
- capitalizing a word at the beginning of a sentence
- skimming, scanning, and using other previewing techniques
- using the title and illustrations to understand a passage

Reading Comprehension
- identifying the main idea and important details
- predicting outcomes/anticipating events

- identifying story sequence
- summarizing and paraphrasing

Critical Reading Skills
- discriminating between fact and opinion
- recognizing cause and effect

Literature Study
- recognizing important feelings and motivations of characters
- identifying the conflict

These are skills which, depending on the language level and developmental level of the students, can be called upon in second-language classes and reinforced through reading in the new language.

Communicating with Mainstream Classroom Teachers

As we address the issues of literacy in a new language we must work with the concerns of classroom teachers. Mainstream classroom teachers of students in the early grades, especially kindergarten and first grade, are often concerned about confusion if students see print in two languages. Their concerns are understandable, especially if they have had no previous experience with how children learn new languages. In fact, however, in some schools the reading specialist is one of the most enthusiastic supporters of a foreign language program in which reading and writing are introduced early. For example, Kathy Sthokal, a reading specialist in Appleton, Wisconsin, has seen benefits to the reading skills of second graders who began learning Spanish in the first grade with an approach that includes reading and writing.

In the early grades foreign language instruction does not focus on new reading skills; rather, we work on building the oral language base that provides the foundation for literacy in the second language. The print environment that we provide supports the oral language the students already have. We can reassure classroom teachers that we will not spend our time focusing on reading skills, but instead we will take advantage of the skills students have already acquired in their first language. We use literacy as a tool for interpersonal or interpretive communication in the new language, rather than focusing on teaching the reading skills and subskills.

Schema

One of the most important aspects of literacy is background knowledge. The process of understanding written language involves drawing on experiences and information already stored in memory. For example, if a person does not have a schema for the term *carburetor,* he or she would need a lot of scaffolding in order to understand a text about carburetors. Considerable visual support and other explanations would help that person to understand the meaning of the text. In the same way, learners who are approaching a text in any language need to have enough background knowledge so that they can make sense out of it. This is especially true in second-language literacy. There must be intensive work before, during, and after reading the text to ensure that the students will comprehend what they read, because in second-language literacy there are two elements to deal with: the concept itself and the label for the concept in the new language.

Reading and Writing as Tools for Communication

In the language classroom we want to use reading and writing primarily as tools for communication in the interpersonal, the interpretive, and the presentational modes, and not as ends in themselves. Isolated fill-in-the-blank exercises do not provide meaningful reading and writing experiences. A focus on reading subskills and isolated exercises puts students who are already having difficulty in the first language at a special disadvantage, and reduces their chances for success. In a standards-based early language program, these students can have an opportunity to begin anew with success-building reading and writing experiences in their new language.

In an integrated standards-based approach to language learning, listening, reading, speaking, and writing activities do not take place in isolation, but are interrelated and flow out of the communication task that the learners are performing. The amount of time devoted to reading and writing experiences will vary according to the grade level of the students and the amount of time available for instruction.

Building Blocks of Second-Language Literacy

In this section, we will examine what meaningful reading and writing experiences might look like in a standards-based classroom. As with native-language classrooms, it has sometimes been the case that working on literacy in a foreign language classroom has been limited to drill and practice, with a focus on spelling and grammatical accuracy. Within a meaning- and standards-based curriculum, however, reading and writing can be much more. Copying isolated letters and words has no purpose except for drill and practice. We can find ways to put even necessary drill and practice into a communicative context that makes literacy activities more meaningful for the learners.

First Steps in Reading and Writing for Communication

In preschool and primary school classrooms, beginning reading experiences can focus on teacher storytelling and story reading, with incidental exposure to the written language. This means that the classroom and school can be labeled and that students will see, posted around the room, the written version of the vocabulary and structures that they are learning. A simple way for the teacher to include literacy in the early start language program is by *modeling* the processes of reading and writing during the class. For example, the teacher might write a message to the students to be read at the beginning of class. Most children at grade three and above already have well-established literacy skills in the first language. Once these skills are established, we can use and reinforce them in the new language. With students in second grade and above who are beginners, we may be able to proceed more quickly with written language than with beginners in earlier grades.

Key Words and Word Banks

The key vocabulary words and word bank strategy was initiated by Sylvia Ashton-Warner, in her seminal work *Teacher* (1963). Key words are sets of words requested by students, which are thus of personal interest for them. These students keep a *word bank*—the words they have requested are written on cards that can be saved and referred to when needed.

Students can store their *word banks* in a notebook or in a small file box for index cards. Key words of interest to the entire class can be posted around the room. Word banks can also be developed by a whole class and posted in the classroom in preparation for a specific written or oral activity.

These strategies are used in first-language classrooms to help students make a transition to literacy through their own experiences. In the early language classroom they help students to acquire and use the language that will be most valuable to them in dealing with their own needs and interests.

Environmental and Functional Print

Many children in their native language become readers naturally as they begin to make sense of environmental and functional print—the words on the milk carton or their favorite brands of cereal or candy; names of buildings, stores, and products of interest; traffic and information signs. Foreign language programs usually do not exist in an environment that is rich with public written information in the target language; however, filling the classroom with opportunities for reading can create some of the same opportunities. Environmental print, for this purpose, includes *all* the second-language print that exists in the classroom:

charts	lunch menus
bulletin boards	signs
displays	calendars
passwords	lesson plans on the board
language ladders	class rules
posted Gouin series	and many more

Environmental and functional print also includes the type of written information found in authentic materials from the target culture, writing that communicates needed information that is of immediate value to the reader. Such print might include labels and directions on packages, ads, CD covers, and TV and radio guides.

Teachers can use environmental and functional print to add a dimension of written language to learning activities, even if they are not necessarily literacy-focused activities.

The Language Experience Approach to Reading

A third building block for meaningful literacy experiences in early language classrooms is the Language Experience Approach to reading. This approach incorporates all the communication skills—speaking, listening, writing, and reading—and moves from the interpersonal mode to the interpretive mode and possibly to the presentational mode.

The Language Experience Approach to reading is based on the idea that children will be able to read printed words if these words are part of their everyday language and experience. Familiar experiences are translated into oral expression, then recorded and read. When a visual symbol is connected to the spoken word and the word is part of the learner's experience, the meaning is readily understood and has immediate relevance. The students are not asked to read material for which they have no background knowledge.

Initially, the teacher elicits language from the students through group discussion of an experience. Such an experience might be one in which the teacher, students, and parents in a language class go to a restaurant specializing in that culture's cuisine. In order to write a language experience story about this activity, the teacher might proceed as follows: After the restaurant activity is over, the teacher and the class talk together about what they have experienced. The teacher speaks only in the target language, but the students may volunteer some information in their native language. As the activity progresses, the teacher writes down the students' words and ideas, usually on a large chart or on the chalkboard. The final story for a Japanese class's visit to a Japanese restaurant might be something like this:

We went to the Tokyo Sushi Restaurant.
We took off our shoes.
We sat down on the floor.
We looked at the menu.
We ordered sushi.
We ate with chopsticks.
Our parents ate with chopsticks, too.
We like sushi.

The story might be shorter or longer, or more or less complex, depending on the age and language level of the students, but it is written in the target language.

After the story has been written, the teacher and the students read the story aloud together. Then the story can be copied and illustrated by the students and read and reread at school and at home. In later stages of elementary school language programs, where there is considerable contact time, students might write their own stories and share them at a class story table or in the library.

This approach to beginning reading makes the task easier and less frustrating because reading materials match oral language patterns and draw on personal experiences. We are not asking the learners to try to decipher the unfamiliar or confusing language of texts that are not yet meaningful. In spite of the students' marginal control of the oral language, the introduction to print by way of the language experience approach ensures that learners will understand what they are reading and will find it meaningful.

The Language Experience Approach can be used successfully with both first- and second-language learners. There are some differences in how it is conducted in the two settings, however. While the steps in the process are similar for both groups, the language teacher spends much more time structuring the experience and guiding the dictation process. In first-language classes the teacher writes down anything and everything the children say, with little editing. In second-language classes, the teacher usually has to prompt language and supply vocabulary. The actual language dictated by the children is usually modified (rephrased correctly, where necessary) and sometimes translated by the teacher at this step.

The Language Experience Approach must be adapted somewhat for second-language classrooms to allow for firmer direction from the teacher, but the central concept remains the same—using the students' own background of experiences and their own words, as much as possible, to create the reading text.

Shared Reading

A last building block for literacy experiences in the early language classroom is shared reading: teachers read books aloud to language learners, thus giving them oral language input and a bridge to literacy in the new language. Big books have become a popular way for teachers to engage students in story reading. A big book is an enlarged piece of commercial or student-made literature, intended to recreate the intimacy and good feelings of one-on-one "read-aloud" sessions with an entire class. These are sometimes referred to as "extended lap" experiences. They are labeled "big books" because they are large enough so that the entire class can see and share in the experience. Most big books have a predictable story line with strong rhythm, rhyme, repeated patterns, logical sequence, and supportive illustrations.

Students follow each word in the big book as it is read, thus reinforcing the reading skill of directionality. Students in native language literacy development programs begin to "read" by reciting and memorizing, recognizing sight words, and decoding the text. Students in early language programs can used shared reading experiences to begin matching oral language with the written word. Being able to see the text easily along with the teacher and the other learners helps students to make the connection between the oral language and the print. Reading to students in the new language is a very valuable experience, even if the students do not have access to the text, as in shared reading, because it provides them with the valuable input they need in order to begin to construct meaning in the new language.

Building Literacy in the Early Language Classroom

In this section, we will examine a selection of literacy-building activities that can be done at various levels of language and literacy. We'll start with the most basic: visual discrimination and directionality.

Visual Discrimination and Directionality

Visual discrimination and directionality are some of the most basic literacy experiences. Students need to be able to discriminate shapes and also need to know in which direction the eyes move in order to follow the print within the text. Does the print move horizontally from left to right, or from right to left? Does it move vertically? Books in Arabic open from what we would call the "back," for example. Teachers in Arabic programs who are adapting materials often have to reformat books so that they open in the proper direction. When students are reading in Arabic, Hebrew, and other non-European languages, they must learn that directionality is relative.

Figure 5.1 shows a page from a Japanese class book written by Lynn Sessler-Schmaling and her students from Menasha, Wisconsin. Each student contributed to the book by making an origami fish, pasting it on the page, and then embellishing the page with artwork. Lynn added the word for fish, *sakana,* along with each child's name, to every page. Lynn uses this book to help her students with visual discrimination. She has created an activity that helps them to match up the word for *fish* with its occurrence on their page. The book has a string attached to it with a paper fish on the other end, on which is written the Japanese word for fish. Students take the fish and match what is written on the paper fish with the same word on each page of the book. The other word on each page of this class book is the name of the student who created the page. Lynn also has students match up their names with a card. Lynn is helping her students to make the connection between oral language and print in Japanese.

As we have seen, students in Japanese programs and programs in other less commonly taught languages often have to start at the very beginning with visual discrimination, since they are learning a totally new writing system or systems. Of course, students are also working on visual discrimination and figuring out sight words when they put together a word bank, or participate in a language experience or shared reading activity.

Literacy Building Activities at the Word Level

Most young language learners are familiar with the process of reading and writing and have probably already had the experience with both in their first language. At very early stages, much of the children's activities will be in the form of reading, copying, and labeling, especially at the word and sentence level. It is possible that even at the word and sentence level the students are able to communicate meaning.

FIGURE 5.1   Students match the Japanese word for fish in their class book.

Labeling.   There are many ways to begin second-language literacy activities with labeling. Students can label real objects, either with a label they write themselves or with a label prepared by the teacher. They can hold up labels in response to questions asked by the teacher. They can label diagrams and graphic organizers. They can label the classroom, including not only the objects and furniture, but expanding the effort into such areas as labeling the walls with the cardinal directions—north, south, east, and west. Students in early language programs are often engaged in labeling activities in which the basic objective is that they connect printed language with the oral language they have learned.

Other Word-Level Literacy Building Activities

Here are some other examples of word-level activities:

- Match the written word with a picture on the whiteboard or magnet board, or in a game such as concentration or dominoes.
- Respond to true-false questions about familiar stories.
- Given a list of items sold in a store, make a list of things to buy for a parent, for friends, for a party, and so on.
- Create collages with visual representations of specific vocabulary.
- Pick a movie from the movie page in a target language publication and write down information to share with a friend.
- Given a list of jobs written in a "job" jar, pick out and list the ones they hope to draw.
- Complete graphs, charts, and maps to give personal information or show preferences.
- Write the names of people in a family picture.
- Make as long a "word snake" as possible—write strings of words in which the last letter of one word is the same as the first letter of the next.
- Label items in a picture.
- Write a menu for a restaurant, choosing items from a list.
- Write a restaurant take-out order, choosing from items listed on the menu.
- "Shop" out of a target language catalog, making a list of items to buy and filling out an order form (simplified for beginning students).
- Given a chart on which foods are listed by food groups, write a menu for a balanced meal.
- Make a list of items in a picture and sort them according to category.

Sorting and Classifying as a Word-Level Activity.   Sorting and classifying is an inherently meaningful activity because it is cognitively engaging. When students sort and classify words, they must attend to them carefully so they can put them in the correct categories. Each time a word is repeated in a different categorizing exercise, the students must attend to it again. Each repetition forces the brain to deal with that word again, and after enough repetitions, sooner or later the word will "stick." Here is an example of how this might work. Given a set of vocabulary words related to food, we can ask the students to sort them in various ways. For example, which foods grow above the ground? Which grow below the ground? For which foods do we eat the stem, the root, and the leaf? Which foods do we eat cooked or raw? There are many more possibilities: foods I like or don't like, hot or cold foods, processed or unprocessed foods, salty or sweet foods, and so on.

Sentence-Level Activities

- Read and write songs, rhymes, and poems that have been learned orally.
- Write weather reports and include pictures.
- Compare weather in two countries.
- Write action (TPR) commands for students to give to each other or to the teacher.
- Rewrite a TPRS story.
- Write mathematics problems.
- Fill in balloons in a comic strip with very simple captions.
- Supply simple dialogue for pictures or picture books.
- Write simple captions for pictures in a class or personal album.
- Have students keep their own journal, or notebook of classroom requests, and classroom-centered survival vocabulary.
- Write recipes.
- Write and deliver a note in a classroom mailbox or on a classroom message board.
- Write questions for interviews about favorite television shows, pets, travel, favorite foods, teachers, subjects, et cetera.
- Write invitations.
- Write birth announcements.
- Write a reading action chain (see Chapter 14) or a Hear-Say (see Chapter 6) activity.
- Write learning logs using memorized chunks of language.
- Write questions to an historical figure about his or her place in history.
- Fill in the end to a sentence that begins with a prompt such as: "I feel happy when . . . I feel sad when . . .)

Paragraph-Level Activities

- Create pattern stories according to a model that students have heard and seen.
- Draw a picture and write about how you are dressed now, draw a picture and write about what you will be dressed like when you are grown up.
- Describe the house you live in now, describe the house you will live in when you grow up.
- Write class experience stories.
- Write introductions (to people, places, books, etc.).
- Write daily journals.

Hildegard Merkle has enjoyed using a literacy-building activity from Germany in a game-like context. She gives these directions for a *Laufdiktat,* or walking dictation:

Goal/Purpose:	To read and write from memory
Materials needed:	Teacher: Different cards/strips with the target vocabulary
	Students: Paper and pencil

Procedure:	After reading a picture book, telling a story, cooking following a recipe or any language activity, write the target vocabulary on cards and hang the cards facedown in different locations in the room. To ensure high success, review the target vocabulary by helping the learners to imagine the items with closed eyes and then drawing them in the air, on a partner's back, on their own arms, or something similar. Using TPR commands, instruct the students to take paper and pencil and draw the target vocabulary items.

Then **model** (don't just describe it!) the walking dictation carefully:

1. Put down paper and pencil. Pick up your imaginary camera.
2. Go around the room, looking for a card. Turn one card over.
3. Take your imaginary camera and take a picture of the writing on the card; "exposure time" can vary as needed by the student.
4. With the picture in your mind, go back to your place, pick up your pencil, and write the word(s) you see in your mind to label the picture you have drawn.
5. Look carefully at what you have written, put down the paper and pencil, go back to the card, and compare the writing with your mental picture.
6. If it is incorrect, go back and correct your writing. If it is correct, go to the next card and repeat.

Set a time limit and instruct learners to begin.
Closure: Read the story again and allow learners to compare their work with the original.
Suggestions for intermediate and advanced students:
Instead of single words, write a story or a poem in several sentences on the cards. Follow the same procedure as above. The students first write all the sentences in random order and then sequence them. Closure would be the reading of the story or poem. It is more interesting if there are several possibilities with surprise endings!

Phonics and Grammar

Using phonics methods alone is not sufficient for young language learners. Younger students who are not yet at the stage of abstract thinking are not able to focus on grammatical rules and reading and writing activities based solely on grammar. These students need reading and writing experiences that are connected to their lives in a natural way. They also need to have real-life experiences or experiences with interesting books in order to develop a base of interesting things about which to write. It is very difficult to make the connection between reading and writing if the only experiences students have with writing are connected to isolated drills and practice exercises in workbooks.

What about Accuracy?

Young world language learners may not yet be accurate spellers in their native language since accurate spelling is something that does not develop until the late elementary grades. It is important to have flexibility, so that in some early writing experiences the focus is on communicating important and meaningful messages and not necessarily on accuracy for everything that is written. Accuracy will increase as the students progress toward accuracy in their native language and as they develop skills over time in the second language.

Students who are dyslexic in their native language will experience similar difficulties in a second language. A reasonable accommodation can be found by not holding them to a higher standard in the second language than they can show in their first language.

Round Robin Reading

One practice that is not beneficial to early language learners is commonly called "round robin" reading: (students reading from a selection one after the other in a predictable order.) Reading should be approached first of all as a process for deriving meaning from the printed word and not for using the printed word as a stimulus for speaking, or a kind of recitation. "Round robin" reading, often seen in elementary school language classrooms, is not an appropriate strategy for developing reading skill in a second language.

Round robin reading tends to encourage students to respond to the surface features of the language and not to the message. Many students master the "trick" of sound-symbol association without developing skill in comprehension or communication. Because reading aloud is a practice with such a long tradition, it gives many teachers a sense of security to use it as a strategy; however, current understanding of the reading process does not support its continued use.

Reading aloud can be very useful when it is done for meaningful communicative purpose, such as:

- sharing a part of a story that students especially liked
- reading part of a story that they have written or something that they want to share
- reading parts of a play practicing for a performance
- reading to a child in a younger grade
- reading to a partner in order to practice for reading the same book at home to their parents
- practicing reading to a partner in order to prepare for reading in another setting.

Summary

In this chapter on literacy in early language programs we have explored the building blocks of literacy in a second language. While there is sometimes controversy about the issues of when reading and writing in a foreign language should begin, experience has shown that language learners can be exposed to written forms of the language from the beginning of the language learning experience. Students transfer the literacy skills they have learned in their first language to their new language, although this process is more complex when writing systems in the new language are very different from those the students have already learned. As we communicate with classroom teachers and reading teachers, we can reassure them that we will be building on language and literacy skills that are already in place, and that literacy skills in the first language will not be threatened by the process.

First steps in reading and writing in a new language include the use of key words and word banks, enriching the classroom environment with environmental print in the target language, the Language Experience Approach to reading and writing, and regular shared reading experiences. Helping students to build literacy skills in their new language requires many meaningful opportunities to read and write, at the word, sentence, and even the paragraph level.

A few strategies found in some first-language classrooms are not useful in the foreign language setting. A phonics focus is not as effective as reading and writing experiences that are directly connected to students' lives and interests. An emphasis on accuracy in spelling and grammar is not appropriate in early stages of learning a new language.

FOR STUDY AND DISCUSSION

1. Imagine that you are a K–1 foreign language teacher in a new program. It is your job to explain to the classroom teachers how the new language program will work. You know that concerns are bound to arise about possible interference between the writing system of the new language and the emerging literacy skills in the native language. Prepare yourself for one of these conversations by outlining the message you plan to deliver.

2. Choose one of the first steps in reading and writing and build a lesson plan around use of this step.

3. Round robin reading, as described in this chapter, does not seem to be a very useful strategy in an early language classroom. Describe some possible alternatives that would involve meaningful experiences in reading aloud.

4. Choose a story book and develop a walking dictation activity to use as a follow-up to reading the story aloud several times.

FOR FURTHER READING

The following sources are recommended for additional information about material covered in this chapter. Chapter citations are documented in *Works Cited* at the end of the volume.

Cloud, Nancy, Genesee, Fred, & Else Hamayan. *Dual Language Instruction: A Handbook for Enriched Education*. Boston: Heinle and Heinle, 2000.

Peregoy, Suzanne, and Owen F. Boyle. *Reading, Writing and Learning in ESL: A Resource Book for K–8 Teachers*. 3rd ed. Boston: Allyn and Bacon, 2001.

Yopp, Ruth Helen, and Kallie Kay Yopp. *Literature-Based Reading Activities*. Boston: Allyn and Bacon, 1996.

6 Interpersonal Communication

Partners and Small Groups

Cooperative Structures: Cooperative Learning and Interactive Language Tasks

Interaction is the key to language development for second-language learners, and interactive language tasks are among the most important means by which this communication can be accomplished. Part of the challenge for the early language teacher is giving students sufficient opportunity for interaction and interpersonal communication within the limits of a short class period.

In the elementary or middle school language classroom that is oriented toward communication, the traditional large-group, teacher-led structure has severe limitations. Communication flows primarily in one direction, from teacher to students, and learners have few opportunities to test their own use of the language for personal communication. Yet both cognitive learning theory and second-language acquisition theory tell us that for children to learn, it is important for them to express themselves orally. Expressing concepts, putting them in our own words, explaining them to others and speculating about them aloud, making applications of concepts to new situations, and finding creative and personalized ways to remember new concepts or language materials all contribute to genuine, successful learning.

Cooperative learning in the form of partner activities and small-group work holds much promise for the early language classroom. When children learn to work cooperatively in small groups or in pairs, their opportunities for language use are multiplied many times over, as are their opportunities for active participation in concrete and meaningful experiences. Small-group and partner activities, as contrasted with large-group, teacher-fronted activities alone, have numerous advantages for the language learner:

- many opportunities for language use
- a chance for natural language practice
- more student talk
- a higher percentage of student talk in real communicative activities
- a "safe" environment for communication, more like one-on-one conversation
- two-way communication—a chance both to ask and answer questions

In addition to the language benefits, partner activities specifically provide other benefits:

- variety in class routines and activities
- opportunity for students to practice social skills
- students are "center stage" rather than the teacher
- more on-task behavior, according to Nerenz and Knop (1982)

Nancy Foss, from Concordia College in Moorhead, Minnesota, has researched the interaction between learning styles and foreign language proficiency. According to her studies, partner activities in the foreign language classroom may be the only type of speaking activity that is comfortable for every learning style (2002). For the learning style that likes groups, pairs are almost as good, and for other styles, pairs were preferred to groups.

It is important to emphasize here that partner and small-group activities are not a strategy for teaching language. They are a very effective strategy for practicing language that has already been learned through a variety of other activities, and for using that language to achieve important goals. When partner and small-group activities are introduced prematurely, before the needed language is readily available, students will be frustrated and they are likely to revert to English in order to achieve the task. One teacher observed that the more engaging the activity is, the more likely the students are to complete it in English, especially if they are not comfortable with the language needed for accomplishing the task.

Developing Cooperative Skills

Children need just as much guidance in developing cooperative skills as they do in developing communication competencies. The early language classroom is a natural setting for this growth.

Small groups and pairs, in order to function successfully, require that certain elements of cooperative learning be in place (Johnson and Johnson 1987):

1. *Positive interdependence* means that everyone depends on one another and that no one feels exploited, unnecessary, or left out.
2. *Face-to-face interaction* is possible only when children are in a physical setting in which they can talk with one another and work together easily, without raising their voices.
3. *Individual accountability* is in effect when each child knows that she or he may bear full responsibility for the information or the skills being learned by the group. There are no hitchhikers—only full participants.
4. *Social skills training* is an integral component of all the work in the cooperative classroom. The teacher helps children to understand the skills they will need to work successfully together and helps them to practice and monitor them. As is the case with language skills, a few specific cooperative skills will be highlighted at the beginning, such as making sure everyone has a turn to speak, giving encouragement, and listening when other group members are talking. Additional skills can be added after practice of the first skills has become habitual. Only development of the skills of working and living cooperatively can make communication possible, in either the target language or the native language.

5. *Group processing* of the cooperative skills is just as important to the classroom routine as are quizzes and other strategies for determining progress in the subject content. The teacher helps children analyze what is working well in their group and what can be improved, offers suggestions when individual groups are having specific problems, and focuses the attention of the entire class on a limited, manageable number of skills at a time. Much of the group processing can take place in the target language, providing an additional area for meaningful communication within the classroom. At the end of an activity the teacher might ask, for example, "How did your group do today about making sure everyone had a chance to speak? Hold up three fingers if you feel you did great, two fingers if you need some improvement, and one finger if you need to really work at this." As an alternative, the responses could be written, or decided on by the group and then reported.

Proponents of cooperative learning indicate that roles have an important place in the development of social skills. They also have an important place in the development of language; that is, functions, since many of the roles develop language functions that are an integral part of the second-language curriculum. Some of the roles that could be assigned include:

Encourager/Praiser
Reinforces group members for performing well or staying on task.

Manager/Timekeeper/Supervisor/Checker
Organizes the group, keeps the group on task, makes sure everyone contributes.

Recorder/Secretary
Records group answers.

Spokesperson/Speaker/Reporter
Reports back to the whole class

When roles are explained, the teacher might teach and practice the language needed for each of the roles, possibly posting it on the wall as a reminder. For example, the encourager might say, "That's a good idea. Good job, Mary! We're doing a great job of getting this done." The manager might need to say, "Do you have any ideas, Dave? We just have three minutes left. What shall we do first?" The recorder would need to be able to ask for clarification and repetition. The spokesperson and reporter would need to check for clarity. Roles should shift with each task, so all group members have the opportunity to perform all the roles. Before each task begins, the teacher might ask, "When I come around to listen to you work, what will I hear the encourager say that will show me that that person is doing a good job? What will I hear the manager say?" and so forth. This should all take place in the target language.

Winn-Bell, Olsen, and Kagan (1992) present a useful list of group and task roles that are valuable in themselves, but in addition carry with them an important language component. Learning how to interact in a group will have both short-term benefits in the students' own cultures and long-range benefits, should they have the opportunity to travel to the target culture. This kind of experience will enable them to be more open and receptive to speakers of the target language. Some of the group-related social skills for which the teacher will provide language and support include the following:

asking for help
complimenting
sharing courtesy
following directions
listening
talking in turn
using first names
acknowledging others' contributions
praising others
recognizing others
verifying consensus
keeping the group on task
mediating disagreements of discrepancies

Some of the task-related social skills are:

asking for clarification
asking for explanations
checking for understanding
elaborating the ideas of others
explaining ideas or concepts
giving information or explanations
paraphrasing and summarizing
maintaining eye contact (a culturally based behavior)

Managing Small-Group and Partner Activities

Some teachers have not had a lot of experience with small-group and pair work and may have concerns about placing students in a situation in which they have more independence than in traditional large-group instruction. They may also have anxiety about classroom noise and the potential for off-task behavior and disruption, but if partner and small-group activities are carefully planned for, the benefits to student learning will far outweigh these challenges.

Classroom management changes dramatically in the implementation of cooperative learning activities. Traditionally, class activities are relatively simple, and students do little talking and interacting. In fact, the goal is often to keep students from talking at all. Cooperative learning activities are more complicated and do not offer the simple, quiet classroom found in other types of classroom management. Cooperative activities can be noisy, the rooms need to be arranged differently, and the teacher may have to function as a resolver of conflicts, especially among students who are resistant to working with others. Most of all, the teacher has the role of a facilitator rather than that of a manager.

Organizing Small Groups

Students in a classroom might be divided into long-term groups by "family," with each family seated around its own table. This allows children who are going to be given target language names to have a last name as well as a first name. Within the small group each member might be assigned a role: mother, father, sister, brother, grandparent. The teacher can use the family groupings to assign tasks within the group: today the mother will be the leader, the father will be the recorder, and so forth. The small group could form the basis for a simulation in which one family encounters another family on an outing and introductions are made all around. This type of simulation allows for meaningful use of language in an imaginary setting.

Organizing small groups for short-term activities can be done in a number of ways. Rita Gullickson keeps a basket of plastic-colored clothespins near her classroom door. As students enter the room they take one of the pins and clip it to their clothing. For example, all those wearing purple clothespins work in one group and all those with yellow pins work in another. Colored pieces of paper, colored toothpicks, colored teddy bear counters, colored candies, or any other manipulatives could function in much the same way. Deborah Roberts (2002) takes this strategy one step further by having the students choose a group name based on the color—for example, yellow might be the sun group.

Roberts offers a number of other interesting ways to form groups. She suggests that students can be given a simple arithmetic problem on a notecard, and they form a group with others whose arithmetic problem has the same solution: 12×5, $30 + 30$, 15×4, and so on. Students can be grouped in categories, and items belonging to those categories are written on index cards. For example, one student has food and others have hamburger, bread, grapes. In a similar strategy, the teacher might use countries and cities: Deutschland, Berlin, Frankfurt, München. Another variation of this strategy would be for students to receive index cards, some of which have single letters. Other students have combinations of letters that, when combined with the single letter, form a word. For example: C/offee/andy/old.

Groups can also be formed by counting off. The teacher first decides how many students will be needed in each group for the planned activity. Then the teacher divides the number of students in the class by the number of students planned for each group, and students count off by that number. For example, for groups of five in a class of thirty-five students the students would count off by seven—students count from one to seven and then begin again with one, counting until everyone has received a number between one and seven. With young children especially, it is helpful to have each child hold up their fingers for their number until all the counting is completed—so they don't forget their number. After the number is finished, all the number six students form a group, as do all the twos, and so on.

Groups can be organized by putting together the pieces of a cut-up shape or a puzzle to make a whole, or simply by drawing names of other class members. Groups could be organized by historical figures, for example: the kings and queens of France could be one group, French musicians another, French artists another, French sports figures another, and French scientists another group. Food in various parts of the food pyramid could constitute another method of grouping; or animals in different habitats might be another grouping strategy.

Some ways to organize students into groups require little preparation and can be language activities in themselves. For example, students can organize into groups by make of family car. Those who have the same family car form a group. If there are unbalanced numbers, the teacher can intervene and quickly make two or three groups out of a very large one, or send a few students to another group. Other ways to organize include:

number of hours they slept last night, or time they went to bed

number of siblings/family members

number of syllables in their name

shoe styles

shoe size or color (the teacher can form groups with various sizes together in same group)

Organizing Partner Activities

In most cases it is desirable for students to work with a variety of partners over a period of time, and not choose their own partners. Classes can be organized for pair activities in a variety of ways. Partners can be organized informally, simply by saying: "Turn to the person next to you, turn to the person in front of you, go to another person in the room who is wearing the same color you are," and so on. One middle school teacher gives students ten seconds to make eye contact with a partner and get together with that person—silently. Counting off works for partners, too—in a class of twenty students, students could count from one to ten twice, or using letters A–J twice, for example.

Inside-outside circles (Figure 6.1) is another effective way of organizing the class so that students have a chance to work with several partners in succession. The teacher divides the class into two groups, perhaps by having them count off by twos. Ones form a circle and face to the outside of the circle. Twos form another circle around the first circle and face to the inside. Each student should be facing a partner. In this situation the students can practice a conversational exchange, such as a simple greeting, asking age, something about favorites, or whatever interaction needs practice at the time. It is most effective if the students are actually learning something of interest about their partners. As soon as the exchange has been completed, on a signal from the teacher, students in the outside circle move one partner to the left around the circle. Only one circle moves, and always in the same direction. The conversation is repeated with a new partner, and on signal the outside circle moves again. The circle keeps moving until it returns to the place it started.

A variation on the circles theme is to use two lines of students facing each other, which is especially useful when there isn't room to create circles. One of the lines rotates, with the person at the head of the line moving to the end of the line each time (Figure 6.2). Sometimes students in both lines can move, with the students on each end moving to the other line after each exchange (Figure 6.3). This gives students a greater variety of partners to work with.

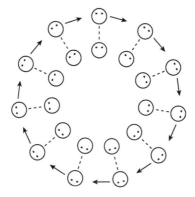

FIGURE 6.1   Inside-out circles.

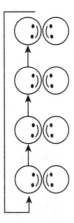

FIGURE 6.2   One line rotates, the other stays in place.

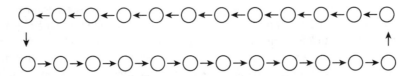

FIGURE 6.3   Both lines move, and new partners face each other.

This use of rotating lines is especially useful if partners are practicing two lines of a dialogue, because it feels more like real communication when students work with different partners.

Partners can be organized more formally. The teacher can prepare sets of cards with identical matching pairs and distribute them to the class; the students circulate until they find the person who has the matching picture card (numbers, shapes, animals, foods, and so on). For example, a student who has the number three must find a partner who also has the number three, or a student who has a picture of an animal must find the person who has the same picture. Alternatively, the teacher might prepare card pairs in which one card has a picture or a numeral and the other card has the word written out.

The teacher can prepare and distribute sets of cards with pairs that are matched by relationship; students find their partner by locating the person who has the related card. In this way the matching of partners becomes a learning experience in itself. For example, one partner has the name of a country, the other the name of the capital, or one partner has one half of a proverb from the target culture and must find the partner with the other half. Matches can be organized using many different categories, such as:

- first names and last names of artists or historical figures
- various forms of a verb
- singular and plural forms of nouns
- opposites
- synonyms

- subject with appropriate verb form
- matching puzzle pieces of pictures or words (art pictures and proverbs and common sayings also add a cultural dimension)
- matching common expressions, such as "Happy/Birthday," "Good/Morning"
- two-line conversational exchanges or dialogues
- associations, such as hammer/nail, hospital/nurse, red/apple

Another way to organize partners is to use a procedure in which partners are assigned for a period of time. One such procedure is called "partners around the clock." Each student has a piece of paper with a blank clock face large enough to write names next to each hour on the clock (see Figure 6.4). The teacher might draw a line on which students can sign their names. The teacher gives directions for the activity and sets a time limit. Students arrange to meet a different classmate for each hour on the clock, so that there is a different name written next to each number. They cannot arrange more than one meeting per hour. Students arrange their meetings by moving around the classroom asking each other questions, such as: "Are you free at one o'clock? At three o'clock? Are you busy at noon? Can we meet at five o'clock?" After the designated time period is over, the teacher makes sure that each student has a partner for each hour by quickly asking who still needs a partner for each hour in turn. Those who are missing certain hours can then make appointments with each other. This is especially helpful for those students who are shy or who may not be the first ones asked by other students.

If at the end there are still some students without partners, those students can "double book" and make some groups of three. It is important that each student be represented in the activity, even absent ones. Students can make appointments with the clock on the absent students' desks, for example. Roberts (2002) suggests the possibility of having students

FIGURE 6.4   A large clock can be used to organize communication among partners.

make two dates for some of the times on the clock, in order to make groups of three (or three dates for groups of four).

Once all the times have been filled in, the teacher can then use the clock as the basis for organizing interviews or for any other language tasks. For example, "For the next activity you are going to be working with your three o'clock partner"; "Discuss with your ten o'clock partner the solution to the puzzle on the chalkboard." The students can keep their clocks for use over several days or weeks, or for the duration of a unit. The teacher could collect the clocks and distribute them the next time they are needed. If students keep the clocks, it is a good idea for students to make an extra set of the clocks for the teacher, in case one or more students lose them.

This activity can take on a greater cultural dimension by using a map of the target language country or city with lines for signatures drawn in various places. For example, students with a map of Japan can ask another student, "Can I meet you in Tokyo? Can we see each other in Kobe? Do you have free time in Kyoto?" Using a variety of devices such as this for organizing partners over a specified period of time frees the teacher from always having to find a different way to get the students to work together. Geography connections could be emphasized by using a world map and arranging meetings on every continent.

Deborah Roberts (2002) uses an engaging activity called "Snowball" to bring partners together. The teacher gives every person in the class a piece of paper, preferably recycled. The class then forms a circle, crumples the paper into a "snowball," and tosses the snowballs up into the air toward the center of the circle. Each student then picks up a snowball, opens it up, and looks for a person in the group who has the antonym (or synonym) of the word on the paper. Together they make a sentence including both words.

Planning Small-Group and Partner Activities

In order to plan for cooperative learning activities and to effectively manage student behavior, several factors must be taken into account. The following guidelines are helpful in developing successful activities and in choosing appropriate activities from a variety of sources. A suggested planning format is found in Figure 6.6.

Not all of these criteria will be applicable to every activity, but each of these items should be considered as the activity is developed.

1. What is the source of the message(s) to be exchanged? What motivates the communication?
   - Is there an information gap?
   - Is there an opinion gap?
   - Is there a reason for the students to want to know the information?
2. What language will be required to complete the activity? How much of it will need to be practiced or reviewed?
3. What will be the product that results from the activity? Can this product be shared or evaluated?
4. How is the language to be used guided, controlled, or scaffolded?
   - Is there a natural limitation because of the task itself?
   - Is most of the language provided in written form?

FIGURE 6.5 Children develop both language and human-relations skills when they work in cooperative groups.

5. How will partners or group members take turns?
   - Is there a built-in indicator for taking turns, like an asterisk in front of the item for the partner who is to ask the question, or have roles been assigned to group members?
   - Does each partner or group member have an opportunity to participate approximately equally?
   - Is there a means to prevent either partner or any group member from dominating the conversation?
6. Can the partners or group members find out immediately whether they have been successful?
   - Is the activity self-correcting?
   - Is there a way for the partners to monitor their own accuracy or success?
7. How can the teacher follow up on the activity in a communicative way?
   - Can the teacher ask questions about the activity to which the answers are not already known? For example, can she or he ask, "What did you find out about your partner or other group member that you didn't know before?" or "Which of the problems did you have the most trouble with?" "Which response or idea surprised you the most?"
   - Will the follow-up to the activity be interesting to the students as well as holding them accountable?
   - What potential exists for oral or written follow-up or homework?
8. If partners or groups finish their task early, how can the activity be extended so that they will be engaged while the rest of the class is finishing?
9. What is the plan for dealing with a student who does not have a partner?
   - Will the teacher take the role of the extra partner? Though tempting, this role removes the teacher from the important role of monitor, and makes it hard to

determine how the task is progressing and what kind of intervention might be needed.

■ Will the teacher prepare one set of materials for three students instead of two, so that the extra student will be accommodated smoothly?

Guiding Small-Group and Partner Activities

Although one of the advantages of small-group work is that it takes the spotlight off the teacher for a period of time, it can only be effective if it is carefully organized and consistently monitored. Especially for the first few times, preparing and conducting such activities may actually require more teacher effort than the traditional teacher-centered classroom style. But the many benefits make partner and group work more than worth the extra effort. The following guidelines, adapted from Knop (1985), Johnson and Johnson (1987), and Kagan (1990), will help the teacher plan effectively for pair or small-group activity in the classroom.

1. *Keep the group size small; start with pair activities.* It is easiest to start with pairs for the first experience with group activities. Cooperative groups are usually most effective when they are comprised of no more than five people, and they should never be larger than seven.

2. *Set the stage; motivate the activity.* When the teacher sets the context for the activity dramatically, using actions and visuals, it enhances motivation. It is also helpful to give each activity a name, making it easier for students to request it again and to recall the rules the next time the activity is introduced.

FIGURE 6.6   Planning format for cooperative learning and partner activities.

Topic/Theme:

Grade Level:

Language Level (Beginning, Intermediate, Advanced):

Title:

Type of Activity (jigsaw, finding differences, following directions, arrangements . . .):

Objective/Outcome:

Product:

Receptive Vocabulary (Vocabulary teacher will use):

Productive Vocabulary (Vocabulary and structures students will practice during the activity):

Directions (Exact wording of directions that will be given to the students):

Time limit:

Communicative Feedback/Processing:

Procedures:

Source (If activity is not original, source for the original idea. Here also should be listed where needed visuals can be found):

3. *Set clear goals; describe the outcomes clearly for the students.* Students should understand how the language task relates to the context provided by the teacher and recognize the outcome as satisfying some purpose or interest. Included in the goals should be clear expectations about the use of the target language during the activity.

4. *Make sure the students have the target language they need to accomplish the activity, that they know how to say what they will need to say.* Review and practice the language needed by each partner in order to complete the activity successfully. For many activities the actual language to be used can be printed on the task sheet, so that students can focus on communication and practice accurately at the same time.

5. *Give exact directions for every step of the task.* Carefully prepare and sequence the instructions for the activity so that they are as simple as possible and can be presented in the target language. To appeal to different learning styles, directions should be both oral and written, perhaps provided on the activity itself, or written on the overhead projector or chalkboard.

Model the sequence of the activity in precise steps, so students know exactly what is expected of them at every step of the way. You may model both parts yourself, or begin by working with the whole class so that the teacher plays the part of Partner A and the rest of the class plays the part of Partner B. An individual student might play Partner A while you play the role of Partner B, or you might bring up two students and have the class watch them go through the steps of the entire activity.

Get student feedback on all the steps to be sure students know how the activity will proceed and will not waste time during the activity itself:

Teacher:

Who begins the activity?

What does Partner A start with?

What does Partner B do?

What else does Partner B do?

What if Partner B doesn't agree?

What does Partner A do next?

6. *Set a time limit.* Set a time limit to help students feel accountable and to make the best possible use of the time available to them. It is effective to use a kitchen timer with a loud bell or buzzer to provide a neutral timekeeper and a clear signal for the end of the activity. Adjust the time limit if necessary during the activity, to allow for less time if students are finishing early or more time if the activity takes longer than expected.

7. *Circulate among the students throughout the activity.* Circulating allows you to monitor use of the target language, language problems the students are having, and success or failure in the use of cooperative skills. You can also show interest in the students' conversations and give suggestions when they need help. Moving among the students, especially if you have a clipboard in hand, is also a form of control for on-task behavior. Provide positive feedback and give attention and special recognition to the teams that are most on task.

8. *Establish a system for getting the attention of the students back to you.* Establish a way to get the noise level down when it is necessary. Many teachers use a hand signal such as a raised right hand to get the students to give their full attention to the teacher and to keep their hands and bodies still. The teacher initiates the signal by raising the right arm in the air. The students respond by stopping their activity, becoming quiet, and showing the signal back to the teacher and to the other students with whom they are working. (This helps to give some of the responsibility for control back to the students.)

9. *Elicit communicative feedback and process group effectiveness at the end of the activity.* Not every pair or every student needs to be reached after every activity, but call for responses at random so students always feel accountable. Rather than simply checking only for the correct solutions for the task, use communicative feedback techniques that extend the language used in the task. This can be interesting to the whole group. For example, in an activity related to foods, the teacher might ask: "Is the dinner your partner planned one you would eat?" "Did your partner or group members say anything surprising?" Also, regularly use the feedback period to assist students in evaluating the effectiveness of their groups.

A number of resources for small-group and partner activities are listed at the end of this chapter.

Sample Cooperative Group Activities for Beginning Language Learners

Students can work together in a small group to solve a problem or develop a response to a situation the teacher designs. There are many types of interactive language tasks. A pair or small group might design a series of commands to give to another small group or to the teacher, orally at first and perhaps later in writing. The members of the small group might rehearse with one another to make sure that everyone in the group is able to ask to go to the bathroom or to sharpen a pencil, to ask to have something repeated, to agree or disagree. The shared teaching task creates a kind of validity for the communication in and of itself, because it is being directed toward a goal and being managed and monitored by the students themselves.

Jigsaw.   In a pair or small-group setting of three to four students they might work with a "jigsaw": each has a certain amount of information that, when combined with the information from the rest of the groups, will lead to the completion of an assignment. In a jigsaw activity, for example, each student might be given part of the information necessary to find a location on a map, to choose an appropriate gift for a parent, to identify another member of their class, and so on. As they share the information orally, the students solve the problem and also practice the language involved.

In the jigsaw activity in Table 6.1, each student has a piece of information about an animal from the unit just completed about the African continent. Each student reads the information on the sheet that they have been given, one animal at a time. Students proceed through each person's description until they figure out, as a group, which animal is being described.

TABLE 6.1 Jigsaw Activity Identifies Animals in Their Habitats

Student A	Student B	Student C	Student D
1. It's an African mammal.	1. It has stripes.	1. It's black and white.	1. It ends in A.
2. It has black spots.	2. It lives in forests.	2. Found in Africa and Asia.	2. It's in the cat family.
3. It lives in the savanna.	3. It has a long neck.	3. It's up to 5.5 meters tall.	3. It eats from trees.

Let's Have a Dinner Party.   The following cooperative learning activity, appropriate for early language learners, is called "Let's Have a Dinner Party!" (Table 6.2). In this activity students are assigned various roles and tasks and work in a cooperative group to plan a meal. Students are given food options (in their target language) and are helped with the language they may need in order to accomplish the activity. Each group member is responsible for making sure that one food group is represented. The menu must include a variety of colors, shapes, and textures *and* every member must agree to the entire dinner and enjoy eating it! This activity adds a kinesthetic dimension since the students must draw (using crayons or markers) the dinner they have planned on a paper plate. As follow-up the class

TABLE 6.2 Task Sheet for Cooperative Activity "Let's Have a Dinner Party!"

Tasks:
Create a dinner menu with your group.

The menu must include a variety of colors, textures, and shapes.

If necessary, you may use foods not listed on this sheet.

Every member must agree to the entire menu and enjoy eating it!

Roles:
Each group member is responsible for making sure one food group is represented.

One member is recorder. The recorder will draw the menu on a paper plate so that you can present it to the rest of the class, and then write the menu down.

Language to be used
Let's serve. . . .

I really like. . . .

I don't like. . . .

We need a different (shape, texture, color).

Fat, Oil, Sugar Group

butter	deep-fried onion rings
chocolate cake	pecan pie
French fries	potato chips

TABLE 6.2 Continued

Dairy Group

milk	ice cream	custard
Swiss cheese	yogurt	cheddar cheese
cottage cheese	chocolate pudding	

Bread/Cereal Group

French bread	whole-grain bread	popovers
rice	pancakes	white bread
blueberry muffins	sourdough rolls	
tortillas	cornbread	

Meat Group

beef steak	veal	salmon steak
pork chop	meatballs	baked chicken breast
sausage	lamb	roast turkey
hamburger	frankfurter	fried chicken
beef roast	shrimp	
ham slice	walleye fillet	

Fruit Group

fruit cup	melon	strawberries
peach sauce	orange slices with coconut	cherries
grapes	pears	pineapple chunks

Vegetable Group

French fries	spinach	carrot sticks
fresh grapes	green beans	acorn squash
cole slaw	cauliflower	sliced tomatoes
broccoli	mashed potatoes	tossed green salad

can vote on their favorite dinner of those presented, students can write about the dinner their group has planned, or write about a dinner that they would like to plan for themselves. As a variation to this activity, students can plan a trip with the clothes they will take and the itinerary they will follow. In order to integrate mathematics, they can be given a certain budget to work with.

Sample Partner Activities for Beginning Language Learners

Because of the power of partner activities in the development of communication competencies, especially the interpersonal mode, there are a growing number of resources commercially available for older learners. Many high school and college textbooks incorporate partner activities, for example, and some books of activities focus on one-on-one interaction. Partner activities can be fully as effective and useful with young learners, as the following examples will show.

Partner activities can range from "drill in disguise" to a meaningful exchange of information, depending on the degree to which the participants have real motivation to complete the task, the degree of investment in the outcome, and the level of autonomy in setting up the task. When the students see a clear purpose for the activity and it results in a product or a solution that has individual meaning, it is more likely that real interpersonal communication is taking place. For example, in the dinner party group activity described earlier, the decision about a meal that every member would eat reflected a real-world challenge and called for genuine communication to negotiate a result—the "real" answer was not predetermined by the teacher. The resulting menu was shared with others as a culmination of the task.

The jigsaw task relating to animals in Africa was predetermined by the teacher, but the puzzle context was more motivating than a simple drill. In the examples below, there is a range of activities from "drill-in-disguise" to more communicative tasks. All types of partner activities have value. Those on the drill end of the spectrum give needed practice in a sheltered setting. More communicative, personally motivated activities help students to develop their interpersonal language competencies. As teachers we can work toward increasing the level of communication in our partner and group tasks and regularly raise for ourselves the nagging question from Kieran Egan: "Why should it matter to children?"

Informal Pairs: Students Working Together to Complete a Task

In an informal pair, partners work together to get a task finished or to share information that is available to both of them. Informal pairs can be as simple as "turn to your partner and say 'good morning.'" "Turn to your partner and tell your partner your favorite color." "Tell your partner the first step in this activity." This use of pairs is a kind of sheltered practice that helps to create a climate of cooperation and to move the focus from the teacher back to the students.

Partners can show each other their answers to a problem or a question in order to check it. They can turn to each other with greetings at the beginning of the class and say good-bye at the end of the class. In Tara Kraft-Mahnke's Spanish class in Appleton, Wisconsin, the students greet three fellow students each morning and exchange one polite comment, such as "How are you?" Informal pairs might take turns reading from a text or reading to each other the stories they have written. They might work together on a task assigned by the teacher.

Patty Ryerson Hans does partner work even with her pre-kindergarten and kinder-garten students, but she notes that the teacher is nearly always the leader in the activity, guiding the children in the process of sharing, cooperating, and taking turns (Partner A, hold up the bag; Partner B, take the red block out of the bag . . . and so on).

For early stages of language development, a back-to-back TPR partner activity can be both fun and useful. After learning a number of colors, for example, students might stand back to back with crayons in their hand for all the colors they have learned. Partner A might call out, in the target language, "Show me red!" at the same time pulling out the red crayon and holding it out. Partner B also finds the red crayon and holds it out. Together they count to three in the target language, and then they turn to see if they have chosen the same color. Then the partners go back to back again and Partner B gives the command. The same type of activity could be used with body parts, emotions, or any vocabulary to which a gesture has been attached. It might be especially useful with TPR Storytelling. This activity is self-correcting in that the person giving the command is unlikely to choose something about which they are not certain themselves, and it could be used as a sponge activity when there are only a couple of minutes left in a class.

Information Exchange Tasks

In contrast to informal pairs activities, information exchange tasks require students to inter-act in order to exchange information to accomplish a task. These exchange-of-information tasks are sometimes referred to as "information gap" or "opinion gap" activities. One part-ner has information or an opinion that the other partner needs or wants to find out. After the task is completed, each partner will have obtained new information from the other and will have completed some type of informational objective.

Several common variations of information exchange tasks are:

- interviewing or surveying
- finding differences and/or similarities
- following and giving directions
- finding and giving information

Interviewing or Surveying. In interviewing or surveying activities, each partner inter-views the other, or interviews other members of the class one at a time in order to gain information. Here are two examples, each of which could serve as a model for others on different themes, and with different structural emphases.

Find Someone "Find someone" is an interview activity that can be used again and again. It is often used as in ice-breaker activity but it can be used in many other ways. In Figure 6.7 Marianne Soldavini, an ESL teacher in the Milwaukee Public Schools, uses it as part of a nutrition unit.

Figure 6.7 Worksheet for Find Someone Who.

Find someone who likes to go to McDonalds.	Name _____
Find someone who ate breakfast this morning.	Name _____
Find someone who can name a protein.	
_____ name of protein	_____ Name
Find someone who can cook something.	
_____ what they can cook	_____ Name
Find someone who can tell you one of the food groups.	
_____ a food group	_____ Name
Find someone who hates to eat broccoli.	Name _____

Marianne Soldavini, Milwaukee Public Schools

What's Your Pastime?   For this interview students are given a list of pastimes, all of which have been studied recently in class. Their task is to find a student in their class who does each of the activities in the list. The interview sheet would look like the one in Figure 6.8 (written in the target language, simplified as necessary).

The activities here would be chosen from among those the teacher knows the students enjoy, based on activities earlier in the learning sequence. After the students have finished the interviews, the teacher will follow up by asking:

Who plays tennis? (Someone will give the name of a person whose name they have written down.)

Who else plays tennis? (Other names will be read.)

Does anyone else play tennis? Raise your hand. (Possible hands are raised.)

Who plays the piano? (One student says, "Mary plays the piano.")

Who can tell me something else about Mary? (Some students may have Mary's name listed for another activity, so the teacher gets a description of Mary's interests.)

Mary, do you play anything else? (Mary may add something.)

The follow-up can continue in this manner until the teacher is satisfied that the students have achieved the purpose of the task and their curiosity has been satisfied.

How Was Your Weekend?   This activity (Figure 6.9), designed by Nancy Foss of Concordia College, is a "missing information pair activity" that combines a personal interview

FIGURE 6.8 Surveying activity related to pastimes.

The principal has just announced that several students from Switzerland will be visiting our school for two weeks. Their teacher provided us with a list of interests and hobbies for these students, in the hope that there would be students in our class with whom they would have something in common. Interview the other members of the class until you find at least one person interested in each activity—no more than one activity per person, please. Conduct the interview using the following format:

Hi, Mary.

Hi, Johnny.

Do you (like to) play _____

Yes, I do.

Good. Write your name on the line.

When you have all the blanks filled, see if you can find additional people for some of the activities. You will have ten minutes to complete this survey.

Do you play tennis? _____

Do you play the piano? _____

Do you play chess? _____

Do you play soccer? _____

Do you play jazz music? _____

Do you play classical music? _____

Do you play cards? _____

Do you play the violin? _____

with a kind of jigsaw, in which each partner has different information. The first step is for each partner to answer the questions for himself or herself, using a + sign for yes and a – sign for no. Then the partners ask each other what they ate/drank/did on the weekend. The third step is to ask about Ludovic, a young boy from France with whom the teacher has contact. Each of the partners has different information about Ludovic, so they have to ask yes-no questions to determine how his weekend went. The partners, and later the class, can then compare their weekends with that of Ludovic. The addition of a real French boy adds a valuable cultural connection to this activity. Of course, when used in the classroom, the interview sheets would be written entirely in the target language. This template can be used with any topic, and the column for Ludovic could be replaced with the teacher, the music teacher, or a real contact from the target culture.

ESP! This activity is adapted from Dr. Constance K. Knop, who has presented many helpful workshops about partner activities. The activity is called "ESP" because it gives

On the Weekend... A

This weekend did you...	Ludovic	You	Your Partner
Eat an apple			
a pizza	-		
a sandwich	-		
rice			
pâté	+		
gruyère cheese			
Drink water	+		
Coca Cola			
milk			
café au lait	+		
wine	+		
Go to a soccer match			
Spend 5 hours eating with your family	+		

On the Weekend... B

This weekend did you...	Ludovic	You	Your Partner
Eat an apple	+		
a pizza			
a sandwich			
rice	+		
pâté			
gruyère cheese	+		
Drink water			
Coca Cola	-		
milk	-		
café au lait			
wine			
Go to a soccer match	-		
Spend 5 hours eating with your family			

FIGURE 6.9 On the weekend . . .

Source: Designed by Nancy Foss

students a chance to test their extrasensory perception. The key factor in this activity is the fact that students predict their partner's answers, thus intensifying their own involvement in the activity and making them more interested in the answers to their questions.

Each student receives the same list of forced-choice questions about her or his preferences, based on theme vocabulary from recent class work. Each partner decides on her or his own choice for each item, and then looks intently at his or her partner in order to see if she or he can sense what the partner has decided for each item. Then each partner writes down a prediction for each item for the other person. The partners take turns asking the printed questions in order to determine whether their predictions were accurate. The number predicted correctly is the ESP "score." If students finish early, they can predict the teacher's answers, or the teacher might give the list to the principal or another familiar school figure ahead of time and then ask students to predict that person's responses. The answer sheet might look like Figure 6.10.

As a variation on the ESP activity, the teacher might collaborate via e-mail with a teacher in a classroom in the target culture and use a student from that classroom as the third person to predict.

The ESP activity is especially versatile, because it could be redesigned to use the concepts in nearly every unit. The process would continue to be engaging because the information would be new each time, and probably the partner would be different as well.

FIGURE 6.10 ESP activity.

¡¡ESP!!

Do you know your partner? Can you read your partner's mind?

1. Decide how you will answer each of the questions. You must choose one answer.
2. Look at your partner. What will your partner answer?
3. Write down what you think your partner will answer for each question.
4. Partner A asks the questions first. Score one point for each correct prediction.
5. Partner B asks the questions second. Score one point for each correct prediction.

Who has the most ESP?

If you have time, work with your partner to predict how the principal would answer.

	Partner	**Principal**
Do you prefer soccer or football?	_____	_____
Do you prefer popular or jazz music?	_____	_____
Do you prefer movies or concerts?	_____	_____
Do you prefer cards or board games?	_____	_____
Do you prefer to watch tennis or golf?	_____	_____
ESP Score: _____		

Interviews like these are usually intrinsically interesting, because students want to know what other students think, or what other students have to say about a topic. Some topics that could be developed into interesting interviews include:

number of brothers and sisters
favorite TV shows
favorite/least favorite foods
favorite animal
names of pets
tasks that are liked/hated
profession in the student's future

Finding Differences and Similarities. A typical pair activity for elementary school learners is based on the idea that each partner has different information and the partners must find the differences in order for the pair to reach a common goal. For example, each partner might have a sheet of paper with pictures arranged in the following order. This activity comes from a unit on animals and their habitats (Figure 6.11A and 6.11B).

Partner A begins the activity, because Partner A has an asterisk next to number one on the first set of pictures. Partner A names the pictures in number one in order, and Partner B compares what Partner A reads with what is found on her or his sheet of paper. If they match, Partner B says, "It's the same." If they don't match, Partner B says, "It's different." Just to be sure, Partner B might name the animals in the order found on her or his sheet. When the partners decide they have a match, they place a plus sign on the line following the item. If they decide they don't have a match, they place a zero or a minus sign on the line. Then Partner B names the animals in order as they are found in item number two on her or his sheet, because Partner B has an asterisk beside that item. The activity continues until the students have made decisions on all six groups of pictures. Only then do the partners compare sheets to see if all their decisions are correct.

This activity can be a two-level activity, because after students have decided whether each of their rows is the same or different, they can take another step. Do all of the animals in number 1A and number 1B actually live in the same habitat? This activity could become more of a puzzle and less of a drill if part of the task was to find the misplaced animals—that is, animals in the wrong habitat—and determine to which habitat they all belong. Then the directions might be something like this:

"After we made these lovely groups of matching animals for you, some animals wandered into rows where they don't belong. Tell your partner the names of the animals in each row that has an asterisk, and see if it is the same or different from your partner's row. If it is different, decide which animal doesn't belong in the habitat and write down that animal's name (or draw a circle around that animal). When you have finished comparing your rows, decide what habitat all those wandering animals belong to and draw a picture of it."

The type of matching activity described above can have endless variations, depending on the language skills of the students and on the goals of the activity. Students working on reading skills might match a picture with a word, or a more complex picture with a written description.

In another finding differences activity, students compare single pictures that have relatively small but noticeable differences. Each student has a different version of the same picture, and students have to find the differences between them without looking at each other's pictures. This activity is considerably more difficult than the activity above, because partners must use descriptive language and questions as they try to determine how their pictures differ. To avoid frustration, it is helpful to tell the students how many differences there are to find. Another variation might be to set a time limit and challenge students to see how many differences they can find. This version of finding differences, in which each partner has a single picture, is a template for practice of any language, culture, or curriculum concept. All that is needed is a black-and-white picture of the items to be practiced and a bottle of Wite-Out so that the picture can be slightly changed.

In another variation of finding differences, one partner has a single picture and the other partner has two or more similar pictures. The first partner describes the picture and the other partner tries to determine, from the description and by questioning, which of the pictures is the same as the one being described.

Following and Giving Directions

Block patterns. In another common type of pair activity, one partner gives instructions and the other partner carries them out. For example, Partner A has a picture showing an arrangement of colored blocks. Partner B has actual colored blocks, which she or he must

FIGURE 6.11A   Animals and habitats: Partner A.

arrange to match the picture, based on instructions given by Partner A. If the instructions are not clear, Partner B can ask questions to clarify the task. After the task is successfully completed, the partners switch roles and build an arrangement based on a new picture. Variations of this activity include giving directions for placing furniture in a room, moving a token on a map, or arranging a variety of shapes to form a picture. (Figure 6.12)

FIGURE 6.11B Animals and habitats: Partner B.

As a cultural variation for this activity, the teacher could download a series of pictures by one or more artists from the target culture from the Internet and duplicate small copies so that each student has an envelope with eight or more pictures. The task is for one partner to arrange a display of pictures, using some but not all of the pictures, as if it were to be a school hall display. They imagine that the partner is in the hall, getting ready to mount

FIGURE 6.12   Not all pair activities have to involve reading or paper-and-pencil tasks. These children are helping each other to arrange blocks in a predetermined pattern.

the display, and the first partner has to use an imaginary cell phone to describe how the display is to be put together. After the second partner arranges the pictures, they compare to see if the communication was effective.

Mystery Dots.   This activity involves a "dot-to-dot" picture in which the numbers have been scrambled. One partner has the picture, and the other partner has a card with the correct sequence of numbers that must be followed in order to connect the dots properly. The student with the card tells the partner how to connect the dots, number by number, to complete the picture. (When the teacher puts the activity together, it is helpful to add "distractor" numbers and dots so that the picture being drawn is not immediately apparent.) One way of increasing student motivation is to ask students to write down or circle the dot number at which they first thought they knew what the picture was going to be. Then in the feedback phase the teacher can find out when pairs of students figured the puzzle out, or ask whether the first guess was right or wrong, and so forth.

Dress the Bear.   Each partner has a picture or figure of a bear and a variety of pieces of clothing to place on the bear. Partner A dresses the bear and then tells Partner B how to dress the bear. Partner B can ask questions for clarification. After the directions are completed, the partners compare bears to see if they are identical (Figure 6.13).

This activity could also be extended into a "finding differences" activity. After partners each dress their own bears, they interview each other to find out how the bears are the same and how they are different.

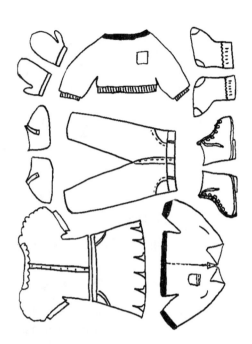

FIGURE 6.13   Dress the Bear

Finding and Giving Information

Let's Make a Sandwich.   Visuals are cut out and each partner receives an envelope that contains small food pictures, including two pieces of bread. Each partner has the same visuals (Figure 6.14).

First each partner individually "makes a sandwich" (using the paper bread and food cut-out pictures) with a specified number of items in it. The partners should not be able to see each other's sandwiches. After each has made a sandwich, they each predict how many things they think will be the same in their two sandwiches, writing down the number secretly. They then interview each other to find out how many things are the same and how many things are different in their sandwiches.

Communicative feedback involves asking questions such as: Did your partner have anything in the sandwich that you would never eat? Did your partner make a sandwich that surprised you? What was in it? How many of you would eat that sandwich? And so on.

As a variation of this activity, students can make "sandwiches" with culturally appropriate bread products and fillings. Some teachers have given students half sheets of paper, folded, and had them write or draw the fillings for their sandwich, and the appeal still seems to hold. Curriculum connections can be made by adding prices, calories, or food groups, and asking students to make sandwiches within a certain budget, a certain calorie

FIGURE 6.14   Let's Make a Sandwich

content, or representing certain food groups. This task has great appeal because it has a kinesthetic dimension. Students can manipulate the pictures in the envelope in different ways. And, of course, many different kinds of pictures with language, culture, and curriculum connections can be put into the envelope.

What's in My Backpack?   Each student draws a picture of a backpack or bookbag on a half sheet of paper or construction paper, folded over (Figure 6.15). Students draw and label a specified number of items in the backpack, consulting a list of possible items posted on the bulletin board or on the chalkboard. The students then consult with their partners to determine what things are in each other's backpacks, keeping a list of what each partner has and doesn't have. At the end of the activity, students can give an oral report to the class about their partner. For example, "Maria has a ruler, she doesn't have a pencil," et cetera.

As a variation, students could go among their classmates looking for students who have chosen the same items to put in their backpack. At the end of the time period, the teacher could determine which student located the most identical backpacks. As another option, students might chart the number of duplicates they find for each of the items in their own backpack.

Using the same idea, students might pack their suitcase for an imaginary trip, pack a picnic basket, or collect any other logical combination of items to compare.

What's on Your Shopping List?   Similar partner activities can be done with written language. Students learn to write by writing, and this occurs first at the word level. In this activity, students choose from a posted list of possible items to create a five-item shopping list for their trip to the beach. They then compare their list with that of a partner, or they could interview other classmates to find someone who has the same list. Better yet, each student might seek someone with a completely different list, so that he or she could share products at the beach!

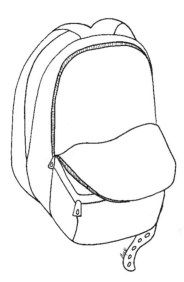

FIGURE 6.15   What's in My Backpack?

Where's the Teddy Bear?   Each partner has a large picture of a house with various rooms like the house in Figure 6.16. Each partner has some small object or party favor, for example a teddy bear counter, which he or she can "hide" in the house.

Partner A places the teddy bear counter or other small object in a room of the house and Partner B must ask questions to find out where the object is hidden. The counter can be hidden in the middle of the room in order to make the questioning and vocabulary easier, or the counter can be hidden "in," "on," "under," or "next to" a certain object in the house, thus increasing the amount of vocabulary being practiced. When Partner B has found the object, then Partner A must look for the missing object that Partner B will hide. The house visual can be used as the basis for other class activities; for example, a next step would be to guess or describe what the teddy bear is doing in the house.

The beauty of this activity is that the teddy bear or other object could be hidden any-where. There is an endless variety of language, curriculum, and cultural connections that can be made as the teddy bear is "hidden" on a picture of a monument, a map, a painting, or in one of the layers of the rain forest. Patty Hans, PK–4 French teacher at the Wellington School in Columbus, Ohio, has her first graders draw a picture of *"mon jardin"* (my garden), adding to the yard or garden gradually as they develop language about animals, fruit, fruit trees, and the prepositions for on and under. Then they use the yard scene as a game board and one student "hides" a token representing an animal "on" or "under" one of the trees in the drawing. The second person guesses where the animal is.

Hear-Say Activity.   This is an activity that calls for careful listening and speaking. Each partner has a grid arranged in two columns, one with an ear or other symbol or words to indicate "I hear" at the top. The other column has a mouth at the top, or another symbol or words to indicate "I say." Partner A begins by saying the word in the "I say" column that has

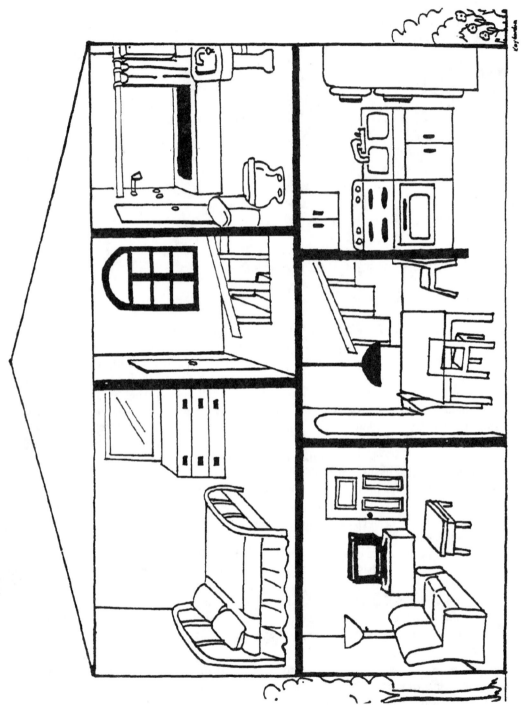

FIGURE 6.16 Where's the Teddy Bear?

an asterisk beside it. Partner B finds that word in the "I hear" column and says the word next to it, in the "I say" column. Partner A looks for that word in the "I hear" column and says the word next to it, and so on, until the process works its way back to the language item with the asterisk. See the example in Figure 6.17. This activity can be repeated with any language items, including pictures, and can be used at any language level. Students might listen to whole sentences, or even descriptions, or put stories in sequence. Once students have done an activity like this several times, they might work as partners to create a "hear-say activity" for their classmates, using familiar vocabulary or concepts.

Corners.   This activity, adapted from Spencer Kagan (1990), provides a valuable and flexible format for early language communication tasks. The teacher posts visuals in each corner of the room (or other appropriate places) and asks the students to think about why they might want to go to that corner, or what kinds of things they might want to do there. The activity is most effective if it takes place within a context. For example, the teacher might explain (in the target language):

> "Imagine that we have just received approval for a class vacation trip later this year. We have four options: the seashore, the mountains, the woods, or the lake. Think about which one of these you would most like to visit on a class trip, and what you would like to do at this location."

> "In a moment you are going to walk to the vacation spot you would choose. When you get there, find one partner and raise your hand silently. Now walk to the picture of the vacation spot you would choose."

> "Now that you have a partner, tell your partner one thing that you would like to do at that vacation spot. Raise your hand when you have both had a chance to speak."

> "Now find another partner and tell your new partner what you would like to do. Raise your hand when you are finished."

> "Now find a third partner and tell that partner what your first two partners want to do."

> "Who can tell me what Mary wants to do at the beach?"

> "Tell me what Richard wants to do in the mountains."

And so on.

The visuals in the corner could represent any number of topics, such as seasons, food, months, days of the week, clothing, cities, countries, continents, occupations, places in the city, types of houses, types of museums, and activities.

The language for this activity can be carefully controlled and teachers can plan for the grammatical structures they would like to highlight. Here is the procedure summarized.

- The teacher announces the corners. It is helpful to have visuals—either pictures or words posted in each corner.
- Students are given time to think about which corner they would like to go to and why. (Some teachers ask students to write the name of the corner to which they are going on a piece of self-stick notepaper. This ensures that students will think for themselves and not go to the corner to which their class friends may be going.)

Hear-Say   Primary Plants A

	A
Plants make our world beautiful.	A seed is a plant.
Animals carry seeds.	People plant seeds.
Seeds need sunlight.	The roots come first.
Then the fruit grows.	A plant can be a bush.
Wind blows seeds.	Water carries seeds.
A plant can be a tree.	Plants are food for us.
The leaves grow next.	Flowers come.
Seeds need good dirt.	Seeds need water.

Hear-Say   Primary Plants B

	B
Plants are food for us.	Plants make our world beautiful.
Flowers come.	Then the fruit grows.
People plant seeds.	Seeds need good dirt.
Seeds need water.	Seeds need sunlight.
A seed is a plant.	Wind blows seeds.
The roots come first.	The leaves grow next.
A plant can be a bush.	A plant can be a tree.
Water carries seeds.	Animals carry seeds.

FIGURE 6.17   Hear-Say Activity Plants

Source: Created by Marianne Soldavini. Milwaukee Public Schools, 2000

■ Students go to their chosen corners and find a partner with whom to share the language task. For example, the teacher may post pictures of the four seasons, and the students may be asked to tell the partner their favorite activity during that season. They may say: "I like swimming."

■ Students then find a second partner with whom they share the same information.

■ Students then find a third partner and tell that third partner what the first two students they have spoken with have said.

■ There is then a feedback period and the results are shared with the class.

Other ideas for corners are posting pictures of different types of shoes or clothing in each corner and asking students where they like to go wearing that shoe or that article of clothing. Scenes or art prints from the target culture could be posted and students could go to the corner of their favorite one and tell their partners why it is their favorite.

This activity can have a greater narrative structure if students are also asked to make a prediction. For example, at the beginning of the class trip activity the students might be asked to think about which vacation spot their teacher would choose, based on what they know about the teacher or the enthusiasm with which the teacher described each of the corners. At the end of the activity, the students could be asked to predict which of the spots the teacher would choose by pointing to that corner. The teacher could end the activity by going to that corner and telling what she or he would do there.

Although there are increasing numbers of commercial sources for partner activities, some of them with copying rights for the teacher, many teachers will find these sources to be useful primarily as models for their own creations. Partner and group activities will be the most successful when they are designed specifically for the interests and the curriculum of a specific group of learners.

Summary

Partner and small group activities are effective and motivating tools for encouraging interpersonal communication. Although these activities take the teacher off of "center stage," they require, if anything, even more careful planning than traditional teacher-fronted instruction. The teacher needs to plan for developing the social skills, as well as the language skills, that are necessary for effective interaction and use of time in partner and small-group activities.

Organizing the class into groups and partners should be part of the learning experience, and can take place in a variety of ways. Activities themselves can range from being "drills in disguise" to highly personal and communicative, but all have the advantage of giving students language practice in a sheltered small-group, interpersonal setting.

With all the activities presented, the importance of meaningful context is evident. These activities can be games, puzzles, or opportunities to learn more about fellow students, but all of them encourage motivation that goes beyond just "the teacher said so." Each activity presented in this chapter is intended as a starting point, or a template, for teacher-designed activities that will build on the language skills and the interests of each teacher and each class.

FOR STUDY AND DISCUSSION

1. What different concerns would you anticipate in planning partner activities for students in the middle school, as compared with students in first grade?

2. How would you explain the purpose of partner- or small-group activities to a parent or a principal who walked into your classroom in the middle of an activity? Assume that the person is somewhat taken aback by the fact that students are not sitting in rows.

3. Design two different types of partner activity for a thematic unit that you have designed, or one that you find in other resources. Use the planning template on page 108.

4. Create a hear-say activity that summarizes the most important guidelines for conducting small-group or partner activities.

FOR FURTHER READING

The following sources are recommended for additional information about material covered in this chapter. Chapter citations are documented in Works Cited at the end of the volume.

Dreke, Michael, and Sofia Slgueiro. *Wechselspiel Junior. Bilder & Mehr.* Munich: Langenscheidt, 2000.

Johnson, David W., Robert T. Johnson, and Edythe Johnson Holubec. *Cooperation in the Classroom.* Edina, MN: Interaction Book Company, 1990.

Kagan, Spencer. *Cooperative Learning, Resources for Teachers.* San Juan Capistrano, CA: Resources for Teachers, 2002.

Klippel, Friederke. *Keep Talking. Communicative Fluency Activities for Language Leaching.* New York: Cambridge University Press, 1984.

McConnell, Mary. *Español En Pareja.* Munich: Langenscheidt, 1991.

McDonnell, Wendy. "Language and Cognitive Development through Cooperative Group Work," in *Cooperative Learning: a Teacher's Resource Book,* edited by Carolyn Kessler. Englewood Cliffs, NJ: Regents-Prentice-Hall, 1992.

McGroarty, Mary. "The Benefits of Cooperative Learning Arrangements in Second Language Instruction." *NABE Journal* 13, no. 2 (winter 1989): 127–183.

Putnam, JoAnne. *Cooperative Learning in Diverse Classrooms.* Upper Saddle River, NJ: Prentice-Hall, 1997.

Sánchez, Juana, and Carlos Sanz. *Jugando en español.* Munich: Langenscheidt, 1993.

7 Integrated Thematic Planning for Curriculum, Unit, and Lesson Design

Why Thematic Instruction for the Early Language Curriculum?

Thematic planning and instruction are among the most important elements of an effective early language program. Our standards orientation calls for integrated learning, with connections to other content areas and to new information through the use of the new language. Our growing insight about brain-compatible learning supports thematic instruction, as well. As we teach new languages to children, our focus is making meaning, rather than making accurate new sounds or grammatically correct sentences (important though these may be). Eric Jensen (1998) suggests that for meaning-making to take place, we should evoke three important ingredients in our general practice: emotion, relevance, and context and patterns (96). A carefully designed theme can incorporate emotion, one of the most powerful channels for learning; relevance, a critical motivator for language learning; and rich context, an element that brings language learning to life and activates the pattern-making functions of the brain.

Much of elementary school curriculum in all content areas is built around themes, often as a means of integrating several subjects during the school day. Middle school curriculum is also growing ever more theme-based, as schools respond to the intellectual, social, and developmental needs of the early adolescent learner. As the language teacher connects language instruction to existing themes or creates language-specific themes, the language class is clearly an integrated part of the school day, and languages are perceived to be meaningful components of student learning.

1. Thematic planning makes instruction more comprehensible, because the theme creates a meaningful context.

In a thematic unit, students can interpret new language and new information on the basis of their background knowledge. They are not just learning vocabulary in isolation; they are using words to identify which animals are endangered in South America, or which foods came from Europe in the Columbian exchange (the goods and foods that were exchanged as a result of Columbus's encounter with the Americas).

Thematic instruction makes the learning more relevant to the learner. When themes are well chosen, students will be more engaged with the learning because they can see its purpose and find it interesting—and fun.

2. Thematic planning changes the instructional focus from the language itself to the use of language to achieve meaningful goals.

In thematic instruction we focus on using the language to communicate something related to a theme, rather than repeating words in isolation with no connection to the classroom or the student. Instead of focusing on how to say or write something, thematic instruction shifts the focus to communicating a message for a reason.

As we shift the focus to what language means and can do, students become motivated to acquire language and to be accurate, because they want to communicate about information that is of interest to them.

3. Thematic instruction provides a rich context for standards-based instruction.

One of the important features of the *National Standards for Foreign Language Learning* is their emphasis on working toward a goal, and focusing on the "big picture"— or the "big idea." A German teacher who helped to pilot the standards commented that with the standards orientation she began planning in bigger "chunks"—essentially, developing themes that worked toward an important goal, over a longer period of time. Many of the scenarios found in the Standards document are also examples of integrated thematic units.

4. Thematic instruction offers a natural setting for narrative structure and task-based organization of content.

Wiggins and McTighe (1998) suggest that the story structure is an ideal curricular design, in which meanings unfold as a unit works its way from beginning to middle to end. Stories make learning easier because the brain is naturally structured to use narrative to organize memory. Task-based learning also has a narrative structure, as students work through the challenges of the unit in order to complete an important final task. Both of these powerful strategies for structuring learning are natural components of a thematic unit.

5. Thematic instruction involves the students in real language use in a variety of situations, modes, and text types.

Thematic instruction, especially when it is organized in a story structure, gives students the opportunity to use language in a variety of situations, including simulations of cultural experiences. A theme lends itself to all three of the communication modes: interpersonal, interpretive, and presentational. Text types within a thematic unit can range from preparing and reading poetry to reading headlines to creating or listening to a description to participating in a conversation to listening to a play—and the list goes on and on.

A thematic unit is organized in terms of meaningful experiences with language, focused on a theme and on theme-related tasks. These experiences prepare students to use the language for a variety of purposes—their own purposes—beyond the classroom.

6. Thematic instruction involves activities or tasks that engage the learner in complex thinking and more sophisticated use of language.

Even though learners may have very little language at their disposal, they are still capable of using that language in a complex and sophisticated way, if they have the opportunity and the interest. An engaging theme built around endangered animals, for example, led one student to use simple vocabulary to make a very sophisticated statement. On a picture of a leopard, the student wrote the caption *"No soy un abrigo"* (I am not a coat). This is a far more sophisticated and meaningful use of the verb "to be" than the obvious statement "I am a boy" or "I am a girl."

7. Thematic instruction avoids the use of isolated exercises with grammatical structures, practiced out of context, that tend to fragment language at the word or sentence level and to neglect the discourse level.

The thematic unit provides many opportunities for students to hear and use language in a variety of meaningful contexts. We have learned from brain research that manipulation of vocabulary and grammar in a drill setting is less efficient than the meaningful use of language in rich contexts. Students need contexts for extended listening, for conversations in which real information is exchanged, and for oral and written presentations of information and ideas. Fragmented language is not as memorable as language learned in context—and it certainly isn't as usable.

8. Thematic instruction connects content, language, and culture goals to a "big idea."

What is really worth understanding? Is it the past tense of the irregular verbs? Is it the names of six modes of transportation? Wiggins and McTighe (1998) advocate the organization of curriculum around "big ideas": ideas, topics, or processes that reside at the heart of the discipline and have enduring value beyond the classroom. These are ideas, topics, or processes that are not obvious, about which students may even have misconceptions, so that learning can become a process of discovery or "uncovering." Topics like these are likely to be of great interest to students, especially when they are approached as questions, issues, or problems (10–11).

Glastonbury Public Schools has developed a curriculum based on the principles of *Understanding by Design,* the curriculum design principle developed by Wiggins and McTighe (1998). The Spanish curriculum is organized around key "big ideas" at each grade level, and these are developed through the use of guiding questions that focus each unit. For example, the grade one curriculum is focused on the question, "How do we name things in a different language?" The "big idea" question in grade 3 is, "Why is my day the way it is, and is it different from other countries?" The guiding questions include, "What is school for? How is my family different from others?" In grade four the central question is, "Why do we explore and what do we find?" Some of the guiding questions are, "What is an explorer? What influences have the explorers left on the types of homes we have today? What types of transportation do explorers use?"

Thematic instruction helps students to go beyond knowledge and skills in their language use and bring them to the point of actually *using* these skills to gain access to important ideas that are worth understanding. These important "big ideas" have enduring value, beyond the classroom and beyond the context in which they were learned.

For example, learning the terms for a variety of foods is typical content for the early language classroom. By itself this food vocabulary is static knowledge, easily forgotten. When it is encountered in the context of a unit about the Columbian exchange, however, the same vocabulary takes on relevance and importance as a tool for learning about something of lasting value—and thus the vocabulary becomes more memorable. This thematic unit begins to uncover the "big ideas" of what happens when cultures interact with one another, and how things change over time.

Another common early language topic is animals, and sometimes this topic can also result in limited, static knowledge. Jackie Dove's fourth grade students in a beginning French class, however, used the animal vocabulary they had learned to uncover and share information about endangered animals. This experience gave these Burleigh Elementary School students a connection with the "big idea" of the interaction of all living things with their environment.

Curriculum and lesson planning are the most important components of an early language program. Each day's lesson fits into a larger framework of planning, which makes it a part of long-range goals and unified, sequenced objectives. A planning process organized around standards, communicative principles, and the framework introduced later in this chapter will develop experiences for students that enable them to function effectively in a variety of situations and modes of communication. This planning process will first attempt to give children control over their immediate environment and then move outward, enabling them to discuss interests, needs, and concerns in the school beyond their classroom, in their families, and in their community. At the same time, students will acquire and use the new language in contexts that are planned to be rich with cultural meanings and associations.

Thematic Planning for K–8 Classrooms

In order to achieve and maintain high student interest and motivation in the early language classroom, planners must organize the curriculum and the everyday activities of the classroom around the needs and interests of students. In the elementary school, perhaps more than at any other level, this is an individual challenge from school to school and from class to class. Faced with a perpetual lack of published materials, the elementary school language teacher will no doubt always have to develop a great many materials personally, and existing materials usually require adaptation to meet the needs of a specific school or class. Middle school language teachers often find that published materials are not appropriate to the language level or the developmental levels of their students. A commitment to thematic planning can free the language teacher from the limitations of existing materials and lead to more interesting lessons and greater learning on the part of their students. Whether at the elementary or the middle school level, planning for foreign language instruction should be standards based, thematic, and multidisciplinary, addressing the needs and the development of the whole child. Close cooperation with classroom teachers can lead to an effective integration of languages with the emphases and the goals of other content areas. Several tools to assist the teacher are described in the following sections of the chapter.

Framework for Curriculum Development

The *Framework for Curriculum Development for FLES Programs* (Pesola 1995) was developed to help teachers make sense of the competing demands for time and attention in

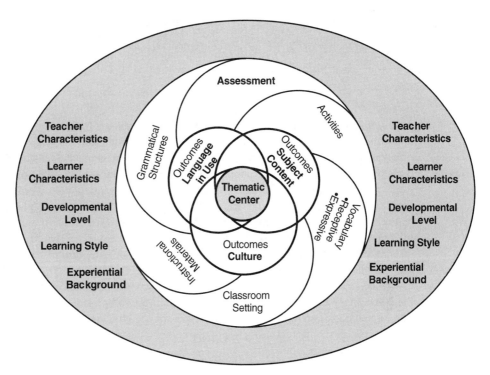

FIGURE 7.1 A Framework for Curriculum Development for FLES Programs (Foreign Languages in Elementary Schools).

curriculum planning. It is a visual representation of priorities and relationships among elements of curriculum design (see Figure 7.1).

This framework is designed to guide decisions encountered in the process of curriculum development and to inform the process of curriculum and program evaluation. It is an effort to capture a dynamic relationship among elements that are in constant and continuously changing interaction with one another. Each of these elements is addressed below:

Learner and Teacher Characteristics. The characteristics of the learner guide and constrain all curriculum decisions. All elements of curriculum planning and evaluation must take into account the developmental level of the learners, and the presence among learners of a variety of learning styles. Previous language learning and the experiential background of the learners will also have significant influence in curriculum planning. The urban child who encounters public transportation, museums, and street vendors on a daily basis will likely be motivated by somewhat different themes and activities from those that are successful with rural students, whose world is very different.

Teacher characteristics are also significant factors in curriculum planning. The teacher's language skills and experiences with the target culture will influence all aspects of instruction. The classroom should be a comfortable place for the teacher, as well as for the student. Teachers will be most effective if they teach their strengths and their interests. The teacher who has spent several years in Quebec, for example, and who loves French-Canadian music and history, will probably—and appropriately—design curriculum that reflects those interests. The teacher who loves to sing will infuse the curriculum with music.

Thematic Center. This framework establishes the *thematic center* as the focal point for curriculum development. The thematic center includes the theme, the targeted standards, broad unit outcomes, and a culminating performance assessment. Choice of a thematic center is based on interests of the pupils and the teacher, relationship to the goals of the curriculum for the grade level or age of the class, potential for integration with the culture of the language being taught, and potential for the application and development of appropriate and useful language functions and communication modes. The focus of a thematic center might be a topic from the general school curriculum or it could be drawn from the literature or culture of the target language. The thematic center could be designed to use a guiding question that focuses all the activities of the unit.

The curriculum for a school year consists of several thematic centers, each related to the others by systematic reinforcement of the unit just completed, and by careful preparation for and transition to the units that follow. Language functions and basic vocabulary are encountered and reinforced from unit to unit, due to the spiral character of the general elementary school curriculum.

Targeted Standards. An important element of the thematic center is the standards that will be targeted during the unit of study. Both national and state standards will play a role here. Not all standards will be addressed in every unit, but each unit should take into consideration the range of possibilities that the standards suggest. In addition to targeted standards, the thematic center may also include some standards of secondary emphasis.

Outcomes. Three major groups of outcomes give substance to the thematic unit:

1. *Outcomes for language in use, or functional language outcomes.* This is the language necessary for dealing appropriately with the theme. These outcomes are not grammatical categories or vocabulary lists, but rather the uses of language: asking permission, explaining, giving directions, describing, and so on (see Table 7.1). These outcomes reflect the communication goal in the *Standards for Foreign Language Learning in the 21st Century.*

2. *Subject content outcomes.* This is the reinforcement and extension of concepts and goals from the general elementary school curriculum, reflecting the connections goal in the Standards.

3. *Culture outcomes.* These reflect experiences with patterns of thinking and behavior that are distinctively representative of communities in which the target language is used— the products, practices, and perspectives of the cultures goal in the Standards.

TABLE 7.1 Communicative Functions, Notions, Topics, and Contexts Australian Language Levels Stages A → C (Junior Primary)

Communicative Functions/Language in Use	Notions/Vocabulary Areas
(involving both initiating and reacting)	**Categories** people
Socializing using different modes of address greeting introducing thanking	places things actions/events qualities presence/absence
Exchanging information identifying asking for/giving information describing narrating personal experiences inquiring about or expressing knowledge inquiring about or expressing opinions asking for/giving permission stating necessity and need inquiring about or expressing likes/dislikes/preferences inquiring about or expressing wishes	**Time** present time past time beforehand/afterwards/at the same time **Space** location **Quantity** numbers expressions of amount expressions of degree
Getting things done requesting suggesting making arrangements reacting to offers, requests, suggestions inviting instructing	**Characteristics** shape physical appearance color sound taste smell age
Expressing attitudes expressing admiration expressing approval/disapproval expressing interest/disinterest expressing friendship expressing regret expressing apology	**Evaluation** price evaluating things seen, heard, done, eaten, etc. truth/falsehood correctness/incorrectness
Organizing and maintaining communication attracting attention expressing lack of comprehension asking for repetition or rephrasing asking how to say something in the target language	**Relationships between units of meaning** comparison possession negation

TABLE 7.1   Continued

Communicative Functions/Language in Use	Notions/Vocabulary Areas
Organizing and maintaining communication	**Suggested contexts/roles/relationships**
asking how to spell something mentioned	school
asking someone to explain what they just said	home
	local area
	self as learner in class with teachers and other
Some suggested themes/topics	learners
self	self to friend (peer/adult)
family	self to stranger (peer/adult)
friends	
home	
school	
free time	
world of fantasy/imagination	

Source: Adapted from *Australian Language Levels Guidelines, Book 2: Syllabus Development and Programming.* Woden, A.C.T.: Curriculum Development Centre (1988), 69.

Making choices in these three areas and maintaining a balance among them is the fundamental work of curriculum development. Like a three-legged stool, each of the goals areas should carry equal weight in order to provide a solid foundation.

Each of these three categories for decision making overlaps with the others in significant and sometimes problematic ways. For example, at the intersection of functional language and culture, the close relationship between language and culture is evident. This relationship is so deeply and tightly established that it is sometimes difficult to separate language and culture in instruction. Such a close relationship can lead to the inappropriate assumption that whenever the language is being used, the culture is inevitably being taught. At times this assumption has resulted in a failure to identify specific cultural outcomes and content for language curriculum. This framework represents visually the idea that even though there may be significant overlap between two of these areas, each of them also plays a distinctive and valuable role in instruction that must be planned for separately and carefully.

Both culture and subject content serve as opportunities for meaningful use of language. Subject content is the integrative component that melds language learning with the immediate, relevant world of the learner. Culture is the distinctive contribution of the language classroom to the general education of the child. As balance is sought among these three essential components of the curriculum, it is important to avoid choosing trivial or superficial cultural and subject content elements simply to provide a token representation in the plan.

Performance Assessment   The final element of the thematic center is a culminating performance assessment. In a standards-based curriculum, the final assessment (or cluster of assessments) is the opportunity for students to show that they are able to use the language and concepts from the unit in a setting that reflects real-world language use. ACTFL recommends that the culminating assessment include the interpersonal, interpretive, and presentational modes. This culminating performance task pulls together the goals of the unit and guides all the other planning choices that have to be made.

Additional Decisions.   Once all the elements of the thematic center have been established, the teacher begins to plan the unit that will lead to the outcomes and the assessment, and thus address the standards that have been selected. These decisions relate to the *vocabulary,* both receptive and expressive, necessary for interacting with the content of the unit and for successful completion of the final performance; the *grammatical structures* necessary for dealing appropriately with the unit; the *materials and activities* that will be used to advance the development of the unit; the *classroom setting* in which the teaching and learning will take place; and the *assessment strategies* that will be used during the course of the unit to measure student progress toward the final performance. The teaching of *grammatical structures* is understood to take place through usage and practice, rather than through analysis and drill.

Each of the decisions in this framework interacts with all earlier decisions and with one another to create a dynamic planning process that can be responsive to the particular environment of each individual setting. The framework is also intended to reflect a flexible planning process. The planner can begin with any of the elements in the process, and make decisions in any order, but all those decisions are held together with the focus of the thematic center and with the ultimate performance task(s) in mind.

The Framework and the Standards.   The Framework for Curriculum Development is fully compatible with the *Standards for Foreign Language Learning in the 21st Century.* Each of the outcomes circles ties directly to one of the goals in the Standards. "Language in Use" could also be named "Communication"; "Culture" and "Cultures" are fully compatible; and "Subject Content" could easily be renamed "Connections." The remaining Standards, Comparisons, and Communities interact with the framework outcomes at several points, as illustrated in the diagrams in Figure 7.2. Standard 4.1 deals with comparing languages, and Standard 4.2 addresses comparison of cultures. The communities goal brings the learning of language, culture, and curriculum content beyond the classroom, and engages the learner with the language and the culture for lifelong learning.

Narrative as a Design Principle

Narrative structure is emerging as one of the most valuable of all teaching tools. Cognitive researchers such as Bruner (1990, 1996), Schank (1995), and Sylwester (1995) have identified narrative, or story form, as one of the most significant cognitive tools available to us. The brain is wired for narrative, and as humans we use narrative as a means of organizing our own experience. The emotional component of narrative colors experiences of all kinds and makes them more memorable. Wiggins and McTighe (1998) go so far as to suggest that planners use the logic of narrative as a principle of curricular design (139).

Story form, or narrative structure, is much more than just using stories as part of a unit or a lesson. The principles of a good story are found in a count-out rhyme, in an experiment in which students predict whether a vegetable or fruit will sink or float, in a game, a

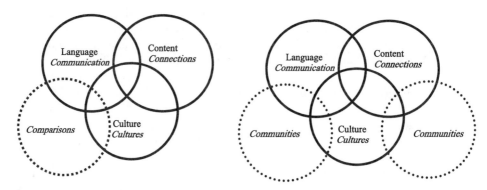

FIGURE 7.2   Interactions of Framework for Curriculum Development with *Standards for Foreign Language Learning.*

puzzle, or a problem to solve. One of the key elements in a unit, lesson, or activity developed with story form is the presence of a clear-cut beginning, middle, and end. Task-based learning and problem-based learning are other examples of story form in curriculum.

Several strategies can help teachers to design or redesign activities in story form. One way to think about it is to structure every unit and lesson toward some kind of culminating activity—and every activity toward a sense of completion and accomplishment. Like the gymnast "sticking" a landing, the learner can experience a sense of accomplishment and the "aha!" of understanding.

Prediction can be one of the most powerful tools for engaging student attention, and it is often overlooked. If students predict the outcome before they begin an activity, they are likely to have greater motivation to carry the activity through to the end. In doing a count-out rhyme with the whole class, for example, the teacher might stop when five children are left standing and ask the class to predict who will be the winner. Before beginning an activity in which students build a graph based on the birthday month of each class member, students might predict which month will have the most birthdays. This kind of activity can lead to more language use and also intensify the story form structure.

Sometimes a unit—or an activity—can work toward a performance. Music teachers have a big advantage here—every rehearsal can be working toward a performance. But so can classroom work—it could be a play, a skit, or a conversation with a native speaker. Performance of a song, a dance, or a rhyme is a powerful motivator for accuracy and attention.

A unit that works toward a product, like a storybook, an art display, or some other tangible and sharable product, is almost guaranteed to be in story form—and to motivate learners! Sometimes the product might be a publication, like a class newsletter or an announcement on local cable TV.

The story form strategy might be a puzzle, or a problem to solve—the popularity of computer games like "Where in the World is Carmen San Diego" is a great example of this strategy. Some teachers have built entire units on a search for a "stolen" or disappeared item. The search takes them from one country to another where the target language is spoken, or from one place to another in a city in the target culture. The simple, popular activity "I see something that you don't see" is a much simpler example of the puzzle strategy. In this game the teacher (or later a student) describes something or someone in plain sight and students try to identify it. Another example is the jigsaw strategy in cooperative learning, in which each student holds a different piece of information and the group must communicate in order to solve a problem or complete a task.

The strategy might be like many children's picture books—establishing a repetitive pattern and then culminating with a surprising break in the pattern.

What all of these strategies have in common, and those the reader might be able to add, as well, is the fact that they give *purpose* to the unit, the lesson, and the activity. They have a clear-cut beginning, middle, and end. The story form, and the anticipation of the outcome, add an emotional component to learning that increases the probability that it will find a place in long-term memory.

Kieran Egan Frameworks.   One effective tool for organizing both the thematic unit and the daily lesson is Kieran Egan's *Story Form Framework*. His suggestions for organizing instruction take into account the educational characteristics of learners at different developmental stages (see Chapter 1). He invites the teacher to pose the following questions in the process of planning for the *mythic layer* (1986, 41), ages five or six to nine or ten, and the *romantic layer* (1992, 94), ages eight or nine to fourteen or fifteen.

Story Form Framework for the Mythic Layer (Primary School Years)

1. *Identifying importance.* What is most important about this topic? Why should it matter to children? What is affectively engaging about it?
2. *Finding binary opposites.* What powerful binary opposites best catch the importance of the topic?
3. *Organizing content in story form.*
   3.1 What content most dramatically embodies the binary opposites, in order to provide access to the topic?
   3.2 What content best articulates the topic into a developing story form?
4. *Conclusion.* What is the best way to resolve the dramatic conflict inherent in these binary opposites? What degree of mediation of those opposites is it appropriate to seek?
5. *Evaluation.* How can one know whether the topic has been understood, whether its importance has been grasped, and whether the content was learned?

The first step in this story form framework includes three key questions that are relevant to any grade level and to every unit, lesson, or activity we might teach:

What is most important about this topic?
Why should it matter to children?
What is affectively engaging about it?

These questions help to define the thematic center of the Framework for Curriculum Development, and they address the basic purpose of everything we do. See figure 7.3 for an example.

A Planning Framework for the Romantic Layer (Middle School Years)

1. Identifying transcendent qualities
   - What transcendent human qualities can be seen and felt as central to the topic?
   - What affective images do they evoke?
2. Organizing the content into a narrative structure

   2.1 Initial access
   - What content, distinct from students' everyday experience, best embodies the transcendent qualities most central to the topic?
   - Does this expose some extreme or limit of reality within the topic?

   2.2 Structuring the body of the unit or lesson
   - What content best articulates the topic into a clear narrative structure? Briefly sketch the main narrative line.

   2.3 Humanizing the content
   - How can the content be shown in terms of human hopes, fears, intentions, or other emotions?
   - What aspects of the content can best stimulate romance, wonder, and awe?
   - What ideals and/or revolts against conventions are evident in the topic?

   2.4 Pursuing details
   - What content best allows students to pursue some aspect of the topic in exhaustive detail?
3. Concluding
   - How can one best bring the topic to satisfactory closure, while pointing on to further dimensions or to other topics?
   - How can the students *feel* this satisfaction?
4. Evaluation
   - How can one know whether the topic has been understood and has engaged and stimulated students' imaginations?

Egan's planning frameworks are intended for teachers in all subject areas, but they do not specifically address the teaching of another language. In planning a daily lesson or a unit based on a thematic center, the foreign language teacher might ask an additional series of questions:

1. What communication needs will the student be able to meet through the activities of this unit, and in what kinds of situations should the student be able to meet those needs?
2. What kind of activities will help the student to meet those needs?
3. What can I do as a teacher to motivate the student to feel the need and to want to meet the need?
4. What kind of materials will help clarify the new information and make the experiences come alive for the children?
5. What language will the children need to practice in order to experience success in meeting their communication goals?
6. What will the payoff be? What performance tasks will bring resolution to the story of the unit and show the teacher and the students themselves that the goals of the unit have been met?

FIGURE 7.3   Sample ideas for using story form framework with a thematic unit based on animals.

Use of this framework for a unit based on animals might result in some of the following ideas:

Important concepts (potential):

Content	**Language in Use**	**Culture**
Animal habitat	Expressing needs	Animal sounds
Animal characteristics	Expressing fear	Common animals in culture
What animals eat	Describing	Cultural animal song(s)
Relationships	Suggesting	Cultural animal story

Binary opposites:
Hungry ↔ Satisfied
Threatened ↔ Secure
Alone/Isolated ↔ Connected
Unwanted/Unloved ↔ Wanted/Loved
Useless ↔ Useful
Homeless ↔ At Home
Sad ↔ Happy
Good ↔ Bad

**Story form: sample activities incorporating story form
(One story? Series of story-form activities?)**
- Bremen town musicians.
- Fantasy animals: What does this baby animal need to eat to live?
- *Are You My Mother?* book or equivalent.
- Stories of animals in need in various settings: How can the "Superkid" help?
- Story of one endangered species, perhaps nearby.

Conclusion
- Draw pictures of animals children care about and show how they get what they need.
- "Superkids" reunite mother and baby animals that have been "separated" from one another around the classroom.
- Design fantasy animals and tell what they need to eat, what makes them happy, where they live, what threatens them.

Evaluation/Assessment
- Can children participate in problem-solving with fantasy animal in need?
- Designing fantasy animal.
- Responsiveness in group activities and fantasy situations.

Both a unit plan and a daily plan must include a variety of possible activities for meeting each goal.

Backward Design

In their landmark book *Understanding by Design,* Wiggins and McTighe (1998) describe an approach to curriculum development that builds on and enriches the educational focus on standards and performance assessment. They describe the design process in three stages.

Stage one is the identification of desired results. The questions they ask bear remarkable similarity to those listed by Kieran Egan: "What should students know, understand, and be able to do? What is worthy of understanding? What enduring understandings are desired?" (11).

In stage two the planner determines acceptable evidence that students have achieved the desired results and met the standards. The assessment possibilities range from informal checks for understanding to a performance task or project. The unit will be anchored by performance tasks or projects (13).

At stage three the teacher plans learning experiences and instructional activities. At this stage the planner needs to identify enabling knowledge and skills that students will need; to identify activities that will equip students with this knowledge and these skills; to determine what needs to be taught and how it should best be taught; to decide on materials and resources; and to determine whether the design is coherent and effective.

As with the Framework for Curriculum Development, the details of planning follow the identification of the instructional focus, or desired results, and decisions about final performance assessment.

This template for unit design for French, Latin, Spanish, and Japanese in Glastonbury Public Schools applies the principles of backward design and the insights of *Understanding by Design.* Notice how each of the planning stages is carried out.

(*Select Language*) Curricular Unit

Unit title: **Grade:**   **Level:**

Subject/Topic Area(s):

Key Words:

Standards:
  Major standards:
  Supporting standards:

Brief Summary of Unit (including curricular context and unit goals):

Number of days for activity:

Materials and resources (including technology and multimedia):

Identifying Desired Results
  ■ What essential questions will guide this unit and focus teaching/learning?
  ■ What enduring understandings are desired?
    Students will understand . . .

- What key knowledge and skills will students acquire as a result of this unit? (include all relevant structures, grammar, vocabulary, etc.)

     Students will know . . .   *Students will be able to . . .*
- What do they already know that will help them learn new information? Where and when did they learn it?

Determining Acceptable Evidence
- What evidence will show that students understand?
     - *Performance Tasks:*
     - *Quizzes, Tests, Prompts, Work Samples:*
     - *Unprompted Evidence (observations, dialogues):*
     - *Student Self-Assessment:*

Lessons:
     - Lesson 1:
     - Lesson 2:
     - etc.

Links to Relevant Web Sites:
     - www.site1.com
     - www.site2.com
     - etc.

Assessment Blueprint (Performance Tasks)

Task Title:

Approximate Time Frame:

Standards:

Purpose: (*check those that apply*)
     ☐ Formative
     ☐ Summative

Description of Task:

Evidence of desired understanding:

Criteria of judgment:

Evaluative Tools: (*check those that apply*)
     ☐ Analytic Rubric
     ☐ Holistic Rubric
     ☐ Criterion (performance) list
     ☐ Checklist

Assessment Blueprint (Other Evidence)
- What is being assessed?
- Describe the assessment
- What is the purpose of the assessment?
- Criteria of judgment/evaluative tools:

Planning Integrated Thematic Units

Thematic teaching, as described in the Framework for Curriculum Development above, provides context for concepts and activities through their relationship to a thematic center. One significant function of the theme is to focus on meaningful and interesting information and experiences as reasons for learning and using language. It also helps to connect ideas and information to make them more understandable and easier to remember. Possible themes might be selected or rejected on the basis of their potential for appropriate language in use, for salient and child-appropriate culture experiences, or for reinforcement of important concepts or skills from the general curriculum.

Resources for Thematic Planning. The first step in thematic planning is to assemble the resources and guidelines available for the planning process. At a minimum, this should include the following:

1. *Standards for Foreign Language Learning in the 21st Century,* state and local foreign language standards.
2. An inventory of language-in-use (language functions) appropriate for the language level of the students. In some cases this will be provided in a scope and sequence already existing for the program. State curriculum guidelines or a textbook series may offer inventories of language functions, or the teacher might draw from a list such as the one provided in Table 7.1 (Drawn from the Australian Language Levels [ALL] Guidelines).
3. A set of outcomes for culture, drawn from a program scope and sequence or from a source such as the Montgomery County scope and sequence (see Chapter 10), or the Framework for Cultural Competence from the American Association of Teachers of French. The culture resources might also include a locally developed collection of *cultural symbols, products and practices,* as described in Chapter 10.
4. Outcomes and standards for the content areas of the general curriculum, including mathematics, science, language arts, social studies, health, music, art, and physical education. In general, related content for thematic units can successfully be drawn from concepts and skills at grade level and from at least the two earlier grades. Although many curriculum concepts and skills in preschool and primary grades can be communicated successfully in the target language at grade level, language skills of students in FLES programs may not be equal to the more sophisticated content of some curriculum areas in the middle and upper grades.
5. ACTFL Performance Guidelines for K–12 Learners (see Appendix).

Choice of Theme. Choice of a thematic center should take several factors into consideration:

- the interests of the learners and the teacher
- relationship to the goals of the curriculum for the grade level or age of the class
- potential for integration with the culture of the language being taught
- potential for story form; that is, an interesting, unfolding story line and a clear beginning, middle, and end
- a meaningful response to the question posed by Egan: "Why should it matter to children?"
- potential for the application and development of appropriate and useful language functions and communication modes
- potential for a meaningful culminating performance assessment with links to real-world language use

Other factors influencing the choice and development of a theme might include schoolwide or across-the-curriculum emphases, holidays or special school or community events, available materials and resources, or the presence of individuals in the school or the community with special background they can bring to the language classroom.

The focal point for a thematic center may be a topic from the general school curriculum or it may be drawn from the literature or culture of the target language. Broadly based thematic units may be designed to last for several weeks—*explorations,* for example, or *change.* Other units may have more focused themes, based on a single story, a holiday, or a special occasion like a birthday celebration.

From Topic to Theme.   There are many possible starting points for this process. For example, you might start with an idea or a topic based on a curriculum concept; a poem; a story; a book; a school or grade focus; a piece of art, or an artist; music, or a composer.

Deciding on a topic is really only the first step. Our next step is to move from a topic to a theme. A theme is a richer basis for a unit, one that has greater potential for meaning and purpose. While a topic usually involves just a loose collection of ideas, a theme suggests a "big idea" and more focus for the unit. It provides a goal, or a destination for the learning, resulting in a planned culminating activity. We often express this goal or destination by means of a focus question that guides the activities of the unit, as we saw in the examples from the Glastonbury curriculum. We might think of the theme as a way of "putting clothes on" the topic, to make it more appealing, more colorful, and to give it more personality—and a much stronger affective impact.

The topic of "house," for example, has very little potential for the richness of a theme that will really matter to learners and to their teacher. Here are some possibilities for a theme that are developed from the topic "house," each of which suggests a possible story line and many connections:

My house of the future
The enchanted castle
The haunted house
A house of hedgehogs

Brainstorming a Web of Ideas.   Once a theme has been established, it is very effective to begin a brainstorming process that yields a web-like organization of ideas related through meaning to one another and to the central theme. A web is a cognitive organizer, a visual representation of concepts and their relationships. It allows the planner to extend the theme in many directions and to flesh out the topic with meaningful categories and subcategories (Pappas, Kiefer, Levstik, 1990, 51). Although not every element from the web may find its way into the unit, information gathered in this way forms the basis for further planning. Some planners find it helpful to build their webbing around pre-selected categories, such as culture, geography, and mathematics (see Figure 7.4). Many planners use a web based on multiple intelligences, such as that found in Figure 7.5. Others prefer to let the brainstorming run free, screening the information later for the inclusion of elements of language, subject content, and culture.

Organizing the Planning Information.   The next step is to choose targeted standards, broad unit outcomes, and a culminating assessment for the theme. Together these constitute the thematic center for the unit.

These elements and those that follow could be organized on a *Unit Plan Inventory,* Table 7.2, beginning with the top section, where the targeted standards, the performance assessment, and the outcomes for the unit help to focus all planning.

The planner chooses and organizes information from the web that will become the actual content of the unit, beginning with the *Language Functions, Subject Content,* and

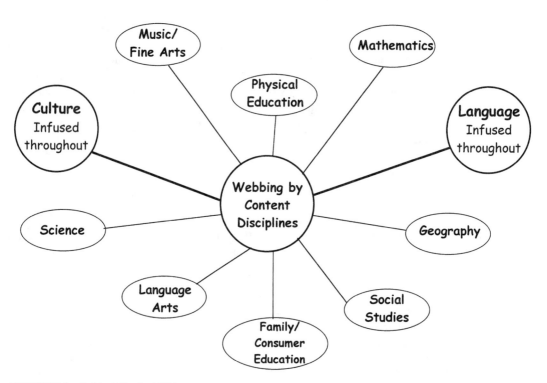

FIGURE 7.4   Subject Content Web

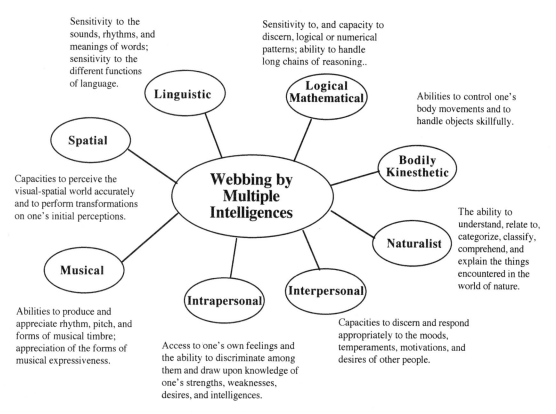

Sensitivity to the sounds, rhythms, and meanings of words; sensitivity to the different functions of language.

Sensitivity to, and capacity to discern, logical or numerical patterns; ability to handle long chains of reasoning..

Abilities to control one's body movements and to handle objects skillfully.

Capacities to perceive the visual-spatial world accurately and to perform transformations on one's initial perceptions.

The ability to understand, relate to, categorize, classify, comprehend, and explain the things encountered in the world of nature.

Abilities to produce and appreciate rhythm, pitch, and forms of musical timbre; appreciation of the forms of musical expressiveness.

Access to one's own feelings and the ability to discriminate among them and draw upon knowledge of one's strengths, weaknesses, desires, and intelligences.

Capacities to discern and respond appropriately to the moods, temperaments, motivations, and desires of other people.

FIGURE 7.5   Multiple Intelligences Web

Source: From *Multiple Intelligences,* by Howard Gardner. Copyright © 1993 by Howard Gardner. Reprinted by permission of Basic Books, a member of Perseus Books, L.L.C.

Culture. Once these key elements have been chosen, and a relative balance has been achieved among them, decisions can be made about the remaining components of the planning process: vocabulary, grammatical structures, activities and ongoing assessments, and materials. The Unit Plan Inventory serves as a chart for organizing information from the web. The final step in the preliminary organization may be to reexamine and refine the student outcomes for the unit.

It is important to emphasize that all these categories relate to our thematic center; that is, they flow from our choice of themes, standards, outcomes, and culminating assessment. Essentially, these are all the planning elements listed on the Planning Framework, except for classroom setting, which would likely be indicated under activities.

Laying things out on the Unit Plan Inventory helps us to see the balance among our choices and to make sure that we are emphasizing the elements that we have decided are most important.

The process we have described here is not a linear process—it is more of a spiral. At every step along the way, we need to monitor and adjust our work, so that it reflects the

TABLE 7.2 Unit Plan Inventory

Targeted Standards:

Outcomes (Objectives):

Performance Assessment:

Language Functions	Subject Content	Culture	Vocabulary	Grammatical Structures	Essential Materials	Major Lesson Topics, Performances (Assessments)
(Language in Use)						

characteristics and content of good unit design. Throughout the planning process, it is important to monitor at each step for:

- unit focus
- culture elements related to outcomes
- subject content elements related to outcomes
- functional language related to outcomes
- vocabulary and grammar to support functional language
- Standards-related content and activities
- opportunities for general student growth
- accommodation for:
  - learning styles
  - multiple intelligences
  - thinking skills
- feasibility
  - classroom setting
  - materials
  - time
- strong beginning, middle, end
  - for unit
  - for activities within unit (story form)
- engaging culminating task/activity/performance

The next step in the planning process is to organize the activities and assessments in a logical sequence, to ensure that there is a careful progression and a well-developed beginning, middle, and end. At this point it is time to begin planning the daily lessons.

Planning the Daily Lesson

The importance of a written plan cannot be overemphasized. There is a remarkable correlation between the presence of a detailed written plan and the ability of a teacher to be creative and flexible in the actual class setting. Many early language programs have a very limited amount of class time in which to give children experiences with the target language. Only careful planning can prevent the loss and misuse of time, which is already in very short supply.

Objectives/Outcomes

The careful formulation of written objectives (sometimes called *outcomes*) will help the teacher to plan relevant activities and coherent lessons. Effective objectives always describe what students will be able to do at the end of the lesson. The statements include action verbs that represent a student activity that is observable. Verbs such as *teach, learn,* and *understand* are not useful because they describe process rather than outcome, and because they are essentially unobservable. It is often helpful to think of each objective as beginning with the phrase "The students will be able to . . ."

Here are some examples of objectives for a beginning elementary school foreign-language class.

Students will be able to do the following:

1.   Respond to the teacher with an appropriate greeting
2.   Point to a day of the week on the calendar when it is named
3.   Identify numerals 0 to 5 when they are not in sequence
4.   Respond correctly to the following commands, individually and in a group:
— stand up   — sit down
— point to . . .   — touch . . . (color, number, body part)
— walk   — turn around

5.   Respond with name when asked "What is your name?" (Some children will also say "My name is . . .")

Elements of the Daily Plan

The daily lesson plan should provide the teacher with easy reference to the key elements of the day's instruction. One format that works well in connection with the *Framework for FLES Curriculum* is as follows (see Figure 7.6):

FIGURE 7.6   Sample format for daily lesson plan.

Lesson Plan Format

Theme:

Lesson Title or Topic:

Standards Addressed:

Outcomes or Objectives: Language   Culture   Content

Assessment:

Lesson Building Blocks:
Language Emphasis *(functions, vocabulary, structures, modalities)*

Subject Content Emphasis *(math, geography, etc.)*

Culture Emphasis *(products, practices, perspectives)*

Materials:

Lesson Outline:
Warmup

Introduction

FIGURE 7.6   Continued

Lesson Activities or Procedures

Options for Recording Student Performance

Closure

Follow-Up/Homework:

Reflection:

Special Considerations:
How does the lesson address

  learning styles

  multiple intelligences

  special needs of individual students

  learning strategies

Theme.   We start by listing the theme. This helps us to keep in mind where we have been and where we are going with the theme on which we are working. It's also helpful to list a lesson title or topic. This title, of course, refers back to the theme.

Standards.   Here we list the foreign language standards that we are targeting in this lesson, and possibly other standards that support the goals of the lesson. It isn't realistic to try to include all eleven standards in a single lesson, but communication standards should always be represented.

Outcomes or Objectives.   Here we identify observable student outcomes for the lesson. They describe student behavior at the end of the lesson. For each of the outcomes we determine whether they incorporate language, content, or culture. In many cases the outcome will include more than one of these three major goals. Sometimes we might use a check-off, as indicated on the lesson plan format. As an alternative, we might simply write the classifications at the end of the outcome. In this way we can make sure to pay attention to all aspects of language teaching. It is possible that not every lesson will incorporate all three components, of course, but just as in the Unit Plan Inventory, our lessons themselves should reflect a balance among Language, Content, and Culture. We list them on the lesson plan as a reminder of their importance and as a way to keep them in balance over the course of the unit.

Assessment.   The assessment category describes any procedures for determining student performance during this lesson. If we are doing a formal assessment, the needed rubrics or checklists are provided on separate pages at the end of the lesson. This would also be a place to indicate names of students for whom we intend to do an informal assessment.

Lesson Building Blocks.   In this section we identify the building blocks of the lesson, those elements that lead to the student outcomes. We list for ourselves what we are addressing within this lesson:

- Language emphasis: the language functions, vocabulary, grammatical structures, and communication modes that are the focus of this lesson
- Content emphasis: academic skills and processes in the lesson, and connections with the general curriculum
- Culture emphasis: culture products, practices, and perspectives; comparisons of cultures

Materials.   It is valuable to indicate on the lesson plan which materials we need for the lesson, so we can see at a glance what we have to bring with us to class or to prepare in advance. For traveling teachers this is especially important.

Lesson Outline.   Here the teacher provides a step-by-step description of activities and procedures, with a time designation for each one. As we plan for the class flow, it is important to keep in mind what we have learned from cognitive theorists. The first five minutes and the last five minutes of a class period are prime learning time. We need to use this precious learning time very carefully, and make sure that it isn't wasted in routine or unchallenging, undirected activity.

Within this step-by-step lesson outline we will plan for

- Warm up, to help students make the transition from their previous activity to the language class. Often the warm up consists of an opening routine.
- Introduction to the lesson for the day, and informing the students so they know the objectives of the lesson.
- Lesson activities or procedures, a step-by-step guide to how we present the main part of the lesson and how students will practice the lesson components. We want to make sure that there is sufficient variety in the activities we have planned. Early language learners need variety and are unable to stay on task if an activity is too long. Eric Jensen (1998) suggests a maximum of five to seven minutes of focused attention time for K–2, eight to twelve minutes for grades three to seven, and twelve to fifteen minutes for grades eight to twelve (49).
- Closure, how we will bring the lesson to a close. This could be the culminating activity of the lesson, or an opportunity for students to demonstrate their new learning.

Follow-Up/Homework.   How will we follow up on this lesson? If we assign homework we list it here and indicate whether handouts will be needed.

Reflection.   How did the lesson go? Here we make notes on items to remember for the next time that we teach the lesson, or the next time we meet with this class. Observations about individual students might also be listed.

Other Considerations.   It is important to plan in advance for strategies within the lesson to help us meet the needs of the diverse student populations in each of our classes. This includes attention to the areas of:

- learning styles,
- multiple intelligences,
- needs of special students,
- or possibly learning strategies.

Sharing the Lesson Plan with Students.   Actually writing a lesson plan or a lesson outline on the board helps students to anticipate the variety of activities they will experience and to feel a sense of progress through the lesson or through the material. The plan itself can become the object of meaningful communication and language practice, as the teacher asks children to remind her or him of the next activity, or invites them to choose an activity from those remaining. Teachers in some advanced classes write the day's schedule in sentences on the chalkboard, and it becomes a class activity at the end of the lesson or the day to rewrite the sentences in the past tense to show that the activity has been completed. Rather than talking about changing the tense of the verb, the teacher says, "This sentence isn't true anymore; how can we change it to make it right?" In some classes, especially immersion classes, the revised daily schedule is written in a class diary, illustrated, and used to maintain a class history.

Factors to Consider When Planning the Lesson

Warm-up.   Each early language class period, regardless of its length, should begin with a brief warm-up. This is a time for communicative use of completely familiar language. The warm-up has several purposes:

1. It provides a review and a basis for new material to be introduced.
2. It provides a transition from the instructional time the students have just experienced in their native language to an intensive experience of learning and thinking in the target language.
3. Because of the relatively easy level at which the warm-up is conducted, it helps students to build or regain confidence in their ability to work with the target language. At some point in the warm-up every child should have the opportunity to say something in the target language, either individually, in a small group, or in the larger group.
4. It provides a time during which teachers and students alike can share dimensions of their personality and their interests—as they talk about likes and dislikes, families, weather (and how they deal with it)—and they can personalize applications of material they have learned earlier in a more structured setting.

The warm-up does not "just happen." It must be carefully planned to include different material and strategies each day.

Balance of Old and New Material.   Learners need a great deal of practice with new material before they are able to appropriate it for their own functional, communicative purposes. Every class period should contain some new and some familiar material; the exact balance will vary from day to day. One of the teacher's tasks is to make the old material seem new and the new material seem familiar. The teacher must plan for many different contexts within which to practice, in order to prevent boredom with the practice and to provide the children with a sense of progress—the old always seems new, because the message to be communicated has a new context and the need to communicate that message is also new. For example, when children are first introduced to numbers, they might count objects, participate in a count-out rhyme, guess which number the teacher has hidden in her or his hand, participate in a concentration game with numbers, play a "Go Fish" game with number cards, roll giant dice and call out the numbers, sing a song based on numbers, and so forth. Each activity presents a new context and a new challenge, but in the process the children have practiced the numbers vocabulary enough for it to become automatic.

Introducing New Material.   When introducing new material, the teacher tries to build on what students have already learned so they have maximum security and reason for self-confidence. For example, on the first day of class, the teacher might point out, if appropriate, some relationships and cognates between the native language and the target language, and show how many of the target-language words the student may already be familiar with without realizing it. When the class hears a new song, poem, story, or another message for the first time, the teacher may invite the students to identify familiar words and phrases. In order to facilitate this task of making the new seem familiar, the teacher will consciously "seed" or plant material in the lesson for Monday which will appear in a larger context on Wednesday or Thursday, so that the later, longer message will not seem entirely new: familiar material is already present.

For example, the German teacher has decided to introduce a birthday song because one of the students has a birthday on Thursday:

> *Zum Geburtstag viel Glück!* (Good luck/happiness on your birthday!)
> *Zum Geburtstag viel Glück!* (Good luck/happiness on your birthday!)
> *Langes Leben und Gesundheit!* (Long life and good health)
> *Zum Geburtstag viel Glück!* (Good luck/happiness on your birthday!)

On Monday, the teacher introduces the exclamation *Viel Glück* (Good luck!) in the course of a game, demonstrating the contrast between the American gesture of crossed fingers and the German gesture of pressing thumbs to symbolize a good luck wish. The exclamation is reentered at every opportunity during the course of the week. On Tuesday the lesson includes the opposites *kurz* and *lang* (short and long), applied during a TPR exercise at the chalkboard in which children draw monsters with long and short hair, long and short arms and legs, long and short ears and noses. On Wednesday, the teacher pretends to have a cold, sneezing frequently, and the children are taught to wish the teacher and one another *Gesundheit,* which is already somewhat familiar to them. By Thursday, the only new words in the birthday song are the word for birthday itself, *Geburtstag,* which the teacher explains by means of a visual showing a birthday cake and presents, and the word for life, *Leben,* which the teacher may explain by contrasting a long life of someone who is ninety-six years old with a short life of someone who is two years old. After listening to the song one or two times (and with a minimum of repetition) the students are ready to sing the birthday song.

Planning from day to day should incorporate these linkages. The teacher should constantly be helping students to recognize these links, so that students discover language learning as a cumulative process, in contrast to what seems so often to be the case in other classes, where learning for the test (and later forgetting) seems somehow to be acceptable and inevitable.

Routines. Every class period, especially in the primary grades, should include a certain number of regular, predictable classroom routines that make heavy use of language repetition and patterned teacher-student interaction. Show-and-tell and the calendar activities that begin the day in many primary classrooms are examples of such routines. These routines provide children with a sense of security, and they also help to give meaning clues to the content discussed in the course of the activity. Special routines are common for lineups to leave for another classroom, or for changing activities within the classroom. Passing out or turning in papers becomes an opportunity for routine use of language for many teachers.

Variety. Each class period should also include a number and variety of activities. In general, the younger the children in a class, the greater the number of different activities planned for each class period. The attention span increases with the age of the child, but even in the middle school/junior high, activities should rarely last longer than ten minutes, and they should usually be planned to last from five to eight minutes.

Activities should be developed with attention to high and low energy requirements on the part of both the teacher and the students. The teacher might think in terms of planning for peaks and valleys of excitement, of movement, or of physical and verbal involvement. The early language teacher should plan activities at the end of the class period that leave the children ready to go on to work in other classes. Closing a class period with a game that leaves the children excited, unmanageable, or noisy will not earn the appreciation or the future cooperation of their next teacher.

Each lesson should include a balance of active and quiet activities, of large-group and small-group or partner activities, of one-way and two-way communication. It is very important for learners to have the opportunity to ask questions as well as to answer them and, especially in the TPR-oriented classroom, to give directions as well as to respond to them. It is also wise to plan for a change of pace and activities that involve movement outside of the desk or the learning circle. Songs, games, and rhymes with actions can change the tempo and the emphasis of a class period, while continuing to further communicative goals.

Interactive Homework. Some teachers have found it very useful to use homework as a means of connecting the language classroom with the home. When they give children tasks to complete at home and ask for parent signatures on the work, parents become more aware of what is happening in the classroom, and this can translate into greater support for student learning. Children can read a book or a story that they have written or copied, name all the foods at a meal, teach their family a series of TPR commands, perform a TPR Storytelling variation, label the objects in their bedroom—the list is virtually endless. Teachers in Pinellas County, Florida use a system of interactive homework as an assessment tool (see Chapter 13, Gilzow and Branaman 2000). In programs that have very limited class time, interactive homework can be a means of extending the students' amount of exposure to their new language.

Planning for Immersion, Bilingual, and Content-Based Instruction

Planning in an immersion or a bilingual, content-based classroom will focus on and take its direction from the goals of the subject content area. One major difference between the classroom in which a second language is the medium of instruction and the native-language classroom is that planning focuses on language development and on subject content goals at the same time in the second-language classroom. While the organizing principle for instruction will be the subject-matter content, the language skills necessary to progress in communication about subject matter content must also be intentionally developed through the planning process. This suggests that it will sometimes be necessary to do language development activities in preparation for or as a component of a lesson directed toward subject content goals. The teacher of subject content in a second language must always be aware of the language skills demanded by the concepts and the activities involved in the subject content goals. The teacher must also plan carefully for the concrete experiences and the visual reinforcement that will make the academic language of instruction comprehensible to the students and help them to develop the linguistic skills necessary for dealing with the subject content material.

A further difference found in the immersion or content-based language classroom is the added priority of providing cultural insight, information, and experiences as an important part of the curriculum. The time and effort required to deliver significant components of the general curriculum in a second language can sometimes result in a shortchanging of culture goals in a content-based curriculum. Like language development, culture must be systematically incorporated into each unit and lesson in order to provide students with the best possible learning experience.

Summary

Careful planning can help the early language teacher to make the most of the limited time available for instruction in the target language. One meaningful approach to planning curriculum is the development of integrated thematic units that incorporate the key elements of language-in-use, subject content, and culture. Effective planning takes into account the educational development of the students and draws on such approaches as story form and backward design to make learning more meaningful and more memorable. The careful preparation of student-oriented objectives and a written plan can free the teacher to be flexible and creative during the class period, responding to the needs and interests of the children as they develop without losing the direction and focus of the lesson. Each plan should be organized around the needs and development of the whole child and take into account the child's need for both variety and routine.

FOR STUDY AND DISCUSSION

1. How can the preparation of student-oriented objectives and a carefully written plan free the teacher to be creative and flexible during the class period?

2. Choose a potential theme for a unit in your language and develop a web of possible concepts and content for the unit. Share the web with a colleague and check for the presence of language-in-use, culture, and subject content. Select the content from the web and lay it out on the unit plan inventory.

3. Using the web in question 2, follow the Glastonbury framework for unit planning to design a unit for a class in one of the primary grades (K–2). Consult the standards for other content areas on the Web or from your curriculum library to help identify subject content connections.

4. Create an example of a thematic language unit for the *romantic layer,* using the Egan Planning Framework for Middle School Students.

5. Choose a song or a game you would like to teach to your class because it reinforces or anticipates basic concepts that are a part of the curriculum. Analyze it for unfamiliar vocabulary, and build a plan for "seeding" that new vocabulary over a period of several days.

6. Write a set of objectives, phrased in student terms, for teaching the song or game in question 5.

FOR FURTHER READING

The following sources are recommended for additional information about material covered in this chapter. Chapter citations are documented in Works Cited at the end of the volume.

Egan, Kieran. *Teaching as Story Telling.* Chicago: University of Chicago Press, 1986.

———. *Primary Understanding.* New York: Routledge, 1988.

———. *Imagination in Teaching and Learning: The Middle School Years.* Chicago: University of Chicago Press, 1992.

Gilzow, Douglas F., and Lucinda E. Branaman. *Lessons Learned. Model Early Foreign Language Programs.* McHenry, IL: Center for Applied Linguistics and Delta Systems Co., 2000.

Glastonbury (CT) Public Schools Foreign Language Curriculum Documents. Available on-line at http://foreignlanguage.org/curriculum/

Sandrock, Paul. *Planning Curriculum for Learning World Languages.* Madison, WI: Wisconsin Department of Public Instruction, 2002.

Wiggins, Grant, and Jay McTighe. *Understanding by Design.* Alexandria, VA: Association for Supervision and Curriculum Development, 1998.

8 Using Assessment to Help Students and Programs Grow

Student Assessment

When elementary or middle school language teachers gather at conferences and in-service meetings, or when they communicate on listservs, there is a constant flow of good ideas. They exchange games and activities, suggestions for songs, patterns for visuals, recipes for in-class food activities. They rarely exchange ideas for assessment, record keeping, reporting, or grading.

The tendency to focus on ideas and innovations for presenting material and developing activities is not found exclusively at the elementary and middle school level, nor exclusively among classroom teachers. Assessment of student performance has received far less time and attention in many methods classes and methods books, in conference programs, and in teacher in-service sessions than techniques for motivating students, planning curriculum, and managing the classroom. Methods for measuring student achievement within the communication-oriented classroom have not kept pace with methods for presenting materials and for giving students the opportunity to use language in communicative ways.

Assessment of student learning has acquired new relevance, however, in a world language community focused on standards, proficiency, and communication. Instead of being the last priority for consideration in planning curriculum and instruction, standards and assessment have become the starting point for "backward design," a process of working from final student products and performances back to content and activities.

The reorganization of the curriculum around standards and communicative goals requires a similar radical reorganization of assessment philosophy and practices. The results of communicative, standards-based programs can no longer be assessed with the same philosophy and using the same methods that have been used for decades. The popular and familiar discrete-point test, which measures grammar and vocabulary items in isolation, unrelated to meaningful context, is clearly an inappropriate measure for the achievement of communicative goals. It may have been somewhat more appropriate for assessing student performance in programs with a grammar-translation emphasis or based on the behaviorist principles of the audiolingual method. Yet because these methods of assessment have both the security of familiarity and the illusion of objectivity, they continue to play a dominant role in many classrooms.

The discrepancy between what is taught and what is tested threatens both the credibility of communicative goals as they are stated and their chance of being realized. When students and parents perceive a discrepancy between the stated goals of a course and the contents of achievement tests, they invariably—and appropriately—believe the message of the testing. Sandra Savignon (1997) summarizes the problem very effectively:

> The most important implication of the concept of communicative competence is undoubtedly the need for tests that measure an *ability to use language* effectively to attain communicative goals. Discrete-point tests of linguistic structures of the kind developed in the 1960s have not only failed to sufficiently take into account the complexity and dynamic quality of the communicative setting. In some cases, they have also served, in their emphasis on grammatical accuracy, to discourage the strategies needed for communicative competence and thus to hinder the development of more communicative curricula. A language course that sets out to "cover" all the points of grammar presented in a basic textbook, and then tests learners on their "mastery" of these points, has little time left for communication (223).

Discrete-point tests are particularly inappropriate as a means of measuring the richness and diversity of the language acquired by the young learner in a communicative, standards-oriented classroom. As we grow more sophisticated in our ability to capitalize on the meaning-making ability of the learner, as we allow students to draw from a rich target-language environment in individually meaningful ways, as we encourage learners to build their own structures of meanings and expression in the target language, we lose control of the bits and pieces that are easily measurable by traditional means. At the same time, the obligation to assess, the need to describe learning in a meaningful way, takes on even greater importance. Both the pressure toward accountability to standards and the requirements of effective articulation from one program level to another demand meaningful assessment practices and clear means of communicating student achievement within the profession, the school, and the community.

This kind of pressure can lead us to embrace familiar assessment measures, and perhaps even to compromise our goals for early language programs in order to make them more easily measurable by available means. The performance of a learner who is participating in a meaning-filled, communicatively oriented, developmentally appropriate early language program must be assessed and reported by meaning-filled, communicative, developmentally appropriate means. Otherwise the entire basis on which new programs are developed is threatened. As Kieran Egan notes (1988, 240): "We must be wary of the temptation to make learning cruder, so that we can measure it more securely."

Importance of Assessing Student Performance

In many early language programs the problem is not so much inappropriate assessment as it is an absence of formal assessment measures altogether. Because of the nature of program goals and the large number of students each teacher sees in a day or in a week, assessment of student achievement may receive little priority in these programs. Some teachers are concerned that testing or assessment of any kind will raise anxiety levels and lower motivation in their classes, especially among students who have been unsuccessful in much of the traditional school curriculum. Yet children and their parents often take seriously only those subjects for which there is regular assessment and reporting; any tendency to regard the language class as an "extra," or as a subject area of less than equal status with the rest of the curriculum, is reinforced by the absence of regular, careful student assessment and reporting.

In fact, assessment is just as essential to planning and instruction as are the choice of theme, identification of targeted standards, and selection of language, content, and culture goals. The culminating performance assessment is a critical component of the thematic center, and the assessment circle is the largest in the third layer of the *Framework for Curriculum Development* (see Figure 7.1), suggesting that it is the first of these six categories to be considered, the doorway to all other planning considerations. In fact, every step in the decision-making process is linked to assessment, from theme selection to decisions about standards and content to be addressed. Well-written outcomes contain or imply an assessment strategy, and the first step in structuring any lesson is to ask the twin questions, "What do I expect students to be able to do as a result of this instruction?" and "How will I know if they have met this goal?" The answers to these questions are of interest and importance to students as well as to the teacher, to parents, and to all other stakeholders in the educational setting.

One reason for the uneasiness often felt by early language teachers about the topic of assessment may be common perceptions of testing and reporting that most of us have encountered in our own educational journeys. Often testing is experienced as something teachers—the empowered—do *to* students for purposes of rendering (often negative) value judgments about the students' work. It is not surprising that teachers who place a high value on motivating students and helping them to feel competent and successful are uncomfortable with the idea of testing; they might even put it off and try to avoid it altogether.

Some of this uneasiness can perhaps be overcome if all parties in the assessment process change the emphasis in assessment from *making judgments* to *gathering information*. This information can be used to recognize and celebrate progress, identify areas for more intense effort, and describe levels of proficiency for the benefit of planning and articulation, among many other possibilities.

It is important to keep in mind, then, that assessment is more than simply giving and grading quizzes and tests and then marking report cards. Effective assessment is a complex and ongoing process.

Assessment Process

Discussion of the assessment process brings to mind a cartoon in which a little boy comes up to the teacher after class and asks, "What did I learn today, Miss Jones? My mother will want to know."

That cartoon is a good reminder that determining what has been learned in the classroom is important—for the teacher, of course, but also for the parent. And probably most important of all, our students also need help in recognizing their own progress in language learning. Before we begin the assessment process, we must identify what information we need in order to determine whether our goals have been met. This question comes at the beginning of the planning process, when we set the goals for our unit or our lesson. Asking this question during initial planning helps us to decide on the performance tasks—the products and performances—that will focus the unit, and to determine the evidence we will need to find out what the students have learned.

Our focus in the assessment process itself, then, is finding out and reporting what has been learned. This process has three major components: assessment, evaluation, and grading.

Assessment.　Assessment, the first component of the process, is the gathering of data or information. Our question here is: What information do I need to gather in order to find out if the goals for this segment of learning have been met? And how will that evidence best be gathered?

Evaluation.　The second component is to consider the interpretation of the data or information that has been gathered. The critical issue is to determine what criteria I will use to judge the *quality* of the student work. There are many questions at this step, including the following:

> What are the most important aspects of the performance on which I will be providing students with feedback?
>
> Have I prepared my students to be evaluated on these criteria (have they had sufficient practice and preparation to hold them accountable on these criteria)?
>
> Are the evaluation criteria focused on the quality of the performance or merely on the completion of the task?
>
> How does the information compare with other information I may already have?
>
> How important is it, in relationship to other information?
>
> What other information do I need?

Grading.　The last element of the process is grading, the process of transforming assessment data or information into a symbol that communicates the results of an evaluation.

Performance Assessment

Much of education in the twenty-first century is moving toward standards-based education and alternative forms of assessment, in an effort to match the goals of curriculum more effectively with the assessment evidence we gather. In addition, the effort is to link the assessment tasks with student activity in their world, and to measure achievement of these goals in terms of application of knowledge rather than rote learning. The focus on performance assessment is particularly appropriate for world languages, since proficiency in the use of the language—performance—is the true measure of what students know and are able to do.

This emphasis on performance is a very good fit with both the goals and the practices of standards- and communication-based, integrative curriculum in the elementary and middle school language program. Wiggins (1992) offers several suggestions for the design of tasks for performance assessment (27–28):

1. *Contextualize the task.* Provide rich contextual detail.
2. *Aim to design "meaningful" tasks—not the same as "immediately relevant or practical" tasks.* A context, a problem, or a task can be invented as well as be of actual, direct relevance to a learner's surroundings. Helping to identify an alien's home planet through a series of questions and answers could be a meaningful and interest-

ing way to see if students recognize descriptions, although it is not immediately relevant or practical.

3. *Design performances, not drills. A test of many items (a drill) is not a test of knowledge in use.* Performance is not about desired bits of knowledge, but about "putting it all together" with good judgment.

4. *Refine the tasks you design by building them backwards from the models and scoring criteria.* Students should know the target and the standard in advance.

As with language acquisition itself, the most authentic and potentially the richest source of meaningful context for the young learner is the language classroom. Several possibilities for gathering meaningful information about student performance within the classroom setting are suggested below.

What Did I Learn Today?   It is a challenge for teachers—and students—to gather information about what has been learned during a class, a unit, or a marking period, especially when classes are short and the teacher sees many students in a day. The early language teacher needs many different strategies for gathering this kind of information, and the most meaningful and reliable of these strategies are performance tasks, a form of performance assessment.

Performance Tasks

Performance tasks differ significantly from traditional paper-and-pencil approaches to assessment. Like the Standards themselves, they focus on what students can do with language, rather than what they know about language or their ability to manipulate bits of knowledge about language. A performance task is a product or a performance that calls for the student to use the competencies and the vocabulary from a unit of instruction in a meaningful context, preferably a context that replicates the challenges of the "real world."

The following performance task was developed for middle school students at the novice-high or early intermediate level, after several years of language study. It was designed to be the culmination of a unit on weather, and it assumes earlier units on clothing and seasons. Notice that there is a careful description of the task and considerable student support for each of the steps along the way. There are elements of all three modes of communication in the task: interpersonal, interpretive, and presentational. This task also incorporates story form: there is a clear-cut beginning, middle, and end for the activities. The directions for the task would probably be written in English, but it could also be written in Spanish if the student language skills were sufficiently sophisticated and if the task were introduced with sufficient modeling and careful explanation.

Performance Task: Deciding on a Destination.   An anonymous donor has offered to fund a trip for this class to the capital of any country we choose in the Spanish-speaking world, at exactly this time next year. Our job is to decide which city we would like to visit.

Each member of the class will research the climate of one of the cities that we might like to visit, as well as some of the attractions. Your job is to find the information that will help us to decide which city we will choose. This project includes two tasks:

1. Visit a Spanish-language Web site for your city on four different days during next week, keeping track of the weather conditions on the chart below. Web sites will be distributed in class. We will assume that this is typical weather for the city for this time of year. Prepare a weather report for the class, in which you do the following:
   - give the average high and low temperatures over the time period you researched (Reminder: divide the total of all the temperatures by the number of days in the report)
   - explain the sky conditions, wind conditions, and precipitation, if any
   - describe what the weather would feel like and suggest what clothes we would need (something about the humidity would help us here)
   - prepare a visual that would help us to understand your weather report
   - tell something else interesting or important about the weather and the city

   Use the weather vocabulary we have studied during this unit, and present your information in complete sentences. It will be more effective if you do not read from a script, but you may use a script if you prefer to do so. Be prepared to answer questions from your classmates, and to ask them questions about their presentations.
2. Using the same Web site, or other links to Spanish-language sites about your city, identify at least five special characteristics or attractions of the city that you think your classmates would find interesting and worth visiting. Then prepare a two-minute "commercial" using PowerPoint or another multimedia format, giving the reasons why this city should be our choice for the trip. If you prefer, you could develop a brochure about the city, either with the computer or by hand.

After all the presentations have been made, the class will vote on the city we would most like to visit. As a class, we will write a letter to our anonymous benefactor explaining our choice.

Accompanying this description of the task is the weather chart that students will use in recording the weather. This chart would be written entirely in the target language (see Table 8.1).

Evaluation of Student Performance

Sometimes teachers shy away from using performance assessments because of the fact that they must make judgments based on criteria rather than on an answer key, and they are concerned about treating students fairly. A checklist or a rubric can help us to be consistent and relevant with our observations, so that we are not distracted in a skit, for example, by the clever props the student may have designed, and overlook some major problems with the actual language used.

Checklists. A checklist for a performance task is simply a listing of the qualities expected or required in a quality product or performance. For example, a checklist for the student oral weather report in the performance task just described might look like the one in Table 8.2.

When students have a checklist like this in advance, they know what is expected and can compare their own level of performance with that expectation. This checklist has the

TABLE 8.1   Worksheet for Student Weather Research. Weather Chart for _____

Date					**Averages**
High Temperature	____ °C.	____ °C.	____ °C.	____ °C.	____ °C.
High temperature feels: • freezing • cold • cool • warm • hot • very hot					
Low Temperature	____ °C.	____ °C.	____ °C.	____ °C.	____ °C.
Low temperature feels: • freezing • cold • cool • warm • hot • very hot					
Precipitation • light/heavy rain • snow • sleet • hail • mist • thunderstorm					
Wind Conditions • windy • light breeze • still					
Sky Conditions • sunny • cloudy • partly sunny • partly cloudy					
Humidity					

first four items listed as non-negotiables (Sandrock 2002). These are factors that must be completed before the performance can be evaluated, based on the remaining criteria. It is helpful for students to understand that meeting the non-negotiable criteria is the ticket to presenting work for evaluation.

Some teachers use checklists in a slightly different way. They give students a list of the outcomes for each unit when the unit begins, so that students can keep track of their own progress. This becomes a checklist for the use of both students and teacher. Table 8.3 is such a list used by Hildegard Merkle with her German students at Holy Childhood School in St. Paul, Minnesota.

One way that Hildegard uses this checklist is to have students demonstrate mastery of each item on the list as they complete it—probably with the exception of the last two items

TABLE 8.2   Checklist for Student Oral Weather Report

In my weather report I will remember to:

* ___ include information about temperature and humidity

* ___ include information about sky conditions and precipitation, if any

* ___suggest appropriate clothing for the weather in the city

* ___use visuals that clarify weather terms or other information

___ pronounce the important vocabulary words correctly

___use sentences to describe the weather

___ add interesting and relevant information

___look at my audience and be enthusiastic

___answer questions carefully and clearly

* Non-negotiable. Performance will not be evaluated until these requirements for the task are completed.

on the list. The student goes first to a partner, who monitors the performance and checks it off if it is acceptable. After successful performance with a partner, the student goes to the teacher for a final check.

Jessica Haxhi uses the format in Figure 8.1 as a summative checklist at the end of a grading period. Students assess their own progress and then the teacher checks their performance using student interviews.

TABLE 8.3   Unit Checklist: It's My Birthday!

Please check off (√) what you can do in German.

Now I can:

☐ ☐ State my own age in German.
☐ ☐ Tell the ages of my family members.
☐ ☐ Say all the months and seasons.
☐ ☐ Tell time and the days of the week.
☐ ☐ Tell and measure my height.
☐ ☐ Write a shopping list with the things I want for my party.
☐ ☐ Count money in German.
☐ ☐ Name the stores I have to go to for doing my shopping.
☐ ☐ Write an invitation to one of my friends.
☐ ☐ Sing at least one birthday song and congratulations in German.
☐ ☐ Have fun the German way! (Tells favorite activity from unit)
☐ ☐ Bake a cake following a recipe. (Done at home)

FIGURE 8.1   Summative checklist for third-grade Japanese students in Waterbury, CT.

Name _____   December 3rd grade

Things I Can Do in Japanese

Think about what you can do in Japanese. Make a checkmark under the appropriate column for each sentence. After our testing, Jessica-sensei will write a red "O" in the correct column according to how you do on the test.

	Yes!	With help	Not yet
Communication Skills			
I can say whether I have something using "_ ga aru."	○	✓	
I can ask for things using "kudasai."	⊘		
I can say "here you are" and "thank you."	⊘		
I can count to 100 by tens.		○	✓
I can count to 1,000 by hundreds.	✓		○
I can read all the hiragana we learned so far (35).	All ✓	Many ○	Few ___
Culture Skills			
I can recognize three kinds of Japanese writing: Kanji, hiragana, and katakana.	✓	○	
I can recognize different Japanese coins.	⊘		
I can play rock-paper-scissors in Japanese.	⊘		
Connections to Other Subject Areas			
I can find Japan and the U.S. on a globe and a map. (geography)	⊘		
If you give me a price, I can "draw" the correct amount of money I need using 1, 5, 10, 50, 100, and 500 yen coins. (math)		⊘	
Comparisons (of language and culture)			
I know the difference between Japanese and American money and I can tell you about how much each Japanese coin is worth in American dollars.	⊘		
Communities (Japanese Beyond the School)			
I have done at least two homeworks for Japanese so far this year.	Yes! ⊘	No ___	
I have told someone outside of school about the things I learned in Japanese class.	Yes! ✓	No ___	

Source: Reprinted by permission of Jessica Haxhi.

Checklists should represent clearly the goals and objectives for a unit or a performance task. They need to be written in language and vocabulary that is clear and understandable to students and free of educational jargon, as is the case with the examples just provided. It is often the case that the goals of the unit or a task become clearer to the teacher when they are translated into a checklist designed for students.

Checklists can be used at the end of a project or a unit so that students can assess their own work. They are usually most valuable when they are given to students at the beginning of a unit or a performance task, so the students have guidance with regard to the teacher's expectations and with regard to what constitutes quality work.

The Home Assessment System.   Spanish teachers in Pinellas County, Florida, have developed an assessment system that makes parents and classroom teachers partners in assessment. The language teachers send parents each a sheet of performance activity cards, attached to an explanatory letter. Activities are at ten different language levels, with ten performance activities for each level. When a child can accomplish one of the activities, the parent signs the card and sends it back to school with the child. The child files the card in a pocket chart in the classroom, where the classroom teacher reviews the cards with the children who have completed them. The Spanish teacher may check a few children at the beginning of the class period, as well.

Children are proud to see the cards accumulate, and the cards form a permanent record of their language development. Children can complete the cards in each set in any order, depending on their interest and their individual learning styles. New students can use the cards to catch up on what they have missed. This system helps to develop excellent ties between home and school, as well as between the language teacher and the classroom teacher.

The cards are carefully developed to incorporate all the important objectives and competencies of the program in the performance tasks. Some sample cards are shown in Table 8.4 (Gilzow and Branaman 2000, 23).

Using Rubrics for Evaluation

The rubric is another very valuable tool for evaluating student products and performances. The rubric and the checklist are similar in that they both describe the characteristics of

TABLE 8.4   Examples from Pinellas County Home Assessement System

I can say what I ate for breakfast.	I can describe (order) a well-balanced dinner.
Name _____	Name _____
Date: _____	Date: _____
Parent Signature _____	Parent Signature _____
I can name the four seasons in Spanish.	I can name five modes of transportation.
Name _____	Name _____
Date: _____	Date: _____
Parent Signature _____	Parent Signature _____

quality performance. A rubric is somewhat more complex, however, in that it also describes levels of performance. Two of the main types of rubrics are analytic and holistic.

Analytic Rubrics.   An analytic rubric scores several different components of a performance or a product. Typically the teacher chooses the three or four most important elements of a quality performance to evaluate. It is important not to overload one rubric with components, or the evaluation task becomes cumbersome. These elements are listed in the first column down the left side of the rubric.

Across the top there are usually three or four scoring categories. On a three-point scale, there would be descriptions for performance that is somewhat below standard, for good performance that meets all the criteria, and for outstanding or exemplary performance that even exceeds some of the criteria. Four categories might be termed "Not Yet Successful"; "Successful"; "Highly Successful"; and "Outstanding." These categories could also be given number values, but these numbers are not easily translatable into letter grades by percentages alone. A student who receives all threes in the rubric in Table 8.5, for example,

TABLE 8.5   Analytic Rubric for Weather Report

Criteria	Getting Ready to Try Out (1)	Intern at the Local Channel (2)	Weekend Weather Reporter (3)	Ready for the Weather Channel (4)
Appropriate Information	Weather information is present. Added information inappropriate.	Required weather information is present but not clear. Added information is sketchy or not relevant.	Includes all required weather information. Added information is present, not relevant or interesting.	Includes all required weather information. Added information is interesting, relevant.
Appropriate Clothing Suggestions	Suggestions are very unclear or inappropriate.	Suggestions are unclear or not entirely appropriate. Relationship is made to weather conditions.	Suggestions are clearly related to weather. Clothing vocabulary is limited.	Suggestions are interesting, use familiar vocabulary, clearly related to weather conditions.
Use of Visuals	Visual is made but not clear.	Visuals are sloppy or missing, or not clearly related to the presentation.	Visuals are present, but not entirely clear, or not effectively used.	Visuals are highly effective, help to make the information clear.
Presentation	Some single words, mixed with English. Language is hard to understand.	Very dependent on notes. Little eye contact. Makes some pronunciation errors, but still understandable. Enthusiasm is lacking.	Able to look away from notes at times. Some eye contact. Pronunciation correct with a few errors. Shows enthusiasm part of the time.	Presents with little or no reference to notes. Maintains good eye contact with audience. Consistently correct pronunciation. Enthusiasm is obvious.

is at the "Successful" level, and yet the point total of 12 is only 75 percent of the possible 16. On a strict percentage basis, this would be a barely passing score.

It's fun to give these categories theme-related titles, such as those shown in Table 8.5 for the weather report task.

A checklist can take on some of the qualities of an analytic rubric if there is a rating scale for each item on the checklist. A three-point scale might indicate these characteristics:

1. Somewhat below the standard of quality.
2. Meets the standard.
3. Exceeds the standard.

When non-negotiables are present on the checklist, they should be indicated simply with a yes or no rather than a scale.

Jessica Haxhi does oral testing twice a year with her first and second grade Japanese students at Maloney Magnet School in Waterbury, Connecticut. She records their performance using the checklist shown in Table 8.6, which combines a simple checklist format with quality categories. The checklist/rubric in that example is used for oral testing at the end of December.

Obviously, the description of the points on the scale can vary, according to the preferences of the teacher.

The same rubric or checklist can be used to guide self-assessment and peer assessment of student skits or other student presentations performed in front of the class. When the rubric/checklist is used this way, some teachers add at the bottom a line like this:

I want to present/show to the class the following item(s) without help: _____.

TABLE 8.6   Checklist with Elements of a Rubric

Name_____   Second Grades/December 200x

Student is able to:

	Yes!	With help	Not yet
Say the class rules according to pictures	___	___	___
Express needs such as, "Can I get a tissue?"	___	___	___
Identify the classroom objects	___	___	___
Name various Japanese and American foods	___	___	___
Tell the difference between *hiragana* and *katakana*	___	___	___
Talk about school lunch in Japan in English	___	___	___
Identify the characters in Momotaro	___	___	___
Act out the verbs give/take, go/return, eat, meet	___	___	___

This acts as a check on honesty, because the student now knows that he or she must be ready to prove that the task can be done without any help (and may erase the check in the first column and move it to the second column!) (Sandrock 2002).

Once teachers and students have had regular experience with rubrics, it can be valuable to construct the rubric together for a major product or performance. As teacher and class consider together what constitutes good work, the students are likely to have a much greater investment in the quality of their own work.

Holistic Rubrics. Holistic rubrics are most appropriate for summative evaluation; that is, they summarize the overall success of a product or a performance, based on the categories and guidelines provided in advance. Unlike the analytic rubric, they do not break the evaluation down into specific feedback on important points; thus, they provide less detailed feedback and are less effective in helping students to improve.

The Articulation and Achievement Project in New England (Jackson 1999) developed a very useful rubric for holistic scoring, shown in Table 8.7. This rubric uses three categories that serve as a very useful backbone for rubrics and checklist rubrics of all kinds:

1. Does not meet expectations.
2. Meets expectations.
3. Exceeds expectations.

When students have checklists to provide guidance in the development of a project or a performance, the holistic rubric is both more meaningful to the students and more usable by the teacher. The checklist, in that case, serves as a developmental tool, and the rubric is a summative evaluation. A sample holistic rubric for the weather report task is found in Table 8.8.

A checklist can be combined with the categories of a three-point rubric to form another convenient means of evaluating a student product. When the three-point scale is always understood to mean the same thing, it can be used effectively for many different products and performances and save the teacher time. The weather report checklist, when converted to a checklist/rubric, would look like that shown in Table 8.9.

The teacher can provide for student self-assessment by having students complete their own copy of the checklist/rubric, or they could fill in their own rating in the blank on the left of the checklist.

Rubric Development. Development of either an analytic or a holistic rubric will follow approximately the same steps:

1. Decide on the key elements that will be taken into account. In the case of the analytic rubric, these elements will be listed on the left side of the rubric, and will usually number either three or four. In the case of a holistic rubric, these characteristics will be described at each level of performance, in a parallel manner.
2. Decide on the levels of performance—usually three to four, but sometimes more. In the case of an analytic rubric, these might be labeled in a way that reflects the theme. For the analytic rubric, these will probably be listed across the top of the rubric chart.

TABLE 8.7   Rubrics for Holistic Scoring

3   Exceeds Expectations
- Message very effectively communicated
- Rich variety of vocabulary
- Highly accurate, showing no significant patterns of error
- Content supports interest level
- Self-correction increases comprehensibility

2   Meets Expectations
- Message generally comprehensible
- Vocabulary is appropriate, with some groping
- Accuracy appropriate to the stage, although some patterns of error may interfere with comprehensibility
- Content is predictable, but adequate
- Occasional self-correction may be successful

1   Does Not Meet Expectations
- Message communicated with difficulty and is unclear
- Vocabulary is often inappropriate, leading to miscommunication
- Significant patterns of error
- Content repetitious
- Self-correction is rare and usually unsuccessful

0   Unratable Sample
- No consistent use of target language, only isolated words in target language
- Off task

Note: Evaluators applying these rubrics must refer to the *Language Learning Continuum* for verification of expectations at each stage. Because this is a criterion-referenced scoring, student work samples should be held accountable to the specific criteria rather than to each other.

Source: From *Articulation and Achievement: Connecting Standards, Performance, and Assessment in Foreign Language,* page 36. Copyright © 1996 by the College Entrance Examination Board. Reprinted with permission. All rights reserved. *A Challenge to Change: the Language Learning Continuum,* page 102. Copyright © 1999 by the College Entrance Examination Board. Reprinted with permission. All rights reserved. www.collegeboard.com.

3. Describe the performance at the highest, exemplary level. For the analytic rubric, this will involve descriptions for each of the elements being evaluated. For the holistic rubric, this will involve a single description that takes into account all of the important elements of the product or the performance. This description should be achievable, but challenging. Be sure that your descriptions include only observable behaviors, so that students can easily understand the rubric.
4. Describe unacceptable performance, the lowest end of the scale. Students who do not complete the task will receive no credit, but unacceptable, or the lowest level of performance, implies that the task has at least been completed.

TABLE 8.8   Holistic Rubric for Weather Report

3	**Exceeds Expectations**

- All required information is presented and organized in an interesting way.
- Spanish is used consistently, with complete sentences and varied sentence patterns.
- Visual strongly supports the message; relationship to the content is clear and helpful.
- Information is mostly presented without reference to the text, using good expression and accurate pronunciation.
- Student makes eye contact with the audience and adjusts the presentation according to their response.

2   Meets Expectations

- Presentation includes all required information and is organized in a satisfactory way.
- Spanish is used consistently, mostly with complete sentences.
- Visual generally supports the message; relationship to the content is generally clear and helpful.
- Information is mostly read from the page, with good expression and pronunciation.
- Student makes some eye contact with the audience.

1   Needs Work

- Presentation includes all information but is poorly organized.
- Spanish is used, but mostly single words and short phrases.
- Visual is not clear, or not closely related to content.
- Information is read from the page with many stops and inaccuracies.
- No eye contact with the audience.

0   Unratable Sample

- No consistent use of Spanish, only isolated words in Spanish.
- Off task.

---

5. Describe the level(s) of performance that are acceptable but not exemplary. As you do this, go back to the "exceeds" and "unacceptable" descriptions and adjust to make sure you are comfortable with the quality of the "meets expectations."
6. Assign a value to each of the levels of performance in the rubric. Be sure that the line between unacceptable and acceptable is clear. Be sure that the differences between one level and the next are fair and equal. For example, the difference between a two and a three should not be greater or less than the distance between a three and a four. Be sure that there is an expectation of quality in the acceptable level(s).
7. Check the rubric to make sure that it really addresses the most important characteristics of the product or the performance, and that it reflects the priorities of instruction.
8. Check the analytic rubric to see if all the characteristics are equally important. If you are recording accumulated points from the rubric, you may wish to give greater

TABLE 8.9   Checklist/Rubric Gives Information about Quality of Performance

The student is expected to:

___include information about temperature and humidity	y = yes		n = no
___include information about sky conditions and precipitation, if any	y = yes		n = no
___suggest appropriate clothing for the weather in the city	y = yes		n = no
___use visuals that clarify weather terms or other information	1	2	3
___pronounce the important vocabulary words correctly	1	2	3
___use sentences to describe the weather	1	2	3
___add one piece of interesting and relevant information	1	2	3
___look at the audience and show enthusiasm	1	2	3
___answer questions carefully and clearly	1	2	3

1 = needs improvement   2 = meets expectations   3 = exceeds expectations

value to characteristics that are more important. In the case of the weather report, for example, "Appropriate Information" or "Presentation" might be more important than "Use of Visuals," so the teacher might give two points for each level of quality for the more important categories and only one point for "Use of Visuals."

Rubric for Gouin Series Activity.   Vicki Welch Alvis (2002, 3) describes a helpful assessment sequence for a hands-on class activity based on a Gouin series:

1. Students act out a Gouin series to make and describe skeleton sweets using Brach's Dem Bones candy (sold in grocery stores in October).
   - I put a napkin on my desk.
   - I put a cracker on top of the napkin.
   - I spread frosting on the cracker with a Popsicle stick.
   - I open the package of candy.
   - I place the candy on top of the frosting.
   - I describe my skeleton.
   - At last, I eat it all up!

2. Teacher assesses comprehension with a silent assessment: Students close their eyes and listen to and act out each step of the Gouin series.
3. After completing (and eating!) the activity, the teacher assesses student recall of the steps of the Gouin series by having them create a storyboard. They draw pictures and write sentences to reproduce the Gouin series on paper. The teacher uses the rubric shown in Table 8.10 to communicate progress:

TABLE 8.10   A Rubric Giving Students Feedback about Their Progress

Criteria	¡Fenomenal!	Bien hecho	Necesitas más esfuerzo
Meaning	Drawings accurately match written steps.	5 of 7 drawings match steps.	Drawings do not match steps.
Accuracy	Steps are written correctly and in order.	Some misused words or phrases.	Many misused words or phrases; steps not written in order.
Completion of task	Illustrations and written sentences for all 7 steps.	Illustrations and written sentences for 5 of 7 steps.	Less than 5 of the steps are written and illustrated.

Sample Products and Performances. Rubrics and checklists are most useful for students when they are accompanied by examples of quality student work. When students can see several examples of successful products, as in the case of a menu or a travel brochure, and perhaps one or two less successful examples, they have a clearer idea of what they are working toward. When these examples are shown before the development of a rubric, they can help to guide student thinking as they plan rubric categories and descriptions. When examples are shown after a rubric is already in place, they can be used for practice in evaluating the product examples. Effective student performance can be shared by means of videotape and used in the same way.

When providing samples of finished products and performances, it is important for the teacher to include a variety of successful examples, preferably very different from one another. If a single good example is shown, students may feel compelled to follow that example as closely as possible. When a range of successful possibilities is shown, students are more likely to express their own ideas and to exhibit creativity. Usually it is best when examples are not identified with student names—especially less successful examples.

Observation as a Source of Assessment Information

Much of the assessment for many teachers, especially at early language learning levels, is done through observation, either of performance in class or of a performance task. In order to gather information successfully and reliably using this strategy, teachers need to consider two major factors: (1) a rubric or checklist to help them focus on the most important elements of what they observe; and (2) a method for recording the information they gather through observation.

Observation is one of the most natural and appropriate ways to gather information about what early language learners know and can do. For some aspects of learning, it may be enough for a teacher to gather information just about whether a student can perform a task or not.

Can the student point to at least three colors when asked to do so?
Can the student describe a partner's clothing?
Can the student choose and name a piece of clothing?

These are all tasks for beginning students, where observation is a very common assessment strategy.

Strategies for Recording Observed Performances. Well-designed activities that reflect the outcomes of an integrated, thematic unit or lesson are inherently also tools of assessment. Many teachers record observations of individual students after each class session, using a format that lists unit outcomes and names of class members.

Of course, it isn't possible to record observations about every student every day. Most observation takes place over time; thus, it is imperative that the teacher have a careful recording procedure, to keep track of who has performed and who has not. It is practical, even for the teacher who sees many classes in a day, to record observations of three to five selected students each day, including any students whose performance was especially outstanding or notable, with some observation recorded for each student at least once a week. This procedure serves not only to develop a record of actual student performance, but it also is a reminder to the teacher of students who need more attention or who might otherwise be overlooked.

Some teachers keep a grading sheet on a clipboard, one sheet for each class, and take notes on student performance as it occurs each day. An example of this is shown in Figure 8.2.

Jennifer Roth, a K–5 French teacher in Chapel Hill, North Carolina, has a sheet like this for each class every week (Figure 8.7). Every student's name is listed. She can summarize performance in each category weekly, and make note of any special information each day in the boxes at the bottom.

Other teachers use a pad of sticky notes together with a clipboard. A planned assessment is written on top of a sheet of paper, one for each class. When a student successfully performs an assessment, the teacher writes his or her name on the sticky note and puts it on the class sheet. At the end of the day the teacher can transfer the information from each class sheet to the grade book, or to folders that are kept for each student.

The "Boxes" Strategy. Alisha Dawn Samples developed a useful assessment and recording strategy when she was teaching French in a K–5 program in Dahlonega, Georgia. She begins with two recipe boxes of different colors, for example, one blue and one green. She has colored index cards in the blue box, one color for each class, with an individual card for each student. In her lesson plans she writes what the goal of the assessment with the boxes will be for each day. At the end of a class period she regularly plays the game of "Boxes" with the students, and students are eager to participate.

At the beginning of each unit all students' names are in the blue box. She draws a name from the blue box and asks a question or asks the student to perform an action that was taught in that day's lesson. Students know that if they were good listeners they will have a chance to show it by completing a task like one that was part of the day's lesson. If the student is successful, Samples moves the card to the green box and places it on end. If

Class_____Week of __*10/2 - 10/6*____

Theme/Objective_____

Name	P	C	D	W
John Smith				
Jane Doe				
Alice James				
Hannah Adam				
Josh Cook				
Kim Burns				
Britney Top				
Sandra McVeigh				

P = Participation

C = Content

D = Discipline

W = Assigned
      Work

S = Satisfactory

N = Needs
      Improvement
      (Not yet)

U = Unsatisfactory

General Observation

lundi	mardi	mercredi
Alice ↑participation *Sandra ✓ talk*	*John - not following* *Sandra ✓ removed* *from group, own seat*	*Assembly 9 a.m.* *Sandra ✓ excessive* *talk (phone call)*
jeudi *Class very loud,* *talkative*	vendredi *Jane very verbal*	other *Britney moved* *10-2*

FIGURE 8.2   This form is used weekly to record a variety of information about student performance.

Source: Jennifer Roth, Coweta County, Georgia.

the student is not successful she puts the card back in the blue box and places it on end. At the end of the day she records the successful performance of the students whose cards were transferred to the green box and the unsuccessful attempts made by the students whose cards were put back into the blue box. The students understand that they will have another opportunity to get the task completed successfully if their card goes back into the blue box. They do not perceive this as a failure but rather as a first attempt.

Students also understand that once their card is in the green box it will stay there until everyone else's card joins them. At that time Samples returns *all* the cards to the blue box to begin again. Some units have multiple assessments of all the students using "boxes" and some have only one. When all the cards have been moved from one box to the other, the assessment for that unit or task is completed. The class celebrates their success and eagerly moves on to another round. It is important to note that this activity only takes about five minutes total of class time. All students are not assessed on exactly the same task or on the same day. Sometimes only five to seven students are assessed on a given day. At the end of each day Samples records their responses in her grade book and replaces the cards in the box they were moved to during that day's assessment.

If students still have their names in the blue box at the end of a unit and have not been able to move to the green box, the task level of difficulty can be adjusted (and noted) so that the remaining students can respond and feel successful. At the end of a unit Samples is able to look back over her students' overall performance of physical and/or oral language responses to gauge their progress. This is only one of several means of assessment that Alisha uses in her classroom.

Some teachers have altered the boxes strategy slightly by using tongue depressors or ice-cream sticks and small plastic boxes or cans. The sticks have names of the children written on them with a permanent marker, and they are color-coded by class with a color on only one of the sticks. Successful performance is indicated by moving the stick from one box to the other and placing it upside down until it has been recorded. Unsuccessful performance is indicated by placing the stick upside down in the original box until it has been recorded. One teacher has three plastic boxes attached together so the sticks can be placed in the appropriate box to indicate shaky, satisfactory, and outstanding performances. Of course, if a child is unable to perform at all, the stick would go back into the pile so the child can try again.

Recording and Grading with the "Boxes" Strategy.   Alisha Dawn Samples uses both her lesson plan book and her grade book in order to accumulate and evaluate the assessments in her classroom. In her lesson plan, under "Assessment," she writes what the assessment task of the day will be (as a reflection of what the lesson was on). For example:

> Boxes—R task (receptive). Students will be able to identify the colors of the described item by pointing or jumping from item to item. Or
>
> Boxes—P task (productive). Students will be able to describe the shape of the house in each picture (using big, small, medium, triangle, square, circle, or rectangle). Or
>
> Students will complete the activity by placing the correct number called out next to the correct item on the handout (8/8).

In her record or grade book she uses the following key for recording data:

+ —Answered correctly	MC—multiple choice
– —Answered incorrectly	HO—handout
P—Productive response	D!—Discipline/behavior issue
R—Receptive response	Abs—Absent
NP—Would not participate when called on	T—Test

Presentations—oral or written will be represented according to the rubric determined in class.

In her record book Samples records the date and a one- or two-word description of the assessment. She can go back to the plan book to see what the assessment was in greater detail and to review progress later. She records the student responses according to the key above. She can later tabulate the progress of each student using his or her marks in receptive versus productive language and their "written" or other verbal responses. She can also note the effects of their behavior and/or absenteeism on their progress. Going from left to right she can determine over time which students are both responsive and verbal, which ones are able to understand but not yet speak very much, and also those who are not able to perform due to absences, lack of participation, or poor behavior. She is not able to evaluate every objective with each student, but she can see their language ability as a whole. She also includes anecdotal notes in her record book, as well as samples of student work. A sample from Samples's record book is shown in Table 8.11.

Peer Assessment

Peer assessment can be valuable both to the student being assessed and to the students completing the assessments. It can be a valuable step toward recognition of quality and honest

TABLE 8.11   Sample from Alisha Dawn Samples's Record Book

	11/4 color id (R)	11/6 color id (R)	11/7 color id (P)	11/10 color id (P)	11/11 review colors (P)	11/13 color id HO 6/6	11/15 shape id (R)	11/16 house/shapes (R)	11/17 shapes game (R)	11/18 shapes game (P)	11/19 shapes story (P)	11/21 shapes/house HO 8/8	11/22 shapes song (P)
Erica	+R		+P	+P		6/6	+R	+R	+R	+P	+P	6/8	+P
Michael		+R	–P		–P	2/6	+R		+R	–P	–P	4/8	+P
Ashley	+R			+P		5/6	+R	–R	+R		–P	6/8	+P
Nick	–R	D!	–P		–P	0/6	D!		Abs		–P	2/8	+P
Stephanie	Abs		Abs		–P	Abs	NP		+R	Abs		Abs	–P

4 ☺ ☺	We understand you easily.
3 ☺	We understand you when the teacher or other students help a little.
2 ··	We understand you a little when the teacher or other students help a lot.
1 ⌣	You try a little but we don't understand you.

4 = excellent   3 = good   2 = satisfactory   1 = needs improvement

FIGURE 8.3   Easy-to-use format for giving students feedback on a presentation.

self-assessment. Clear guidelines, usually in the form of a rubric, are the essential element in peer assessment.

Vicki Welch Alvis (2002, 3) uses the simple "student friendly" oral assessment rubric shown in Figure 8.3 for a variety of oral topics and presentation:

Alvis uses the rubric in Table 8.12 to assess participation. It would be suitable for the use of the students themselves, the teacher, and the students' partners or other group members (5).

Hildegard Merkle uses peer assessment with middle school students to keep them alert and on task during presentations. The assessment in Table 8.13 was used to evaluate the final product of a unit on famous Germans. Each student chose a famous German person from a list, did research, and prepared a class presentation accompanied by a poster. The rubric/checklist shown in the table was given to the students in German.

TABLE 8.12   Rubric for Assessing Participation

Participation		Grade_____
Score	**Criteria**	**Comments**
4	√ Takes initiative to see that group completes project	
	√ Works enthusiastically	
	√ Begins and ends tasks promptly	
	√ Completes own share of the assignment	
3	√ Takes initiative to complete own share of assignment	
2	√ Completes own share of assignment with encouragement from teacher or partner	
1	√ Completes some of assignment with insistence from teacher or partner	

4(A) = excellent   3(B) = good   2(C) = satisfactory   1(D) = needs improvement

TABLE 8.13 Rubric for Assessment of a Final Oral Project

Directions: Take a new evaluation form for each presenter. Fill in the top portion. At the end of the presentation, circle the points given. At the end, after all questions have been answered, fill in the last two lines, give a comment, and hand in the evaluation sheet.

My name:

Name of presenter:

Famous person presented about:

	1 point	2 points	3 points
Language	Hard to understand. Sentences not complete. Past tense missing/ incorrect. Some English mixed in.	I understood almost everything. I learned some new words. Grammar mostly correct. Past tense used.	I learned so much! Excellent German! Easy to understand. Grammar correct.
	1 point	**2 points**	**3 points**
Information	Hard to stay awake. I learned only a little. Little of the required information is given.	Quite interesting! The facts are clear. Some information is missing.	Simply fascinating! I have a picture of the person's life in my head. I need to learn more!
	1 point	**2 points**	**3 points**
Answering of Questions	Unable to answer many questions. Not enough research done.	Answered briefly. Information is correct. Enough research done.	Answered all questions in detail! Able to tell stories about the person. An expert!
	1 point	**2 points**	**3 points**
Presentation	Read most facts. Not loud or clear enough.	Spoke freely with some reference to notes. Loud, clear voice.	Enthusiastic speaker! Captures audience! Want to listen more!
	1 point	**2 points**	**3 points**
Visuals/Poster	Sloppy and unimaginative. Did not help presentation.	Did not really fascinate me. Not much detail given.	Gave me insight. Illustrated the presentation.

Length of presentation:

Points given:

Comments:

Participation

The frequency and accuracy of the students' class participation is an important gauge of student understanding and progress. To encourage and keep track of participation, as well as to reward it, a number of teachers have used a system in which they award students a slip of paper for each contribution to class or for individual performance of a teacher-directed activity, as in TPR. The student places all of the tokens earned in a class period in their designated place on a bulletin board or in their notebook. At regular intervals the teacher records the accumulated points for each student. As a variation of this procedure, the students might use similar means to keep track of their success with specific outcomes—for example, using the target language to request permission from the teacher to go to the bathroom.

Comprehension Checks

Comprehension checks are quick ways to see what students understand, before a more formal assessment is used to see how well students are doing. We need to see if students truly understand before we assign practice activities! Here are several examples of quick comprehension checks.

1. Learners demonstrate understanding, or lack of understanding, by physical responses such as:
   - hold up your hand for one answer, your elbow for the other answer
   - touch your ear for yes, your nose for no
   - nod your head for yes, shake it for no
   Any number of familiar TPR commands could be used for this purpose.
2. Learners demonstrate understanding, or lack of understanding, using objects:
   - hold up yes-no cards in the target language
   - hold up objects, such as a pencil, a pen, a ruler, or a crayon
   - hold up tongue depressors that have one end painted one color and the other another color (using felt-tip markers)
3. Learners demonstrate understanding by writing an answer on a small chalk slate or a dry-erase board. This is an especially good strategy for small-group responses.

Portfolios

Development of a portfolio by each student has become one of the most popular and widespread of the non-traditional means of assessment. One of the special advantages of this approach is the collaboration between the teacher and the students in assembling and reflecting on the information in the portfolio.

Portfolios are more than just scrapbooks to be stored away with other childhood memorabilia. They should contain examples, selected by the students, that illustrate growth in language learning. The students and the teacher can also select items to place in the portfolio together. Sometimes the teacher might suggest to the whole class, for example, "This project would be an excellent item for you all to place in your portfolio, because you are really using some new skills and information here." On other occasions a teacher might suggest, "Choose one of the writing projects that you completed in this unit to keep in your portfolio at school. The others you may take home to share with your parents."

With each item placed in the portfolio, the student should write a short statement to accompany it, in English or the target language. This statement should include the student's reason for choosing the item for the portfolio, perhaps what the student is proud of, and what the item shows about student learning. It might also include a statement about what the student still needs to work on. Especially with early portfolio experiences, the teacher will need to provide a form for the student to use in supplying this information.

It would be important to include evidence from all three of the communication modes from the communication standard: interpersonal, interpretive, and presentational. A good selection of information in a portfolio might include the following:

- drawings or photographs that the student can explain or describe
- written products such as individual versions of a class Language Experience story
- poetry or other expressive writing
- letters, invitations, greeting cards, or other "writing for publication"
- photographs or slides of skits, puppet plays, simulations, or other activities in which the student participated, together with an audiotape of the student contribution, if possible
- journal entries relating to class or other experiences
- audiotapes or videotapes documenting oral participation in a meaningful group or individual activity
- visual products (or photos of them) developed through class activities: maps, charts, displays, bulletin boards

Paul Sandrock and Donna Clementi suggest a number of possibilities for student products to collect in portfolios. Here are a few of them:

Written Presentations
- expressive (diaries, journals, writing logs)
- transactional (letters, surveys, reports)
- poetic (poems, stories, plays)

Performances
- role playing, drama
- dance/movement
- reader's theater
- mime
- choral readings
- music—instrumental and choral

Representations
- maps
- graphs
- dioramas
- models
- mock-ups
- displays
- bulletin boards
- charts
- replicas

Visual and Graphic Arts
- storyboards
- drawings
- posters
- cartoons
- mobiles

Media Presentations	*Oral Presentations*

- videotapes
- audiotapes
- slides
- photo essays
- print media
- computer programs

- debates
- discussions
- interviews
- speeches
- storytelling
- oral histories
- poetry readings
- broadcasts

Evaluating Portfolios. One strategy for using portfolios is to have students select the best example of what they have learned for separate assessment (or comment, or showing off to parents and others). Short (1991) recommends the following criteria for evaluating portfolios. She emphasizes the importance of establishing and announcing these criteria in advance, and suggests the possibility that students and teacher might decide the criteria together. Some possible criteria include:

- Variety—selected pieces display the range of tasks students can accomplish and skills they have learned.
- Growth—student work represents the students' growth in content knowledge and language proficiency.
- Completeness—student work reflects finished products.
- Organization—students organized the contents systematically.
- Fluency—selected pieces are meaningful to the students and communicate information to the teacher.
- Accuracy—student work demonstrates skill in the mechanics of the language.
- Goal-oriented—the contents reflect progress and accomplishment of curricular objectives.
- Following directions—students follow the teacher's directions for selecting pieces for the portfolio (i.e., if a teacher requests eight items, student provides eight, not six).
- Neatness—student work is neatly written, typed, or illustrated.
- Justification or significance—students include reasonable justifications for the work selected or explain why selected items are significant (54–55).

The portfolio's ultimate value is that it shows that students have engaged in self-reflection, and that this has resulted in greater learning. At the end of the year, the portfolio should highlight what the student has learned, and where the student is on the continuum of proficiency. In this way they can serve as a valuable means of informing teachers at the next level of language instruction about the skills and progress of the students with whom they are about to work.

Portfolios should be housed in the school and distributed and collected for student use, so that this valuable information doesn't disappear on the trip to or from school, or serve as a nibbling exercise for the family puppy!

Grading

After all the assessment data has been accumulated and evaluated, the final step in the assessment process is grading—transforming the assessment data into a number or a symbol to report the results of evaluation. Grading policies differ from school to school, and from program to program. Some programs have decided to avoid the issue altogether and simply not give grades to students. They cite the rationale that grading can serve to discourage some students, and they prefer to have students just enjoy the program. This approach may well be problematic, for at least two reasons.

First, as we have shown, students want to know what they have learned and how good their progress is—and so do their parents.

Second, when students are receiving grades for other subjects in school, but not for languages, there is a strong tendency to believe that languages are not as "serious" or important as the other content areas. This definitely leaves the program vulnerable when budgets and programs are being cut.

Grading is a far less difficult and uncomfortable task when the teacher has sufficient information—that is, assessment data—to work with. Number values can be assigned to rubrics and checklists. Results of observations, systematic student checks, and achievement testing can be tallied. Results of all these measures can be weighted and averaged in a variety of different ways.

There are a number of questions a teacher can ask at the point of arriving at a grade. How much does completion of homework count toward the final unit, semester, or quarter grade? What weight will class participation carry? How heavily does the final performance assessment count toward a final grade? These are questions that only the individual teacher can answer, based on the priorities for that unit, that class, and that specific school setting. These decisions should be made at the beginning of planning, however, and not as the teacher sits with the grade book the night before grades are due.

How the grade itself is expressed is largely a matter of school or district policy. It might be a scale of A to F, or a percentage, or "Satisfactory/Unsatisfactory." The most important consideration is the amount of information available to parents. Some school systems use an anecdotal report card in the elementary grades. The anecdotal report can be a good opportunity to communicate program information along with the individual student report.

Jessica Haxhi's semester report to parents includes, on one side of the form, a list of the content covered in the class over the semester. The third grade, for example, covered the following:

Communication
- saying the numbers one to one hundred
- building and community helpers
- describing a scene using "there is/are" (___*ga aru*), and "there is/are not" (___*ga nai*)
- naming Japanese foods and their ingredients
- reading the forty-eight *hiragana* characters

Culture
- New Year's Day in Japan
- all about Tokyo and the flight to Japan
- Mt. Fuji
- sumo wrestling

Connections to Other Subject Areas
- using calculators to convert measurements
- solving addition and multiplication problems in Japanese

Comparisons
- knowing basic differences between Tokyo and Waterbury, and Tokyo and other American cities and towns

On the other side of the form is the individual student report. One student, whom we will call Mary Jones, received this report:

Communication	*Effort/Attitude*
Uses learned vocabulary to communicate with occasional hints.	Excellent

Culture
Develops age-appropriate knowledge of cultural practices and products.

Connections
Performs tasks from other subjects in Japanese with accuracy.

Comparisons
Demonstrates ability to compare Japanese language and culture to their own.

Comments Regarding Mary
Mary is a solid student in Japanese classes and her language skills are developing steadily. Nice work!

Even in situations where the language program is not a part of the regular reporting system, the teacher can initiate a method of sharing student progress similar to this one, in order to help both parents and students feel that progress in the language class is noticed and valued.

ACTFL Performance Guidelines for K–12 Learners

One of the most important tools for the language teacher in designing realistic goals and assessments for the classroom is the ACTFL Performance Guidelines for K–12 Learners

(Swender and Duncan 1998). These guidelines provide the performance levels for students working in a standards-based program beginning in kindergarten and continuing through grade twelve. (See Appendix.)

Performance indicators are given in six areas:

Comprehension—how well do they understand?

Comprehensibility—how well are they understood?

Cultural awareness—how is their cultural understanding reflected in their communication?

Communication strategies—how do they maintain communication?

Vocabulary use—how extensive and applicable is their vocabulary?

Language control—how accurate is their language?

Performance indicators are organized according to three levels:

Novice Learner Range
grades K–4, 5–8, or 9–10

Intermediate Learner Range
grades K–8, 7–12

Pre-Advanced Learner Range
grades K–12

Within each level, performances are listed according to the communication modes—interpersonal, interpretive, and presentational. These guidelines will help us all to set realistic goals for our students and choose appropriate performance assessments to measure our students' success. Thus, for example, the teacher in a third grade early language program might consult the "vocabulary use" category. If the students have been learning the new language since kindergarten, they will be nearing the benchmarks identified in the novice learner range (K–4). The teacher can read the descriptions to see what her students are working toward in the areas of interpersonal, interpretive, and presentational communication, as shown in Table 8.14.

After examining these guidelines, the teacher realizes that performance tasks will be most useful and realistic if they prompt students to use memorized vocabulary and phrases in familiar contexts. The teacher also realizes that extended writing or speaking in sentences will not be a realistic expectation. It will be important that activities and tasks directed toward vocabulary in the interpretive mode should use familiar contexts and be accompanied by gestures, pantomime, props, and visuals (oral) or illustrations (written) and other contextual clues.

Examination of performance indicators in the other five areas should give the teacher a basis for realistic and appropriate lessons and tasks for these third grade students.

Teachers working with beginning language students in grade three would have to recognize that students in their classrooms are at very early stages of development toward

TABLE 8.14   Novice Learner Range Grades K–4 or Grades 5–8 or Grades 9–10

Interpersonal:

- Comprehend and produce vocabulary that is related to everyday objects and actions on a limited number of familiar topics.
- Use words and phrases primarily as lexical items without awareness of grammatical structure.
- Recognize and use vocabulary from a variety of topics including those related to other curricular areas.
- May often rely on words and phrases from their native language when attempting to communicate beyond the word and/or gesture level.

Interpretive:

- Recognize a variety of vocabulary words and expressions related to familiar topics embedded within relevant curricular areas.
- Demonstrate increased comprehension of vocabulary in spoken passages when these are enhanced by pantomime, props, and/or visuals.
- Demonstrate increased comprehension of written passages when accompanied by illustrations and other contextual clues.

Presentational:

- Use a limited number of words and phrases for common objects and actions in familiar categories.
- Supplement their basic vocabulary with expressions acquired from sources such as the teacher or picture dictionaries.
- Rely on native language and phrases when expressing personal meaning in less familiar categories.

meeting these performance levels, but the performance goals are still the same. Teachers working with eighth grade students in a 5–8 program would also find their students in the novice learner range, but their topics and familiar contexts would likely be different from those of the third or fourth grade child.

Taken together, the performance indicators in the six domains provide a snapshot of learner performance at each of three points along the K–12 continuum: novice, intermediate, and pre-advanced. Teachers can use the performance guidelines to help focus their planning and assessment, no matter how many years of previous language experience their students may have had.

ACTFL Integrated Performance Assessment (IPA)

The final step in the standards initiative of the American Council on the Teaching of Foreign Languages (ACTFL) is the development of an assessment document to assist teachers in designing effective measures of student performance. The *ACTFL Integrated Performance Assessment* (American Council on the Teaching of Foreign Languages 2003) is intended to serve as "a prototype to assess students' progress toward the K–12 standards as well as students' language proficiency within the framework of the *ACTFL Performance Guidelines for K–12 Learners* (9)." The ACTFL Integrated Performance Assessment (IPA) is considered a "cluster assessment" that incorporates three linguistic tasks, each featuring one of the three modes of communication described in the Standards: interpersonal, interpretive, and presentational. The designers of the IPA envision a seamless connection between the performance assessment and standards-based curriculum and instruction.

The tasks of the IPA take place within a single, meaningful context and are designed to build upon one another. They are intended to reflect real-world uses for the language that students have learned during the course of a given unit of study. Students are motivated because the tasks are interesting and relevant to their world and their interests. Teachers prepare students for the assessments with ongoing feedback on performance during classroom instruction, as well as by providing rubrics and models of excellent performances for the IPA itself.

Together with the *Standards for Foreign Language Learning in the 21st Century* and the K–12 Student Performance Guidelines, the ACTFL Integrated Performance Assessment provides teachers and curriculum developers with a clear path toward meaningful, communicative foreign language instruction for learners of all ages. Teachers now have access to all the critical resources necessary to make the significant shift to standards-based, performance guided communicative language teaching.

Program Assessment

Program assessment is a concern both separate from and related to the development of classroom testing measures. Elementary and middle school language programs, especially when they are new to the curriculum or are experiencing extensive revision, need to provide evidence that program goals are being met. Classroom achievement testing may provide one component of this evidence. There may also be a need or a desire to demonstrate the impact of the program on student performance in other content areas, on self-concept, on attitudes, or on cognitive or social development. This type of assessment requires careful advance planning and the cooperation of administrators, classroom teachers, and assessment personnel, where available. In the case of programs established with funding provided by a government agency or by a private foundation, external evaluators may be involved in developing an assessment plan.

Assessment of Student Performance as Part of Program Assessment

One of the problems encountered in the process of program assessment is the difficulty in measuring student performance appropriately and reliably. In an educational climate that measures program success in terms of standardized test scores, elementary and middle school language programs have not had any tools available to obtain comparative information. Existing standardized tests of language skills, like the MLA Coop test, were designed for secondary school students taught in an audiolingual or a grammar-based methodology, and norms were available only for older students.

Two useful measures of student language attainment have been developed by the Center for Applied Linguistics, with a specific focus on young learners. The Student Oral Proficiency Assessment (SOPA), is designed for students in grades three through five who have had at least four years of language instruction. Originally developed for immersion students in 1991, it was adapted for FLES programs in 1996. Validity and reliability testing were completed for both versions in 1999. The ELLOPA, Early Language Listening and Oral Proficiency Assessment, was developed for children ages four to eight learning a foreign or second language in a school setting.

Student Oral Proficiency Assessment (SOPA).   The SOPA interview is fifteen to twenty minutes in length, depending on students' proficiency levels. Students participate in the interview in pairs, to reduce anxiety and create a more natural assessment situation. There are two assessors, one to conduct the interview and another to serve as a rater. Sometimes the interview is audiotaped or videotaped.

After an initial warm-up period the students perform several tasks that focus on their listening skills, using a bag of colorful and appealing manipulatives, such as plastic fruits or animals. Once the students have been successful in the listening phase, the interviewer moves on to ask simple questions about numbers, colors, and favorites. These tasks are followed by additional tasks, some of them calling for students to interact with one another. Depending on their ability, the students are given the opportunity to give directions, describe, retell a story, or persuade. After the assessment tasks are completed, students participate in a wind-down activity that leaves students feeling successful. The entire interview is designed to assess student ability in oral fluency, grammar, vocabulary, and listening comprehension.

The SOPA makes it possible for schools and school districts to assess their students' performance holistically, using the criteria based on the ACTFL Proficiency Guidelines for Speaking (revised in 1999) and the Performance Guidelines for K–12 Learners. The rating scale typically consists of nine levels, from "junior novice-low" to "junior advanced-high."

SOPA training is available through the Center for Applied Linguistics. It is offered at several language conferences and it is also available to individual school districts, on request.

Early Language Listening and Oral Proficiency Assessment (ELLOPA).   "Cow Talk," as the ELLOPA is sometimes called, consists of a series of game-like activities that are appropriate for children in pre-kindergarten through grade two. Two or three children at a time participate in a series of five language games in which they interact with a Spanish-speaking cow puppet, Señora Vaca, who speaks only Spanish. Of course, for other languages the cow would go by another target language name. This assessment focuses primarily on listening skills and only secondarily on speaking skills. Topics covered include family members, colors, numbers, size, food, songs, animals, and weather.

Student performance is rated holistically, on a scale that measures listening comprehension, fluency, vocabulary, language control (grammar), communication strategies, and cultural awareness.

Resources for Program Assessment

While a full description of program assessment is beyond the scope of this chapter and this text, it must be taken seriously by every elementary and middle school language teacher.

Schinke-Llano (1985), Heining-Boynton (1991), and Rosenbusch (1991) offer suggestions and formats for program assessment to assist teachers and program coordinators in developing an effective assessment process.

Student Achievement Testing

Of course, there is still a place for quizzes and tests, even within the performance-based mindset that we have developed as a profession. Written tests and quizzes can demonstrate mastery of specific skills at a specific point in time. They are probably most useful as guideposts along the way, like the comprehension checks described earlier in this chapter. They help the teacher and the students themselves to know what building blocks to pay closer attention to before the language can be successfully used in meaningful performance tasks.

Tests and quizzes can be made much more meaningful if they are contextualized, or made to resemble some real-life situation. For example, a multiple choice test could tell the story of a teddy bear's trip to the rainforest, and students could choose appropriate vocabulary or responses to make the story "make sense."

The following guidelines are offered for the use of teachers who wish to develop a program of student achievement testing, in addition to the performance-oriented assessments above, that is congruent with both their own goals and with the needs of the children in their classes.

Guideline One: Use the Achievement Test as an Opportunity for Children to Discover How Much They Know, Not How Much They Still Have To Learn

Many teachers, like their students, recall testing experiences in which it seemed clear that the test was designed to trick and confuse them, and to demonstrate that they didn't know as much as they might have thought. No matter what grade may eventually have been awarded on the test, the feeling of frustration and inadequacy lingered long after the test items had been forgotten.

In an early language classroom that has focused on providing students with successful experiences in communication, the testing situation can be an extension of the same principle. Just as the teacher attempts to reduce students' anxiety and to enhance their motivation and self-confidence for language activities in the classroom, so can the teacher reduce anxiety and enhance motivation to help students to achieve success in demonstrating what they have learned. For example, teachers can schedule short testing sessions on a regular basis to prevent children from becoming anxious and to avoid placing unwarranted importance on the role of testing in the class.

Guideline Two: Test What Has Been Taught in the Way It Has Been Taught

There should be no surprises on a test designed to help students discover what they know. All the skills that have been used in activities during class should be included in the test in some way. Skills and specific materials should be tested using the same type of communicative activity by which they were practiced. For example, if a teacher wishes to use a paper-and-pencil test to determine whether students understand commands that have been practiced in the classroom, that teacher can prepare the students to feel comfortable with the test item by introducing a game-like partner activity. In one game, students choose a picture that matches a command given by the teacher or by one of their classmates; in another game they draw stick figures to represent a command and compare their results with one another. If listening has been emphasized in the class, it should be emphasized in the testing situation. If speaking has been practiced during class, it should be a part of the assessment in approximately the same proportion as it was in the class, and using similar speaking situations.

The teacher who plans each lesson on the basis of carefully worded, student-oriented objectives has already laid the groundwork for the activities that will be a part of the assessment. Each objective that appears on the test should bear approximately the same weight of importance that it carried in the development of class activities.

While performance assessment in its great variety may have the most to offer the foreign language setting at the elementary and middle school level, there continue to be times when more traditional paper-and-pencil measures will also be helpful. These approaches are familiar to students and parents, as well as teachers, and thus can provide valuable corroboration of information gathered by other means. Hadley (2001) makes a case for, and suggests strategies for developing "hybrid classroom tests," in which traditional classroom tests are revised to give them a more communicative orientation. One of the key components in this revision is the idea of providing a context for all test items; for example, a series of ten questions would all refer to the same familiar story and actually develop an idea or a narrative sequence. This allows the learner to use all the information available, both on the page and in her or his own memory, to complete the task.

The best source of ideas for assessment are the activities and contexts used in daily class sessions, since these are the settings within which meanings and understanding have been developed. Additional suggestions are provided below, most of them especially appropriate for early levels of language acquisition, when assessment seems to be the most difficult.

Suggestions for Testing

Interpretive Mode: Listening

1. *True-false tests.* In advance, prepare answer sheets numbered from 1 to 10 (or 1 to 15, or 1 to 20, depending on length desired), with *true* and *false* given for each number. With no additional preparation the answer sheet shown here may be used for any of the test items described below.

1. True	False		1. oui	non		1.	
2. True	False		2. oui	non		2.	
3. True	False		3. oui	non		3.	
4. True	False		4. oui	non		4.	
5. True	False	OR	5. oui	non	OR	5.	

6. True	False		6. oui	non		6.
7. True	False		7. oui	non		7.
8. True	False		8. oui	non		8.
9. True	False		9. oui	non		9.
10. True	False		10. oui	non		10.

a. Show the class a picture that includes more than one item of information (for example, different types of weather and their effects, a scene with individuals performing a variety of actions, and so forth). Then read statements about the picture, and have the students respond with true or false.

b. Read a short paragraph or dialogue to the class. Then make several statements about the content of the selection or probable outcomes of the situation. The students respond *true* or *false* on the basis of the correctness of each statement.

c. Read a command and perform the action commanded, or show a picture of the action being commanded or described (see Figure 8.4). Have the students indicate *true* if the command or statement and the action agree; have the students indicate *false* if they do not agree. Link the actions in a meaningful, story-like sequence to provide maximum context.

d. Base some true-and-false statements on reasonableness or logic. For example, if you read, "The turtle says bow-wow," the students would mark *false*.

(**CAUTION!** *Never* include a negative in a statement used for a true-false item.)

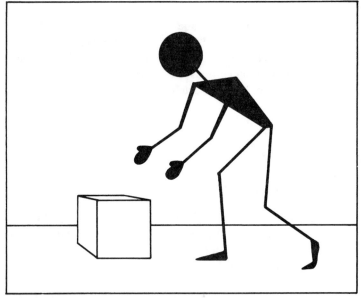

He is going to lift the box.   T   F

FIGURE 8.4 Sample true-false item.

2. *Listening/picture stimuli tests.* In advance prepare answer sheets with 1 to 10 questions (or more) and the choices of (a), (b), (c), (d), or (e) for each question. This type of answer sheet lends itself to a variety of question techniques, which are described below.

1. (a)___   (b)___   (c)___   (d)___   (e)___
2. (a)___   (b)___   (c)___   (d)___   (e)___
3. (a)___   (b)___   (c)___   (d)___   (e)___
4. (a)___   (b)___   (c)___   (d)___   (e)___
5. (a)___   (b)___   (c)___   (d)___   (e)___
6. (a)___   (b)___   (c)___   (d)___   (e)___
7. (a)___   (b)___   (c)___   (d)___   (e)___
8. (a)___   (b)___   (c)___   (d)___   (e)___
9. (a)___   (b)___   (c)___   (d)___   (e)___
10. (a)___   (b)___   (c)___   (d)___   (e)___

a. Show students several pictures, each of them numbered. When the students hear a statement, have them place the number of the appropriate picture next to the letter for that statement. For best results, the pictures should be related to one another in a meaningful way, perhaps placed in a sequence showing development of a sequence or a story line.

b. Give the students a picture showing several activities. Read sentences describing each of the activities, and have the students place the number of the sentence on the part of the picture that depicts the activity described. As an alternative, show a picture that has numbers on it, and have the students place the number of the activity next to the letter of the sentence read. Make the picture as rich with connections and even humor as possible—for example, an item for a German class combining culture and activities might be as follows: "The *Heinzelmännchen* have stolen into the home of the sick family to help out. Each of the workers has found something to do, but some of them have chosen very strange tools for the job. Mark the number that shows the activity being described. Number one is washing the dishes."

c. Present classroom objects or other learned vocabulary in individual pictures, either on the students' papers or on cards in the front of the class. Read statements containing the individual vocabulary items, and have the students number the items to correspond to the sentences (or place the number of the object beside the letter of the sentence that you read). The sentences should be in a connected, meaningful narrative. This type of item tests (and encourages) the students' ability to perceive known language embedded in unfamiliar language (see Figure 8.5).

d. Give a "labeling" exercise: have students place numbers corresponding to the correct identification of a part of a picture (body parts, table setting, countries, and so forth) when they hear you read the identification, *or* when they hear you read a statement containing the label. This could be developed as a description of a fantasy creature, which will help to find the creature hiding in the closet.

e. For more advanced students, prepare a short connected story using sentences that the students have learned, but in a different context. Place a collection of large pictures on the chalkboard tray, flannel board, pocket chart; or display pictures on the

FIGURE 8.5   Sample multiple-choice test item.

overhead projector. Have the students look at the pictures while listening a second (or third) time to the narrative. Then ask the children to write on their papers the letters of any pictures that represent a part of the story, or perhaps to list the letters in order to show the sequence of the story.

3. *Carrying out commands*. For a classroom in which TPR is an important tool, carrying out commands is one of the most natural of all types of assessment techniques. Berty Segal (n.d.) suggests establishing a list of commands that incorporate the key learning elements for each unit of instruction. While other students are working at their seats, working at learning stations, or developing group projects, Segal tests students in groups of three by giving the commands and having the students carry them out. She uses the same list of commands for all student groups, varying the order in which they are given. The teacher uses a grid to check students who do *not* perform the command accurately. Other options include the following:

a. Make a picture test containing balloons, either in numbered squares or in a picture format on which each balloon itself is numbered. Ask students to color the balloons according to instructions. You can construct other tests in which you ask students to identify some elements of a picture with numbers or colors, or in which students draw a picture or construct figures on command (for example, the monster drawings).

b. Have individual students carry out your commands, either orally or by writing on slips or cards. You can devise these commands to show comprehension of other vocabulary in addition to the verbs involved.

Interpersonal Mode: Speaking

If all instruction in speaking has been in context and communicative, the assessment function should also be contextual and communicative. The scheme of assessment should reflect the ongoing goals of the program rather than focusing on detail and grammar (which often seem easier to evaluate). In many cases interpersonal contexts are genuine, naturally occurring opportunities for performance assessment. Interpersonal activities that could form the basis for assessment include the following:

1. *Personal question-answer.* Have students discuss a familiar topic, something often discussed in class in the same manner, with you or with one another.
2. *Dialogue.* Two (or several) children may perform a dialogue they have created, memorized, or adapted.
3. *Rejoinder.* Make a statement to which students respond appropriately: for example, if you say, "I feel terrible today" the student says, "That's too bad."
4. *Picture reaction.* Give students a picture; have them respond either by telling about it, or perhaps by giving the command suggested by the picture (at an earlier stage). See the example in Figure 8.6.
5. *Narrative or dialogue completion.* Give the students part of a familiar narrative or dialogue, and ask them to complete it, either by choosing the completion learned in class or by providing a new one created for the occasion.
6. *Role reversal.* You may use role reversal as a means of evaluating the individual student's development of speaking skills, but neither the teacher nor the student should view it primarily as an assessment tool. When role reversal has become a standard and comfortable part of class procedure, you may begin to incorporate some elements from this activity into the assessment format.
7. *Oral identification and/or description of familiar objects.* Have students draw familiar objects from a sack or from a "magic box" and identify or describe them aloud. (This may also be a good opportunity to work with requests, politeness vocabulary, and other components of the rituals that have been established in class.) This strategy could be structured as a game, in which students describe items to the class and the class tries to guess which familiar object has been drawn.
8. *Puppet show.* Have children work in pairs or in small groups to develop puppet shows that may serve as a demonstration of what they have learned.

Interpretive Mode: Reading

Creating means of assessing reading as a communicative function can be challenging, but such means are possible. Asking students to perform written commands is a natural first step, and these commands can take on greater complexity as students progress.

1. Adapt items suggested in the listening section to evaluate reading by changing the stimulus from the spoken to the written word. (Many of the listening items are readily adaptable.)

FIGURE 8.6 Sample Picture Item. Teacher says: "Tell me something about this picture," or "Give a command that would fit the action."

2. Ask students to perform commands delivered in writing, either individually or as paper-pencil responses done by the entire class at one time.
3. Have students read parts of stories written by the group and react to them in some way—true-false items, multiple choice items, and so forth. They may fill in blanks with words chosen from a list at the end of or on the side of the reading passage (cloze procedure).
4. Have students match labels with pictures or parts of pictures.

Writing: Interpersonal and Presentational Modes

Much writing will be copying in the early years of an early language program, but some assessment of writing, in addition to listening, speaking, and reading, will leave students with a sense of achievement in all four skills.

1. *Labeling*. Have students label pictures or parts of pictures with the appropriate target language term (see Figure 8.7).
2. *Cloze or completion*. Have students fill in blanks in a familiar passage, or complete an anecdote without an immediate model. In this kind of an assessment the context is very important, so students will be filling in the blanks to make the meaning clear.
3. *Commands*. Have students write commands to be performed by the teacher or by a classmate.

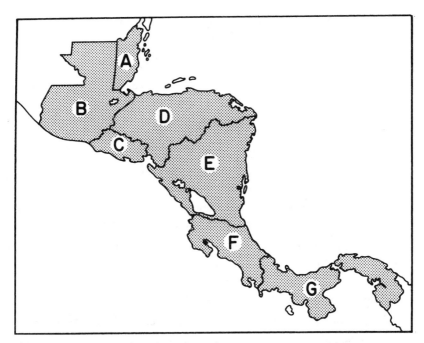

FIGURE 8.7   Teacher says: "Label the countries on this map from which we have had guests in class."

Teacher Evaluation

The teacher is the most important part of any classroom, in any subject area. Teachers who are committed to personal and professional growth and to providing the finest possible learning environment for their students can be the best evaluators of the teaching and learning that take place in their own classrooms. The assistance of supportive peers and administrators can also help teachers to achieve new goals and to develop new dimensions of their teaching skills. Teachers can work together to give one another feedback and support as they experiment with new approaches and techniques. The reorientation of language teaching toward communication and performance is a major step away from the traditions within which most language teachers have themselves learned languages and have been trained to teach them. Ongoing support and encouragement from peers will play an essential role in making this significant reorientation.

The checklist of teaching behaviors that follows is oriented toward communicative language teaching in the elementary and middle school. It is intended to assist teachers who wish to evaluate their own teaching and to be helpful observers of one another. It will also assist administrators in giving support and feedback to language teachers working in their schools. The observation guide can be used most successfully over an extended period of time, for a series of observations.

The Effective Elementary and Middle School Language Teacher

Use of the Target Language

___ **1.** Teacher uses target language as the normal and expected means of classroom communication.

   ___Uses natural speed and intonation

   ___Uses gestures, facial expressions, and body language

   ___Uses concrete referents such as props, realia, manipulatives, and visuals (especially with entry-level students)

   ___Uses linguistic modifications when necessary to make the target language more comprehensible for the students

___ **2.** Teacher keeps use of the native language clearly separated from use of the target language.

Communicative Language Teaching

___ **3.** Teacher provides students with opportunities for extended listening.

___ **4.** Teacher uses authentic communication to motivate all language use.

___ **5.** Teacher practices sensitive error correction with primary focus on errors of meaning rather than on errors of form.

___ **6.** Teacher provides hands-on experiences for students, accompanied by oral and written language use.

___ **7.** Teacher accelerates student communication by teaching functional chunks of language.

___ **8.** Reading and writing for communication are integrated with listening and speaking experiences.

___ **9.** Reading and writing are based on student-centered experiences, including experiences with literature.

___ **10.** Questions and activities provide for a real exchange of information and opinions.

___ **11.** Students ask as well as answer questions.

___ **12.** Grammatical structures and vocabulary are introduced and practiced in meaningful contexts.

___ **13.** Classroom routines provide students with clear clues to meaning.

Lesson Content

___ **14.** Lesson/unit is clearly standards-based, with both targeted and supporting standards.

___ **15.** Lesson/unit shows relationship to a guiding thematic idea (thematic center).

___ **16.** Lesson/unit shows a balance of language, culture, and subject content goals.

___ **17.** Language components of lesson/unit emphasizes language in use.

___ **18.** Grammar is presented through and for usage rather than analysis.

___ **19.** Lessons incorporate global and multicultural awareness.

___ **20.** Lessons contain links to the general school curriculum.

___ **21.** Lessons contain information and experiences drawn from the target culture(s).

___ **22.** Culture activities include experiences with children's literature from the target culture(s).

___ **23.** Lessons avoid and attempt to counter cultural and other stereotypes.

Lesson Planning

___ **24.** There is evidence of detailed planning.

___ **25.** Lessons incorporate both new and familiar material.

___ **26.** Plans include experiences with both oral and written language.

___ **27.** Individual activities are part of an overall plan that includes careful preparation and follow-up.

___ **28.** Lesson content and activities are appropriate to age and developmental level of the class.

___ **29.** Plans incorporate activities from a variety of cognitive levels.

___ **30.** Plans address a variety of cognitive styles and intelligences.

___ **31.** Activities provide students with successful learning experiences.

___ **32.** Teacher provides smooth and logical transitions from one activity to another.

Lesson Implementation

___ **33.** Teacher uses a variety of classroom techniques.

___ **34.** Teachers and students use visuals and realia effectively.

___ **35.** Teacher uses many and varied concrete materials and realia.

___ **36.** Teacher gives clear directions and examples.

___ **37.** Teacher allows ample wait time after questions.

___ **38.** Teacher maintains a pace that has momentum and a sense of direction.

___ **39.** Teacher changes activities frequently and logically.

___ **40.** Students are active throughout the class period

___individually   ___ as part of groups.

___ **41.** There are varied groupings of students and varied interaction patterns

___teacher/student   ___ student/teacher   ___ student/student.

Classroom Climate

___ **42.** Teacher appears enthusiastic and motivated.

___ **43.** Teacher shows patience with student attempts to communicate.

___ **44.** Teacher uses varied and appropriate rewards.

___ **45.** Environment is attractive and reflects the target culture.

___ **46.** Discipline is positive, prompt, non-disruptive.

Monitoring and Assessment

___ **47.** Teacher constantly monitors student comprehension, avoiding reference to the students' native language.

___ **48.** Teacher assesses language development in meaningful contexts.

___ **49.** Teacher uses a variety of formal and informal performance assessment tools.

Summary

A careful and systematic assessment process is an essential component of the early language program. The most powerful assessment tools are performance tasks that allow students to use the language they have learned in a meaningful and purposeful way. The culminating performance assessment focuses the unit and guides the planning of all unit components and activities. Checklists and rubrics can help teachers to evaluate performance on these tasks and help develop student skills in self-assessment.

Students can also benefit from achievement testing that gives them the opportunity to demonstrate what they have learned in a supportive, positive atmosphere designed to help them succeed. The most effective assessment tools will test what has been taught in the way it has been taught. Only when the means of testing appropriately reflect the goals of the curriculum can those goals most effectively be achieved.

Student performance assessment can be an important component of program assessment. Two useful tools, the SOPA and the ELLOPA, have been developed by the Center for Applied Linguistics to assist schools and programs in evaluating student progress.

Evaluation of teacher performance is another important component of the effective elementary and middle school program. It is most valuable when the teacher is a critical self-evaluator who receives support and encouragement from colleagues and administrators. The communicative, standards-based reorientation of language teaching is a dramatic change in approach that requires a cooperative effort from all members of the teaching team.

FOR STUDY AND DISCUSSION

1. In your department meeting, a discussion has developed about the current policy of giving children in the elementary school language program a grade of "Satisfactory/Unsatisfactory" and basing the assessment on observation of the degree of each child's participation and enthusiasm. You have been in the department only a few weeks, but you have some insight to add. What suggestions would you make to the department, and why?

2. You and your fellow teacher have decided to develop some of your tests together in order to be able to write more effective assessments. However, now she is complaining about the tests you write. She claims that if you give the children only material that you are sure they can succeed with, and test them in the same way you taught them, then the results of your tests aren't worth anything. How do you respond to her?

3. Choose a series of lessons from FLES materials that you know, from observations you have made, or from lessons found on the Internet. Design a short test for one or two of the objectives covered in the lessons, no more than five questions, keeping in mind the testing prin-

ciples identified in this chapter. What activities in the lessons have prepared the children to be tested in this way? Or what activities would you have to incorporate in the lessons in order to use the testing items you have written?

4. Examine carefully the K–12 Performance Guidelines for the novice level, including all six of the categories described (see Appendix). Design a performance task that would allow students to show their ability to use the language at this level in interpersonal, interpretive, and presentational modes of communication, and indicate which of the guidelines are being addressed. Create a checklist and a rubric to assist you in evaluating this assessment.

5. Use the teacher checklist in this chapter to evaluate your own teaching performance in the class setting with which you are most familiar. Write a goals statement in which you set objectives for your continued growth as a teacher. Use that personal goals statement to list four things you would like to have your favorite colleague watch for and give you feedback about on her or his next visit to your class (make them very specific).

FOR FURTHER READING

The following sources are recommended for additional information about material covered in this chapter. Chapter citations are documented in Works Cited at the end of the volume.

Blaz, Deborah. *A Collection of Performance Tasks and Rubrics. Foreign Languages.* Larchmont, NY: Eye on Education, 2001.

Boyles, Peggy. "Scoring Rubrics: Changing the Way We Grade." *Learning Languages* 4, no. 1 (1998): 29–32.

Gilzow, Douglas F., and Lucinda E. Branaman. *Lessons Learned. Model Early Foreign Language Programs.* McHenry, IL: Center for Applied Linguistics and Delta Systems Co., 2000.

Goodman, Kenneth S., Lois Bridges Bird, and Yetta M. Goodman, eds. *The Whole Language Catalog:*

Supplement on Authentic Assessment. Santa Rosa, CA: American School Publishers, 1992.

Heining-Boynton, Audrey. "The FLES Program Evaluation Inventory (FPEI)." *Foreign Language Annals* 24, no. 3 (1991): 193–201.

National Capita Language Resource Center. *Portfolio Assessment in the Foreign Language Classroom.* Interactive module available on-line at: www.cal.org/nclrc/portfolio/modules.html

O'Malley, J. Michael, and Lorraine Valdez Pierce. *Authentic Assessment for English Language Learners. Practical Approaches for Teachers.* United States: Addison-Wesley Publishing Company, 1996.

Sandrock, Paul. *Planning Curriculum for Learning World Languages.* Madison, WI: Wisconsin Department of Public Instruction, 2002.

9 Managing the Successful Early Language Classroom

Every teacher steps into a classroom with the intention of being effective, although we may not always have a clear idea of how to achieve that goal. Based on their research, Good and Brophy (1994) identified three characteristics of effective teachers (376–377): they have classroom management skills, they teach for lesson mastery, and they practice positive expectations.

These characteristics are clearly closely related, and much of this book supports effectiveness in all three areas. This chapter focuses on the first of these characteristics: managing an early language classroom. Classroom management involves all of those procedures and routines that make our time with our students as productive as possible. Without effective management skills, a teacher's repertoire of units and activities is useless.

Just as we plan the content of the lesson and unit, we must also plan for the management of the class: rules and consequences, procedures and routines. Just as we have objectives and outcomes in our lesson and unit plans, we have goals and plans for student behavior in our management plan.

Factors beyond the Teacher's Control

There are a number of factors involved in classroom management over which the teacher has virtually no control. We have to develop our management strategy by taking these factors into consideration, factors that differ from school to school and even from class to class. This section describes some of these factors.

Time of Day

In the morning classes may be full of energy, and many elementary school teachers regard morning as prime learning time. On the other hand, an early morning class in the middle school might be difficult to wake up. During the last hour of the day, students tend to be tired—or sometimes all wound up such as on a Friday or just before a holiday.

Lunch presents another issue. Before lunch students may be hungry and preoccupied, or restless and watching the clock, especially in middle school. After lunch some students may be sleepy, and others may be especially excitable if they had a high-sugar meal.

We need to take into account where students were immediately before the language class. They may have come from outdoor play, or from physical education, and they will need activities and encouragement to help them cool down so they can make the most of class time. They may have come from a relatively quiet activity, or from a long stretch of sitting or concentrating. Then they may need the teacher to energize them and refocus them on the language tasks.

Where the Language Class Is Held

It's possible that elementary school language teachers work in their own classrooms. It is even more likely, however, that they will be teaching from carts and traveling from one classroom to the next. Those teachers have to work within the management styles of the classroom teachers, and they may need to negotiate some of their own management system with other teachers. Here the key to success is establishing good relationships with fellow teachers.

Moving from class to class means adjusting to the mood of each new classroom, and sometimes having to wait until the classroom teacher is ready to turn the class over to the language teacher. Once in a while a classroom teacher returns to the class late, causing the language teacher to be late and perhaps breathless for the start of the next class.

Sometimes language classes are held in choir rooms, on stages in the gymnasium, or in a corner of the library. Each of these non-typical class settings has its own challenges and requires specific management planning.

Social and Emotional Factors: Nature of Children

The last and most important of the factors beyond our control is the nature of the students that we are dealing with. They are just kids! And they carry all the developmental characteristics of students their age.

Teachers need to be knowledgeable about how children develop and about what constitutes typical and predictable behavior for each of the ages we teach. The language teacher who is determined to have kindergarten children sit still for fifteen minutes at a time will misinterpret the five-year-old's need to move around as misbehavior and treat the child accordingly. The teacher who uses regular and frequent partner activities because she recognizes the need for middle school students to interact with their friends has learned to turn a developmental characteristic into an advantage for language learning.

These kids we teach tend to be fun-loving and enthusiastic, and they show their enthusiasm and their sense of fun in different ways at different ages. They can be amazingly perceptive and unbearably wise. They can be stubborn and frightened. They can be easily hurt, and sometimes those who seem to have the toughest shell are the most fragile inside.

We may have troubled students who need every bit of our skill to help them manage themselves in our classrooms. We may have students with physical and emotional needs beyond our expertise, but our class needs to be a special place for all of them.

Frank Smith (1988, 1997) has described language learning as a social gift, not a genetic gift. Learning another language is becoming a member of the club, the community of people who speak that language. We can invite all students in.

Factors within the Teacher's Control:
Classroom Management Basics

Advice to new teachers almost always centers around classroom management issues: "Be organized." "Be prepared." "Be firm." "Be consistent." "Be fair." The number of books addressing classroom management could fill one whole wing of a library. The best place to start in developing a plan for classroom management, however, is within the school itself. To plan an effective program of classroom management for a specific school setting, the teacher should:

- Be informed about all school procedures and follow them carefully.
- Find out which classroom teachers have the best reputation for well-managed classrooms—then visit with them and visit their classes. They will have the best understanding of the students in this school and at these grade levels. The observation suggestions in Table 9.1 will help to make the most of such a visit.
- In the elementary school setting, visit all the classes she or he will be working with before beginning language instruction, if possible, in order to understand the way each of the classrooms functions and to get a feeling for how students behave generally in their regular classes. This is especially important for teachers who are new to the level they will be teaching.
- Talk with other language teachers in the school or in another school in the same community, if there are other language programs.
- Read books on successful management, such as those suggested at the end of this chapter.

The following major guidelines for classroom management will help teachers to organize and evaluate the advice they receive and to build their own management plan that will be effective specifically for the early language classroom.

1. Maintain a positive environment.
2. Establish clear procedures.
3. Plan for every single moment—and beyond!
4. Be proactive: involve parents and the school community.

Maintain a Positive Environment

The Teacher—Who am I? The essential element in a successful classroom is the teacher. Every study of methodology or student performance eventually concludes that the single most important factor in student success is the teacher. Teachers need to ask themselves: "Who am I? What are my strengths? What are my weaknesses? Am I aware of them so that I can build on my strengths and compensate for my weaknesses? What are my reasons for being a teacher?" If we have a realistic picture of ourselves and feel confident that we have the skills we need to be successful early language teachers, we can also be successful in creating positive feelings in our classrooms.

Haim Ginott (1972) makes an eloquent statement about the significance of the teacher in the classroom environment:

TABLE 9.1   Observation Suggestions for Elementary/Middle School World Language Classrooms

Take notes on the sheet below and use them as a basis for discussion after class.

Grade level observed _____ date _____ time _____ to _____

What did the teacher do to gain attention?

What strategies did the teacher use for beginning and ending activities, and for making transitions from one activity or topic to another?

What did the teacher do to motivate pupil interest and engagement?

What kinds of activities did you observe in the class (teacher presentation, partner or small group work, individual seat work, problem-solving, etc.)? How often did activities change?

What topics and activities seemed to be especially motivating to these pupils?

Did there seem to be any class routines that were followed, patterns pupils knew to follow? What rules or expectations do pupils seem to understand in this classroom? Explain.

What types of non-verbal communication did the teacher use (eye contact, hands, proximity, etc.)?

How do these pupils behave when they are bored? Excited? Under stress?

What behaviors (individual or group) surprised you? Bothered you? Impressed you? Were there any behaviors that bothered you but didn't seem to bother the teacher? Or that she or he seemed to ignore?

What did you learn about pupils of this age during this visit to their classroom?

> I've come to a frightening conclusion. I am the decisive element in the classroom. It's my personal approach that creates the climate. It's my daily mood that makes the weather. As a teacher, I possess a tremendous power to make a child's life miserable or joyous. I can be a tool of torture or an instrument of inspiration. I can humiliate or humor, hurt or heal. In all situations, it is my response that decides whether a crisis will be escalated or de-escalated, and a child humanized or de-humanized. (15–16)

Mission.   Another way we build a positive focus is by remembering our powerful and important mission. We are giving our students the beautiful gift of another language, in a country in which that opportunity has not always been available. We are opening the door to new ways of thinking, a door that links us to the rest of the world. Many of us have come to believe that this is an important step toward peace.

Sense of Humor.   We need to activate our sense of humor, because it is such a help in maintaining a positive atmosphere. If we remember to keep it with us at all times, we may be amazed at how far it will take us. Approaching a situation with humor and patience can defuse many tense moments.

A classroom filled with laughter is likely to be a healthy classroom. It is important to remember, however, that laughter should never be at the expense of the dignity of any student, and laughing at another student should be promptly confronted and stopped.

Keeping Our Cool. Anger has no place in the classroom. Allowing oneself to lose control and to shout is simply inappropriate. And tempting though it may be at times, striking back at a student with a put-down or sarcasm damages everyone in the classroom—including the teacher. These are the same behaviors that we are trying to discourage our students from using. Even though we might be seething inside, maintaining a calm and supportive manner is an essential part of keeping a positive atmosphere.

Motivating Students. Another key to maintaining a positive environment is to motivate our students. Motivation is important both for the content of our lessons and units and to help students understand the value of learning another language. We need to explain the reasons for an early start and a long sequence and why the language they are learning is important. In this way we can empower them to participate more fully.

Availability and Visibility to Students. We can also nurture a positive atmosphere by being available to students before and after school, for help, and on occasion just to talk. We can share a bit of ourselves during our classes, so that they recognize us as people with interests and with interesting experiences. We can greet students by name when we meet them in the classroom and when we see them in the halls or in the world beyond the classroom.

One of the most meaningful ways to be visible and supportive to students is to attend their activities and chaperone their field trips and parties. When we can tell a student "I really enjoyed your play last night" or "The band concert was very enjoyable," we are affirming them and supporting them in important ways. The additional benefit for the teacher is the discovery of talents and aspects of personality that are not always revealed in the language classroom.

Establish Clear Procedures

Our second classroom management basic is to establish clear procedures. This means that we have clear and concrete expectations for academic performance and for how the classroom functions, and that we present these expectations to the students in a clear, step-by-step fashion. Many students do not transfer behavioral expectations from the English language setting, where there is relative silence much of the time. The language class is sometimes a real contrast, and students need clear guidance as to what is expected.

Establish Rules. Establishing and communicating a set of classroom rules is an extremely important element in helping the classroom to function smoothly. We can help to maintain a positive environment when we state classroom rules positively and reinforce positive behaviors.

When establishing our rules in the elementary school setting, we must also consult with the classroom teachers and set up ground rules for how we will operate together. For example, the language teacher will need to make clear who will do the disciplining during the language class and how well the language class rules will mesh with those of the classroom teacher. Of course, all rules will be consistent with school policies.

The first step in developing a set of rules is to decide which behaviors are important to us in the classroom. Next we put those behaviors into short and simple statements or commands in the target language, so that the students will be able to understand them.

These statements should be positive; for example, instead of "Don't Run" state "Walk." Instead of "Don't touch your neighbor" state "Keep hands and feet to yourself." Effective rules should be:

1. observable
2. enforceable
3. non-judgmental
4. an expression of behavior that is important to the teacher in order to teach effectively
5. in the target language

Audray Weber's rules for her K–5 Spanish classes are: *¡Paren, Miren, Escuchen!* (Stop, Look, Listen!) When she wants attention she sings those three words in a familiar pattern and the students respond immediately.

Jo Ellen Hague's rules for her French classes are: Look, Listen, Participate (by raising your hand), and Speak French!—*Regardez, Ecoutez, Participez, Parlez français!* She writes each of these rules on a paddle, and when students need to be reminded of one of the rules she holds up that paddle. She also reviews the rules daily by holding up the paddles.

Jessica Haxhi has four rules for her Japanese students: Listen, Raise your hand, Keep hands to yourself, Speak Japanese! She also has an important silence signal: when she wants students to stop whatever they are doing and be quiet, she places both hands on top of her head with her elbows raised. When students see this they put their hands on their heads, too, stop talking, and pay attention to the teacher.

Once the teacher has decided on the rules, the next step is to plan how to teach the rules using the target language. The most effective way to go about this is to do a lot of modeling and then to involve student participation. When teachers incorporate a motion with each rule the students remember it more easily, and the teacher can later use TPR as a form of practice for the rules. In the case of Jessica's four rules for Japanese, for example, she has the students cup their hands behind their ears for "Listen." They raise their hand dramatically for "Raise your hand." They cross their arms and hold their hands above the elbow for "Keep hands to yourself," and for "Speak Japanese" they make speaking motions with their hands and repeat a Japanese greeting. Many teachers post their rules in the target language after they have taught them, usually with a picture or other symbol to help students connect the words with meanings.

Jessica is able to communicate to the students exactly what they may and may not do in the class when she demonstrates what it looks like to break the rule and then points to the rule or shows the gesture for the rule. Some teachers have a puppet misbehave and ask the students to point to the rule, or show the motion for the rule, or call out the rule, once they have learned the language for doing so.

One of the most important things to remember about establishing and implementing rules in a classroom in which only the target language is spoken is *modeling*. In fact, some educators say that this is the key to all good teaching. We need to show students in a step-by-step fashion exactly what it is they are supposed to do. Management problems are much reduced when all students are on task and understand how they are expected to behave.

Establish the Connection between Behavior and Consequences—Positive and Negative.

Hand in hand with establishing the rules is determining the consequences for breaking the rules. We need to make sure that students understand the connection between a behavior and the consequence attached to that behavior. Consequences will be determined to a certain extent by school policies, but the teacher needs to have a plan for the steps to take when students break the rules.

Some teachers link their consequences with rewards. For example, Jessica Haxhi and her colleague Kazumi Yamashita use a Japanese toy to implement consequences. There are four layers stacked together to make up this toy. When someone disobeys a rule, the teacher removes the lowest layer. For each disruption another layer is removed. At the end of the class, the number of remaining layers is entered on a chart as the class score for the day. There is competition among the classes for the most points over a specified period of time, and when points reach a certain predetermined number the class qualifies for a party or some kind of special day.

Laura Igarteburu described a similar management strategy on the Ñandu listserv. She gives each class a sticker if the whole class follows her three rules: "Listen. Raise your hand. Speak Spanish." At the beginning of the class period she writes a word in Spanish on the board, and whenever any student breaks a rule she erases a letter from the word. If there are no letters remaining in the word at the end of the class, there is no sticker for the day. As the year progresses, she uses shorter words each month, until by the last month the "game" is played with a one-letter word! Penny Fields uses a similar strategy with numbers. At the beginning of each class period she writes the number ten on the board, and after the first breaking of a rule she erases the ten and replaces it with a nine, usually without comment, so that peer pressure can work its magic. This process continues throughout the class. The number on the board at the end of the class is recorded, and whenever the class total reaches one hundred points they may have a special day in which they select favorite games or other activities.

Sometimes individual behaviors persist and do not respond to group consequences, especially with students who have recurring behavior problems. In that case additional measures are called for. For many teachers the first step to take is "the look." Every teacher needs the skill of looking directly at a student, without smiling, and silently communicating the message "I see what you are doing and we both know you need to stop." For some students and some situations, this is all the student may need to resume the expected behavior.

Teachers often follow this step by "moving in on" the offending student, without interrupting the lesson or calling attention to the student. When the teacher moves close enough, this may stop the behavior altogether. Proximity can also be used to prevent behavior problems from starting, when the teacher senses a potential problem in some part of the room.

Sometimes just calling the student's name will serve as a good reminder, although this strategy must be used carefully. Calling the name as a reprimand also calls attention to the student and that may be just what the misbehavior is intended to accomplish. It is best to use the student's name as a kind of invitation: "Fabian, did you get a good look at this?" or "Claire, I want you to notice this picture especially." Using the student's name in an example can also be a good way to pull a student back in: "Let's imagine that Roberta is walking down the street in Germany looking for a good place to buy a loaf of bread." Calling on the student next to the offending student can sometimes achieve the same purpose.

Calling on an inattentive student to answer a question, primarily for the purpose of "catching the student out," communicates the message that questioning is more of a punishment than it is an invitation.

Many teachers find that a disruptive or inattentive student can be best handled by temporarily moving them out of the group or to another part of the room until they are ready to participate more fully. With a very young child, this time-out should be short. When we place a student outside the group, we must be certain to monitor their behavior closely and to remember to call them back to the group as soon as they seem ready. We are responsible for every student in our class, all the time.

With repeated misbehaviors, it is time to start keeping a written "log" of behaviors and the steps we have taken to deal with them. If misbehaviors persist, a call home is often a helpful step, and we need to be prepared to give a detailed history of the behavior when we consult with the parents. Persistent or troubling misbehavior should also be discussed with the principal in early stages, so that there can be a team approach to helping the student resolve the problems. For any of these steps, a carefully dated log with simple descriptions of behavior can be invaluable.

Here are some helpful tips put together by early language teachers in Georgia:

- Know the process that works in your school and grade level.
- Do not plan for a consequence you will not be willing to apply.
- Make sure students know the consequences.
- Make sure parents know the consequences.
- Be consistent, impartial, and fair.
- Follow through with consequences.
- Don't make threats—use your system.
- Remember that the child makes the choice to break the rule, receive the consequence.

Rewards.   There are consequences for good behavior as well as poor behavior, of course—we usually call these rewards. There has been a great deal of professional discussion about the benefits and the risks of rewarding performance or behavior, and about intrinsic and extrinsic motivation. While we focus on intrinsic motivation for positive behavior and for learning in the long run, in the short term many teachers find it useful to use extrinsic systems for motivating positive behavior and performance.

Many teachers give stickers for good performance or for especially good behavior; these stickers seem to be valued by students in the whole K–8 spectrum. That depends on the sticker, of course; no eighth grader would feel rewarded by a Barney sticker, for example. Some teachers also use small pieces of candy as occasional rewards. Stickers can be awarded to individuals or to a whole class, as in the Igarteburu strategy described earlier. Similar rewards can be given for target language use, or for other forms of excellent performance.

Some teachers use a visual challenge to motivate behavior—for example, children in a Spanish class move one step higher on an Aztec pyramid whenever they have earned the step through good behavior or good performance. Other teachers keep track of points on a chart, or marbles or coins in a jar. When the goal is achieved, there is a celebration—a party, or some other special event. For Penny Fields and Laura Igarteburu, the special event is a day on which students are allowed to pick favorite games or activities, in the target language—not a vacation from the language or an expensive party for which the teacher would have to pay.

It is important to keep in mind, however, that extrinsic rewards are a temporary measure, a bridge to positive performance that we want to encourage for its own sake. We should plan to wean our students from these extrinsic rewards once the behavior has been well established.

There are intangible rewards that may be even more powerful than stickers and candy. Sometimes classes or individuals feel rewarded just by the fact that the teacher is pleased, or happy, or even excited by a certain performance. Students can feel rewarded when they are given the opportunity to lead a class. Some teachers lead group applause whenever a student has done a good job on an individual performance.

Students also feel rewarded when they are given a special responsibility for the class or the classroom. Most children love to help, and the teacher needs only to identify specific tasks. Tasks are also a good way to help some children develop a sense of responsibility. Some possibilities for "rewarding" tasks include: erasing chalkboards or whiteboards, acting as line leader, passing out materials, leading some familiar group activity, or acting as messenger for items that need to be delivered to the office or to another classroom.

Our ultimate goal is for students to feel rewarded and motivated by their own success. Our role is to praise, support, and encourage along the way.

Establish Procedures for All Classroom Routines. We need procedures for making sure that students understand what we want them to do and how we want them to do it. We need procedures for beginning the class, for ending the class, and for maintaining and refocusing the attention of the class as the lesson is in progress. We also need procedures for other aspects of classroom routine, such as asking to sharpen a pencil or to get out of one's seat. With such procedures students know what to expect, and they feel safe and comfortable within the routines we have established.

Beginning Class. Many teachers begin their classes with a song or a chant or a routine greeting—or sometimes all three. Students need a signal for when it is time to begin the language class and give the teacher their full attention. In many cases when the traveling teacher pushes the cart through the door the class starts with a greeting and a song, giving the teacher a chance to take out materials and set the stage for the lesson about to begin. When students come to the language classroom, there have to be procedures for quickly taking assigned places, followed by a teacher-led greeting or another opening routine.

After the opening song, teachers often continue with a calendar routine or song. Naming the day and date, with the use of a large calendar in the target language, gives practice with numbers as well as the names for the days of the week. Another common component of the calendar time is to check the weather and record it. Students enjoy leading this portion of the class and can often do so quite early in the year. Once the students get to a certain point in their language development, calendar time can change so as to incorporate different types of language—if teachers still use a daily calendar routine in a third grade class, for example, it should look very different from the routine used in a kindergarten or in a fifth grade class.

Researchers tell us that the first five minutes and the last five minutes of any class period are prime learning time. We need to be careful not to let opening routines and calendar activities drag on too long or else we fail to take advantage of this prime learning time for important work with the main objectives of our lesson.

Ending Class Routines.   The responsibility for ending the class period belongs to the teacher, not to the students. This is of special concern in schools with bell schedules. We need to teach students that the teacher is the one who dismisses the class, not the bell or the second hand on the clock.

As we approach the end of the class period, it is important to be conscious of how we leave the students for the next teacher. If we have engaged the class in some very lively activities, we will make sure that that we have a cool-down activity before we close. When students leave our class they have to be ready for the next teacher to continue with their learning.

When students leave our language classrooms, they need a routine for lining up at the door and leaving the room quietly and in an orderly fashion. Teachers often dismiss students by table, choosing the most cooperative table first, or the table that was ready the fastest. Sometimes a teacher dismisses by clothing colors, hair color, or some other characteristic, so that this portion of class is a continuation of language learning time.

Many ending routines are similar to opening routines in that they include a good-bye song or a chant and, of course, saying good-bye to the teacher. Japanese teachers usually incorporate a traditional bow at the beginning and end of class. Traveling teachers sometimes include a "heads-down" component at the very end of the class. That is, the last thing students do as part of the language class is to put their heads down on their desks or tables, until the next teacher arrives to "wake them up."

Routines for Maintaining and Refocusing Attention.   Elementary and middle school language teachers use various routines for maintaining the focus of the class or getting back attention if it is wavering. These routines are especially necessary with younger students. The younger the students are, the more easily they will be distracted.

There are various options for focusing student attention, including hand signals, rhythmic clapping, songs, and other activities. It is important to be consistent with these signals and not to introduce too many at one time.

One common quiet or attention signal is sometimes called the "zero noise signal" or the "universal cooperative learning signal." The teacher raises her or his hand, and students raise their hands as soon as they see the teacher's hand raised. When they raise their hands, students must also stop the activity, stop talking, and show the hand signal to their teacher and to their classmates. This routine puts some of the responsibility for quieting down the classroom on the students themselves. Students need practice in responding to these signals, too, until they become habitual—otherwise the signals won't have any effect on their behavior!

Some teachers use a system of counting down or counting up to indicate that the class may be exceeding the bounds of the rules, usually with a raised hand and counting from one to five or five to one in the target language. By the time the teacher has reached the end of the sequence, or the lowest number when counting down, the students must be ready to continue the activity or to begin a new activity. Some teachers use rhythmic clapping to help refocus the students. When Audray Weber needs to regain attention, she might interrupt an activity by singing her three class rules until students are silent and ready to begin again.

Some teachers use special routines when beginning or ending an activity. Audray Weber calls the names of the students who are ready to begin an activity, putting others on notice that they need to get ready themselves. Tara Kraft-Mahnke indicates the start of an activity by calling out *"Luces! Camera! Acción!"* (lights, camera, action), accompanied by dramatic gestures reflecting the excitement of movie making.

Teachers can also help students by signaling the end of an activity. When students are engaged in group work, hearing or seeing that they have three minutes left can help them to focus and finish the task. When everyone is engaged with a successful game, the teacher can end the game more easily by indicating (in the target language), "Two more turns," or "We'll play one more time," and then sticking to that format. Jessica Haxhi often wears a thematically appropriate hat when she monitors a class activity such as partner work, interviews, or a simulation. She signals the end of the activity by removing her hat.

Procedures for Performing Other Class Activities. As the teacher creates a management plan, the more carefully procedures are developed for the recurring activities in the classroom, the more successful the plan is likely to be. The teacher should design a procedure and a plan to teach students how to do each of the following.

- Ask permission to leave their seats (to sharpen pencils, get materials, go the bathroom, and so on). Passwords can be helpful tools for these procedures.
- Pass out and collect materials. Teachers must show students the procedures for picking up and returning materials when they are working in groups, or when materials such as papers, craft materials, or books need to be distributed during class. A few minutes spent practicing these procedures will ultimately save hours of class time over the course of a year.

  Many teachers build the collecting of the materials into the class activity itself so that by the time the activity is over, the teacher has the materials back. TPR is a useful strategy to use for this purpose. "Put all the red animals into the basket. Put all the green animals into the basket. . ." and so on.

  Instead of doing everything themselves, some teachers choose student assistants to serve as materials helpers. Students usually feel rewarded by the opportunity to help in this way, and their assistance is especially valuable because of short class times and a need to move quickly from one class to another in an elementary school program.
- Transitions from one activity to another.

  When activities change, when students need to move from one place to another, when the focus moves from the large group to individual or partner work, the teacher needs to plan for an efficient transition. For example, transitions involving movement can be facilitated by means of a chant or a familiar song that relates to the next activity or the one just completed. Teachers can describe exactly what behavior is expected during the change from one group configuration to another, perhaps making a game of finding a partner within ten seconds or being in the assigned seat and ready to work before the class has completed the singing of a favorite song. The teacher should examine each lesson plan to discover where transitional activities will be needed and then plan for them.

Procedures for Calling on Students Efficiently.   Deciding which student to call on can be a difficult process for the teacher, and sometimes it contributes to wasted class time. So many hands are waving in the air! How can we remember who last had a turn? Or whose turn is next? We also know that our field of vision sometimes causes us to favor one side of the group over the other. One strategy is to move our students (or ourselves) so that the same students are not always to our left or to our right during class activities. Another simple strategy for making sure that all students have been included is to begin an activity with all children standing, and then have each child sit down after participating.

A further technique involves writing student names on individual notecards or craft sticks. The teacher draws a card or a stick from the pack and calls on the student whose name is written there. This ensures that students will be called on at random, and it also makes calling on students much more efficient, since no time is lost in deciding who will be called on among the sea of hands that might be raised. The teacher continues going through the pack until each student has had a turn. This technique can also be used for assessment purposes as we go through the pack over the course of several days.

A second way to use the cards or sticks is to put the student's name back with the others, once the student has had a turn. In this way the students who have already been called on will remain alert since they do not know if or when their name will be called again. Used in this way, however, there is no assurance that every student will have a chance to participate. Another strategy for retaining attention would be to occasionally draw a name from among the students who have already recited, so that no student feels they can afford to let their attention drift.

Another factor to consider when calling on students is wait time. Research tells us that students need three to five seconds of thinking time in their native language in order to give a good answer to a question. They are likely to require more time to think of a response in a new language, except for quick memorized responses. Allowing students enough time to think will generate more responses and higher-quality responses.

Plan for Every Single Moment—and Beyond!

Our third basic for classroom management involves: *planning, planning, planning.*

The teacher must have a detailed plan for each lesson. There can be no downtime, because if there is an unplanned moment, or if the teacher has to stop and think about what to do next, the students will begin to make plans of their own! It is better to have too many activities planned rather than too few.

The teacher needs to adjust the classroom activities to fit the students' attention span. For kindergarten students, activities must be changed every few minutes, while sixth through eighth grade students can stay on one topic for longer periods of time. Some researchers suggest that most children can focus for a number of minutes equal to their age plus two. Thus a seven-year-old can focus for no more than nine minutes under the best conditions.

The teacher's plan must provide activities in which each student can experience a measure of success and satisfaction, consistent with his or her ability. This principle requires attention to diverse learning styles and to each of the multiple intelligences identified by Howard Gardner (1983, 1999), as well as to the differing academic abilities among our students, and the presence of physical and emotional obstacles that some students have to overcome. Our goal should be that each student is able to succeed with at least one thing in every class period.

Effective planning will involve the students in directing their own activities. Students should have a chance to lead the group, make decisions, and assist the teacher in meaningful ways. The class is usually far more attentive when a student leads a familiar activity like the calendar or a song than they would be if the teacher were the only leader. Older students can check for the completion of homework, monitor attendance, or take responsibility for other important tasks.

Lesson planning must also provide for a balance between movement and quiet, sitting-at-desks tasks. It is important to remember that K–1 students have a physical need to move. It is more stressful for them to sit quietly for a long period of time than it would be for them to run around the track for the same amount of time. The same can also be said for middle school students.

Some teachers provide for this variety by moving their students from one side of the classroom to the other when they change activities. This helps to keep the class interested and focused. Sometimes a quick TPR sequence can serve as a transition from one activity to another and provide a needed energy lift. A song or a chant, accompanied by movement, can also provide a needed change of pace.

Procedures for Using Every Bit of Class Time. There is so little time in a language class, especially in the elementary school, that every minute is precious. Teachers work hard to take advantage of every moment. A teacher might sing while a student is taking a long time to make a decision. Sometimes students themselves can sing to mark time, or while materials are being distributed or collected.

Effective teachers simply don't waste a single minute. For example, when students are engaged in a group activity, the teacher is busy monitoring the group and intervening whenever there is a need for assistance, or for correction of behavior. Sometimes a teacher will also use part of the group time to organize materials for the next activity.

Sponge activities are important resources to have available to make the most of class time. These sponges are used to soak up any extra class minutes with productive student activity. A well-planned teacher has a repertoire of these activities ready whenever they are needed—such as at the end of a class when there's not enough time to start a longer activity but there is a minute or two before the students leave. Sponge activities can also serve as options for students when they have finished their individual or group work.

The following activities are examples of useful sponges for different language levels:

Playing the game "I spy," or "I see something that you don't see and it is (description). . . .

"I'm thinking of a person who is wearing . . ."

How many questions can you think of to ask a person from Germany who might come to visit the class?

A simple back-to-back partner TPR activity, in which partners take turns giving commands and then face each other to see if their actions match. For example, "Touch your nose, 1–2–3."

In two minutes, write down as many jungle animals (farm, savanna, ocean) as you can think of with your partner. Did anyone write down anything that no one else thought of?

"I'll say a word and see if you can give me the opposite (or as many synonyms as you can think of, etc.).

"I'm thinking of an animal that starts with the letter ___"

The Proactive Manager: Involving Parents and the School Community

An early and very important step in management planning is for the teacher to develop a close relationship with the school principal, or with the administrator who is responsible for student discipline. We can share our management plan with this person and invite suggestions. If we make the administrator aware of problems that arise before they become crises, we can work together as a team.

We also need to enlist parent support. Parents need to be informed about class policies and class activities, so that there will be no surprises if we have to contact them about a problem situation. A letter home at the beginning of the year is a good starting point in building this relationship. Then we can send notes and make phone calls regularly, with more "good-news" messages than negative ones. Regular newsletters are another important vehicle for keeping parents informed about classes, expectations, and the philosophy of the program. A single page sent out at the beginning of each new unit, or on a regular basis every two to four weeks, can prevent misunderstanding and build parent support for the program.

Children should know that we will follow up on problems that arise in school. When we call a parent, we need to make sure that we talk with parents in person. It is usually best not to leave a phone message that could be intercepted, or that might be misinterpreted before it can be clarified. The phone call itself should be in the spirit of enlisting parent cooperation and inviting their insights about the student who matters to both of us. We should try to follow up negative messages with positive ones as soon as possible. We also need to be aware of family circumstances before sending out negative reports—in some cases a bad school report could have serious unintended family consequences.

Interactive homework is another powerful tool for connecting home and the classroom. Students take home examples of their work in class, with the expectation that they will share it with some adult in their lives who will sign it, comment on it, and return it to school. This practice gives parents a much better gauge of what their students are learning than if they periodically ask "What did you learn in Japanese today?" or "How do you say _____ in French?"

The best method of all for building parent understanding of the language class is to invite the parents into the classroom itself. Then they can see for themselves how the class functions and how their children behave and perform. They may even become interested enough to volunteer assistance for special projects and activities.

Special Issues Affecting the Traveling
Teacher—*à la* Cart

Many teachers in early language programs live a mobile life and travel from classroom to classroom using a cart. While most early language teachers would prefer to have their own room, which they could decorate thematically and set up to match their teaching style, there are also some benefits in the traveling situation. In a discussion of the traveling teacher on the Ñandu listserv, several advantages were mentioned.

Mary Sosnowski points out that traveling to the children's space makes it possible to incorporate the posters, bulletin boards, and current student work in the daily lesson. Communication with the classroom teacher is regular and natural. When the language teacher comes to the classroom, there is less disruption of the students' day and the language feels like a more integrated part of their learning.

Susan Fomento teaches in her own classroom in one school and travels in another. She notes that students have their basic tools close at hand when she comes to them, so she doesn't lose time by having to distribute scissors, markers, rulers, or other things that students normally have in their desks. Maintaining a room of her own requires considerable time and effort, and she also notices that she sees far less of her colleagues when she teaches in her own room. On the whole, of course, she prefers to have her own room.

Usually teachers don't have a choice as to whether they will teach in their own room or from a cart. When it is necessary for the teacher to travel, there are a number of ways to make the most of the situation, beginning with the cart itself.

Teaching from a Cart

The cart has to serve as a storage place for all the materials needed for the day's classes and also as a staging area for most of the classroom activities. Because the cart is so important, design of the cart and planning for its use are crucial decisions for the traveling teacher to make. Some traveling Georgia FLES teachers made suggestions for the design and use of the cart, shown in Figure 9.1.

Working with Many Different Classroom Teachers

A second challenge for traveling teachers is the fact that they must work closely with a number of different classroom teachers, moving from room to room and from one environment to another. Sometimes they have very little time between classes to make the transition. A close relationship with the teachers whose classrooms they share can make this challenging situation much more manageable. Here are some ideas for working closely with classroom teachers and enlisting their help.

How the Language Teacher Can Support the Classroom Teacher.   Planning together with classroom teachers is extremely important, because cooperation improves the quality of instruction. Joint planning inspires shared goals and motivates integration of the language into the classroom. If the program should come under threat, the language teachers are regarded as part of the team, and other teachers become advocates for the program.

FIGURE 9.1   Suggestions for design and use of a traveling cart.

Keep the cart carefully organized. You will need:

- baskets
- plastic storage boxes and cases
- plastic bags

Attach posters to edges of the cart:

- place velcro on edge of cart and posters
- use jumbo bag clips to attach posters and other items to cart

Use sides of cart for:

- poster storage and display
- whiteboard
- cork board/bulletin board
- felt board

Use small easel on top of cart for display.

Be sure cart is enclosed so materials don't drop off when you go over a bump in the floor.

Use hook(s) on side of cart to attach posters (use hole punch and reinforcement rings on posters before laminating).

Design a drop-leaf table from one side of cart for use in simulations.

Design/add fold-out arms from top of cart to allow for up to 3 posters side by side.

Designate a space on the cart for each grade level you teach.

Use desk letter-stacker for collecting and organizing student work (by teacher).

Color code classes and class work.

Have a special place for the tape recorder/CD player (easy access and use).

Use hook-and-loop material on inside of cart door to attach needed audiocassettes and keep them handy.

Have a space reserved for a clipboard and pen, or other record-keeping materials.

Have a covered space/place to keep items that are meant to be "surprises" for the class.

Keep stickers and other rewards and prizes very accessible.

Have laminated games easily available, as well as other materials for sponge activities.

Create routines to have children assist in repacking the cart at the end of class (or at the end of activities).

Get cart ready for the next day before you go home each afternoon.

Whenever possible, get to class early in order to get set up before instruction begins.

Wheels of the cart are important. If they roll well, the teacher's back is less likely to be strained. It is helpful if they can be locked. Keep them oiled so you don't squeak in quiet halls.

(continued)

FIGURE 9.1 Continued

When you leave the cart parked, place the open end toward the wall (or leave in the room for your next class).

Ask the classroom teacher for a drawer or other storage space in each classroom you visit.

Know the rules and consequences of each classroom you visit; adapt to them as necessary.

There are many ways for the language teacher to make links with the rest of the curriculum. For example, the language arts series may contain stories set in Spanish-speaking countries, and the Spanish teacher might focus a unit on one of the same countries, or teach similar stories in Spanish. The social studies curriculum is often a source of ideas for integrating the language with the rest of the students' day. The classroom teacher will be happy to recognize that the language program can connect with and enrich the existing curriculum.

As language teachers, we need to be prompt in arrival for class and in ending the class. We leave the students ready for the classroom teacher at the end of our lesson, just as we expect them to be ready for us to begin class when we arrive.

We need to leave the classroom the way we found it. We should try to rearrange the classroom as little as possible, but if we change things around, we need to put furniture and equipment back in its place.

We can provide classroom teachers with a written lesson plan, or with written vocabulary for their use, as well as written copies of songs, chants, and rhymes. Most teachers are geared to an adult's more visual or reading style of learning and no longer have the child's quick ability to learn languages orally.

We can supply classroom labels in the target language for use with calendars, bulletin boards, and items in the classroom.

If the teacher and students wear target language nametags during the language class, the classroom teacher should have a target language nametag to wear, as well.

If we need the classroom teachers to provide any special materials for the language lesson on a given day, such as scissors, crayons, or paper, we can notify the teachers at least a week in advance, if possible, and put another short reminder in their mailboxes the day before. We must also be sure to collect those materials at the end of class so the teacher doesn't have any extra work.

Classroom teachers come to rely on the language class at a certain point in their day, and when we are absent they sometimes feel imposed upon. We need be sensitive to this issue and to provide lesson plans and materials for days on which we know we must miss school. Some teachers also create simple learning stations for each classroom, for students to use during their free time or for use when the language teacher is gone. Parents are sometimes willing to help create games or other self-correcting activities that will allow students to work with the new language on their own.

How the Classroom Teacher Can Support the Language Teacher. One of the most important ways the classroom teacher can support the language teacher is by being positive about the role of language in the curriculum. The message the classroom teacher sends to the students can make a world of difference! Comments like "You are so lucky to be able to study a foreign language at a young age" or "Knowing a foreign language will certainly help you in the future" are powerful motivators. If a classroom teacher is enthusiastic about the study of a foreign language, it will make a positive impression on the students that is, of course, very helpful to the language teacher when that teacher enters the classroom.

Language teachers can encourage their classroom colleagues to have the students ready for class when the language teacher arrives. This means having other work completed and put away, having desks arranged for the language class, and perhaps having nametags on the desks or around the students' necks. These simple steps will save valuable minutes for language learning.

Sometimes classroom teachers are supportive of the program and want to help in any way they can. One of the first ways to help is by avoiding the temptation to translate what the language teacher says for the students. Experiencing the language through the language itself and not through English will increase students' language skills. Classroom teachers who are familiar with our philosophy of language learning will be in a much better position to support the program in positive ways. For example, the classroom teacher could coordinate the distribution of a language-related book bag that children sign out to take home. Inside the book bag could be books with tapes, maps, language activities for students to complete with parents, and a comments sheet for parents to fill out.

Teachers who feel comfortable with using the new language could work with the students in the following small ways:

- Have the students write the day and date in the target language.
- Give page numbers in the target language.
- Do part of the morning calendar routine in the new language.
- Use numbers and give math answers in the target language.
- Label the bulletin board in both languages.
- Encourage students to give responses or otherwise use the target language they know.

When the Classroom Teacher Is Not Interested or Not Supportive.   One language teacher wrote the following to the Ñandu listserv: "I teach 2nd and 3rd grades, and out of the 16 classes that I go to, about 6 do not reinforce what I teach. As a result the students of those teachers do not pick up as much as those where the classroom teacher reinforces what is being taught. I see this a lot especially at the time of evaluations. I feel bad for those students because I know they would do better if the classroom teacher showed some interest herself."

Sometimes, despite our best efforts at cooperation and collaboration, we must work with teachers who are not supportive of what we do. These teachers may require special attention and even some education about program goals and outcomes. The following suggestions, many from teachers on the Ñandu listserv, may help to improve the situation.

We can assure teachers that we will not be adding to their workload, and that we will support and reinforce what they are doing in class. Once they see our program in action they may become as excited about the program as we are. We might do a short demonstration for them in the target language, in which we incorporate information or content that the students already learn in their regular classes. For example, we could do something as simple as counting by tens, or teaching cardinal directions, or locating several countries where the target language is spoken by using latitude and longitude. At the end of our presentation, we can assure the teachers that we will be using the new language as a tool to reinforce and review skills and concepts from regular classroom, in addition to our focus on language and culture.

One way to help classroom teachers feel ownership in the program is to enlist their opinions and their expertise. This can be done either formally or informally. We might use the following survey with the teachers in order to obtain information:

- What are some ways that you would be willing to be more involved in the language program?
- What are some special topics, projects, or teaching methods you would like to see us incorporate into the program?
- How can we improve communication and planning with you?
- What are some of your general ideas and recommendations on how the program could be improved?

Finally, in our efforts to win over a reluctant classroom teacher, we need to be flexible, but not so flexible that we lose our sense of purpose and our own curricular goals.

Summary

Managing a successful early language classroom is a complex process in which planning is the essential element. Teacher plans always have to adjust for factors beyond the teacher's control, such as the time and place their classes meet and the developmental and individual characteristics of the children in those classes. As teachers begin the planning process, they can prepare themselves by learning about the school climate and the successful strategies of classroom teachers for the age level they will teach themselves, as well as by reading about classroom management theories and strategies.

The management plan should include strategies for establishing and maintaining a positive classroom environment, establishing rules, consequences, and routines for the management of all classroom procedures. Part of management is making a detailed plan for every class period that uses every available minute of class time and takes into account the students' need for variety, movement, and clear directions for every activity. The effective manager is also proactive, building bridges to administrators and parents that will create a climate of cooperation when it is necessary to confront a problem.

Teachers who must travel from room to room with a cart face special issues in classroom management. The quality of the cart itself is a significant factor in teacher effectiveness, and careful planning can make the cart an efficient and valuable tool. Working in another teacher's classroom can be challenging at times, but the effort spent to establish a good working relationship can yield very positive results that benefit planning, scheduling, and student learning.

FOR STUDY AND DISCUSSION

1. Plan five rules for your class, worded positively, that are
   a. observable
   b. enforceable
   c. non-judgmental
   d. expression of behavior that is important to you in order to teach effectively
   e. in the language you teach
   Word these rules carefully so that they are clear to students.

2. Design a poster for your rules that you can place in your language classroom (or on your cart!). Be sure there is a visual that helps convey the meaning of the rule.

3. List consequences for your rules, both negative and positive. Your consequences should be:
   a. logical
   b. reasonable

   c. designed so they do not require you to stop the lesson

4. Identify and describe at least three procedures that you will use to make your class run smoothly. Design a plan for teaching one of these procedures to your class.

5. Develop a lesson plan for your first day of class, in which you:
   a. introduce your rules and procedures
   b. establish a positive classroom environment
   c. give students some "chunks of language" to take home with them the first day

FOR FURTHER READING

The following sources are recommended for additional information about material covered in this chapter. Chapter citations are documented in Works Cited at the end of the volume.

Ginott, Haim G. *Teacher and Child: A Book for Parents and Teachers.* New York: Macmillan, 1972.

Good, Thomas, and Jere Brophy. *Looking in Classrooms.* New York: HarperCollins, 1994.

Kohn, Alfie. "The Risks of Rewards." ERIC Digest EDO PS 94 14. ERIC Clearinghouse on Elementary and Early Childhood Education, December 1994.

Wong, Harry K., and Rosemary T. Wong. *The First Days of School. How to be an Effective Teacher.* Mountain View, CA: Harry K. Wong Publications, 1998.

10 Language, Culture, and Curriculum Interact

Experiencing Culture in the Classroom

Even fifty years ago, when language classes were usually taught using a grammar-translation method and students didn't learn interactive or communicative language skills, culture was a part of the standard curriculum for language classes. At that time the culture goals tended to be primarily what some have called "big C" culture—historical figures, geography, literature, music, and fine art. Since then the curriculum for culture has expanded to include patterns of everyday life of the people who use the target language, as well as folklore, contemporary media, and countless other facets of the life and thought of the people who speak the target language.

As our world has grown smaller and our society more diverse, language programs have become an important curricular area for teaching our young people to be empathetic toward people from other cultures. The language courses also help learners to develop a global awareness necessary for a world that is both smaller and more complicated than it was even ten years ago.

Culture and the Standards

The *Standards for Foreign Language Learning in the 21st Century* (1999) have redefined the relationship of culture to all aspects of language learning, raising it to new prominence and importance in the curriculum. Not only does culture have its own separate standards, 2.1 and 2.2, but it also serves as a unifying thread throughout the other four areas of the Standards document. Effective communication is defined by cultural appropriateness and sensitivity (1.1, 1.2, 1.3); cultural connections enrich the links made to the general curriculum (3.1); and the new language gives access to information, ideas, and opinions that are embedded in another culture (3.2). Comparisons of languages (4.1) uncover a host of culturally defined patterns of expression and ways to view the world, and comparisons of cultures (4.2) bring students to greater understanding of both the target culture and their own. The communities standards encourage direct and ongoing application of language and culture competencies in the world beyond the classroom.

The Standards have reminded us of what we instinctively knew: Culture is the most important context for language learning. As Lange points out (1999), "The new standards put culture at the core of foreign language learning as a major content." The Standards themselves put it clearly: "In reality, then, the true content of the foreign language course is not the grammar and the vocabulary of the language, but the cultures expressed through that language" (1999, 47–48).

Cultural topics to be included in an integrated and communication-based elementary and middle school foreign language program are often chosen at least in part on the basis of their potential for enabling students to communicate through the target language and for their inherent ability to motivate students to use the target language. Interest in the culture in which the target language is spoken can motivate language acquisition and practice. In addition, the cultural dimension of the language class can assist the learners in better understanding their own culture, as they make comparisons and begin to understand a point of view that is based in the target culture and expressed in the target language.

Even more important than the potential for communication, the interests and developmental level of the students in the class must guide the choice of cultural information selected for instruction. There may well be parallels between the acquisition of a second language and the acquisition of a second culture. Many similar criteria could be said to apply. Students will not understand or be open to cultural information and practices that are so divorced from their own experiences as to seem funny or even bizarre, any more than they will learn language that is not directed to their interests and built on their own experiences. They are also unlikely to "acquire" cultural information that primarily affects adults in the target culture, since they have yet to penetrate the adult culture of their own world and often find it confusing. Perhaps most significantly, just as children do not acquire a language primarily by being told about it, but rather through meaningful, communicative experiences with the language, so also do children penetrate a new culture through meaningful experiences with cultural practices and cultural phenomena that are appropriate to their age level, their interests, and the classroom setting.

The Culture Triangle

With the cultures goal, the Standards have given us an additional, more challenging set of lenses to use when planning to integrate culture with our language classes: gain knowledge and understanding of other cultures. While the goal itself seems quite general, the two standards associated with it turn our thinking sharply in a new direction.

The Standards define culture to include the philosophical perspectives, the behavioral practices, and the tangible and intangible products of a society. The diagram shown in Figure 10.1 represents the close relationship among these three elements.

Standard 2.1: Students demonstrate an understanding of the relationship between the practices and perspectives of the cultures studied.
Standard 2.2: Students demonstrate an understanding of the relationship between the products and perspectives of the cultures studied.

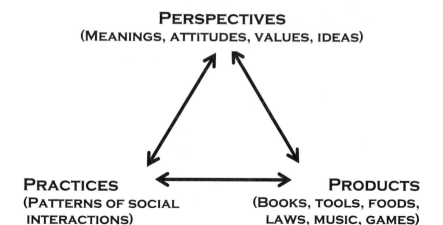

FIGURE 10.1   The Culture Triangle

Source: Standards for Foreign Language Learning in the 21st Century. Yonkers, NY: National Standards in Foreign Language Education Project, 1999, p. 47. Reprinted by permission of ACTFL.

An example may help to illustrate the relationship among the three elements of culture. The *drum* is a product and a familiar artifact of Native American culture, sometimes a tourist item bought as a plaything for children. The drum is also a practice, a group of drummers sitting around a large drum and playing or chanting for a powwow. The product and the practice reflect the perspective, or the value and importance, of community gathered around the drum to share traditional ritual, rhythm, and dance. To present only the drum product without the context and the values in which it holds an important place is to miss the meaning of the drum entirely.

Another example comes from a German setting. American visitors to a large German city are likely to be struck by the fact that many of the cars are very small, in comparison to most vehicles driven in America, and that cars are parked on the sidewalks all over the city. The Smart Car, a very small car, is particularly adept at parking in these tiny spaces. Here the product is the Smart Car, and the practice is parking on the sidewalk. The perspective emerges when we realize that many German inner cities have been retained or restored to the way they were centuries ago, so valuing of the past might be one of the perspectives represented here.

The relationship among products, practices, and perspectives might not always be so easy to trace, especially with young learners, but this goal and these standards challenge us as teachers to be aware of the perspectives represented in the cultural products and practices we incorporate into our classes, and to build our plans around these perspectives. In early language classrooms we are laying the groundwork for perspective through experiences with the products and practices that infuse every aspect of our language program.

Jessica Haxhi and her fifth grade students developed this summary of some of the things they had learned about Japanese culture, based on the culture triangle (see Figure 10.2). Although normally the Japanese class is conducted entirely in Japanese, this discussion took place in English.

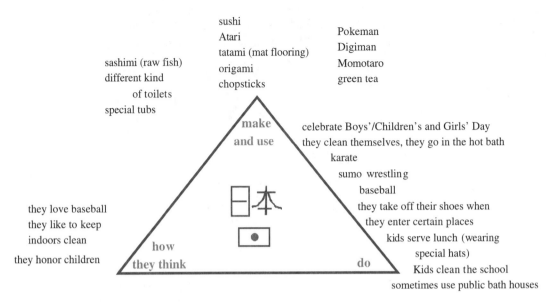

FIGURE 10.2   Brainstorming the Culture Triangle

Source: From Maloney Magnet School, Waterbury, CT. Reprinted by permission of Jessica Haxhi, Japanese Teacher.

Notice that Haxhi renamed the points in the triangle to be more child-friendly: what they make and use, what they do, how they think. An examination of these brainstorming results shows how many rich experiences with products and practices have led to the perspectives the students were able (with some prompting) to identify.

Creating Experiences with Culture

Experiences with the products and practices of culture in the target language can begin with the first language class and infuse all classroom activities. For example, children in a German classroom can learn from the first day that a greeting is accompanied by a hand-shaking ritual (2.1). Young students beginning Spanish can learn first the colors of the Mexican flag and then learn how to place the flag on Mexico on a map of North America (2.2). Learners beginning French can celebrate April Fool's Day with fish shapes placed on one another's backs (2.1). A teacher of Japanese might greet students with a bow and expect them to greet one another in the same way (2.1). Children learning any European language can learn to count on their fingers starting with the thumb representing the number one (2.1). Students in a German class can learn very early to press their thumbs for good luck, or to knock on their desks instead of applauding to show approval (2.1). None of these experiences requires an elaborate explanation, but each is a step toward identification with another way of thinking and another way of behaving in everyday situations (see Figure 10.3).

Many cultural practices blend easily with regular classroom routines. Choice of the next person to recite or to participate in a game can be made using a culturally based counting-out

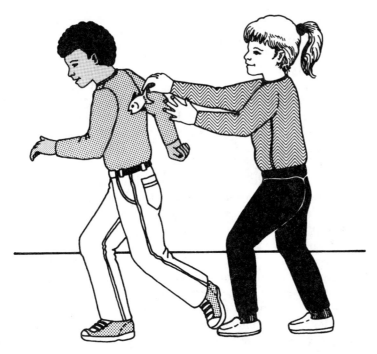

FIGURE 10.3 Playing a fish game on April 1 gives children learning French an experience with French culture.

rhyme. A tie in a Japanese class could be broken with the traditional rock-paper-scissors game. Children in the French classroom might learn to raise two fingers rather than waving a whole hand when they want to be called on.

Simple crafts and food activities can provide experiences with products of the target culture that extend over a longer period of time, and some of them address both Standards 2.1 and 2.2. An activity such as building and later breaking a class *piñata,* or perhaps individual *piñatas* made with paper bags, can be both an opportunity to apply language to a new activity and an experience in preparation for a celebration common to the target culture. Mask making can be a prelude to the celebration of an in-class version of a festival specific to the target culture, such as the pre-Lenten carnivals observed in several German-, French-, and Spanish-speaking cultures. A Japanese class could learn to follow directions in an *origami* paper-folding activity and then decorate the classroom with their creations. A food activity such as preparing an open-faced sandwich in a German class, and then eating it with a knife (in the right hand) and a fork (in the left hand) provides an opportunity for experiencing several cultural contrasts in food presentation and eating behavior. A food activity for a Chinese class could include cooking noodles and then eating them using chopsticks.

These crafts and food activities can later become the focal point for language experience stories and for writing or copying activities. They can serve as the central feature of simulations or the starting point for student-prepared skits or presentations to parents. Preparations for a festival, including making such crafts as *piñatas,* paper flowers, or masks, might culminate in a festive celebration, either within the class or as a joint experience with other classes or invited guests.

The use of a variety of visuals representing the target culture can help to relate interests of the children to the wider world in which the target language plays a role. Posters and bulletin boards can create an awareness of the cultural settings in which the target language is spoken. Magazines and comic books from the target culture can be used to illustrate vocabulary items or to communicate a bulletin board message. Coins from the culture used as counters for math activities or as playing pieces in a board game bring a reality to these everyday cultural objects. Board games, puzzles and picture books, when made available to children in a learning center or in a special foreign language corner of the classroom or the library, open doors to the daily life of the child in the target culture and invite the learner to experience a small portion of that culture.

When Jo Ellen Hague visited Paris, she developed a wonderful cultural resource for her classroom. She took along the class mascot, Gustave the frog, and took pictures of him in many different situations—for example, Gustave with the Notre Dame cathedral in the background, Gustave eyeing a beautiful French dessert. Reiko Aya, a Japanese immersion teacher from Portland, Oregon, had a similar idea when she took her class mascot, Barney, to Japan, and photographed him in Japanese settings. Seeing the familiar mascot in the target culture brings a special kind of credibility and reality to the pictures of these unfamiliar places (see Figure 10.4).

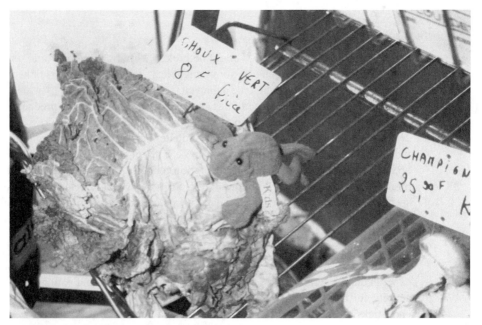

FIGURE 10.4   Gustave inspects the lettuce in a French market.
Source: Reprinted by permission of JoEllen Hague.

Comparing Cultures: Standard 4.2

As teachers and students work with the practices, products, and perspectives of the target cultures, it is natural that students should begin to compare these new cultures with their own. The teacher can encourage and invite these comparisons and help students move toward the understanding that cultural behavior is systematic and governed by the perspectives of a culture. With enough experience and guidance, the students can begin to hypothesize about cultures in general and to reflect on their own culture as one among many.

One simple example of this kind of comparison can be accomplished by the use of contrasting maps of the world. A map printed for an American audience almost always has North America at the center. A map printed in Europe for a European audience almost always has Europe at the center, and a map printed in Asia has Asia at the center. Drawing students' attention to these contrasts can lead to questions about why each orientation is appropriate for its audience.

Jessica Haxhi uses a popular Japanese children's movie, *Totoro,* to draw out a number of cultural comparisons. The movie is about a furry creature that is only visible to children, and the creature's adventures with two little girls. One of the class activities is to compare some interesting cultural contrasts between suffixes on names in Japanese. Later the class makes a comparison chart with the "Girl's home from the movie" on one side and "my home" on the other. Students draw pictures of beds, baths, tables, eating utensils, and so on, for each side, taking from what they saw in the movie. This is a good way to compare without making broad generalizations about "Japanese homes" and "American homes."

Jeanette Borich (2001) developed a unit rich with opportunities for cultural comparisons, although her primary goals were cultures and connections. As second grade students participated in an imaginary trip from their home in Iowa to the Yucatan Peninsula, they had the opportunity to compare many cultural elements: concepts of spring and other seasons because of contrasting climates, celebration of birthdays, typical foods, housing in villages and cities. Through a journaling activity the children were encouraged to reflect on these cultural experiences: "Mérida is a large city and Tinum is a small town in Yucatán. What did you notice about the houses in those places? Tell how María celebrated her birthday in Yucatán" (19). The entire experience helped the children to become observers of differences and similarities and tended to discourage quick judgments based on first impressions.

The guided and thoughtful reflection about cultural experiences and observations, conducted in the target language as described in the examples above, gives students the opportunity to construct meaning. Genuine, personal understanding of culture cannot be "transmitted" through a lecture or a multimedia presentation by someone who already has that understanding. It comes through personal experiences with products and practices, recognition of differing perspectives, and thoughtful comparisons of all three dimensions of culture. It may be that this comparisons standard holds the key to real culture learning.

Identifying Resources for Integrating Culture

Many teachers find the integration of culture and cultural experiences to be among their most challenging tasks, because they lack the firsthand experiences that would give them a rich background on which to draw. Even for teachers who have spent considerable time in a foreign country, or who were raised in a foreign setting, it is often difficult to know where to begin with cultural instruction. The following are intended as starting points for integrative culture planning.

Identifying Cultural Information for an Integrated Plan

When considering what culture one might draw into a thematic unit, it can be useful to think in terms of cultural symbols, other cultural products, and cultural practices. Some examples follow.

Cultural Products
Cultural symbols such as:
- flags, insignia related to children's interests
- significant national or geographic monuments
- symbols associated with holidays
- good and bad luck symbols
- symbolic meaning of animals
- heroes from history or myth

Other Cultural Products Such As . . .
- significant examples of the visual arts (and artists)
- significant examples of the musical arts (and composers)
- important characters, events, and themes from folk literature
- traditional children's songs, rhymes, games
- traditional stories and legends
- examples of folk arts
- currency and coins, stamps, and other realia
- traditional and holiday foods

Cultural Practices
- forms of greeting
- celebration of holidays
- use of gestures
- meals and eating practices
- shopping
- favorite playtime and recreational activities
- home and school life
- patterns of politeness
- types of pets and attitudes towards pets
- how children and families move from place to place (Pesola 1991, 339)

Any of the above items might serve as the starting point of a thematic unit or as a component of instruction.

Children's literature—folk and fairy tales, contemporary children's books, songs, rhymes, and finger plays—provide an especially valuable resource for cultural information.

Use of literature designed for children in the target culture allows learners of the target language to share cultural experiences and attitudes in a very direct way, thus offering an experience very similar to that of a child growing up in that culture. Location and use of culturally authentic stories may be among the most valuable and successful of all cultural activities.

Story and Culture

Story, or narrative, is a powerful vehicle for experiencing culture. Values and concepts of the culture that are embedded in myths and folktales can be shared through storytelling, story reading, and dramatization, and in this way they become part of the childhood experience that is a foundation for later understanding on a deeper level. In addition, stories, as we have seen in Chapter 7, have special effectiveness in giving children access to ideas and feelings. Stories about historical figures or legendary heroes are infused with the personal qualities and behaviors valued in the culture. In fact, stories may be one of the best ways of bridging the relationships among products, practices, and perspectives—they are, quite simply, an expression of the perspectives of the culture. As is the case with the native language and culture, experiences with these stories in childhood lay the groundwork for cultural insights and culturally sensitive behaviors.

One of the ways to give greater meaning to objects, or realia, from the culture is to weave them into a story, often linking them to a practice. For example, Jo Ellen Hague, a French teacher in Douglas County, Georgia, built a story around the king's cake tradition in France that her kindergarten students will never forget. Instead of just telling the students about the cake and the tradition that are part of the Celebration of the Three Kings, the students "bake" an imaginary king's cake. Students take turns placing imaginary ingredients in a two-dimensional bowl, pushing down the "beaters" and "whirring" as the ingredients mix. Every child is involved, as they pass each ingredient around the class before it is added to the batter, singing a song about a cake. The last ingredient to be added is the all-important bean. Jo Ellen pours the imaginary batter into a two-dimensional cake pan and places it in a cardboard oven with a hinged door.

The cake "bakes" while the children sing another song, and anticipation builds. When the cake comes out of the oven, it has magically baked—thanks to a bit of sleight-of-hand on the part of the teacher, who has placed a tagboard cake shape in the pan while manipulating the oven door. There are four large pieces of the cake, which is now placed on a tagboard picture of a table with four people sitting around the cake: the father, the mother, the sister, the brother. The family member who finds the bean in her or his piece of cake will be king or queen for the day.

The teacher asks children to predict which piece of cake is hiding the bean, calling for a show of hands with each piece of cake and writing down the number of votes. Then they look under each piece of cake in turn to see where the bean is hidden. When the bean is found, a crown is placed on the head of that family member, and everyone applauds.

Art and Artists

The visual arts can draw students into the culture in a number of ways, and art can play a role in almost every kind of language activity. For example, we could use reproductions of famous paintings to illustrate vocabulary or concepts, or as props in a corners activity (see Chapter 6). The stories of famous artists often draw students in and can encourage them to learn more about the artist's work, life, and environment. Some teachers have focused on the work of a single artist, such as Franz Marc, Claude Monet, or Pablo Picasso, and had their students copy the artist's style in their own creations. This focus could serve as a thematic center for an entire unit that integrates study of colors, descriptions, shapes, and artistic techniques.

As a first step in an artist unit, the teacher would introduce the artist, perhaps by telling a story that captures something of her or his spirit, and then show a number of the artist's creations. This would lead to many opportunities for student language use: description of what they see, and identification of specific objects or elements of the work. In the case of a realist painter, the students might describe or identify those things that contribute to a sense of reality in the work. In other cases the students might explain what clues they used to identify what is represented in the picture. During this phase students become acquainted with the vocabulary needed to discuss basic elements of artistic design.

After they have seen and discussed many examples of works by Franz Marc, for example, the students are ready to create their own art works in the same style. The culminating activity for this kind of unit might be a gallery showing. Each picture should be given a title by the student artist, and then each student might give a brief oral description of the painting and its most important characteristics, as if it were part of a gallery tour.

Some artists seem particularly appropriate for this kind of an activity. Franz Marc produced a large number of pictures of animals, many of them in bright colors. Joan Miró uses a style of drawing that would be easy for children to imitate. Matisse has many images that could be imitated creatively as an art project. The teacher does not need to be an art expert in order to develop activities like these. Many art books for young readers provide engaging and useful information that can guide the development of such a unit.

Never has locating artwork for use in classrooms been easier. Museum stores often have books of art for children; calendars often feature the work of a specific artist—and they are best bought on sale in January or February. And of course the Internet can provide pictures by almost any artist with whom a teacher would like to work.

Culture Scope and Sequence

If culture is to play a significant role in the integrated language curriculum, as described in Chapter 7, it must be planned for as carefully and in as great detail as are the language and the subject content elements of the program. To address the serious need for more guidance in planning and implementing culture instruction, the Montgomery County, Maryland, public schools applied the resources of a grant from the National Endowment for the Humanities to the development of a culture scope and sequence for foreign language programs in kindergarten through grade eight. The document identifies core competencies, which are to be developed by students in all types of foreign language programs at the grade level; FLES competencies appropriate primarily for FLES programs; and immersion competencies expected only for students in immersion programs. Several outcomes from the kindergarten level are listed below (Met and Lorenz 1993). All of these are core outcomes, expected for learners in every type of program.

Literature

Students will:

- Understand short narratives and/or folktales from the target cultures read aloud by the teacher.
- Recite traditional rhymes from the target cultures used by caregivers with preschool and young children.
- Use illustrations in children's literature from the target culture as context for the story line of short narratives and folktales.

Music

Students will:

- Sing songs, including lullabies, from the target cultures used by caregivers with preschool and young children.
- Use authentic instruments and/or replicas of authentic instruments to explore music and rhythm from the target cultures.

Art

Students will:

- Recognize colors using artifacts and works of art and illustrations in children's literature drawn from the target cultures.
- Recognize and appreciate artifacts and works of art as creations from the target cultures and use them to discuss topics that are a familiar part of the daily world of kindergarten students, that is, family, pets, holidays, et cetera.
- Create their own artwork related to target cultures.

Festivals/Holidays

Students will:

- Describe how peers in the target culture celebrate birthdays.
- Recognize the day, date, and month using a calendar, organized as it is in the target cultures.
- Make and taste selected foods from the target cultures related to holidays and seasons of the year.

Fantasy Experiences

It is possible to create more extended experiences with culture in the classroom, even for students who have very limited language background. By combining fantasy, culture, story form, and elements of Total Physical Response, the teacher can create a vivid, living connection between the children in the classroom and the target culture. Like simulations, fantasy experiences can place students in a setting that replicates important elements of the target culture and offers the opportunity to experience new feelings, new combinations of circumstances, and new solutions to familiar problems. The fantasy experiences described below are highly structured and teacher controlled, designed for use in early stages of language instruction, when it is often considered very difficult to deal with culture in the target language. Variations and adaptations of this technique can be used at every level of language instruction.

Fantasy Activity for the First Day of Class

Experience with fantasy can begin as early as the first day of class. With Baroque-style string music playing softly in the background, the teacher explains to students that they are to imagine themselves as children in the target culture and to choose a name by which they will be called during the course of the class. They close their eyes and listen as the teacher reads a list of names expressively, then a second time in an angry voice, so students know how a name might sound in case the teacher should ever become angry during class. Finally the students open their eyes and listen as the teacher reads the names a third time, raising their hands when they hear a name they would like to use. When two or more students choose the same name, the teacher goes on, continuing through the list until only one child chooses each name. In the case of very popular names, which several children want, the teacher might either give more than one child the same name, or simply remove the name so that children make other choices.

This activity establishes the connection between background music and use of the imagination. It also gives children an opportunity to take the first step toward identification with a new culture, a new way of thinking, even a new way of being addressed.

Fantasy Activity for Early Stages of Language Acquisition

The following is a plan for a simple fantasy experience that can be used in early stages of instruction. With music in the background, the teacher talks about being very tired and directs the children to stretch, to yawn, to lay their heads on their arms, to close their eyes, and to sleep (perhaps even to snore). The teacher counts off the hours of the night, reminding the children to sleep, perhaps to snore (or *not* to snore). At seven o'clock the teacher plays a recording of church bells (reflecting German culture) or sets off an alarm clock, and then directs the children to wake up, to stretch (again), to wash their faces, brush their teeth, dress, make their beds, and sit down for breakfast. The culminating portion of this fantasy might be a small continental breakfast, if the class can include food experiences; or the pantomiming of leaving home to go on to other activities.

Airplane Fantasy

A longer fantasy experience is popular in summer classes for children at Concordia College in Moorhead, Minnesota. Children are issued passports and airline tickets and prepare for a "trip" to Germany, Canada, Colombia, or any other destination appropriate to the language being taught. In addition to the Baroque music in the background, the teacher prepares an "aircraft" with a masking tape outline on the floor. This takes up much of the room, especially in a large class, with chairs placed side by side, in twos or in fours depending on the size of the class, and labeled with letters and numbers, as in a real aircraft. In the Concordia experience there are actual airline ticket folders, luggage tags, and air-sickness bags, as well as some in-flight magazines and other realia typically found in an airplane. Children are directed to show their tickets and their passports to the flight attendant, to find their seats, to buckle their imaginary seat belts—and of course they are told to refrain from smoking and to participate in all the other activities associated with the beginning of any flight. During the course of the flight, children are directed to look out their imaginary windows at drawings of clouds and of other aircraft. Turbulence comes, and they are led by the teacher in jiggling up and down and back and forth. The teacher exclaims over the unease in the stomach that they all feel, and many children discover an imaginary use for their real air-sickness bags. In an extended fantasy, the teacher might distribute in-flight meals, consisting of a half sandwich, a pickle, fruit, and a mint or a cookie assembled on small trays from a meat department wrapped in plastic food wrap. The children are directed to close their eyes and sleep as the teacher counts off the hours and notes the change of time because of the passage through time zones. The children finally arrive at their destination and exclaim over large pictures of the city in which they have landed, as they are directed to look at and point to special landmarks they should note. Classes that have shared this experience often remember a feeling of actually having traveled in an airplane to a distant place. As a follow-up to the airplane trip, classes might write a language-experience story together or draw pictures of the trip on postcard-sized tagboard and write messages from their destination to send home (see Figure 10.5).

When Jo Ellen Hague wanted to transport her kindergarten students into a Paris environment, she had the class mascot, Gustave, do the flying. In fact, one of the children took on the role of the airplane and Gustave, fastened to the child's clothing, rode around the room from Georgia to Paris!

Steamer Trip Fantasy

Another example of a fantasy, this one taking place in Germany, is a trip on a Rhine steamer, again to the accompaniment of Baroque music, using inexpensive sunglasses and a simple box camera as props, and with the outline of a Rhine steamer taped to the floor. Children are directed to exchange coins for tickets, to give their tickets to a ship attendant, and to board the steamer. As the steamer progresses down the Rhine, the children are directed to go to the left and the right on the deck, to look at and point to castles and other landmarks as they go by, and to pass the camera back and forth to "take pictures" of the special features along the Rhine. If a snack is desired, it might be some kind of finger food,

FIGURE 10.5   Just a few props can create a fantasy environment with great potential for culture and language acquisition.

an ice cream bar, or some juice. A day or two after the Rhine trip the students might view slides of an actual Rhine trip, once again point to the special landmarks they have seen, and perhaps even pick out themselves and their classmates in pictures of Rhine passengers. (Although of course they are not actually present in the pictures, children usually have no problem in "finding" themselves in a large group of people from an actual Rhine photo.)

Other Fantasies

Other examples of potential fantasy settings might include a bus trip or a walking trip around Paris, Mexico City, Madrid, Tokyo, or Berlin, with important tourist attractions along the way to look at and point to. It could be a canoe trip down a river in Canada, during which animals from the woods appear and disappear on either side of the masking-tape river "flowing" through the center of the classroom. The boat trip could be on the Loire, or a tourist boat in Paris, a raft on the Amazon River, a pirogue on the Niger River, a junk in Hong Kong, and so on. Fantasy subway rides can also be fun and instructive, especially if accompanied by actual tape-recorded subway sounds.

In some fantasies, all children can take part at the same time, as in the airplane trip and the simple morning fantasy. In other fantasies, a few students may take part and the rest of the class serves as observers. There can be several episodes of the same fantasy, involving different members of the class. In each repetition the script might change so that children never know exactly what to expect and thus remain attentive through several repetitions. In a fantasy that takes place in Berlin, for example, several students stand in line, press the call button outside the elevator, choose the correct floor, and press the button to reach the observation tower. Many variations are possible in this fantasy: the door might fail to open or become stuck partway, one student might be left behind, a child (or the teacher) might get a hand or a piece of clothing caught in the door; thus children will be directed to perform different activities in each variation of a similar situation. For the elevator fantasy, only a masking tape elevator, the up-down buttons on the outside, and the floor buttons on the inside of the elevator are required as props. (The elevator door "opens" when the masking tape door is temporarily lifted from the floor.) Passengers in the elevator might discover their stomachs growing queasy, as the elevator goes very high very fast (see Figure 10.6).

Planning a Fantasy Experience

Some of the key components to be considered by a teacher wishing to plan a fantasy experience include the following:

1. Precede major culture-bearing fantasies with shorter experiences.
2. Choose background music that is regular and unobtrusive. (Baroque string music works very well.)
3. Set the scene in a physical way, using masking tape, chair arrangement, or other physical means.
4. Choose cultural features that have dramatic potential.
5. Choose topics that include possibilities for movement, props, and sounds as a part of the dramatic sequence.
6. Plan the sequence to include a beginning, a middle, and an end.
7. Build in elements of humor and surprise.
8. Choose a few appropriate props; do not use too many props.
9. Use familiar commands with new content *or* introduce new commands carefully in advance.
10. Plan for natural communicative follow-up during succeeding class periods.

Fantasy activities such as those described here can provide very vivid, memorable experiences with the target culture. Since fantasy requires the suspension of disbelief, it is important that major or extended fantasies not be overused, or they will lose their special quality. Student willingness to suspend reality for extended periods of time will also diminish if elaborate fantasy experiences are planned too frequently.

Classroom Exchanges

A classroom twinning project is a particularly effective means of combining linguistic and cultural goals, as it offers children the opportunity to experience aspects of the target culture in a very direct and personal way. First described by Jonas (1969), this idea can be used

FIGURE 10.6   Even a school classroom can include an elevator—at least for the purposes of fantasy.

as the core of the foreign language curriculum for a period of time or as an effective supplement to any program model.

The elementary or middle school language teacher establishes a relationship with a teacher, preferably an English teacher, at a comparable grade level in a school in the target culture. Together they set goals for a variety of activities involved in an exchange of class projects. Setting up individual pen-pal relationships is not part of the early stages of this program, since the emphasis is on group work within each class. The program takes place in two phases; during the first phase each school plans and prepares the projects they will send to their partner school, and during the second phase they interpret and respond to the project they have received from their partner school.

A fourth grade class in a parochial school in Northfield, Minnesota, developed a classroom exchange with a fifth grade group in Hamburg, West Germany, in a project designed by Dahlberg. As a first step the two groups exchanged group photographs of class members, class lists, and school schedules. Then the Northfield group discussed the best way to show their partner group what it meant to be a fourth grade child, in their school, in Northfield, in Minnesota, in the United States. At the same time they began to generate questions about the life of the German children. The project resulted in the following activities:

1. A questionnaire based on students' questions about life in Hamburg was developed. The questions reflected interest in family and pets, modes of transportation, size of families, hobbies, and favorite film, TV, and pop music stars. The children also took the questionnaire themselves and analyzed the results to gain insight into their own lives. Because these students were beginners, the questionnaire was developed in English and translated by the teacher before it was sent to Germany. With more advanced learners the same activity might be conducted in the target language.

2. Materials containing information about the community and aspects of the children's daily lives were collected. This involved visits to the local chamber of commerce, letters to the state tourist agency, and visits to many local businesses and service organizations. The final collection of materials included these items:
   - TV and movie schedules
   - mail-order catalogs
   - telephone book
   - weekly food ads and coupon pages
   - comic books
   - brochures about the city and the state
   - colorful information about community businesses
   - seed catalogs and packets for favorite garden products
   - circus flyers
   - school student handbooks
   - copies of the school paper and of the local paper

3. Photographs of selected aspects of the children's daily lives were taken. Different children's homes were selected for each room of the house; other children had pets or hobbies photographed. The final slide collection included pictures of the following:
   - all possible rooms in a home
   - a school bus
   - the school, the classroom, the gymnasium
   - stores and businesses familiar to the children
   - pets and children engaged in hobbies
   - the cafeteria
   - school athletic, music, and drama events the children liked to attend
   - individual pictures of the children with a favorite pet or toy

4. Music and other information that held meaning for class members was recorded. The recorded information included the following:
   - favorite songs from German class and music classes
   - school song and cheers
   - favorite pop or rock music (determined by class vote)
   - self-introductions by each child in German

   (The German partner class also made recordings of the material the American children were learning in their German classes, but there was no interest in having American children return the favor, because at the time an American accent was not considered acceptable in the partner school.)

5. To see how the climates compared, the weather was charted day by day over a period of several months, and later compared with information sent from Hamburg.

The period of preparation for the exchange lasted about six weeks and was an experience with inquiry and interdisciplinary involvement that resulted in better knowledge of the children's own class and environment and heightened interest in life in German-speaking countries. The activity would have been valuable even if nothing had ever been received from Hamburg. When the Hamburg projects actually arrived, there was considerable excitement throughout the school.

Many of the Hamburg contributions had been prepared by individual children, who enclosed drawings, favorite rhymes and games, family pictures, postcards, maps, and short descriptions of favorite activities. The responses to the questionnaire provided material for investigation and discussion for the rest of the school year—why would so many American film stars appear in the list of favorites? Where were the Saturday-morning cartoons on television? The contact with authentic materials and the awareness of the lives of real children of about their own age provided a context for the study of language and a springboard for a continuing interest in culture.

Finding a Partner for an Exchange

Teachers wishing to develop a classroom exchange project may find a potential partner teacher in several ways. Several of the professional associations and journals have teacher pen-pal opportunities with fellow teachers abroad, and these contacts can be developed into classroom exchanges. Many colleges and universities have programs of study abroad, and students in these programs are often willing to serve as liaisons in setting up such a program. The best route for developing a program is a personal contact with a teacher or a school during a trip to a country of target culture. The goals of the project should be fully discussed and agreed upon before the project begins, and the project should begin in the fall, to allow enough time for materials to be developed, to reach their destination, and to receive a response before the end of the school year.

Many variations on the classroom exchange are possible. Technology would now permit exchange of digital photos and even movies, as well as e-mail questionnaires and electronic bulletin boards. Developing exchange relationships with several different countries in which the target language is spoken, and focusing on a different country each year, would help students to appreciate the variety of approaches to daily life that can be discovered through the use of a single language. Exchanges between students learning the same language in different parts of the United States or different parts of the world can be motivating and revealing, as learners discover that lifestyles and customs are not identical even where others speak their own native language.

Classroom exchanges can go even further, of course. Sometimes an exchange like the one described above can precede an actual exchange of visits between groups of students. Several teachers have pointed out the advantages of bringing pre-adolescent youngsters on trips abroad. While in some cases they may be more likely to experience homesickness than older students, they may also be more likely to welcome the family experience and be less resistant to the necessary rules and restrictions that a trip abroad entails. Teachers report success in exchanging visits with children as early as the end of fifth grade, provided that there is a close working relationship between the teachers involved, as well as close cooperation with parents. While exchange programs involve a great deal of preparation and supervision, they provide powerful opportunities for language use and cultural contact that cannot be obtained any other way.

Placing students in contact with students of their own age in the target culture makes it possible to address several of the national standards in a meaningful way. Much of the information exchanged invites comparisons, especially cultural comparisons (Standard 4.2). Students become more aware of their own culture as they explain it to others and see similarities and contrasts with their partner school. They have ready access to information and opinions in the partner class (Standard 3.2), and they are clearly moving their language learning beyond the classroom walls (Standard 5.1).

Flat Stanley—Where Have You Been?

Flat Stanley, a book for young readers by Jeff Brown, has sparked the imagination of teachers and children all over the country and even spawned several Web sites. It tells the story of a little boy who is flattened by a falling bulletin board so that he is a mere half-inch thick. Being flat has some advantages, as Stanley discovers when he travels through the U.S. mail in a very large brown envelope to visit a friend across the continent.

In the Flat Stanley project, students make a paper or electronic Flat Stanley to exchange with other classrooms. Sometimes they use a copy of the "Stanley" from the book, and sometimes they use their own faces on the flat paper figure. The recipients treat the visiting Stanley as a guest and record events from Stanley's visit in a journal and through photographs, postcards, and so forth. These are then returned to the original group of students. Some classes mail Stanleys to relatives and friends all over this country. A few language classes have used Flat Stanley as a way of exchanging with young learners in other cultures and other countries. The potential for geographic and cultural learning through a project like this one is almost endless. The Web site for the Flat Stanley project has extensive information, photos, and stories about successful projects: www.flatstanley.net.

Education for Global and Multicultural Awareness

The early language classroom provides an especially favorable setting for introducing the learner to the whole world of cultural diversity. When the language teacher limits the attention of the class to a single country, or even to one region of a country in which the target language is spoken, an important opportunity is being missed. Almost all of the languages most commonly taught in elementary school in the United States are used in a number of countries with customs and lifestyles that vary greatly from one to another. The classroom experience will be much richer if this variety is brought into the classroom through activities, visual representation, and specific songs, games, crafts, foods, and other experiences reflecting a variety of cultures.

Global awareness can be further enhanced when teachers use every opportunity to show relationships between countries where the target language is used and other nations around the world. The presence of many Germans in South America, the trade of a local business with Japan, and the role of French explorers in America and in other parts of the world can all become a part of the information exchanged in an early language classroom.

The teacher can invite speakers of the target language who have had experiences in any part of the world to show the class slides and to discuss the countries they have visited—in the target language. In more advanced classes, the teacher and students together can discuss implications of events in any part of the world, both for countries in which the target language is spoken and for the students themselves.

Broadening culture study to include ideas and practices from a more global perspective can also help students to see the contrasts they experience between their home environment and the target cultures in a wider context. Instead of perceiving a conflict or a set of either-or choices, learners can begin to see the options in their own and another culture as simply two of many alternatives within a rich variety of possibilities.

Language teachers, like teachers in all other areas of the curriculum, have a responsibility to plan lessons with sensitivity to the racial and ethnic diversity present in their classrooms and in the world in which their students live. The early language classroom that incorporates the goals of global and multicultural education into carefully developed culture instruction can help students to take on a new and broader perspective. By learning to appreciate the point of view of someone living in the target culture, they can also learn to value the points of view of many others whose life experiences are different from their own.

Rosenbusch (1992b) describes a process for developing thematic units for FLES classes that are based on global education concepts and incorporate insights and information from the target culture. She maintains that foreign language teachers can be leaders in helping students to develop a global perspective and in preparing them for responsible world citizenship. This may be just what H. Douglas Brown had in mind when he wrote: "Language is a tool for overcoming powerlessness. Our professional commitment intrinsically drives us to help the inhabitants of this planet to communicate with each other and to negotiate the meaning of peace, of goodwill, and of survival on this tender, fragile globe" (1991, 257).

Additional Activities

Early language teachers who are committed to providing cultural experiences for their classes will be constantly in search of authentic games, music, crafts, foods, and customs to share with them. In addition, many of the following activities will contribute to developing the standards described above.

1. Invite foreign visitors or target language speakers to visit the class and share their experience, using visuals, slides, and as many concrete materials as possible (2.1, 2.2, 5.1).
2. Learn and perform folk dances and singing games from the target culture (2.1).
3. Celebrate holidays and festivals of the target culture in the class, especially those that do not have an American counterpart (2.1, 2.2).
4. Where possible, make field trips to a neighborhood, restaurant, museum, or store that reflects some aspects of the target culture (2.2).
5. Invite children to bring to class any items from the target culture or samples of the target language that they may come across in their homes. Many students become very good at finding the target language on directions, store labels, and advertisements.

These items can become the stimulus for a great deal of language when the child or the teacher shares them with the class (2.2).

6. Identify local or regional place names that may be derived from the target language and investigate the reason for the choice of name. Some communities may have namesakes in the target culture, or sister cities in another country, and these relationships can be the source of many activities (2.2).

7. Ask students to skim target language newspapers or magazines to find illustrations for concepts they are learning in the foreign language class or in subject content classes (2.2).

8. Tell or read fables, folktales, and legends that come from the target culture or from other cultures around the world (all in the target language) (2.2, 3.1).

9. Read to students from picture books written for children in the target culture and reflecting that culture (2.2).

10. Students can view videos made for children in the target culture.

11. Visit a supermarket or a gourmet shop and list foods that are imported from countries where the target language is spoken (2.2).

12. Encourage students to read fiction and nonfiction books about children in the target culture. The school media center director is often willing to help develop a list or a collection of these books for each grade level (2.2, 5.2).

13. Use collections of games from around the world to locate suitable games played in the target culture, and incorporate these into units and lessons (2.1).

14. Establish contacts through e-mail or professional channels with language teachers and their classrooms in the target culture. Use these contacts to answer teacher and student questions about life in the target culture, and to exchange cultural products, children's literature, and up-to-date cultural information (2.1, 2.2, 3.2).

15. Subscribe to magazines written in the target language and produced in the target culture, both those intended for young people of the same age as the language learners and those intended for parents and caregivers. These can provide students with direct contacts with authentic cultural materials and can give teachers insight about life and concerns affecting young people in the target culture (2.2, 3.2, 4.2).

16. Incorporate animal sounds in the target language into any unit dealing with animals. These sounds are fun to use and reinforce the differences among languages (4.1, 4.2).

Summary

The elementary school foreign language classroom is an ideal setting for the development of cultural awareness and understanding. Cultural goals can best be met by giving children experiences with the culture rather than by talking about cultural facts and artifacts. Many of these experiences can be part of daily classroom activity, integrated with the use of language in an authentic, communicative setting. Teachers may identify cultural information to integrate with language and subject content by considering the categories of *cultural symbols, cultural products,* and *cultural practices* and considering the *perspectives* they represent. Teachers may also turn to resources such as an existing scope and sequence for culture. In all cases culture requires careful and systematic planning, to provide developmentally appropriate information and experiences at each developmental level and a well-designed sequence of instruction.

As teachers plan lessons that incorporate cultural products and practices, they are also building a foundation for awareness of the perspectives of the culture. Although perspectives may not always be overtly taught, the teacher needs to be aware of the perspectives underlying the cultural experiences of the classroom. Guiding students in the comparison of cultures helps them to develop a deeper and more personalized understanding of both the target culture and their own culture.

This chapter also describes two types of extended cultural experience—the fantasy and the classroom exchange. The fantasy makes use of a few props and the child's imagination to bring the child together with the culture in a fantasy setting. In the classroom exchange, two cultures actually meet, as a language class exchanges projects and information with a partner class in the target culture. The classroom exchange requires extensive preparation and continues over a period of time.

Global awareness and multicultural education are additional goals that have special importance in the elementary school foreign language classroom. The target language can be used as a point of departure for making connections with the entire world, and gaining access to the perspective of the target culture can help learners to appreciate other perspectives in their community and their world. The chapter closes with a series of additional activities that can give children experiences with the target culture or with global concepts.

FOR STUDY AND DISCUSSION

1. Explain to a colleague why you have chosen to spend a considerable amount of time seeking out authentic songs, games, rhymes, and stories for use in your primary school classes, rather than simply retelling or translating the things children are already familiar with in English.

2. You have invited a native speaker to speak to your class of sixth graders, who are in their second year of learning the language you teach. Based on what you know about language and culture, what instructions and help will you give your speaker in advance to ensure that the experience will be valuable for the children in your class?

3. Together with a classmate or a native speaker of the language you teach, develop an inventory of cultural symbols, cultural products, and cultural practices that you can draw from as you develop integrated thematic instruction. Can you iden-

tify the perspectives reflected in the items you have written down?

4. Choose a feature of the target culture that you feel would be suitable for the development of a classroom fantasy experience. Follow the guidelines in the chapter and plan a fantasy for the grade and language level with which you are the most familiar.

5. You have made contact with a teacher of English in an elementary school in the target culture, and the teacher is eager to take part in a classroom exchange but has no idea how to begin. Write a letter in which you describe the mechanics and the potential of the idea.

6. List seven ideas for meaningfully linking the target language that you teach with worldwide cultures, beyond the limits of the countries in which the target language is spoken natively.

FOR FURTHER READING

The following sources are recommended for additional information about material covered in this chapter. Chapter citations are documented in Works Cited at the end of the volume.

Bosma, Betty. *Fairy Tales, Fables, Legends, and Myths: Using Folk Literature in Your Classroom.* New York: Teachers College Press, 1987.

Brown, Jeff. *Flat Stanley.* Steve Björkman, Illus. New York: HarperTrophy, 1996.

Crawford-Lange, Linda M., and Dale L. Lange. "Doing the Unthinkable in the Second-Language Classroom: A Process for the Integration of Language and Culture." In *Teaching for Proficiency, the Organizing Principle,* edited by Theodore V. Higgs, 139–177. Lincolnwood, IL: National Textbook Company, 1984.

Electronic Magazine of Multicultural Education. www.eastern.edu/publications/emme

Flat Stanley Project Web site: www.flatstanleyproject.com

Lange, Dale L. "Planning for and Using the New National Culture Standards." In *Foreign Language Standards: Linking Research, Theories, and Practices,* edited by June K. Phillips, 57–135. The ACTFL Foreign Language Education Series. Lincolnwood, IL: National Textbook Company, 1999.

Pesola, Carol Ann. "Culture in the Elementary School Foreign Language Classroom." *Foreign Language Annals* 24, no. 4 (September 1991): 331–346.

Rosenbusch, Marcia. "Is Knowledge of Cultural Diversity Enough? Global Education in the Elementary School Foreign Language Program." *Foreign Language Annals* 25, no. 2 (April 1992):129–136.

Seelye, H. Ned. *Teaching Culture. Strategies for Intercultural Communication.* 3d ed. Lincolnwood, IL: National Textbook Company, 1993.

Strasheim, Lorraine A. "Language is the Medium, Culture is the Message: Globalizing Foreign Languages." In *A Global Approach to Foreign Language Education,* edited by Maurice W. Conner, 1–16. Skokie, IL: National Textbook Company, 1981.

11 The Connections Standard

Content-Related Instruction

Regarding language as a medium of learning naturally leads to a cross-curriculum perspective. We have seen that reading specialists contrast learning to read with reading to learn. Writing specialists contrast learning to write with writing to learn. Similarly, language education specialists should distinguish between language learning and using language to learn. Outside the isolated foreign language classroom students learn language and content at the same time. Helping students use language to learn requires us to look beyond the language domain to all subject areas, and to look beyond language learning to education in general. Therefore we need a broad perspective which integrates language and content learning.

—Mohan 1986: 18

Making Connections between Language and Content

The connections goal of the *Standards for Foreign Language Learning in the 21st Century* emphasizes the role that languages can play in extending and enriching student learning in all content areas. Languages give students access to information, opinions, and ideas that would be otherwise inaccessible. The Standards-based language classroom gives students the skills and the practice needed to acquire information in their new language, and it connects the foreign language curriculum with other parts of students' academic lives.

Content-related instruction ties directly to the connections goal in the Standards document: Connect with Other Disciplines and Acquire Information. There are two standards under the connections goal:

Standard 3.1: Students reinforce and further their knowledge of other disciplines through the foreign language.

This standard recognizes that foreign languages can be used to acquire new knowledge by making connections between other subject areas and the foreign language. An important benefit of this connection is that the new language is used as a tool for thinking and learning.

Standard 3.2: Students acquire information and recognize the distinctive viewpoints that are only available through the foreign language and its cultures.

In this standard students use the new language to gain access to information and points of view that are not available to some other students who do not know the language. This standard reminds us that a second or third language broadens our students' horizons and resources for all aspects of learning.

Some of the main purposes of content-related instruction are:

- to integrate language development with content learning
- to provide a vehicle for reinforcing the academic skills and processes and the cognitive skills required by the regular curriculum
- to enrich concepts learned in other content areas with the unique experiences and insights available through language study

Programs that Relate Language and Content

The goals of foreign language teachers and content area teachers have not always been congruent. Too often the foreign language curriculum was conceived and taught independently from, and to the exclusion of, the content area curriculum. This situation accounts in part for the resistance classroom teachers sometimes raise to the addition of a language program to an already crowded school day.

The integration of subject content and academic skills with language and culture is a positive step toward meeting the goals of both language teaching and content teaching, and toward identifying a place for languages in every student's program. In fact, integration of language and subject content is already being successfully accomplished in several types of programs, including the following:

- immersion programs
- two-way immersion/bilingual programs
- content-based FLES and partial immersion programs
- content-based teaching models at the university level
- sheltered English programs for English Language Learners (ELL) students

In all of the above programs students succeed not only in acquiring another language, but also in acquiring subject content knowledge at the same time.

Immersion programs have demonstrated for more than three decades that students can learn subject content and language simultaneously and successfully. As discussed in Chapter 12, immersion students achieve at the same level with, or often at higher levels than, students in English-only classes on standardized tests administered in English (Swain 1984).

Two-way immersion programs, also known as dual language or two-ways bilingual are content-based programs that are similar to the immersion model, except that the students are both native and non-native speakers of the second language.

Immersion programs are not alone in providing successful content-based instruction for second language learners. Sheltered English programs, when used as a component of bilingual education, have also proved to be very effective in this regard. Sheltered English programs are designed to teach English and subject content to English language learners using specially adapted (but not watered-down) curriculum and materials. Students in these classes learn the subject content in the target language, but they are not required to compete with native speakers nor to work with the same linguistic tools that are used by native speakers. In the sheltered English class, as in the immersion class, language is a tool through which subject content is learned and not primarily the object of instruction.

In content-based FLES programs or in partial immersion programs, students receive some subject content instruction in a second language in addition to formal instruction in the language. Content-based FLES programs teach the language and take responsibility for some content; thus they require more scheduled time than a FLES program, but less than 50 percent of the school day.

Partial immersion programs, such as those found in Cincinnati; Minneapolis; Anchorage, Alaska; Portland, Oregon; and Fairfax County, Virginia, provide English-speaking students with at least half the day of classroom instruction in a foreign language. Programs vary in terms of whether the same subjects are taught from day to day and from year to year in the new language, or whether the languages of instruction change at specified intervals.

Ways to Integrate Language and Content

Bernard Mohan (1986) has outlined three types of relationships between language teaching and content teaching. They are as follows:

1. Language teaching *by* content teaching, in which the focus is on content, and the language competencies develop almost incidentally. The intention is that the student will learn the second language by participating in the content instruction. The belief is that students will learn language through exposure to modified content alone.

2. Language teaching *with* content teaching, where the focus is on teaching both language and content. In such an approach the language and content objectives are in close alignment. Language learning in the language classroom can further the goals of content teaching by giving learners help with the processes of content learning.

3. Language teaching *for* content teaching, in which students learn the specific language needed for success in various subject areas as quickly as possible.

Immersion and two-way immersion/bilingual programs focus on the first area of language and content teaching—language teaching *by* content teaching. Content-based early language programs, partial immersion programs, and sheltered English programs focus on the second area—language teaching *with* content teaching. English Language Learner (ELL) programs, in some cases, focus on the third area—language teaching *for* content teaching.

Content-Related FLES Programs

In Chapter 18 the distinction is made between content-related and content-based programs. Content-*related* programs use the regular curriculum as a vehicle for making language activities more cognitively engaging, but they do not commit to teaching a specific portion of the general school curriculum. A standards-based language program at the elementary or middle school level will always be content-related, because it incorporates the connections goal into the curriculum. Integration of curriculum content is an important factor, but it does not overbalance the other goals.

Use of curriculum content in this way provides a rationale for fitting the foreign language program into an already crowded school day. Content-related programs reinforce the curriculum and may or may not use content directly associated with the grade level of the students. More and more school districts are recognizing curriculum integration as a powerful vehicle for convincing parents, school board members, and regular classroom teachers of the value and viability of second language instruction.

Reasons for Content-Related Instruction

The reasons for having content-related instruction are twofold. First of all, the movements toward communicative competence, proficiency, and Standards all support the use of meaningful content in the language classroom. In order for communication to take place, some knowledge or information must be shared. Communicative competence can be developed as students feel the need to exchange information with one another or with the teacher in a setting that has significance for all of the participants in the communication. Incorporating subject content instruction into the elementary school world language classroom provides a meaningful context for language use, and encourages language use for interesting and engaging purposes.

The second area of support for content-related instruction comes from what we know about second language acquisition and what we know about the brain. Subject content instruction fills the need for "comprehensible input" as described by Stephen Krashen. When providing subject content instruction, the teacher surrounds the students with language to which they can relate by means of a concrete experience, or on the basis of their previous experiences with the information.

Lessons on mapping and graphing, estimating, measuring, endangered animals, the solar system, or the rain forest provide rich opportunities for making language input comprehensible through meaningful visual and tactile experiences. The language used is comprehensible to the students because teachers make sure that ideas and concepts are being communicated clearly and concretely in language the students understand. The language is supported by contextual clues, often in the form of visuals or concrete objects.

Content-related instruction supports what we know about how the brain makes connections and how learning takes place. Students are actively engaged in constructing meaning and making sense of the interesting world presented to them through the vehicle of the target language.

Another source of support for content-related instruction relates to the notion of how time is allocated in the elementary school day. The perennial question asked by administrators and classroom teachers is: "What will we have to take out of the curriculum in order to include language instruction? There is currently not enough time in the curriculum for us to accomplish our existing goals." A language curriculum that introduces or reinforces some mathematics, social studies, or science concepts, and that also makes activities cognitively engaging by focusing on academic skills and processes, provides a powerful rationale for justifying a stable place in the curriculum for elementary language instruction.

Curricular Areas with Potential for Content-Related Instruction (Standard 3.1)

A careful examination of the curriculum and the standards for each of the content areas of the K–8 curriculum will yield many ideas for making connections with languages. Several of the areas with the greatest potential are the social studies, mathematics, and science.

Social Studies

The social studies curriculum for the elementary school deals with many of the same concepts traditionally taught in language programs in a less systematic way. Such topics as home, family, community, social patterns, and comparative cultures are natural choices for the foreign language curriculum. Geography and map skills are also easily incorporated into content-related instruction, and there is a natural culture connection. It is also true that U.S. students lag far behind those in other countries in the area of geography. Learning geographical concepts in another language can reinforce a weak curricular area and perhaps heighten student interest.

Many of the techniques and resources used for the teaching of social studies are also appropriate for presenting the same concepts in another language. For example, the use of media; the inquiry method; the use of photos, pictures, and study prints; the use of historical artifacts; and reference to colorful periodicals all provide rich stimuli for meaning-based language instruction.

Although the social studies, especially geography, offer a wealth of language and materials for content-related instruction, there are both advantages and disadvantages to using social studies as a basis for early language learning programs. On the one hand, there is the potential for a great deal of meaningful language and vocabulary use in topic areas that are closely related to the language and cultures curriculum. On the other hand, there may be more vocabulary and language proficiency required for the content and processes of social studies than novice-level language students can adequately develop. This problem becomes evident beginning as early as grade three in a K–5 curriculum. Many important geography concepts, however, such as identification of places, use of maps, and map directions, work well with novice learners even though they may be cognitively complex.

Mathematics

Abstract concepts at higher levels of mathematics instruction may pose difficulties, but computation and concrete problem-solving situations can be very useful in content-related instruction. Concepts of size and shape are easily communicated in the target language, and elementary school language teachers have long used simple computation as a means of practicing number concepts. We have included here some of the components of the elementary school mathematics curriculum in order to illustrate in just one subject area a sampling of a few possible curriculum connections that could be made in the language program.

Measurement
- Learn to measure—in inches/feet/centimeters/meters.
- Estimate measurements with reasonable accuracy, using appropriate unit (length, mass, area, volume, time, temperature).
- Identify standard measures and intra-system equivalencies.

Statistics
- Read, interpret, and construct graphs.
- Given a set of data, determine the mean or average of that data.
- Classify numbers as prime or composite.
- Tell, read, and write time to the nearest minute.

Arithmetic
- Make simple calculations, using the foreign language to review and reinforce math "facts" and measurement.
- Read, write, and say whole numbers 0–100 billion.
- Round numbers to nearest 10, 100, 1,000, 10,000 or 100,000.
- List multiples of a given number.
- Find products and quotients of whole numbers.
- Multiply mentally by 10, 100, or 1,000.

Graphing Activities

Graphing is an excellent mathematics-related activity that can be used with many different themes in a language classroom, even when children have relatively limited expressive language ability. Graphing is also an essential concept in science and social studies. Graphing the weather, for example, can be part of the daily routine (see Figure 11.1).

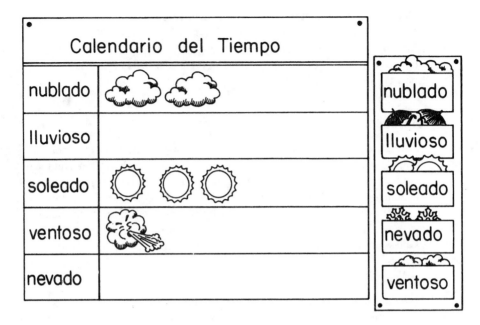

FIGURE 11.1   A chart of the daily weather can also give children experience with a bar graph.

A first experience with graphing might be entirely teacher directed and involve only physical responses on the part of the children. (Children have already learned to understand colors and various items of clothing when the teacher describes them.)

TEACHER: Everyone who has brown shoes on, stand up.
Hold up your left foot so we can see your brown shoe.
(Walks around class to check for shoes and to comment.)
Yes, Mary has brown shoes—they look new, Mary!
Look, Tom has brown shoes.
Let's see how many people have brown shoes (counts).
1–2–3–4. . . (or children may count along).

(Goes to prepared chart on overhead projector, chart paper, or chalkboard).

Seven children have brown shoes.

(Colors in graph—seven squares, perhaps with brown marker, or places colored shoes on the graph.)

Everyone who has brown shoes, sit down.
Everyone with black shoes, raise your hand.
Wave your hand back and forth!
Lift up your feet so we can see your black shoes.

(Continues in this way, changing things slightly with each color).

At the end of this activity there will be a completed graph that the children can talk about. If the activity is used with more than one class during the day, the graphs for the different classes can be compared, and concepts such as more and less can be practiced.

With very young children, a graph is more meaningful if it is created with real objects. In the shoe graph activity, a first step with kindergarten children might be to have each child place her or his own shoe in the appropriate space on a graph outlined on the floor. As a next step, the child might trade the shoe for a piece of paper in the color of his or her shoe, thus making the connection between the number of papers and the number of shoes.

Measuring and graphing heights of class members using centimeters has a cultural "shock value" for students of all ages—even college students find this experience to be engaging. The heights of the class can then be graphed, following a procedure similar to that of the shoe graph.

Another type of graphing activity involves food (or other item) preferences. Pictures of different foods might be placed on each of the walls of the room, and children "vote" for their favorite first by pointing to it and then by walking to that section of the room. (In a class in which children are already doing a lot of speaking, they might express their preferences orally.) The teacher counts the number of students at each of the options and colors in the results on the graph. As an alternative, the students themselves might place a square representing their choice on the chart, perhaps with their name printed on it, to help build a graph. Once the graphing activity has been completed, it can be the basis of discussion and used for comparisons, for recalling favorite foods of individual classmates, for games, and for a variety of other communicative activities.

At more advanced speaking stages, children might take surveys among their classmates about topics that interest them and graph the results, using their graphs to help explain their discoveries to their classmates. Some sample topics would be: number of sisters and brothers, number or kind of pet(s), favorites (colors, day of the week, season of the year, vegetable, and so on).

Science

Science is especially well suited to content-related foreign language instruction. Hands-on science activities involve many opportunities for interaction and meaningful exchange of language. Activities such as formulating hypotheses and reformulating them when the outcomes vary are important opportunities for the exchange of real information with learners beyond the novice level. Science instruction incorporates the use of many graphics and charts that contribute to understanding.

One of the most powerful strategies in science instruction is the use of prediction. Students encounter a puzzling situation or develop an experiment and predict the results they expect, thus investing personally in both the project and the solution. This strategy can be implemented even when students still have very limited expressive language skills, if the teacher surrounds the experience with language and uses carefully designed questioning techniques. The following example illustrates how the student involvement might be guided:

T: Who believes that the pear will float? Raise your hand. Who believes that the pear will not float? Raise your hand. Let's see—*counting*—sixteen believe that the pear will float, and twelve believe that the pear will not float. *Teacher or student records responses on the chalkboard or on a graph.* I wonder who is right. Does anyone want to change your mind? Raise your hand if you want to change your mind.

* * * * * *

T: X, do you believe that the pear will float? Yes or no.

X: Yes.

T: X says yes. Let's mark yes for X. *Asks one child after another, and records the response on a graph, or has a student recording responses.*

* * * * * *

T: Y, do you believe that the pear will sink or float?

Y: Sink.

T: Y believes that the pear will sink. Let's put one mark by "sink." *Asks one child after another, and records the response on a graph.*

Other Curricular Areas

Other curricular areas, such as physical education, family and consumer education, health, art, and music have potential for content-related instruction. Because they deal with highly experiential, often very visual learning, the use of a second language in communicating the concepts could be a natural and successful alternative for instruction.

Using the Language to Acquire Information and Insight That Is Only Available through the Target Language (Standard 3.2)

While the focus of Connections Standard 3.1 is integration with the school curriculum, Standard 3.2 pushes the student beyond the classroom and beyond the general curriculum in search of information and opinions that have personal importance to the learner: "Students acquire information and recognize the distinctive viewpoints that are only available through the foreign language and its cultures" (*Standards for Foreign Language Learning in the 21st Century,* 1999, 56).

Young language learners have many experiences inside a world language classroom that they could not have anywhere else. They hear and read folktales, stories, poems, and music written for native speakers, or sometimes adapted to their language level. Sometimes fantasy experiences such as those described in Chapter 10 can help them to better understand a point of view or a piece of information that would otherwise seem inexplicable.

When teachers work with world maps from the target culture, learners discover that other cultures place their own country or continent in the center of the world—not North America, as U.S. students are accustomed to seeing in the central position. Country names are different in another language, and many familiar cities go unrecognized in the language of the country where they are located.

All of these experiences lay the groundwork for greater independence in seeking out new information from the target culture and in the target language. Jessica Haxhi in Waterbury, Connecticut, builds a unit around the Japanese movie *My Neighbor Totoro*. Children identify many characteristic cultural features in the movie and contrast them with their own homes and lives. While these are activities closely related to the cultures and the comparisons goals, they also build a foundation of experiences and understandings that would be inaccessible to them any other way. Because the movie was designed for peers in the target culture, it is an especially valuable experience for these learners of Japanese.

Children who use the target language to sing songs and play games from the target culture are also gaining insights that would be unavailable to them outside the language classroom. These games and songs, like the picture books and stories that enrich early classrooms, or the Japanese movie mentioned earlier, give students a foundation that only young children can receive, because childhood is a natural time for such experiences. The ability to express understanding of information and distinctive viewpoints available through these experiences will come with time.

If teachers in early language classrooms have established a partner relationship with a classroom in the target culture, they are in a good position to guide student inquiry about the target culture and the lives of their peers. The class might develop a questionnaire or a survey for their peers in response to an international event, or to check information in a storybook they have read or in a textbook. They might request information about birthdays or other celebrations in the target culture, and then share their own customs. What the teacher carefully structures and guides in early stages can blossom into interesting and meaningful independent or group projects.

Older learners who have had more experience with the language and the culture will be more independent in accessing information and opinions. Students in middle school will be able to use such sources as key pals, Web sites, and magazines written for young adolescents in the target culture to prepare reports on topics of personal interest. They may even become motivated to research such topics as popular music, movies, and teen pastimes on their own.

This independent research is truly the goal of Communication Standard 3.2—motivating students to seek out information that goes beyond the limits of the curriculum and often beyond the teacher's own expertise. The role of the teacher and the language classroom is to give students the skills and the language foundation that will allow them to do so. As Met points out (1999), Standard 3.2 links closely with the communities standards (5.1—students use the language both within and beyond the school setting; 5.2—students show evidence of becoming lifelong learners by using the language for personal enjoyment and enrichment). It can also provide the opportunity for students to develop the perspectives called for in the cultures standards, often in areas that are well beyond the teacher's own expertise (see Chapter 10). The new perspectives may also be compared with the students' own worldview, thus addressing the Comparison Standard 4.2: "Students demonstrate understanding of the concept of culture through comparisons of the cultures studied and their own." As Connections Standard 3.2 moves students beyond the classroom, teachers and students can become co-learners within the classroom.

All of the activities in this connections standard have the goal of giving students a "new window on the world," and helping them to achieve ever greater independence in the use of their new language for personally meaningful purposes.

Considerations for Implementation of Subject Content Instruction

Context-Embedded and Context-Reduced Language Tasks

The work of Cummins (1981) continues to be very helpful in explaining some of the strategies that are useful for subject content instruction. Cummins states that first- or second-language proficiency can be looked at in terms of the degree of contextual support available for expressing or comprehending through a language. He describes "context-embedded" language, which is supported by a wide range of clues, and "context-reduced" language, which has very little extra support, so that everything depends on the words themselves. Cummins also says that language proficiency can be viewed in terms of cognitive involvement, or the amount of information a person must process simultaneously or in close succession in order to accomplish a task.

According to Cummins's model, tasks involving language use can be classified into four categories, as seen in the four quadrants in the chart in Figure 11.2. These categories are as follows:

A. cognitively undemanding and context embedded (embedded in context that helps to make the meaning clear)
B. cognitively undemanding and context reduced (little context provided)
C. cognitively demanding and context embedded
D. cognitively demanding and context reduced

The chart in Figure 11.2 helps to illustrate the level of contextual support and academic complexity found in various areas of the curriculum. They range from quadrant A, in which the activities are context embedded and relatively simple, to quadrant D, where the activities are more language dependent, context reduced, and relatively difficult.

As concepts characteristic of quadrant B and quadrant D emerge in the course of instruction, the teacher can make them more accessible to students through the incorporation of extensive visual and concrete referents and through the careful establishment of a context.

The teacher can make the math story problem from quadrant D intelligible through visual or graphic representation. Conceptual explanations can be made more vivid with the addition of appropriate graphs, charts, illustrations, and hands-on experiences. With the addition of context, materials that would otherwise be unintelligible in the target language can contribute to student learning.

The Cummins grid has clear implications for teaching in early language programs, as described below.

Make new concepts less language dependent
1. Make increased use of visuals and realia.
2. Provide for hands-on involvement of learners.
3. Increase the number and vividness of examples and analogies.
4. Establish a clear, meaningful context.
5. Draw on learners' past experience and previous learning from the curriculum.
6. Make generous use of rephrasing and repetition.

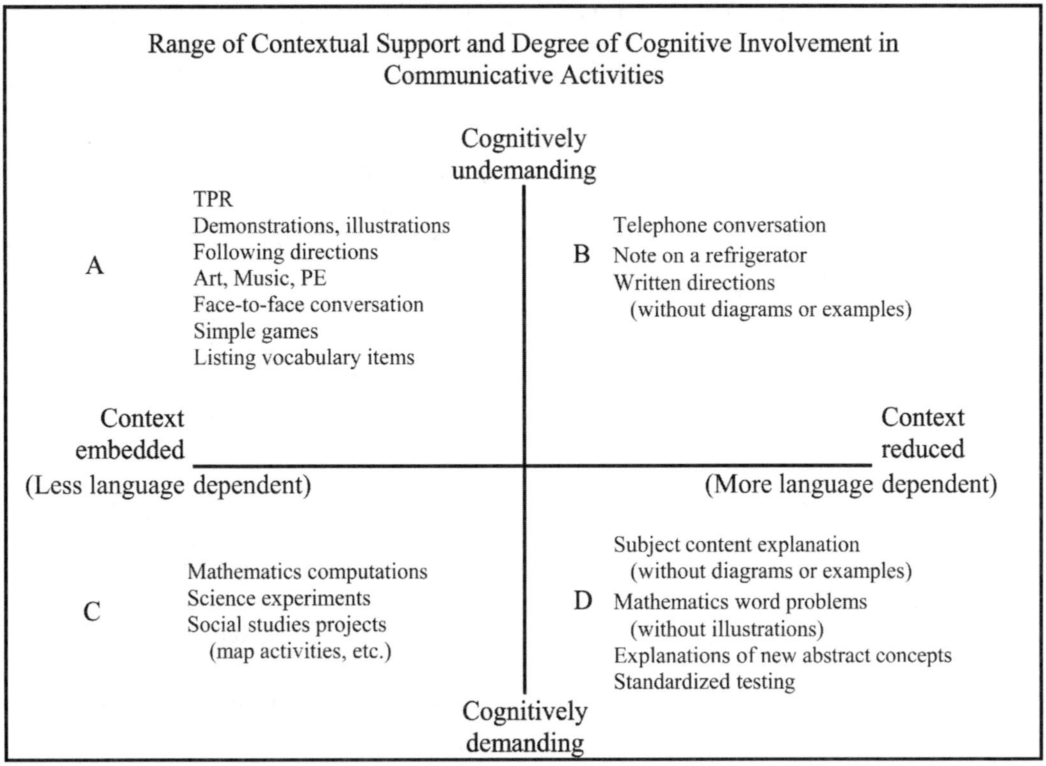

Range of Contextual Support and Degree of Cognitive Involvement in Communicative Activities

Cognitively
undemanding

A

TPR
Demonstrations, illustrations
Following directions
Art, Music, PE
Face-to-face conversation
Simple games
Listing vocabulary items

B

Telephone conversation
Note on a refrigerator
Written directions
   (without diagrams or examples)

Context
embedded
(Less language dependent)

Context
reduced
(More language dependent)

C

Mathematics computations
Science experiments
Social studies projects
   (map activities, etc.)

D

Subject content explanation
   (without diagrams or examples)
Mathematics word problems
   (without illustrations)
Explanations of new abstract concepts
Standardized testing

Cognitively
demanding

FIGURE 11.2 Range of contextual support and degree of cognitive involvement in communicative activities.

Source: Adapted from Cummins, Jim. 2000. *Language, Power and Pedagogy. Bilingual Children in the Crossfire.* Clevedon, UK: 68.

Make language tasks more cognitively engaging

1. Relate foreign language curriculum to the concepts in the general school curriculum.
2. Make use of academic skills and processes to engage learners at higher cognitive levels, even when the language itself may be quite simple: classifying, categorizing, graphing, estimating, predicting, comparing, sequencing, identifying patterns.
3. Create opportunities for learners to practice new language in communicative and problem-solving situations, including games, rather than relying on imitation and drill.

Application of General Academic Skills

As world language teachers begin to incorporate content teaching into the class period, their planning will take on a three-dimensional character. They will design lessons to develop the students' skills in the content area, their understanding of and experience with the culture, and the language necessary for them to achieve both of the preceding goals. Cutting across all three dimensions are intellectual or general academic skills.

One of the useful contributions of cognitive psychology to teaching and learning is a new attention to learners' thought processes. Like language, thinking skills are best developed in context, in the process of grappling with an important idea or decision. At the same time, purposeful implementation of a variety of academic skills and processes can also add to the meaning-making potential of their new language. Teaching children these skills enables them to manipulate information in order to plan, make judgments, decide, and solve problems. Learners need to be able to use academic skills and processes so that they can raise questions as well as support possible answers. Children also need to become aware of their own mental processes and to assess what they know so that they can determine what they still need to learn.

Inventories of thinking skills can be useful to language teachers as a reminder of the need to make activities more cognitively engaging by increasing the sophistication of the thinking required. Bloom's Taxonomy of Thinking Processes (Bloom 1956) is a helpful tool that is familiar to many educators.

Bloom's Taxonomy of Thinking Processes

Bloom outlines six levels of skills, including knowledge, comprehension, application, analysis, synthesis, and evaluation (see Table 11.1). The chart outlines the levels and possible teacher and student activities associated with each level of thinking. This taxonomy should be helpful to teachers as they seek to incorporate academic skills and processes into their teaching. Another chart, shown in Table 11.2, outlines the skills that are needed in various subject areas. Both charts provide teachers with helpful information needed for addressing cognitive process in their teaching.

Learning Strategies.   Young learners can become more skilled at monitoring their own learning through attention to learning strategies. Some students use these strategies naturally, while for others they must be taught. Learning strategies are usually divided into three groups:

- *Metacognitive Strategies*—Strategies for planning and reflecting on the learning process, such as previewing the main ideas, or planning what is going to be expressed orally or in writing.
- *Cognitive Strategies*—Strategies learners apply directly to the task itself, for example:
  outlining
  summarizing
  using context clues
  grouping and clustering
  compensation strategies, such as use of gestures
  memorization strategies
  study skills
- *Affective and Social Strategies*—Learners use these strategies to reward and encourage themselves, to lower anxiety and frustration, or to ask for help. Some examples are:
  questioning for clarification
  self talk
  asking for help
  working with other students

Jill Bergren, a middle school French teacher in Fargo, North Dakota, has successfully taught ninth grade students to be intentional in their use of strategies. Her students especially like using memorization strategies, study skills, compensation strategies, and affective strategies. She started her strategies instruction as an action research project, after reading that only older students could make effective use of strategy instruction. Based on her experience, she would not hesitate to use strategy instruction with students beginning in grade six, if they had already had several years of language.

TABLE 11.1 Bloom's Taxonomy of Thinking Processes

Level	Definition	What the Student Does	Useful Verbs for Designing Activities
Knowledge	Recall or location of specific bits of information. Remembering. Bringing to mind the appropriate material.	responds, absorbs, remembers, recognizes	tell—list—define—name—recall—identify—state—know—remember—repeat—recognize
Comprehension (Understanding)	Understanding of communicated material or information. The lowest level of understanding, without necessarily relating ideas.	explains, translates, demonstrates, interprets	transform—change—restate—describe—explain—review—paraphrase—relate—generalize—summarize—interpret—infer—give main idea
Application (Using)	Use of rules, concepts, principles, and theories in new situations. The use of abstractions in particular and concrete situations.	solves problems, demonstrates, uses knowledge, constructs	apply—practice—employ—use—demonstrate—illustrate—show—report
Analysis (Taking apart)	Breaking down information into its parts. The breakdown of a communication into its constituent elements so that the relations between the ideas are clear.	discusses, uncovers, lists, dissects, classifies, determines sequence and consequence, compares and contrasts, sees cause and effect relationships, makes associations, verifies	analyze—dissect—distinguish—examine—compare—contrast—survey—investigate—separate—categorize—classify—organize, order

(continued)

TABLE 11.1   Continued

Level	Definition	What the Student Does	Useful Verbs for Designing Activities
Synthesis (Creating new)	Putting together of ideas into a new or unique product or plan. The putting together of elements and parts so as to form a whole. Production of a unique communication.	discusses, generalizes, relates, contrasts, decision maker, makes inferences and draws conclusions, hypothesizes, creates, imagines, predicts	create—invent—compose—construct—design—modify—imagine—produce—propose—what if. . .
Evaluation (Judging)	Judging the value of materials or ideas on the basis of set standards or criteria. Quantitative and qualitative judgments about value.	judges, disputes, forms opinions, debates, assesses value, makes judgments and formulates reactions based on personal experience or available facts, persuades, problem solves	judge—decide/select/justify—evaluate—critique—debate—verify—recommend—assess

TABLE 11.2   Process Skills across the Curriculum

Science	Reading	Math	Social Science
Classifying	Comparing and contrasting characteristics	Sorting, sequencing	Comparing ideas
Collecting data	Taking notes	Collecting data	Collecting data
Interpreting data	Organizing facts, recognizing cause and effect	Analyzing	Interpreting data
Communicating results	Logically arranging information	Graphing, constructing tables	Making maps
Predicting	Predicting	Predicting	Predicting

From *Instructor Magazine,* March 1991 issue. Copyright © 1991 by Scholastic Inc. Reprinted by permission of Scholastic Inc.

Techniques for Helping Students Access Content

Marzano, Pickering, and Pollock (2001) have suggested several important strategies that help students to access content, which can be especially helpful when that content is presented in a new language. Two of the research-proven strategies they suggest are identifying similarities and differences and using non-linguistic representations.

Identifying Similarities and Differences

Presenting students with explicit guidance in identifying similarities and differences, or asking students to identify similarities and differences independently, enhances students' understanding of and ability to use knowledge. Strategies for identifying similarities and differences include comparing, classifying, using metaphors, and using analogies. These strategies can be extended into the language curriculum as well, of course. For example, students might compare a birthday celebration in the target culture with their own; they might classify clothing vocabulary according to whether the item is worn in the winter or the summer or both. Students might create writing projects based on a metaphor: winter is a polar bear, for example. More advanced students might create more sophisticated products. Creating analogies based on combinations of old and new vocabulary could be an interesting way to intensify the understanding and the memorability of the words. Even at the single-word language level students could play word games with analogies like: Dark is to light as night is to . . . ?

Non-Linguistic Representations

Non-linguistic representations represent a second system of storage for knowledge, an imagery form, that is different from linguistic forms of representation. When students use both systems, they are better able to think about and to recall knowledge. Marzano et al. (2001) identify the following non-linguistic representations as ways to aid student learning.

- Making physical models, such a using math manipulatives to solve a story problem, can make otherwise abstract concepts more concrete and more meaningful.
- Generating mental pictures can create a story-like or emotional connection to vocabulary or information. A teacher who describes the setting in detail before telling a story to the class is helping them to generate a mental picture that will aid comprehension.
- Drawing pictures and pictographs could be a means of anchoring vocabulary in the new language. Students might create an individualized picture dictionary, for example.
- Engaging in kinesthetic activity is a popular means of helping students to understand and remember language. TPR, TPR Storytelling, the Gouin series, and songs and rhymes with actions all capitalize on the value of connecting language and ideas with motion.
- Creating graphic representations can help to clarify relationships among ideas and concepts.

In the next section we will focus on using graphic representations to help students access content knowledge through the new language.

Using Graphic Representations as Cognitive Organizers

A graphic or cognitive organizer is a visual that displays words or concepts in categories to show how they relate to one another. This organizes the information in such a way that it can be easily understood, remembered, and applied. Cognitive organizers connect linguistic and visual information, thus facilitating both learning and retrieval of what has been learned.

For the novice language learner, who finds listing and naming to be the most natural ways to use a new language, graphic organizers provide an ideal and cognitively engaging context for using and practicing vocabulary. The teacher who uses a variety of cognitive organizers is moving language instruction from area A in the Cummins grid, cognitively undemanding and context-embedded, to area B, cognitively (more) demanding and context-embedded. At the same time, the student is experiencing vocabulary in a variety of meaningful contexts and will be much more likely to store that vocabulary in his or her long-term memory.

Charts, graphs, time lines, flowcharts, tables, maps, Venn diagrams, and many other types of organizers are used to help students place vocabulary and information in a comprehensible and engaging context. Cognitive organizers can be used to list concepts in various ways. One of the ways to classify the many different types of organizers is in terms of how they structure information.

- simple listing/mapping/webbing/clustering
- time sequence/chronology
- compare and contrast
- process/cause and effect

We will examine examples of each of these four types in turn.

Simple Listing, Mapping, Webbing, Clustering

This type of organizer presents information or clarifies and categorizes information in a structured way. These organizers can be linear or non-linear depending in the relationships being described. They are used to describe and list attributes or patterns or to organize information about specific events, settings, or people. They can organize information into general statements with supporting examples or clarify concepts relating to a word or phrase that represents entire classes of people, places, things, and events.

Clustering/mapping/webbing organizers might be used to list everything the students can think of related to a central concept, such as a geography concept, an animal, or a specific person. The word can be placed in the center of the map with the other ideas listed as spokes coming out from the central concept. A picture map of Africa helps students to visualize the range of various animals that are native to the continent. Other organizers, such as the brace map, the tree map, and the topic category organizer, show how ideas and concepts are related to one another in a hierarchical fashion. A family tree is a simple example of this kind of organizer. Figure 11.3 is a tree map organizer for foods.

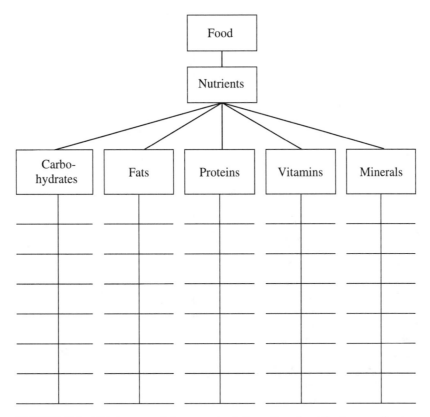

FIGURE 11.3   This tree map helps organize information about foods according to basic nutrients.

Sequence/Chronology

This type of cognitive organizer categorizes information according to some kind of sequence or chronology, as in a time line or a flowchart. Flowcharts can be linear or cyclical. A cycle flowchart shows how a series of events can produce the same results again and again, as with the water cycle or the life cycle of a butterfly or a frog (see Figure 11.4b).

Sequence/chronology organizers could also show a chain of events, the stages of an event, the steps in a procedure, or the actions of a character. A story map fits into this category of organizers. (See the section on story maps in Chapter 5.) Another way to graphically organize a sequence or chronology is with a continuum that shows the beginning and ending points of a process, or the range of some quality, such as student heights within a class, between extremes. Figure 11.4a is a chronology in the form of a foods time line that could become an interesting part of a nutrition unit.

FIGURE 11.4A   Foods timeline   **FIGURE 11.4B**   A cycle flow chart

4000 B.C.	Oranges and watermelons
3600 B.C.	Popcorn
2000 B.C.	Marshmallows
490 B.C.	Pasta and macaroni
200 B.C.	Potatoes
1395	Gingerbread and Lebkuchen
1484	Hot dogs
1544	Tomatoes in Europe
1553	Potatoes in Europe
1762	Sandwiches
1781	Tomatoes in the Americas
1819	Spaghetti
1830	Soft drinks in America
1869	Campbell's soup
1894	Hershey bars
1941	M & M's and Cheerios
1947	Betty Crocker cake mix
1954	TV dinners
1955	McDonald's restaurants
1965	Gatorade
1998	Grape tomatoes

Cycle

Source: Adapted from: The Food Timeline (www.gti.net/mocolib1/kid/food/html).

Comparison and Contrast

A third way the graphic organizers can classify information is by showing comparisons and contrasts. These types of organizers help students to display similarities and differences. The chart comparing the Mayas of Mexico and Central America and the Tainos of Puerto Rico shows the similarities and differences on a simple chart (Figure 11.5). The first column lists the elements to be compared while the second and third columns specify how each group manifests this element.

The Venn diagram is frequently used for comparison and contrast. A Venn diagram consists of two or more intersecting circles that graphically depict logical relationships between or among concepts. The Venn diagrams pictured here show two overlapping circles, each circle representing one of the concepts to be compared. One circle lists the characteristics of the first item while a second circle lists the characteristics of the other item. The segment where the two circles overlap in the middle shows the similarities between the two items, while the characteristics outside of the center show the differences. This activity serves as an exercise in logical thinking, and it can also be the basis of a meaningful writing exercise with each area of the diagram serving as the starting point for a separate paragraph. Figure 11.6 shows two Venn diagrams that help students organize information. The first deals with climate and clothing and the second deals with the life cycle of a frog.

FIGURE 11.5 This comparison/contrast worksheet can reveal similarities and differences.

	Tainos	**Mayas**
Food Supply		
Shelter		
Division of labor		
Social structure		

Venn diagrams can also be used for simple sorting activities conducted entirely orally. Two large hula hoops or two jump ropes laid out in adjoining circles could form the diagrams. Children could be asked to sort a group of objects into things that are blue in one circle, for example, and things that are round in the other. The teacher would include some items that are both round and blue. When students realize that these items should go in both circles, they are faced with a problem. They can usually solve the problem by moving the circles so that they intersect, leaving a space in the middle for items that have both characteristics. If students do not arrive at this solution within a reasonable time, the teacher can help with hints, or actually make the circles intersect herself or himself.

Cause and Effect

This last type of organizer shows the logical relationships between causes and effects. These organizers can be used to show relationships among events within a story, for example, or steps in a process. The causes and effects must be specifically labeled "cause" or "effect" in order to make the relationship clear (see Figure 11.7a and b, and c).

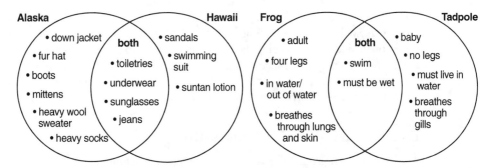

FIGURE 11.6 Venn diagrams show similarities and differences between items being compared.

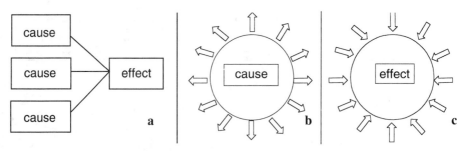

FIGURE 11.7   Cause and effect organizers can have many uses.

Special Considerations in Planning for Content-Related Instruction

There are numerous factors to consider when planning connections with the content curriculum for an integrated thematic curriculum, unit, or lesson. Most of the same considerations apply for the teacher in an immersion, partial immersion, or content-based program:

- the content-area skills and concepts that can interrelate most effectively with the language goals
- the language competencies needed to work with the content selected
- the cognitive skills necessary to perform the tasks in the lesson
- the potential for integration with cultural concepts and goals

It is important to emphasize the point that when teachers incorporate general curriculum content into a thematic unit, they should not ignore the balance among language, content, and culture goals. While there may be some lessons in a unit that emphasize subject content, elements of the cultures standard and the communication standard should always be present.

Both authors of this book have had the experience of working with school districts where content-related instruction is the primary emphasis in a FLES program, at the expense of other goals. In these situations, other dimensions of the curriculum appear to suffer. Students are still learning, of course, but the full potential of an early language program is not being realized. When this happens, it is often because school administrators seized on the idea of reinforcing the regular curriculum to the virtual exclusion of the other important elements of language teaching. In our enthusiasm for content-related instruction, we must remember that our vision is shaped by the interrelatedness of language, content, and culture, and by all five of the national standards, not by the connections standard alone.

Focus: Content-Based or Content-Related?

A *content-related* program draws from the regular curriculum as a vehicle for making language activities more cognitively engaging. Content-related instruction reinforces the regular curriculum and may or may not use content directly associated with the grade level of the students. *Any standards-based FLES or exploratory program with an integrated, the-*

matic curriculum can be described as content-related. However, a content-based program actually takes responsibility for a specific portion of the regular curriculum for that grade level. In this case, more time is needed for instruction so that a balanced language program can be provided.

Curriculum Resources

The best resources for the teacher who is interested in content-related instruction are the curriculum documents for the elementary and middle school level of the school district in which the second-language program takes place. If such materials are not current or are not available, the state department of education will have available standards for instruction at various grade levels. National standards for each subject can also provide guidance. Language teachers may find, when they examine school curriculum documents, that they are already addressing some of the concepts but in an unsystematic way. For example, the teacher who regularly teaches the location of French-speaking countries in a fifth grade class may choose to expand these lessons to include locating capital cities on simple maps using elementary grids, thus reinforcing additional map-reading skills taught at this grade level.

Teachability through the Target Language

The language teacher looks for concepts that lend themselves especially well to the kind of concrete, hands-on, activity-oriented teaching that is necessary in the early language classroom. Thus the teacher must ask: Can these concepts be taught using the simple language that novice-level learners are able to understand and use? Or do they require more abstract, complex, and sophisticated language?

For the fourth grade science curriculum of a partial immersion program in Minneapolis, for example, the staff chose a unit on rocks and charts as a likely candidate for Spanish instruction. They chose this topic because so many of the activities involved handling and observing characteristics of rocks and then classifying the rocks according to visual criteria.

They decided, however, that a unit on magnetism would require an inappropriately sophisticated command of the target language because of the expectation that conclusions would be evaluated and discussed in great detail.

Content-Compatible and Content-Obligatory Language

Identify the language needed—include both content vocabulary for the particular subject area and the other new language the students will need to know in order to understand the lesson. Decide how much subject content language can reasonably be taught in the second language.

Content obligatory language is the language that *must* be taught in order to teach or reinforce the curriculum concept, drawn from content curriculum. Content-compatible language, drawn from the language curriculum, is that language for which the curriculum concept or information provides a convenient context. For example, although the teacher knows that the basic language functions that will be needed for a rain forest unit are probably identifying and describing, the teacher recognizes this as an opportunity to work on other language functions such as asking for and giving information, or expressing admiration. Students could conduct role-play tours of the rain forest and ask about the animals in various levels, or express admiration for the beautiful colors of animals and flowers.

The teacher could decide to develop a fantasy theme in which the animals take on personalities. Then content-compatible language could even extend to socializing. Perhaps the teacher could have the animals greet each other like this:

> **STUDENT A:**   Hello, I'm Mrs. Jaguar, I live in the understory, and I am pleased to meet you.
>
> **STUDENT B:**   Hello Mrs. Jaguar, I'm Ms. Hummingbird. I live in the middle layer. I'm pleased to meet you.

Availability of Relevant Materials

Early in the planning process it is important to identify the instructional materials you will use. Are sufficient materials available in the target language or will most materials have to be translated? If materials are available in the target language, how much adaptation is necessary?

It may be necessary to simplify the instructional materials if the print involved is too difficult, or amplify them if they do not provide enough comprehensible input for foreign language students. Also, make sure that the materials needed to teach the lessons you have chosen are readily available (and that they are easily portable if you are a traveling teacher and do not have your own classroom).

Adapting Materials

Echevarria and Graves (1998) have developed a useful list of techniques for adapting materials (67). While some of these are primarily directed at the content-based or immersion setting, many of the ideas can be used by FLES or exploratory teachers, as well.

1. Use graphic depiction:
   - Venn diagrams
   - maps
   - time lines clusters
   - webs
2. Outline the text.
3. Rewrite the text:
   - organize material in manageable, sequential steps
     - use shorter, simpler sentences without watering down content
     - use bullets or lists
4. Use audiotapes:
   - record material so that students may hear it "come alive"
5. Provide live demonstrations:
   - use realia whenever possible
   - videotapes

- hands-on demonstrations of processes
6. Use alternate tools: texts with similar concepts but an easier reading level—"high interest low vocabulary"—to focus on concepts.
7. Send students to appropriate Web sites.

Active, Hands-On Teaching Strategies for Helping Students to Understand the Concepts

These strategies should not demand heavy verbal involvement of the students but should focus on receptive language. Surround the activity with language, and use visuals, demonstrations, and vocabulary the students already know to explain the new content vocabulary. Make sure the components of the lesson are observable and manipulable. Total Physical Response and Natural Approach activities can help to provide the meaningful context necessary in content-based classes (see explanations in Chapter 3). Close communication with classroom teachers will be helpful in evaluating these teaching strategies and rethinking those that may need improvement.

Challenges in Integrating Language and Content

A great challenge inherent in the integration of language and content instruction, especially for immersion and other content-based programs, is that not enough attention will be paid to the other crucial elements involved in elementary school language teaching—namely, language and culture. Incorporating content alone does not ensure that effective language learning will take place. Content-related instruction incorporates concepts and activities from the general curriculum to enhance the language class, because they provide meaningful, motivating, and intrinsically interesting experiences upon which to build language learning. Foreign language teachers who are attempting content-based or content-related instruction for the first time often lack a strong professional preparation in specific content areas. As a result they need to focus most of their attention on the content aspects of planning and, given the limited planning time available, they may not plan as carefully for the language and culture components.

Another danger, especially for immersion and other content-based programs, is the possibility that some of the problematic practices from first-language teaching will be carried over into second-language instruction. A traditional content class might consist of a series of teacher questions about what students have read, or to elicit students' background knowledge. The teacher often asks rapid-fire questions that require a specific answer, perhaps only a one-word or very short answer. The follow-up to the teacher questions during class might be a worksheet with more questions that students answer individually. In this example, there is a lot of teacher talk and little opportunity for students to process what has been learned or to engage in extended discourse. If these practices are used in the world language class, it is likely that there will be no opportunity for students to use their new language in a meaningful way. When they do use the second language, under these circumstances, their teacher may focus only on errors of content and never address—or even notice—errors in syntax, grammar, or pronunciation.

Solutions to these challenges could include designing a systematic plan for language development; providing purposeful, theme-based activities that give the student opportunities to present a product to an "important audience"; and providing opportunities for students to engage frequently in extended discourse thorough cooperative learning and interactive tasks. Ideas and activities presented in this book can be directly useful in addressing many of these challenges. The solutions lie in a meaning-based, thematic curriculum that purposefully and continually integrates the teaching of language, content, and culture.

Summary

The value of integrating subject content instruction with foreign and second languages is clearly evident in the success of immersion programs, sheltered English programs, and other content-based programs in which mastery of the content curriculum is a major goal. The insights and gains from these experiences can be extended into all foreign language programs, at elementary, middle school/junior high, and high school levels. Including content from the general curriculum and paying attention to general academic skills, while also teaching students to communicate in another language and culture, can increase the intensity of the language learning experience, thus enhancing motivation, accelerating language development, and contributing to the overall academic achievement of the learner. Especially in elementary school programs, the incorporation of content-related instruction can give increased impetus to language study at that level, not only because of the more effective language learning it will bring, but also because it offers a solution to the perennial problem of how to find time for elementary school foreign language instruction. When subject content is integrated with elementary school foreign language curriculum, the classroom teacher who struggles to schedule a multitude of curricular areas into a limited amount of time may see the elementary school foreign language teacher as an ally in this effort, rather than as a competitor in a zero-sum game for control of instructional time in the school day. Integrating subject content with foreign language and culture instruction can be a powerful way to build a stable place in the curriculum for foreign language programs.

Content-related instruction, properly implemented, gives us a valuable source of cognitively engaging and intrinsically interesting activities with which we can enrich our programs. It connects the foreign language curriculum with other parts of students' academic lives, and it extends their access to meaningful information through the target language.

F O R   S T U D Y   A N D   D I S C U S S I O N

1. Examine an elementary or middle school foreign language curriculum to identify concepts from other subject content areas that are already present there. What role do they play? How could the teacher increase their importance within the existing curriculum?

2. Locate a curriculum guide for social studies, science, language arts, mathematics, health, or physical education at the elementary level with which you are most familiar. What concepts do you find that are already touched on in foreign language classes? Which concepts lend themselves to instruction in a second language?

What criteria did you apply for choosing these concepts? List five of the concepts that you feel have the best potential, and give reasons for your choice.

3. Using the curriculum guide in number two (above), choose two concepts that are located in quadrant D of Cummins's chart shown in Figure 11.2 (context-reduced, cognitively demanding) and explain how you would develop lessons and materials to move them to quadrant C (context-embedded, cognitively demanding) in order to include them in a foreign language curriculum.

4. Which of the advantages of integrating subject content with language and culture instruction do you think would be most important in the elementary school language situation you know best? What obstacles will need to be confronted in order to implement it?

5. Design an activity in which you use a cognitive organizer to help students understand and remember vocabulary for a thematic unit. What other cognitive organizers could you use with the same vocabulary?

6. Plan two activities addressing the Connections Standard 3.2, one for a middle school classroom in which students have already had six years of language study, and one for a class of second grade students.

FOR FURTHER READING

The following sources are recommended for additional information about material covered in this chapter. Chapter citations are documented in Works Cited at the end of the volume.

Echevarria, Jana, and Anne Graves. *Sheltered Content Instruction: Teaching English Language Learners with Diverse Abilities.* Boston: Allyn and Bacon, 1998.

Echevarria, Jana, Mary Ellen Vogt, and Deborah Short. *Making Content Comprehensible for English Language Learners: The SIOP Model.* Boston: Allyn and Bacon, 2000.

Caine, Renate N., and Geoffrey Caine. *Education on the Edge of Possibility.* Alexandria, VA: Association for Supervision and Curriculum Development, 1997.

Chamot, Anna Uhl, and J. Michael O'Malley. *A Cognitive Academic Language Learning Approach: An ESL Content-Based Curriculum.* Rosslyn, VA: National Clearinghouse for Bilingual Education, 1986.

Gibbons, Pauline. *Scaffolding Language, Scaffolding Learning: Teaching Second Language Learners in the Mainstream Classroom.* Portsmouth, NH : Heinemann, 2002.

Hyerle, David. *Visual Tools for Constructing Knowledge.* Alexandria, VA: Association for Supervision and Curriculum Development, 1996.

Marzano, Robert J., Debra Pickering, and Jane Pollock. *Classroom Instruction that Works.* Alexandria, VA: Association for Supervision and Curriculum Development, 2001.

Met, Myriam. "Learning Language through Content: Learning Content through Language." *Foreign Language Annals* 24, no. 4 (1991): 281–295.

———. "Making Connections." In *Foreign Language Standards: Linking Research, Theories, and Practices,* edited by June K. Phillips, 137–164. The ACTFL Foreign Language Education Series. Lincolnwood, IL: National Textbook Company, 1999.

Rhodes, Nancy, Helena Curtain, and Mari Haas. "Child Development and Academic Skills in the Elementary School Foreign language Classroom." *Shifting the Instructional Focus to the Learner,* edited by Magnan, Sally S., 57–92. Middlebury, VT: Northeast Conference on the Teaching of Foreign languages, 1990.

WEB SITES OF INTEREST

Although the following Web sites are focused on English Language Learners, they include a variety of valuable resources on the topic of teaching language through content.

The Center for Applied Linguistics
www.cal.org
The Integrated Language and Content page of the Center for Applied Linguistics' (CAL) Web site includes a complete listing of CAL projects and products:
www.cal.org/topics/ilc.html
Content ESL Across the USA: A Training Packet
www.ncela.gwu.edu/miscpubs/cal/contentesl/ howare.htm
Designed by the National Clearinghouse for Bilingual Education and the Center for Applied Linguistics, this instructional guide provides background information on teaching language through content, guidelines for designing and implementing a content-based ESL program, and sample lesson plans for content-based programs at the elementary, middle school, and high school levels.

The National Clearinghouse for English Language Acquisition and Language Instruction Educational Programs (NCELA)
www.nceela.gwu.edu/
NCELA (formerly the National Clearinghouse for Bilingual Education) offers many resources for teaching language through content, such as the "In the Classroom Toolkit," with sample activities for teaching grade-level content in K–12 educational settings:
www.ncbe.gwu.edu/library/curriculum/index. htm

12 What We Can Learn from Immersion

Immersion: What Is It? What Makes It Work? What Are the Results?

In the chart listing in chapter 18 foreign language program goals (Table 18.1), immersion is presented as the program model that has the greatest success in terms of language outcomes. Students in immersion programs become functionally proficient in the second language at a level appropriate to their age and grade in school. Immersion students not only become bilingual but also master the subject content of the regular elementary school curriculum that is taught through the second language. As an approach to elementary school language education, immersion is easily able to provide a holistic language learning experience for learners of a new language, since the teachers and students are able to communicate throughout the entire school day on topics spanning the full range of the curriculum.

The purpose of this section is to expand on the overview of immersion given in Chapter 18, to provide answers to the most frequently asked questions about immersion, and most important, to relate what is known about immersion to other types of early language programs. Characteristics and strategies common to immersion programs are presented in the latter half of the chapter. This group of characteristics and strategies represents some of the features of immersion programs that make them so successful. The same concepts can provide insight and direction for the reexamination of other types of early language programs to make them even more effective.

Focus of Instruction

In immersion, the focus of instruction is on the curriculum (social studies, science, mathematics, language arts, health, art, music), and the second language is used as a tool to teach the curriculum. It has been said that immersion teachers are elementary teachers 100 percent of the time and are also language teachers 100 percent of the time. Language arts is approached in an immersion classroom very much as it would be approached in a regular monolingual classroom, except that it is taught in the target language. Since the syllabus is oriented toward the regular curriculum of the school district, and since the students need their new language to communicate on a daily basis, immersion programs are usually able to avoid the pitfalls of many second language programs that are grammar-driven. They are truly able to base language learning on real communication needs.

Immersion students are generally monolingual English speakers who are learning another language for enrichment purposes, and immersion teachers are elementary-certified teachers who are native or near-native speakers of the second language.

As outlined in Chapter 18, there are several variables in immersion program design. Programs can vary as to the entry point (early, middle, or late immersion), as to the amount of time each day that is spent using the second language, the point at which English reading is introduced (total or partial immersion), and the nature of the student population (two-way immersion).

Immersion Goals.   Immersion program goals may be summarized as follows:
1. Functional proficiency in the second language.
2. Maintenance and development of English language arts skills comparable to or surpassing the achievement of students in English-only programs.
3. Mastery of subject content material of the school district curriculum.
4. Cross-cultural understanding.

How Did Immersion Start?

The idea of immersing second-language learners in an environment in which they must use the language is certainly not a new one. Immersion programs have appeared throughout history and can be found in many private schools throughout the world. The first North American public school immersion program in recent times began in 1965 with a kindergarten in St. Lambert in Quebec. It was prompted by a group of English-speaking parents who were concerned that traditional French programs were not sufficient to meet their children's needs for greater comprehension of and fluency in French, at a time when bilingualism in French and English had become a necessity in Canada.

As research information from Canadian immersion programs began to be disseminated, and as immersion programs were spreading rapidly in Canada, similar programs began to be established in the United States, where a different set of realities regarding second-language learning existed. Whereas Canadian immersion programs were developed because of a demonstrated need for bilingualism, immersion programs in the United States were established for a variety of reasons, most of which centered on a search for alternative approaches to successful second-language teaching for young children.

The first immersion program in the United States was started in 1971 in Culver City, California, with the help of professors at the University of California at Los Angeles (Campbell 1984, Cohen 1974). They had observed the St. Lambert Elementary School immersion program, were familiar with the Lambert and Tucker research on that program (1972), and were excited by the possibilities of establishing such a program in the United States. The Culver City Spanish program, like many immersion programs in the United States, is modeled after the St. Lambert program.

The number of immersion programs in the United States grew slowly: in 1974, a total immersion program in French was started in Montgomery County, Maryland, near

Washington, D.C.; in 1974 a partial immersion program in French, German, and Spanish began in Cincinnati, Ohio; in 1975 a total immersion program in French was started in Plattsburgh, New York; and in 1977 the Milwaukee Public Schools opened the German component of its immersion program, and San Diego Schools began a program in Spanish. Immersion programs have continued to spread. In 1987 there were a total of 50 school districts offering such programs in the United States in 101 schools, involving approximately 16,000 students in ten languages in locations ranging from small rural areas to large urban school districts in 23 states. By 1999 these numbers had grown to 278 schools in 72 districts, ten languages, and approximately 46,000 students in 29 states plus the District of Columbia. Canadian programs have also continued to grow, so that by 1999–2000 there were over 300,000 students involved in French immersion programs alone. The charts in Table 12.1 summarize the locations of immersion programs in the United States according to a 1999 survey by the Center for Applied Linguistics.

Immersion programs in the United States have been initiated in a variety of ways: in some cases the school principal; in other cases parents, teachers, or the district foreign language coordinator have been the most influential at early stages. An interesting historical note is that at least three of the citywide immersion programs were developed as part of voluntary desegregation efforts. District administrators in large urban school districts such as San Diego and Milwaukee planned the immersion programs as magnet schools to attract students from all over the district.

Two-Way Immersion

A distinctive U.S. contribution to the inventory of immersion program models is the two-way immersion program, also known as two-way bilingual, dual language, or developmental bilingual education programs. These programs have been developed in a number of American cities with the support of funding from Title VII, as an alternative to transitional bilingual programs. They provide education opportunities in two languages for English language learners (ELL), while at the same time giving native speakers of English the opportunity to learn a new language.

San Diego was the site of the first such program, in 1975 (Genesee 1987). In 1992 the Center for Applied Linguistics (CAL) identified 124 schools in 69 districts offering two-way immersion programs in 13 states. Languages offered include Spanish, Portuguese, Cantonese, and Haitian Creole. By 2001 another CAL survey identified two-way immersion programs in 260 schools in 135 districts in a total of 23 states. Languages listed included Spanish, French, Chinese, Korean, and Navajo.

These programs contrast with transitional bilingual programs that feature homogeneous native language classes, in which minority language students begin their studies in their native language until they have learned enough English to be transferred to a mainstream classroom. In these transitional classes, students study English as a second language (ESL), but do not benefit from language reinforcement through interaction with native-English-speaking peers in the classroom. In contrast, a two-way program targets both language minority and language majority students. In each half of the day one of the groups is receiving instruction in their native language and one of the groups is learning in their new language. This format provides ELL students with the opportunity to learn English without

TABLE 12.1   Summary U.S. Immersion Programs—1999–2000*

State	Elem.	M.S.	H.S.**	Language	Number of Programs
Alaska	7	2	2	Spanish	131
California	12	3	2	French	71
Delaware	1			Hawaiian	25
D.C.	3	1		Japanese	19
Florida	11	3		German	13
Georgia	1			Arabic	1
Hawaii	21	2	2	Cantonese	1
Illinois	1			Inupiaq	1
Indiana	2	2		Russian	1
Kentucky	3	1	1	Yup'ik	1
Louisiana	14	6	2		
Maryland	7	6	1	**Number of Languages**	**10**
Massachusetts	8	2	2		
Michigan	3	1			
Minnesota	9	4	3		
Missouri	8	1		29 States + DC 72 Districts 278 Schools	
Montana	1				
New Jersey	2			Approximate total number of Immersion Students = 46,000	
New York	3				
N. Carolina	5	2	1		
Ohio	5	2			
Oklahoma	1	1			
Oregon	14	5	5		
Pennsylvania	9	1	1		
Tennessee	0	2	1		
Texas	1	1			
Utah	6	1			
Virginia	21	14	1		
Washington	1	1	1		
Wisconsin	3	1	1		

*For a complete directory of immersion programs by state, see www.cal.org/cal/db/immerse/

**Eleven of the schools have two-way immersion programs, where classes include both native English speakers and native speakers of the target language.

Source: Based on Total and Partial Immersion Language Programs in US Elementary Schools, 1999. Developed by the Center for Applied Linguistics, 1118 22nd St. NW, Washington, DC 20037–1214.

lagging behind academically, and it gives native-English-speaking students the chance both to learn a second language and to develop an understanding of another culture.

Two-way programs share with one-way immersion programs the basic assumption that a new language is best learned not as the object of instruction, but rather as the medium of instruction, through a content-based curriculum. Immersion programs have traditionally been designed as language enrichment programs for language majority students. Two-way programs in the United States, on the other hand, are designed to serve the needs of both language majority English speakers and ELL populations. In a two-way program, native English speakers are not separated from ELL students during instruction; the two groups are in the same class. Such a model takes advantage of the fact that children learn new languages most naturally and effectively when they have peers—classmates and playmates—as language models (Dulay, Burt, Krashen 1982).

Program designs vary from district to district, but three typical designs are described in detail by Christian et al. (1997) in Table 12.2. This CAL publication profiles Key Elementary School in Arlington, Virginia, River Glen Elementary School in San Jose, California, and Inter-American Magnet School in Chicago. Two of the variables among these three programs are percentage of instruction in Spanish and English, and initial reading instruction. Table 12.2 shows two of the differences among the three programs studied.

TABLE 12.2 Program Design by Grade Level and School Site: Percentage of Instruction in Spanish and English

Grade Level	Key	River Glen	IAMS
Kindergarten–First	50–50	90–10	80–20
Second	50–50	85–15	80–20
Third	50–50	80–20	80–20
Fourth–Fifth	50–50	60–40	60–40
Sixth	50–50	50–50	60–40

Initial Reading Instruction by Grade Level and School Site

Grade Level	Key	River Glen	IAMS
Kindergarten–First	ALL: English and Spanish	ALL: Spanish	English Proficient: English Spanish Proficient: Spanish
Second			ALL: add L2 (approx.)
Third		ALL: Add English	

Source: Christian, et al. 1997. *Profiles in Two-Way Immersion Education.* Washington, D.C.: Center for Applied Linguistics and Delta Systems, Inc., 97–98.

The distinctive goals of two-way language development programs are as follows:

- Language minority students will become literate in their native language as well as in English.
- Language majority students will develop high levels of proficiency in a second language while making normal progress in first-language development.
- Both language groups will perform academically at their grade level, develop positive attitudes toward the two languages being learned and toward the communities they represent, and develop a positive self-image.

Two-way immersion programs are most appropriate for communities that have a large and fairly stable population of native speakers of the target language. Ideally, approximately equal numbers of the students should be native speakers of each language. When language majority students outnumber language minority students, there tends to be greater in-school use of English, the language that is already reinforced outside of school.

Both the National Clearinghouse for English Language Acquisition and Language Instruction Educational Programs (NCELA) and the Center for Applied Linguistics (CAL) serve as rich sources of information regarding two-way language development programs.

How Does Immersion Work?

In early total immersion programs students begin their study of the new language in kindergarten or first grade. When the children arrive at school in the morning, they hear the teacher speak only the new language, and all classroom conversation and instructions are in the target language. In this way the children acquire the new language in play and work situations that are related to meaningful communication. The emphasis is on the learning activity (reading, mathematics, social studies, art, etc.) and not on the language. Even though the teacher is constantly using the target language, the students may use English among themselves and also in speaking to the teacher. This reduces anxiety and frustration and allows the children a period of time in which they can build up comprehension skills in the second language. Within one to two years in the program, the children move rather automatically into speech production.

Since most of the students in an immersion class are monolingual, they begin on an equal footing with each other with regard to competence in the new language. The children tend to show little anxiety or frustration about learning in another language because the things they learn are within their experience and because every effort is made to put messages into a meaningful context. For example, they learn to speak and write about things they understand: in kindergarten a lesson on objects that sink and float, in first grade a trip to the fire station, in second grade a lesson on magnets, in fifth grade a lesson on geography, and so forth. In the beginning stages of the program they learn to say things like "I have hot lunch today," "Can we go out for recess?", "I want to be first," and "Give me the ball."

Children in total immersion programs learn to read through the second language rather than through the first. They read about things they have been exposed to through various experiences and can already speak about. This approach is markedly different from that used in most bilingual education programs, in which reading is always introduced in the first language. Parents of kindergarten and first grade students in immersion programs are advised that they should feel free to encourage any natural interest in reading expressed by their child, but that they should not try to formally teach English reading at home.

After two or three years in a total immersion program, formal English language arts is introduced for about thirty minutes to an hour each day—in the second or third grade, depending on the school district. A few districts wait until fourth or fifth grade to introduce instruction in English. Children continue to study the remainder of their subjects through the new language. Once children begin to read in English, the many skills that transfer from the second language enable most of them to "catch up" in English reading within one or two years. In some immersion programs, as the students progress through the middle grades, the amount of English is gradually increased until by fifth or sixth grade, there is a balance of instruction in the target language and in English. In other immersion programs, such as the one in Milwaukee, once students have been exposed to English for one hour per day, the amount of English continues at one hour per day for the duration of the program. The result is that 80 percent of the student's day is spent in the second language and 20 percent of the day is spent in English through the sixth grade. Variations in program design reflect the needs, desires, and resources of the individual school district.

What Are Immersion Results?

Initially, parents and school administrators may express fear that immersion students will not achieve well in the basics and will fall behind their peers in monolingual English classes. Abundant research reports on immersion programs in Canada have thoroughly described and documented the positive effects of the immersion approach since the original St. Lambert study (Lambert and Tucker 1972).

Immersion students acquire remarkable proficiency in the second language compared with students in other second-language programs. But it must be noted that this proficiency is not native-like in every aspect. Immersion students are able to communicate on any topic appropriate to their level of intellectual development, but they do make grammatical errors, and they have to use circumlocutions and other strategies to express themselves when they are lacking the appropriate vocabulary.

One reason that immersion students do not have native-like speech in every respect is that they do not usually have the opportunity to interact with native-speaking peers. Often the only native speaker model that the immersion students have available to them is their classroom teacher. The other models that they hear constantly are their non–native-speaking classmates. Immersion students who have moved into a native-speaking environment, however, have been able to adjust their speech successfully. This issue is far less frequent in two-way immersion classrooms, since there are native speakers among the learner's peers in addition to the teacher.

- *English Skills*
  Research results (Swain 1984) show that students in early immersion programs perform as well as, or often out-perform, their English-educated peers on tests of achievement in English. Immersion students are initially behind in their English skills but catch up within a year after the English component is introduced into the curriculum.

- *Subject Content Mastery*
  Immersion students perform as well as or better than their monolingual English-speaking peers on tests of subject-content mastery in mathematics, science, and social studies. It is interesting to note that these achievement tests are administered in English even though the students have been taught through the second language.
- *Cross-Cultural Understanding*
  Results from research show that Canadian immersion students "develop more friendly and open attitudes toward French-Canadians" (Lambert 1984).

Differences between Partial and Total Immersion Programs.   As would be expected, the language competencies of students in partial and total immersion programs are found to differ: the more contact hours students have with the second language, the better their second-language proficiency (Campbell, Gray, Rhodes, Snow 1985).

Results from Late Immersion Programs.   The outcomes from late immersion programs with respect to subject content mastery, maintenance of first-language skills, and development of second-language skills are difficult to summarize because of the large variation in formats that are available. For example, Swain (1979) states that if there is sufficient core French instruction prior to the program, and if sufficient additional courses are taken in French following the program, high levels of French proficiency can be attained, with no loss to the mastery of content material or native language proficiency.

Benefits of Early Immersion.   One of the most obvious benefits of early immersion education is the long sequence of time it allows the student to achieve proficiency in the second language. Early immersion prepares students to survive communicatively in a native-speaking environment, with the expectation that the student's speech will become more and more native-like. Early immersion makes bilingualism possible for the largest number of students, because functional proficiency in the second language at that level is not necessarily tied to literacy skills.

Since early immersion develops proficiency in the second language very quickly, it is possible for children to acquire the fluency they need to deal with subject content areas without any difficulty. This is not the case in partial or late immersion programs, in which the level of language required in a subject content course may be beyond the language ability of the students. In early immersion much less time is required than is required in partial immersion programs to develop the equivalent results on tests of achievement in English.

A final point in favor of early immersion programs that should not be discounted is the apparent enthusiasm and aptitude of young children for language learning. Swain (1979, 26) characterizes this as "feelings of ease, comfort and naturalness in using the second language." In contrast, older students may have had experiences or may have formed negative attitudes that could jeopardize second-language learning (Genesee 1984). Also, since early immersion programs are an integral part of the elementary school day, they do not compete with other activities for prominence or student participation.

Principles for Communication:
What We Have Learned from Immersion Programs

The immersion program model offers optimum results due to the amount of time available, the ease of integration with the remainder of the elementary school curriculum, and the limitless opportunities for meaningful communication. It comes as no surprise that the study of children in immersion, partial immersion, and FLES programs by the Center for Applied Linguistics (Campbell, Gray, Rhodes, Snow 1985) found immersion and partial immersion students to be far ahead of FLES students in listening, speaking, reading, and writing. Furthermore, their speaking skills were much more flexible and wide ranging than were those of the FLES students, to a degree not measurable with the test instrument used for the study. The impact of this report in some circles has been for teachers, parents, and administrators to question the value of other types of early language programs, since the results appear to fall so far short of those experienced in immersion. They have sometimes chosen to offer no language at all, when immersion was not feasible or desired.

This is a very unfortunate decision, for several reasons. First, while immersion is a powerful and very successful way for children to learn languages, it will never be able to reach every child. Immersion will continue to be an elective program, often very popular and competitive, but it will not be implemented in every school or in every community. The shortage of qualified teachers alone precludes this possibility. If every child is to have the opportunity of acquiring a second (or third) language in the elementary school, there must be a variety of high-quality options available.

Second, a well-designed, successful FLES program can prepare a school or a community for a stronger commitment to foreign language learning. Once children have demonstrated their interest and ability in a FLES program, parents and administrators may be willing to consider adding an immersion option to the program, or they may choose to support language learning in other significant ways, such as planning trips and developing exchange programs or building short-term immersion opportunities into the extracurricular schedule.

Third, and most important, a well-planned and skillfully taught FLES program can produce significant language outcomes. Children can acquire an impressive amount of a new language of high quality in well-taught FLES programs, even under the severe time limitations that often characterize them. Graduates of such programs can have a stable foundation on which to build further competencies in their second language, as well as an enriched cultural understanding and a broader perspective of the world.

The amount of time available is both the most obvious and one of the most important differences between immersion and other early language programs. One example of the influence of time can be seen in the fact that in most immersion programs known to the authors, the children are not given new names in the target language, although this practice is common in FLES programs. It may be that a FLES teacher has to use every moment and every possible opportunity to model and reinforce the target language in the short teaching time available, whereas time for immersion teachers is an ally rather than a constraint—they do not have to contrive uses of the target language. As teachers in FLES and exploratory programs seek to make the best possible use of their limited class time with students, examining other features of immersion that contribute to its remarkable success may be helpful. These teachers may find it practical to organize their teaching around the key characteristics that follow.

Characteristics and Applications
of Immersion Programs

Characteristic One: Communication
motivates all language use.

- There are myriad opportunities to communicate throughout the school day.
- The need to communicate is strong and ongoing.
- Pupils are encouraged to communicate in the target language, using vocabulary and structures they know.
- Communication results from a need to bridge an "information gap" or an "opinion gap."

This may be the single most important and distinctive feature of an immersion classroom. In contrast to the recitation orientation of traditional FLES classrooms, the language activities in immersion are based on the exchange of information. Prominent in the thrust toward communicative language teaching is the idea that for communication to take place there must be either an "information gap" or "opinion gap" (Morrow 1981). That is, for real exchange of information, there must be information or an opinion that one person has and another does not. Communication takes place in order to bridge that gap. In the immersion classroom these conditions are continually present, a natural and normal part of the entire school day.

Applications to FLES.   In the FLES classroom, by contrast, the need to communicate must usually be created, and the teacher must take full advantage of every naturally occurring communicative situation. Giving directions, disciplining, and performing standard classroom routines are all recurring opportunities for communication. When access to the drinking fountain, the bathroom, and the pencil sharpener is dependent on conversations in the target language, the need to communicate is strong and genuine. Many teachers have found that Total Physical Response strategies, in which children respond to teacher commands, are a useful first step in creating a climate of communication.

Characteristic Two: There is natural use of oral language.

- Language use is not grammatically sequenced.
- Program design takes into account natural stages of second-language acquisition.
- There is an initial listening period when students are not expected to respond in the target language.
- The ability to speak emerges and develops in a predictable manner.
- The target language is used for all classroom management.
- Classroom routines provide students with clear clues to meaning.

Applications to FLES.   The elementary school language teacher has often felt obligated to restrict the language used in the classroom to that which the students can understand fully and attempt to produce themselves. When teachers follow the immersion approach, they enrich the language environment and surround the activity of the classroom with speech. Instead of calling for immediate imitation of words and patterns, they allow for an initial period when students are not expected to respond in the target language, thus encouraging the children to listen for meaning rather than listening for speaking. As children accumulate a stockpile of language meanings, they will also begin to speak, using vocabulary and structures drawn from the treasury of their own experience to express personal meanings. The teacher has already demonstrated that the target language has real value for expressing important ideas by using the language for discipline and for praise, for routine and for change of pace, for venting frustrations, and for teasing and joking.

This exchange of personal meanings in natural situations is very difficult to achieve in the limited setting of the FLES classroom. If it is to occur at all, it must be a planned part of classroom activity, and it will no doubt displace some traditional "learning" activities.

Characteristic Three: Language is a tool of instruction, and not just the object of instruction.

In the immersion classroom this characteristic is clear from the first day, when the language used with the children is based entirely on practical needs—how can we communicate about the ideas and the routines of the classroom? Language becomes the object of instruction only when students have acquired enough language for the teacher to be able to approach it in the same way that language arts is approached in the English track.

Applications to FLES. While this characteristic may seem difficult to translate fully into the FLES setting, it does suggest the possibility of choosing initial language content based on utility for the classroom, school, and community setting rather than on grammatical sequencing or other factors.

Characteristic Four: Subject content is taught in the target language.

One of the clearest implications of immersion for all other forms of language programs is that of the value of subject content instruction. Dulay, Burt, and Krashen (1982) suggest that the addition of even one area of subject content taught in the target language can have a dramatic impact on the rate and quality of second-language acquisition. Simply adding a class in mathematics, music, art, social studies, science, health, or physical education taught in the target language could multiply the effects of a FLES program several times over.

Applications to FLES. Within the FLES class itself, the implementation of this characteristic is somewhat harder, but very rewarding. One of the best features of teaching subject content in the target language is that it provides something meaningful and real to talk about. Cultural concepts are in themselves subject content and can be taught effectively in the target language. Close cooperation with teachers in other content areas will suggest concepts that can be reinforced or enriched in the language classroom. In FLES programs, the willingness of the language teacher to take responsibility for specific concepts from another subject area may ease the problem of finding time in the school day for the second language.

Characteristic Five: Grammar instruction does not follow any set sequence, or may be dictated by communication needs.

Teaching of the target language structure in an immersion program is integrated into the rest of the curriculum and is not presented in isolation. Structures are modeled and introduced as they are needed to express meanings important to the children and to the content being addressed. This is a very different approach to grammar from what has been the practice in most language classrooms at any level—in fact, grammar has frequently been the primary basis for curriculum and daily activities.

Applications to FLES.   There is very little emphasis on formal grammar instruction in a FLES program. When it occurs, it should be presented as a means for communicating messages that have importance to both the speaker and the listener.

Characteristic Six: Error correction at the beginning stages is minimal and focuses on errors of meaning rather than on errors of form.

- Correction should not interrupt the student flow of talk.
- Classroom activities should be developed to address recurring errors.

In the immersion classroom children are exposed to a great deal of meaningful, natural, accurate language modeling before they are expected to speak, in a setting that focuses on meaning rather than on form. When children begin to speak they naturally make errors, but early correction efforts also focus on meaning rather than on form. Teachers work with individual children to help them clarify their messages, but they do not interrupt with corrections when the child does not request assistance. Frequently, in the process of reflective listening, the teacher uses indirect error correction in the form of recasting what the student has said:

STUDENT: I eated at McDonald's last night.

TEACHER: Oh, you ate at McDonald's? What did you have?

The day-to-day need to clarify the grammatical errors that children make will be addressed in the interest of communication, by working with children individually or in a group to correct recurring problems that prevent them from getting their ideas across to others. See Lyster, 1999 for more information on error correction in immersion programs.

Applications to FLES.   Formal error correction has little place in the FLES classroom, especially in the first several years. That does not mean that teachers cannot occasionally plan activities in which the focus is on the form of the language rather than on the meaning of the language. Such activities will be most successful when their goals are made clear to the students and when they take place in a communicative context.

Characteristic Seven: Use of the native language is kept clearly separate from use of the target language.

In many Canadian immersion programs, the separation of languages is made very clear: classes in French are taught by a French teacher, classes in English are taught by an English teacher. In most adaptations in the United States the classroom teacher is responsible for both the target language and the English parts of the curriculum. Evidence from bilingual classrooms in the United States reinforces the idea that a clear division between the use of the native language and the use of the target language results in significantly improved second-language acquisition (Wong-Fillmore 1983, 1985). Many teachers in the United States have found the simple device of using a sign to indicate the present language of communication to be very successful in maintaining a clear separation of languages. The sign, for example, reads "English being spoken now" on one side, and "On parle français maintenant," on the other. Whenever the language of classroom communication changes, the sign is flipped over.

Applications to FLES.   Elementary and middle school language teachers will find that creating a tangible, visible reminder, like a sign, or raising a flag, or putting on a "French" apron, will encourage cooperation from the children—and even reminders from them when the teacher or a fellow student slips. Teachers who have tried this technique have found it to be very effective.

Characteristic Eight: Reading and writing experiences accompany the development of oral language.

As is the case in first-language instruction, children in immersion programs learn to read and write about things they can understand and respond to orally in the target language.

Applications to FLES.   In early language classrooms in which language use has been determined by the communication needs of the immediate environment, literacy skills will develop with the same emphasis: Reading will be a natural reinforcement of the spoken word, presented and nurtured as a form of communication. The kind of delay in reading in the target language that has sometimes been suggested for the FLES program—up to several years, according to some sources—is not compatible with the lessons learned from immersion programs. This emphasis on integration of oral and written language is also reflective of the holistic approach to language arts found in many primary school programs in the native language.

Characteristic Nine: Literacy skills are transferred from the language in which they first are learned to the next language.

Applications to FLES.   The tasks of the immersion teacher and of the FLES teacher are clearly very different in the area of reading. In early total immersion programs students learn to read first in the target language. The FLES teacher is not responsible for teaching the child to read, since literacy has already been developed in the first language. It is the role of the FLES teacher to assist the child in the transfer of reading competency from the native language to the target language, and then to develop reading as an additional tool of communication. Reading and writing will be used to extend and reinforce the oral material from the classroom experience and will be integrated into the total FLES curriculum.

Characteristic Ten: Culture is an integral component of language learning.

The presence of cultural content in every aspect of curriculum may be more common in French-Canadian immersion programs than those programs found in the United States, at least in part because of the intimate relationship between French-Canadian culture and the Canadian identity. In programs in the United States, considerable energy must be directed toward developing a curriculum that reproduces the English-language concepts taught in other schools in the district. Under these circumstances it can sometimes happen that culture becomes an overlay rather than an integral program component. Many programs have recognized this danger and taken steps to make cultural learning and experiences an important component of curriculum and planning.

Applications to FLES.   The message of immersion for FLES is that culture must be embedded in the curriculum, infusing instruction at every point along the way—from the choice of the content that will be discussed to the use of gestures and exclamations in dealing with everyday events. As children acquire language through meaningful experiences surrounded by language, so also do they acquire cultural awareness and the ability to function in a new cultural setting—also through meaningful experiences surrounded by language.

Characteristic Eleven: The second-language atmosphere permeates the classroom and the school.

The immersion classroom provides a rich visual environment for the language learner, much as the primary classroom uses wall, hall, and ceiling space to reinforce the concepts and the relationships being developed there. This atmosphere also reinforces the importance of the group and enhances the attractiveness of being a part of the group: "We belong to Mrs. Nelson's second grade, and that's a good place to be!" "We are all learning Japanese, and that's a good thing to do!"

Applications to FLES.   This target language environment can also be developed through a FLES program—and as this atmosphere develops, so does the perception of the program's importance. Labeling classroom objects in the target language, developing displays for the classroom and the hallways, celebrating target culture holidays, publishing the school lunch menu in the target language, labeling items all over the school building in the new language— all these techniques and many more may be used to reinforce the idea that the target language is something valuable, and that learning a language is an important activity.

Characteristic Strategies of Immersion Teaching

The above characteristics of immersion offer a rich resource for the elementary school language teacher, but willingness to apply them may be overcome by questions and uncertainties: "How can I make my students understand? Shouldn't I have them talking right away? Will I really know they have the right concepts if I don't check in English? Is everything I've been doing wrong? Why should I change when the children like things just the way they are—and so do I?!" The immersion strategies listed below are intended to respond to some of those anxieties. Another listing of immersion strategies is found in Figure 12.1, an observation checklist from the Center for Advanced Research on Second Language Acquisition at the University of Minnesota.

Strategy One: Teachers make regular use of contextual clues such as gestures, facial expressions, and body language; and of concrete referents such as props, realia, manipulatives, and visuals (especially with entry-level students).

Kindergarten and first grade teachers are natural users of body language and manipulatives, even in native-language instruction. These techniques link language very clearly to its meaning, and the use of the native language to clarify meaning becomes an unnecessary intrusion in the concrete situations most commonly encountered in early second-language instruction. Use of extensive body language and a variety of props and realia also appeals to the right hemisphere of the brain, according to some educators (Grady 1984, Caine and Caine 1991), thus adding to the impact of the information for the learner at any stage of language instruction.

Applications to FLES.   This strategy can be adopted fully by teachers in FLES programs, with the confidence that it is an extension of the natural mode of learning for elementary school children.

Strategy Two: Teachers provide hands-on experiences for students, accompanied by oral and written language use.

Language acquisition in the immersion classroom is based on experiences the children share in the course of a school day rich in activity. Teachers surround these experiences with language, and language and content skills grow at the same time.

Applications to FLES.   The choice and range of available experiences is much more limited within the time constraints of the FLES program. This fact suggests that teachers need to be deliberate about planning experiences that have the maximum potential for language use.

Strategy Three: Teachers use linguistic modifications when necessary to make the target language more comprehensible for the students in the beginning stages of the program, such as:

- controlled, standardized vocabulary
- controlled sentence length and complexity
- slower speech rate
- restatements, expansions, and repetitions

The special modifications of language used by immersion teachers in order to make the target language comprehensible represent the natural use of language by a fluent speaker who takes into account the limitations of a conversation partner in order to help the partner understand. A slower speech rate in this context, for example, does not mean exaggerated slow speech, which distorts the natural features of the language. The speaker simply operates at the slower end of the normal range for that speaker. (See Chapter 2 for a more extended discussion of use of language.)

Applications to FLES.   The FLES teacher can make conscious application of these modifications in order to avoid translation, on the one hand, or to avoid overwhelming the learners with a stream of language, on the other.

Strategy Four: Teachers accelerate student communication by teaching functional chunks of language.

Immersion teachers in Milwaukee developed an extensive list of "passwords," phrases that are necessary for students to use in the normal course of day-to-day school life such as "Please may I go to the bathroom," or "I need to buy a lunch ticket" (See Chapter 3 for a partial list). One such phrase is taught each day, with a clear indication of the need it will resolve for the children, and then the phrase is posted on the bulletin board. In order to leave the room at any time during the day—whether to go to lunch, the playground, or the bus—each child must be able to say the password of the day. Motivation to learn these chunks of language is high, because they obviously will meet a specific need in the child's daily school life. While much other language is acquired through experience surrounded by language, these high-frequency items are directly taught and practiced. Other chunks of language can be found in songs, rhymes, poems and Gouin series. (Teaching these specific chunks of language is addressed in Chapter 3.)

Applications to FLES.   This procedure is clearly applicable to the FLES classroom, where it will hasten the active involvement of the children in classroom communication.

Strategy Five: Teachers constantly monitor student comprehension through interactive means.

Interactive methods teachers may employ include the following:

- checking comprehension with non-verbal responses
- personalizing questions
- using a variety of questioning types

Many of these strategies are drawn not only from immersion teaching, but also from effective teaching strategies in general. The immersion teacher must do far more monitoring of student comprehension than is usual in the content teaching of the first-language classroom, because the immersion teacher must determine whether the student understands both the concept and the language in which the concept is communicated. This careful monitoring may be one reason for the impressive record of immersion students in tests of content area mastery.

Applications to FLES.   The principle of checking comprehension by means of application, when adopted for the FLES classroom, will eliminate the temptation to check if the student "really" understands by asking for translation.

Strategy Six: Teachers use a holistic approach to literacy instruction.

The Whole-Language Approach to reading, common in many American elementary schools, is an extension of the principle that language acquisition grows out of experiences that are surrounded by language. It is fully as applicable in FLES programs, in which the task is to assist students in transferring reading skills from their native language, as it is in immersion programs, where students are learning to read for the first time. In the Language Experience Approach, one tool of holistic language instruction, the teacher guides children in their description or narration of an experience they have shared and then writes the children's sentences as a record of the event. Children read and later copy these sentences, associating the content with their own words and their own experiences. A more extensive discussion of the Language Experience Approach is found in Chapter 5.

Applications to FLES.   Students in FLES programs will require more extended oral discussion of an experience, with indirect correction and guidance from the teacher, before they are able to provide the language for an adequate written record.

FIGURE 12.1   Immersion Teaching Strategies Observation Checklist

Teacher _____ School _____ Grade Level _____ Number of Students _____ Date _____

Observer _____ Lesson Observed _____ Start _____ Finish _____

Each of the following seven category labels identifies a key pedagogical goal in immersion settings. The subsequent descriptors illustrate what the effective immersion teacher does in the classroom to achieve these goals.

The Immersion Teacher Aims To: _(Observed Not Observed Not Applicable)_	O	NO	NA	Comments:
1. Integrate language, content, and culture				
■ Contextualizes and organizes curriculum around content-based thematic concept(s)				
■ Specifies content-obligatory and content-compatible language objectives for each lesson/unit				
■ Identifies theme-related culture learning goals to introduce products, practices, and perspectives				
■ Selects appropriate language and culture learning objectives that follow from content goals				
■ Uses authentic songs, poems, literature, rhymes, artifacts to teach language and culture				
■ Evaluates language, content, and culture learning for each lesson/unit				
2. Attend to continuous language growth and improve accuracy				
■ Elicits and holds all students accountable for self and peer repair				
■ Attends to errors in both oral and written language				
■ Uses a variety of effective feedback techniques including elicitation, metalinguistic clues, clarification requests, repetition, recasts, explicit correction, and non-verbal cues				
■ Differentiates between feedback on form versus meaning, e.g., "I like that idea. How might you say it more precisely?"				
■ Creates opportunities and activities to assist students in noticing and producing less frequently used, accurate language in oral and written form				
■ Focuses corrective responses on pre-determined language objectives based on the lesson and the developmental level of the learners				
■ Balances use of feedback with flow of lesson				
3. Make input comprehensible				
■ Uses body language, TPR, visuals, realia, manipulatives to communicate meaning				

(continued)

FIGURE 12.1 Continued

The Immersion Teacher Aims To: *(Observed Not Observed Not Applicable)*	O	NO	NA	Comments:
■ Solicits and draws upon prior knowledge and experiences with new themes				
■ Uses a variety of pre-reading and pre-writing activities to make language and content more accessible, e.g., advanced organizers, etc.				
■ Breaks complex information and processes into component parts				
■ Makes frequent use of comprehension checks that require learners to demonstrate their understanding				
■ Selects and adapts instructional material for learners' developmental level				
■ Establishes routines to build familiarity and allow for repetition				
4. Create an L2-rich learning environment				
■ Extend students' language repertoires by teaching synonyms and antonyms				
■ Displays a variety of words, phrases, written text throughout classroom and hallways				
■ Invites native speakers to participate in the classroom				
■ Makes available a variety of target language reading and resource materials such as dictionaries, thesaurus, encyclopedia, etc.				
■ Surrounds learner with extensive oral and written language input				
5. Use teacher talk effectively				
■ Articulates and enunciates clearly				
■ Slows down and simplifies language when developmentally appropriate				
■ Rephrases and repeats messages in a variety of ways				
■ Varies intonation to mirror messages				
■ Recycles past, present, and future vocabulary and language structures consciously				
■ Models accurate use of language				
■ Limits amount of teacher talk				
6. Promote extended student output				
■ Plans for and employs questioning techniques that encourage extended discourse and foster higher-order thinking				

FIGURE 12.1   Continued

The Immersion Teacher Aims To: *(Observed Not Observed Not Applicable)*	O	NO	NA	Comments:
■ Structures and facilitates high-interest, student-centered activities				
■ Uses output-oriented activities such as role plays, simulations, drama, debates, presentations, etc.				
■ Makes use of a variety of grouping techniques such as dyads, think-pair-share, small groups, etc.				
■ Promotes learning from and with peers, e.g., peer editing, peer tutoring				
■ Communicates and consistently reinforces clear expectations about language use				
■ Creates a non-threatening learning environment				
7. Attend to diverse learner needs				
■ Includes a range of language abilities in student groups				
■ Uses cooperative group learning				
■ Plans for diverse learner needs based on linguistic and cultural backgrounds				
■ Surveys student interests to allow for student choice				
■ Invites students to share different problem-solving approaches and learning strategies				
■ Makes use of a wide variety of activities through learning centers where students can work at a level that is appropriate for them				
■ Reinforces concepts and language considering a variety of learning styles such as visual, auditory, tactile, kinesthetic, etc.				
■ Fosters development of multiple intelligences				

Source: Checklist created by Tara Fortune, Ph.D., Immersion Projects Coordinator, Center for Advanced Research on Language Acquisition, University of Minnesota. Reprinted by permission.

Strategy Seven: Teachers draw classroom techniques primarily from elementary school methodology.

The overwhelming impression from visits to immersion schools is at the same time the most obvious and the most unexpected: *Good immersion teachers are good elementary school classroom teachers* who happen to be teaching in another language. The same qualities observed in teachers and student teachers in native-language elementary schools are evident in immersion classrooms. Successful immersion teachers use the finest elementary school methodologies; less successful immersion teachers would probably have just as much difficulty teaching students in their native language. Immersion teachers need to be as up to date as possible about current first-language methodology for elementary school subject content and language arts. Immersion teachers are full-time language teachers— and also full-time elementary school teachers.

Applications to FLES.   The early language teacher who wishes to develop the strongest possible program will draw heavily on the ideas and the methodology of the elementary school, such as literature-based reading, the process approach to writing, and cooperative learning.

Starting Points for Applying the Insights of Immersion

The above list does not exhaust, by any means, the strategies used by immersion teachers that might enhance the teaching of FLES, but it establishes a direction in which to search for ideas and resources for developing ever more effective programs. Met and Lorenz (1991), Snow (1987), and Cloud, Genesee, and Hamayan (2000) provide more extensive descriptions of immersion strategies and techniques.

Where do we start in applying immersion strategies to FLES programs? It seems clear that the first requirement is the conviction that the insights of immersion teaching can be applied even in a more limited setting. For some teachers and administrators this may require a firsthand experience such as a visit to an immersion school. For others it may be enough to develop as much background as possible through reading and conference sessions and consultations. The language teacher with a limited elementary school background will also find it helpful to read extensively about first language methodology in the language arts and other content areas. Visits to kindergarten and first grade classrooms will yield valuable insights about strategies for using contextual clues and for tying language to experience. Classroom visits at other grade levels will suggest subject content appropriate for the second-language classroom. Immersion materials obtained from programs in the United States and Canada may serve as a resource for developing classroom activities and approaches in the FLES classroom.

Immersion Issues

While the numerous benefits of immersion are gratifying and exciting, immersion programs are not without their own set of issues and problems. In order for these programs to meet the needs of the students for whom they have been developed, basic standards need to be met. The following questions summarize the conditions necessary for immersion programs in the United States to realize their potential for the children enrolled within them. Readers interested in other models of early language programs will find many of these issues to be familiar, and will see applications to their own setting. A more extended discussion of these immersion-specific issues can be found on this book's companion Web site.

   1. Is the program design based on the developmental, social, and academic needs of children?

- Varied instructional experiences
  - Accommodation for children with learning difficulties
  - Consistent use of the immersion language
  - Materials at an appropriate level of language and academic development
2. Does the program take into account the child's need for development of the native language?
3. Does the program take into account the child's need for proficiency in the immersion language?
- Many opportunities for students to speak
  - Opportunities for extended discourse
  - Systematic and sensitive error correction
  - Varied language use by teachers to provide helpful language modeling
4. How does the factor of time affect the development of proficiency in both the native language and the immersion language?
5. Does the program design call for rigorous separation of languages, so that the child can construct meaning in each language *separately*? Is the plan for separating languages is clearly stated?
6. Does each teacher in the program have a repertoire of strategies for building the child's first and second language?
- explicit language teaching strategies
- strategies for integrating language and content
7. Does each teacher in the program have a repertoire of strategies for building the child's knowledge of academic content?
- attention paid to integrating language and content
- experiential, concrete, hands-on curriculum in every subject area
8. Does each program use a framework that defines language outcomes and helps keep track of language development for each student?
9. Does each teacher in the program have a repertoire of strategies for addressing issues related to linguistic, cultural, racial, and ethnic diversity?
10. Are the child's parents supportive of the program? Have they been informed about all aspects of the program?

It is important for present and future immersion teachers to be aware of these questions. Even more importantly, immersion teachers should be given the time and the training that will empower them to address these issues themselves. In this way teachers and programs can be accountable to the children they serve.

Summary

Immersion programs place children in a school environment in which all subject content is taught in a new language, beginning as early as kindergarten or grade one. Carefully designed immersion programs in Canada, the United States, and other countries have produced remarkable results, both in terms of the amount and quality of the second language acquired and in terms of the level of achievement in subject content and native-language competencies. Children who are given the opportunity to learn in an early total immersion program can achieve a degree of fluency in the target language that would otherwise be attainable only through an extended period of study in the target culture. In addition, their performance in first-language basic skills and their mastery of subject content is as good as or better than that of their peers who are studying in an English-only curriculum. Research results in Canada have been replicated in immersion programs in the United States.

While intensive, long-term exposure to a second language is available only in an immersion program, other distinctive components of immersion instruction can be applied in every early language classroom. Eleven characteristics and seven strategies are listed in this section as key to the concept of immersion, with suggested applications to other program models. In addition, ten challenges facing immersion education are presented. These challenges, too, can bring insight to the development of non-immersion language programs.

Even though immersion instruction will always be a limited program option, available only to some students in some school systems, insights gathered from the experiences of immersion can contribute to improved language instruction for all students.

FOR STUDY AND DISCUSSION

1. As the new curriculum coordinator for your district, it is your job to present an information session for parents who are considering enrolling their children in a new immersion program in your language in the district.
   a. Outline the information you will include in your presentation.
   b. What questions do you expect the parents to raise? How will you answer them?

2. Despite the compelling research evidence of success, immersion programs are found in relatively few locations in the United States. Why do you think this is the case? What steps might you recommend for increasing the number of immersion programs?

3. Adaptations and change in teaching practice never happen all at once. Teaching a FLES class according to the insights of immersion may have to proceed as a step-by-step process, especially for the experienced teacher who has been relatively successful using a more traditional methodology. As a consultant to the early language teachers in your district, choose one or two of the characteristics and strategies of immersion that you think would be important first steps toward teaching within the immersion philosophy, and explain how you would present them to the teachers. Use concrete examples in your explanations.

4. What implications would the implementation of an early immersion program in one elementary school in a midsized American city have for the language offerings in other schools and at other levels in the same school system?

5. What benefits can two-way immersion programs provide that are not available through traditional bilingual education or immersion programs? Under what circumstances would you recommend that a school or district consider instituting such a program?

6. Which of the issues and challenges facing immersion education have the closest corollaries in FLES or exploratory programs? What suggestions could you offer for meeting these challenges?

FOR FURTHER READING

The following sources are recommended for additional information about material covered in this chapter. Chapter citations are documented in Works Cited at the end of the volume.

General Resources: Immersion

Canadian Parents for French. *The State of French Second-Language Education in Canada 2001*. Canada, 2001. Accessed on-line at www.cpf.ca, 4/14/2003.

Center for Advanced Research on Second Language Acquisition (CARLA). University of Minnesota, Minneapolis. Available on-line at http://carla.acad.umn.edu/

Center for Applied Linguistics. *Total and Partial Immersion Programs*. Washington, DC: 1987, 1999. Available on-line at www.cal.org.

Cloud, Nancy, Fred Genesee, and Else Hamayan. *Dual Language Instruction: A Handbook for Enriched Education*. Boston: Heinle and Heinle, 2000.

Cummins, Jim, and Merrill Swain. *Bilingualism in Education: Aspects of Theory, Research and Practice*. Burnt Mill, Harlow, UK: Longman Group, 1986.

Day, Elaine M., and Stanley M. Shapson. *Studies in Immersion Education*. Clevedon, UK: Multilingual Matters, 1996.

Directory of Two-Way Bilingual Immersion Programs in the U.S. Washington, DC: Center for Applied Linguistics, 2001. Available on-line at www.cal.org/twi/directory/

Fortune, Tara, and Helen Jorstad. "US Immersion Programs: A National Survey." *Foreign Language Annals* 29, no. 2 (1996): 163–190.

Genesee, Fred. *Learning through Two Languages: Studies of Immersion and Bilingual Education*. Cambridge, MA: Newbury House, 1987.

Lyster, Roy. Immersion Pedagogy and Implications for Language Teaching, 64–95. In Cenoz, Jasone and Fred Genesee, eds. *Beyond Bilingualism: Multilingualism and Multilingual Education*. Clevedon, U.K.: Multilingual Matters, 1999.

Snow, Marguerite Ann. "Instructional Methodology in Immersion Foreign Language Education." In *Foreign Language Education Issues and Strategies*, edited by A. Padilla, H. Fairchild, and C. Valadez, 156–171. Newbury Park, CA: Sage Publications, 1990.

Swain, Merrill. "Manipulating and Complementing Content Teaching to Maximize Second Language Learning." *TESL Canada Journal* 6, no. 1 (1988): 68–83.

———. "French Immersion Research in Canada: Recent Contributions to SLA and Applied Linguistics." *Annual Review of Applied Linguistics* 20 (2000): 199–212.

Swain, Merrill, and Robert Keith Johnson. "Immersion Education: A Category Within Bilingual Education." In *Immersion Education: International Perspectives*, edited by Robert Keith Johnson and Merrill Swain, 1–16. Cambridge, UK: Cambridge University Press, 1997.

Two-Way Bilingual/Two-Way Immersion/Dual Language programs

Christian, Donna, Christopher L. Montone, Kathryn J. Lindholm, and Isolda Carranza. *Profiles in Two-Way Immersion Education*. Washington, DC: Center for Applied Linguistics and Delta Systems, 1997.

Lessow-Hurley, Judith. *The Foundations of Dual Language Instruction*. 3rd ed. White Plains, NY: Longman, 2000.

13 Stocking the Early Language Classroom with Materials and Resources

Useful Supplies, Materials, and Equipment

Materials represent a significant portion of the time and resources invested in an early language program, no matter what program model has been chosen. This chapter describes materials that will provide the means for creating the concrete context that is so necessary for meaningful communication. Because young learners require hands-on learning experiences with concrete objects, the early language classroom must have a wide variety of objects and materials available, as many of them as possible from the target culture. Such materials offer a richness and texture not available even in the most carefully designed textbook. This need for a wide range of materials is one of the most marked differences between teaching elementary or middle school/junior high school children and older students. While high school and university teachers often emphasize the written word and written homework early in the learning experience, the early language teacher works with the development of oral language skills over an extended period of time.

The need for a wealth of materials creates special problems for the traveling teacher, who must devise practical ways of transporting props and realia that are often bulky and unwieldy. Some teachers have devised a traveling cart especially for this purpose, and many other early language teachers have become well known for the large bags and satchels they carry with them. Some types of materials, especially those used for crafts and projects, are already present in the regular classroom, but they must be specially ordered and stored in a classroom that is being equipped for foreign language instruction.

You can tap many sources in the process of stocking the early language classroom. You can arrange for the short-term loan of some items with preschool and elementary school teachers, or teachers in the ELL or the bilingual program. Some types of visuals and media resources are available through the school media center, especially videos, audiotapes and CDs, and equipment. School supply houses are good sources of most basic classroom supplies, and many other materials listed in this section are available from distributors of curriculum materials, supplies, and equipment for early childhood and elementary education. Early language teachers will find it useful to be on mailing lists for as many of these catalogs as possible. Browsing through such catalogs often suggests new activities and new uses for materials already present in the classroom.

Locating authentic materials from the target culture is usually more difficult and more time consuming. A number of companies specialize in importing realia and materials for foreign language teachers, but these materials are often chosen to appeal to older students. The foreign language teacher traveling in a country where the target language is spoken can find many teaching materials in toy stores, bookstores, record stores, and novelty and souvenir shops. Cassette tapes or CDs of children's stories, songs and rhymes, and simple picture books for storytelling are especially valuable "finds" for the classroom. Toys, books, and music can sometimes be located on the Internet, when local sources fail and a trip to the country is not an immediate option. Language teachers who are able to travel abroad collect items ranging from empty packaging for candy and soft drinks to menus, coins, and ticket stubs. Those who do not have regular opportunities to travel must find other sources for child-appropriate authentic materials and realia.

One of the best ways to obtain teaching materials from the target culture is to correspond with an elementary school English teacher in one of the countries where the target language is spoken. This type of relationship can make it possible for teachers to exchange pictures, music, and realia spontaneously, either to complement a theme of interest or to serve as a focus for an entire unit of instruction. Technology now makes it possible to exchange materials like these very quickly, once a relationship has been established. This type of cooperative exchange provides the opportunity for both teachers to obtain meaningful materials at a reasonable cost, although there is usually considerable delay in receiving any materials that cannot be transmitted electronically.

You can sometimes obtain posters and travel brochures without cost from embassies, consulates, or tourist agencies representing countries in which the target language is spoken. As a starting point for contacting such agencies, teachers can search the Internet and write letters requesting materials to all possible sources. A letter or e-mail requesting posters and city information from the visitors' bureau in capital cities or other cities in the country where the target language is spoken can also yield valuable resources. Multinational businesses sometimes make materials developed for another country available to teachers; posters and travel brochures can also be obtained from travel agencies and airline companies that are sometimes willing to provide such material to foreign language teachers.

There are also less formal sources for obtaining materials and resources for classroom use. Garage sales and rummage sales are often good places to find plastic fruit, flowers, and other replicas, as well as toys, costumes, puppets, and other realia. Children themselves enjoy sharing favorite toys or helping to create a visual or a device that will bring classroom instruction to life. Always on the lookout for a new way to make a concept or a communicative situation more vivid, many early language teachers are regular customers at toy stores, variety stores, and souvenir shops.

The time and the budget devoted to developing the materials and resources available to the early language teacher will have a significant impact on the quality and the success of the elementary school language program. Some of the items that are valuable to the elementary or middle school language teacher include the following:

Butcher/Chart Paper, 1,000-foot Roll
Because this paper can be cut to varying sizes as needed, it can be used for classroom collages, art projects, tracing body shapes, and making life-size paper dolls.

Butcher/Chart Paper (precut), Chart Tablets, Flip Charts
These are used for language-experience stories, developing charts and graphs, demonstrations, and explanations. Chart tablets are excellent for displaying the results of small-group projects or brainstorming.

Construction Paper
This should be available in at least twelve colors, and in at least two different sizes, $9'' \times 12''$ and $12'' \times 18''$.

red	blue	white
black	green	yellow
brown	gold	purple
pink	orange	gray

Construction paper can be used for craft projects, visuals, and games.

Tagboard, Oaktag, Posterboard
Available in $9'' \times 12''$, $12'' \times 18''$, and larger pieces, these are useful for mounting pictures and for making flashcards, posters, signs (such as passwords), language ladders, and classroom charts.

Self-Adhesive Plastic, in Clear and Assorted Colors/Patterns
This is used for preserving visuals, classroom crafts, game boards, and teacher-prepared materials.

Paper Plates
These are a basic supply for the early language classroom, and they are usually less expensive than tagboard. They can be used as a background for almost any picture; to display meals using food pictures; as a basis for crafts, visuals, clocks, masks, mood faces, weather pictures, and mobiles; as well as for serving snacks.

Masking Tape
This can be used for changing the environment by creating shapes and defining spaces on the floor; it also has many commonplace uses such as attaching labels and attaching posters and visuals to walls by making a circle out of masking tape. (When attaching masking tape to pictures and posters, first place a strip or two of tape on the item itself, at each point where the masking-tape circle will be applied. Then, when the masking-tape circle is removed, the picture or poster will not be damaged.)

"Easy Release" Tape and Notes
This is good for labeling anything on a temporary basis. (This tape sticks but does not remain permanently and does not damage surfaces.)

White Glue
This is especially suitable for adhesive jobs that are similar to model building and for putting a magnet or pin on the back of an object. It is used mainly for crafts.

Glue Stick

This is a handy item for quick jobs or for non-permanent stickups and paper crafts. (For some tasks, a glue stick is easier for children to handle than white glue.)

Paper Fasteners

These are for making clock faces and jointed figures and for joining booklets.

Paper Punch

This is for making nametags, clock faces, and many crafts.

Colored Chalk

Color adds variety to chalkboard activities. Some chalkboards do not tolerate colored chalk well, so be sure to check with a custodian before using this chalk extensively.

Whiteboard Markers and Erasers

Where whiteboards are available, the use of color is very engaging.

Colored Tissue Paper

Many crafts call for tissue paper, including paper flowers, piñatas, mosaics, papier-mâché figures, mobiles, and many crafts.

Chenille Stems or Pipe Cleaners

These can be used for paper flowers and other crafts.

Yarn in Assorted Colors

Crafts and game activities often require yarn, as well as nametags, mobiles, minibooks, and other projects.

Notecards: 3″ × 5″, 4″ × 6″

These are useful for making games, and for multiple other uses, including activities with flags (4″ × 6″ cards are the same size as silk flags that are commercially available).

Portfolios or Other Carrying Cases

Artist portfolios or other means of carrying posters and large teaching visuals are essential for helping the teacher to stay organized. Using different portfolios for each theme is also helpful.

Zip-Closure Plastic Bags of Various Sizes

These bags can keep materials organized and prevent small pieces from becoming lost. They are used for the teacher's materials and also to keep manipulatives for partner and other student activities sorted and organized.

Stickers in a Colorful Variety

Many teachers use stickers as a reward for performance, or as a way of brightening student work when it is returned. These kinds of rewards are most effective when they are unpredictable celebrations of student work or effort, and when they relate to the theme of the class.

Craft Sticks, Tongue Depressors, Dowels

Craft sticks or tongue depressors can be used for randomly calling on students or creating groups or teams, as well as for craft activities. They can also serve as the basis for several kinds of puppets.

General Resources

Folk and Fairy Tales (Books, Videos)

These are good for reading aloud, planning units, or student browsing at a reading table or in a learning center.

Songbooks

A selection of songbooks from the target culture will make it easier for the teacher to choose songs that reinforce specific topics and vocabulary in the curriculum. Teachers should not overlook target language songs in the music series currently being used in the school district.

Coloring Books and Dot-to-Dot Books

These are a good source for visuals and activities, especially when they come from the target culture.

Paper Dolls

For individual student use at a learning station with recorded instructions on how to dress the doll, or in a partner activity in which one student tells the other how to dress the doll. Large dolls can be used for whole-class activities.

Books of Simple Rhymes, Finger Plays

Regularly used with preschool and primary level students, finger plays are rhymes with corresponding actions. Using rhymes from the target culture rather than translations of English rhymes can be a way to provide more cultural experiences in the early language classroom.

Duplicating Master Books

Available from various publishers, these books are useful as sources for visuals and student-activity sheets. Activities developed from these sources must be meaningful and must be an integrated part of the curriculum.

Flannel Board Manipulatives

Available from various publishers, they are used as props for telling fairy tales and other stories and are also available in sets depicting various vocabulary categories such as the house, family, foods, clothing, weather, opposites, and animals. Magnetic sheets can be used in the same way on a chalkboard or a whiteboard that has a steel core.

Rubber Stamps and Ink Pads

For creating realia (coin, clock, shape stamps), for incentives and rewards, and for creating pair or partner activities.

Peel and Stick Plastic Activity Kits

These cutout vinyl shapes adhere to a glossy surface. They are valuable for learning center activities and for TPR activities with individuals and small groups. The teacher can put together a scene, take a picture of it, and record directions for constructing the scene on an audiocassette. The child re-creates the scene, following the directions, and uses the photograph to check for accuracy. If the vinyl pictures are large enough, they can be used for TPR activities with the whole class.

Board Games

Some board games from the target culture are useful for small group and learning center work. Certain native-language board games can be adapted to activities conducted entirely in the target language.

Bingo and Lotto Games

Many commercial games are available to reinforce vocabulary of all kinds. Games specifically keyed to vocabulary and concepts of an individual lesson can be made by the teacher and laminated, often with student help in a class project.

Realia

Plastic Fillable Eggs in Several Sizes

Eggs can be hidden one inside the other for discovery activities. They can also be used to hide various objects, to hold scrambled sentence parts, pictures for sequencing, or objects for guessing games. Graduated sizes in various colors are available at Easter time.

Magnetic Numbers, Letters

These are used on the magnet board or chalkboard for manipulating number concepts or creating words.

Foam Numbers, Letters

These provide a different texture and an alternative way of dealing with the same vocabulary. Children love to touch soft letters and numbers.

Math Counters or a Gross of Any Small Objects Such As Erasers

Counters can be used for math activities, of course, and also for games of many kinds.

Empty 35mm Film Cans

Useful for storage, for guessing games, as containers for surprise vocabulary items, these are very handy to have on hand.

Magnetic Mirror
Use as a prop on a magnetized chalkboard for pantomime and action chain activities. For example, the teacher might draw a sink on the board and have students go there individually to pretend to comb their hair and wash their faces, looking in the mirror while performing the actions. The simple prop of the mirror makes the activity more meaningful.

Oversized Combs, Toothbrushes, Sunglasses, and Other Props
The use of exaggerated sizes for props dealing with any relevant vocabulary adds to the feeling of play and fun and incorporates an element of surprise.

Inflatable Figures (Dolls, Animals, Skeletons, Globes)
Inflatable figures can be foils in classroom activities or serve as giant-sized manipulatives.

Clocks with Movable Hands
This is a necessary prop for activities dealing with time. These are available commercially in both individual student and large teacher sizes, or students can make their own as a craft activity.

Large Dice
Dice are available with dots, numbers, or blank faces for adding pictures. These are useful for practicing numbers, creating math problems, and developing vocabulary games of many kinds.

Wand, Baton, or Pointer
Teacher or students can direct chants or singing with a "magic" wand or baton. These items can also be used for pointing out objects in a game, choosing students, and creating fantasy transformations.

Jump Ropes
Jump ropes are useful for TPR activities such as jumping a specified number of times, jumping forward, backward, sideways, fast, slow, high, low. Jump rope rhymes from the culture are a good way to move the language beyond the classroom. Two jump ropes laid on the floor in circles side by side can become a Venn diagram.

Hoops (Hula Hoops or Mathematics Hoops)
Use hoops for sorting activities and creating Venn diagrams with actual objects. They can also be used as props in TPR activities designed to illustrate terms such as "into, over, out of, next to." (Jump over the circle; sit down in the circle; step out of the circle, and so forth.)

Balls
Sponge balls can be thrown around the classroom with no danger of injury or breakage. They can be thrown to the person who will respond to a question, provide the next question, or be the partner in some kind of exchange. The ball can also be used for various games and for a number of "New Games" (Fluegelman 1976) activities.

Bouncing balls can be used for TPR activities that are similar to the jump rope activities described above. The balls can be bounced high and low, fast and slow, a specified number of times.

Colorful Fabric Backdrops with Thematic Illustrations
Available by the yard from fabric stores, a yard or more of these thirty-six- or forty-five-inch-wide fabric pieces can set the tone for a unit and sometimes become part of unit activities.

Puppets, Stuffed Animals, Dolls
Puppets, stuffed animals, and dolls can be partners in modeling a conversational exchange. Puppets can be the stimulus for getting information: they can have a secret, speak for a shy child, or be part of an impromptu skit in which the puppets themselves are the characters. Puppets can be the desired objects in a classroom activity in which students ask to hold or to play with certain things. If they are of the right size and design, a large number of them can be placed in the "magic box" to surprise everyone when all the puppets appear.

Puppets can be of various types: hand puppets, stick puppets, paper bag puppets, folded paper puppets, sock puppets, finger puppets, and others. The children can make many types of puppets themselves.

Plastic Fruit, Vegetables, Flowers, Toys
Especially when they are life-sized, plastic models are the next best to the real thing for vocabulary of all kinds.

Suitcase Full of Clothing for Dress-Up, Games
Children enjoy dressing up for games or role plays. Oversized clothing in adult sizes is the easiest to use because students can put it on and take it off quickly and easily. Activities such as relay games and fashion shows are especially effective. The suitcase itself can be a prop in simulations.

Blindfolds
Blindfolds are useful for games, and for changing drill to communicative activities by removing the obvious stimulus from sight.

Brightly Patterned Tablecloth or Scarf, Preferably from the Target Culture
The cloth spread out on the floor can define the stage, or set the scene for a story, for classes that sit on the floor. Activities and materials can be laid on the cloth, and the students stay in a relatively well-defined circle around it.

Portable Electronic Keyboard, Rhythm Box
The teacher can choose a rhythm as a background for practicing rote material like numbers, lists, or rhymes. Providing a background rhythm changes the character of the activity, making it more fun and adding a right-hemisphere dimension.

Silk Flags (4″ × 6″)
These are a colorful reminder of the variety of places where the target language is spoken; children will learn to identify flags with geographic locations. Flags are also useful for

work with colors. Flags for almost any target language country are also available on the Internet, or in many software drawing packages.

Dollhouse and Furniture
These are useful props for vocabulary dealing with household items and everyday activities.

Sequencing Materials
Pictures and manipulatives designed for sequencing activities in early childhood education can be used as the basis for simple storytelling and vocabulary reinforcement as well as for sequencing practice.

Playing Cards
There are many kinds of commercially available playing cards, including games such as Go Fish and Old Maid, many of which can be labeled over for the elementary or middle school world language classroom. Target language card games such as the German Quartett or French Jeu de la famille games are valuable for small-group activities because they put students in physical touch with objects from the culture. Regular playing cards can be used for a variety of games that involve reviewing numbers. Cards can also be made with clip art, a copier, card stock, and a paper cutter.

Mathematics and Numbers Flash Cards
Flash cards for addition, subtraction, multiplication, and division facts, as well as for numbers and fractions, reinforce the regular mathematics curriculum while providing practice in the target language.

Individual Chalkboards or Whiteboards
These can be used for comprehension checks and for listening comprehension and TPR activities. They can also be used for a variety of games. Whiteboards can be made inexpensively by cutting up large sheets of the same material purchased at a builder's supply store. Sometimes the store will even cut up the smaller boards for the teacher.

Beads, Blocks, Rods, and Counters
These are manipulatives for listening comprehension and communicative language activities. They are also useful for dealing with mathematics concepts such as patterns. Students might organize the blocks or beads according to the teacher's directions, then hold them up to confirm that they understood. They can also be used for partner work in which partners take turns giving directions.

Toy Telephones
These make good props for skits and simulations. Toy coin telephones into which plastic coins can actually be inserted are available, making them a good prop for a Gouin series. (Some telephone companies will lend or donate real telephones for classroom purposes.)

Picture Books and Easy Readers in the Second Language
Picture books with very simple texts, if they are well illustrated to provide the necessary visual reinforcement, can be read aloud to a class or a small group or used for beginning

reading experiences. It is difficult to find books with the right text-to-picture ratio. Some schools have taken English books and labeled over them in the second language; however, this results in a loss of cultural exposure for the learners.

Elementary School Second Language (Picture) Dictionaries
These resources help children develop early skills in dictionary use and provide target language visuals for important concepts.

Toy Money
This is useful for simulations and for reinforcing mathematics concepts. (It is preferable to use toy money from the target culture.) Teachers can also duplicate replicas of actual money used in the target culture by using actual currency or models available on the Internet.

Toy Cash Register
This is for simulations, making change. (It is preferable to use one from the target culture or one that doesn't have a dollar sign.)

Menus from the Target Culture
These are useful for pair work, for stating preferences, in simulations, for room decorations, and for reinforcing vocabulary.

Thermometer (Demonstration)
The classroom demonstration thermometer should have both Fahrenheit and Celsius scales and a movable temperature indicator. It is used for temperature reports and comparisons with temperatures in foreign countries. (Using thermometers reinforces science concepts and knowledge of the metric system.)

Metric and Balance Scales
Both a small food scale and a larger scale for weighing people are useful. Scales are especially valuable for cooking activities reflecting cultures in which ingredients are weighed rather than measured with a cup. Simple balance scales are useful for a number of science activities.

Meter Stick or Measuring Tape
These are for measuring activities and reinforcing the mathematics and science curricula.

Postcards, Letters, and Stamps
These can serve as classroom decoration, props in simulations and partner work, and for cultural inquiry activities.

Newspapers and Magazines
When written in the target language, these provide browsing and early reading activities, material for art projects, bulletin board backdrops, and props. English language magazines can also be a source of materials for visuals and collages, but they lack the cultural perspective.

Empty Food Packaging

Preferably from the target culture, these are useful for simulations and as props and decorations. Some teachers set up a "store" in part of the classroom as a part of the regular classroom environment.

Table Settings

Flatware, dishes, glasses, cups, napkins, and tablecloths are useful for practice in table setting. Real food, food replicas, or pictures for nutrition lessons and simulations provide the finishing touches.

Rhythm and Orff Instruments

Simple instruments are useful for developing accompaniments to songs and rhymes and for creating sound effects for simulations and fantasy experiences.

Coins from the Target Culture

Coins are useful for role play and simulations and are a good source of cultural information. Coins can also be used to make rubbings, as counters in board games, and for mathematics activities.

Sporting Goods

Sports equipment from the target culture is useful for games and demonstration purposes. For example, boule in a French class or bocce in an Italian class provide an authentic cultural experience for the students. These games are best played outside, since enthusiastic participation might alienate a teacher in a classroom below!

Calendars

When made in the target culture, these show different customs for formatting the date and the month, and they provide attractive pictures reflecting the culture. Other calendars can be useful sources for visuals and student projects. Some software can create calendars in several languages.

Picture Visuals

Pictures provide context and stimuli for a variety of classroom activities. For use with the entire class, they should be mounted and should be large and clear enough (at least $8'' \times 10''$) so that all students can see them. Smaller pictures are appropriate for small-group and pair work. When used to illustrate a concept, pictures must not be cluttered or confusing; only one thing should be represented by each picture.

Pictures are very helpful in keeping the classroom in the target language. They should provide the focus for meaningful, communicative activity, and not just be used to elicit one-word responses and naming. For example, students can sort a series of pictures into the categories of the food pyramid, or arrange them to plan menus. Other pictures might be used to classify types of clothing by appropriate season, color, or degree of formality or informality. In the beginning stages, pictures help the teacher to convey meaning, but later the same or similar pictures can be used as cues for partner activities or group work so that they become aids to communication as well as to vocabulary.

Picture Files

It is important to have a variety of materials so that students do not become bored with the same picture used over and over. A variety of visuals for the same concept or vocabulary term can help to ensure that students understand the concept itself, and do not simply have an automatic reaction to a single picture. Picture files can be developed from magazines, postcards, calendars, catalogs, brochures, posters, wall charts and commercially available flash cards, among many other possibilities. Pictures and clip art available on-line and in software packages can also be useful resources for pictures.

Travel Posters and Brochures

Posters and travel brochures provide an especially colorful point of reference for the target culture in the classroom, and they can sometimes be used to set the stage for a fantasy or a culture activity. They should be changed periodically so that they do not lose their appeal for students. Posters, maps, and charts should be laminated before they are displayed if they are to be used for an extended period of time.

Flash Cards

Flash cards can be either commercially produced or teacher prepared. They provide picture or symbol stimulus for a wide range of vocabulary and for sequencing activities. Tagboard, oaktag, or poster board is a good base for making flash cards. It is helpful to make all flash cards in a series the same size for convenience in storage and in dimensions that can be easily held and manipulated by small hands if they are intended for individual or small-group activities; or viewed by an entire class if they were meant for work with large groups. If the flash card is rectangular it is also helpful to have each flash card oriented the same way vertically or horizontally so that the pictures do not have to be constantly rotated from horizontal to vertical when they are shown in a sequence.

Art Works that Represent Significant Artists or Folk Arts from the Target Culture

Fine arts and folk art are important facets of the target culture that can be a part of the learning environment from the first day of class. They can also be the focus or components of thematic units. Prints are available commercially from museums, in calendars and books, and in study prints (see below). There are also numerous Web sites from which teachers can download both the artworks themselves and information about artists and their times.

Study Prints and Charts

Many curriculum libraries and school libraries have files of study prints and charts that can be borrowed for a period of time. These pictures are centered around a theme, such as "Children Around the World," or "Community Workers." They are especially useful for content teaching.

Visuals Available from Computer Clip Art and on the Internet

Visual materials have never been so abundant as they are now, given the availability of clip-art software at reasonable prices. Libraries of clip art are often included with word processing and other software programs. The Internet offers numerous sites with downloadable free images, and many Web pages offer visual materials for teachers, as well. Use of a search engine such as www.google.com will often yield Web sites that have visuals available for exactly the topic the teacher needs to illustrate a concept or enrich a theme. Teachers often exchange information about these sites on listservs such as Ñandu, or some teachers have built links to useful sites from their own Web pages.

Classroom Equipment

Chalkboard

This is probably the most used classroom aid. Using both colored and white chalk on a chalkboard or Whiteboard makes it more effective, provided that the board surface can handle colored chalk. Walking up to the board is a change of pace for the students. In some schools, the board has a steel core, making it possible to use it like a magnet board.

Pocket Chart

The pocket chart is a standard tool for reading instruction in the primary grades. Charts are made of sturdy cardboard or vinyl and contain pockets that are useful for holding word cards and picture cards. Pocket charts are available from school supply sources, or teachers can develop their own. A long pocket chart with only one pocket can be placed along the chalkboard for use with unscrambling sentences, creating time lines, organizing pictures to retell a story, and so on (see Figure 13.1).

Flannel Board

Flannel boards are commercially available or can be made by stretching a piece of cotton flannel or felt over a backing such as stiff cardboard, wood, or styrofoam. They should be about $3' \times 2'$ in size if they are to be used with the entire class, or they may be smaller if they will be used by small groups or individuals.

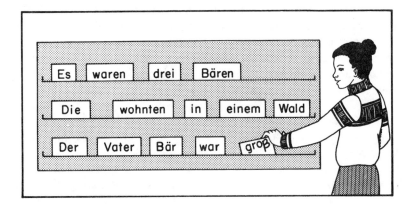

FIGURE 13.1 A pocket chart.

Lightweight items with a piece of flannel, felt, or sandpaper on the back will stick to the flannel board so that scenes can be put together and changed easily. Pieces of dress-stiffening fabric or interfacing can also be cut out and colored for use on the flannel board. The flannel board provides an excellent device for storytelling and manipulating objects. The board can be divided into rooms of the house, roads, farms, calendars, and many other spaces with felt strip dividers. Other materials that adhere easily to the flannel board include paper with flocked backing, pipe cleaners, string, yarn, suede, and sponges. Many flannel board manipulative materials are available from school supply stores and catalogs.

Magnet Board

Magnet boards are commercially available in sizes similar to those available for flannel boards, and they can be used in much the same way. Magnets can be placed on top of figures to hold them in place, or they can be glued to the back of objects or figures to be used. Magnet strips with adhesive backing are available from school supply stores and stationery stores. Magnetic letters, numbers, pictures, and other magnetized items can also be obtained commercially. Some teachers have bought sets of words designed for "refrigerator poetry" in countries where the target language is spoken, to be used in learning centers or for special projects. Sheets of magnetized paper suitable for use with a computer printer make it possible for the teacher to create words and pictures for use on a magnet board. Teachers can create their own magnet boards using a large cookie sheet or a piece of sheet metal. Many chalkboards and some whiteboards have a steel core and can be used as a magnet board.

Peg-Board

The Peg-Board consists of a sturdy board perforated with a regular pattern of holes and with a series of fixed or movable pegs or hooks that protrude from it. The pegs or hooks can be used to hang flash cards, numbers, pictures, or letters that have a hole punched in them. The items can be moved from peg to peg. Boards with hooks can be used to display three-dimensional items or to mount shelves for storage and display.

Hook and Loop Boards and Strips

Hook and loop material—commercially known as Velcro®—is sometimes used for fasteners in sewing. It consists of two different types of surfaces that attach very tightly to one another. Hook and loop boards can be used for displaying three-dimensional materials because the system creates a very strong bond. Even without a hook and loop board the teacher can attach a strip of the hook and loop material along the side of a chalkboard or bulletin board and use it to mount various items. Some teachers use hook and loop pieces to attach and remove visuals from charts, calendars, and other games or displays.

Chart Stand, Easel

These are useful for displaying large visuals and maps and for supporting chart tablets and flip charts. When teachers read "big books," the easel is a very helpful aid.

Globes, World Maps, Maps of Countries Where the Target Language is Spoken

Frequent reference to globes and world maps will help students to put learning into a global context. Ideally, these resources will be printed in the target language, although first-language maps and globes can also be useful. Inflatable globes are available in English and in some target languages. These can be tossed around the classroom and used in a very personalized way; they are usually less expensive than traditional classroom globes.

Audiovisual Equipment

Overhead Projector

The overhead projector allows the teacher to control the focus of class attention by turning the projector off and on and by revealing only one part of the transparency at a time. The overhead projector is especially valuable for the traveling teacher, provided that there is a projector in every classroom the teacher visits, or room on the cart for a portable projector. Many instructional materials can be prepared ahead of time and projected when they are needed during the class; this saves class time that would otherwise be spent in writing on the chalkboard.

Transparencies are especially effective when they include color, which may be added even to commercially prepared transparencies with transparency pens. Transparencies for use with color printers make it possible for the teacher to create excellent color transparencies that are suited precisely to the current theme. Figures on transparencies can be cut out and moved around on the glass projector stage to achieve a variety of effects. (A number of additional activities for the overhead projector are listed in Chapter 14.)

Videocassette Recorder-Player/DVD Player

Videocassete recorder-players make it possible to view commercially prepared lessons or supplementary materials, many of which provide an image of the target culture that is nearly impossible to achieve in any other way. Some classrooms also exchange videotape "letters" or projects with children studying or speaking the target language in other parts of the country or with children living in the target culture. Multistandard equipment is essential for use with videotapes or DVDs made in some other countries.

Audiocassette Recorder/Player or CD Player

These can be used for learning stations as well as in the whole-group setting. Students can read a book and listen to an accompanying tape, or they can listen to a set of instructions for performing activities such as completing a scrambled dot-to-dot puzzle or dressing a paper doll. There are many possibilities for individual listening activities in which there is a product at the end and the opportunity for self-check.

The cassette player is also useful for playing accompaniments to songs, providing background music for a variety of classroom activities, and for recording and playing back special songs or skits done by the class—either for their own enjoyment or for sharing with other classes through a tape exchange. When the teacher plans to play the same song repeatedly in a class, or in a series of classes, it is helpful to record the song several times on the same tape, so there is no need to rewind and try to find the starting point for each repetition. Some teachers dub the song they plan to use onto a very short tape, available from many radio stations. Then they can rewind quickly without having to look for the beginning of the segment.

The CD player has several advantages for teacher use in the classroom. It is easy to find the beginning of a recorded segment, and the sound quality is often better than with an audiotape. It is practical for the teacher to have a combination CD/audiotape machine in order to have maximum flexibility.

Sound equipment should have a good-quality speaker that does not distort the sound when played at a volume high enough to be heard by the entire class.

Magnetic Card Reader

Cards of varying lengths with magnetic strips at the bottom are used for short recorded messages that relate the word(s) or picture on the card to the spoken language (see Figure 13.2). Primarily an individual tool at a learning station, this provides both an audio and visual stimulus for students to help them practice everything from individual vocabulary items to a conversational exchange. While these are no longer popular in most schools, language teachers have found them to be very useful, especially for individual or remedial work. If there is one on the shelves of the media center, you can put it to good use.

Slide Projector

Slides can be useful for imparting cultural information, especially when they have been taken by the teacher in the target culture. Some teachers have children illustrate a play with drawings for each scene, and then photograph the drawings on a copy stand to create a slide sequence telling the story. Children then record a dramatization of the play and present the

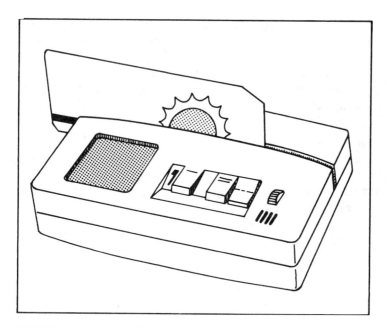

FIGURE 13.2   A magnetic card reader

slide-tape story to parents or other students. A similar process could be used to create a PowerPoint or other multimedia presentation. The drawback to slide projection is the fact that the projector must be set up in advance and the room has to be darkened for the best viewing of the slides.

Computer, Modem, Scanner, and Printer

The computer has a lot of potential for providing interactive and communicative practice. There are increasing numbers of interesting and useful programs that allow children to use the language in a game-like setting, or that provide review and practice. Word processing in the target language offers creative writing opportunities for early language classes. With a modem and telephone line, the computer provides electronic links for powerful class-to-class and student-to-student exchanges.

If the teacher has a scanner and a color printer available, as well as Internet access, the job of developing materials and activities is much more efficient. Scanners with slide adapters make it possible for teachers to make computer images from selected slides in their collection. Internet resources can simplify teacher preparation by offering downloadable lessons, worksheets, activities, visuals, and authentic materials of all kinds. Clip art and visuals from Web sites in the target culture make it possible for teachers to provide students with authentic materials and experiences that have previously been accessible only by a visit to the country itself. See Chapter 15 for a more extended discussion of technology.

Visual Reinforcement in the Early Language Classroom

Labels

All classroom furniture and classroom features can be labeled in the target language (chalkboard, desk, door, erasers, electric outlets). It is also effective to label other parts of the school with target language names—toilets, offices, specialty classrooms, exits, and so forth (see Figure 13.3). Where there is more than one language taught in the school, labels from all languages may be used side by side.

Nametags

Nametags can be an effective reinforcement of the second-language atmosphere if the students have chosen names in the target language. Nametags may be placed on the desks for the language period every day or they may be hung around the neck or pinned on an article of the students' clothing. Some teachers create classroom rituals around the distribution of nametags every day; others prefer to have the students keep the nametags in their desks and take them out as a sign of the beginning of class. Nametags may not be needed beyond the first several weeks of the year; although, for teachers who see many students in a day or in a week, the nametags may be necessary for a much longer period of time. Nametags permit teachers to call students by name, even when a target language name has not been assigned, in a situation where it is otherwise very difficult to learn all the names of the students.

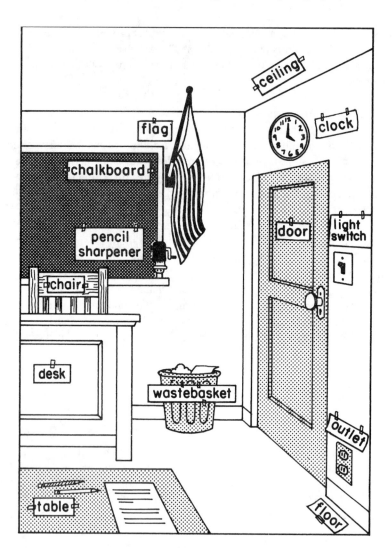

FIGURE 13.3   The classroom can be labeled in the target language.
Here is a classroom labeled for English language learners.

Calendar

Having a calendar in the target language is an easy way to have the target culture present in the classroom at all times. For some teachers an opening routine for each class involves the calendar and the weather. They use the same calendar format as the base, and then they have month headers and calendar numbers (different ones for each month). Many teachers add the new calendar number each day, attaching it with a hook-and-loop tab or with masking tape.

Weather Cards, Chart, or Weather Wheel

As part of the calendar opening for class, students identify the weather for the day and post it with the calendar. Some teachers keep a weather chart on which the class records the weather over the course of a week or longer.

Lynn Sessler-Schmaling, Japanese teacher in Menasha, Wisconsin, uses weather pictures for each type of weather likely to be encountered in the local climate. She attaches a hook or a link to the bottom of each picture. Each day the students decide on the weather—in Japanese, of course—and add a link to the chain under that weather picture. At the end of the week, or the month, the class has a graph of the weather conditions and can use it to describe the weather over that period of time.

Signal Indicating Language Being Spoken

This signal can be a sign or a flag or an apron or some other device that indicates whether English or the target language is being used. The teacher changes the signal when the language of the classroom is changed.

Symbols to Hang from the Ceiling

Signs with specific vocabulary items, such as weather, months, or time of day, can be hung from the ceiling in various parts of the room. They can be used as a way of organizing children or as a part of TPR activities. Passwords or Language Ladders might also be hung from the ceiling instead of being placed on the wall. This possibility assumes that the language is always taught in the same room.

Mobiles

Coat hangers are the easiest base for creating classroom mobiles that reflect some aspect of the thematic unit. Directions for making mobiles can be found in many classroom craft books.

Reference Charts

Charts can be student or teacher made, or they can be obtained from commercial sources. They visually represent the concepts taught in class. For example, a food pyramid might be used in conjunction with a food unit.

Other charts are teacher or student made and used for the maintenance of classroom routines. Following are some additional examples.

Helper Chart

This is a list of classroom jobs performed by students, with visual cues to make the meaning clear (see Figure 13.4). This is obviously appropriate for a classroom devoted to the target language, but sometimes classroom teachers are willing to use a target language chart for the helpers each week, instead of an English language chart.

Classroom Rules Chart

Classroom rules should be spelled out in the target language with a visual cue to make the meaning clear.

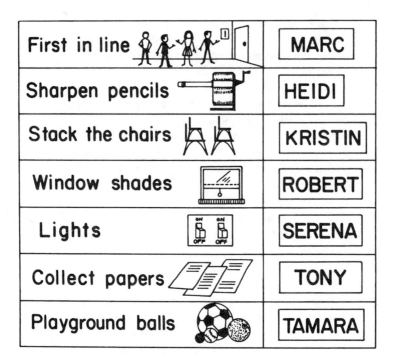

FIGURE 13.4   A sample helper chart.

Color and Number Charts

In primary and early elementary school language classrooms, these are helpful reference points for early activities with colors and numbers.

Bulletin Boards

Bulletin boards captioned in the target language and reflecting the target culture can be a source of cultural stimulation in the classroom, and they can also serve as valuable teaching tools. They should be changed frequently, often with the help of the students themselves, and they should reflect the concepts and the vocabulary being taught in the classroom. Bulletin boards in hallways and entryways of the school provide an opportunity to gain attention for the language program. Some classroom teachers are willing to devote one portion of the classroom board space for the traveling language teacher.

Teacher-Produced Materials

Teacher-made materials are among the most effective means in communicating a concept, structuring an activity, or motivating a lesson, because they are usually tailored to the special needs and interests of a specific class and situation. Both the teacher and the students value the extra effort that has gone into making these materials and use them with special pleasure. Supplementary materials like most of those represented here should contribute to the goals of the lesson and not become a separate entity in themselves.

Many of these items can also be produced by students or with student assistance. All items prepared for the classroom should be of good quality, carefully prepared, durable, and colorful. Edges should be straight and squared, cut with a paper cutter. Pinking shears should be used to cut any cloth with a tendency to ravel, or to provide a decorative edge to paper or fabric.

Protecting Teacher-Made Visuals and Game Boards

Three methods for protecting a visual are *binding, mounting,* and *making surface coverings*. Binding (with masking tape or other strong tape) protects the edges and makes for longer wear.

Mounting a visual keeps it flat and makes it easier to handle and file; mounting material must be sturdy so that the pictures are not flimsy and do not become dog-eared. Two effective techniques for mounting involve using the dry-mount heat press and spray adhesive. Visuals should be mounted on backings of similar sizes so that they are easier to store.

The surface of visuals can be protected through lamination or by use of clear self-adhesive plastic. Lamination tends to enhance the colors of the visuals and to give a more professional, long-lasting finish. It is frequently no more expensive than other techniques, but it may sometimes be a source of glare, making it difficult for some students to see the visual under certain lighting conditions. With clear self-adhesive plastic there is often a loss of vividness of color, but no machine is necessary, so projects can be completed at home. Do not use permanent ink pens to mark materials that will be laminated or covered with clear contact paper, as the color may bleed; instead, use water-based pens.

Magic/Mystery Box

This resource can conceal or reveal vocabulary items and can be a recurring source of surprises and motivation in the classroom (see Figure 13.5). Specific suggestions for its use are found in Chapter 14.

Here are the directions for making a magic box:

1. Cover the bottom and sides of a 42-ounce (large) oatmeal box with two layers of self-stick plastic covering. If patterned covering is not used, decorate the box with symbols cut from contrasting plastic.
2. Cut away the heel and the foot from a large heavy sock, or use a portion of a leg warmer. Pull the sock over the top of the oatmeal box until the entire sock is stretched around the box.
3. Staple the sock around the top edge to fasten it to the box.
4. Place a strip of the self-stick plastic around the top edge of the box, covering the staples and the top edge of the sock.
5. Pull the sock up from the bottom, inside out, to form a "handle" for the box.

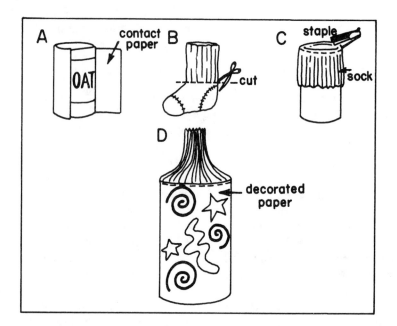

FIGURE 13.5   A magic box.

Laminated Circles and Numbers
Make large- and small-colored circles (at least one set of each, 12 inches and 6 inches in diameter) out of construction paper for every color to be taught. Other laminated shapes are useful for mathematics concepts. Make large numbers out of $9'' \times 12''$ colored tagboard. Laminate or cover with clear self-stick plastic. These materials are all useful for TPR activities, creative play, and subject content instruction.

Floor Maps and Pattern Games
Use a sheet of heavy-gauge vinyl table covering (preferably without texture) to make a floor map of countries, continents, or cities. (If the vinyl is white on both sides, each side can be used for a different map or activity). It also works to use a heavy shower curtain. Attach the vinyl to the chalkboard or the wall and project a copy of the map using an opaque projector or an overhead projector. Trace the map onto the vinyl using a permanent felt marker or a laundry marker. For additional interest add colored markers to indicate bodies of water and other features of importance.

This teaching tool can be used for teaching geography concepts by TPR as children step, sit, or jump on a country, a city, or a physical feature. (Additional teaching suggestions are found in Chapter 14.)

Use the back of the map or another piece of vinyl to create a game board, a chart, or a geometric grid for use with TPR activities associated with a variety of concepts.

Nametags
Punch holes in the two top corners of a piece of tagboard, pull yarn through the holes and tie it, write the student's target language name on the tagboard, and hang it around the student's neck. The nametag can be shaped to represent elements of the culture being learned, such as berets, flags, and pretzels. (If nametags are laminated, they will last much longer. They must be laminated if they are made out of construction paper.)

Booklets, Theme Books, and Shape Books
Use booklets or theme books as initial, developmental, or culminating activities for just about any topic. When you create a booklet that represents concepts just learned in pictures (and perhaps also in words), the students have something tangible to take home with them and share with their parents, and the second-language learning becomes more concrete for them. You can prepare the illustrations for the booklet, or the booklet pages themselves, before class, and have students complete them as a classroom activity. Typical booklet topics include weather, feelings, the alphabet, a group trip, foods, and animals.

For variety you can prepare the cover and the pages for a theme book or booklet in the shape of the topic of the booklet, and have students assemble the booklet and use it to record information about the topic. For example, an experience with a rabbit might be recorded in a booklet shaped like a rabbit, or a nutrition experience might be described in a book shaped like an apple or an egg. These experiences give students both tactile and verbal reinforcement of the concepts under discussion.

Clothesline
A clothesline provides an easy way to display visuals or student work in the classroom. For example, the teacher might hang paper or doll clothing on it, use it as a time line, or hang up weather signs or other symbols.

Wheel of Months, Seasons/Weather
This teaching tool provides a way of looking at the months of the year and the seasons as a whole and associating them with distinctive characteristics representative of the target culture. The teacher uses heavyweight tagboard or poster board to cut two large half circles that will be hinged together to form a complete circle. The circle is divided into twelve equal segments, each representing a month of the year and identified by a picture reflecting special activities or occasions for that month and with the name or initial of the month. The board can be used for teaching months of the year, locating class birthdays, and for songs and rhymes dealing with months and seasons.

Clothespin Matchups (Self-Correcting Activity)
To create clothespin matchups, use the following materials: a large circle (or other shape if preferred) made of cardboard or tagboard divided into eight to twelve sections, and wooden clothespins—enough so that there is one pin for each section of the wheel.

There are many varieties of activities with clothespin matchups. The circle can contain pictures of vocabulary words, and the clothespins can have the correct word written on them; the activity can deal with rhyming words, opposites, various tenses, or many other topics; students must match the clothespin with the section of the wheel that has the correct picture. To make the activity self-checking, place a number or symbol on the back of the clothespin and the same number or symbol on the back of the correct section of the wheel (see Figure 13.6).

Dominoes (Number or Picture)
You can create domino games using colors, numbers, or pictures representing current vocabulary. Use the dominoes for small groups or whole-class activities on the chalkboard or on the floor. Commercial domino games are also useful for many activities.

Yarn-Board (Self-Correcting Activity)
To make a yarn-board use these materials:

- an 8½″ × 11″ piece of tagboard divided in half lengthwise, and into four to six sections horizontally

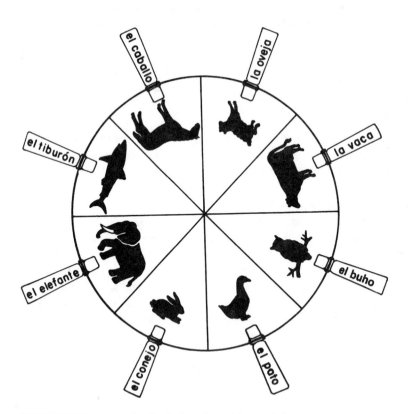

FIGURE 13.6   A sample of a clothespin matchup activity.

- colored yarn (either enough pieces of one color or a different color for each horizontal section)
- hole puncher
- reinforcements for three-hole-punched paper

Arrange various pairs for matching practice so that one member of the pair appears in the left-hand column and the other member of the pair appears in a random position in the right-hand column. Attach one piece of the yarn to each segment on the edge of the left-hand column and punch one hole on the edge of each segment in the right-hand column. The student places the yarn in the hole representing the correct match. Many items can be matched: vocabulary pictures with vocabulary words, opposites, and so forth (see Figure 13.7). This activity can be self-correcting in the following ways:

Variation 1: Cut the yarn various lengths so that each piece can fit into only the hole with the correct answer.

Variation 2: Use multicolored yarn strands all the same length and color-code the correct answers on the back of the hole by placing a round reinforcement for three-hole-punched paper over the hole. Color-code the reinforcement the same color as the yarn.

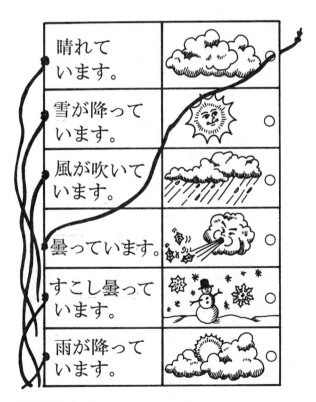

FIGURE 13.7 A sample yarn-board.

Game Boards

You can make simple game boards similar to those popular with children and create games to reinforce concepts that you are teaching. Game boards can be of any shape and design.

Felt Beanbags in a Variety of Colors

Here are instructions for making beanbags:

1. Cut two pieces of felt in a circle shape with a 5″ diameter.
2. Stitch them together with a ⅜″ seam around the edge, leaving about 1½″ opening for filling the bag.
3. Use light cardboard to make a funnel for beans.
4. Fill bag with a rounded ¼ cup of navy beans.
5. Sew shut.

Beanbags can be used for TPR activities, in games involving a floor map or game board, and in other common children's games.

Lotto-Color Board

Out of a piece of white or beige 9″ × 12″ construction paper, make a lotto or bingo grid divided into nine squares or rectangles with the title "Colors!" in the target language. Next, cut out squares of construction paper in the colors that the students will learn, probably twelve or thirteen in all, including white. Arrange the squares systematically so that each of the game boards is different from the others, and affix the squares to the boards using a spray adhesive or a glue stick. Laminate each of the game boards for permanence. Using a water-based transparency pen or a wax pencil, write in the numbers "1, 2, 3" above each of the columns. (These numbers may be changed for more advanced students.) Prepare game pieces to be drawn out of a hat, a magic box, or another device, three of each color, marked 1, 2, and 3, respectively.

Play the game by having the teacher draw game pieces and call out the color and the location, as in Bingo: "1 blue, 3 red," and so forth. The game may be played in any of the usual Bingo ways, including filling the whole board. This can become a more speaking oriented game if the students call back the numbers to the leader when they have won a round. When students are ready to begin speaking, they will volunteer the number. With only nine squares in the grid, the game does not go on endlessly, and many different children have a chance for success.

Scrolls

Scrolls can be used as a dramatic way of telling a story or presenting a sequence of events or steps, and they are often student produced. They are made by rolling a long strip of paper from one stick or dowel to another. They can also be used as a way of keeping a class or individual record of language learned or experiences shared.

Choosing and Using Materials Wisely

The materials and realia described in this chapter constitute a significant investment of time and resources. They are important, because they make the classroom come alive and they meet the developmental needs of our students. They are also precious. As we create materials and consider their purchase, we must be sure that our time and funds are wisely spent. Materials should be usable in a variety of ways, not purchased or made for a single activity on one day and then never used again. Busy teachers don't have hours to spend on visuals or on manipulatives that can only be used once, for a single purpose; nor do they have budgets large enough to purchase a costly manipulative that will likely only be used once.

For example, a teacher created a large two-story house from poster board, using hook-and-loop tabs to place furnishings in the house, and creating fold-out walls and doors so that the rooms could be revealed one at a time. During one class session she introduced the rooms of the house by opening the doors to each room and having the class pantomime the kinds of activities that would take place in that room. On another day she removed the furnishings from the rooms and used TPR commands to have students place the furniture in the appropriate room. On another day she hid family members in different rooms of the house and the class tried to guess where each family member was hiding. There are many more variations that could take place with this one, labor-intensive visual, and with each variation the students' language development grows.

Another way to make the most of valuable materials is to share them within a team of teachers. Especially when there is more than one teacher per grade level, sharing materials and ideas makes everyone's load lighter and enhances learning for all the students.

Criteria for Evaluating Non-Textbook Materials and Realia

Whether they have been prepared by hand, commercially produced, or obtained directly from the target culture, materials will be most effective when the following questions can be answered affirmatively:

- Are the materials durable? Can they stand up to repeated, ungentle handling?
- Are the materials culturally authentic? (Some items, such as balls, numbers, shapes, animal replicas, and models of uncooked food, are culture free.)
- Are they free of non-essential detail?
- Are they brightly colored?
- Are they safe for use by children?
- Is their size appropriate to their intended use?
- Are they appealing to the intended age and developmental level?
- Do they have a versatility that lends itself to multiple use?
- Are they free of gender and racial bias?
- Do they collectively incorporate a variety of textures (soft, hard, rough, smooth)?
- Are the materials functional and simple to use?
- Are they easy to keep clean?
- Are they aesthetically pleasing?
- Do they reflect quality workmanship?
- Is the cost within the budget?

Choosing a Textbook and
Other Curriculum Materials

Choosing a textbook is one of the most important tasks for the foreign language teacher at any level. In the elementary school the process is made much more difficult by the fact that there are few text series from which to choose. A number of programs that are still available were written in the 1960s or soon thereafter and do not reflect the insights about communication and language acquisition that have been achieved since then. Other materials have been developed for specific purposes and are not completely transferable to the early foreign language classroom. Spanish materials from bilingual education, for example, are designed for children who already speak Spanish, at least to some extent, and who function at least some of the time in a Spanish-speaking environment. Thus, the linguistic level of these materials is inappropriate for English-speaking children who live in an all-English setting. Materials developed for French immersion and core French programs in Canada are often too advanced and proceed too rapidly for many program settings in the United States. German materials developed for the non-German speakers in Germany or the children of German-speaking families living abroad present similar problems when they are used with American speakers of English.

Many early language programs develop a curriculum that is not dependent on the use of a text series for at least the first year or two, but it is extremely difficult to maintain a well-articulated local curriculum over a long period of time without reference to a professionally developed text series. In the absence of satisfactory commercial text series, some school systems have invested the funding and the effort necessary to create successful locally developed materials for an entire elementary school sequence. Short-term exploratory programs, designed to offer an experience with a language that lasts no more than a year, usually work with a locally produced curriculum, since textbook publishers have produced little material appropriate for this type of program. Current curricula and program descriptions can be located using the Educational Resources Information Center (ERIC) database and the resources of the National Network for Early Language Learning.

As the interest in elementary and middle school foreign language programs continues to grow, publishers are producing curriculum materials to add to the small number of contemporary early language text series already developed for the American market, and some of these materials use videotapes as a core component. Many of these will be welcome resources that can provide a useful core for the language program.

Special Considerations at the Middle School Level

Awareness of the distinctive characteristics and learning needs of early adolescents has led to significant changes in the middle school curriculum and organization. Middle school philosophy permeates curriculum and planning for students in grades five through eight, and hands-on integrated learning has begun to replace classic textbook-driven instruction. For language programs beginning in the middle school, it has been common practice to choose foreign language materials designed for high school students and "slow them down" for the middle school, often covering the materials for the first high school year over a two-year period. This practice is intended to prepare middle school students for a smooth integration into the high school sequence, but it fails to address the special needs and interests of the early adolescent at the romantic layer of educational development (see Chapter 1).

Language programs that continue an elementary school FLES or immersion program require materials that build on earlier learning and extend it in developmentally appropriate ways. Few foreign language materials have been developed specifically for the middle school level, except for some exploratory programs, and teachers must revise and adapt extensively. The middle school student will be best served with a continued emphasis on integrated thematic units, with reference to textbook materials only when they are appropriate to the goals of the curriculum and the learning needs of the students.

Even when satisfactory curriculum materials are available, they represent only one of the tools for curriculum development. Standards-based, thematic planning is the core of any early language program, and curriculum materials need to support these integrated thematic units. Materials and activities chosen or devised by the teacher respond to the interests and needs of students in each specific school setting, and they constitute the most dynamic part of early language instruction.

The materials described in this chapter and the sample activities discussed in Chapter 14 are intended to serve as useful components of both those programs that draw on the resources of a text series and those that have been developed locally.

Criteria for Evaluating Textbooks and Other Printed Curriculum Material

As early language teachers evaluate text series or curriculum materials developed in other districts, the following questions are recommended for the screening process:

Goals
- Are the materials standards-based and oriented toward student performance?
- Are the goals of the program or authors clearly stated? Are these goals compatible with local program goals?
- Is the scope and sequence for the entire series carefully developed and clearly presented?
- Do the materials reflect authentic use of language? Is this the way people in the target culture *really* express themselves?
- What is the intended grade level for the materials? Are the materials suitable for the interests and maturity level of the proposed audience?

Communication
- Does *communication* rather than *grammar* serve as the organizing principle? Does work with grammar concentrate on functional use rather than on analysis? Do the activities focus on meaning rather than on form?
- Is the use of English avoided in student materials and discouraged in the activities described in the teacher's manual?
- Do the materials reflect an understanding of the use of current methodology?
- Is the material oriented to activity and experience rather than to exercise and drill?
- Do the materials provide opportunities for meaningful, purposeful language use in the interpersonal, interpretive, and presentational modes?

- Are the materials designed to develop a solid oral language base upon which to build reading and writing skills?
- Do the materials provide for a variety of types of classroom organization (pairs, small groups, individual work)?

Culture

- Is culture integrated into the program materials? Is there emphasis on *experiencing* culture rather than on learning *about* culture?
- Is culture presented from a global perspective rather than focusing on a single country, region, or ethnic group?
- Are the situations and language presented culturally authentic and up to date?
- Do the materials promote an appreciation of the value and richness of cultural diversity?
- Are there resources provided or suggested for authentic songs, games, and children's literature?

Subject Content and Thinking Skills (Connections)

- Is there provision for the teaching of grade-appropriate subject content in the target language? Are there suggestions for *interdisciplinary* content and activities?
- Are the materials conducive to the development of higher-order thinking skills, and not restricted to rote learning?
- Are there opportunities for students to personalize both language, culture, and content learning?
- Are there opportunities for students to seek out new information using the target language?

Bias

- Are the illustrations and text free of racial, gender, and cultural bias?

Flexibility

- Are the materials adaptable to different program models and time allocations?
- Do the materials provide options for a variety of student learning styles—visual, auditory, kinesthetic?

Physical Characteristics

- Are the student materials visually oriented and colorful?
- Are there color photographs and other visuals clearly linked to the printed material?
- Is the size of print in student materials the same as that used in subject content textbooks used at the same grade level?
- Are the materials durable? Can they withstand handling by many children over the period of time covered by a textbook adoption?

Support Materials

- Is there a teacher's manual with abundant suggestions for the teacher? Does the teacher receive adequate guidance in the use of the materials?
- Are there relevant and effective charts, transparencies, flash cards, pictures, tapes, and other support materials available in addition to the basic program?

■ If taped materials are available, do they feature native-speaker voices speaking naturally in the presentation of songs, rhymes, and stories? Are there tapes available that include program-relevant sound effects and background music?

Budget
■ Are the materials affordable?

Summary

The early language teacher works with the whole child in the whole-classroom learning environment. Every aspect of the classroom and all of the materials and realia have potential for contributing to the language experiences from which language acquisition develops. An ample inventory of supplies will encourage the development of craft and other activities and will make it easier for teachers to prepare materials tailored to classroom communication needs. A good selection of manipulatives and realia makes it possible to vary the contexts within which students communicate, giving them the practice that they need while maintaining high motivation. A variety of picture visuals to supplement the realia helps students to stretch the concepts they have learned to include a variety of occurrences. A classroom that is well equipped with display boards and equipment makes it easier for the teacher to draw on all the resources available to create a target language "island." Audiovisual equipment can make it possible for children to have a direct visual or auditory experience with the target culture and with speakers of the language, and it can also facilitate many types of individual instruction. The classroom environment can illustrate that a foreign language is an important part of the curriculum, through bulletin boards, charts, calendars, and other vivid evidence. Even when the early language teacher must travel to several rooms in a day, each classroom should be able to find a place for some evidence of the new language and its culture. Teacher-produced materials and visuals add a personal quality and investment to any lesson, and they are often the most effective of all teaching tools. Equipment and materials necessary to conduct in-class food activities provide for some of the most motivating and memorable of all classroom activities.

Textbook series appropriate for American elementary and middle school language programs are more difficult to find than are locally produced curriculum materials, but they are of great assistance in developing an integrated and articulated program that spans several grade levels. All materials must be carefully chosen and evaluated, with the goals and philosophy of the local program serving as the main criteria. The guidelines suggested in this chapter will assist teachers and supervisors in making choices of materials and curriculum and in communicating with textbook publishers.

FOR STUDY AND DISCUSSION

1. What special advantages might be expected from the use of teacher-made visuals and realia? What are the drawbacks of their use?

2. Choose an item from one of the materials lists and describe four different ways in which you could use it in the early language classroom.

Identify the grade and language level of the children for whom you plan the activities.

3. Choose a textbook series or a teacher-developed curriculum designed for an early language program and evaluate it in terms of the criteria questions found at the end of the textbook section of this chapter.

4. How do the criteria for choosing and evaluating materials for elementary and middle school language classes differ from criteria used in other content areas?

5. One of the exhibitors at a foreign language conference has announced the publication of a new textbook in your language for children in kindergarten through grade six. Write down seven questions you would ask the publisher's representative to help you determine whether or not the series is worth a closer look.

FOR FURTHER READING

The following sources are recommended for additional information about material covered in this chapter. Chapter citations are documented in Works Cited at the end of the volume.

Praktische Ideen für den Deutschunterricht.
Ideas practices para la clase de español.
Idées pratiques pour la classe de français.
Idee pratiche per lezioni d'italiano.

All are available from EMC/Paradigm Publishing, 875 Montreal Way, St. Paul, MN 55102.

14 Bringing Language to Life

Choosing and Creating Classroom Games and Activities

Games and game-like activities are among the most natural means available for developing a context for communication with children. Play is often described as a child's work, and games form a natural part of the child's most important work setting, the classroom. Middle school students are also very responsive to games—in fact, playing with language is a powerful tool no matter what age the learners may be. Games and game-like activities might be credited with carrying the largest role in the acquisition of language in the early language classroom. While some educators make a distinction between games and activities, it is often very difficult to draw a clear line, and the differences between them are far less important than is the impact they have on the motivation and the language acquisition of the children in the class. Many early language teachers have discovered that students regard any well-designed, successful activity that they enjoy as a "game." This chapter treats activities and games as a single category and makes no distinction between them. The suggestions and guidelines presented are applicable to all classroom activities.

The most successful games are very simple, requiring a minimum of explanation and rules. The simple addition of a competitive factor, or an element of mystery or surprise, can convert an otherwise meaningless but necessary practice activity into a game. Most games should flow naturally within the class period from the topics and vocabulary being worked on, and only rarely will they be set apart as major events in themselves.

The most important requirement for a game is that it should be fun for the students to play. Before planning a game activity, the teacher should consider whether the students would enjoy the topic and the game outside the classroom. Some additional guidelines for choosing and using games in the language classroom are detailed in the next section of the chapter.

Guidelines for Games and Activities

1. Choose games or adjust them so that the students need to understand the language and express themselves in it. Then they will realize that the language is useful and they will be motivated to communicate. It is to be expected that the teacher will produce most of the language during the early stages of language acquisition; this is

perfectly natural and acceptable, but the language must play an important part in every game. Some games, such as dominoes and certain board games, include important concepts being covered in general education classes, but they can be played successfully with virtually no use of the target language by the students or the teacher. These games need not be abandoned, however, if the teacher can devise a playing routine or a variation that will necessitate language use in them. If the language is not truly required, however, students will choose to use it only when the teacher is within hearing.

2. Provide maximum opportunity for students to participate. All children should be engaged in the activity all of the time. Some activities, like "Simon Says," are designed so that children who miss are "out," which leaves many children inactive for most of the game. These games can be redesigned to allow for students who are "out" to contribute to the game in a new way, such as by taking turns at giving commands to other children, or to give them a method for reentry into the competition by paying close attention or by completing a special performance of some kind.

3. Organize and score the game so that most of the playing time can be spent communicating in the target language.

4. Add an appealing element of suspense or competition, but structure the game to avoid intense individual competition that could carry over into bad feelings outside the classroom. The healthiest type of competition takes place when teams or groups are evenly matched and have equal opportunity for success. It often works well, when a higher level of competition is desired, to pit the class against the teacher or against an imaginary villain, like the ghost in some computer games. That way the entire class works together to "win," and when the class wins, so does the teacher.

5. Choose a game that is easy to play so that it will move quickly. In most cases short games that can be repeated in several rounds during one class period are preferable to longer games, which may not be completed by the time the language class is over.

6. Stop the game or the activity at a point when the class still wants more, rather than continuing it until interest begins to flag.

7. Do not repeat successful activities, except those designed to be played with several rounds, during the same class or on the following day, even when children request them. Using any specific game sparingly helps to keep it fresh and motivating.

8. Structure activities when possible in the spirit of New Games (Fluegelman 1976, 13), in which *everybody* plays to the level of her or his ability: "Play Hard, Play Fair, Nobody Hurt!"

9. Give games a name, especially if they are likely to be used again in a similar form. Children regard the game as something special if it has a name, and a name makes it easier for them to talk about the game outside of class or to request it at a future time.

10. Incorporate games played in the target culture or in other cultures around the world whenever possible. Several sources for games with global roots are listed at the end of this chapter. The physical education teacher may have suggestions for references on international games and may also be willing to include such games in the physical education curriculum at the teacher's suggestion. Other possibilities for locating games include the following:

- Games books for elementary school teachers, especially those with a theme of games around the world.
- Teacher's manuals for early language textbook series, even in languages other than the ones taught in your school.
- The ERIC database, under the descriptors *FLES Programs and Materials* or *Games.*
- *Learning Languages,* published by the National Network for Early Language Learning.
- Professional journals for early childhood and elementary school teachers, as well as those for language teachers.
- The Ñandu listserv and FLTeach listserv, together with their archives, are rich resources for exchange of games and activities.

Classroom Games and Activities

The games and activities that follow have been gleaned from many sources; they represent only a sampling of the kinds of activities that are possible in an early language classroom. Two types of activities with special value for the early language classroom receive specific attention and suggestions within the chapter: the role of puppets and stuffed animals, and the use of songs.

This collection includes many activities with an emphasis on listening, although games and activities in which children play an active speaking role are also featured. Awareness of the importance of a listening stage is a recent development in the teaching of foreign and second languages, and materials for the early stages of language acquisition are often difficult to find. In games and activities in which children do a minimum of speaking or do not speak at all, it is important for the teacher to surround the activity with meaningful, communicative language. Every game in the early language classroom is a language game; every activity is a setting for language acquisition.

The activities that follow do not include every content for the language classroom. Rather, they are templates that can be used to create a game-like activity to develop concepts or information from any content area or any target culture.

Name Games

Names or Numbers Concentration.   Sit with the students in a circle, if possible, and set up a rhythm, slowly at first, as follows:

   slap, slap (knees)
   clap, clap (hands)
   snap, snap (left hand)
   snap, snap (right hand)

On the left-hand snaps call your own name, and on the right-hand snaps call the name of one of the students. On the next left-hand snaps, have the student call her or his own name and on the right-hand snaps the name of another student. The chain continues until someone misses a turn or loses the rhythm, at which point the teacher begins the game again. When this game is introduced, it is often helpful if you tell students to practice by always responding with the teacher's name on the right-hand snaps for the first few times, until the rhythm and the name-calling have become coordinated. As students increase their confidence and ability and begin to call on one another, you can speed up the rhythm. You can also play with numbers, letters of the alphabet, or any other vocabulary by placing the visual representing each child on the floor in front of her or him.

Another variant for older children who already know one another is "Hollywood Rhythm." Use categories such as animals, countries, foods, and so forth. Students name an item that hasn't been mentioned yet from within the category, without breaking the rhythm.

Spin the Plate.   With children sitting in a circle, if possible, set a metal pie plate on its edge in the center of the group. Spin the plate and call the name of one of the children. If the child reaches the plate and catches it before it stops spinning, the child takes your place. If the child does not reach the plate in time, you take another turn spinning the plate. The game continues, with each successful child taking the role of plate-spinner and calling another child's name, until most or all names have been called at least once. This game can also be played with numbers, colors, or any other set of vocabulary.

Seven-Up.   Here is a variation of a favorite elementary school game: Call seven children to the front of the room, and the rest of the children in the class place heads down on their desks with their eyes closed. The seven children move around the room and each touch one child on the shoulder, after which they return to the front of the room. You can recite (or have the seven children recite in chorus) a routine such as "1, 2, 3, eyes open!" The children whose shoulders were touched take turns guessing which child touched them. If they guess correctly in a single try, they trade places with the child in the front of the room. Children who are not correctly guessed stay in the front of the room for another round.

Chalkboard or Whiteboard Activities

Total Physical Response with Chalk or Marker.   Ask the students to respond to commands such as the following:

- Walk (jump, run, crawl, walk backward) to the board.
- Pick up the _____. (color, chalk, marker)
- Write _____.
- Circle _____.
- Make an x on _____.
- Draw (part of a face, body, and so forth).
- Take the eraser and erase _____.

(This is an especially good activity for giving children practice in remembering a series of commands.)

Chalkboard Monster.   Have a child or two children go to the chalkboard and create a monster by following your directions, preferably using colored chalk. In more advanced situations, the monster might develop from the joint commands of the class. For example, you might say, "Draw a big head; draw an ear," and then ask the class, "Do you want large ears or small ears?" so that students can contribute to the development of the monster in various ways, depending on their language level. If more than one child is at the chalkboard at the same time, it is interesting to compare the efforts of each child in a class discussion, always being careful to avoid comparative judgments.

What's the Weather?   Draw a window on the chalkboard. Direct the children to go to the board and draw the weather in the window as you describe it. (Variation: Use a felt or magnet board and have children choose elements to place in the window.) To activate the language, you might lead a discussion about what time of year this weather represents, whether children like or dislike this kind of weather, and what kinds of activities they enjoy in this weather.

Activities with a Magic Box (Bag, Backpack)

(See directions for making a magic box in Chapter 13.)

1. Remove items from the box, describe them, and have students ask for them.
2. Pull familiar items from the box, revealing a little bit at a time, and have children take turns either guessing each item or describing it.
3. Have students describe and/or guess an item in the box from touch alone.
4. Stuff the box with a number of items; have each student pull out one item and use it as a speech stimulus.
5. Use the box and the items it contains with physical-response activities such as *take, put, give, throw.*
6. Have students pull words or phrases from the box and string them together into a narrative or combine them into a command.
7. Play "I'm going on a trip and I'm taking . . ." with items (or pictures of items) pulled from the box. Each student repeats all previous items before they say their own.
8. Stuff food items—real or artificial—into the box. Have students remove three to five items, construct a menu, and identify the meal.
9. Play "Twenty Questions" about an item or group of items in the box.
10. Place items in the box that suggest a specific person and have students guess who it is as each item is revealed.
11. Place items in the box that represent two different categories, such as water creatures and animal creatures. As students take turns removing the items, they classify them using a Venn diagram.

12. Seat children in a circle. Place a number of familiar items in the magic box and pass it around the circle until a bell rings, the music stops, or some other prearranged signal is given. Have the student holding the box draw out one of the items and identify it. The game proceeds until all the items have been removed. Variation: Place items that were incorrectly identified in the center of the circle. When the box stops, the child holding it has the option of drawing an object from the box or choosing one from the center of the circle. The reward for correct identification is the opportunity to hold the object (and perhaps to play with it) during the course of the game.

Activities with Laminated Circles, Shapes, and Numbers

(See Chapter 13 for directions.)

Total Physical Response Commands
1. For giving commands at the beginning stages of learning, use short specific directions, such as:

Take red!

Touch red!

Give me red!

Sit down on red!

Jump over red!

Jump from red to blue!

Lay red on Mary's head, arm, leg, knee, hand, stomach, et cetera.

Lay red under the chair, in front of the chair, beside, behind, left of, right of, et cetera.

Take the colors of the German, United States, Puerto Rican et cetera, flag, and lay them on the flag.

Make the numbers nineteen, twenty-one, et cetera (by placing two numerals together)

2. *Clock Face:* Lay numbers out in a circle to make a clock face; have children move large, laminated hands to tell time or lie down and make their own arms tell the time.

3. *Number Match:* Pass out a set of numbers from zero to nine to each of two teams (or more, as class size suggests). Call (or have another leader call) a number; the first team whose "number" stands up gets a point; if more than one child stands, the team cannot win a point.

4. *Who Has It?* Use this at the end of an activity, when each child has either a number or a color. Tell the children to lay their number or color in front of them on the floor or hold them up so everyone can see. Set rhythm as for concentration: slap knees, clap hands, snap left fingers, snap right fingers. Ask a question in rhythm; have students answer in rhythm. If they cannot answer, either repeat the question or give the answer.

TEACHER:	Who- has- sev- en?
STUDENTS:	(slap) (clap) Sus- an.
TEACHER:	Loud- er (snap) (snap)
STUDENTS:	(slap) (clap) Sus- an!

This activity also works with using items from the magic box.

Activities with Floor Map (Shower Curtain Map)

(See Chapter 13 for directions for making a shower curtain map.)

1. Using the floor map, direct children to do the following:

- Step from country to country or area to area or lay various parts of their own body on different countries.
- Lay flags on the appropriate countries.
- "Swim" in rivers, lakes, or oceans; "ski" in the mountains, et cetera.
- Jump over rivers or borders.
- Locate capitals.
- Lay maps of political subdivisions on the larger map (as in a jigsaw puzzle).
- Place geographical features such as mountains or major cities or other geographical features on the maps. For example, direct students to put various sizes of colored plastic drinking cups and thick blue yarn on the map in order to indicate the mountains and rivers.
- Place products on the region where they originate.
- Trace routes from place to place using a toy car, boat, or train.

This kind of activity can make geographical and cultural concepts very concrete (see Figure 14.1).

2. Using a geometric grid or randomly placed numbers, children can be directed to:

- step from number to number or shape to shape
- toss beanbags or lay objects on various parts of the board
- perform on the board in response to commands
- lay vocabulary flash cards on various parts of the board
- perform other activities similar to those described for the floor map

Carol Meyer, from Bennington College, uses a shower curtain map for a number of geography activities in her Spanish classes. They would be adaptable to any language, with just a few changes. She posted these ideas to the Ñandu listserv in April 2002:

1. With the map itself you can ask students to go to a certain country, in stocking feet. I find that this is difficult, given the small size of some of the countries, so I prefer activity 2.
2. With the cutouts, I can give the students commands to go, pick up a country, and put it in its place.
3. With the cutouts, ask "What color is Chile?" and so forth.
4. With the cutouts, a student has a country that they describe, and the other students have to guess the country. As an alternative, the rest of the students can play 20 questions about the country the student is hiding (depending on the amount of language that the students have).

FIGURE 14.1   Floor map activity.

5. With the cutouts, give each student a country and have them form Central and South America. They can then describe their relationships using south, north, and so forth.
6. With the cutouts, play "What's missing (from among the cutouts on the map)?"
7. With the cutouts students can compare the sizes of the countries, for example, Country X is twice the size of Country Y. Or you can use language like bigger than, smaller than. The teacher can ask, "How many countries can fit into Argentina, and which ones are they?" Any kind of compare and contrast activity that has the students work with the countries will help to make the content memorable.

8. With the cutouts have the students sort them into categories such as Central America and South America (North America if you include it), countries that speak Spanish and countries that don't, countries from which we import goods, and so forth, depending on the content studied.

Paper and Pencil Activities

Dot-to-Dot Puzzle.   Modify a simple dot-to-dot puzzle by renumbering the dots randomly. Call out the numbers in the prearranged order for students to connect the dots to complete the puzzle. (Note: Be sure you have solved a copy of the puzzle for yourself, so you do not forget which numbers to call and in which order!) Success is measured by whether the completed puzzle looks as it is supposed to look! You can make this activity more challenging by adding several numbered dots to the puzzle that are not used in the completion of the picture.

Variation.   As a reading and writing exercise, write out the numbers in the target language; for example, *uno, tres, ocho.* Students can then solve the puzzle as an independent reading activity.

Monsters.   Give each student a blank piece of paper and have them take out their crayons, pencils, or markers. Direct the children to write their names on one corner of the page and then to draw a head *only.* Then have the children pass their papers a specified number of times to the left or right (or front or back) and tell them to draw another part of the body (or of the face). Keep adding face and body parts and move the papers around after each new part has been drawn. The result is the product of listening comprehension and a series of works of "group art."

Variation.   Have the children take turns telling the class which parts of the anatomy to draw.

List Bingo Game.   Have the students choose five to six words from a list of eight to twelve previously learned vocabulary words written on the chalkboard, an overhead projector, or on a handout. Have the students write the words they have chosen in a list on a piece of paper. Then call out words from the large list in random order and have students cross off the words on their own lists as they are called. The first student to cross out all the words on her or his list is the winner.

Activities with Playing Cards or Small Flash Cards
(Use numbers one to ten only, no jack, queen, or king)

Group children in circles of three to four. Lay one suit of cards with numbers from one to ten faceup in the center of each group. Call a number—the first child to *cover* the number with an open hand keeps it. If two or more children touch the number at the same time, no one gets to take it. The successful child holds the number up for all to see (and for you to check comprehension). Identify who has the most at the end of each round, asking in the target language: "Who has three?" "Who has four?" and give congratulations. As a variation, you can have each group work with two suits of cards, one black and one red. You can then call both numbers and colors. This game can also be played with cards from any other number or color game.

Colors and Shapes Variation.   Glue shapes in various colors on playing cards or notecards, approximately ten to twelve cards for each small group. Lay them faceup in the center of each group of three to five children. Call a color and a shape (it works best if there are at least two colors per shape and at least two shapes per color). The first child to cover the number gets to take it and hold it up (so you can check for comprehension). At the end of the game, count who has the most cards and give congratulations. (This can also be played on Peg-Board, transparency, chalkboard, pocket chart, or masking taped grid.)

Use one red suit and one black suit, each numbered from one to ten. With masking tape, attach matching pictures, flags, numbers, or other information to the *back* of each card—being sure that every card has a match. (It could be a flag and its country name or two of the same flags.) Place cards in four-by-five-inch rows, number side up, in the center of the circle. Have the children take turns around the circle: each child calls for two cards to be turned over, one at a time (one-red, five-black). If the cards match, the child keeps the cards and takes another turn. If not, the cards are turned over again and play goes on to next player. This game can be played with any set of vocabulary items, synonyms, matching words and pictures, opposites, or mathematics operations.

Variation.   The child must name the item on the first card in order to call a second card.

Go Fish.   Have children play in groups of three or four. Each child receives five cards, and the remaining cards are placed in a pile in the middle of the group. The child to the left of the dealer begins by asking for a card from any other player, in the hope of finding a matching card to one in her or his hand. If the player has the card, she or he must give it to the player requesting it, and that player places the pair on the table (or floor) in front of her or him and receives another turn. If not, the player says "Go fish!" (an equivalent phrase in the target language), and the first player draws a card from the pile. If the first player draws the card for which he or she asked, that player lays down the pair and receives another turn. The winner is the player who completes the most pairs.

Variation.   The children seek to accumulate groups of four rather than two. German Quartett or French Jeu de famille games are cultural examples of these games. The teacher can make sets of cards with groups of four, using whatever vocabulary the class needs to work on—for example, four chairs, tables, and so forth if the unit is the home; four hats, shoes, coats, and so forth if the unit is clothing. See suggestions for making these cards in Chapter 13.

Ugly Monster.   This game is played like Old Maid but with an "ugly monster" as the extra card. Any category of vocabulary sets can be used.

Changing the Classroom Environment with Masking Tape

Masking tape can be used to create shapes, games, and imaginary settings on the classroom floor. Children might respond to such commands as, "Jump backward from the triangle to the square!" or "Sit down in the middle of the rectangle!" Human tic-tac-toe, hopscotch, and many other play environments can be created. Masking tape will peel off most floor surfaces, including a carpet, without damaging them, provided the tape is removed promptly.

You might lead the class on an imaginary trip with the help of a large airplane (or boat or train) taped in outline to the floor. Other fantasy environments might include the floor plan of a house, an elevator with "up" and "down" and floor buttons, a map with rivers and mountains indicated. (See Chapter 10 for more details.)

Tic-Tac-Toe.   Use masking tape to create a large tic-tac-toe board on the floor. Make large *X*s and *O*s out of laminated tagboard, about the same size as the giant numbers described above.

Variations.   Many variations are possible. Place different colors or numbers in the squares, and hand out smaller versions to the class. Call a color or number; the child who has it chooses the *X* or the *O* to place in the square, or sits on the square holding the symbol.

Variations on "Safe Tag."   In an open area of the classroom or the gymnasium, outline several rectangles on the floor using masking tape. Within each of these possible "safe zones" place a different color. The person who is "it" must begin and return to a designated spot. The game begins when you (or a child, later) call out "Go to (a color)!" As of that moment, the person who is "it" is free to tag anyone not touching the indicated safe zone. The first person tagged becomes the new "it." As soon as every player is touching the correct safe zone or there is a new "it," call a different color, creating a new "safe zone." The beauty of this fast-paced game is that it demands immediate recognition of vocabulary items.

Variations.   (1) taping different geometric shapes instead of just rectangles to the floor; (2) giving more complex commands, such as "Everyone wearing tennis shoes go to the blue!" or "Hop backward to red!"; (3) substituting numbers for colors and indicating the "safe zone" with numbers or with simple equations; (4) using features of the classroom environment as "safe zones," such as the chalkboard, the door, and so forth.

Games Focusing on Body Parts

Life-Sized Paper Dolls.   You will need the following materials: butcher paper and crayons or markers.

1. Working with one child at a time, instruct each child to lie down on her or his back on a piece of butcher paper and to shut her or his eyes.
2. Trace around the child's body using a marker.

3. Have the children write their names at the top of their outlines.
4. If children are at the pre-writing or pre-reading stage, instruct them with commands such as, "Take your red color crayon and write a number five in the thumb" or "Take your black color and write a seven in the foot."
5. Use these giant paper dolls later for clothing Lotto:
   - Provide each child with an identical number of pieces of clothing, including, for example, pants, socks, hats, and shoes.
   - Call out random commands: "If you have a skirt, put the skirt on your paper doll." See who can be the first child to put all of the clothing on her or his doll by following commands.

Living Statues.   Give commands to one child at a time, such as, "Put your left hand on John's right elbow and kneel on your right knee." Use a number of children (in a small class, the entire group) and build a "living statue" of class members connected to one another. As a final, interesting, and dramatic gesture, take a photograph with an instant camera and display it on the bulletin board. (Be careful to avoid "connections" that are potentially embarrassing, and avoid placing children together who have a strong antipathy for one another.)

It can be even more effective to have the rest of the students, who are not in the picture, be the picture takers with imaginary cameras.

Shell Game from Cameroon.   Have one student leave the room and another student lie down while classmates outline that student's shape with shells or stones (large uncooked pasta shells work very well). Direct the activity with such suggestions as "Put the shells around the left arm, the right leg, the head." The returning student must guess which student is outlined by the shells or the rocks. If you desire more language use, give the student the opportunity to ask a limited number of questions in order to improve the chances of a correct guess.

Body Collage.   Cut individual arms, legs, eyes, noses, mouths, and ears from magazines so there are many options for each child. Have children ask for their choice of individual body parts in the target language. They then glue them to construction paper and draw in their own heads, hair, torsos, and clothing. You or the students may label the creations; or give the students captions written on self-stick labels and have them select the appropriate label for each body part.

Variation.   As an alternative version for a comprehension emphasis, direct children to choose different body parts one at a time.

Balloon Bounce.   Give each child a balloon; for younger children the balloon should be already blown up, while for older children blowing up the balloon could be part of the chain of commands used. Have the children toss the ball into the air on command, then continue to bounce it in the air, using various parts of the body as you direct: "Hit the balloon with the head, with the knee, with the elbow, with the back, with the little finger of the right hand." There is almost no sound from the children, so the listening opportunity is excellent. There is no winner or loser—the challenge of keeping the balloons in the air is sufficient.

Finger Twister.   Marie Consuelo Lopez shared an interesting game for practicing colors and fingers on the Ñandu listserv:

> I pass out color wheels and tell the students that we will be playing *"twister de dedos."* The students are immediately interested in this game. I begin by introducing the names of the different fingers in Spanish and then explain that I will tell them which color to put each finger on. The object of the game is to be able to put all fingers on all of the colors and keep them there. I begin by telling them to put their *pulgar* (thumb) on *rojo* (red). The students keep their thumb on the red section while placing other fingers on the sections as they are instructed to do so. We play the game several times and each time I speed the commands up. By the last time I am giving chain commands rather than individual commands. While playing the game I observe that the students' affective filters have gone down and they are focused more on the physical challenge than on the language.

Activities Related to Curriculum Content

Geography of Central America.   Julie Barros described these activities for fourth grade students on the Ñandu listserv. They are a good illustration of the idea that any of the games in this chapter can be used to bring any of the subject content areas to life.

> I just finished teaching the countries of Central America. We played, and still play, several games using a colored map of Central American countries (drawn on a shower curtain and colored in) labeling the countries first so that students learn where they are. Then I drew blank maps of Central America on index cards and colored in one country. I asked *¿Donde vives?* and the student had to stand on the country that they received and say *"Vivo en . . ."* Then we take the labels off and see how many the students can remember. The cards were also color coded with the shower curtain so that we could give hints like . . . *Nicaragua es azul. La Republica Dominicana es amarillo y es parte de una isla.*
>
> We played a game using a song to the tune "This is the way we wash our clothes": *asi asi camino, camino, camino* (This is how I walk), *asi asi camino por america central* (This is how I walk in Central America).
>
> We walk around the map singing this song until I clap. Then they stop and I pick a student and say "(child's name) camina por Honduras." The student then has to walk through Honduras.
>
> We also played *"¿Qué pais tengo?"*. We put the shower curtain map on the board and one student picks a country out of the bag. The students have to ask yes or no prepositional questions to find out what country it is. Of course I listed the questions on the board and went over them first. I used: *Está encima de, está abajo de, al lado de,* and also the locations east, west, north, and south (in Spanish) (also, *¿Es una isla?*).
>
> We also divided into three teams and had a timed race to see who could label the countries fastest. They loved that one too!

This same game could easily work with Francophone Africa, or the countries of the European Union.

The Compass Rose.   Kathy Siddons teaches the Compass Rose in her Spanish classes with a lot of imagination, and she shared this strategy on the Ñandu listserv.

In our district, *la rosa naútica* is taught in third grade in the regular classroom curriculum—not second. Therefore, I find that once the regular classroom teacher has covered the material, the reintroduction is very easy. My goal is to have the children experience the concept of north/south/east/west through a simulation.

To review the directionals, I place four children as markers, holding signs for north/south/east/west in the correct spots according to the real compass—which takes some thinking as I am in eleven different classrooms daily in two schools! I display the Spanish flag and use Almirante Cristóbal Colón and his sailors as the main characters. Colón marches in with great authority, holding a telescope under his arm and wearing a small Italian flag, and greets his *marineros*. Then he says, *"Marineros, miran al norte."* The children as sailors turn in that direction and receive commands from him to turn to the other directions. The children learn *"noroeste"* too. The children love it and beg to take a turn being Colón.

I transition from this simulation about directionals, to a similar scenario where the sailors experience different weather and physical conditions on board the *carabelas*. When it rains a lot, Colón says, *"¡Marineros, llueve mucho! Hay mucha agua en la carabela!"*, and they have to bail water. When the weather is good, the sailors raise the sails and say, *"Hace buen tiempo. Almirante, tengo hambre."* When it is hot, they cry, *"¡Hace mucho calor! ¡Almirante, tengo sed!"* When it is foggy, *"¡Hay mucha neblina! ¡Tengo miedo!"*, someone rings a bell. When it is very windy, *"¡Hace mucho viento!"*, the sailors hold on to the sides of the boat and pantomime being blown around. The children really ham it up here, of course.

The game character of this activity could be intensified by using cards or dice to change the weather arbitrarily on every turn.

Science and Art Activities.   Sara Palacio has used this project in grades one through four to help teach the science concept that water and oil don't mix. She shared it on the Ñandu listserv.

Marbling and Silhouettes Art Project
   a. I buy two different colors of oil-based paint (I've used blue and green). Pour some of each color into a shallow pan covered with about 1–2 inches of water. Swirl the paint with a stick; it should float on top of water. Place a white piece of paper gently on top of water. Pull off. And you should have a cool swirly design. Let dry.
   b. Have students cut out 3–4 different animal shapes on black construction paper—ocean animals whose names they have learned.
   c. Glue on top of the marbled paper. You now have an ocean scene! This project can stand on its own, be framed by black construction paper, or serve as a cover to an Ocean Portfolio or Ocean Alphabet book!

I usually follow up the art activity with an Oil Spill Activity. I get some used motor oil and put it in some tubs, and I gather a variety of items found around the ocean: egg (hard-boiled!), feathers, sand, fur (fake), hair, dirt, leaves, bushes, wood, and so on. Then the students work in small groups and test to see what happens to the items in the oil. It's a great vocabulary builder and motivational as well.

Action Games

Command Chairs.   Give many commands in a row, sending children as a group all over the room touching doors, walls, jumping, and so forth. In the meantime remove one chair, so there is one less chair than there are students. When the command "Sit down on your chair" comes, the students scramble for a chair and the one left standing is "out." The game goes on until the last person is "out." After the students are "out," they can assist you in giving commands to the rest of the class.

A Game for Hands—and Plurals.   Silvia Pontaza posted this activity, adapted from the Global Child program, on the Ñandu listserv:

> To practice plurals, have students trace their hands on a piece of paper. Make sure both hands are traced on one side of the paper. Ask them to put their hands on the hands that are traced on the paper. When you say *"La mano"* they hold one hand up. Then you say *"El papel"* they put the hand back on the paper. Then you say *"Las manos"* and they have to hold both hands up. Always to go back to the normal position (hands on hands traced) you say something like *"el papel,"* or *"abajo,"* or whatever works for you. You play this game saying *la mano la mano el papel las manos . . .* They love when you try to trick them, and they listen for the difference when the word is plural (you can add *arriba la mano, arriba las manos, cierra el ojo,* or *cierra los ojos* and so forth).
>
> Another option is to play Duck, Duck Goose. Students are in a circle with both hands behind them. The person walking around touches each child's hand saying *la mano, la mano . . .* When he or she touches both hands, saying *las manos,* that's when it's time to chase.

Clothing Race.   Have the children form two (or more) teams. Give each team a pile of clothing, the names of which have been learned in the class. Command the first person on each team to put on selected items of clothing. The list and order of clothing changes each time. The team members can help by reminding the contestant of items they have forgotten, but only in the target language. The first contestant to put on all the right clothing (and only the right clothing) wins a point for the team. (It is helpful if all the clothing is a little too large for the participants, so it can be easily put on and removed.) Lists of clothing can grow longer with successive rotations, to stretch the listening memory.

Story in Third Person.   As a variation on a fantasy (see Chapter 10), give each person a role in a narrative, preferably with a prop for each character. As you read the story, the students act out their parts. If there is dialogue, the characters simply repeat their lines. This is most effective if there is considerable action and emotion involved, such as laughing or crying. (This technique can also be used with a familiar story, but it is perhaps most effective when only the teacher knows what will happen next, so everyone has to listen carefully.)

Color Walk, Number Walk.   This is an adaptation of the old carnival Cake Walk. Place laminated colored circles or numbers in a circular pattern on the floor and have one student stand on each circle or number. Turn on the cassette player or record player (or music keyboard) and have the students walk around the circle until the music stops, when they will stop on the circle or number nearest them. Draw a color or a number out of a box and ask the class, "Who is standing on ___?" The student standing by that color or number wins and receives applause. You can set up more than one "cake walk" in the room so that all of the children can play at one time. As a variation, pictures or written vocabulary words could be used instead of numbers and colors.

Numbers Game from Austria.   The children form a circle around a child chosen as "it." That child is blindfolded and stands; the other children are seated. Give each child a number, beginning with one. When the child who is "it" calls out two of the numbers, the children who have these numbers must trade places immediately and silently. Should their movements be detected by the child who is "it," she or he must try to catch one of the children and exchange places. If their movements go undetected and the two reach their new places safely, everyone in the circle claps hands (or calls out a predetermined phrase in the target language), and whoever is "it" tries once again by calling two other numbers.

Variation.   Instead of numbers, use names of animals, colors, foods, or other current vocabulary.

Going Fishing.   Place numbers, colors, or pictures of vocabulary on small paper fish with paper clips attached to them. Children "catch" their fish with a fishing pole that has a string and a magnet attached to the end. If the child names the number, color, or picture, that child may keep the fish; if not, the fish goes back into the "pond."

Variation.   Attach individual words or familiar commands to the fish. If the child can label the correct object with the word or perform the command, that child may keep the fish. Or, if reading and speaking are well established, the child may repeat the word or give the command to another child in order to keep the fish.

Follow the Footpath.   Place footprints in a variety of colors and sizes around the room, forming a path that the children can follow. Have the children proceed along the path by placing their own feet on one print at a time, naming the color, and then proceeding to the next print. The goal is to follow the path to its destination.

Variations.   (1) Place pictures or symbols for familiar vocabulary on the footprints and tell the children they must name the vocabulary before proceeding further; (2) Point out prints of various sizes and have the children respond with their guesses as to who might have left such a print: the principal, a bear, a well-known young sibling of one of the children, and so forth. The teacher might ask, "Do you think this print was made by the principal? By a bear? By Mr. Jacobson or by Tommy? By a lion or by a mouse?"

Typewriter.   Have students holding letter flash cards arrange themselves to spell words, or have students holding numeral flash cards arrange themselves to form several-digit numbers. Distribute the flash cards to a group of students and then call out the word or the number they are to form.

Pierre's Clothes.   Have several children stand in front of the class, each of them holding a picture from a group of related vocabulary items. Begin the game by saying, "Pierre is going to school, but he doesn't have any cap." The child holding the cap responds by saying, "Oh, yes, he has a cap, but he doesn't have any shoes (picture held by another child in the group)." The child holding the shoes continues the game using the same pattern, and the game continues until one child misses after being called on or until a player mentions an item that no one has a picture of. If a child misses, he or she names another child from the class to take her or his place in the group in the front. The class may play this game with any type of vocabulary by changing the situation established in the "frame" sentence.

Calisthenics and Fitness Path.   Use commands to lead children in regular calisthenics movements, using many of the same exercises that they perform in physical education classes, if possible. This makes a good change of pace when children become restless, and as they become more verbal they may wish to lead the exercises themselves.

On the playground, in the gymnasium, or in a nearby park, if there is one, prepare exercise stations at various points around a walking path, using illustrations to help students understand what they are to do in each case. For the first several times, lead the class around the course, directing the students to perform the activity for a specified number of times at each station. The stations need not all be typical of an authentic fitness path. Some possible stations might include the following:

- Do ten jumping jacks.
- Touch your toes six times.
- Do four windmills.
- Join hands and form a circle.
- Take four large steps forward.
- Raise your hands high.
- Take six small steps backward.

Variation.   Students may wish to prepare stations themselves, in small groups, and take responsibility for giving the directions when the class arrives at their station. With older children, these stations might imitate activities from the Olympic games.

Aerobic Dance.   Obtain an aerobic dance record or tape in the target language, preferably one with directions that are clearly pronounced and easy to understand. First teach the children the actions without music, and then spend a few minutes every few days doing the aerobic dance exercises with the music.

Ducks Fly/Birds Fly.   Have the players stand in aisles or beside their chairs. Have the person who is "it" (you may be "it") stand in front, facing the group, and call out "Ducks fly!" "Birds fly!" "Horses fly!" and so forth. When whoever is "it" names an animal that does fly, the players go through the motions of flying, raising their arms high above their heads and lowering them to their sides. When whoever is "it" names an animal that does not fly, they must not "fly." Anyone who "flies" when a non-flying animal is named, or anyone who does not fly when a flying animal is named, becomes "it" (or gives a forfeit).

Yarn Games.   Hang very long strands of yarn in a variety of colors from a hook in a corner to be used when there are a few minutes to spare or as a central activity. Have children work individually or in small groups on the floor to make figures such as these:

- a circle, square, or triangle
- the numeral five, eight, or nine

- a dog, horse, or lion (or "make an animal" and students can guess which animal was made)
- a map of a familiar place
- a boy, girl, man, or woman

Use these figures for physical response activities such as "Jump into the circle"; "Put your left foot in the triangle"; and "Jump backward over the eight."

Variation.   You can make similar figures on the floor or have students use jump ropes as well as yarn. The same types of activities can be performed.

Scrambled Eggs.   In this activity the students exchange conversation with one student at a time. Once the conversation has been exchanged, the student who has initiated the conversation must sit in the second student's seat. The second student then must go to find a third student, initiate the same conversational exchange, and sit down in the third student's seat once the exchange is finished. The third student then finds another student, and so on. The activity is completed when each student is sitting in someone else's seat.

Variation.   Three or four students begin initiating conversations at once so that several students are talking at the same time and the activity progresses at a faster pace.
    The conversational exchange could be on any topic. Here is an example:

First student
1. Hello my name is _____.
    My favorite _____ is _____.
    What's your favorite _____?

Second student
2. My favorite _____ is _____.

Bear Hunt.   Sit in front of the class and narrate the following sequence in the target language, accompanying each statement with an appropriate motion. Have children copy the motions throughout. With each retelling, you might change the order or add new complications, in order to maintain suspense and surprise. Eventually the children will want to repeat the statements, echoing you, and some may even volunteer to lead the bear hunt.

"Let's go on a *bear hunt!*"
"Everybody ready?" (Class responds "Yes!" or "Yes, ready!")
"Let's go!"
"Look at the *big* woods!" (Make hand gesture for *big,* point to visual of woods.)
"We can't go *around* it!" (Make hand gesture for *around.*)
"We can't go *over* it!" (Make hand gesture for *over.*)
"We have to go *through* it!" (Make hand gesture for *through,* or straight ahead.)
(Slap hands on legs rhythmically to represent *walking* through the woods.)
"Look at the *tall* grass!" (Make hand gesture for *tall*; point to visual.)
"We can't go *around* it!" (Make hand gesture.)

"We can't go *over* it!" (Make hand gesture.)

"We have to go *through* it!" (Make hand gesture.)

(Rub hands together rhythmically, fingers pointing forward, to represent walking through the tall grass.)

"Look at the *big* lake!" (Make hand gesture for *big,* point to visual.)

"We can't go *around* it!" (Make hand gesture.)

"We can't go *over* it!" (Make hand gesture.)

"We have to go *through* it!" (Make hand gesture.)

(Move arms rhythmically in a swimming motion.)

"Look at that *tall* tree!" (Make hand gesture; point to visual.)

"Let's climb it!" (Pantomime hand-over-hand climbing motion.)

"Look for the bear!"

(Pantomime looking, hand over eyes, and moving head slowly from side to side.)

"Do you see a bear?" (Class responds, "No!" or "No, no bear!")

"Climb down the tree!" (Pantomime.)

"Look at the thick vines/bushes!" (Make hand gesture; point to visual.)

"We can't go *around* them!" (Make hand gesture.)

"We can't go *over* them!" (Make hand gesture.)

"We have to go *through* them!" (Make hand gesture.)

(Do rhythmic motion with arms, pushing vines or bushes aside.)

"Look! I see a cave!" (Make dramatic pointing motion.)

"Let's go inside!" (Pat cheeks with mouth open to get hollow sound.)

"It's cold [hug arms and shiver] and dark." (Pass hands over eyes.)

"Let's feel around with our hands." (Make groping motions with hands in all directions.)

"I feel something!" (Touch tentatively, withdraw hand, touch again.)

"It's furry!" (Stroke as with an animal.)

"And wet!" (Withdraw hand quickly.)

"IT'S A BEAR!" (Pantomime shock and horror.)

(Pantomime each of the actions from above in the reverse order, quickly, as the narration proceeds.)

"Run out of the cave!"

"Run through the vines/bushes!"

"Climb up the tree!"

"Look around!"

"Is that the BEAR?"

"Climb down the tree!"

"Swim the lake—fast!"

"Run through the tall grass!"

"Run through the woods!"

"We're home!" (Relax and slouch in the chair.)

"Lock the door!"

Reading Action Chain.   This activity provides silent reading practice in a communicative setting. Give each student a card describing an action they are to perform and the action they will observe that triggers their response. (An example of a series of such cards follows.) Instruct students not to show their card to anyone else, to listen and watch very carefully, and to wait to start their action until at least two seconds after the preceding action has been completed. The object of the game is to proceed through the entire series without making mistakes and without leaving anyone out.

You will need to have a list of the actions in the correct order so that if the chain is broken, you will know what went wrong. If the chain breaks, the entire sequence starts over from the beginning, and the suspense grows.

This activity is easy to create, although it appears complicated; and it can be tailored to the personalities and special characteristics of each individual class and classroom. Write commands on three-by-five-inch notecards, one command on the bottom half of each card; make enough cards so that there is one card for each member of the class. Place the cards in an interesting sequence, including a beginning, an end, and surprises. Then write the first half of each card in the form of a subordinate clause referring to the card just preceding it (see below). Type out the directions for reference during the game and for future use, mix the cards, and distribute them for the game. You can make the game more complicated and longer if you make two cards for each student in the class. This game is very flexible and can be adapted to any thematic unit.

If students have good writing skills, they often enjoy working in groups to create their own games. Group one might write the first five commands for the game and give a copy of its final command to group two. Group two uses that command as the cue for the first command in its series, then give a copy of their final command to group three, and so on, until the commands of all the groups are linked into a complete chain.

Here is an example of a master plan for a reading action chain:

- After the teacher says "Begin," stand up and say "Good morning."
- After someone says "Good morning," go to the chalkboard and draw a triangle.
- After someone draws a triangle on the board, clap your hands slowly four times.
- After someone claps her or his hands four times, jump to the teacher's desk and back to your seat.
- After someone jumps to the teacher's desk and back to her or his seat, count backward from five to one.
- After someone counts backward from five to one, say "Blast off!" (appropriate target language equivalent) very loudly.
- After someone says, "Blast off!", stand up, turn around two times, and sit down.
- After someone stands up, turns around two times, and sits down, turn off the lights.

- After someone turns *off* the lights say, "It's dark in here."
- After someone says "It's dark in here," turn *on* the lights.
- After someone turns *on* the lights, go to the teacher and shake hands.
- After someone shakes hands with the teacher, go to the chalkboard and write the numbers one to ten under the triangle.
- After someone writes the numbers one to ten on the chalkboard, jump four times beside your desk.
- After someone jumps four times beside her or his desk, get up, go to the pencil sharpener, and sharpen your pencil.
- After someone sharpens her or his pencil, go to the board and erase numbers one to five.
- After someone erases numbers one to five from the board, meow like a cat.
- After someone meows like a cat, say "Stop that!"
- After someone says "Stop that!", erase the triangle and numbers six to ten from the board.
- After someone erases the triangle and numbers six to ten from the board, say "That's all—good job."

Guessing Games

What's Missing.   Place any number of objects, animals, colors, and so forth on a tray and make sure that all the students have a chance to see the contents of the tray clearly. Let them study what is there and explain that you will remove something and that they must guess what it is. Remove one item and hide it while the children's eyes are closed. Use a cover cloth for "peekers" (and to add a touch of drama). Repeat with a different item. Adapt the game to desired vocabulary.

Overhead Projector Variations: Place small items with a clearly identifiable silhouette on the overhead projector. Turn off the projector, remove an item, and turn it on again. Have the children guess what is missing. Or make color or black-and-white transparencies of pictures or words. Cut them up and do the same activity by removing one item.

With any of these variations, students love to have the chance to move items around on the overhead projector themselves.

Hot and Cold.   One student leaves the room and something is hidden in the classroom. The student returns and must find the hidden object. The rest of the class gives clues as to the location of the object. When the student is near the object they say "hot" and when the student is far away from the object they say "cold" (or anything else you decide.)

Variations.   Have the children count slowly, or repeat the name of the hidden item, or repeat a rhyme or other memorized material as a group. When whoever is "it" comes nearer to the hidden object, they recite louder; when that person moves away from the object, they recite more softly.

I'm Thinking Of . . .   Begin the game by saying, in the target language, "I'm thinking of a child in the third row." The children guess the names of children in that row, saying in the target language, "Is it Juan? Is it Marie? Is it Fritz?" until they guess the correct child. Continue with another child. (The game can include more language if you choose from the whole class and describe a student a little at a time until the class guesses who it is. Of course, you will start with details that many students share and withhold the clear identifiers until the end.)

You may play this game with clock times, numbers, objects in the classroom, cities in the target culture, or other suitable vocabulary. Examples of starter statements are: "I'm thinking of a time to meet my friend. What time is it?" "I'm thinking of a number between seven and thirty. What number is it?" "I'm thinking of a city in South America to visit on my vacation. What city is it?"

Variation.   The student who makes the correct guess becomes the leader for the next round.

Game variation.   Students in small groups can develop descriptions of class members not in their group.

How Many Do I Have in My Hand?   Play this game with beans, buttons, seeds, marbles, candy-covered chocolates, coins from the target culture, or any other object that comes in handfuls. Reach into a container and take a number of the objects into your hand (not the one you write with), asking "How many ___s do I have in my hand?" The children guess the number and you write the guesses on the chalkboard. After the children have guessed ten or twelve numbers, you and the students count the objects together and determine if anyone guessed the exact number—or who made the closest guess.

Variation.   Play the game with a known number of items in the hand. With each guess the leader tells whether the guess is "more than" or "less than" the correct number. This adds the element of logical thinking to the game.

Shoe Guessing Game.   Blindfold one child who is "it" (or simply have her or him close eyes). Then individual children from the class come up to whoever is "it" and allow him or her to feel their shoes. After feeling each shoe, he or she guesses who the person is by asking, in the target language, "Is your name ___?" Variations include having children switch shoes or having them bring in a big, funny pair of shoes.

ESP Guessing Game.   Penny Fields shared this guessing game on the Ñandu listserv:

> The ESP Game is something I got from someone on either this or another listserv, so I will not take credit for it. It is a good game for reviewing different vocabulary. Since I have small picture flash cards for all the units I teach, I just use those. To play, your class should be in groups of four students. You start with a category of vocabulary, for example colors. Sight unseen you select one of the flash cards and set it aside. Give the students just a short time to decide what color they think the card is. I usually have six groups so I number 1–6 on the board. In turn, you ask each group to report their choice. It is OK for several groups to have chosen the same thing. I write their choice on the board, under their number. When all groups have reported, I reveal the card and give a point to the group or groups who were correct. If no one guessed correctly, no points are awarded. We usually do several rounds with the same vocabulary and then change topics. At the end of the game you count up points for each group and the group with the most points has the best ESP (extrasensory perception).

Hide and Seek in the School—A Version of CLUE. Penny Fields also described this guessing game on the Ñandu listserv. She also gives several stages of activities that work up to the game itself.

> I also teach a unit on places in the school to 3rd graders. My students love to hide a person in a room and work with a partner to guess where he is. I have prepared a sheet with the rooms of the school that we teach (about 7 or 8) and have 2 versions, one with the words and one without. In the early stages, I give them the one with the words and they each put the paper behind their folder and hide the figure of a boy or girl. They take turns guessing—¿*Está en el gimnasio* (is he/she in the gym)? or ¿*Está en la biblioteca* (is he/she in the library)? To tie in our clothing items I will put one clothing item (a small flash card) in a room (behind one of the rooms on a poster in the front of the room). The kids close their eyes while I hide the item and then they must guess where it is.
>
> But the one that they really like is a version of "Clue." I have prepared a sheet with the pictures of the school people at the top, the pictures of the rooms in the middle, and the articles of clothing at the bottom. Then we play. Each student has a sheet. I pick a small flash card from each category and put them in envelopes on the chalkboard tray. Then the kids have to give me a sentence, i.e. *La profesora está en el cuarto de baño con los pantalones.* (The teacher is in the bathroom with the trousers.) The kids have piles of chips and they cover the incorrect pictures. This keeps them from repeating items already given. If one of the items is correct, I display it on the chalkboard. We keep going until the "mystery" is solved.

New Games Activities

People to People.
1. Establish a rhythm and have the students snap or clap the beat, as you say four times, "people [snap] to people [snap]" (translate into desired language).
2. Call out "hand [snap] to hand [snap]" four times.
3. Have each student find a partner and place one hand on the partner's hand, repeating the action four times in the rhythm you set.
4. Return to "people to people" and have the students clap and move around four more times.
5. Call out another body parts combination (elbow to elbow, nose to nose, knee to knee) and have the students match up with a new partner. The game continues until all the body parts have been practiced, in a variety of combinations. Be careful not to suggest combinations that will embarrass the students (see Figure 14.2).

Quick Lineups. Have the children line up by month of birthday, height, color of shirt, pants, shoes, hair, and so forth.

Animal Calls. Give the children the name of an animal whose "call" they have learned, with two children for each animal. They find their partners by making the animal sound, and then complete a language task. This could also be done by having students sing a familiar song or say a familiar phrase and form groups with all of those saying or singing the same thing.

FIGURE 14.2   New Games—People to People.

Board Games

Teacher-created board games are an enjoyable option for reviewing many aspects of language learning. Any simple children's board game can serve as a model, with circles or squares winding around the board from a starting point to a destination. Players advance with the throw of a die, or according to directions on cards. Some game boards may also be downloaded from the Internet. Here are two descriptions of teacher-created board games that were shared on the Ñandu listserv.

Jean Pacheco uses this board game with very young students:

> One of the games that I use with kindergarteners is the game Waggles. Each child has a game board that has been run off on cardstock and laminated. The game board shows a worm. They work in partners and each group of two has a die. The partners take turns throwing the die and saying the number shown in the target language. Then the partner covers that number on her or his worm with a unifix cube. Some numbers are repeated several times on the worm. If the number on the die is already covered on the worm, the player loses the turn. The first partner to cover up all of the numbers on their worm is the winner. This is a good way to practice the numbers 1–6.

Bettina Hoar describes this math and numbers game for older students:

> For the 4th graders at my school we use *"la serpiente de los números"* [see Figure 14.3]. You can use it in different ways: for listening comprehension, read out pre-selected numbers

and students put them in the boxes and see who gets the final tally correct. At the beginning of the year, we just did the numbers 0–20, but later we go up to the hundreds. You can also change the plus and minus signs to multiplication and division (it gets much more complicated, though). Other days, the kids pick numbers out of a hat and have to say the number (at first, they then show the number to the class, but later the kids have to rely on their friend's pronunciation).

Making a Game Board. Kathy Siddons offered some good advice on the Ñandu listserv:

When I create a new game I start work on a blank sheet of $8\frac{1}{2} \times 11''$ white paper. I sketch things out first with a light pencil and then I go over the pencil outlines with a narrow black marker, using a Wite-Out pen as needed to make things perfect. Sometimes I use graph paper with those light blue lines if I really want things to line up exactly by hand. Then I photocopy the final black and white sheet. Then I color in the outlines well and add colorful clip art wherever needed to jazz things up and make it interesting for young children. (Sometimes I am able to complete everything with Microsoft Word and the "AutoShapes" features with color added.)

I then go to a retail copy store and get several copies made, enlarged to $11'' \times 17''$. This size fits nicely on a large piece of oaktag (lightweight poster paper). I use rubber cement for "glue," let it dry, and then laminate before the children use them. I make enough boards so that there are small groups of children (best size of the group is three) at each game board. One child sits in front of the game board and the other two are on the right and left sides of the game board so everyone can see clearly. I try to use small manipulatives that complement the game theme for the individual game pieces that the children move around. But the children's real favorites are small plastic fruits and animals and "plain old beans or buttons."

However, before the game is played by everyone, I devote class time to having a minidemo with a small, hand-picked group of children surrounded by the rest of the class. And I use www.puzzlemaker.com to make exercises to reinforce the necessary vocabulary and symbols that were introduced beforehand, several days before the actual "game day." ("Puzzlemaker" now allows teachers to "file" their created exercises for access later.)

In-Class Food Activities

Experiences with food customs and with preparing food reflecting the target culture provide vivid context and motivation for language use. An ideal early language setting will offer access to a kitchen in which food can be prepared with maximum involvement of the students. If no kitchen is available, many food activities can take place in the classroom itself with a minimum of equipment; for example, making sugar popcorn for students in French and German classes or making a French breakfast with French bread and unsalted butter or with a croissant and hot chocolate drunk out of bowls. German or French language classes might make cheese fondue with buttermilk and Swiss cheese in an electric fondue pot. Crepes are always a favorite with French classes. Spanish classes might prepare tacos, Spanish omelets, or fried plantains. Japanese and Chinese classes could make rice or noodle dishes.

NOMBRE:_____   FECHA:_____

La serpiente de los números:

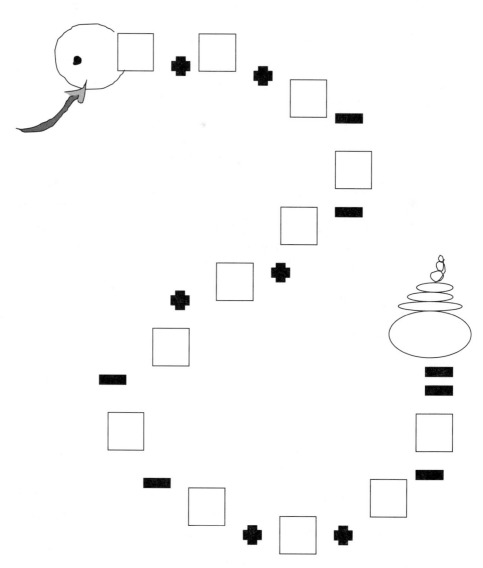

FIGURE 14.3   La serpiente de los números. *Source:* Reprinted by permission of Bettina Hoar.

Food activities add real spark to classes and do not have to require a great deal of class time. For example, crepes for an entire French class can be made ahead of time and kept warm in a Crock-Pot or reheated in a microwave or an electric frying pan; you can prepare just a few during the actual class itself. The teacher can demonstrate all the steps while the students pantomime the actions. (Valuable class time is saved when students do not have to wait while each individual crepe is fried.)

Before planning any food activity, it is essential to have parent permission, in case some child has a dangerous allergy or is diabetic.

Useful Materials for Food Activities
Paper plates
Plastic cutlery
Plastic or paper bowls, cups
Napkins
Electric frying pan
Popcorn popper
Electric fondue pot
Electric coffee maker or hot pot (for heating water)
Crepe maker

A Potpourri of Additional Games and Activities

Common Games
Relay races
Charades
Spelling bee
Hangman
Mystery guest
Twenty questions
Auction
Simon says

Miscellaneous Activities
Go on a treasure hunt, scavenger hunt.
Draw favorite foods on paper plates.
Draw and cut out items for store.
Draw family members.
Draw a community map and label it.
Participate in a play with stick puppets or props.
Do folk dancing.
Make simulated target country currency.
Make rubbings of coins from the target culture.
Make murals.

Make picture dictionaries.

Plan a menu.

Collect simple recipes for culturally appropriate foods.

Cook specialties from the target culture.

Go on a field trip.

Write a class poem.

Dress dolls in native costumes.

Model animals or other figures with clay.

Make clocks.

Make paper bag puppets, dolls, and/or masks.

Draw faces on paper plates to show feelings.

Make mobiles on many topics: five senses, food groups, pets, family.

Make a home or school floor plan.

Pantomime feelings, illnesses.

Make or wear costumes from other countries to learn about clothing.

Make dioramas in a shoebox.

"Shop" from a target language catalogue.

Using Puppets in the Early Language Classroom

There are few teaching aids in the elementary school as versatile and appealing as puppets and stuffed animals. Puppets can take on the role of personalities otherwise not present in the classroom, such as an adult male if the teacher is female, a person who is much older or younger than members of the class, a foreign visitor, a pet, or a special friend to all. A puppet can serve as an alter ego for the teacher, performing exaggerated or foolish actions that the teacher can react to or build on. Puppets can become the second fluent speaker in a conversational exchange, modeling the kind of interaction that the students can someday hope to achieve. Sometimes a puppet becomes the "difficult student" who can't do anything right, or who repeatedly gets into trouble by forgetting to obey the rules. These personalities make every class member feel proud of what they know and how they behave, and the puppet misbehavior gives the teacher a chance to model the rules in a very effective way— and the consequences of breaking them.

Because puppets can be so colorful and often have such distinctive personalities, they provide the ideal subject for descriptions that go beyond simple clothing, size, and colors to include disposition, family, and imagined background. The puppet can also take on the role of teacher, modeling the process of role reversal for the class and encouraging the students to try being the teacher. While the puppet is the teacher, the actual teacher can demonstrate actions or behaviors that will later be expected from the class (see Figure 14.4).

A puppet is an ideal foil for many minidramas that help to create a meaningful classroom context. One favorite puppet character, a colorful frog with a tongue that can be made to pop out of its opened mouth, helps to teach a class to say "please" in the following situation:

TEACHER: (holds up frog as if talking very seriously to it) "Show us your tongue, Mr. Frog!"

FIGURE 14.4 Puppets are a useful tool.

FROG: (shakes its head)

TEACHER: (pleadingly) "Please?"

FROG: (shakes head)

TEACHER: (more emphatically) "Please?"

FROG: (shakes head vehemently)

TEACHER: (even more urgently) "Please? PLEASE?"

FROG: (shakes head almost violently)

TEACHER: (conspiratorially to class) "*You* say please." (Implying, "Maybe he'll listen to *you*.")

CLASS: "Please!"

FROG: (shakes head less emphatically)

TEACHER: (to class, in a stage whisper) "Say please—louder."

CLASS: "Please!"

FROG: (shakes head again)

TEACHER: (to class, in a stage whisper) "Say please twice."

CLASS: "Please, please!"

FROG: (pauses, looks at the class, shows the tongue)

TEACHER: (to frog, beaming) "Thank you, Mr. Frog!"

In any such exchange it is always important for the teacher to play the "ham," over-acting from beginning to end.

Students, as well as teachers, enjoy working with puppets and bringing their personalities to life. In early stages, the desire to hold a puppet or a stuffed animal can motivate even a very shy student to tell the teacher or a classmate, "Please give me the frog." In one popular activity, the teacher draws puppets, stuffed animals, and other items from a magic box or from a large bag and hands them to students who volunteer to hold them. When it turns out that there are not enough items to go around, the children are invited to request them from one another, using the phrase the teacher has already used dozens of times in class to collect objects after a circle activity: "Please give me the _____." A lively exchange of puppets and animals inevitably results, all triggered by language use.

In certain activities the puppet can "take the place" of the student, just as sometimes a puppet takes the teacher's place. Many students who are hesitant about speaking in class will do so much more easily if they are speaking through the new personality of a puppet, especially if the puppet has an established classroom personality to maintain and if all class members are familiar with the routines in which the puppets take part. Some class periods might begin with the call for volunteers (in the target language, of course): "Who would like to be Mr. Frog today? Who would like to be Schnick-Schnack, the witch?" As children develop more speaking skills and come to know their puppet friends well, they may wish to work together to plan conversations between the puppets, or even short puppet plays.

Sources of Puppets

Puppets can be obtained from commercial sources, or they can be teacher made or created by the students in the class. A few puppets that specifically reflect elements of the target culture are especially precious participants in the class, but any puppet with personality is a good choice. It is wise to avoid choosing puppets with high commercial visibility, such as those representing popular cartoon characters, so that children are free from prior associations and can participate fully in the imaginary lives of their friends in the language class.

Treatment of Puppets

When we invest puppets or other props in the class with personality and "feelings," we are creating an illusion that can be very powerful. This illusion can build a magical atmosphere in the classroom and serve as an important support for student learning. In order to sustain the illusion, it is important to treat these "personalities" with respect, even when they are not the focus of attention. At the end of an activity, for example, the puppet or other prop should be placed carefully in a special spot, sometimes referred to as a puppet tote, rather than being dropped carelessly onto the desk or the floor. When we take our creatures and our minidramas seriously, they are more likely to be meaningful and memorable to our students.

Using Exaggeration

A very small comb or tiny sunglasses might be hidden in an egg or in a magic box or somewhere else in the room. The exaggeration lends a sense of excitement and enjoyment to a "seek-and-find" activity. In a Gouin series or a TPR sequence in which a child goes to the mirror to comb her or his hair, using a huge comb adds humor to the activity. A regular comb or an imaginary comb does not have the same appeal. When an activity is repeated with the added factor of exaggeration, it becomes a new activity for the class, and the children will participate with enthusiasm.

Songs in the Curriculum

Music is one of the most appealing and effective entry points into a new language and culture. When used for background or listening experiences, music from the target culture adds to the authenticity of the language setting. Songs learned in the target language have the double benefit of giving children experience with an important dimension of the target culture and helping them to internalize the sounds, the vocabulary, rhythms, and structures of the new language. Children can often sing with a better accent than they can speak with at first.

Songs can play an important role in every unit and every class period. They are most effective when they are an integrated part of the curriculum, selected for their relationship to all of the activities and vocabulary in a class period and not regarded as an add-on, or filler, should there be extra time available.

Choice of Songs

Choose songs with a vocabulary that is limited and compatible with the language being used in the classroom so that the words and concepts in the song reinforce or introduce material used for many other activities in the curriculum. Some children's songs from the target culture have a greater vocabulary load than children in the first several years of an early language program can manage with understanding and enjoyment.

Choose songs with a limited musical challenge, especially in the primary grades. A song that is musically very difficult will require considerable time just for learning the music, and the language objectives will be overshadowed. Consult with the music teacher about the skills of a specific class, but in general be aware that a simple song moves step-wise from note to note, rather than including wide melodic leaps, and it should have a limited range of notes from low to high. The rhythm should be straightforward and repetitive. Even when they are very simple, songs should be *interesting* in both melody and rhythm. Also, the topics for songs should be within the experiences of the children in the class and of real interest to them.

Choose songs with a potential for actions, dramatization, rhythm accompaniment, or performance (such as a round or canon). Children in elementary school grades have great difficulty singing rounds, but they participate enthusiastically in songs accompanied by actions, and the actions help children to remember the words and their meanings.

Especially in the early stages of instruction choose songs that are highly repetitive in their text, rhythm, and melody. It is also very helpful to use songs that have a refrain. As a teaching strategy, you can introduce the refrain first, so that as verses are learned the singers can always return to something familiar when they reach the refrain.

The best song choices are those that are popular in the cultures of the target language, because they reflect the target culture and provide children with an experience in common with native speakers. Songs translated from English have the advantage of familiarity, but they lack cultural authenticity.

Teaching a Song

Teachers do not have to be solo singers to be effective in presenting a song to their students. If teachers know a song they can present it to the class. A less-than-perfect voice can be an especially good model for children, because it is easier for them to identify with, and even shy singers may feel that they can safely participate.

Some highly repetitive songs that accompany games or dramatic play can be presented informally, with the teacher singing alone at first. Children, especially at the elementary school level, are motivated to participate in both the activity and the singing, and they often learn the words and melody of the song with little formal teaching.

Middle school learners may seem reluctant to sing, but they can often be enticed by an engaging contemporary song that is popular in the target culture. They often respond well to hearing a recording of the song while reading the text for the song. One good strategy for learners at this level is to give them the text with blank spots for significant vocabulary that they should be able to recognize (a variation on a Cloze procedure). They will listen to the words more carefully as they try to fill in the blanks and eventually learn the song quite well.

In most cases, however, especially with older learners, systematic teaching of the song results in the most efficient learning.

The teaching of a song will proceed more smoothly if a careful sequence is followed:

Step One—Prepare the Students

Prepare the students by telling them what the song is about, preferably in the target language, making heavy use of visuals and gestures. Motivate the students to learn the song by sharing something about the setting of the song, the possibilities for actions or dramatization, or when or how it is sung in another country. Play a recording or sing the entire song so that students know what they are working toward. Note that some recordings made by children's choirs in the target culture are pitched so high that they cannot comfortably be used to provide an accompaniment for classroom singing, even though they may be very successful in motivating the activity.

Step Two—Go through the Words

Go through the words to make sure the students understand them, or at least that they understand the key words necessary for singing the song meaningfully and with enjoyment. Have the class listen for vocabulary they already know, and ask them to recall the context in which they have used it before. For example, if there is a vocabulary item they know, they can recall a song, game, or situation in which they used it and perhaps some of the things they know about the item. This helps learners to appreciate the cumulative nature of language acquisition and to listen for known vocabulary and meanings even in new material. Place new vocabulary in context and illustrate with gestures and visuals, using English only as a last resort. There should be very little new vocabulary in any new song, as most of it should have been introduced in other contexts several days before you introduce the song.

Step Three—Speak the Song Line by Line

Speak the song line by line and have the students repeat the words. This step may be skipped, depending on the nature of the group, the degree to which the language is already familiar, and the difficulty of the song.

Step Four—Sing a Line at a Time

Sing the song a line at a time and have the students sing it back. Practice each line several times, until the children can sing it independently. Then practice it two lines at a time (for a song that has about four lines), and then put the entire song together.

Four lines of a song is a good amount to teach during a single class period. If the song is longer and if it has a refrain, teach the refrain first, so that there is a sense of closure even though the entire song cannot be completed in one day.

Step Five—Add Rhythmic Accompaniment

After the students have learned the song and enjoy it, begin to add rhythmic accompaniment such as clapping, finger snapping, foot stamping, or hand shuffling. Use Orff and rhythm instruments to make the background even more sophisticated. Consult the music teacher for additional suggestions.

If the song includes motions, teach them together with the words and the music; learning each part of the song will reinforce learning the others. If the song can be used for a game or dramatic play, the students can use it for its real purpose as soon as they have learned the words and music thoroughly.

If the song is a round, perform it first with the class taking one part and the teacher the other. Then divide the class into two parts, then three or more, as the round dictates. Rounds are especially satisfying when they end on a chord rather than just by having groups drop out at the end. If the first group holds the final note and the second group holds the note at the end of the next-to-last phrase, and so on, then the final sound is sometimes very impressive.

Step Six—Create New Verses for the Song

After the song has become familiar, students often enjoy creating their own verses for a song. Lauren Schaffer of Portland, Oregon, uses Matt Maxwell's song "Café Crocodile" in this way. Her students brainstorm other animals not mentioned in the song and create additional lines to fit into the song's rhythm and structure, incorporating old and new vocabulary. This activity is similar to student creation of pattern books based on well-loved stories, and it could be extended into a writing activity in much the same way.

Step Seven—Enjoy Singing!

Enjoy singing a growing repertoire of lively, interesting songs with children in your classes!

Here are some suggestions if you consider yourself to be a non-singer:

- Ask a friend or an advanced student in your language to record the song for you, line by line, just as you will teach it.
- Use an electronic keyboard; program the melody or have someone do it for you; play the melody line by line in class.

- Use a tape or CD that comes with a songbook and play the song line by line during the teaching phase.
- Play the melody on a recorder or another instrument.

Don't Sing? Won't Sing? Try Chants and Raps

Rhythmic speech has many of the same benefits as song for making language memorable and enjoyable. Almost any content or occasion can find its way into a chant. Following are some examples.

Lois Ann Folliard uses this chant when her French students do something special:

Fabuleux! *(arms cheering in the air)*
Fantastique *(arms cheering in the air)*
Excellent *(arms cheering in the air)*
Trés bien *(clapping the two syllables)*
Bravo *(clapping the two syllables)*

Lynn Sessler-Schmaling uses a Japanese chant to reward her students for good performance:

Yoku dekimashita.
Yoku dekimashita.
Shu goy! Shu goy!

Here is a German chant to celebrate something well done:

Toll! Toll! *(Clap, clap)*
Prima! *(rap on the table)*
Toll! *(clap, clap)*
Das ist ausgezeichnet! *(wave hands in the air)*

Rita Gullickson developed the following chant to introduce her unit on the Columbian exchange. It is accompanied by finger-snapping and gestures.

1. Cristóbal	2. Cristóbal	3. Cristóbal
Cristóbal Colón	Cristóbal Colón	Cristóbal Colón
pidió permiso	pidió permiso	pidió permiso
permiso de navegar.	permiso de navegar.	permiso de navegar.
La reina Isabela	La reina Isabela	La reina Isabela
dijo que ¡no!	dijo que ¡si!	dijo que ¡si!
El rey Fernando	El rey Fernando	El rey Fernando
dijo que ¡no!	dijo que ¡no!	dijo que ¡si!
Cristóbal Colón	Cristóbal Colón	Cristóbal Colón
dijo ¡ay caramba!	dijo ¡ay caramba!	dijo ¡bravo!

This chant in Italian was developed by Italian teachers in Ohio:

Pasta! Pasta! Pizza! Pizza!
Chi mangia la pasta? Chi mangia la pizza?
Tutti! Tutti! Tutti! Tutti!
Alti! Bassi! Italiani! Americani!
Biondi! Bruni! Francesi! Cinesi!
Tutti mangiano la pasta! Tutti mangiano la pizza!

This French chant is recited to a marching rhythm:

À gauche À gauche
à droite à droite
à gauche à gauche
à droite à droite

J'ai mal au dos J'ai mal au ventre
J'ai mal aux pieds J'ai mal au genou
Zut alors j'ai mal au nez! Zut alors j'ai mal au cou!

This Spanish chant could be a nice review of clothing vocabulary—with variations, for any other set of related vocabulary items:

Me pongo el sombrero. I'm wearing a hat.
¿Qué te pones tú? What are you wearing?

Me pongo el suéter. I'm wearing a sweater.
¿Qué te pones tú? What are you wearing?

(Go on to shoes, socks, etc.)

Raps and chants are contagious. Many of them start out in an echo form, in which the teacher says a line, usually with body motions and snapping fingers or clapping, and students echo the line. It isn't long before the rhythm carries the chant or the rap and everyone is performing together. When introducing the chant, it is important to keep the rhythm going throughout, rather than stopping at the end of each line. Repetition will help students pick up all the words, and the rhythm will make the experience fun.

Some teachers make chants out of vocabulary words themselves—perhaps representative foods from a certain layer of the food pyramid could become a chant:

Milk, milk, ice cream, yogurt
Cheese, cheese, (clap) cottage cheese.
Buttermilk, buttermilk, yum, yum, yum.

The "Hollywood Rhythms" game described at the beginning of the chapter could be used as a chant as well as a game.

Craft Activities

Students enjoy the opportunity to create crafts that reflect the target culture, as well as participating in other art-related experiences. These activities sometimes challenge the teacher to develop new areas of vocabulary and to perfect the skills of giving directions and modeling. The art activity is an extension of the lesson or unit, not a vacation from it, so planning needs to include both the language that will be used and practiced and the craft activity itself.

A number of challenges await the teacher who plans an art or craft activity for the early language classroom. Because class periods are short, it is difficult to complete an activity of any complexity within a single class period. Children of different ages differ greatly in their ability to handle tasks like gluing, cutting, and assembling projects, and it is wise to check with a classroom teacher about the feasibility of an intended project. We always have to keep in mind that the art or craft project is an occasion for using the target language and not allow the complexity of the project to overshadow the language objectives.

Kathy Siddons, Spanish teacher at Goodwin School in Storrs, Connecticut, manages to do successful projects with her second through fourth grade students in fifteen-minute classes, and she has learned how to accomplish this very efficiently. She shared this advice on the Ñandu listserv:

> The more I teach FLES, the more strongly I feel about giving children hands-on experiences of creating their own projects to reinforce what's taught in the classroom.
>
> 1. Pre-cut as much as possible! Super-large paper cutters are wonderful, since large sheets of paper generally cost less in bulk. Also invest in some really good, sharp scissors and don't be afraid to cut several sheets of construction paper at a time. Just trace the pattern on the top sheet only and cut away at six or more sheets. Your cutting doesn't have to be perfect, you know. Pre-measure exactly what size you need and order/cut accordingly.
>
> 2. Copy designs right onto construction paper instead of plain copy paper. We have a copier that makes wonderful copies onto construction paper, fast and inexpensively. The "art" project will last longer and seem more special than on plain paper. White construction paper works very well here.
>
> 3. Always allow some part of the project to be designed their own way so you won't end up with cookie-cutter projects. Offer different colors of paper or a choice of texture or placement. One project I did called "La Flor Multicolor" was a flower in a pot with different colors of petals. The children had to color the petals according to the word in Spanish that appeared on the petals. But the children added a disc with a paper fastener in the center that they colored the way they wished, and they put designs on their pots that made each flower look completely different. (We did this the first day of spring.)
>
> 4. Use commercially made paper trimmers, sheets from designed notepads, paper fasteners, stickers, "Scotch" invisible tape, and staples to eliminate the mess and drying time of gluing. I have successfully used PURPLE glue sticks, however. These allow the children to see exactly where they have placed the glue so they don't use more than they need. Too much glue takes forever to dry, and nothing is worse than having beautifully done projects stuck together in piles!! I ask the classroom teachers to share their staplers or tape dispensers for project day. I borrow a cafeteria tray and collect all I can. I fill them with staples/tape and carry my tray [from] class to class. The children love to do their own stapling and taping. (I am even contemplating trying a project with the use of

double-sided tape.) Prompt return of staplers and dispensers to the teachers is necessary to keep good relations going. To keep track of my own, I put special toucan stickers or "flags" of colored masking tape on my own supplies.

5. Regarding trimmers, notepads, and stickers, take your time to order and peruse catalogues. Some educational firms offer a wide, wonderful selection of cleverly designed trimmers, notepads, and stickers. Working with themes in your curriculum helps you to eliminate unusable ones and think about how to use ones that go along with your theme creatively. Don't shy away from "office-type" stickers at office supply stores. I use the large dot stickers available in many colors that are ordinarily used for files. Also, take the time to estimate just how much of a particular material you will need; you don't want to be short, and you don't want to spend money if not needed. If the catalogue doesn't offer the information you need, such as size and count, call the Customer Service Department.

6. Days before the "art" project, ask the classroom teachers to have the children super-ready on project day—desks cleared, pencils sharpened, crayons, scissors ready, etc. A cute reminder in their mailboxes on the morning of project day is a nice touch, too. Plan to stay a few minutes extra if possible to help in any cleanup. With pre-cutting the cleanup is really minimal, which classroom teachers appreciate.

7. Use pre-cut shapes from a commercial source, or make your own using a die-cut machine, available in many teacher work centers or resource centers.

8. Colored masking tape and crepe paper for your "art" are inexpensive, quick, and easy ways to add color and different textures. Consider also using the more expensive "fadeless" construction paper, which doesn't tear easily and cuts beautifully, for special situations and crafts.

9. Work out the sequencing of construction of the project ahead of time. Make several mock-ups (for display) at adult speed. I even make a super-size one for display. Time it and then double or triple the time, depending on grade level. I find if I can't make up the project in less than five minutes, then it's not suitable for a fifteen-minute class. (Sometimes a simple enlargement of the pieces will speed things along for little hands.) If your schedule allows, let your first class of the day be "guinea pigs." By the last class, you will have techniques down pat. The children are always anxious to take their projects home immediately, so I really avoid things that cannot be finished in less than fifteen minutes. Passing out pieces in large manila envelopes, or clipped together with a large paper clip, saves passing-out time.

10. Last, but not least, I just came across a catalogue by way of my school's art teacher that has potential for fifteen-minute FLES "art" projects. If you already have access to an Ellison die-cut machine to cut out letters and numbers for bulletin boards, be aware that dies in other designs are available as well. The dies are expensive but I plan on asking the other members of the district's FLES team to share the cost so we can start building a collection year by year. Just to give you an idea, there are llamas, outline maps of Mexico, North America, Puerto Rico, and South America, sombreros, a woman from Spain, and palm trees. (I haven't even considered what dies would pertain to other languages and themes.) Next year I hope to have one or two in the system to try out. At first glance, they would serve nicely as attractive backgrounds for lyrics of songs just learned or to display poetry. Again, the emphasis is on quickness. *¡Buena suerte!*

The possibilities for art and craft activities in classroom are endless. A book of elementary school craft activities should get the thought processes going, and those focused on a variety of cultures are especially helpful.

Overhead Projector Activities

You may project visuals on the screen using a variety of techniques:

- Cover the transparency with a piece of paper and gradually reveal the entire transparency.
- Use a "peep show" technique to show only selected parts of the transparency. Make a mask with "windows" by cutting and hinging doors in an overlay made of stiff paper or card stock. Open the windows to reveal parts of the picture, and allow the students to guess what the picture is or what story lies behind the picture. As an alternative, make a single hole in an overlay mask and move it around the transparency at the request of class members, so that they can see various small parts of the picture and come to conclusions as to what the picture is about.
- Use overlays to put together a picture in various stages, or to uncover or reveal various parts of an image in a step-by-step sequence.
- Project the outlines of three-dimensional objects by laying them on the glass stage.
- Make shadows on the screen using hand motions. This is especially effective when the projector is placed behind a sheet or translucent screen and the shadow play takes place between the projector and the screen.
- Make silhouette stories by cutting out shapes from stiff paper and moving the shapes around on the projector stage to animate a story or dramatize a point in a lesson.
- Play "what's missing" games by putting a collection of physical objects or pictures of objects on the overhead projector. Turn off the projector and take away one object at a time; then turn on the projector and have the students identify which object is missing.
- Draw simple maps and add paper cutout figures to indicate streets, houses, landmarks, people, and so forth.
- Use the overhead projector to model partner activities. The students serve as one partner and the teacher uses the projector to demonstrate the task of the other partner.

Summary

Games and activities are important classroom means by which the communicative goals of the early language program are achieved. They involve the students and the teacher in meaningful, motivating situations within which real information is exchanged. Guidelines are presented to assist the teacher in choosing and devising games and activities that will be both successful and communicative, and a selection of classroom-tested games illustrates principles from the guidelines. Among the most important of these guidelines are the requirements that a game or activity should be enjoyable, that the use of language must play an important role in the activity, and that all students should be involved or engaged at all times.

FOR STUDY AND DISCUSSION

1. Choose a game recommended in a teacher's manual, or one you have actually used or observed in an early language classroom. Evaluate it according to the guidelines for games discussed in this chapter.

2. Choose a game from among those described in this chapter that call for little or no spoken language to be used by the students. Write a script for the teacher role in introducing and conducting this game, demonstrating how the teacher surrounds the activity with language and provides the class with comprehensible input.

3. Respond to a secondary-school language teacher who complains, "All you do in the elementary school is give them fun and games. When they get to our program and find out that really learning languages requires some work, they are disillusioned and they drop out. I'd rather just wait and start them out when they get to high school."

4. Choose a song for a class of young learners that meets the guidelines suggested in this chapter. Explain how it might fit into a specific unit of instruction; describe the vocabulary and concepts it can be used to teach or reinforce; and discuss the preparation that would take place before you begin to teach the song. Then demonstrate actually teaching the song to the class, using the target language.

5. Plan a lesson in which you use a puppet to introduce an important concept or a portion of a common conversational exchange. Refer to the conversation with the frog in this chapter as an idea-starter. Demonstrate the lesson to your class. Caution: Keep it simple!

FOR FURTHER READING

The following sources are recommended for additional information about material covered in this chapter. Chapter citations are documented in Works Cited at the end of the volume.

The following should be available from school or university curriculum libraries:

Books of craft activities, especially those from a variety of cultures.
Books of games from around the world.
Songbooks for children from the target culture.

Archives from the Ñandu listserv, and membership in the listserv itself, available at **www.cal.org/earlyorg.**

15 Choosing and Using Technology Resources

Technology is a tool. Sometimes the technology resources that early language teachers have at their disposal seem more like a magic carpet or a magic wand, capable of transforming teaching and curriculum in ways that would have been unimaginable less than a generation ago. But technology is just a tool, like a chalkboard, a copy machine, a rolling cart, an overhead projector, a magic box, or a CD player. The skilled teacher, like the skilled craftsman, matches the tool to the task in order to accomplish an important purpose. In this chapter we will examine a number of dimensions of the technology tools we have at our disposal.

At the same time as we consider our own uses for technology, we need to focus on our students and their need to be able to use technology effectively. Technology, especially the Internet, can provide access to authentic sources of language that are simply unavailable any other way. When we integrate technology with our lessons and create opportunities for our students to use technology meaningfully, we are supporting them in the development of two essential tools for lifelong learning: skill in the use of another language and the ability to make discerning and effective use of technological tools.

National Educational Technology Standards for Students and Teachers

The International Society for Technology in Education published a set of technology standards for students in 2000, in cooperation with the U.S. Department of Education and a number of curriculum organizations, including the American Council on the Teaching of Foreign Languages. These standards can help teachers to plan technology components for their lessons to give students experiences with language and cultures that would be unavailable any other way. As students become proficient with the technology tools at their disposal, they can be more independent language learners, pursue their own interests and needs using the target language, and develop skills that will be useful in all dimensions of their education. Technology can bring the cultures, connections, and comparisons goals to life, even as they allow students to use their communication skills to participate in a wider community of speakers of the language they are learning.

ISTE National Educational Technology Foundation Standards for Students

1. Basic operations and concepts
   - Students demonstrate a sound understanding of the nature and operation of technology systems.
   - Students are proficient in the use of technology.
2. Social, ethical, and human issues
   - Students understand the ethical, cultural, and societal issues related to technology.
   - Students practice responsible use of technology systems, information, and software.
   - Students develop positive attitudes toward technology uses that support lifelong learning, collaboration, personal pursuits, and productivity.
3. Technology productivity tools
   - Students use technology tools to enhance learning, increase productivity, and promote creativity.
   - Students use productivity tools to collaborate in constructing technology-enhanced models, prepare publications, and produce other creative works.
4. Technology communications tools
   - Students use telecommunications to collaborate, publish, and interact with peers, experts, and other audiences.
   - Students use a variety of media and formats to communicate information and ideas effectively to multiple audiences.
5. Technology research tools
   - Students use technology to locate, evaluate, and collect information from a variety of sources.
   - Students use technology tools to process data and report results.
   - Students evaluate and select new information resources and technological innovations based on the appropriateness for specific tasks.
6. Technology problem-solving and decision-making tools
   - Students use technology resources for solving problems and making informed decisions.
   - Students employ technology in the development of strategies for solving problems in the real world. (International Society for Technology in Education 2000a, 14–15)

The technology standards for teachers parallel those for students, offering guidance for teacher development on the part of college and university departments of education, school districts, and teachers themselves.

ISTE National Educational Technology Standards (NETS) for Teachers

I. TECHNOLOGY OPERATIONS AND CONCEPTS
   Teachers demonstrate a sound understanding of technology operations and concepts. Teachers:
   A. demonstrate introductory knowledge, skills, and understanding of concepts related to technology (as described in the ISTE National Educational Technology Standards for Students).
   B. demonstrate continual growth in technology knowledge and skills to stay abreast of current and emerging technologies.

II. PLANNING AND DESIGNING LEARNING ENVIRONMENTS AND EXPERIENCES

Teachers plan and design effective learning environments and experiences supported by technology. Teachers:

A. design developmentally appropriate learning opportunities that apply technology-enhanced instructional strategies to support the diverse needs of learners.

B. apply current research on teaching and learning with technology when planning learning environments and experiences.

C. identify and locate technology resources and evaluate them for accuracy and suitability.

D. plan for the management of technology resources within the context of learning activities.

E. plan strategies to manage student learning in a technology-enhanced environment.

III. TEACHING, LEARNING, AND THE CURRICULUM

Teachers implement curriculum plans that include methods and strategies for applying technology to maximize student learning. Teachers:

A. facilitate technology-enhanced experiences that address content standards and student technology standards.

B. use technology to support learner-centered strategies that address the diverse needs of students.

C. apply technology to develop students' higher order skills and creativity.

D. manage student learning activities in a technology-enhanced environment.

IV. ASSESSMENT AND EVALUATION

Teachers apply technology to facilitate a variety of effective assessment and evaluation strategies. Teachers:

A. apply technology in assessing student learning of subject matter using a variety of assessment techniques.

B. use technology resources to collect and analyze data, interpret results, and communicate findings to improve instructional practice and maximize student learning.

C. apply multiple methods of evaluation to determine students' appropriate use of technology resources for learning, communication, and productivity.

V. PRODUCTIVITY AND PROFESSIONAL PRACTICE

Teachers use technology to enhance their productivity and professional practice. Teachers:

A. use technology resources to engage in ongoing professional development and lifelong learning.

B. continually evaluate and reflect on professional practice to make informed decisions regarding the use of technology in support of student learning.

C. apply technology to increase productivity.

D. use technology to communicate and collaborate with peers, parents, and the larger community in order to nurture student learning.

VI. SOCIAL, ETHICAL, LEGAL, AND HUMAN ISSUES

Teachers understand the social, ethical, legal, and human issues surrounding the use of technology in PK–12 schools and apply that understanding in practice. Teachers:

A. model and teach legal and ethical practice related to technology use.
B. apply technology resources to enable and empower learners with diverse backgrounds, characteristics, and abilities.
C. identify and use technology resources that affirm diversity.
D. promote safe and healthy use of technology resources.
E. facilitate equitable access to technology resources for all students.

(International Society for Technology in Education 2000b, 9)

Computer-Assisted Projects

For teachers who have computer-equipped classrooms, or access to computer laboratories, student projects can include use of the computer. Depending on the age and language experience of the students, many of the following possibilities can enhance learning in a thematic unit:

- Create a menu using a word processing or a drawing program.
- Create a greeting card in the target language using clip art with a cultural element.
- Students use scanned or digital photos to design a poster with which to introduce themselves to a new student, a student teacher, or to parents for parent night.
- Create a story, an episode from a story, or a poem and illustrate with clip art or using a drawing program. All projects are printed and compiled into a class book.
- Develop a book report by creating a book jacket that includes a front cover designed to reflect book content, flaps to summarize the story, and information about the author on the back cover.
- Create a class newspaper or newsletter.
- Create a brochure about a city or a country in which the target language is spoken—to encourage visits from classmates and their families. Information might come from research on the Internet, and be enhanced with images downloaded from the Web.
- Create an advertisement for a culturally significant product, using scanned or clip-art images to illustrate the text.
- Develop a personal "picture dictionary" of words (or phrases) in the target language, using clip art or scanned images to illustrate the meanings rather than translations into English.
- After researching information about a famous figure from the target culture, using a variety of resources, create a "Who am I?" puzzle, illustrated with clip art and written in the first person. Place the answer on the back of the page, at the bottom, so it can be folded up to reveal the answer.
- Use interactive CD-ROMs in library study areas, the computer lab, or as a learning station in the classroom. Many "storybook" CDs are available in several languages.

Other CDs give learners vocabulary practice or listening opportunities supported by visuals and animations. A few game-like drill and practice programs are also appropriate at the K-8 level.

■ Students create a PowerPoint or HyperStudio presentation about themselves (or any other topic), using learned vocabulary and following a format provided by the teacher. The students illustrate the presentation with scanned photos and clip art.

■ Middle school students work in small groups to create "talking storybooks" for elementary school students, using the scanner or clip art to illustrate original or traditional children's stories. They read the stories aloud as they create a multimedia program in the target language that elementary school students listen to again and again.

This list offers just a few of the many possibilities for using the computer as a tool for communication in the target language. Most of these examples address Standard 1.3: "Students present information, concepts, and ideas to an audience of listeners or readers on a variety of topics" (9).

Using Computers to Enhance Teacher Productivity

When Alisha Dawn Samples of South Carolina Instructional Television presents technology workshops for language teachers she demonstrates the following ideas for teacher use of the computer. She suggests that teachers can:

■ Create their own roll/record/plan books (especially the FLES teachers since their needs are so different). This makes it much easier to go back another year and make modifications to lessons, activities, and anecdotal notes. It's also easier to share with colleagues this way!

■ Create visuals for games using clip art! Teachers may not have to stay up all night coloring if they have access to a color printer—it's a great time saver. You can also make "mini" visuals in black and white for students to use in booklets or centers, to take home or for homework, etc. . . . with visuals that look just like the ones they are using in class.

■ Include authentic pictures in visuals and materials. This works well if you have pictures taken with a digital camera or scanned photographs. It's a great way to provide authentic culture in games, books, and so forth, and it saves the originals from being destroyed!

■ Create an e-calendar by inserting numbers and clip art into a calendar created in PowerPoint. The clip art can come up as the teacher and/or students count (and click). This works well for sequencing and repeating holiday/thematic vocabulary on a daily basis. You can also print it out for students, or include it as a link on your Web page for viewing from home and for practice away from school!

■ Produce newsletters for parents. Include pictures from class, sites to visit at home with students, information about upcoming and completed themes, and so on. The newsletter may be printed out and/or posted on the Web page, where visuals in color will make the newsletter even more enjoyable.

- Create e-games! Several devices are available that allow everyone in the classroom to see what is on the computer screen by means of a television screen or a projector in the classroom. Everyone can see and participate in whatever activity is being done on the computer. This is a great one for the computer classroom and for teachers who want to do things on the computer with the class as a large group.
  - Many games can easily be converted to an electronic format by using links in PowerPoint. This allows students to take turns as they usually do but also manipulate the mouse and click (student NETS).
  - Matching games, multiple choice games, Jeopardy-type games, and question-and-answer games can all be done with PowerPoint slides and links.
- Creating e-books in PowerPoint is Alisha Dawn's favorite use of this technology, because she likes to introduce themes and units with books. The teacher can create an e-book using any visuals—clip art, scanned images, or digital photos—and then easily print the visuals that go with the book for games, activities, worksheets, and centers for the whole unit. PowerPoint allows the user to print in "hand-out" mode—different-size squares that are great for using in games or as manipulatives. Use small photo albums purchased at a dollar store to create "books" for use with activities such as paired reading and in centers. For these books, choose the option of printing two slides to a page, cut them out, and put them into the photo album. The teacher can also print out more slides to a page and run them off so that students have their own books to take home and read to parents . . . just like the one the teacher made for class. The teacher can read the class book by projecting the PowerPoint for large groups, or print out each slide and make a large book.
- When the teacher creates and presents a book with PowerPoint, it can include sound effects and music. You can make a book to "read" to students of the songs you plan to teach them, so the students learn the meaning and words to a song first by having a literature experience. Then add the music and the students will realize they already know the song.
- CD-ROMs have many possibilities. The materials a teacher makes electronically might be used only as print materials in the classroom, at least initially. If the teacher has access to a CD burner, however, the possibilities multiply. Electronic games, lessons, and materials can be stored on CD-ROMs to be shared with other teachers, or easily taken from home to school or from one school to another. Since the resources are electronic, the CD-ROM format provides easy ways to make multiple copies, or to make subtle changes in a resource for use in different schools or different classes. CD-ROMs are also valuable because you can record your own voice (or that of native speakers) to go with the materials. A CD-ROM could be a good resource for newcomers or for those who just want a little extra practice. Students might check out the CD-ROM from the teacher or the media center, or it could be made available in learning centers in each of the classrooms where the language is taught.

Using the Resources of the Internet

The Internet has expanded the resources available to language teachers and learners to an almost incredible degree. Teachers and students alike can access information about the countries where the target language is spoken and learn from and about the people who speak the language. Authentic sources of language are just an Internet connection away. Teachers can use the Web to download pictures, ideas, activities, and units to support their teaching, as well as to initiate and maintain contact with other teachers. The resources available to teachers on the Internet are almost overwhelming, and they make it possible to incorporate cultural information in our lessons in a multitude of ways. It is just short of miraculous to have access to books, teaching activities, virtual greeting cards in the target language, games to print, coloring pages based on famous painters, writing and pre-writing activities—the list is endless. One French-language Web site even provides lined paper in the French style, with a place for the student to write in his or her name and date. (See www.momes.net/education/ecriture/modeles/pagevide.html.)

Students can access Internet resources, under teacher guidance, to answer questions, research topics of interest, and use their language skills for personal enrichment and enjoyment. Use of the Internet can expand the students' community of target language speakers beyond the classroom and the neighborhood to the world.

There are growing numbers of sources of ideas for Web-based activities, some of them on listservs such as FLTeach and Ñandu (see "For Further Reading" at the end of the chapter). Teacher idea Web sites abound, and many of them offer ideas for activities using Internet resources. As teachers consider these ideas for their own classrooms, the evaluation form in Figure 15.1 will be helpful in assessing the quality of the activity and its potential for success in their own classrooms.

Many teachers have created their own Web pages, which they use to provide resources for students and their parents, as well as to share ideas, lessons, and favorite links with colleagues. In some cases the teacher's Web page can be a tool for advocacy for early language learning. Some teachers post homework assignments on their Web page, or links to Web sites of special interest to students in their classes. Some examples of teacher Web pages, active as this book went to press, are listed at the end of the chapter.

Anything and everything the teacher creates in class can be posted to the Web site for students to review, revisit, or share at home: classroom games, activities, e-books, calendars, collages of student work, or pictures of students in action. If the materials are created electronically they can be modified to go on the page according to how the teacher wants students to use them. There might even be some things that students did not experience electronically in class, but if they were created electronically they can be shared on the Web page. This includes newsletters, classroom management rules and procedures, information about the teachers and how to contact them, and program information.

Strategies for the One-Computer Classroom

Although teachers who have access to only one computer for classroom purposes may be limited, there are still a number of ways to take advantage of Internet resources under these circumstances. Teachers can download resources from the Internet to make hard copies for the classroom, or to use in making transparencies that will be visible to the whole class. Of course, the same copyright laws pertain to Internet materials as do those for other published information. Sometimes teachers download information at a remote site to a zip disk or a CD-ROM so they can display it in a classroom that doesn't have an Internet connection.

FIGURE 15.1   An evaluation form for web lessons.

Lesson name _____   Intended language level _____

Web address _____

Circle all that apply.

Type of instruction:

| Individual at computer | Small group at computer | Whole class—one computer |

Skills addressed:

Listening   Speaking   Reading   Writing

Thinking skills:

Recall   Comprehension Application   Analysis   Synthesis   Evaluation

Which Standards are addressed:

| Communication | Cultures | Connections | Comparisons | Communities |
| 1 2 3 | 1 2 | 1 2 | 1 2 | 1 2 |

Which intelligences are addressed:

Verbal-linguistic   Logical-math   Visual-spatial   Bodily-kinesth.   Musical-rhyth.   Interpersonal   Intrapers'l

Senses utilized:

Auditory   Tactile   Olfactory   Visual   Gustatory

Type of communication required:

Interpersonal   Interpretive   Presentational

Reading strategies employed:

Pre-reading activities:

During reading   Skimming   Cognates   Guess meaning   Careful   Other
in context   reading

Application

Type of lesson:

Form-based: Language
learning

Meaning-based   Simulation   Role play

Uses authentic   Scavenger   Research   Guided
document   hunt   reading

(continued)

FIGURE 15.1 Continued

Circle one: 1 = minimal, poor; 5 = maximum, exemplary

Appropriateness for level	1	2	3	4	5	Very appropriate
Integration into curriculum	1	2	3	4	5	Integrates perfectly
Use of target language	1	2	3	4	5	Exclusive/very appropriate
Enjoyment level for students	1	2	3	4	5	Very enjoyable
Advance preparation by teacher (compared to student benefit)	1	2	3	4	5	Minimum teacher prep; maximum student benefit
Appeal to a diverse student population	1	2	3	4	5	Very appealing to all students
Overall rating	**1**	**2**	**3**	**4**	**5**	**Exemplary lesson**

Would you use this in your classroom? _____

Could this lesson be presented as well or better in another medium (book, computer program, tapes, etc.)?

_____

How would you modify it?

_____

_____

Other comments:

_____

Source: Internet Activities for Foreign Language Classes. Reprinted by permission of California Language Teachers Association and California Foreign Language Project. Available online at www.clta.net/lessons/evalform.html

When there are projection capabilities available, the teacher or students can use the computer to access Web pages that can be seen by the entire class. This is an effective way to use Internet resources to enhance a unit of instruction with authentic documents and pictures. If students have worked individually or in pairs in the computer lab to become familiar with one or more Web sites that relate to the current class topic, they can demonstrate what they have learned to the entire class.

A single computer in the classroom can also function as a learning station for students working alone or in pairs during a designated study time on Web-based projects or assignments.

Electronic Mail: Key Pals

Electronic mail is perhaps the most accessible of all Internet tools. Electronic pen pals, or "key pals," can provide a motivating and effective opportunity for students to interact with native speakers or other learners of the target language. A key pals project gives experience with written communication in the interpersonal mode for learners who already have language skills, keyboard skills, and sufficient computer experience. There are also important personal benefits, especially for middle school students. As Barnum puts it, "E-mail offers the students the possibility to tell someone their own age in another land with a different culture about themselves, to ask questions and at the same time, to become aware of who they themselves are" (2001, 1).

Any key pals project requires careful preparation and organization. The first step is finding a partner class in which the students are approximately the same age, at the same level of language study, and about the same number of students. These partner classes might be students of English in the target culture, students of the same target language from a different part of their own country, or students of the same target language from a country in which neither English nor the target language is spoken natively. This last option has the special advantage of illustrating the fact that a second language can open doors to many, sometimes unexpected parts of the world. Since some students inevitably turn out to be poor correspondence partners, Robb (1996) recommends pairing up each student with two or three in the opposite class.

The language teacher should work carefully with the partner teacher to make sure that they have agreed upon:

1. who writes to whom
2. content of the letters
3. corrections—how many?
4. number of letters
5. time line
6. evaluation
7. use of other media
8. what the teachers want to achieve by the end (Barnum 2001, 3)

The next step is preparing the students. The teacher must be sure that the students have both the language skills and the technical skills to participate in the project. At the beginning of the project it is useful to brainstorm with the class what they already know about the country or the area of their partner class and what they would like to learn. These lists can then be used to focus the content of messages during the project and to help students assess what they have learned when the project is completed.

The teacher will need to supply students with appropriate phrases for salutations and endings, as well as for other recurring functions in the letters: thanking for previous messages, asking questions, appropriate responses, e-mail etiquette ("Netiquette") such as avoiding the use of all capitals (screaming) except for important emphasis, or using emoticons to indicate the tone of a sentence: :-) or ;-) or :-(for example. Experienced e-mail users will need to be reminded not to use common e-mail acronyms that represent English phrases, such as BTW (by the way) and IMHO (in my humble opinion). See Web sites at the end of this chapter for several Netiquette sites.

Students will need to see samples of appropriate letters and practice sending e-mails to one another, in the target language, before they are ready to make their first e-mail contact. Topics for the letters will vary, depending on the brainstorming session at the beginning of the project, but initial letters will undoubtedly exchange information about such topics as name, sex, age, birthday, nationality (if appropriate), maybe height, color of hair and eyes, school name—and always some questions for the partner.

One effective strategy for maintaining focus in a key-pals project is to brainstorm each of the communications before students begin to write their letters. The brainstorming session might result in a word bank that provides support for students as they write their own letters. It is wise to avoid the temptation to give students a template for each letter— students in the receiving class will not enjoy letters that are virtually identical! A checklist can help students self-monitor for quality. Barnum (2001, 11) suggests the following:

1. Does the letter begin with the place and date?
2. Is the address correct?
3. Have you thanked your partner for the last letter you received?
4. Are all your nouns capitalized? (Checklist is for a German class.)
5. Did you use the correct verb endings?
6. Did you use the correct possessive adjective?
7. Have you answered all your partner's questions?
8. Did you ask at least two questions?
9. Have you used the correct salutation and ending?
10. Are you satisfied with your letter?

The teacher will also need some method for tracking the progress of the key-pals project for each student. Robb (1996) suggests that students copy the first, crucial letter to the teacher and then keep a log of messages sent and received, including the number of lines in each message. For really personal communication, the goal of the project, copying all letters to the teacher would be intrusive and would inhibit real communication. If each new topic for the letters is brainstormed in advance, each student might summarize the information received on each topic as a part of the assessment process.

Deby Doloff (1999) developed a charming variation of key pals for elementary school students. She sent a brown stuffed bear, Tito, to six participating elementary school programs to experience adventures in Spanish. Tito wrote an e-mail letter in Spanish when he arrived at each school, explaining what he was looking forward to doing at the new school. At the end of his visit he e-mailed again to tell the children at home what he had done and where he was going next. Over a three-year period, Tito had visited schools in ten states in the United States, as well as Argentina and Spain, some of them several times. When he returns home at the end of the year, he has numerous souvenirs picked up along the way!

In an article in *Learning Languages,* Jean Pacheco (2001) describes a key-pal project with students from Russia who were studying English. Although the communication was entirely in English, the ideas for the various technologies used in the exchange and the insights gained are easily transferable to a target language exchange. Pacheco explains how her fourth grade students developed Web pages as a part of the project.

WebQuests: A Focused Strategy for Accessing the Internet

The Internet is a rich and wonderful resource, seductive in its color and diversity, unorganized, inconsistent regarding quality, commercialized, uneven in its reliability, and sometimes even dangerous—in short, much like the "real world." As teachers we can send our students to the Web in search of authentic sources of information in the target language, about weather conditions and forecasts, restaurant menus, famous people, on-line shopping, museums, movies—the list is almost endless, and it now includes access to music videos and real-time radio broadcasts. These kinds of searches among target language Web sites provide valuable experiences with communication in the interpretive mode, and many opportunities for gaining insights about cultures, as well as making comparisons between the target culture and the student's home culture. Given the nature of the Internet, however, a more focused and carefully designed approach to the Internet can give students more meaningful and memorable learning experiences.

WebQuests were developed in 1995 by Professor Bernie Dodge at San Diego State University with the goal of helping teachers to integrate the power of the Web with student learning. Since that time WebQuests have become a widely used tool throughout the country and at every learning level. According to Dodge (1997) and Kuck and Lietz (1998), the WebQuest consists of at least the following components:

1. An introduction to set the stage for the activity, provide background for the topic, and engage the learner. The introduction often places the learner in some sort of role-playing situation.
2. A task that describes learner expectations and may take the form of a multimedia presentation, a classroom presentation, a written report, or a classroom demonstration, to name a few mediums.
3. A description of the process students are expected to follow, in a step-by-step format. The task is divided into subtasks, roles or perspectives for each learner are described, and learning advice is offered in the form of guided questions and directions. Formats such as time lines, concept maps, or cause-and-effect diagrams may be offered for the students' use.
4. A set of information resources needed to complete the task. Most of these resources will be Internet based, although resources such as books, documents, and personal interviews may also be included. This list of sources helps to discourage aimless "surfing" and directs the learning experience.
5. Evaluation/Assessment strategies are described to measure the knowledge gained by the learner. Benchmarks and rubrics are often included here. A sample rubric for a WebQuest product is found in Table 15.1. The WebQuest "Lions and Tigers and Bears, Oh My!" was developed for a social studies class by Susan McGuan of Shawano, Wisconsin, and Gail Cole of Gillett, Wisconsin.
6. The conclusion summarizes the experience, encourages reflection about the process, and brings closure to the quest.

The WebQuest is usually designed as a group activity, encouraging the development of cooperative skills. WebQuests often assign roles to students (biologist, adventurer,

TABLE 15.1   Example: Rubric for One of the Products from a WebQuest about Hmong Culture

SAMPLE RUBRIC—WEBQUEST

	Advanced	**Proficient**	**Adequate**	**Minimal**
Mechanics	No more than 5 mistakes are acceptable	No more than 8 mistakes are acceptable	No more than 10 mistakes are acceptable	No more than 15 mistakes are acceptable
Research	Accurate, well presented, and very creative	Accurate and well presented, creativity good	Accuracy and presentation need work	Lack of concern for accuracy and presentation
Slide Presentation	Graphics and text are well presented and very appropriate for the telling of the story	Graphics and text are appropriate for conveying the story	Graphics and text adequate for telling the story	Graphics and text need much improvement
Delivery	Excellent eye contact and vocal delivery in presenting PowerPoint presentation	Good eye contact and vocal delivery in presenting your PowerPoint presentation	Adequate eye contact and vocal delivery in presenting your PowerPoint presentation	Much work needed on eye contact and vocal delivery when presenting
Adapted Story	Adaptation was excellent and the moral was consistent, held to the original	Adaptation was very good and was consistent with the moral of the original	Adaptation was adequate but did not convey the meaning of the original story	Adaptation did not have any connection to the original story
Group Dynamics	Students worked well independently researching, and worked well together using that research to write their story	Students worked well either independently researching or writing. But there were a few problems working cooperatively.	Students had some problems working independently and in their group	Students did not do well researching or working in their group

Source: Rubric for Hmong WebQuest, created by Susan McGuan, Shawano Community High School, Shawano, Wisconsin, and Gail Cole, Gillett High School, Gillett, Wisconsin. Reprinted by permission. Available on-line at www.cesa8.k12.wi.us/teares/it/webquests/Hmong/Hmong%20index.htm

photographer, journalist) and suggest a scenario that reflects a real-world use of the information that will be located in the WebQuest. For example, "You have been hired to do consumer research for a new product about to be introduced in Germany. Your employer wants you to develop an ad campaign that will reflect the values of the new customers and demonstrate qualities that similar products already on the market do not have."

The task is the most important element of the WebQuest, the dimension that raises the cognitive level of the activity and makes it meaningful for the learner. In general a WebQuest involves taking information located through multiple sources—on the Web and elsewhere—and recombining it, organizing or summarizing it in a creative way, or otherwise using the information to achieve a purpose. Some of the task categories identified on the San Diego State University WebQuest Web site include:

- retelling tasks—sharing information in a new form (PowerPoint or HyperStudio), not simply cutting and pasting
- compilation tasks—a cookbook, a time capsule
- mystery tasks—the task is wrapped in a puzzle or a detective story
- persuasion tasks—the student takes a position based on research and tries to persuade others to take the same position

These are just a few of the possible tasks that could focus a WebQuest. For a complete introduction to the construction of WebQuests and links to examples from all subject areas, see the resources listed at the end of this chapter.

Electronic Portfolios

An electronic portfolio is a purposeful collection of student work stored digitally on a computer hard drive, on a zip disk or CD-ROM, DVD-ROM, or on the World Wide Web. Unlike bulky portfolios stacked in closets or corners, the electronic portfolio takes up little space and provides convenient access to a record of student progress. HyperStudio is often the format of choice in elementary and middle schools.

As with the portfolios described in Chapter 8, student selection of materials and reflection on their own work are key elements in effective portfolio compilation. Portfolio activities can be used to encourage students to review their own work, analyze their own learning strategies and assess their collaboration with others. The teacher and the students together can make decisions about what should be included. Students gain valuable technology skills as they create or edit their own portfolios.

The following components for the portfolio are suggested on the Tammy's Technology Tips for Teachers Web site (2002):

- Title card that shows the name of the student, the year, and the teacher, as well as a photo or video of the student.
- Table of Contents Card. Buttons can be used to link this page to the contents of the portfolio.
- Information cards that hold information and student self-reflections for chosen subject areas. For a foreign language student these cards might include items such as the following:

- Writing sample.
- Recording of student reading aloud, or a dialogue with another student.
- Illustrated Gouin series.
- WebQuest.
- Short poem or story.
- Work entered into the portfolio should always be dated, and the task should be described (from Alphabet Superhighway, www.ash.udel.edu/ash/teacher/portfolio. html).
- Letter to the viewer, thanking the viewer for looking at the portfolio and pointing out things for the viewer to be sure to notice.
- Viewer response card, so that the teacher and other viewers can write responses to the student.

For the most sophisticated portfolio options, the same Web site suggests that the following equipment should be available (www.essdack.org/port/how.html):

- Computer with video input and output. The more RAM the better!
- Color flatbed scanner.
- Digital camera.
- Multimedia software program such as HyperStudio.
- Or a commercial Web authoring program.

The teacher may choose to set up a template for students to use when entering their information. One of the great advantages of the electronic portfolio is the fact that it can store information using a variety of media, thus reflecting various intelligences and learning styles and the whole range of target language applications. Use of electronic portfolios will demonstrate clearly the progress of students as they move from one grade level to another, or from elementary to middle to high school language classes.

Using Video in Early Language Teaching

Not all applications of technology take place on the Internet or using a computer. Videotapes (and more recently DVDs) have played a role in the classroom for many years, often to supplement classroom instruction. Videos made for children in the target language culture are valuable sources of both language and culture experience, if they are carefully chosen and the class is prepared ahead of time for the viewing experience. A videotape might also be the product of a student project, or the teacher can videotape student presentations to share with other classes or with parents.

Alisha Dawn Samples (2002) encourages teachers to tape some of their lessons as a way to provide "take-home" lessons for those who are newcomers, and as a method of providing lessons for substitutes or classroom teachers when the language teacher has to be absent. She suggests taping several generic review lessons every year that pertain to different topics or themes in the curriculum; they can be kept on hand in case of illness or special circumstances. Video lessons work best when the lesson is taped as direct instruction *to the camera*—not when simply taping a class. Students respond better to lessons that are taught straight into the camera (to them, the audience) than watching another class passively. Little children respond to the TV and are much more interactive when the lesson is taught like this. Taping a class is useful for other purposes, however: to demonstrate teaching for the teacher's portfolio, or to use for assessment of student progress.

Video and Television Lessons as Curriculum

Videos and television lessons have been used as part of the language curriculum since the 1960s, often in situations in which a full-time language teacher is not available. With the increasing demand for early language programs, the growing shortage of qualified teachers, and inadequate budgets for these programs, school systems are turning to video-based programs as a possible vehicle to providing instruction to large numbers of children.

Video programs are used in one of four ways (Rhodes 2002):

- as the foreign language curriculum by a classroom teacher (or other non-specialist) who does not speak the language and learns it along with the students
- as the foreign language curriculum by a classroom teacher who may or may not speak the language, with reinforcement by a foreign language teacher on a weekly basis
- by a language teacher as a supplement to the foreign language curriculum
- as the foreign language curriculum by a language teacher (not common)

It is important to remember that the quality of language learning in a video-based program will be dependent on several important factors. First, the video must meet a very high standard of quality, making consistent use of the target language in engaging and child-appropriate situations, and the pedagogy must be consistent with current understanding of second-language acquisition. There must be full and informed cooperation by classroom teachers and all assisting personnel involved with the program.

When Wyoming legislators mandated foreign language programs in K-2, beginning in the fall of 2002, Ann Tollefson applied for a federal grant to support the development of a video-based Spanish curriculum taught by classroom teachers, most of whom did not speak Spanish. The project was designed to give the teachers sufficient training and support so that they could supplement the videos confidently, using appropriate methodology. The group meets regularly, either in face-to-face sessions with national experts or using video teleconferencing. There is a research component of the project that will assess the effectiveness of three different delivery systems: classroom teacher alone, classroom teacher plus an aide who is a native speaker of the target language, or a language specialist who delivers all the instruction.

Rhodes and Pufahl of the Center for Applied Linguistics (CAL) have identified pros and cons of video-based foreign language teaching, according to teachers (2002, 5).

PROs
- is cost effective
- facilitates lesson scheduling

- can substitute during absence of the foreign language teacher
- native speakers and different accents challenge listening comprehension
- appeals to children; gets their attention
- provides ready access for (new) students who have missed part of the program
- allows students who have missed a lesson to review it
- creates visual contextualization
- could incorporate culture not available to local teachers
- appeals to different learning styles

CONs
- requires video technology
- experience may be passive/boring if overused
- lack of feedback/reinforcement if the teacher does not speak the language
- lack of interaction among students and among students and teacher
- lack of control over content and vocabulary

Almost all of the available video-based programs are in Spanish, and it is clear that the quality of the video is the determining factor in student learning and program success. Rhodes and Pufahl (4) identified characteristics of a good language video for children, based on teacher comments. These characteristics should be met whether the video is intended as the curriculum for the language or as a supplement:

What Makes a Good Language Video for Children?
- *extensive* use of the foreign language
- *authentic* use of the foreign language
- clear pronunciation by native speakers
- catchy tunes
- lots of repetition
- humor
- characters are fun to watch (puppets, cartoons, and/or people)
- engaging story line
- profiles of Spanish-speaking communities (abroad and in United States) from a child's point of view (or profiles of communities that speak the language of the video)
- national/state standards are addressed

Using Videotapes or Television Lessons in the Classroom

The effectiveness of any viewing experience in the classroom, whether of a supplementary video, a videotaped lesson, or a television lesson, will be determined in large part by how well the teacher prepares the experience and follows up on it. Alisha Dawn Samples, in her presentation for classroom teachers, makes the following suggestions:

Before Viewing

- Preview and prepare the program(s) prior to classroom viewing.
- Select segments from the video that are most relevant to the lesson topic and specifically target lesson objectives.
- Provide a focus for the students for viewing—what are they looking for?
- Have students sit where they can all see and have access to writing materials and something firm to write on.
- Keep the lights on.

During Viewing—Use the "Pause" Button Frequently to

- Check comprehension.
- Highlight or underscore a point.
- Invite student inferences or predictions.
- Have students make connections to other topics or "real-world" applications.
- Ask a student to come and point to something on the screen.
- Have students define a word based on contextual clues.
- Decipher a situation or solve a problem.
- Enhance students' observation and memory skills.
- Control the viewing pace and amount of information to be digested.
- Provide students time to reflect on what they have seen.

After Viewing

- Tie the lesson objectives to the video students have just viewed.
- Allow students to respond to the program.
- Recognize the validity of divergent reactions.
- Help students relate the program to their own experiences and feelings.

Material and information from any viewing experience will soon be forgotten if they are not incorporated into later instruction by means of hands-on experiences, related projects or instruction, or by some other means. Videotape or television instruction holds great promise for presenting language experiences in an interesting and meaningful way, provided that the program is of high quality and meets class objectives. Only if the material is an integrated part of the language curriculum, however, will viewing experiences contribute effectively to the language development of our students.

Summary

Early language teachers have more technology resources at their disposal than at any time in history. These resources are tools that must be matched carefully to the outcomes of instruction and chosen because they are the best means available for reaching a specific goal.

The National Educational Technology Standards for Students and for Teachers can serve as a guide for us as we choose technology applications for our classrooms. Because technology can extend the reach of the language classroom into the world of the target culture, there is tremendous potential for integrating foreign language curriculum with technology goals and standards. The Internet, when it is used well, may be one of the best resources for our students as lifelong learners and users of the language we teach. Therefore, it is our task to help our students use it effectively.

A number of specific technology applications are highlighted in this chapter. Key pals can provide opportunities for written interpersonal communication that helps students understand the cultures of the language we teach. WebQuests can develop thinking and presentational skills at the same time as they guide students through useful research processes. Finally, electronic portfolios can help students to gather and reflect on the evidence of their learning during the language class, while they develop and use important skills in technology, such as scanning documents, recording their own speaking of the language, and using a digital camera.

Videotapes and other visual media such as CD-ROMs and DVD-ROMs can support language teaching, and can sometimes, under the right circumstances, even provide language instruction when a qualified teacher is not available. These materials, like all other teaching materials, must be carefully evaluated before they are adopted.

FOR STUDY AND DISCUSSION

1. Read the National Educational Technology Standards carefully. For each of the standards, identify one project or activity in your language classroom that would also address the technology standard. Identify the foreign language standard(s) being addressed, as well.

2. If you have ever had a pen pal or a key pal, what were the benefits and the frustrations of that situation? What could you do in your own classroom to build on the benefits and avoid the frustrations in a key pals project?

3. Access several of the WebQuests available online from one of the Web pages listed in the "For Further Reading" section. Describe a WebQuest that you would like to design for a thematic unit that you plan to teach in your language class.

4. Electronic portfolios are valuable for students who are learning a new language. They are also valuable for teachers to develop as a way of reflecting on their own teaching and sharing their philosophy and their teaching experiences with potential employers. What are some of the elements that you would include in a teacher portfolio, based on the experiences you have had thus far?

5. View a video that is designed for teaching a foreign language at the elementary or middle school level. Evaluate it using the criteria listed by CAL. Would you use this video? If so, how? If not, why not?

FOR FURTHER READING

The following sources are recommended for additional information about material covered in this chapter. Chapter citations are documented in Works Cited at the end of the volume.

California Language Teachers Association, California Foreign Language Project. *Internet Activities for Foreign Language Classes.* Available on-line at www.clta.net/lessons/evalform.html

Creating and Using Portfolios on the Alphabet Superhighway. www.ash.udel.edu/ash/teacher/portfolio.html

Green, Anne. "A Beginner's Guide to the Internet in the

Foreign Language Classroom with a Focus on the World Wide Web." *Foreign Language Annals* 30, no. 2 (summer 1997): 253–264.

International Society for Technology in Education (ISTE). *National Educational Technology Standards for Students. Connecting Curriculum and Technology.* Eugene, OR: ISTE, 2000.

Kost, Claudia R. "Enhancing Communicative Language Skills through Effective Use of the World Wide Web in the Foreign Language Classroom." *Foreign Language Annals* 32, no. 3 (fall 1999): 309–320.

LeLoup, Jean W., and Robert Ponterio. "Enhancing Authentic Language Learning Experiences through Internet Technology." *ERIC Digest,* 2000. Available online at www.ed.gov/databases/ERIC_Digests/ed442277.html

Pacheco, Jean L. "A Successful Keypal Project Using Varied Technologies." *Learning Languages* 7, no. 1 (fall 2001): 10–14.

Tammy's Technology Tips for Teachers, Web site for Educational Services and Staff Development Association of Central Kansas. www.essdack.org/tips/ (electronic portfolios, other technology information) Accessed November 2002.

WEB SITES OF INTEREST

E-mail Resources

Doloff, Deby. *"Te Quiero, Tito"*—FLES Email Project." *Learning Languages* 4, no. 3 (spring 1999): 21–23.

E-Pals Dot Com:
www.epals.com

E-Pals and On-line Projects:
http:members.tripod.com/the_english_dept/epals.html

Harness E-mail: Smileys:
www.learnthenet.com/english/html/25smile.htm

Intercultural E-Mail Classroom Connections (IECC):
www.stolaf.edu/network/iecc

Kidlink:
www.kidlink.org/index.html
A global networking portal for kids around the world.

Lawrence, Geoff. "A Touch of . . . Class!" *The Canadian Modern Language Review* 58, no. 3 (March 2002): 465–472.

Online Netiquette.com:
www.getnetiquette.com

Robb, Thomas N. "E-Mail Keypals for Language Fluency." *Foreign Language Notes* (Foreign Language Educators of New Jersey) 38, no. 3 (fall 1996): 8–10. Accessed on-line November 30, 2002, at
www.kyoto-su.ac.jp/~trobb/keypals.html

Smileys and Emoticons for Effective Communication:
www.windweaver.com/emoticon.htm

WebQuests

CESA 8 site, Wisconsin—Teacher Resources
www.cesa8.k12.wi.us

San Diego State University WebQuest site:
http://webquest.sdsu.edu

WebQuests for Learning.
www.ozline.com/webquests/intro.html

Listservs and Archives (Subscribe to the Listserv from the Archive Page)

FLTeach:
www.cortland.edu/www/flteach/flteach.html

Ñandu, Early Language Listserv:
www.cal.org/earlylang

Early Language Teacher Web Pages

Doug Shivers, Spanish Songs and Games for Children:
www.hevanet.com/dshivers/juegos/

Foreign Language Teacher Web Pages for Many Languages. Some Special Topics:
www.geocities.com/paris/leftbank/9806/f/teacherpgs.html

Lori Langer de Ramírez, Herricks Public Schools, New Hyde Park, NY:
www.miscositas.com

Japanese language teachers, Maloney Magnet School, Waterbury, CT:
www.teacherweb.com/ct/maloneymagnetschool/japanese/

Kathleen Siddons, Goodwin School, Storrs, CT:
www.anacleta.homestead.com

Language-Specific Sites for Student Use

www.boowakwala.com
Site for young learners in several languages. Once a language is chosen, everything that follows is in the target language.

www.blinde-kuh.de
German site with many games, resources, and information for young learners.

www.mome.net
French site with many options, designed for francophone children.

www.chicos.net.ar
Spanish-language site.

www.jinjapan.org/kidsweb/
Source of kid-friendly information about Japan, in any of nine languages, including English and Japanese.

CHAPTER

16 Making the Case for Early Language Programs

Rationale and Advocacy

For world languages, as for any content area seeking a secure place in the school curriculum, offering a convincing rationale holds a high priority. School boards and parent organizations need reasons and evidence before making a commitment of time and resources to a new program, and existing programs can be called into question at any time. Almost every "public" occasion—from class or program coverage by the media to party conversation—holds the potential for the common, recurring question, "Why should children learn new languages in elementary school?"

Perhaps the best response to this question is to rephrase it into a larger and more important one: "Why should foreign languages become a K–12 experience for all students?" This is a question that better reflects the vision of language education expressed in the *Standards for Foreign Language Learning in the 21st Century*. Establishing and maintaining language programs in the elementary school, and then articulating them carefully through middle school and high school, will make it possible to provide all of our citizens with the precious gift of other languages, cultures, and perspectives. Another way to rephrase the "Why?" question might be to ask, "What academic and cognitive benefits are the students not receiving if they do not learn another language?"

A rationale, like a program philosophy, must be developed to meet the needs and priorities of the local school and of the community that it serves. It will address the reasons and goals for language learning, as well as the basis for choice of language(s) to be taught; it may also deal with the methods selected for instruction. The teacher or group developing a rationale can draw from a variety of resources to complete the task; one purpose of this chapter is to give direction to the search for resources and to give guidance for the shaping of a rationale that is both consistent with the national vision and meaningful to the community for which it is developed.

During the surge of popularity for elementary school language programs in the 1960s, it was common for schools to launch programs before setting rationale and goals. As a consequence, many programs gained public support for the wrong reasons: "catching up" with the Russians, taking advantage of government money available, providing a program like that of a neighboring school, trying to produce fluent speakers quickly because learners were thought to be at an optimal age for language learning. Many administrators, parents, and teachers had unrealistic expectations of student performance. Those who had jumped onto the language bandwagon out of fear or because foreign languages were a fad, or who expected fluency in weeks or months, were bound to suffer disappointment. In their eagerness to expand their offerings into the elementary schools, language teachers sometimes did not discourage such expectations. Disillusionment and lack of clear direction combined to bring an end to programs that had been too hastily begun.

At the beginning of the twenty-first century there are both a resurgence of interest in early language learning, as a component of the K–12 sequence, and an abundance of information that supports an early start and a long sequence of language study. Clarity in purpose and rationale can be an important first step in the development of an effective and enduring program.

Where to Look for a Rationale for Foreign Languages

Cognitive Science and Brain Research

Parents and teachers often comment that children are much better language learners than adolescents or adults and that we should make the most of this special ability before it is lost. The research of Penfield and Roberts (1959) offered a psychological and physiological basis for starting second-language learning as early as possible, and this research was frequently cited in FLES program rationale in the 1960s. Donoghue (1968, 11), in her ground-breaking methods text for elementary school foreign languages, makes this recommendation: "Ideally, the age for beginning the learning of a second language is at birth. But when considering language learning in relation to schooling, the optimum age for beginning the continuous learning of a second language seems to fall within the span of ages four through eight. . . . In this span of ages, the brain apparently has the greatest plasticity and specialized capacity for acquiring speech. This capacity includes the ability to mimic properly all the speech sounds, intonations, and stresses and to learn readily all language patterns."

Some later research evidence suggested that older learners have specific advantages over children in many areas—with a small advantage for children in the area of native-like pronunciation—at least in most classroom settings (Krashen et al. 1982, Harley 1986, Singleton 1995). Many of the reasons that children are such successful language learners may lie in other factors, of course, such as the amount of time available for learning the language and the teaching methodology used. The brain research of the 1990s and beyond, however, has tended to support the instincts of parents and teachers, as well as those early research claims.

Since the mid-1990s there has been a flurry of publication of new information emerging from the study of the brain and cognitive functioning. This research has been made accessible to a wider public through articles in *Newsweek* and *Time*. J. Madeline Nash, in an often-quoted article (1997, 56), pointed out that "The ability to learn a second language is highest between birth and the age of six, then undergoes a steady and inexorable decline." Among the conclusions she draws from the research is this: "What lessons can be drawn from the new findings? Among other things, it is clear that foreign languages should be taught in elementary school, if not before."

Very much the same message was presented in the public radio program *Gray Matters: The Developing Brain*. An article in *Learning Languages,* Language Learning and the Developing Brain (1996) summarized some of the key findings from that program (17). According to Dr. Michael Phelps, chairman of the Department of Molecular and Medical Pharmacology of the UCLA School of Medicine, the child's brain is different from the adult brain in that it is a very dynamic structure that is evolving. A two-year-old child has twice as many synapses (connections) in the brain as an adult. The young brain must use these connections or lose them.

Thus, failure to learn a skill, such as a foreign language, during a critical or sensitive period, has important significance. The learning experiences of the child determine which connections are developed and which will no longer function. That means that what is easy and natural for a child—learning a language—can become hard work for an older learner.

Another piece of evidence comes from the work of Dr. Susan Curtiss, professor of linguistics at UCLA, also cited in the *Learning Languages* summary (17). She has found that the four- or five-year-old learning a second language is a "perfect model for the idea of the critical period." According to Dr. Curtiss, "the power to learn language is so great in the young child that it doesn't seem to matter how many languages you seem to throw their way . . . They can learn as many spoken languages as you can allow them to hear systematically and regularly at the same time. Children just have this capacity. Their brain is just ripe to do this . . . there doesn't seem to be any detriment to . . . develop(ing) several languages at the same time."

These conclusions were reinforced by researchers at Dartmouth College, who looked at children who had been exposed to different combinations of languages in both natural and school settings at various ages. As reported in *News in Science* (2002), researcher Laura-Ann Petitto addressed the annual meeting of the Society for Neuroscience on this topic. She reported that children exposed to two languages from a very early age "grow as if there were two mono-linguals housed in one brain." She added that there is no contamination of either language by the other. The researchers concluded that "the earlier and more intensively the languages are introduced, the better" (1).

National Reports, Policy Statements, and Studies

Beginning with the appearance of *Strength through Wisdom,* the report of the President's Commission on Foreign Language and International Studies (1979), a series of studies and reports on education have highlighted the need for improvement of opportunities for language study in the schools. The importance of language study has been tied to national security: "A nation's welfare depends in large measure on the intellectual and psychological strengths that are derived from perceptive visions of the world beyond its own boundaries" (2). Language study has been related to the success of the United States in the international marketplace and to the skills required for happy and productive living in a future of increasing global interdependence. The commission specifically recommended that language study begin in the elementary school and continue throughout the student's education. Paul Simon's book, *The Tongue-Tied American: Confronting the Foreign Language Crisis* (1980), provides a wealth of material for the construction of a rationale for language learning.

In *A Nation at Risk,* the Report of the National Commission on Excellence in Education (1983), the study of foreign language and culture was placed alongside the five "basics" of English, mathematics, computer science, social studies, and the natural sciences as a fundamental component of a sound education.

Other commission reports, while focusing on the general decline in the quality of the nation's schools, have also addressed the need for studying foreign languages at the elementary school level. The National Commission on Excellence in Education (1983) maintained that achieving proficiency in a foreign language takes from four to six years of study and suggested that this begin in the elementary grades: "We believe it is desirable that students achieve such proficiency because study of a foreign language introduces students to non-English-speaking cultures, heightens awareness and comprehension of one's native tongue, and serves the nation's needs in commerce, diplomacy, defense, and education" (26).

The National Advisory Board on International Education Programs, in a report to the Secretary of Education (1983, 9), stated that language instruction should start as early as possible. In its report, "Critical Needs in International Education: Recommendations for Action," the board recommended that local school districts provide every student with the opportunity to begin the study of foreign language in the earliest years of formal education and to continue study of the same language until a functionally useful level of measured proficiency has been achieved.

These views are reiterated in a study by the College Board (1983) that emphasized the importance of expanding the concept of basic skills to include foreign language instruction for all students. More specifically, the report credits knowledge of a foreign language with helping students to prepare for careers in commerce, international relations, law, science, and the arts. Furthermore, the report emphasizes that the development and maintenance of foreign language skills is a valuable national resource.

The Goals 2000: Educate America Act includes foreign languages in the list of critical areas for which students should demonstrate competence when leaving grades four, eight, and twelve. In 1996, the American Association of School Administrators listed knowledge of foreign languages as one of the most important skills for K–12 students in the twenty-first century. On September 15, 1999, Secretary of Education Richard W. Riley suggested that foreign language instruction would be a valuable way to raise education standards. He stated: "I believe that in this new economy every high school student should be close to fluent in a foreign language when he or she graduates. We should begin teaching foreign languages in our elementary schools, and then in middle schools and high schools."

Three years later, and under a different administration, U.S. Department of Education Secretary Rod Paige announced new priorities and initiatives for International Education on November 20, 2002. In his news release (Office of Public Affairs, U.S. Department of Education 2002), Paige wrote, "We are ever mindful of the lessons of Sept. 11—one of which is that all future measures of a rigorous K–12 education must include a solid grounding in other cultures, other languages and other histories." He continued, "In other words, we need to put the 'world' back into 'world-class' education." Among the initiatives included in this announcement was support for international education in K–12 schools, including partnerships with states to provide new resources for high-quality, K–12 programs "that provide international knowledge and skills in our nation's classrooms" (2). He also announced plans to honor teachers for outstanding work in helping young learners to understand world issues and other countries, cultures, and languages. These initiatives were announced at the annual meeting of the American Council on the Teaching of Foreign Languages on November 22, 2002 (Office of Public Affairs, U.S. Department of Education 2002).

General Rationale for Teaching Languages

The rationale for elementary and middle school programs is embedded in the rationale for languages generally, but it must also take into account some special characteristics of languages at those levels.

1. One of the most important factors influencing the development of language proficiency is the amount of time spent in working with the language. When language learning begins earlier, it can go on longer and provide more practice and experience, leading ultimately to greater fluency and effectiveness.
2. Every skill and outcome that is important to society is introduced through the elementary school curriculum. The lists of curriculum requirements in almost every state attest to the importance of reading, math, social studies, science, music, art, and physical education. The introduction of computers into nearly every elementary school program clearly reflects the values of our electronic, information age. Not until world languages become a secure part of the elementary school curriculum will language learning begin to meet the needs and challenges of the twenty-first century.
3. The age of ten is a crucial time in the development of attitudes toward nations and groups perceived as "other," according to the research of Piaget, Lambert, and others (Lambert and Klineberg 1967). Children are in the process of moving from egocentricity to reciprocity, and information introduced before age ten is eagerly received. Carpenter and Torney (1974) suggest that exposure to a foreign language serves as a means of helping children move toward intercultural competence. The awareness of a global community can be enhanced when children have the opportunity to experience involvement with another culture through a foreign language.

A Vision for Language Competence in the World of the Twenty-First Century

Organizations for foreign language professionals and many of our leaders have expressed compelling reasons for language learning. Savignon (1997, 169) describes the importance of languages as follows: "Learning to speak another's language means taking one's place in the human community. It means reaching out to others across cultural and linguistic boundaries. Language is far more than a system to be explained. It is our most important link to the world around us. Language is culture in motion. It is people interacting with people."

The National Council of State Supervisors of Foreign Languages (NCSSFL), in a position paper entitled "A Rationale for Foreign Language Education" (2002), endorses foreign language education in the curriculum for all students, prekindergarten through grade twelve and beyond" (1), and identifies foreign language education as an important part of basic education.

Cloud and Genesee (1998) argue that basic education in the new millennium must include second and third languages if the United States is to cope with the diversity within its borders and compete successfully in the global marketplace. They cite both cognitive and sociocultural benefits of language study. They conclude, "Linguistic and cultural competence will be the mark of the well-educated citizen of the 21st century" (65).

The *Standards for Foreign Language Learning in the 21st Century* make a strong claim for the importance of language in the "Statement of Philosophy" (1999, 7): "Language and communication are at the heart of the human experience. The United States must educate students who are equipped linguistically and culturally to communicate successfully in a pluralistic American society and abroad. This imperative envisions a future in which ALL students will develop and maintain proficiency in English and at least one other language, modern or classical. Children who come to school from non-English-speaking backgrounds should also have opportunities to develop further proficiencies in their first language." In support of these ideas, the philosophy includes three basic assumptions, two of which point directly toward language learning for all learners, beginning in the elementary school:

> All students can be successful language and culture learners, and they
> - must have access to language and culture study that *is integrated into the entire school experience* [emphasis added];
> Language and culture education is part of the core curriculum.

Basic Elementary School Skills and Goals

Some of the most powerful sources of rationale for foreign languages in the elementary and middle school are the curriculum guides of the schools themselves. Planners who truly understand both the goals of the elementary school and the potential of foreign languages can demonstrate the value of languages very convincingly by showing the relationship between the two. The local curriculum and philosophy provide the best information about the values and priorities of the school and the community in which the language program will take place.

Among the goals and philosophical positions commonly encountered in local curricula and in references about elementary school curriculum, some of the following themes have particularly high potential for the developer of a rationale for languages:

1. Basic Skills. This is certainly not a new concern for elementary school languages. Much of the research done during the banner years of elementary school language programs, the 1960s, was concerned with the relationship of language learning to skills acquisition in English language and mathematics. The concern at that time was almost always to demonstrate that these skills areas had not suffered because of the time "lost" to foreign language instruction. The evidence was consistent: there was no sacrifice of basic skills when time was given to learning a new language (Donoghue 1968).

In "Tangible Benefits of the Study of Latin: A Review of Research" (1977), Rudolph Masciantonio published a survey of research that made a stronger case for languages. Latin instruction in the elementary grades had been shown to result in significant and dramatic gains in standardized test performance in basic-skills areas. In a similar study, gains were also reported for students of French and Spanish. Studies of immersion programs in Canada and the United States show that students taught *by means of* a foreign language achieve at similar *or higher* levels than their peers who are taught only in English, even when testing is done in English. Parents in Chicago, Cincinnati, and Milwaukee, for example, are known to choose metropolitan magnet schools offering languages because of the outstanding record of children in those schools on tests of English basic skills—not always primarily because of the language offerings themselves (Estelle 1985, Anderson 1982, Met 1982). A study in Louisiana (Rafferty 1986) showed that third, fourth, and fifth graders studying French for thirty minutes per day achieved significantly higher scores on the 1985 Basic Skills Language Arts Test than did a similar group of non-participants. In addition, by fifth grade the math scores of language students were also higher than those of non-language students.

Later studies have confirmed the findings of this research. Armstrong and Rogers (1997), for example, showed that third graders who were taught Spanish for thirty minutes three times per week showed statistically significant gains on their Metropolitan Achievement Test scores in the areas of math and language after only one semester of study. It is particularly interesting that one class of students in the experimental group had actually received one and a half fewer hours of math instruction per week, and still outperformed the students in control classes in math.

Saunders (1998) examined the performance of third grade students enrolled in the Georgia Elementary School Foreign Language (ESFL) model program. She compared students who had not received any foreign language instruction with students one year younger who had received four years of foreign language instruction, five days each week, for thirty minutes per day. She found those students in the ESFL program scored significantly higher on the math portion of the Iowa Test of Basic Skills than the older students had scored. They also performed better on the reading portion, but the difference was not statistically significant.

2. Communication. Part of the impact of foreign language study on basic skills performance can be explained by the greater understanding that students gain of their own language when they see it from the perspective of a new language. Vygotsky, a significant contributor to contemporary developmental theory, writes in *Thought and Language* (1986, 160):

> Goethe clearly saw it [reciprocal dependence] when he wrote that he who knows no foreign language does not truly know his own. Experimental studies fully endorse this. It has been shown that a child's understanding of his native language is enhanced by learning a foreign one. The child becomes more conscious and deliberate in using words as tools of his thought and expressive means for his ideas. . . . The child's approach to language becomes more abstract and generalized. . . . The acquisition of foreign language—in its own peculiar way—liberates him from the dependence on concrete linguistic forms and expressions.

Foreign language study has been shown to enhance listening skills and memory (Ratte 1968), and the development of second-language skills can contribute a significant additional dimension to the concept of communication.

Cummins (1990, 1) observes: "research suggests that bilingualism enhances children's understanding of how language itself works and their ability to manipulate language in the service of thinking and problem-solving." The research that Cummins cites is primarily in the field of immersion education. He also indicates that bilingual children learn additional languages much more quickly and efficiently than do monolingual children.

3. Creativity. Many of the activities common in elementary school language programs—emphasis on movement, imagination, and role play, for example—stimulate the right hemisphere of the brain, which is often underplayed in the formal school setting. Foreign language instruction can make a contribution to "whole-brain" education, and one consequence can be enhanced creativity. Elementary school students attending a FLES program were reported to have greater skills in divergent thinking/figural creativity than did those who were monolingual, according to research conducted by Landry (1973).

A number of studies show that people who are competent in more than one language outscore monolinguals on tests of verbal and nonverbal intelligence (Bruck, Lambert, Tucker 1974, Hakuta 1986, Weatherford 1986). Students learning another language can show greater creativity in complex problem solving, according to Bamford and Mizokawa (1991). Rosenbusch (1995, 5) summarizes current research to indicate that "the length of time students study a foreign language relates directly and positively to higher levels of cognitive and metacognitive processing."

4. Self-Concept. Second-language learning in the elementary school, especially in its beginning stages, is less dependent on previous verbal learning than are most other elements of the curriculum. This factor allows some students to succeed who have otherwise experienced repeated failure in school. Evidence from a California study shows language students to have a significantly higher self-concept than do non-language students (Masciantonio 1977). Students in Cincinnati have also shown such success. In a 1987 study (Holobow et al. 1982) working-class students did just as well in French as middle-class students even though their English skills were not as good.

5. Societal and Career Benefits. The rationale white paper published by the National Council of State School Officers of Foreign Languages (NCSSFL) identifies significant societal benefits associated with people who can communicate in at least two languages. As American society becomes increasingly diverse, ever more jobs and careers will require skills in interacting with people who speak languages other than English, and in adapting to a wide range of cultural backgrounds. Managers who know how to deal with a diverse workforce will have an advantage in the increasingly multiethnic business community. Four out of five new jobs in the United States are created as a result of foreign trade, and the global marketplace is an ever-growing reality. Our educational system must provide learners with linguistic and cultural skills that will allow them to function effectively in this new business climate, both at home and around the world.

These new expectations and opportunities will be at every level of employment, not only in positions that require a college education. The needed language skills can only be acquired through extended and intensive language study—that is, an early start and a long sequence. As the NCSSFL (2002) white paper puts it, "the United States must have quality foreign language programs in our schools so that all students will graduate with the ability to interact linguistically and culturally with people from many countries. Students who are competent in at least two languages will dramatically increase the U.S. capabilities in diplomacy, in world trade, and in human understanding" (4). It is also important to note that individuals who already can communicate effectively in two languages are in the best position to learn one or more additional languages quickly and efficiently, when new languages are needed for economic, political, strategic—or personal—purposes.

6. Integration of All Areas of the Curriculum. Every area of the curriculum can be reinforced or enriched in the foreign language classroom, and subject content can be taught through the second language. This kind of integration can foster appreciation of other cultures and can add significant dimensions to the content being taught. With close cooperation between language and classroom teachers, the second-language experience can contribute directly to the mastery of first-language concepts in the curriculum.

7. Cultural Enrichment. Most languages taught at the elementary school level can give insight into a variety of cultures, including multicultural elements in the students' own community. The positive impact of cultural information is significantly enhanced when that information is experienced through the foreign language and accompanied by experiences in culturally authentic situations.

Other Sources of Rationale

The Center for Applied Linguistics summarized the benefits of early language learning as follows:

"Learning a second language at an early age . . .

1. Has a positive effect on intellectual growth.
2. Enriches and enhances a child's mental development.
3. Leaves students with more flexibility in thinking, greater sensitivity to language, and a better ear for listening.
4. Improves a child's understanding of his/her native language.
5. Gives a child the ability to communicate with people s/he would otherwise not have the chance to know.
6. Opens the door to other cultures and helps a child understand and appreciate people from other countries.
7. Gives a student a head start in language requirements for college.
8. Increases job opportunities in many careers where knowing another language is a real asset."

Elizabeth Webb, in her summary of research on early language learning (2001), concurs that "many benefits accrue to children who learn a second language. Those include:

1. The ability to speak another language and communicate with people from a different culture.
2. Improved performance in other basic skill areas, as reading and math. (Students of average intelligence seem to make particularly impressive gains in reading skills.)

3. Improved cognitive flexibility, better problem-solving and higher-order thinking skills.
4. Higher SAT and ACT scores.
5. Higher test scores on standardized tests, such as the Iowa Test of Basic Skills, the Metropolitan Achievement Test, and the Louisiana Basic Skillls Test, in reading, language arts, math, and social studies.
6. Gains on measures of performance I.Q.
7. Improved communication skills, including better listening skills and a sharper memory.
8. Enhanced career potential."

Many of the resources listed at the end of this chapter will be useful in locating information and evidence to support a rationale. The brochure "Why, How, and When Should My Child Learn a Foreign Language?" (Marcos, 1997) is particularly helpful. In addition, readers are encouraged to examine rationale statements for languages and for elementary school programs available on the Internet. National reports on education often include information that gives strong support to teaching languages at the elementary school level; and reports on international business and trade also make mention of languages and their value. Even popular magazines occasionally publish features that can be valuable sources of rationale statements and which speak clearly to local audiences.

A rationale for teaching foreign languages at the elementary school level will be the result of many resources combined to address the needs and priorities of the local school and its community. The resources are abundant and varied, and serious program planners will find and use the most attractive and appropriate ones for their local situation.

Advocacy for Early Language Learning

With so much compelling evidence favoring early language learning, it would seem self-evident that foreign languages should be a basic part of the curriculum in the elementary and the middle school. Unfortunately, there are many obstacles to achieving the vision of a K–12 language education for every learner. In the absence of a long tradition of languages for young learners, such as that found in other parts of the world, and given the limited resources available for education at every level, the addition of a "new basic" to the curriculum has not received widespread support. The fact that local control is a significant and valued characteristic of American schools makes it difficult to establish national language policy like that found in other countries with well-developed early language programs (Rhodes and Branaman 1999). The new century has brought a new awareness of a need for advocacy for early language learning at the national, state, and local levels.

State and National Advocacy Efforts

The Joint National Committee for Languages and the National Council for Languages and International Studies (JNCL-NCLIS) serves as an important advocacy arm of the foreign language profession. Based in Washington, D.C., JNCL-NCLIS serves the profession as the liaison between foreign language teachers and administrators and the federal government. They lobby for foreign language goals and inform the profession about dangers and opportunities as they arise. Their Web site (see "Web Sites of Interest" at the end of this chapter) is an excellent source of information about pending legislation, funding opportunities, and grants of all types. This group also provides sound advice for foreign language professionals who wish to make their own advocacy efforts more effective.

The National Network for Early Language Learning (NNELL) has an active Political Action and Advocacy Committee that guides and encourages advocacy efforts for early language learning throughout the country. The Advocacy Packet, regularly updated, is an invaluable resource for information about benefits of language learning, resources, and strategies for advocacy efforts. The packet is available on their Web site, www.nnell.org.

State Initiatives. Many state associations, including North Carolina, Ohio, Texas, and Wisconsin, have formed political action and advocacy committees to promote language study in their states. In many cases these committees have devoted special attention to the elementary and middle school levels. Advocacy at the state level usually focuses on the state legislators, the governor, and the public at large. Two states, Georgia and North Carolina, will serve as helpful examples of how effective advocacy can take place.

Georgia. Georgia initiated a model programs project in 1992; these state-supported programs began with kindergarten students and added a grade level each year through grade five. The fifteen counties chosen for participation in the program guaranteed that language instruction would take place five days per week, thirty minutes per day, and that teachers would have no more than eight classes per day. Because funding for the program was often in doubt, teachers, parents, and administrators found themselves writing letters and contacting legislators on a regular basis to guarantee support for the coming year. In 2002 a group of concerned educators and other interested individuals formed the Coalition for Language Learning to advocate for foreign language programs at all levels of instruction.

Shortly after the coalition was formed, the group was faced with its first crisis. The governor failed to include funding for the model programs in his budget, and the entire program was threatened. Ironically, the governor's action took place soon after the Center for Applied Linguistics had announced that students in the Georgia Elementary School Foreign Language (ESFL) model programs had scored higher than students in any other program they had tested to date nationwide.

The coalition mobilized and began a campaign of information and advocacy that involved personal visits to legislators and the governor, letter writing by students and parents, and even performances by students at the state capitol. One group of students and parents from a Japanese program folded an origami basket for every legislator containing sweet treats and a message: "Save our Japanese program"—in English and Japanese.

The funding for the program was restored by the legislature and finally approved by the governor. This result would not have been possible without the intensive advocacy efforts of the entire foreign language community, led by the Georgia Coalition for Language Learning.

North Carolina. The Alliance for Language Learning was established in late 1998 to promote opportunities for learning languages throughout North Carolina. It serves as an advocate and as a resource for parents, communities, schools, businesses, and policy makers at state and local levels. The advocacy committee within the Alliance responds to requests for advocacy and makes presentations to economic development committees, civic clubs, and others. Decision makers such as legislators and State Board of Education members are regularly provided with information to encourage their support of foreign language study.

One of the most significant projects undertaken by the Alliance is its Vision 2010, a foreign language component of the North Carolina goal to have the best education system in the country by the year 2010. The Alliance goal for Vision 2010 is to establish well-developed K–12 model foreign language programs across North Carolina.

North Carolina's first Vision 2010 Model Foreign Language Program was established in the fall of 2002, with fifty kindergarten students who have daily content-related FLES instruction in Spanish. An assessment component of the project will document the language proficiency attained at the end of each program year. Additional Vision 2010 programs are envisioned across North Carolina. Ongoing support, including teacher academies, will be provided by the Alliance for Language Learning to ensure that each new site will have the resources to develop and maintain a quality, well-developed and articulated K–12 foreign language program.

The Teacher as Advocate

Once a new program is established, successful, and well regarded, it is tempting to believe that the need for advocacy is over. In fact, the early language teacher needs to be a long-term advocate, if the program is to experience continued success. With a new program there is always a "honeymoon" period of varying length, during which time parents and classroom teachers are amazed at the speed and effectiveness of the language learning. Once this period is over, however, it takes effort on the part of the language teacher to demonstrate what students are learning and to sustain public awareness and support of the program. Each program faces articulation issues, student and parent turnover, and ever-present funding issues, and each of these issues requires a specific advocacy or public relations strategy.

Advocacy begins with the language teacher's day-to-day interactions with the rest of the learning community: school and district administrators, parents, and colleagues such as classroom teachers, teachers of music, physical education and other specials, upper-grade teachers of world languages, guidance counselors, and media specialists. The language teacher can build bridges of cooperation and mutual support that will hold up in the face of budget or scheduling crises. It is also important to help students themselves understand the value of the program and of their opportunity to learn another language, since student attitudes and understandings are the main source of information about the program in many parts of the community. Haxhi (2001) suggests advocacy strategies for use with these groups, as well as with the community at large:

■ Keep all "players" informed.
  Regular newsletters to parents, with copies to administrators, school board members, and classroom teachers, can help all the "players" to have realistic expectations of the

program and to understand what children can be expected to do. Haxhi also uses interactive homework as a means of keeping parents informed about student progress.

- Offer opportunities for involvement, observation, and suggestions.
- Be willing to adapt to changes and to improve.
- Identify the most rewarding (advocacy) activities, and eliminate inefficient activities.
- Get involved!

The language teacher who volunteers to help with the third grade play, or to usher for the music program, is indirectly advocating for the language program at the same time. The language teacher who offers to help build the class schedule is perceived as a team player and can help to create an effective schedule that is manageable for all of the teachers involved.

One of the most effective advocacy activities is a presentation for the local school board, perhaps including students or videotapes that show actual student performance. Virginia Gramer (1999) provided an excellent model for a persuasive school board presentation at a meeting of the ACTFL Delegate Assembly in Chicago. Much of the presentation was devoted to success stories of former students who had begun their language study in the elementary school.

It is important for the language program to be represented at school events, such as parent-teacher meetings, carnivals, and seasonal plays and programs. Sometimes the language classes stage an event themselves, such as a festival, an ethnic dinner, or a classroom presentation for parents. Sometimes the language students develop interesting projects that take the language beyond the classroom, such as writing and reading storybooks in the target language to younger learners, or putting on a play for other classes. In any of these cases, media coverage helps to spread the word about the program and the students involved.

Redmond (1998) suggests the following strategies (4–7) for early language specialist teachers to help them become more effective advocates for early language learning, both locally and on the state and national level. These strategies serve as a summary of the many ways a teacher can advocate for early language learning, both within and beyond the school itself.

Strategy 1: Take every opportunity to inform parents, administrators, and the local community about the foreign language program and your students' accomplishments.

Strategy 2: Clarify the nature of the foreign language curriculum and its connectedness to the elementary school classroom.

Strategy 3: Show parents and the community the skills attained and the purposes for the language learned.

Strategy 4: Invite guests to visit your classes to observe the children "in action."

Strategy 5: Assess students' progress both informally and formally and make parents aware of the results.

Strategy 6: Keep politicians, school board members, and other decision makers informed about your program.

Strategy 7: Thank your supporters!

Strategy 8: Change the mindset of those who studied a language unsuccessfully.

Strategy 9: Network with colleagues and unify efforts in grades K–16.

Strategy 10: Establish regular planning sessions with both elementary classroom teachers and K–12 foreign language colleagues.

Strategy 11: Use your state conference to organize advocacy efforts.

There are numerous resources available to assist early language teachers in implementing these strategies, and in developing activities that will highlight both their own programs and the importance of K–12 language learning. The resources listed at the end of this chapter will serve as a helpful starting point. As teachers work together to build and to draw from unified advocacy initiatives, the place of early language learning in the American school curriculum will become ever more secure.

Summary

No single rationale for teaching of foreign languages at the elementary school level will be effective for every program in every setting. Those who develop and seek support for such programs will need to tailor their rationale to the priorities and values of the community that the program will serve. An effective rationale will draw from a variety of recognized sources when building the case for early language learning and the K–12 sequence. Brain research in the last decade of the twentieth century has given strong support to an early start and a long sequence for language study. Many sound reasons for language learning have been advanced by national reports and studies, both for foreign language study generally and for elementary school languages in particular. The level of communication skills in two or more languages that can provide both career benefits and societal benefits can only be obtained through an early start and a long sequence of language study. The goals of the elementary school and the philosophy of the school district are additional resources for building a rationale, as they set the context for a holistic education to which foreign language can make a unique and valuable contribution.

Advocacy for early language learning is an important function of professional organizations at both the state and the national levels. It is also the responsibility of elementary and middle school language specialists to serve as advocates for their own programs and for K–12 language learning opportunities for all students. Numerous resources are available to support teachers in this essential part of their professional role. This chapter has given examples of advocacy in action and suggestions for the language teaching professional.

FOR STUDY AND DISCUSSION

1. What reasons have you most frequently heard for teaching languages at the elementary school level? Which of these reasons do you feel would be good building blocks for a rationale statement?

2. A parent committee has asked for your assistance in convincing the school board to consider developing a foreign language program at the elementary school level. Write a memo advising the committee how they might go about building their case.

3. The curriculum coordinator in your district has recently discovered research indicating that children may not be better language learners than adults, and that they are in fact less efficient learners of the grammar and structure than are older students. How do you respond to her suggestion that languages should not be taught until grade nine, based on this information?

4. Which of the reasons for teaching languages in the elementary school would be the most convincing for the faculty, administrators, and parents of the school district or school setting with which you are the most familiar?

5. Develop a two-minute advocacy presentation in which you summarize the most important reasons for developing a K–12 foreign language sequence in your school system.

6. Read at least one reference from the listing below about advocacy for early language learning. Describe one strategy not already mentioned in the chapter that you could use to advocate for your program with each of the following: colleagues, administrators, the community, parents, and students.

FOR FURTHER READING

The following sources are recommended for additional information about material covered in this chapter. Chapter citations are documented in Works Cited at the end of the volume.

Gramer, Virginia. "Advocacy for Early Language Education: A School Board Presentation." *Learning Languages* 4, no. 3 (spring 1999): 4–8.

Marcos, Kathleen. "Why, How, and When Should My Child Learn a Foreign Language?" Washington, DC: ERIC Clearinghouse on Languages and Linguistics, 1997. Available on-line at www.accesseric.org/resources/parent/languages.html

———. "Second Language Learning: Everyone Can Benefit." *The ERIC Review: K–12 Foreign Language Education* 6, no. 1 (fall 1998): 2–5.

National Network for Early Language Learning (NNELL) Advocacy Packet. http://nnell.org.

Redmond, Mary Lynn. "ATTENTION! Are You Seeking a Position with Excellent Long-term Benefits? Be an Advocate!" *Learning Languages* 4, no. 1 (fall 1998): 4–9.

Robinson, Deborah Wilburn. "The Cognitive, Academic, and Attitudinal Benefits of Early Language Learning." In *Critical Issues in Early Second Language Learning: Building for Our Children's Future,* edited by Myriam Met, 37–43. Glenview, IL: Scott-Foresman-Addison Wesley, 1998.

Simon, Paul. *The Tongue-Tied American. Confronting the Foreign Language Crisis.* New York: Continuum Publishing, 1980.

WEB SITES OF INTEREST

Association for Supervision and Curriculum Development (ASCD) Advocacy Kit:
    www.ascd.org/advocacykit/

News in Science: Bilingual Kids Not Slowed by Second Tongue.
    Available at www.abc.net.au/science/news/stories/s720173.html

Foreign Language Study and the Brain Web site, University of Idaho, Teresa Kennedy.
    http://ivc.uidaho.edu/flbrain/

Joint National Committee for Languages and National Council for Languages and International Studies (Foreign Language Advocacy):
    www.languagepolicy.org

League of Women Voters:
    www.lwv.org

Ñandu Early Language Web site:
    www.cal.org/earlylang/

National K–12 Foreign Language Resource Center:
    www.educ.iastate.edu/nflrc/

National Network for Early Language Learning (NNELL):
    www.nnell.org

17 Learning from the Past to Enhance the Present and the Future

Children have been learning new languages in American schools since colonial times, and the presence of these languages in the curriculum has often been the subject of controversy. Many of the concerns raised a century or more ago sound surprisingly like discussions held at contemporary staff and school board meetings at which districts consider the addition or expansion of an elementary school language program. It is important for the advocate of languages for children to understand past successes and problems, especially those of the heyday for early language programs in the 1960s, in order to plan and implement programs that build on the strengths and insights of the past and avoid its failures.

A Short History of Early Language Learning in the United States

Foreign language instruction has been fairly common in the United States throughout its history; Latin was often taught in the early years, and German was popular after the great waves of German immigration in 1830 and 1848. French and Spanish schools developed in some areas of the country where there were concentrations of immigrants from French- and Spanish-speaking countries.

Objections to the teaching of German and other languages in the elementary schools were raised by state and territorial officials, often on the grounds that the practice was un-American, and that children in private and parochial schools were being taught by individuals who did not even speak English. However, programs persisted and grew, despite the controversies, until the United States entered World War I. At that time there was a strong reaction against everything German, especially the language, and much elementary school instruction in all languages other than English was eliminated.

New Impetus for Language Instruction

In the 1940s a concern for improvement of Latin American understanding led to the development of Spanish-language programs in the elementary schools of the American Southwest. In 1957, after the stunning orbit of Sputnik, public awareness of the value of foreign language education was heightened by the jarring information that the United States could have known about the development of the Russian satellite had American scientists been regular readers of Russian journals. As a result, languages were included along with mathematics and science in the generous funding of the National Defense Education Act (NDEA) of 1958. Among other provisions, the act included matching funds for the purchase of instructional equipment and materials, and it provided for the training of teachers in "critical" languages (German, French, Spanish, Russian) at both the elementary and the secondary school level.

The national sense of urgency explains in part the haste with which many school districts launched language programs at both the elementary and the secondary school level. Years of low priority for languages had failed to produce enough language teachers to meet the new demand, and most of the teachers available had little preparation for the elementary school level. These factors underscored the importance of the training provisions of the NDEA. Institutes were funded throughout the country to prepare teachers in the new aural-oral/audiolingual approach, based on the methods developed for the army during World War II.

These NDEA institutes marked the first time in the United States that there had been a concentrated effort centered on the development of an approach to language teaching. Much of the teaching of modern languages before the 1960s, even at the elementary school level, had been modeled on the teaching of Latin and Greek, and had included an emphasis on reading, translation, and grammatical analysis using the terminology of Latin grammar. That approach may have been intended to earn academic and intellectual respect for modern languages, which had not been valued in a classical education (Grittner 1977).

In contrast, Emile de Sauze directed a program in Cleveland for selected elementary school students from 1918 until 1949. Under the "Cleveland Plan" all instruction was conducted in the new language, and reading and writing were deferred until the sixth grade (Donoghue 1968).

At the end of the nineteenth century some teachers had already begun to break with the Latin-based formula for language teaching, experimenting with the "natural" and the "direct" methods. Each of these methods stressed the spoken word and de-emphasized grammar for its own sake, although the direct method approached grammar more systematically and developed more carefully constructed curricula. Both required a teacher who was fluent in the language and who was willing to use the target language almost exclusively (Zeydel 1961).

Against this background, the audiolingual method of the 1960s represented a dramatic burst of new energy for language teaching. It claimed a basis in the relatively new field of structural linguistics and in behavioral psychology, as it de-emphasized the traditional methods of grammar study and focused on language competence developed through habit formation. Elementary school students were viewed as natural candidates for this type of instruction because they were far less resistant to the repetition and drill required by the method. Oral language served as the starting point of all language study, even for those students to whom reading was a primary goal. Inductive grammar and oral drill replaced grammatical analysis in English; listening and speaking practice in the classroom and in the language laboratory replaced reading and translation exercises.

Thousands of teachers were trained or retrained in NDEA institutes, which gave teachers the opportunity to develop skills in the new method and to improve their speaking skills in the language. Except for pockets of resistance or misunderstanding, a whole generation of language teachers began modeling dialogues, conducting pattern drills, and practicing the art of mimicry-memorization.

Short-Lived Gains

There was every reason to be optimistic that the newly attained place for languages in national priorities and the new method, supported with new opportunities for teacher preparation, would lead to a "golden age" for language programs, especially at the elementary school level. But the ambitions and good intentions of school districts often outdistanced genuine planning and the availability of well-trained personnel. The "boom" for languages in the elementary schools lasted barely five years, as programs at this level were in decline after 1964. Many of the reasons for this short period of popularity are described in "A Survey of FLES Practices," a report written for the Modern Language Association in 1961. After visiting sixty-two communities with reportedly good FLES programs in the spring of 1961, Alkonis and Brophy drew the following conclusions (213–217):

1. A majority of the FLES programs that we observed do not fulfill the primary aim of such a program—teaching the four language skills—even when this is clearly stated as their objective. Sometimes the teacher is weak; just as often the weakness lies beyond the teacher's control, in the materials or the scheduling.
2. Many programs emphasized such aims as "world understanding" or "broadened horizons" to the extent that it is a clear misnomer to call them *language* programs. We saw no evidence of effective evaluation of the teaching directed toward these objectives. . . .
3. There is such a diversity of linguistic content that a general evaluation of results using a single test or series of tests appears to be impracticable.
4. From the widespread emphasis upon learning lists of words, we conclude that a majority of the FLES teachers think of language as words to be learned in isolation and then strung into "conversation." They showed no awareness of the interacting systems of structure or patterns that are basic to each language.
5. Many programs, started without planning and provision for the materials, the instruction, and the eventual integration with junior- and senior-high school courses, are considered "experimental," but there is no clear statement of the conditions and terms of the experiment and no provision for an evaluation of its results.
6. The most obvious weakness is lack of teachers with sufficient skill in the language and training in methods. (This is no reflection on the sincerity, the enthusiasm, or the good will of the instructors. How many of us, with no knowledge of music and unable to play the piano, could successfully teach a roomful of little children to play that instrument?)
7. In many schools—certainly in the majority of those we visited—FLES is conceived of as merely a preview or prelude to "real" language learning (which will begin in

the high school) rather than as a serious, systematic attempt to develop attitudes and skills.

8. Few programs are planned as an unbroken, cumulative sequence from the primary through the junior high school, partly because of the lack of appropriate teaching materials for the junior high school, but more because of the inadequacy of the FLES work itself.

The eight observations made by Alkonis and Brophy effectively summarized the problems that most FLES programs of the 1960s failed to resolve. As budgets tightened and priorities shifted, as promised results failed to materialize, as graduates of FLES programs failed to meet the expectations of junior and senior high school teachers, language programs in the elementary school lost their credibility as well as their value as a status symbol. These programs were among the first to be cut when school systems evaluated their curricula to make room for new trends and emphases.

Although NDEA funding continued through 1968, the last institute designed specifically for elementary school teachers was held in 1965, at which time enthusiasm for the audiolingual method was also beginning to wane. While the combination of structural linguistics and behavioral psychology had focused on the external features of language, a new concern for the internal processing of language was being articulated by the rationalists and the generative grammarians. Emphasis was shifting from the manipulation of patterns that might eventually be used to convey information to the use of language as a means of communication, and from the means by which an idea was expressed to the importance of the idea being communicated.

The decline of interest and support for traditional foreign language programs in the schools, however, first evidenced by the loss of enthusiasm for elementary school language programs, had become widespread by the early 1970s. Unsettling events at home and abroad led to a period of student apathy and low motivation. The war in Vietnam and student protests at colleges and universities became the focus of public attention. School enrollments began to decline, and enrollments in language classes declined even more rapidly. Critics blamed the tedium and irrelevance of the audiolingual method for declining language enrollments, and universities aggravated the situation by dropping language entrance and exit requirements.

New Challenges and Opportunities

Meanwhile, attempts to understand more about language learning and teaching were being made on behalf of language-minority students. An influx of Spanish-speaking families from Latin American countries and the arrival of refugees from Southeast Asia increased the population of non-English-speaking children in the schools in many areas in the United States and created a need for language instruction for these children.

In dealing with the challenge, teachers of English to speakers of other languages found assistance from linguists and psychologists. This alliance has resulted in a growing body of research that shed new light on how language competence is developed. Abroad, the Council of Europe developed an approach to language teaching and learning that was based on the communication needs of the learner. *The Threshold Level for Modern*

Language Learning in Schools (Van Ek 1977), a resource available for several European languages, identifies functions and vocabulary necessary to interact successfully in a variety of specific situations. Together, these developments reinforced the emerging emphasis on the messages being expressed by language and the process of language acquisition.

In Canada, the desire of English-speaking parents to increase their children's proficiency in French led to the establishment of immersion programs, an innovative educational approach in which the language of the school setting is different from the language of the home, and children learn subject content through the new language. The first French kindergarten class for native speakers of English was offered in September 1965, in St. Lambert, a suburb of Montreal. Public school immersion programs spread throughout Canada and have been thoroughly researched and documented. Immersion has also spread to many parts of the United States, and according to the Center for Applied Linguistics, there were immersion programs in at least thirty cities in the United States by 1987, involving 8,000 school children. By 1999 there were approximately 46,000 children enrolled in eleven languages in 278 immersion schools, more than half of them in Spanish (Center for Applied Linguistics, "Total and Partial Immersion Programs" 1987, 1999). In Canada, French immersion programs alone enrolled nearly 50,000 children in 1979, 150,000 in 1985, and over 300,000 by 2000 (Canadian Parents for French, 2001).

Another approach to teaching subject content and language together was developing for the non-English-speaking child in American schools. Beginning with Cuban refugee children in the Dade County schools of Florida in 1963, bilingual programs helped children learn to read and write in their own language as well as introducing them to English. In most such programs subject content material is taught in both languages, with an increasing emphasis on English at each grade level.

Many early bilingual programs also included the opportunity for English-speaking children to learn the second language in the same setting. With this approach, student native speakers serve as language models for one another. These programs, usually called two-way immersion or two-way bilingual programs, grew in popularity at the turn of the century. By 2000 there were 260 programs in 23 states, most of them in Spanish. This model depends on the presence of a stable population of native speakers in both languages, and the growing Spanish population in the United States creates ideal conditions for two-way Spanish immersion programs.

Renewed Interest in Languages for Young Learners

Twenty years after Sputnik, the national interest in languages other than English was again awakened by international events. The rise of multinational corporations, the increasing importance of international trade, and an oil crisis all contributed to a renewed awareness of American dependence on global relationships. The 1979 President's Commission on Foreign Language and International Studies was the first of a series of commissions on education to highlight the serious situation created by the lack of language skills among Americans. Its specific recommendations included the urging of language study in the elementary school and the development of imaginative curricula dealing with other countries and cultures. Subsequent national studies and reports about education, such as *A Nation at*

Risk (D. Gardner 1983), amplified the call for a more international vision in the schools and a higher priority for language learning.

The first calls for early language learning were joined by many more voices. Among others, the National Governors Association task force recommended in 1990 that all students should have the opportunity to learn to speak a foreign language in their early years; the Commission on International Education of the American Council on Education expressed support for long sequence programs resulting in proficiency, recommending in 1989 that foreign language training should begin as early as possible, preferably in elementary school. On September 11, 2001 American awareness was once again jolted into recognition of the importance to national security of citizens who have skills in a variety of languages.

Further impetus for early language learning came from results and interpretation of brain research, brought to popular awareness through reports in *Newsweek* (Begley 1996) and *Time* (Nash 1997). J. Madeline Nash wrote in the *Time* article, "The ability to learn a second language is highest between birth and the age of six, and then undergoes a steady and inexorable decline. . . . What lessons can be drawn from the new findings? Among other things, it is clear that foreign languages should be taught in elementary school, if not before" (56).

Responses from States and Local School Systems

Responses have come in a variety of ways to the call for early language learning and a long sequence of study. Arizona, for example, mandated foreign language instruction for all students in grades one through eight, with full implementation scheduled for the 1998–1999 school year. Since the mandate was not supported with financial resources, however, it produced only a few new language programs and no teacher preparation programs. Hawaii, Louisiana, New Jersey, North Carolina, Oklahoma, and Wyoming, for example, all mandated foreign language study in some form in the elementary school, although not all mandates led to the results envisioned by legislators. In states where there was sufficient financial and professional support for the elementary school initiative, new programs thrived. Where such support was lacking, as in the Arizona example, the mandates led to only a few new programs in districts that could afford to make languages a priority. Other states, such as Georgia and Iowa, offered some types of financial incentives to school districts willing to plan language programs for the elementary school. This list of state initiatives, though incomplete, gives strong evidence of the tremendous interest in K–8 language programs even at a time of financial cutbacks in education. In some states that were not able to provide financial support for their interest in early language learning, new programs were encouraged by state mandates and other incentives.

The variety of language offerings for young learners has also increased. While Spanish programs outnumber all others, French, Latin, and German continue to be taught at the elementary school level. Increasing numbers of programs are being developed in Chinese, Japanese, Arabic, and Russian, as a reflection of world economic and political realities. Sometimes elementary school language offerings reflect the ethnic background of the community, and the desire to continue with heritage languages. Italian, Portuguese, Hebrew, Czech, Korean, Norwegian, Persian, Greek, and Welsh are examples of such language instruction.

In 1997 there were foreign language programs in 31 percent of all public and private elementary schools surveyed by the Center for Applied Linguistics, up from 22 percent in 1987. Spanish was taught in 79 percent of the programs, followed by French at 27 percent. Programs in German, Latin, Japanese, and Spanish for Spanish speakers were also well represented (Rhodes and Branaman 1999).

Response by the Profession

The professional community also responded to the new public interest in early language programs for children. The National Network for Early Language Learning (NNELL) was originally established in 1987 as an informal network of teachers and supervisors interested in K–8 languages, then became a formal organization in 1991. Its newsletter, *FLES News,* reached over five hundred members three times a year. *FLES News* became a peer-reviewed journal, *Learning Languages,* in 1991, and by 2002 the membership and journal circulation had reached one thousand. NNELL has grown to include a large board of directors, vigorous state organizations, and sponsors sessions at nearly every national and regional meeting of language teachers, as well as at many state meetings.

Advocates for Language Learning (ALL), founded in 1985, drew a large attendance at its yearly conference for parents, administrators, and teachers interested in early language learning. The conference on *Second Language Acquisition by Children,* first held in Oklahoma City in 1985, was an opportunity for practitioners and researchers to meet every 18 months around the topic of languages and learners at the K–8 level. As the national organizations for language teachers began to give greater attention to languages for K–8 learners, and with the increasing influence of NNELL, these conferences disbanded and disappeared by the late 1990s.

The three largest language-specific teacher organizations have each developed special projects addressing K–8 languages: The American Association of Teachers of German (AATG) has its *Kinder lernen Deutsch* steering committee, established in 1987, which channels funds from the German government into teacher preparation, materials evaluation and development, and support for program planning and implementation. The American Association of Teachers of French, (AATF), long active in support of elementary school programs, published a series of useful resources through its FLES Commission. The American Association of Teachers of Spanish and Portuguese (AATSP) has also established a commission for programs at this level, and *Hispania,* their professional journal, regularly addresses the concerns of K–8 programs.

Teachers have access to state and national conferences sponsored by these organizations, as well as regional conferences including the Northeast Conference on the Teaching of Foreign Languages, the Southern Conference on Language Teaching, the Southwest Conference on Language Teaching, and the Central States Conference on the Teaching of Foreign Languages. Most sessions at these conferences focus on curriculum and pedagogy for the K–12 level.

The Center for Applied Linguistics (CAL) provides research and information about K–12 language learning, and its ERIC Clearinghouse on Languages and Linguistics offers a wide range of resources in foreign language education. National Language Resource Centers were created in 1990, under Title VI of the Higher Education Act of the U.S.

Department of Education, to serve as resources to improve the nation's capacity to teach and learn foreign languages effectively. As of 2002, there were fourteen such resource centers located throughout the United States and Hawaii. One of these, the K–12 Foreign Language Resource Center at Iowa State University, is focused specifically on issues of curriculum, assessment, and teacher development for K–12 programs, with special emphasis on the K–8 level.

Listservs and their archives provide teachers with the opportunity to post questions about programs, materials, or methodology and share their ideas with colleagues from all over the country. Two of the most popular are FLTeach, used especially by middle and high school teachers, and Ñandu, the early language listserv for K-8 teachers.

The Proficiency Movement and Elementary and Middle School Language Programs

The description of academic expectations, especially at the college and graduate level, and measures of achievement of language goals have traditionally been based on grammar as an organizing principle and on the teaching of discrete points as a standard practice. This may have been one reason for poor articulation in the past between communication-based elementary school language programs and the secondary school programs into which they fed.

The Proficiency Guidelines from the American Council on the Teaching of Foreign Languages (ACTFL), first published in 1986, marked a pivotal change in the teaching of new languages in the United States. They refocused language instructional goals from what learners know *about* language to what they can *do with* the language they have learned, and at the same time they established a common metric for measuring student performance. Emphasis has shifted from grammar and discrete-item testing to a global evaluation of language competencies. Teachers can permit themselves to assess communication of meaning as well as, though not to the total exclusion of, degree of accuracy, and students can be rewarded for a much broader range of language ability and performance.

The proficiency guidelines describe student performance in listening, speaking, reading, and writing at the novice, intermediate, advanced, and superior levels. They define student language performance in terms of function, content, and accuracy of the message being delivered or received. They were adapted from guidelines developed in U.S. government language schools and have made "proficiency-oriented instruction" a part of the vocabulary of every language teacher. The 1986 guidelines were subsequently reevaluated and revised, beginning with "Speaking" in 1999 (Breiner-Sanders, Lowe, Miles, Swender 2000) and "Writing" in 2001 (Breiner-Sanders, Swender, Terry 2002).

Elementary school language teachers may find the ACTFL guidelines difficult to apply directly to the curriculum of the elementary school program. Many of the functions and much of the content described are not closely related to the interests and needs of children. Yet the principle of purposeful language use is clearly held in common at all levels of communicative language teaching. The guidelines can serve the elementary school language teacher very well as a guide to the future uses to which the language taught in the elementary school will be put. This can make the ACTFL Proficiency Guidelines useful in bridging the gaps between elementary school, middle school, and high school programs.

The ACTFL Guidelines give us an important tool for looking at the outcomes of instruction. This tool can help K–8 language teachers to be both more realistic in their goals for instruction and more realistic in their claims for their programs.

Shaping a K–12 Vision for Language Learning

Perhaps the most significant activity within the language teaching profession has been the movement toward the shared vision of a long sequence of language instruction beginning in the elementary school. "Start Early—Stay Long" was the motto of the initiative established in 1992 by the American Council on the Teaching of Foreign Languages (ACTFL), the umbrella organization for language teachers at all levels. The New American: Project 2017 was a joint project with the National Foreign Language Center to lay the groundwork for sound language programs that progress smoothly from elementary school through the university level. The National Foreign Language Center also sponsored a 1999 National Town Meeting on issues surrounding early language learning entitled "Preparing Young Americans for the 21st Century." The Town Meeting was held in Washington, D.C. and attended by lawmakers and policy makers at the national level, as well as by language professionals.

The Project 2017 initiative was superseded by the challenge and opportunity of the federal Goals 2000 project (later named Educate America 2000). In 1993 the language profession became the seventh and final content area to receive funding from the U.S. Department of Education and the National Endowment for the Humanities to develop a series of content standards—what students should know and be able to do—in foreign language education. This three-year grant, and the place for foreign languages in the listing of critical subject areas, came after several years of lobbying by professional organizations and the Joint National Committee for Language (JNCL). ACTFL, together with AATF, AATG, and AATSP, spearheaded the effort to establish goals and standards for language learning, with descriptors and sample progress indicators at grades four, eight, and twelve. The eleven-member Standards task force represented a variety of languages, levels of instruction, program models, and geographic regions. The decision to design the Standards for an extended, K–12 sequence was made after considerable discussion and significant input from professionals who were already active at the K–6 level.

Standards for Foreign Language Learning in the 21st Century

Just as the proficiency movement spawned a whole new way of thinking about language instruction and assessment, the *Standards for Foreign Language Learning in the 21st Century,* first released in 1996 and revised in 1999, provided a significant new focus for curriculum and program planning. In contrast to earlier curriculum documents, the Standards have created the bold vision of a long sequence of language instruction for all learners, beginning in kindergarten and continuing through grade twelve and beyond. For the first time in the United States, the language teaching profession had made a strong statement about the importance of a long sequence of instruction beginning with the earliest years of schooling. By 1999 the language-specific professional organizations had developed supporting Standards documents describing student progress from grades K–16, thus focusing the entire instructional sequence on a unified vision of language education.

Within a short period of time after the appearance of the Standards in 1996, publishers and in-service providers began to focus materials and workshops on the five goals and eleven content standards described in the Standards document. (See the Standards summary on page xxi.) These content standards describe what students should know and be able to do as a result of instruction, and they are the first step in the process of standards development. Sample performance indicators for grades four, eight, and twelve provide examples of how students demonstrate progress in meeting a standard. They also point the way toward performance standards that define how students demonstrate competency in a given content standard. The ACTFL Proficiency Guidelines are an example of performance standards, but they were designed to describe language performance of adult or adult-like language users, regardless of where or how that language was acquired.

ACTFL Performance Guidelines for K–12 Learners

An ACTFL Young Learner Task Force drew on the *ACTFL Proficiency Guidelines* of 1982, the *Standards for Foreign Language Learning,* and classroom experiences to develop a set of performance standards appropriate for K–12 learners. The *ACTFL Performance Guidelines for K–12 Learners,* released in November 1997, focus on students who participate in elementary, middle school, and high school language programs, taking into account the continuous cognitive development of students at these levels and its influence on their ability to perform language tasks. They also recognize the fact that most K–12 language development takes place in a classroom context, with a curriculum that is articulated from one level to the next. (Swender and Duncan, 1998).

The Performance Guidelines provide benchmarks for the novice range (end of the K–4 sequence, or grades five to eight, or any two years in high school), for the intermediate range (end of the K–8 sequence, or grades nine to twelve, or grades five to twelve); or for the pre-advanced learner range (end of a K–12 sequence). Performance descriptors are grouped into six domains:

> **Comprehensibility** (How well is the student understood?)
> **Comprehension** (How well does the student understand?)
> **Language Control** (How accurate is the student's language?)
> **Vocabulary Use** (How extensive and applicable is the student's vocabulary?)
> **Communication Strategies** (How does the student maintain communication?)
> **Cultural Awareness** (How is the student's cultural knowledge reflected in language use?)

Under each of these domains, student performance is described in terms of the communication modes identified in the Standards: interpersonal (1.1), interpretive (1.2) and presentational (1.3) (See Appendix).

These *ACTFL Performance Guidelines for K–12 Learners* can assist language teachers in gauging the performance levels of their students. They can also help teachers to design effective learning and performance tasks that will guide and assess student progress toward local, state, and national content standards.

The chart in Figure 17.1 illustrates the anticipated performance outcomes described in the K–12 Guidelines and shows their relationship to the *ACTFL Proficiency Guidelines.* Note that the pre-advanced level in the Performance Guidelines is equivalent to intermediate high in the Proficiency Guidelines. Once students have attained the pre-advanced level, the ACTFL Proficiency Guidelines can be used to describe student progress through the superior level.

Working Toward the K–12 Vision

The K–12 vision articulated in the Standards and in the ACTFL Performance Guidelines has infused the language teaching profession in a variety of ways. The National K–12 Foreign Language Resource Center at Iowa State University, together with ACTFL, launched a New Visions project with a goal of reevaluating and reshaping the profession in the light of the Standards—including the goals of language instruction for every child and appropriate preparation for every language teacher. Many states shifted their licensing for world language teachers from a focus on secondary school students—the 7–12 or 5–12 license—to preparation for the long sequence of instruction: K-12 licensure. This approach to teacher licensing motivates colleges and universities to reexamine and reshape their teacher preparation sequences. More institutions now provide preparation for teachers in K–12, instead of exclusively for middle school (beginning at grade five, six, or seven, depending on the state) through grade 12, and this change has become an important factor in moving the K–12 vision forward. Unfortunately, a mandate for K–12 licensure alone cannot ensure that there will be college or university personnel available who understand the elementary school level, and some institutions of higher education find it difficult to create meaningful, appropriately staffed programs. Neither licensing requirements for higher education nor language requirements for elementary schools can ensure quality programs without sufficient funding to institute new programs.

As individual states developed their own standards, in response to the Goals 2000 legislation, most have used the national Standards as their model and described a K–12 sequence of language learning. This has been true even in states with very few existing elementary school programs.

Other efforts to support the K–12 vision have developed through the efforts of foreign language educators themselves. In North Carolina, for example, the Vision 2010 project of the Alliance for Language Learning seeks to develop at least one model K–12 articulated sequence in every school district in the state by the year 2010. Other states have language alliances that bring language teachers together from pre-kindergarten through university levels, with a shared goal of advocating for language learning and bridging the gaps in articulation from one school or age level to another.

The K–12 vision challenges the profession to find new ways to communicate across grade levels and new ways to conceptualize curriculum, instruction, and teacher preparation. It will require the involvement of every member of the profession to translate the vision into reality.

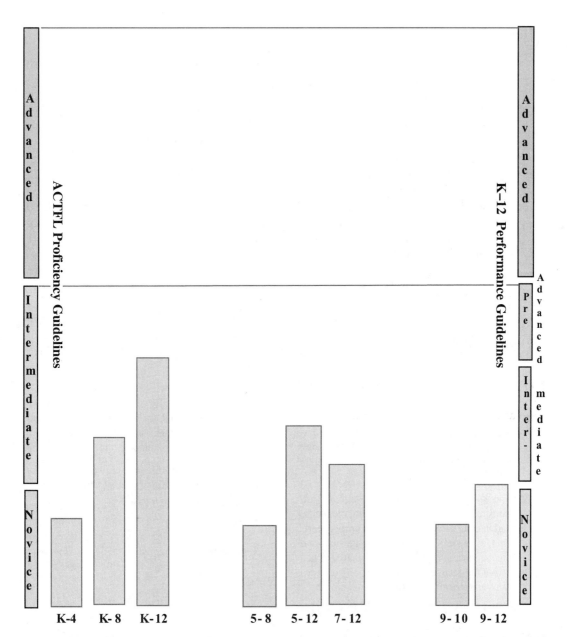

*Descriptors are based on information gathered from foreign language professionals representing a variety of program models and articulation sequences. Descriptors are appropriate for languages most commonly taught in the U.S. Descriptors assume a sustained sequence of Standards-based, performance-outcome language instruction.

FIGURE 17.1   Visual Representation of Anticipated Performance Outcomes as Described in the ACTFL Performance Guidelines for K–12 Learners*

Source: Foreign Language Annals 31, no. 4 (winter 1998): 484. © ACTFL 1998. Reprinted by permission of ACTFL.

Summary

The challenge for the twenty-first century is to learn from the past, to develop programs strong enough to withstand the shifting winds of enthusiasm and fad, and to realize the vision of the K–12 articulated language sequence. Many of the problems that plagued the 1960s still threaten us, especially at the elementary school level: a shortage of qualified teachers, a tendency to establish programs without sufficient planning or careful selection of teachers and materials, a lack of clarity about goals, and a willingness to promise whatever the public wanted to hear. New tools have emerged to meet the challenges: a solid base of research in psychology and linguistics, extensive experiences in immersion and bilingual education, new insights about communication, improved understanding of first- and second-language acquisition, and new standards for judging proficiency and progress. The 1980s and 1990s saw a growing public and professional support for K–8 languages, and the teaching profession has developed numerous initiatives and organizations to assist teachers working at this level. The *Standards for Foreign Language Learning in the 21st Century* have established a new vision for language education as a long sequence beginning in the elementary school. The *ACTFL Proficiency Guidelines* and the *Student Performance Guidelines* provide new ways to look at student language performance and to describe it across programs and levels. Taken together, the problems still in evidence and the tools available for solving them promise a stimulating period of challenge and opportunity as languages in the elementary and middle school become the solid foundation for lifelong language learning.

FOR STUDY AND DISCUSSION

1. What resources does the curriculum planner for elementary school language programs have available today that will help a school system avoid the pitfalls and problems encountered by earlier programs?

2. Supporting elementary school language programs might be considered "getting on another bandwagon," triggered by national reports. What lessons can be learned from the history of language teaching in the United States to help prevent the decline of support for language programs after their "fad value" has worn off?

3. What current national and international events tend to encourage support for language programs at the elementary school level?

4. How might information on the history of foreign language programs be of value when writing a program rationale?

5. What aspects of the history of foreign languages at the elementary school level might have been different if the *ACTFL Proficiency Guidelines* had been available in the 1960s?

FOR FURTHER READING

The following sources are recommended for additional information about material covered in this chapter. Chapter citations are documented in Works Cited at the end of the volume.

Birckbichler, Diane W., ed. *Reflecting on the Past to Shape the Future.* The ACTFL Foreign Language Education Series. Lincolnwood, IL: National Textbook Company, 2000.

Heining-Boynton, Audrey. "Using FLES History to Plan for the Present and the Future." *Foreign Language Annals* 23, no. 4 (1990): 503–509.

Phillips, June K., ed. *Foreign Language Standards: Linking Research, Theories, and Practices.* The ACTFL Foreign Language Education Series. Lincolnwood, IL: National Textbook Company, 1999.

18 Selecting and Staffing an Early Language Program Model

W hen looking at the challenges and opportunities for languages available in the elementary school, school districts are faced with decisions with regard to what type of early language program to offer and how to staff that program. Issues of funding, time available in the school day, staffing, and who will study the language all affect the final decision. The most important issue of all is choosing a program model that matches the goals envisioned for students in the program.

Types of Programs

Elementary school language programs can be classified into two major types: *immersion programs* and *Foreign Language in the Elementary School (FLES) programs*. Each has different goals, a different set of expected student outcomes, and a variety of staffing options, but each can result in significant language outcomes for learners. (Table 18.1 shows typical program formats found within these categories.)

Another type of program related to early language learning is the *exploratory program*. The goals of exploratory programs are usually limited to *introducing* students to language and culture, with the intent of arousing interest in further language study. They are set apart from true language programs in that they usually do not have any degree of language proficiency as an outcome, and they are not always part of an articulated sequence.

Underlying every program description that follows is the fact that language proficiency outcomes are directly proportional to the amount of time spent by students in meaningful communication in the target language. The more time students spend working communicatively with the target language, under the guidance of a skilled and fluent teacher, the greater will be the level of language proficiency that they acquire. Met and Rhodes (1990) suggest that the amount of time spent on language learning and the intensity of the learning experience may be among the most important factors determining the rate of language acquisition and the level of proficiency that can be attained in a language program. Planners should seek to design a program that will result in the highest level of proficiency possible, given the resources they have available.

TABLE 18.1   Elementary School Foreign Language Program Goals

Programs That Are Continuous • Cumulative • Sequential • Proficiency-Oriented • That Are Part of an Integrated K–12 Sequence

Program Type	Percent of Class Time Spent in FL per Week	Goals
Total Immersion Grades K–6	**50–100%** (Time is spent learning *subject matter* taught in FL; language learning *per se* incorporated as necessary throughout curriculum)	To become functionally proficient in the new language To master subject content taught in the foreign language To acquire an understanding of and appreciation for other cultures
Two-Way Immersion Grades K–6 *Also called Two-Way Bilingual, Dual Language, and Developmental Bilingual Education*	**at least 50%** (Time is spent learning *subject matter* taught in FL; language learning *per se* incorporated as necessary throughout curriculum) Student population is both native speakers of English and of the target language.	To become functionally proficient in the language that is new to the student To master subject content taught in the new language To acquire an understanding of and appreciation for other cultures
Partial Immersion Grades K–6	**approx. 50%** (Time is spent learning *subject matter* taught in FL; language learning *per se* incorporated as necessary throughout curriculum)	To become functionally proficient in the new language (although to a lesser extent than is possible in total immersion) To master subject content taught in the foreign language To acquire an understanding of and appreciation for other cultures
Content-Based FLES Grades K–6	**15–50%** (More scheduled time than FLES, less than partial immersion.) Time is spent learning language *per se* as well as subject matter in the FL	To acquire proficiency in listening, speaking, reading, and writing the new language To use subject content as a vehicle for acquiring foreign language skills To acquire an understanding of and appreciation for other cultures
FLES Grades K–6	**5–15%** (minimum 30–40 minutes per class, at least 3–5 days per week) Time is spent learning language *per se;* optimal language curriculum integrates language, subject matter, and culture	To acquire proficiency in listening and speaking (degree of proficiency varies with the program) To acquire an understanding of and appreciation for other cultures To acquire some proficiency in reading and writing (emphasis varies with the program)

(continued)

TABLE 18.1 Continued

Non-Continuous Programs
Not Usually Part of an Integrated K–12 Sequence

Program Type	Percent of Class Time Spent in FL per Week	Goals
Exploratory Grades K-6 Frequent and regular sessions over a short period of time •OR• Short and/or infrequent sessions over an extended period of time	1–5% (Time spent sampling one or more languages and/or learning *about* language—sometimes taught mostly in English)	To develop an interest in new languages for future language study To learn basic words and phrases in one or more new languages To develop careful listening skills To develop cultural awareness To develop linguistic awareness

Source: Nancy Rhodes, Center for Applied Linguistics, 1985. Adapted and revised by Curtain and Dahlberg, 2002. Reprinted by permission.

The best way to understand the differences among various program models is to visit successful programs in action. Thoughtful and thorough descriptions of effective programs can also offer insight and guidance. Gilzow and Branaman (2000) provide descriptions of seven programs from varying program models, and identify key elements leading to their success. All the programs share four key qualities. First, they have been flexible in the face of fluctuating financial support. Second, there is close teamwork among language professionals, administrators, classroom teachers, and parents. Third, each program has had strong leadership that has been key to program success. Finally, the staff has a strong commitment to the program and to the goals of elementary or middle school language education.

The following sections further clarify the distinctions among the various programs:

Immersion Programs

Time and intensity of instruction are two of the great strengths of language immersion programs, in which the usual curriculum activities are conducted in a second language. In this setting the new language is the medium as well as the object of instruction. Children in immersion programs in the United States and Canada are English speakers who are learning to speak a new language such as French, German, Spanish, Japanese, or Chinese. The following goals are most commonly found in immersion programs:

Immersion Goals

1. Functional proficiency in the second language; children are able to communicate in the second language on topics appropriate to their age level.
2. Mastery of subject content material of the school district curriculum.
3. Cross-cultural understanding.
4. Achievement in English language arts comparable to or surpassing the achievement of students in English-only programs.

Immersion programs vary in the amount of time devoted to instruction in the second language (total or partial immersion), in the level of entry (early, middle, or late immersion), and in the population of students who enter the program (two-way or dual language).

The following definitions will clarify terms and concepts associated with immersion in the United States and Canada.

- *Total or Full Immersion*
  The second language is used for the entire school day during the first two or three years. In early total immersion programs, reading is taught through the second language. In some programs instruction by means of English is introduced gradually, often in grade two, and the amount of English is increased until the fifth or sixth grade (the last grade in elementary school), where up to half the day is spent in English and half in the second language. In other programs, once English is introduced (usually at grade two or three) the percentage of time spent in English remains constant throughout the program, at approximately 20 percent. In some other programs the entire day is conducted in the second language for a much greater period of time and English is not introduced until grades four or five.

- *Partial Immersion*
  All instruction is in the second language for part (at least half) of the school day. The amount of instruction in the foreign language usually remains constant throughout the elementary school program. In early partial immersion programs, students frequently learn to read in both languages at the same time; in some programs, notably Chinese and Japanese partial immersion, literacy skills are taught first in the native language.

- *Early Immersion*
  Students begin learning through the second language early in the elementary school sequence, usually in kindergarten or first grade. In some programs, such as some in Milwaukee, immersion programs begin in four-year-old kindergarten.

- *Late Immersion*
  Students begin learning through the second language later in their schooling, either at the end of elementary school, at the beginning of middle school/junior high school, or in high school. Many students entering late immersion programs have had previous instruction (thirty to sixty minutes per day) in the second language. Late immersion programs may involve 90 to 100 percent of the instruction in the second language for the first year and 50 to 80 percent for one or two years after that, or 50 to 60 percent throughout. This model is more common in Canada than in the United States.

- *Continuing Immersion*
  Continuing immersion programs are found at the middle school/junior high school or high school level. These programs are designed to maintain the language skills already developed in total or partial immersion programs and to further develop them to as high a degree as possible.

- *Two-Way Immersion*
  Two-way immersion programs, also known as two-way bilingual, dual language, or developmental bilingual education programs, are similar to one-way immersion programs except that the student group includes native speakers of the target lan-

guage as well as native speakers of English. Thus, all students learn subject matter through their native language as well as through the second language, and both language groups have the benefit of interaction with peers who are native speakers of the language they are learning. The ideal goals of two-way immersion, in addition to subject content mastery, are that the English-speaking students become functionally proficient in the second-language and that the second language speakers become functionally proficient in English. At the same time all students continue to develop skills and proficiency in their native language. These programs have been successfully implemented at both elementary and secondary school levels.

Two-way language development programs promote:
- bilingual education as an enrichment program for all students rather than as a compensatory education mode for English language learners
- better understanding between two linguistic communities in a given district as they work toward a common goal
- access to equal education for all students
- educational excellence

FLES Programs

FLES has sometimes been used as a general term to describe all programs for Languages Other than English (LOTE) at the elementary school level. However, FLES is most appropriately used to describe a particular type of elementary school language program, one that is taught three to five times per week for class periods of twenty minutes to an hour or more. Some FLES classes integrate other areas of the curriculum, and others focus primarily on the second language and its culture. In an effort to establish a set of minimum criteria for the definition of a FLES program, participants in a 1991 "think tank" session sponsored by Goethe House New York recommended the following (Rosenbusch 1992a):

What Is a FLES Program?
- A FLES program is a pre-secondary program that is articulated vertically throughout the entire program sequence.
- In a FLES program, a student studies a single language throughout the program sequence. (This does not imply that only one language is offered throughout the school district.)
- A FLES program results in language proficiency outcomes that involve the production and comprehension of meaningful messages in a communicative setting.
- Teachers in a FLES program have both language proficiency and the professional knowledge and skills necessary for effective foreign language instruction at the elementary school level.
- Classes meet within the school day, throughout the entire school year.

The amount of time allotted to a FLES program is one of the most important variables in its potential for success. The vision of the *Standards for Foreign Language Learning in the 21st Century* calls for an elementary school program that invests the time necessary for students to achieve significant outcomes. In order to achieve the performances described in the *ACTFL Performance Guidelines for K–12 Learners,* committee members advised that elementary school programs should meet no less than thirty to forty minutes per day, and no fewer than three to five days per week (Swender and Duncan 1998). This time allotment should be considered a minimum for an effective early language program on the FLES model.

The curriculum for a successful FLES program incorporates a balance among target language goals, subject content goals, and culture goals. It also helps learners to gain insight into their own language and culture, and makes links with communities of target language speakers.

FLES Goals

As with immersion programs, the goal of FLES programs is functional proficiency in the second language, although FLES students do not attain as high a proficiency level as do immersion students. The level of proficiency varies with the amount of time available for language instruction. Listening and speaking skills tend to be emphasized somewhat more than are reading and writing, and understanding and appreciation of the new culture are consistently identified as important goals. FLES programs are part of a long sequence of language study and lead to continuing courses at the secondary level.

Content-Based FLES

Some FLES programs are *"content based,"* which means that the program takes responsibility for some parts of the general curriculum to be taught at grade level in the new language. In these programs, at least an hour a day (but less than half the day) is spent in the second language. The fact that there is less time spent teaching subject content through the language distinguishes this model from the immersion models. Content-based FLES differs from other forms of FLES in that there is focus on subject content instruction rather than on language instruction alone.

In content-based FLES programs, functional proficiency in the second language is possible to a greater degree than in regular FLES programs because there is greater program intensity, more time actually spent using the language, and a larger range of topics covered in the course of instruction. Mastery of grade-level subject content taught in the target language is an important and distinguishing goal of content-based programs.

An important distinction needs to be made between *content-based instruction* and *content-related instruction,* another term that appears prominently in discussions of the relationship of language instruction to subject content. In content-*based* instruction the curriculum concepts being taught through the new language are appropriate to the grade level of the students, and the foreign language teacher takes responsibility for teaching certain portions of the prescribed curriculum. In content-*related* instruction the language teacher uses concepts from the regular curriculum to enrich the program with academic content, but these concepts are not always part of the curriculum at that grade level. The curriculum content is chosen to provide a vehicle for language learning and to reinforce the academic skills needed by the students, but the language teacher does not regularly assume responsibility for any part of the general curriculum. Most well-designed FLES programs can be described as content-related.

Exploratory Programs

Exploratory programs, sometimes referred to as FLEX (Foreign Language Exploratory or Experience) programs, might appropriately be described as *sampler programs*. While programs may differ in goals and format, they have in common the fact that students do not attain any degree of language proficiency. They are usually self-contained, short-term programs, most often lasting from three weeks to one year. These self-contained programs may occur in the elementary school, but they are frequently found at the middle school/junior high school level.

Exploratory programs have many variations, depending on the goals of the individual district. At one end of the continuum is the course that introduces language primarily through a high-quality language learning experience. These programs are generally successful in giving students an understanding of what it means to learn a new language, and because the students experience progress over time, they are likely to be motivated to continue language instruction. These courses that emphasize language learning experiences hold the greatest implications for program planning. Students learn enough language in such courses to ensure that they will not be total beginners the next time they take a class in the same language, and later teachers in the language sequence will be required to pay some attention to articulation of language content.

At the other extreme in the exploratory model is the course about language, taught mainly in English. These courses can have value for students, but they develop no language competence. It might be more appropriate to consider them as part of the social studies or the English language arts curriculum.

Low-Intensity Exploratory Programs

In some cases a language program continues over a number of years, but at such a low level of frequency and intensity that little or no language proficiency develops for most students. For example, some schools with enthusiasm for a language but inadequate resources have initiated elementary school language programs that meet as little as ten minutes per day, once or twice a week. Based on the definition of FLES programs above, such a program would be classified as an exploratory program. This format for instruction can have unfortunate, unanticipated consequences. When children experience language instruction over a number of years, both they and their parents expect to see progress and increasing levels of fluency. With such low intensity of instruction, however, only very limited language development is likely to be observed, no matter how skilled and dedicated the teaching may be. Students may come to feel that language learning is too hard, or that it is repetitive and boring. When the opportunity comes to study a language more intensively, they may decide against it.

Some districts have recognized this problem and changed the format for their language program in order to provide greater intensity. One solution is to begin language instruction at a later grade level and offer it more frequently during the week—four times at thirty minutes per day beginning in grade three, for example, rather than twice a week beginning in kindergarten. Another approach might be to block language instruction during the school year, so that instead of twice a week throughout the year, students would have language instruction daily for a five-week period, followed by five weeks without the language, and then another five-week block of daily instruction, and so on throughout the year. This type of scheduling would allow for greater intensity during the language instructional block—perhaps the completion of a thematic unit—and there would be better retention of the material learned in each language block. While the language outcomes would not be as great as those obtained in a FLES program beginning in kindergarten, both student language development and their attitude toward language learning would be positively affected.

Exploratory Goals and Program Models

Most exploratory program models share similar goals. The differences primarily involve emphasis of individual goals within a program. Among the most common goals of exploratory programs are the following:

- introduction to language learning
- awareness and appreciation of foreign culture
- appreciation of the value of communicating in another language
- enhanced understanding of English
- motivation for further language study

Exploratory programs generally can be categorized into three basic types, which tend to overlap somewhat in terms of goals and design. These types are described in the following section.

The General Language Course. This course is an introduction and orientation to the nature of language and language learning. This model includes the goals of cultural understanding, but it provides the students with very limited language learning experiences. A general language course often includes exposure to all the modern and classical languages available for later study in the school system, as well as to some related systems such as sign language for the hearing impaired, Morse code, Native American sign language, and computer languages.

The Language Potpourri. This type of course provides limited, introductory experience in the modern and classical languages that will be available later in a sequential program. It may bring several—perhaps all—languages together in a single sequence, as a part of the same learning experience, or it may provide a series of experiences with different languages over the period of a semester, a year, or several years. The language potpourri course is usually team-taught, using specialists in each language. The effectiveness of such a course is likely to be severely limited if the same teacher is responsible for teaching all languages, especially for those languages with which the teacher has little or no experience.

The Single Language Offering.   This exploratory option provides a limited, introductory experience in one language that students may later be able to choose for sequential study. In some cases there may be no opportunity for further study of the exploratory language, or any language, but the experience with the language and culture is valued for itself and its contribution to the elementary or middle school curriculum.

Of course, some exploratory courses combine the features of the general language course, the language potpourri, or the single language course, as school districts draw from several models to meet local goals and priorities.

A comprehensive discussion of exploratory language programs and a list of goals is provided by Kennedy and De Lorenzo in *Complete Guide to Exploratory Foreign Language Programs* (1985).

Non-Curricular Language Programs

When examining non-curricular programs, it is important to note that not all language programs take place within the setting of the school day. Summer camps, immersion weekends, before- and after-school programs, summer day programs, and heritage language Saturday or day schools, among others, all provide opportunities for young learners to be exposed to new languages. When such programs are carefully planned and taught, they can make a positive contribution to early language learning.

Non-curricular programs may be sponsored by the school district, by community groups or parent-teacher organizations, or by tuition-based private education groups. They may be set up in a variety of ways. Some of them have been very successful and have developed sophisticated structures and curricula, while others have limited goals and are of relatively short duration. In many communities the interest generated by non-curricular language programs has led to a place for languages within the school curriculum and the school day. Some programs, such as immersion weekends, extend the school experience into a non-academic setting.

An important strength of non-curricular programs has been their use of community resources that might otherwise remain untapped. In some situations there would be no early language program in the school district without them, and their role as a "foot in the door" is not to be underestimated.

Among the most serious weaknesses of many non-curricular programs is the fact that volunteers in such programs often have little or no training, and there is no agency to regulate the goals and the quality of instruction. Even under the best of circumstances, such programs place languages clearly *outside* the school curriculum and the school day, reinforcing the notion that language learning is "extra" rather than basic.

Staffing Elementary School Programs in Languages Other than English

Staffing is one of the most important components in the elementary school language program. It is vital that teachers working within any of the staffing models described below have excellent language skills and that they have had training and experience in working with elementary school children.

Staffing for Immersion Programs

Immersion teachers are certified elementary school teachers who are native or near-native speakers of the target language. Classroom aides who are also fluent in the target language can provide an additional, authentic model for the students as well as helping with individual and small-group instruction throughout the school day. While it is desirable to have special subjects such as music, art, and physical education taught by specialists who are fluent in the target language, many programs find it difficult to locate staff who are appropriately trained in these areas, so these subjects are taught either by the classroom teachers or by English-speaking specialists.

In early total immersion programs all instruction takes place in the target language, so staffing consists of the classroom teacher, who is a fluent speaker of the target language, and possibly a classroom aide. In partial immersion programs, and in total immersion programs after the introduction of English language instruction, one of the following patterns is usually chosen.

Separate Teacher for Each Language.   The use of the native language and the target language are kept completely separate. All instruction in the target language is given by one teacher, when possible a native speaker of the language, and all native language instruction is given by another.

Strengths
- The native language and the target language are kept clearly separate in the minds of the students.
- The best possible language model is provided for each language.
- In partial immersion programs, one foreign language speaker can provide instruction for two different classrooms of children.

Limitations
- Problems of staffing, scheduling, and curriculum coordination may be aggravated by use of this model, especially when the school day is not divided equally between English and the second language.

The Same Teacher for Both Native-language and Second-language Instruction.
The instructional day is divided into native-language and second-language activities, and the same teacher works with both languages.

Strengths
- The teacher has complete flexibility to adjust the amount of time used for instruction in each language according to the needs of the class on any given day.
- Only one person must be hired for each classroom.
- The classroom teacher can shape the entire classroom environment and climate according to her or his own preference.

Limitations

- The classroom teacher may not be an equally good model in both languages.
- Greater effort is required to establish clear separation between the use of the two languages.

Staffing for FLES and Exploratory Programs

Teachers for FLES programs, or for those exploratory programs designed to be taught in the target language, will need to have considerable fluency in the target language as well as meaningful living experiences in countries in which the language is spoken. Children will not be able to achieve fluency greater than that of their teachers. It is also important that these teachers have education and experience in working with elementary school children and that they have an understanding of teaching and learning second languages.

Language Specialist Model. This is the model that has been employed most often in early language programs. The language specialist usually teaches the new language only, and often has experience with children but certification at the secondary level in a language other than English. The specialist may travel from room to room, or children may come to a special language classroom for early language instruction. Many teachers see from two hundred to four hundred students in the course of a week.

Strengths

- The language specialist usually has good language skills and can provide consistency of instruction.
- The potential for both vertical articulation (from one grade to the next) and horizontal articulation (within the same grade level but possibly taught by different teachers or operating in different schools) is enhanced when the entire language program is in the hands of one or more specialists.

Limitations

- If the language specialist has secondary training only, he or she may have little experience with elementary school students and may require assistance in adapting instruction to their needs and interests.
- The specialist must deal with many students throughout the day, thus limiting the degree of personal involvement and individualization available to each child. When numbers of students mount, teacher burnout is a risk with this model.
- In this model the language program can easily become compartmentalized: the specialist may lack both the time and the opportunity to relate the language program to the rest of the curriculum or to establish ongoing dialogue with all the teachers in all the classes visited during the day or week.
- Salary costs for the language specialist(s) increase the expense to the district for foreign language offerings.

Classroom Teacher Model. In this option, each classroom teacher has the responsibility for teaching the early language program. The program is most effective when designed in cooperation with a language specialist, who also coordinates the program, provides in-service assistance for the classroom teacher, and teaches occasional class sessions in individual classrooms. In some cases, there may be media support—audio and/or video—for the classroom teacher and less actual contact with a language specialist.

Strengths

- The classroom teacher has extensive training and experience in working with the particular age group of students in the class and is in the best position to know their needs and interests.
- The teacher is able to reenter and reinforce the language learning throughout the school day and can also teach some subject content through the new language, as appropriate.
- Except for the specialist-coordinator, there is no extra salary expense for language instruction.

Limitations

- This model is highly dependent on existing language proficiency of the classroom teacher, or the willingness of that teacher to become proficient in the language and to devote the extra time necessary to teach it effectively.
- This model is dependent on the support of a language specialist who knows the language well, understands the schoolchild and the school setting, and can work effectively with teachers and administrators. Individuals with these qualifications may be difficult to locate.
- It is difficult to find classroom teachers with fluency in the second language. This is especially the case during a time of low teacher mobility when the opportunities to replace present staff through natural turnover are infrequent.
- Extensive in-service training may be necessary to help the classroom teacher achieve competence in the language and in language methodology. The teacher may view this as an unwanted and unwarranted burden; the result may be unenthusiastic teaching and hostility toward the program.

Variation on the Classroom Teacher Model.   A variation on the classroom teacher model includes a team approach, in which one of the team members, usually better qualified by training and/or interest, teaches the language in several classrooms; in exchange, other team members offer instruction in other areas. This arrangement often helps to alleviate the morale problem otherwise encountered in this model.

Other Instructional Models

The following are alternatives to the staffing models described above. In most cases they are implemented as stopgap alternatives because of budgetary limitations or because of difficulty in locating teachers.

Media-Based Model

In this model the primary vehicle for teaching the language is some form of media, usually videotape, interactive television, CDs, audiotape, and computers. Follow-up and reinforcement are handled either by the classroom teacher or by a traveling specialist.

Students in our schools are very sophisticated consumers of media products, and they will not likely be engaged with media-based learning materials unless they have meaningful content and high-quality, professional camera work and editing. The target language should be the primary means of instruction, just as in classroom-based programs, and the media presentation should be standards-based and proficiency oriented.

The key to success of media-based programs, in addition to the quality of the media product itself, is the quality and intensity of the follow-up. In a successful program, the media will supplement and not replace time spent with a language teacher. Media-based programs in the past that have not adequately provided for classroom interaction with a qualified teacher have been extremely disappointing in their results. Many have disappeared entirely, leaving behind an extremely negative attitude toward foreign language instruction.

Strengths
- Videotapes and other media-based programs can present some aspects of culture with great imagination, and media programs can use special effects to lighten and enliven the necessary drill and practice sessions.

Limitations
- The success of a media-based program is almost totally dependent on the goodwill of the classroom teacher. Students do not usually have the opportunity to interact with their primary source of instruction, so the attitude of the classroom teacher sets the tone for and establishes the importance of the language sessions.
- Students often feel a detachment from the medium and are adept at shutting it out.
- The cost of buying, maintaining, and upgrading media equipment and software tends to offset the fact that fewer teachers are required for this model.
- High-quality media programs for teaching new languages at the elementary school level are difficult to find.

Distance Learning

In an early language program using interactive television as a vehicle for distance learning, the teacher is located at one site (the base site), usually with a group of students, and one or more groups of students are located at a remote site or sites. Remote sites usually are located in another school building some distance away. Video cameras, monitors, and microphones are located at the base and the remote sites so that the teacher and groups of students can see and communicate with each other. While this model is most frequently used at the high school level, it has been successfully adapted for use with elementary school students when adequate supervision is provided at the remote sites. The National Council of State Supervisors of Foreign Languages (NCSSFL) has published guidelines for distance learning programs (see Figure 18.1).

FIGURE 18.1   National Council of State Supervisors of Foreign Languages (NCSSFL) Guidelines for Foreign Language Distance Learning Programs

1. The foreign language distance learning program uses the *Standards for Foreign Language Learning in the 21st Century* (1999) as a curriculum framework for the distance learning course. The foreign language curriculum incorporates interpersonal, interpretive, and presentational modes of communication.
2. Foreign language distance learning programs are interactive (two-way audio and video, or two-way audio and fax, or computer terminal for interactivity) in the foreign language.
3. The Standards-based curriculum program offers a variety of instructional activities to include listening, speaking, reading, and writing skills, as well as social and cultural information.
4. The program provides frequent (daily, if possible, but at least 2–3 times each week) oral interactions between each student and an adult proficient in the target language (i.e., a certified foreign language teacher, a native speaker, or other individual with training in interactive teaching/learning techniques.)
5. Foreign language distance learning programs offer at least two levels of an articulated and sequential language program.
6. Each distance learning class is formally evaluated each year. The originating site provides data related to the program's effectiveness.
7. The foreign language distance learning program focuses on the instructional needs of the students rather than on the technology itself.
8. Foreign language distance learning classes are limited to no more than 20 students.
9. The schedules of all participating schools are arranged so that there is no conflict with the foreign language program schedule.
10. Local education agencies have the facility and permission to tape programs for repetition and reinforcement of instruction.
11. The distance learning teacher is an experienced master teacher with proven proficiency in the target language. He/She has received hands-on training with the technology used to offer the course.
12. The distance learning teacher is extremely well organized so that classroom facilitators and students are informed of scheduled activities well in advance. A calendar of lesson objectives, test dates, activities, etc., is printed prior to each semester.
13. There is timely feedback on student performance. The teacher at the origination site or a qualified facilitator grades and returns student work (tests, assignments, projects, etc.) within 7–10 school days.
14. The originating site directly involves all schools and students by providing a vehicle (e-mail, website) for networking among all sites.
15. Each distance learning class has a classroom facilitator who is a certified teacher (preferably in another foreign language or a related field).
16. Classroom facilitators have a working knowledge of the foreign language or are committed to learning the language (with students and/or through college/university classes).
17. The originating site provides in-service training in course organization, classroom management, and technical aspects of the program for the classroom facilitators at the receiving sites.
18. In addition to all program printed materials, program source provides classroom facilitators recent research on foreign language learning and foreign language teaching methodology.
19. Each site provides a technical support staff to install, maintain and upgrade equipment.
20. The distance learning teacher and facilitator always prepare a back-up plan in case of technical failures.
21. Text and printed materials correlated with the distance learning class are used for review, drill, practice, and homework to strengthen the concepts being taught.

Source: NCSSFL Guidelines for Foreign Language Distance Learning Programs reprinted by permission of National Council of State Supervisors of Foreign Languages.

Strengths

- Small school districts can combine resources to offer a new language at the elementary school level, or even to offer more than one language.
- A single, talented teacher can reach many more students with this model than would otherwise be physically possible.

Limitations

- It is impossible to engage in as many valuable context-embedded, activity-oriented activities when all of the students and the teacher are not physically in the same place.
- Opportunities for students to produce oral language and teacher evaluation of individual progress are severely limited in this model.
- Teaching on camera requires extensive preparation, skillful planning, and a high level of technical quality. Careful management is required to bring all these factors together. It is critical that the teacher receive adequate preparation time to insure a quality program.
- Supervision of students at the remote site(s) is an additional cost factor.

Staffing Appropriate Only for Short-Term, Non-Curricular Programs

Certain staffing patterns that do not use certified teachers have proved to be successful over limited periods of time for some programs with limited goals, such as after-school programs or summer day camp settings. The option of using non-specialist and volunteer teachers and cross-age tutors can meet the needs of specific programs when the programs are well planned by language specialists who train and monitor the teachers carefully. The staffing options described below are *not suitable for long-term, articulated FLES programs.*

Non-Specialist Teacher/Volunteer

Non-specialist teachers could be college students studying languages, preservice teachers enrolled in teacher education programs, parents, or other interested and qualified adults. They lead short-term language programs, singly or in pairs, under the supervision of a language specialist who assists in planning the program with the capabilities of these teachers clearly in mind.

Strengths

- The use of the tutor in a short-term language experience has possibilities for bringing languages that would otherwise never be considered into the curriculum. For example, an exchange student from Africa might offer a nine-week course in Swahili; a former Peace Corps volunteer might offer a six-week class in Hindi.
- The use of non-specialists identifies and takes advantage of community language resources that might otherwise remain untapped.

Limitations

- Speakers of other languages may not have teaching background or training, and if they are from abroad, they may have difficulty adjusting to the American elementary school setting. They will require carefully planned assistance from language specialists and a well-developed format.
- In some cases, the district language specialist may not speak the language being taught by the volunteer, but the specialist can serve as a resource for the volunteer teacher and help them develop a course framework.
- Finding a dependable supply of qualified and suitable volunteers and auxiliary personnel who are willing to maintain a long-term commitment to a program is an inherent problem.

Cross-Age Tutors

Cross-age tutors are usually intermediate or advanced students in successful middle or high school foreign language programs who work on a short-term basis with students in the elementary school. The programs are developed by a language specialist, usually the secondary teacher, often in collaboration with the secondary students themselves.

Strengths

- Children wish to identify with the cross-age tutors, who thus provide powerful models for future language learning.
- The tutors learn as much as, or more than, the elementary school children, as they go through the process of planning and presenting the lessons.
- This type of very limited, low-cost program can demonstrate interest in and the success of a second-language program; and thus, it can serve as a starting point for consideration of a professionally staffed curricular program.

Limitations

- Success depends on the quality of direction provided by the language teacher and on adequate preparation of secondary students for their role as tutors. Not every secondary school language teacher has the background time, or interest, to provide the necessary training and direction.
- In many school settings the problems of distance and schedule make a cross-age tutoring arrangement impractical or impossible.

Summary

In this chapter, various program models and staffing options have been presented. School districts and program planners must choose among them according to the language proficiency outcomes they desire and the budgetary and staffing circumstances in which they find themselves.

Underlying every program and model description is the fact that *language proficiency outcomes are directly proportional to the amount of time spent by students in meaningful communication in the target language.* The more time students spend working communicatively with the target language, under the guidance of a skilled and fluent teacher, the greater will be the level of language proficiency that they acquire. Planners should seek to design the best possible program, in terms of language proficiency, that they have the resources to implement.

FOR STUDY AND DISCUSSION

1. Discuss which programs described in this chapter you would recommend to school committees for each of the following priorities:
   - maximum, functional fluency in the second language
   - development of interest in languages so students will elect to study them at another level
   - fluency in a language and improved basic skills and subject content skills
   - language instruction for highly verbal gifted students

2. Describe an elementary school level early language program that you know in the greatest detail. Explain how it fits into the categories of this chapter, and identify its strengths and its limitations. What particular aspects of the model account for the program's strengths? What changes in the model might bring about improvements in the program?

3. An influential elementary school principal has taken the position that an exploratory program is too limited in its objectives to justify its inclusion in the elementary school day. Yet, this appears to be the only feasible option for the immediate future for any form of language study at the elementary school level in this district. How would you respond to this principal's objections?

4. Your school district has had a very successful "traditional" FLES program for several years; it is staffed by several traveling specialist teachers, and follow-up programs at the middle school and at the high school are well designed and effective. Many parents and teachers would like to make an even stronger commitment to languages in the elementary school. What options and suggestions would you offer to the parent planning committee?

5. Because there are a number of international companies located in your community, as well as a college with a large population of international students, there is a strong interest in early languages and cultures throughout the district. How might you tap the international resources of the community to provide language learning experiences for elementary school children?

FOR FURTHER READING

The following sources are recommended for additional information about material covered in this chapter. Chapter citations are documented in Works Cited at the end of the volume.

Christian, Donna, et al. *Profiles in Two-Way Immersion Education.* McHenry, IL: Center for Applied Linguistics and Delta Systems Co., 1997.

Cloud, Nancy, Fred Genesee, and Else Hamayan. *Dual Language Instruction. A Handbook for Enriched Education.* Boston: Heinle and Heinle, 2000.

Cummins, Jim, and Merrill Swain. *Bilingualism in Education.* Burnt Mill, Harlow, UK: Longman, 1986.

Gilzow, Douglas F., and Lucinda E. Branaman. *Lessons Learned. Model Early Foreign Language Programs.* McHenry, IL: Center for Applied Linguistics and Delta Systems Co., 2000.

"K–12 Foreign Language Education." *The ERIC Review* 6, no. 1 (fall 1998).

Kennedy, Dora F., and William De Lorenzo. *Complete Guide to Exploratory Foreign Language Programs*. Lincolnwood, IL: National Textbook Company, 1985.

Lipton, Gladys C. *Practical Handbook to Elementary Foreign Language Programs (FLES*)*. 3rd ed. Lincolnwood, IL: National Textbook Company, 1998.

Met, Myriam, ed. *Critical Issues in Early Second Language Learning. Building for Our Children's Future.* Glenview, IL: Scott Foresman-Addison Wesley, 1998.

National Council of State Supervisors of Foreign Languages. *Position Statement on Distance Learning in Foreign Languages.* 2002. Available on-line at www.ncssfl.org/distancelearning.htm

Williford, Mary L. "The Answer: High School Foreign Languages Tutoring Program," *Foreign Language Annals* 12, no. 3 (May 1979): 213–214.

CHAPTER

19 Program Planning, Assessment, and Articulation

Planning Process

Planning is the most crucial element in the success of any early language program, and yet it is often given the least disciplined attention. Programs at this level are frequently initiated because of the enthusiasm of an individual or a group, and in many cases the eagerness to implement the program competes with the need to plan carefully. A thoughtful, thorough planning process that involves all the affected members of the community can build a support system for the program that will help it to weather shifting fads and priorities in the curriculum, the school, and the community.

Pressure to implement programs prematurely was a common problem with the short-lived experiments of the 1960s. As Theodore Andersson pointed out in his thorough account of the history of elementary school foreign language programs (1969, 138),

> Many communities, enchanted by the promise that a FLES program offers, set out with a minimum of preparation, only to find later that, to endure, a FLES program requires hard work, time, money, and expertise. A minimum commitment—a late start, doubtful continuity, too little class time, overloading the teacher, leaving the teacher to work in isolation—leads to almost certain disenchantment.

At a minimum, a planning group should include parents; elementary, middle school/junior high school and high school administrators; language teachers from all instructional levels; and classroom teachers at the affected levels. Other valuable participants include a representative from the teacher's union, a special education teacher, and a reading teacher. Participation by a school board member can also be very helpful. The planning group will make recommendations to the superintendent, who in the end will carry the responsibility for effectively implementing the elementary school foreign language program and the entire K–12 sequence. The planning group should have a budget that will cover purchase of informational materials, duplication costs, and travel to visit existing programs.

The early language program that begins with planning for the entire language sequence, not just for the initial year, is most likely to succeed. Language teachers from all levels can contribute to planning and program development, and they can work together in staff development activities designed to facilitate a smooth transition from one grade to the next. All members of the group should be involved in planning from the beginning so that together they can address these concerns:

philosophy
goals
teachers and teacher recruitment
budget
resources
support of existing staff
choice of language(s)
who should study languages
scheduling
curriculum
integrating second-language learning into the basic curriculum
articulation
building public relations
student assessment
program evaluation
sharing experiences and ideas

Developing Background

The first step for any planning group is to become as informed as possible about articulated K–12 language programs, with a special emphasis on early language learning. Several options for developing this background include the following:

- extensive reading, beginning with resources listed at the end of this chapter
- visits to existing programs representing a variety of program models
- consultations with principals, teachers, and program planners from existing programs
- visits to conferences at which elementary school foreign language programs are the focus of discussion (American Council on the Teaching of Foreign Languages, and state and regional meetings of language teachers)

Reading and consultations are essential elements of the planning process, but planners need to see programs in action. Although this kind of background development can involve weeks or months, the resulting recommendations and decisions will be based on the best available information. The planning group will be in a position to proceed efficiently and confidently in designing a program best tailored to their local needs.

Philosophy

The statement of philosophy for the language program must be congruent with the statement of philosophy or mission statement of the school or the district. This statement of philosophy is the starting point for program planning and will shape many of the responses to the planning considerations outlined in this chapter. The philosophy statement from the *Standards for Foreign Language Learning in the 21st Century* (1999, 7) provides an excellent model, not only because of its content, but also because it served as the basis for the development of the entire Standards document. A portion of this philosophy is reproduced in Chapter 16, on page 396.

The foreign language department of the Glastonbury, Connecticut public schools, site of one of the longest continuing K–12 programs in the country, publishes the following philosophy statement on their Web site, http://foreignlanguage.org/curriculum/philosophy.html.

Departmental Philosophy

1. The study of another language leads to communication. Our goal is to teach all students to communicate beyond their native languages in order to participate effectively in this world.
2. The study of another language leads to understanding other cultures. Our goal is to recognize what is common to all human experience and to accept that which is different.
3. The study of another language leads to critical thinking skills. Our goal is to enhance the ability to analyze, to compare and contrast, to synthesize, to improvise, and to examine cultures through a language and a perspective other than one's own.
4. The study of another language leads to an interdisciplinary view of the curriculum. Our goal is to have every student begin language study as early as possible in an interdisciplinary environment.

Goals

In order to decide which type of program to offer, planners must determine the expected educational outcomes of the program. These goals will flow directly from the philosophy of the program, as demonstrated in the Glastonbury philosophy statement. As outlined in Chapter 18, the broad spectrum of potential outcomes could include, at one end, simply exposing students to foreign language study in an effort to motivate them to study further, and at the other end, a program in which functional proficiency in listening, speaking, reading, and writing is the goal. *The level of language fluency a student will gain in an elementary and middle school foreign language program is directly related to the amount of time students spend learning the language and on the intensity of that language experience.* For example, provided that there is quality teaching, students in a program that meets two or three times a week will not acquire the same level of proficiency as will students who have language instruction five days per week; FLES students who have language classes for thirty to forty minutes per day will not attain the same fluency in the language as will their peers in a total immersion program in which they are using the language intensively for the entire school day. Reading and writing the foreign language are realistic goals only for early language programs that provide 120 or more minutes per week of exposure to the language, and for those programs that involve full or partial immersion. If new programs at the elementary or middle school level are to succeed, their positive features and their distinctive goals must be clearly identified and articulated.

Functional language proficiency means that students are able to communicate in the foreign language on any topic appropriate to their age and grade level. Functional language proficiency is a goal that can only be accomplished in programs where there is sufficient time available and sufficient intensity of instruction. It can be accomplished in total and partial immersion programs in which half the school day or more is devoted to second-language learning. This level of proficiency could not be attained in an exploratory program and would be difficult to attain in most FLES programs. A well-designed FLES program, on the other hand, can provide students with enough intensity of language instruction to achieve a moderate fluency and a strong foundation on which to build further language development.

The community in which the language program is being planned will have a strong influence on the goals that are chosen. For example, it may provide a more favorable climate for one language over another, or community values could very well determine what level of language proficiency is seen as desirable or worthy of support. In some communities a heavy cultural emphasis might seem very important, while in other communities a heavy career orientation might be seen as important giving other directions to the program.

As program goals emerge, specific program models will suggest themselves. At this point, planners can identify existing programs built on models similar to those they are considering. Planners should correspond with people involved in these programs and try to visit them in order to determine whether the goals they are reaching are comparable to the results they hope to achieve themselves. Study and visits of this type will make it clear that *programs must offer languages for a significant amount of time in order to achieve significant goals.* School districts should be encouraged to begin programs that will result in as much language learning as possible for the students.

It is vitally important to set realistic program goals and to communicate them to parents, teachers, administrators, the school board, and the community. *The language proficiency students attain in any elementary school foreign language program is a direct result of the goals of the program and of the amount of time they spend in language study.* The program models chart in Chapter 18 graphically illustrates the variety of goals in elementary school programs; the chart shows that achieving each level of fluency depends on the amount of time available for study.

Paul Sandrock, foreign language specialist for the Wisconsin Department of Public Instruction, has a set of questions he encourages planners to start with as they design a new program (see Figure 19.1).

Staffing

There is no single decision that will affect the success of the language program more than the choice of teachers. School districts will want to ensure that the teachers they select have had training and experience in working with elementary school children, that they have excellent language skills, and that they have had training in the teaching of a foreign language. In states that have a certification category for elementary school language teachers, only licensed/certified teachers should be hired. The best insurance for the success of a language program is the hiring of skilled and talented teachers.

FIGURE 19.1   Foreign Language Program Design

What makes a quality language learning program?

Three key questions to ask when designing a program:

■ Do we want to offer a program to *all* or *some* students? Will the program be required of *or* available to students?

■ What are our goals for the program: for students to become increasingly proficient in **using** the language—or do we really have a Social Studies goal focused on learning **about** languages and cultures?

■ At what grade level can we begin and still sustain the program with quality through twelfth grade: Kindergarten? Third or fourth grade? Sixth grade?

Consider:

■ *Content connection*

Is the content connected to the grade level curriculum and balanced with language and culture goals?

vs.—Is the content separate and isolated?

■ *Frequency of instruction*

Is instruction scheduled at least three times per week?

Does it continue all year?

vs.—Are there long lapses between classes? Is instruction spread too far apart (once a week all year *or* daily for just six weeks)?

■ *Continuity*

Do students continue to learn the language from grade to grade?

vs.—Are there gaps during which no language instruction is available?

Do the same goals continue to be developed throughout the program?

vs.—Do some grades focus only on cultures, some focus on speaking, and others focus on grammar?

■ *Access to district's languages*

Is there a careful balance of the district's language offerings?

Are several world languages being considered?

vs.—Was only one of the district's language options selected for the first experience (elementary or middle school)?

Teacher Skills.   Skills and classroom practices commonly found at the secondary school and college level do not transfer directly into the elementary school classroom. Even teachers who are very successful with older students will require additional background and training before they attempt to work with elementary school children. Successful classroom teachers who are fluent in a foreign language will require some background in foreign language methodology before they can reach the same high level of effectiveness in foreign language teaching as they have attained in other subjects. Because so much of the instruction in the elementary school is oral, and because the teacher is the only model for the children most of the time, it is especially important that the teacher have excellent oral language skills.

Administrators and others sometimes assume that a native speaker of the language is always a better choice to teach in an early language program than is an English speaker who has learned the language. In fact, teachers who have learned the language themselves can be more sensitive to the learning challenges the language presents. They also serve as excellent role models for the learners, who can aspire to be fluent like their teacher but can never become native speakers. Native speakers who were educated in another culture may require considerable orientation and experience before they work comfortably with American students in the American school setting.

A second common assumption is that teachers at beginning levels of instruction do not need to have the same degree of language proficiency as those who teach at more advanced levels. In reality, teachers at all levels need to be fully proficient in the language they teach. Teachers who cannot comfortably use the target language for all classroom purposes will not be able to surround learners with language, an essential component of an effective learning environment in the early language classroom. They will also find it difficult to develop and create curriculum and activities in the target language.

Teacher Availability.   The short-term and long-term availability of teachers will influence the selection of both the program model and the language(s) to be taught. An articulated FLES program in Japanese would be a questionable choice in an isolated rural community that finds it difficult to attract new teachers, while a FLES option in French, German, or Spanish could be realistic in the same community. Searching for a teacher of Japanese might be very manageable in a large, cosmopolitan urban system where the supply of teachers would be more reliable.

Teachers of any language continue to be in short supply, so the planning team should develop a time line and a recruitment strategy for teachers as early as possible. Human resources personnel are often relatively uninformed about the challenges of recruiting world language teachers for early language classrooms, so close cooperation and advice from the planning team will help to ensure that quality teachers are hired for the program.

Immersion Teachers.   Immersion programs require teachers who are fluent in the target language and also certified elementary school teachers. They must be capable of teaching the entire curriculum in the foreign language, and they must understand the process of second-language acquisition. Some school districts with immersion programs have found it necessary to recruit teachers from abroad in order to find staff with adequate background and language skills—and then they have faced the challenge of orienting foreign staff to the realities of the American school and the psyche of the American child. Many teachers in Spanish immersion programs have been drawn from a background in bilingual education, but some readjustment of attitudes and assumptions is necessary before these teachers adapt smoothly to an immersion approach.

Program Coordinator.   The decision to include a program coordinator in the staffing and budget plan is a major step toward insuring that planning and implementation of a language program will proceed smoothly. Rosenbusch (1991, 308) lists a number of qualities this coordinator should have: ". . . is certified K–12, is experienced in teaching foreign language at all levels, is able to work effectively with other teachers, and is able to communicate well with school administrators, parents, and the community. Most importantly, the coordinator must be committed to the expanded foreign language program and dedicated to maintaining a strong program of excellent quality."

Each of the seven programs described by Gilzow and Branaman (2000), in their overview of model early foreign language programs, has the benefit of some type of coordinator position. The program may be guided by a full- or part-time program coordinator, a district foreign language supervisor, or another individual with responsibility for program and curriculum development.

It is important to designate at least a half-time professional position to the role of coordinator of the program, whether this position takes the form of a foreign language supervisor, a lead teacher with released time for supervision and planning, or a resource teacher with administrative responsibility. The coordinator will need time for building the new program; for providing in-service opportunities for language teachers; for developing curriculum, materials, and assessments; and for building school and community support.

Budget

The level of funding that a school system is willing to commit to a language program will be the final determiner of the shape and scope of a program. It is imperative to plan with budget factors in mind, developing a program that will make the best use of the funds available. The most carefully planned "dream" program will suffer if shortcuts and compromises must be made in order to stretch an inadequate budget. A realistic proposed budget will take the following factors into account.

Start-Up Costs

FLES or Exploratory Programs. Start-up costs for FLES or exploratory programs include realia, materials, a collection of resource books and sample programs for teacher use, some audiovisual equipment, and other non-consumable classroom materials. These costs may also include additions to the instructional resource center such as videos, computer software, CDs, and tapes, library books, and displays.

Immersion Programs. In an immersion program the start-up costs are significant, because target language materials must be purchased for all elements of classroom instruction and library supplementation, and some may have to be developed locally.

Media-Based Programs. Media-based formats, such as interactive cable programs, will also have relatively high start-up costs for materials and equipment.

Salaries

Language Specialists. Schools choosing a language specialist model will immediately add the expense of salaries for the language teachers. As the program develops, more teachers will be hired to staff new levels and new sections.

Non-Specialist Tutors.   Programs that use non-specialist tutors will require a professional coordinator to supervise the program at some percentage of a full-time salary.

Immersion Teachers.   Immersion programs have no additional salary costs since the immersion teacher replaces a regular classroom teacher, rather than supplementing that teacher. It should be noted, however, that the most successful immersion models include a native-speaking classroom aide in each classroom, for at least part of each day.

Program Coordinator.   The position of program coordinator may be a full-time position, in the case of a large school system, or it may constitute part of the day for a foreign language classroom teacher. In most cases this should be at least a half-time position.

Curriculum and Staff Development Time

There are few investments that can yield a greater return than planning time for teachers. If at least some of the initial planning is done by an entire language department, both the commitment to the total program and the chances for smooth articulation are improved. Schools should budget to fund at least several weeks of planning time before beginning a new program, and regular summer planning time each year thereafter.

Curriculum Development.   Although commercial materials are available for some FLES programs, most schools will find that they need to develop at least some part of the curriculum to meet the particular needs of the local community. There is very little available commercially for exploratory programs or for the less commonly taught languages, so local planning will consume considerable time and energy. Immersion programs require extensive locally developed materials.

Staff Development.   Teachers in elementary school foreign language programs will need regular staff development opportunities, separately and with secondary school language faculty. Especially with the classroom-teacher model, staff development opportunities should not intrude on regular planning time or on what would otherwise be free time.

Attendance at Conferences.   Because elementary school language teachers often feel very isolated, some of the best staff development support for teachers comes from attendance at foreign language conferences, such as the annual meeting of the American Council on the Teaching of Foreign Languages and various state and regional language conferences. All of these conferences feature workshops and sessions on languages at the elementary school level. A number of states also offer conferences directed specifically at language teaching at the K–8 level. Travel and registration costs for conferences, as well as salary for a substitute teacher, are valuable additions to the language budget.

Materials.   After the start-up costs for materials, there will be ongoing expenditures for the following:

Consumable Materials
- Worksheets, workbooks, crafts materials, and food items fall into this category.
- Language teaching in the elementary and middle school/junior high school relies heavily on visuals and realia, so costs for realia and visuals needed for each language and each level may well be greater than in other curricular areas.

Import costs
- Costs of imported materials may be 10 to 20 percent higher than costs of domestic materials.

Textbook costs
- When texts are available, these costs will increase with each grade level added to the program.

Other Materials Costs
- The costs for photocopying will be proportionally higher in programs for which there is no textbook.
- Hardware and repair costs for all media systems. Media-based programs will have recurring expenditures in this area.
- Video- and audiotapes or CDs, CD-ROMs, and DVDs.
- Cost of laminating and other production of visual materials.

Miscellaneous Costs. There may be various miscellaneous costs to be considered:

- travel between schools for language specialist teachers, when they are assigned to more than one school
- travel from base site to receiving sites in programs that use interactive cable
- travel for the language coordinator for supervision purposes on the part of the language coordinator
- delivery costs, when languages are taught by means of interactive cable, for transporting materials and student work from school to school
- mailing costs for programs that incorporate systematic contacts with schools or children in foreign countries
- admission fees, speaker's fees, and field trips
- costs of making connections with language speakers or other representative elements of the target culture (gift shops, restaurants, museums, festivals, art galleries, etc.)
- food and craft activities

It is sometimes possible for a school system to receive government assistance or a foundation grant for beginning a language program at the elementary school level. While this eases the impact of the start-up costs and initial planning, it is critical that there be a school commitment to a realistic level of long-term funding for the program.

Resources

Interesting and appropriate instructional materials are an important part of any language program, but up-to-date commercial materials for most program models described here may be difficult to find. Many school systems have developed their own curriculum and materials for FLES and exploratory programs, especially in French, German, and Spanish, and these can serve as a starting point for local materials development. Immersion programs in French often draw on resources created for Canadian programs, although these must usually be adapted somewhat for use in the United States. Spanish immersion programs can often make use of some materials developed for bilingual programs, but these materials, too, must be adapted to suit the different language sophistication of the learner. Immersion programs in other languages must rely on locally developed materials and on those developed in already-existing immersion programs. Materials suitable for elementary school children in less commonly taught languages such as Arabic, Chinese, Hebrew, Japanese, and Russian are the most difficult to obtain.

The choice of a program model for which few existing curriculum materials are available requires a commitment to the time and expertise necessary for materials development. Since the goals are so limited, creation of materials for a short-term exploratory program may well be a realistic task for a few teachers working with locally available native speakers during several weeks in the summer. Developing an articulated FLES program, however, will require skilled and experienced teachers and the cooperation of native speakers over a significant period of time, probably including regular released time during the school year. The planning time and start-up curriculum costs for an immersion program that has to be developed locally will represent a major investment for the district.

As more school systems make a commitment to languages at the elementary school level, and as more teachers are able to articulate clearly what kinds of materials they need for these programs, publishers are more likely to produce materials that are usable. That development will make planning a program at the elementary or middle school level an easier and more efficient process.

Space Allocation

Early language programs at the elementary school level are usually housed by one of two methods. Either the language teacher has all classes meet in a special language room, which can be used to create a target language environment for instruction, or the teacher travels from one classroom to another. Teachers have found advantages in either means of organization, although the traveling teacher is severely restricted in terms of extensive use of hands-on materials and realia. When the teacher must travel, it is valuable to have the classroom teacher remain in the room during the language lesson, both to show support and to help ensure that there is no loss of instructional time because of a need to establish behavioral standards. A more extended discussion of these issues is found in Chapter 9.

Support of Existing District Staff

Support of Elementary School Principals and Teachers.   The success of a language program is closely tied to the environment of the school in which it is placed. It is vital that the principal and the teachers in the school be in favor of the program, that they share commitment to its goals, and that they participate in program planning. When planners developed a new elementary school Spanish program in Appleton, Wisconsin, they began with pilot programs in three schools. All interested schools in the district competed for the opportunity to participate in the pilot project. Only schools in which there was clear and unified support from the entire school community were considered as program sites. As a result, the faculty and administration of the pilot schools felt investment in and support for the new program and were willing to work to help it succeed.

In programs using a language-specialist model, classroom teachers who feel themselves to be a part of the language teaching team can extend the language learning into the regular school day. They may suggest curricular areas for reinforcement or vocabulary development in the language classroom, encourage the use of the foreign language during other school activities, and participate in language classes with the children, thus serving as powerful models of interest and enthusiasm.

In programs using a classroom-teacher model, tremendous responsibility for success of the program rests with individual teachers for whom language instruction is only one component in a busy, demanding schedule. Teachers with a commitment to the language program will find ways to use the language communicatively throughout the day and will be in a position to give individual students the special attention they may need in order to succeed to the level of their own potential. Without real commitment to the program, participation may be grudging, and results from the students will be disappointing.

Immersion programs require the coordinated efforts of the principal and all of the staff to create a second-language environment and to work toward unified goals. When immersion programs are housed in the same building as non-language classrooms, considerable effort may be required to make sure that non-immersion teachers understand the immersion program and do not resent the special attention that immersion programs often receive, especially when the program is new. Since considerable funding often goes into the start-up of an immersion program, other teachers may perceive immersion teachers and students to be favorites. Problems like these will not disappear unless there is a focused effort to help the entire school work together and to understand the special characteristics and benefits of the immersion program.

Support of Existing Foreign Language Staff. The success of an early language program also depends to a great extent on the support and expertise of the existing foreign language staff in the school system, who will work with the students from the K-8 program once they reach the high school levels. If teachers at later levels are unsupportive or ineffective, the program at the elementary school will eventually suffer.

A case in point is a medium-sized Minnesota school that taught three languages at the senior high school; one of the languages, French, had very low enrollments and dissatisfied students. In the 1960s an elementary school program in French was introduced by a talented and innovative teacher, and junior high enrollments soared when students reached that level. As soon as these students entered the senior high school, however, they dropped French, sometimes after a week or two, or did not ever register, on the basis of the "grapevine" alone.

After a year or two of this type of enrollment pattern, the school board discontinued the entire French program on the grounds that they could not justify continuing a feeder program without the senior high school culmination. The elementary school program was blamed by some for giving children "false" expectations that language learning would be fun, that the work would be meaningful and enjoyable, and that everyone could learn a language. By the mid-1980s, French had been reintroduced in the district, but no languages had returned to the elementary school.

When students leave a middle school program and are told by the receiving teacher that "fun and games were all very well before, but now you will start real language learning," the entire K–8 program is called into question. Language teachers at every level need to understand and affirm the learning that has already taken place and build their own programs on that learning. This is most likely to happen when teachers from all levels of instruction participate in initial program planning and meet regularly to design curriculum and discuss methodology and articulation issues.

Choice of Language(s)

Deciding which language(s) to offer is often a difficult and emotional issue at the beginning of the planning process. Community interest, availability of materials and staff, and potential for articulation must all be taken into consideration. When none of these factors plays a determining role, many school districts have chosen to advertise a "foreign language" position rather than to indicate a specific language. The best available candidate is hired, regardless of the language, and the quality of the resulting program lays a foundation for long-term success. Compelling rationale can be developed for *any* of the commonly taught languages, and any language, when well taught, can provide children with the benefits of global awareness, enhanced basic skills, identification with other cultures, self-esteem, and communicative language skills.

Planners for a new elementary school immersion program in Moorhead, Minnesota, made their program recommendation to the school board before they had made the decision of which language should be taught. In that way the decision to fund the program could be made on the basis of the importance of early language learning and the type of program recommended—without having issues become clouded by individual preferences for language to be taught. It was clear from later board discussions that this approach had been very helpful in gaining approval for the program.

If the elementary school program is implemented in only one language, a possible adverse effect on enrollments in other languages at the middle school/junior high school and high school levels must be considered. However, implementing an elementary language program in more than one language may fragment the district's program and compound articulation problems. This is one of the most difficult issues to wrestle with. There is some justification for the fear that students will choose the elementary school language for continuation at the high school level, thus crowding out the other languages. In many districts, however, all languages have benefited from an increased interest in learning languages, and students entering high school choose to add a third language, or to explore a different language. It is important to provide more than one entry point into the district's language program in order to accommodate students who would like to study an additional language or who were not able to enroll in the elementary language program.

It is especially desirable to introduce the less-commonly-taught languages, such as Arabic, Chinese, Japanese, and Russian into the elementary school because of their critical importance to the national interest. These languages are more difficult for the English speaker and thus require a much longer exposure before competence can be attained than is the case with the more common school offerings. Their introduction early in the curriculum would make it much more likely that students could develop usable communication skills in them.

Who Should Study Language?

The *Standards for Foreign Language Learning in the 21st Century* (1999) provide a clear answer to this question at the beginning of the "Statement of Philosophy" (7):

> The United States must educate students who are equipped linguistically and culturally to communicate successfully in a pluralistic American society and abroad. This imperative envisions a future in which ALL students will develop and maintain proficiency in English and at least one other language, modern or classical.

The time has arrived to shed the "elitist" image that foreign languages had for most of the last century in the United States. Evidence from the inner-city schools of Philadelphia, Milwaukee, and Cincinnati, among others, supports the idea that foreign language learning must be for all learners of all levels of ability and background. Students with poor skills may even have the most to gain from the opportunity to study languages (Masciantonio 1977, Garfinkel and Tabor 1991). The practice in some schools of reserving foreign language study for children who are reading at or above grade level stands in direct contradiction to the information obtained from the Masciantonio study. Such practices may be taking away opportunities for foreign language study from those children who could benefit from it the most.

Boudreaux (1991) identified sixteen strategies common to immersion teaching that are especially beneficial to the special education student, suggesting that the foreign language learning environment could be a hospitable one for students with learning problems (see Figure 19.2). Andrade, Kretschmer, and Kretschmer (1989) offer both reasons and test results to support the offering of foreign languages to all children. Kretschmer and Kretschmer (1998) also describe the obstacles to learning a new language experienced by learners with various types of disabilities.

Teachers in Chicago (Estelle 1985), New York State (Schnitzler 1986), and in other areas have reported success in teaching foreign languages to learning-disabled and to mentally handicapped students, especially when they employ an oral, communicative methodology. A special education teacher in Glyndon, Minnesota (Bring 1986), verified an observation made by many elementary school language teachers when she noted that some of her students were achieving school success and satisfaction for the first time in their French classes, and that as a result their overall attitude and performance had improved in other school subjects as well.

FIGURE 19.2   Shared Teaching Strategies: Immersion Language and Special Education

1. Provides multisensory approach to teaching/instruction.
2. Pairs visual stimuli with verbalization.
3. Uses manipulatives and hands-on involvement.
4. Calls name to alert student to be ready to listen.
5. Restructures sentences if presentation is not understood.
6. Uses sentences at the level of the students. Begins with short sentences (3–5 words) and moves to longer sentences.
7. Begins with grammatically simple sentences and works toward complex structures.
8. Changes question format if not readily understood. Example: "Who is going to help?" can be changed to "What person is going to help?"
9. Provides many repetitions; demonstrates patterns and redundancies.
10. Uses slow rate of speech.
11. Explicit teacher modeling. A planted sentence/phrase is repeated in various contexts that give meaning and suggest imitation to the student.
12. Uses a controlled vocabulary for specific lessons.
13. Presents new vocabulary just prior to the lesson.
14. Presents question forms based on fact. Then, as abilities develop, the teacher presents questions that involve critical thinking.
15. Advanced organizers (graphs, pictures, outlines) are used by the students during the lesson.
16. Asks another student to retell what teacher stated.

Source: Ellen Boudreaux, M.A., Speech and Language Specialist.

Gifted and Talented Students.   At the other end of the scale, the gifted child is often selected first to be given the opportunity to study a language. Language teachers are caught in a conflict regarding programs for the gifted child. While there is evidence that languages can be of value to every child, and programs offered exclusively to the gifted tend to reinforce an elitist image for languages, it is also true that many language programs that were begun only for the gifted have led to programs for all children because of their success and popularity.

Gifted children are often especially good language learners as a result of certain frequently observed learning characteristics: retentiveness, a high degree of verbal ability, persistent goal-directed behavior, and ability to work independently. For the gifted child, languages can be a key to unlock new dimensions of learning and new perspectives. With the foreign language as a tool, the gifted have the opportunity to explore a new system of thinking, a new cultural context and, at advanced levels, even new literary and political perspectives.

The academically talented are among the nation's most precious resources, the pool from which our strongest leaders are likely to come. In an increasingly interdependent global community, these leaders of tomorrow cannot afford to be monolingual. Programs intended specifically for the gifted must be designed to meet their specific needs and must capitalize on their particular abilities, and they should be supported by appropriate rationale and curriculum. Coordinators of programs for the gifted, working together with knowledgeable language teachers, can design the best possible program for this group.

Scheduling

The way in which the early language program is scheduled may be the determining factor in the ultimate long-term success of the program.

Frequency and Duration of Language Classes.　Will the program be offered once a week, every other day, or daily? How much time will be allotted per class? For optimal learning to take place, *FLES programs should meet for a minimum of thirty to forty minutes per day, five days per week,* with as much additional reinforcement of the language throughout the school day as possible. The *ACTFL Performance Guidelines for K–12 Learners* (Swender and Duncan 1998) describe student performances for grades four, eight, and twelve that can only be achieved if students are enrolled "in elementary programs that meet from 3–5 days per week for no less than 30–40 minutes per class; middle school programs that meet daily for no less than 40–50 minutes; and high school programs that equal four units of credit" (482). For Core French programs in Canada (equivalent to FLES programs in the United States), forty minutes per day is a recommended standard. Programs that do not meet daily will be required to devote a significant proportion of class time to review activity to compensate for the long periods of time between language classes.

Teacher Workload.　A second, equally important consideration in scheduling is the number of classes that the language teacher teaches per day. Curtain and Dahlberg (2000, 2) highlight teacher workload as one of the major potential pitfalls for an early language program:

> ### Pitfall: Planning Schedules and Workloads that Lead to Teacher Burnout
> There is currently a shortage of qualified teachers for early language programs. If we want to rectify this situation, it is imperative that we build programs that are good for children and also good for teachers. With this in mind, the Georgia Department of Education stipulated that FLES teachers in state-supported model programs should teach no more than 8 classes per day, leaving time for the many additional responsibilities of a FLES teacher: interacting with numerous classroom teachers, developing curriculum and materials, communicating with parents and community, and building public relations for the program. Teachers in Bay Point Elementary School (Pinellas County, FL), one of the model programs featured in *Lessons Learned* (2000), also see eight classes per day, and their additional responsibilities are clearly defined (Gilzow and Branaman 2000, 13, 25–26).
>
> If language teachers work under unfavorable conditions, they are likely to burn out and either leave the profession or opt for regular classrooms. There are dangers in the proliferation of early language programs when attention is not given to the stress factors involved in typical teacher workloads. Elementary school language teachers may find themselves teaching as many as 14 classes in a single day, seeing as many as 600 students in a week, or even more. Their classes are often scheduled back to back, with no time in between. They rarely have their own classroom, typically traveling from classroom to classroom—

sometimes from building to building—with all their lessons and materials on a cart. They often lack professional support and opportunities for in-service training. Their schedules rarely allow them time to collaborate with other language teachers or with the classroom teachers in whose rooms they work. Given these difficult conditions, it is not surprising that early language programs have a hard time finding and keeping qualified teachers.

There are other factors that affect the stress level of an early language teacher's schedule. Gilzow and Rhodes (2000) make these recommendations for program staffing (8):

- Do hire at least one foreign language teacher per school so that the teacher is part of the school staff and can communicate and coordinate with regular classroom teachers.
- Do provide adequate workspace. If teachers need to wheel a materials cart from classroom to classroom, ensure that they also have an office or workspace that is their own and that has room for materials, a telephone, and a computer.
- Don't schedule all the language classes back to back. Foreign language teachers need time between classes to gather materials, re-focus on a new group of students, and possibly adapt their lessons to meet a regular classroom teacher's requests.
- Do consider how many students a foreign language teacher will meet with each week. No one teacher can be expected to keep track of—much less really teach—600 students in a week. Fourteen classes in a day is not a reasonable workload; eight 30-minute classes per day is a maximum load.
- Don't expect that the language teacher's number of contact hours will be the same as that of the classroom teachers. Because a language teacher usually meets with a larger number of students and must travel from classroom to classroom, he or she may spend fewer hours per week with students than does a regular elementary classroom teacher.
- Don't require the foreign language teacher to handle multiple grade levels in a single day. Because children's developmental levels are so different in the elementary grades, it is sufficiently challenging for a teacher to work with two grades.
- Do build time in the foreign language teacher's schedule to collaborate with the regular classroom teachers, develop and adapt materials, and participate in meetings and opportunities for professional development.

Relationship to the Total School Curriculum.   Another important point to consider is how the foreign language program fits into the total school curriculum. One frequent obstacle to beginning foreign language programs at the elementary school level is the complaint from classroom teachers and administrators that there is not enough room in the school day for the present curriculum, let alone time to add another subject to it. Many school districts have addressed this problem by allotting some of the language arts or social studies time for the foreign language program. Some districts take a little time from each subject area in order to make a place for languages. When going through the difficult process of finding time for an elementary school foreign language program, it is important to stress the interdisciplinary aspects of foreign language learning and the well-documented benefits to first-language skills.

Another way to deal with the scheduling problem is to plan a content-related curriculum that interfaces with the basic curriculum at various points and is planned in such a way that many objectives from the basic curriculum are clearly evident in the second-language curriculum. Too often, elementary foreign language programs state that the program is interdisciplinary or that subject content instruction is included, but in reality these turn out to be only token activities. (For information on effective use of content in the language curriculum, see the discussion in Chapter 7 and Chapter 11.)

Middle School Scheduling.   Middle school scheduling presents a special challenge because of the variety of scheduling patterns being implemented in schools at this level. Several options have been tried with success, including blocking world languages with the social studies or the language arts component of the curriculum, or building languages into a flexible physical education and arts block. Whatever the solution may be, it is critical that the intensity of the language program be maintained through middle school. Students who have developed meaningful language proficiency in a carefully articulated elementary school program should have opportunity for real language development during the crucial middle school years.

Curriculum

Once the goals of the program have been set, it is necessary to formulate a curriculum to meet these goals. There are three avenues to approaching curriculum development:

1. *Choosing Curriculum*
   The first and easiest approach is to locate already-prepared curriculum that is basically compatible with the program goals and that is suitable for the age level of the students.
2. *Adapting Curriculum*
   The second approach is to locate curriculum that is close to what is desired but that needs to be adapted in some way.
3. *Writing Curriculum*
   The third avenue, and the most difficult, is to begin from scratch to write curriculum.

Each of these three options is discussed more fully below.

Curriculum Sources.   Sources of curriculum for elementary language programs from outside the district include commercial materials and those developed by other school districts. You may locate commercial materials by writing to publishers or by contacting them at foreign language conferences, and through contacts with existing programs. Many materials developed by existing programs to meet local needs are available through the Educational Resources Information Center (ERIC), which can be accessed at most public and university libraries (microfiche and paper copy), by accessing curriculum documents available on the Internet. Two good starting points on the Internet are the Glastonbury, Connecticut, foreign language program, for units and lessons developed as part of an Understanding by Design project, and the Georgia ESFL curriculum for grades K–8. Web sites are listed in "Web Sites of Interest" at the end of the chapter. Many individual teachers share materials on the Internet and in sessions at workshops and conferences.

Other sources of curriculum may include commercial or locally developed materials for ESL and bilingual classes. Many of these materials demonstrate the application of linguistic and psychological research to the language learning process and they can be successfully adapted to a foreign language format. Materials developed for children in the target culture learning in their native language can be useful resources for the teacher in designing content-related lessons and activities with cultural authenticity, but most of these materials are too difficult for language learners in another setting. An exception might be materials designed for children with special needs or for children learning the target language as a second language; for example, non-German speakers learning in a German school, similar to the English language learner in the U.S. context.

Screening Curriculum Sources.   Key factors in determining the appropriateness of materials for adoption in the local program include the following:

- **Standards orientation**
  There should be clear evidence that the materials are designed to address all five of the goals of the *Standards for Foreign Language Learning* (1999) and all eleven standards.
- **Publication date**
  Most materials with publication dates before 1990 do not reflect the insights gained through research and experience in the last years of the twentieth century. It is important to note, however, that a recent publication date does not guarantee that materials have been developed in harmony with current research and practice.
- **Compatibility with the philosophy and goals of the local program.**
  Because goals and circumstances in each local situation differ so markedly, particularly at the elementary school level, the transfer of a curriculum from one setting to another is especially problematic. Publishers find it difficult to produce materials that will meet all the needs of the wide variety of programs being developed.
- **Age-appropriateness**
  In some programs teachers have attempted to solve the problem of materials by adapting high school or college texts, or using texts developed at a much earlier date. We do not recommend the adaptation of high school and college texts because topics and activities covered are inappropriate to the interests of children, and there is often a strong grammatical bias even in beginning-level textbooks of this type.
- **Methodology recommended**
  It is important to determine whether the materials reflect an up-to-date approach in learning languages such as that found in the Key Concepts outlined at the beginning of this book (p. xix–xx), because using materials that do not reflect current pedagogy will detract from the quality of the program being planned. Sometimes the materials themselves may be useful, but teaching recommendations are less compatible with program philosophy. Teachers need to follow their own best instincts and best understanding of effective language teaching, regardless of what suggestions a teacher handbook might offer.

Adapting Curriculum. Whatever curriculum is chosen, be it commercially prepared or developed by another school district, it must be adapted and modified to fit the local situation. For example, a curriculum planned for a daily program would have to be modified to fit the needs of an alternate-day program. A curriculum written for a regular classroom group might have to be modified for use with students in a gifted and talented program, or for a class with a high proportion of special-education students.

Specific interests and priorities of the local school or community must also be taken into account. Children in a rural community will probably not relate well to a program designed to capitalize on the city environment of the metropolitan school system for which it was created. A school in which many children have realistic expectations of traveling abroad will want to incorporate much more information about life and travel in other countries than might be appropriate in another setting. The background and interests of the teaching staff should also influence which countries and which aspects of culture or of the subject content curriculum will be emphasized in a specific program.

Writing Curriculum. Successful local-curriculum writing requires the talents of a skilled teacher, or preferably a team of teachers who are very familiar with the Standards, foreign language proficiency, principles of second-language acquisition, communicative language teaching, curriculum development, and child development. In addition, all materials must be screened for linguistic and cultural content and accuracy by at least one native speaker of the language.

Curriculum writers need to examine a wide variety of available materials, both from commercial sources and from other districts, in order to emulate the strengths and avoid the pitfalls represented there. No curriculum will be in its final form until it has been field-tested and revised as a result of student and teacher reaction.

The development of local curriculum is a time-consuming, costly, and rigorous process. It requires strong support from the district and from the administration, through released time and/or summer writing time; and there must be financial recognition of the high degree of skill and dedication involved in the task. The reward for the district can be an exemplary program that meets local needs in a very precise way, based on a curriculum that can also make a contribution to the development of early language programs in other communities.

Articulation of K–12 Foreign Language Programs

Students leaving the elementary school foreign language program must have an appropriate course available to them in order to continue their language study. One of the reasons that earlier FLES programs failed is that the language ability the children had acquired was not taken into account when the students were programmed into middle school or junior high school language courses. Often elementary school language students were forced to begin the language again when they entered junior high school or high school, because the oral proficiency they had attained was not valued in the grammatically based secondary school program. These experiences discouraged enrollments at the elementary school, discouraged continuation of study at higher levels, and ultimately raised the question of the effectiveness of the FLES programs themselves.

The middle school program for continuing FLES students must be visibly and substantively different from the program for students who are beginning language study at that level. School districts must either establish a separate track for the continuing elementary school language students, or they must ensure that the content of the middle school courses in which these students are enrolled builds on and is complementary to the background they have already obtained. When full or partial immersion has been implemented at the elementary school level, middle school programs must provide some content instruction in the target language as well as advanced language instruction. As students reach the senior high school with extensive foreign language background, curriculum at that level must also change in significant, substantive ways.

One reason that expected outcomes differ among language programs at the elementary school, middle school, and high school levels is that the focus at each level is different. Attempts to describe progress at one level in terms of another level must take into account the differences among programs at each level. Some of these differences are as follows:

1. Elementary school foreign language programs emphasize listening and speaking skills, while an increasing proportion of class time at the middle school and high school is devoted to reading and writing.
2. Elementary school students have very limited experience with grammatical analysis, an area that is addressed more formally at later levels.
3. Language skills at each level are developed to deal with different settings and different interests, in response to the interests and experiences of students at different age levels. The range of vocabulary and situations with which students at various levels can function comfortably will differ accordingly.

Traditionally in American schools the direction of articulation and program development in foreign languages has been determined from the top down. When reform or creative change has developed at the high school level, the expectations of colleges and universities have served as a constraint, even though a minority of the students go on to college study. Junior high and middle school teachers have often experienced criticism from high school teachers who claimed that what incoming students had learned previously was lacking or worse—so middle school teachers often adapt their programs to fit more neatly into the expectations of the teachers who receive their students. It is the challenge of K–12 language programs to turn the traditional articulation pattern on its head—instead of *preparing for* the next level of the program, planners need to give their attention to designing curriculum and experiences to *extend* and *build on* the learning at the preceding level.

The first responsibility of teachers at each level of instruction is to design a program that is congruent with the interests, background, and developmental characteristics of their students. The second responsibility is to design assessment and reporting procedures that are comprehensive and descriptive, so that teachers who receive these students have clear and adequate information upon which to base the goals and learning experiences at the next level. Paul Sandrock of the Wisconsin Department of Public Instruction characterizes the desired movement in articulation as being a "rippling up" of information about student attainments at preceding levels, and using that information as the basis for goals and activities at the next level. He contrasts this with the "pointing down" so familiar to language teachers at every level, in which teachers appear to discount the attainments at earlier levels if they do not fit neatly into the expectations and approaches used with the older age group (Sandrock, 1993).

Middle School Programs

One of the important philosophical tenets in many middle schools is the concept of *exploration*. In some cases this concept has been applied to foreign languages by rejecting the possibility of continuing instruction on a daily basis in the same foreign language students have been studying for several years in elementary school. Exploratory programs are provided, "introducing" learners to the idea of language learning and to several different languages. It has happened that students who have already developed considerable fluency in a language are required to attend introductory classes in that same language, in which they encounter greetings, colors, numbers, and animal names as if for the first time. This is, obviously, a recipe for boredom and frustration, and is likely to discourage later enrollment for that or any other language. But even more serious is the wasted opportunity represented in this situation—students with a solid foundation in one language could be developing a valuable tool during middle school years, which they could apply in learning throughout the curriculum at the senior high school level. It is important to develop curriculum for the middle school level that demonstrates the potential for exploration of the world *while at the same time building additional fluency, skills, and cultural insight in a single language.*

Although some textbook series have been developed or adapted for the middle school level, thematic units can provide the most effective curriculum for the middle school language program. For the continuing language learner, the thematic unit builds on elementary school experiences in a natural way and combines well with the overall integrative nature of the middle school. Beginning language students benefit from integrated thematic units in much the same way, although the language level for the units will be similar to units planned for the elementary school. See Chapter 7 for a complete discussion of thematic planning.

It should be pointed out that graduates of a FLES program who begin a new language in the middle school will be very different learners from those beginners who have had no previous language experience. They are likely to learn much more quickly, and to approach learning with more sophistication and greater motivation.

One of the most vexing problems for planners is the scheduling of foreign languages in the overcrowded middle school day. One option suggested for Wisconsin schools (Sandrock, 1993) is to make foreign language a part of the interdisciplinary team in the humanities block, together with English, social studies, art, music, physical education, and family and consumer education. The technology block includes science, mathematics, technical education and computer education. In this plan English, social studies, foreign language, science, and mathematics meet daily on a flexible schedule planned by teachers in the block; other subjects meet on alternating days. Another option is to schedule the language class in place of the remedial or developmental reading class offered by many middle schools in addition language arts. Yet another option is to completely reconfigure the time schedule, so that a minimum block of forty to forty-five minutes can be made available daily.

North Carolina, the first state in the nation to mandate K–12 foreign language instruction in 1985, has focused intensive effort on articulation at the middle school level. The North Carolina Department of Public Instruction (1991) has produced a document for administrators that addresses the issues in middle-level education in some detail and provides a number of sample schedules to demonstrate options for programs with a variety of program goals. The sample schedules and other information on middle school programs can be found on the companion Web site for this book.

Brown (1995) identifies a number of elements of the long-term success of the foreign language program in Glastonbury, Connecticut, all of which facilitate effective articulation across grade levels:

- Language teachers from all grade levels meet monthly to discuss district-wide events and priorities.
- The curriculum is reviewed with cross representation from all levels of language instruction, including community members, classroom teachers, and administrators from other disciplines.
- Teachers write collaborative departmental examinations for grades five through twelve.
- Teachers have created a common scoring mechanism for grading student examinations.
- Teachers exchange students and tapes for oral examinations in order to assess speaking skills and to ensure a common grading standard.

Successful K–12 articulation, and especially the building of a successful middle school link for a program, can be accomplished only with the full participation of teachers from all levels in careful planning and in ongoing, open communication. Adjustments at every level may have to be made as a K–12 program develops, in order to ensure a continuous opportunity for language development. Teachers who understand one another's goals, visit one another's classrooms, and respect one another's professional judgment will be in the best position to build a strong and vital program that provides a positive environment for learning *and* teaching of foreign languages.

Robert Politzer (1991) developed "Eleven Commandments of Articulation," several of which seem especially pertinent to this discussion. They are provided below:

1. The main principle of articulation is simply a principle of good teaching: Don't (unintentionally) repeat material the student has mastered already; always provide enough new material so that the student is motivated and something new is being learned.
2. Never place students who already know some language in the same class as real beginners.
3. Try and provide a "bridge course" for students who do not fit in an expected level (but do not put them in a beginners class). . . .
4. If in doubt, follow your experience and instinct concerning good teaching. Remember principle number one. If you feel that you are violating this principle, change and adapt the curriculum. *Fight back.*

Building Public Relations

Planning the foreign language program must involve parents, the community, the staff, and the school board in every step of the process. The support of these people will be the decisive factor in the later success of the program. Once the program is in progress, spending the time and effort necessary to develop a broad support base in the school and the community will prove to be very rewarding.

The planning committee for the new program can continue to play an important role after the program has been established. They have the expertise necessary to help the community understand and appreciate the value of language learning, and they can form the core of broader community support. In the event that the new program is threatened in some way, such as a cutback in staffing or in scheduling, there is a strong advocacy team immediately available. Finally, as Tucker and Donato point out (1999), this committee can continue to guide the program and to plan for its expansion.

Leadership from a foreign language program coordinator can be especially helpful in ensuring ongoing and consistent activity to build public support. Some of the activities that can contribute to this support include the following:

- making use of the media to provide publicity
- taking field trips
- inviting parents and others to visit classes
- videotaping classes and specific class projects to share with parent groups and administrators
- reporting class activities to parents, to the principal, and to other teachers
- sending out a monthly newsletter
- taking part in school programs
- putting on a special program for parents and/or for the community
- sending second-language invitations and greeting cards as a class writing activity

These activities give the program visibility and communicate the activities and accomplishments of the elementary school foreign language program. They also serve as an effective recruitment tool for languages at all levels. Additional information about public relations and advocacy is found in Chapter 16.

Assessment

Program Assessment. Assessment must be an integral part of both program and curriculum design. If impact on basic skills, on attitudes, or on performance in other content areas is to be measured, pretests will have to be designed and administered before the beginning of the program. The goals of program assessment should be determined at the outset, so that specific instruments can be developed and a time line for assessment can be built into the school schedule. Types of program assessment include the following:

- pupil language skills performance
- pupil attitudes toward other languages and cultures

- pupil attitudes toward the course
- pupil performance in other content areas
- teacher performance checklists
- teacher evaluation of program
- parent attitudes
- outside consultant observation
- teacher-peer observation and review
- administrator observation and review

The Center for Applied Linguistics has developed the Student Oral Proficiency Assessment (SOPA), appropriate for students in grades three and above, and the Early Language Listening and Oral Proficiency Assessment (ELLOPA) for primary school students. These are designed for assessing overall student performance using randomly selected students, and not for individual student assessment.

Instruments for assessing several of the other areas of program effectiveness have been developed by Heining-Boynton (1991) for use with FLES programs in North Carolina. These resources are shared in her article in *Foreign Language Annals* and they can be adapted very successfully for local program use.

Student Assessment and Grading.   Assessment can be of student performance can be a valuable indicator of program success, and it also provides teachers with essential information about the effectiveness of instruction and the needs of individual students. Meaningful assessment will reflect the goals of the program and the nature of instruction; that is, it will be based on student performance in meaningful, communicative language tasks. Just as traditional paper-and-pencil methods of testing are giving way to performance evaluation and portfolio development across the rest of the curriculum, so, too, will assessment of student performance in foreign language instruction require a variety of non-traditional measures.

Although some school districts have chosen to give students in early language classes a pass/fail grade, or no grade at all, a program that seeks parity with other courses in the curriculum should be treated like other content areas in terms of grading. Both students and parents tend to perceive classes for which grades are not given as less important, as peripheral to the basic curriculum. The basis for assessing student progress and for awarding grades must be compatible with the goals and the philosophy of the program. That is, if oral skills are emphasized, assessment will be based on listening and speaking performance, even though reading and writing skills might be easier to measure objectively. Specific suggestions for effective assessment, evaluation, and reporting of student performance are provided in Chapter 8.

Sharing Experiences and Ideas—Networking

Sharing the experiences and good ideas that you have gained from developing an effective K–12 program will enable others interested in starting a program to build on what has already been done. Your experiences can help to prevent them from making the same discoveries and the same mistakes in isolation. Materials that have been painstakingly developed should be put into the ERIC system or shared on the Internet or in other ways, so that others may take advantage of what has been done. (See the explanation of the ERIC system in Works Cited.) They might also be shared with the state foreign language consultant and with the state foreign language organization. Presentations at local, regional, and national conferences, newsletter articles, and contacts with professional associations are also effective ways of giving program experiences and ideas an impact beyond the local setting.

Characteristics of Effective Programs

Gilzow and Branaman identified ten critical program elements in the model programs described in *Lessons Learned: Model Early Foreign Language Programs* (2000). These elements can help to guide program planning, administration, and evaluation:

1. Implementing National Standards. All seven of the model programs incorporate the Standards in important and curriculum-shaping ways.
2. A Focus on Content. Each program incorporated the general curriculum, using either a content-related or a content-based strategy.
3. Articulation and Alignment. The model programs use a number of different approaches to ensure articulation from one language level to another and alignment across each grade level.
4. Teaching Methods. Language learning is fun in all the model programs, and teachers use a variety of communicative, interactive, age-appropriate activities.
5. Technology. Each of the programs is finding ways to use technology to enhance instruction.
6. Program Evaluation. Among the model programs, Glastonbury is notable for the quality and regularity of its program evaluation.
7. Student Assessment. This is a key component of effective programs, and several of the model programs have interesting and useful assessment strategies.
8. Funding. The model programs typically have benefited from grant funding, especially during the start-up phase, when expenses are particularly high. Secure funding has to be found within the local district for use when grant funding runs out.
9. Professional Development. Professional development is critical in the early stages of a language program, and it continues to be important as the program grows and new curriculum and resources are introduced. The model programs use in-service teacher workshops and professional conferences as effective development opportunities.
10. Advocacy. In nearly all the model programs, reaching out to the community and achieving visibility within the school and the district have been important. Parent involvement is another key element of effective and enduring programs.

Summary

This chapter has outlined the concerns that must be addressed in the planning process for any early language program that is part of a K–12 sequence. There is no factor in the program that will be more crucial to its success than a careful and thorough plan that addresses the key areas of program philosophy and goals, program model, time allocation, budget, staffing, materials, articulation, evaluation, and staff and community involvement and support. A successful plan requires a significant investment of planning time and the unqualified support of the administration and school board. When it is the product of the cooperation, research, and insight of staff, community, and administration, the design of the elementary school program can be carefully tailored to local needs and priorities. Only then is the program likely to become an integrated and lasting component of the basic elementary school curriculum. The following checklist, along with the suggestions in Figure 19.1, provides useful guidelines for applying the principles of this chapter.

Early Language Program Planning Checklist

1. _____ Hold district-wide planning meetings
   _____ Involve community
   _____ Involve classroom and language teachers, administrators, union representatives
2. _____ Complete mission statement, program philosophy
3. _____ Select program model and goals
   _____ Identify students
   _____ Plan for amount of instructional time: days per week, hours per day, years
   _____ Plan for a reasonable teacher workload (eight 30-minute classes per day is optimal)
   _____ Develop patterns of organization for staffing
   _____ Allocate budget for staff, materials, in-service, and miscellaneous costs
4. _____ Identify teachers
5. _____ Select language(s)
6. _____ Develop budget
7. _____ Develop curriculum
   _____ Locate and adapt materials
   _____ Plan scope and sequence, classroom activities
8. _____ Plan articulation with secondary school programs
9. _____ Develop an evaluation plan
10. _____ Design public relations activities
11. _____ Disseminate program information

FOR STUDY AND DISCUSSION

1. Which program-planning considerations might weigh most heavily in each of the following settings?
   - an isolated rural community
   - a community with a rapidly expanding suburban population
   - a small town near a medium-sized city in the American Southwest

- an urban district with many elementary and secondary schools
- a medium-sized city near the Canadian border
- a private school
- a K–12 school housed in a single building

2. You are a middle school foreign language teacher in a system with a strong secondary school program in your language and reasonably successful programs in three other foreign languages, including Latin. You have just been asked to chair a committee to plan an elementary school foreign language program. You have the freedom to choose your own committee and set your own agenda. How will you proceed?

3. An elementary school curriculum coordinator has agreed to support a new foreign language program but he believes strongly that the elementary school day is already too fragmented.

He asks you to design a program that will require the minimum time out of the school day. How will you respond to his request?

4. The curriculum planners in your school district are simultaneously designing a K–12 foreign language program and a new middle school to replace an existing junior high school. You have the opportunity to serve on both committees. What can you do in your role on both committees to help build the best possible K–12 language program and the most effective possible middle school experience for early adolescent learners?

5. One of the elementary school classroom teachers with whom you work comes to you privately and complains that your workload of eight 30-minute world language classes per day is unfair, since she has to teach a full six hours per day. How can you respond?

FOR FURTHER READING

The following sources are recommended for additional information about material covered in this chapter. Chapter citations are documented in Works Cited at the end of the volume.

Brown, Christine. "A Case for Foreign Languages: The Glastonbury Language Program." *Perspective, Council for Basic Education* 7, no. 2 (1995). Available on-line at www.educ.iastate.edu/nnell/glastonb.htm

Byrnes, Heidi. "Curriculum Articulation: Addressing Curriculum Articulation in the Nineties: A Proposal." *Foreign Language Annals* 23, no. 4 (1990): 281–292.

Curtain, Helena, and Carol Ann Pesola Dahlberg. *Planning for Success: Common Pitfalls in the Planning of Early Foreign Language Programs.* Washington, DC: Center for Applied Linguistics, ERIC Digest, December 2000. Available on-line at www.cal.org/ericcll/digest/0011planning.html

Donato, Richard, G., Richard Tucker, Jirada Wudthayagorn, and Kanae Igarashi. "Converging Evidence: Attitudes, Achievements, and Instruction in the Later Years of FLES." *Foreign Language Annals* 33, no. 4 (July/August 2000): 377–393.

Duncan, Gregory. "Administrators and Counselors: Essential Partners to FLES." *FLES News* 2, no. 2 (1988–1989): 1, 6.

Gilzow, Douglas F., and Lucinda E. Branaman. *Lessons Learned: Model Early Foreign Language Programs.* McHenry, IL: Delta Systems Co., 2000.

Gilzow, Douglas F., and Nancy C. Rhodes. *Establishing High-Quality Foreign Language Programs in Elementary Schools.* Northeast and Islands Regional Educational Laboratory at Brown University: Perspectives on Policy and Practice, December 2000. Available on-line at www.lab.brown.edu

Lipton, Gladys C. *Practical Handbook for Elementary Language Programs.* 3rd ed. Lincolnwood, IL: National Textbook Company, 1998.

Met, Myriam. "Decisions, Decisions, Decisions!" *Foreign Language Annals* 18, no. 6 (December 1985): 469–473.

———. "Which Foreign Language Should Students Learn?" *Educational Leadership* 7, no. 1 (1989): 54–58.

———. *Middle Schools And Foreign Languages: A View For The Future.* 1996. Washington DC: Center for Applied Linguistics, ERIC Digest, February. Available on-line at www.cal.org/ericcll/digest/met00002.html

————. *Critical Issues in Early Second Language Learning: Building for Our Children's Future,* see especially Chapters 2, 3, 4, 9, 10, 11. Glenview, IL: Scott Foresman-Addison Wesley, 1998.

National Council of State Supervisors of Foreign Languages and the American Council on the Teaching of Foreign Languages. "NCSSFL/ACTFL Statement on the Study of Foreign Languages in Elementary School." *ACTFL Newsletter* 3, no. 3 (1990). Available on-line at http://ncssfl.org/fles.htm

North Carolina Department of Public Instruction. *Scheduling Foreign Languages on the Block.* 1998. Washington, DC: Center for Applied Linguistics, ERIC Digest, October. Available on-line at www.cal.org/ericcll/digest/blockdigest.html

Pesola, Carol Ann. "Articulation for Elementary School Foreign Language Programs: Challenges and Opportunities." In *Shaping the Future of Foreign Language Education: FLES, Articulation, and Proficiency,* edited by John F. Lalande II, 1–10. Report of Central States Conference on the Teaching of Foreign Languages. Lincolnwood, IL: National Textbook Company, 1988.

Rieken, Elizabeth et al. "Building Better Bridges: Middle School to High School Articulation in Foreign Language Programs." *Foreign Language Annals* 29, no. 4 (1996): 562–570.

Rosenbusch, Marcia H. "Elementary School Foreign Language: The Establishment and Maintenance of Strong Programs." *Foreign Language Annals* 24, no. 4 (1991): 297–314.

————. *Guidelines for Starting an Elementary School Foreign Language Program.* 1995. Washington, DC: Center for Applied Linguistics, ERIC Digest, June. Available on-line at www.cal.org/ericcll/digest/rosenb01.html

Short, Deborah J., and Karen F. Willetts. *Implementing Middle School Foreign Language Programs.* Washington DC: Center for Applied Linguistics, ERIC Digest, June, 1991.

Tucker, G. Richard and Richard Donato. "Designing and Implementing an Innovative Foreign Language Program: Reflections from a School District-University Partnership." *Learning Languages* 4, no. 2 (Winter 1999): 4–12.

————. *Implementing a District-Wide Foreign Language Program.* Washington, DC: Center for Applied Linguistics, ERIC Digest, September 2001. Available on-line at www.cal.org/ericcll/digest/0103implement.html

Walker, Galal. "Gaining Place: The Less Commonly Taught Languages in American Schools." *Foreign Language Annals* 24, no. 2 (1991): 131–150.

Willets, Karen A., and Deborah J. Short. *Planning Middle School Foreign Language Programs.* Washington, DC: Center for Applied Linguistics, ERIC Digest, November 1990.

Wilson, Jo Anne. *Foreign Language Program Articulation: Building Bridges from Elementary to Secondary School.* Washington, DC: Center for Applied Linguistics, ERIC Digest, November 1988.

WEB SITES OF INTEREST

Georgia Learning Connection: Curriculum for K–8 Foreign Languages
www.glc.k12.ga.us/qcc/ancill/fl/ind-fl.htm

Glastonbury, Connecticut, Foreign Language Program and Curriculum
http://foreignlanguage.org

20 Developing Professional Teachers for Early Language Programs

Teachers for elementary and middle school language classrooms of the twenty-first century require a combination of competencies and background that may be unprecedented in the preparation of language teachers. The emphasis on target language use for all classroom purposes calls for strong language skills, and especially for fluent oral language that provides a good model for the learner. In the absence of a textbook as the core of the curriculum, thematic planning demands flexible language and a strong vocabulary base, allowing the teacher to respond to student interests and take advantage of opportunities that arise in the development of a theme. Teachers who do not rely on a textbook need an excellent background in children's literature and in the target culture, so that they can draw these elements into unit and daily lesson plans. Integrative, thematic planning also depends on solid understanding of the general curriculum, in order to relate language instruction effectively with mathematics, science, health, social studies, music, art, language arts, and physical education.

The preparation of language teachers has traditionally taken place in the context of a language and literature major, with education as a secondary emphasis. The typical content of literature classes often does not provide the background most useful for elementary and middle school teachers, and in many cases the culture and language addressed in programs for language majors are not well suited to the future roles of these teachers.

Preparation of teachers for the K–8 language classroom must address four basic areas:

1. Language skills and understanding of the culture, especially the culture of children and young adolescents, within which the language is used;
2. Methodology for and experiences with teaching languages to young learners;
3. Understanding and application of the *Standards for Foreign Language Learning in the 21st Century* and *ACTFL Student Performance Guidelines for K–12 Learners,* as well as their implications for curriculum, instruction, and assessment;
4. Background in the curriculum and philosophy of the elementary and the middle school.

Clients for this preparation come from three basic groups: in-service and preservice K–8 teachers who have language background; in-service and preservice secondary school language teachers who have interest in working with K–8 learners; native speakers of the language whose education and teacher preparation have taken place outside the United

States. Although each group of clients requires a somewhat different pattern of emphasis in their preparation, they can work together very effectively in the same program, each sharing their particular areas of expertise with their colleagues.

The short-term need in teacher preparation is for programs that can facilitate the recertification or relicensure of in-service teachers to staff emerging elementary and middle school programs. A number of intensive summer workshops around the country, including programs in such widespread locations as New York City, Minnesota, Georgia, Florida, and Texas have been designed to meet this challenge. Some local districts provide intensive in-service programs for their own staff, such as the immersion teacher education program developed in Montgomery County, Maryland. More intensive recertification workshops are needed to meet the growing immediate need for teachers, together with the development of licensure programs in colleges and universities nationwide.

For the long term, programs in higher education are needed that will encourage the development of teachers who have dual certification: teachers of language who are fluent language users and are also licensed elementary school generalists or middle school teachers of another content area. Teachers with this kind of background will be able to work successfully with both foreign language immersion programs and intensive, content-related FLES programs. They will be in the best position to provide successful experiences with new languages for young learners of all backgrounds.

The American Council on the Teaching of Foreign Languages (1988, 78) recommended the following guidelines for the preparation of teachers at the elementary school level. These characteristics are listed in addition to those expected of foreign language teachers at other levels.

"Programs provide information about and experience in the elementary educational system to include:

1. an understanding of first language development and its relation to second language learning in childhood;
2. knowledge of instructional methods appropriate to second language instruction in the elementary school;
3. the ability to teach reading and writing as developmental skills to learners acquiring literacy skills in their first language;
4. familiarity with aspects of the target culture appropriate to the developmental needs and interests of students, including children's literature appropriate to the target culture;
5. knowledge of the elementary school curriculum, the relationship among the content areas, and ability to teach or reinforce elementary school curricula through or in a foreign language;
6. knowledge of elementary school principles and practices, and the ability to apply such knowledge to creating an affective and physical environment conducive to foreign language learning."

Preparation of Teachers

The strongest influence on the quality of foreign language teaching in K–12 classrooms is the quality of the teacher preparation programs in which new teachers develop both the skills and the vision for language teaching. Until the fall of 2002, when ACTFL released new teacher standards, the teacher situation for early languages had changed remarkably little since the 1960s: demand has continued to overwhelm supply and many programs continue to be staffed by teachers without specific preparation in teaching world languages to children, by native speakers without any qualification other than language skill, and sometimes even by teachers who have limited language skills themselves. Few states had addressed the issue of special licensure or certification for foreign language teachers at the elementary school level, so there had been little by way of a standard for schools to use in evaluating and employing a potential teacher. Relatively few institutions of higher education have had staff and programs in place to prepare teachers for this emerging field.

Much of the burden of elementary school foreign language teacher preparation has been laid on workshops, summer institutes, and teacher in-service work. Although this "bandage" approach cannot be expected to replace a profession-wide commitment to quality teacher preparation, a number of priorities in teacher background and skills have begun to emerge.

ACTFL Program Standards for the Preparation of Foreign Language Teachers (Initial Level—Undergraduate and Graduate) (For K–12 and Secondary Certification Programs)

Before the fall of 2002 there was little uniformity among states and institutions of higher education regarding standards for teachers entering the profession by way of a teacher licensure program. In August 2002, the ACTFL Foreign Language Teacher Standards Writing Team completed a draft of program standards that was subsequently approved by the National Council for Accreditation of Teacher Education (NCATE), the most widely supported accreditation process for teacher preparation institutions.

The ACTFL/NCATE standards include content standards, supporting standards, supporting explanations, and rubrics for each of the supporting standards. They represent the final step in the process of unifying classroom instruction, teacher preparation, and professional development around carefully designed standards and performances. The following summary of standards shows the breadth and the primary emphases in these program standards. A careful reading of the entire document will give a clear picture of well-prepared foreign language teachers as they enter the profession.

State Initiatives

As the number of K–8 world language programs overwhelms the available teacher supply, those states most affected have developed strategies for meeting the demand for qualified teachers. A number of states have addressed the problem of teacher availability in direct and very different ways. The models that follow suggest a variety of possibilities for other states and other situations.

Standard 1: Language, Linguistics, Comparisons (25)
Standard 1.a. Demonstrating Language Proficiency. Candidates demonstrate a high level of proficiency in the target language, and they seek opportunities to strengthen their proficiency. (Authors' note: This is usually intermediate high or advanced on the ACTFL proficiency scale, depending on the state.)

Standard 1.b. Understanding Linguistics. Candidates know the linguistic elements of the target language system, recognize the changing nature of language, and accommodate for gaps in their own knowledge of the target language system by learning on their own.

Standard 1.c. Identifying Language Comparisons. Candidates know the similarities and differences between the target language and other languages, identify the key differences in varieties of the target language, and seek opportunities to learn about varieties of the target language on their own.

Standard 2: Cultures, Literatures, Cross-Disciplinary Concepts (36)
Standard 2.a. Candidates demonstrate that they understand the connections among the perspectives of a culture and its practices and products, and they integrate the cultural framework for foreign language standards into their instructional practice.

Standard 2.b. Demonstrating Understanding of Literary and Cultural Texts and Traditions. Candidates recognize the value and role of literary and cultural texts and use them to interpret and reflect upon the perspectives of the target cultures over time.

Standard 2.c. Integrating Other Disciplines in Instruction. Candidates integrate knowledge of other disciplines into foreign language instruction and identify distinctive viewpoints accessible only through the target language.

Standard 3: Language Acquisition Theories and Instructional Practices (42)
Standard 3.a. Understanding Language Acquisition and Creating a Supportive Classroom. Candidates demonstrate an understanding of language acquisition at various developmental levels and use this knowledge to create a supportive classroom learning environment that includes target language input and opportunities for negotiation of meaning and meaningful interaction.

Standard 3.b. Developing Instructional Practices That Reflect Language Outcomes and Learner Diversity. Candidates develop a variety of instructional practices that reflect language outcomes and articulated program models and address the needs of diverse language learners.

Standard 4: Integration of Standards into Curriculum and Instruction (47)
Standard 4.a. Candidates demonstrate an understanding of the goal areas and standards of the *Standards for Foreign Language Learning* and their state standards, and they integrate these frameworks into curricular planning.

Standard 4.b. Integrating Standards in Instruction. Candidates integrate the *Standards for Foreign Language Learning* and their state standards into language instruction.

Standard 4.c. Selecting and Designing Instructional Materials. Candidates use standards and curricular goals to evaluate, select, design, and adapt instructional resources.

Standard 5: Assessment of Languages and Cultures (52)
Standard 5.a. Knowing Assessment Models and Using them Appropriately. Candidates believe that assessment is ongoing, and they demonstrate knowledge of multiple ways of assessment that are age- and level-appropriate by implementing purposeful measures.

Standard 5.b. Reflecting on Assessment. Candidates reflect on the results of student assessments, adjust instruction accordingly, analyze the results of assessments, and use success and failure to determine the direction of instruction.

Standard 5.c. Reporting Assessment Results. Candidates interpret and report the results of student performances to all stakeholders and provide opportunity for discussion.

Standard 6: Professionalism (57)
Standard 6.a. Engaging in Professional Development. Candidates engage in professional development opportunities that strengthen their own linguistic and cultural competence and promote reflection on practice.

Standard 6.b. Knowing the Value of Foreign Language Learning. Candidates know the value of foreign language learning to the overall success of all students and understand that they will need to become advocates with students, colleagues, and members of the community to promote the field.

North Carolina Teacher Preparation Project

To meet the need for teachers resulting from the North Carolina state mandate for foreign language study in all elementary schools, the North Carolina Department of Public Instruction, in collaboration with the Center for Applied Linguistics, developed a project to improve the preparation of teachers in North Carolina institutions of higher education. Funded by the Fund for the Improvement of Post Secondary Education (FIPSE), the project built on the experiences of successful teachers already teaching languages in North Carolina's elementary schools. College and university methods instructors worked in teams with elementary school language teachers and collaborated in a project that involved the following activities: (1) an intensive seminar on elementary school foreign language methodology; (2) direct observations of local elementary school foreign language classes; (3) co-teaching in elementary school classrooms; and (4) collaboration in the development of a teacher education curriculum. After completion of the project in August 1992, the teacher educators incorporated the new methods and materials into their teacher preparation programs and began providing methods instruction for undergraduates in their home institutions. The project also resulted in a strong network of language professionals at all levels of instruction that has collaborated in other projects for the support of language education throughout North Carolina. One of these projects is described in detail in Chapter 16.

One of the valuable direct outcomes of this project is a recommended curriculum for preparing foreign language teachers at the elementary school level, *Elementary School (K–8) Foreign Language Teacher Education Curriculum* (1992). Another valuable outcome of the project is the development of a careful and helpful list of competencies for the foreign language teacher at the elementary and middle school level. The major points of this list are reproduced here (1–7).

Elementary School (K–8) Foreign Language Teacher Competencies
1. an understanding of second-language acquisition in childhood and its relation to first-language development
2. knowledge of instructional methods appropriate to foreign language instruction in the elementary school
3. knowledge of instructional resources appropriate to foreign language instruction in the elementary school
4. knowledge of appropriate assessment and evaluation for foreign language instruction in the elementary school
5. ability to develop reading and writing skills in learners who are simultaneously acquiring literacy skills in their first language
6. ability to teach aspects of the target culture appropriate to the developmental needs and interests of students, including children's literature appropriate to the target culture
7. knowledge of K–12 foreign language curriculum and the elementary curriculum, the relationship among the content areas, and ability to teach, integrate, or reinforce the elementary school curriculum through or in a foreign languge

8. knowledge of elementary school principles and practices, effective classroom management techniques, and the ability to apply such knowledge to create an affective and physical environment conducive to foreign language learning
9. proficiency in the foreign language
10. knowledge of child development
11. knowledge of the history of foreign language education in the United States and the rationale for various program models in the elementary school
12. awareness of the need for personal and professional growth
13. an understanding of the need for cooperation among foreign language teachers, other classroom teachers, counselors, school administrators, university personnel, and community members
14. awareness of skills for program promotion

Teacher Preparation and Licensure in Georgia

In Georgia the sequence of program implementation and teacher preparation planning was reversed from that in North Carolina. The State Board of Education approved a new certification standard for languages to begin in July 1989, requiring that all foreign language teachers entering the profession be certified K–12, rather than 7–12 as had previously been the case. As a first step in meeting the challenge of the new standard, the Georgia Department of Education offered an intensive two-week "training the trainers" course in the summer of 1989 to prepare Georgia teacher educators to teach elementary school foreign language methods courses. These professors then returned to their institutions and developed both methods programs for their undergraduates and "conversion courses" for currently licensed 7–12 teachers wishing to receive the additional licensure.

Since that first course was taught, hundreds of Georgia foreign language teachers have been prepared to teach at the K–6 level, and many more are enrolled for class work each year. When the Georgia legislature funded thirteen model programs for languages, beginning in kindergarten, teacher preparation facilities in Georgia were ready to meet the challenge.

Teachers in the Georgia model programs developed and endorsed the following set of guidelines for early language teachers in a FLES program (Georgia Department of Education):

Georgia Model Programs Statements of Understanding
As a Georgia model program teacher, I demonstrate support for the philosophy of the program when I

- teach 98–100 percent of the time in the target language
- use the target language for classroom management as well as for instruction
- avoid using translation as a tool for clarifying meaning
- help learners to clarify meaning and express understanding without translation
- provide learners with a rich target language environment that includes extended listening opportunities such as narration, descriptions, and explanations
- provide learners with meaningful concrete experiences, making extensive use of visuals, props, realia, and hands-on activities

- present vocabulary in chunks and in context rather than as isolated words or lists
- plan and teach around a theme
- seek ways to include meaningful culture content in every lesson and every unit
- seek to integrate concepts from the general elementary school curriculum in every lesson and every unit
- use songs and rhymes to reinforce meaning and practice language
- choose authentic songs, games, stories, and rhymes in preference to translations whenever possible
- incorporate communicative use of reading and writing from early stages of instruction
- plan lessons to include a variety of activities, student groupings, and types of interaction that will appeal to differing learner interests and learning styles
- provide opportunities for learners to express personal meaning from the earliest stages of the program
- encourage growing independence and independent language use on the part of learners, moving them toward increased expression of individual ideas and opinions
- assess learner progress frequently and regularly, using a variety of types of assessment
- use a variety of strategies to maintain frequent and regular contact with parents
- communicate regularly with classroom teachers about student progress and program goals and content
- work closely with other teachers in the program to plan curriculum and resolve issues
- seek frequent opportunities for professional and language development
- maintain open communication about the program and student progress among teachers, administrators, and the general public

The New Jersey Initiative

When New Jersey mandated a world language experience for all learners in 1996, the location of qualified teachers for many new elementary school programs was a serious problem. The New Jersey Department of Education, in cooperation with the American Council on the Teaching of Foreign Languages, developed a series of ongoing teacher institutes throughout the state to prepare teachers for the new level and for the new state student standards, modeled on the national standards. In this way the resources of the entire profession were focused on the needs of a single state, and a new model for professional development was established.

Wisconsin Teacher Institutes

The state of Wisconsin, under the sponsorship of the Department of Public Instruction and with federal funding, began in 1997 to sponsor intensive, four-week summer methods courses as a licensure option for K–8 language teachers, many of whom do not have access to such a program in their own institutions. Other candidates for the course are successful teachers who are already licensed in another area or for another level. These courses are offered in several locations in the state, and university credit is arranged through a participating institution. These courses include methods lecture and demonstration, curriculum development, and actual teaching experiences with young learners.

The K–8 Language Teacher as a Growing Professional

The opportunities for professional growth as a language teacher have never been greater, particularly at the K–8 level. In some states early language teachers have banded together to offer special meetings and conferences to support one another with in-service opportunities. Some of these meetings or organizations are jointly sponsored by the state department of education. Special yearly conferences and meetings for FLES teachers are held in Wisconsin, Kansas, and Connecticut, for example, and the number is likely to grow. At an exciting and rapidly changing period in language education, there is always much more to learn, there are always new strategies and insights to test. Early language teachers no longer have to feel isolated or misunderstood. These possibilities for professional development offer great potential, both for the language teacher and for the students in their classes.

Professional Organizations and Resources

One of the first and most important steps toward becoming a growing professional is active participation in one or more of the organizations that support and unite language teachers. A combined voice is always more effective than a lone voice, and the combined resources of the profession enrich every teacher's classroom.

The founding of the National Network for Early Language Learning (NNELL) in 1987 was a landmark for teachers in K–8 classrooms. The organization provides many opportunities for teachers to become active both locally and nationally, and its journal, *Learning Languages* connects early language teachers all over the country. There is an early language Web site, www.cal.org/earlylang/, and a very active early language listserv, Ñandu, where teachers in all languages ask and answer questions and share curriculum, program, and teaching ideas and experiences.

Each of the languages commonly taught in early language programs has a national organization, and many have state chapters: American Association of Teachers of German (AATG), American Association of Teachers of French (AATF), American Association of Teachers of Spanish and Portuguese (AATSP), Chinese Language Association of Secondary-Elementary Schools (CLASS), American Classical League (ACL), American Association of Teachers of Italian (AATI), National Council of Japanese Language Teachers (NCJLT), and American Council of Teachers of Russian (ACTR). Membership in these organizations brings early language teachers together with other teachers who share many of the same language and culture issues in their classrooms. These groups also offer important cultural resources, Web sites, and contacts that are unavailable any other way. Several of these groups also have national contests, exchange programs, and materials designed for early language learners.

The American Council on the Teaching of Foreign Languages (ACTFL) is the umbrella organization for all language teachers, and a leader in the movement of the profession toward proficiency-oriented, standards-based language learning. ACTFL has a special interest group dedicated to early language learning. Annual conferences, publications, workshops, and many other services make ACTFL a powerful force for change and for uniting teachers of all languages, at all levels.

Membership in organizations listed above; attendance at state, regional, and national conferences; and regular reading of professional journals such as *Learning Languages, Modern Language Journal, and Foreign Language Annals;* as well as language-specific journals connects the language teacher with the wider profession and supports the quality of instruction in every classroom. As teachers grow in their experience with conferences and professional journals, they will be in a position to propose and present sessions and to author articles themselves.

Action Research

As teachers grow in their experience with early language curriculum, classrooms, and learners, they begin to have questions that are not satisfied in conversations with colleagues or articles in professional journals. No one else's answers speak adequately to the issues of *this* classroom or *this* particular group of students. A growing number of teachers are turning to classroom-based action research as a means of answering their own questions about teaching and learning, and also contributing to the professional body of understanding about early language learning.

Briefly stated, research involves identifying a question the teacher would like to have answered, refining that question to make it manageable, collecting and analyzing data or information that may answer the question, and interpreting the information collected. Action research is conducted by teachers, and it may result in changes in curriculum, in teaching practices, or in other aspects of the teaching and learning context.

Chamot (1994) suggests several possible research questions as examples of possibilities for action research in an early language classroom (6):

- What themes or content topics are most interesting to children at particular grade levels?
- What interlanguage features characterize children's L2 [second language] at different points in instructional time?
- What differences exist between successful and less successful language learners in these area(s)? Select one or two only: (a) attitudes toward the target language and culture; (b) access to/use of L2 outside of school (e.g., parents, community, television); (c) use of appropriate language learning strategies; (d) level of achievement in L1 [first language] language arts; (e) transfer of knowledge, skills, or strategies from L1; (f) level of self-confidence in own language learning ability.
- What are students' reactions to/acceptance of particular instructional techniques (e.g., cooperative learning, information gap activities, instruction in learning strategies, grammar explanation and practice, Total Physical Response, teaching to different learning styles)?

- What types of assessment measures (e.g., oral interviews, role plays, multiple choice, cloze exercises, writing samples, portfolios) are best suited for assessing children's language proficiency in a particular area or in general?

Some of the methods used for collecting information include diaries, think-aloud interviews, stimulated recall, structured interviews, questionnaires, and classroom observation. All of the suggested topics are researchable by classroom teachers, and the information this research could yield would be a valuable contribution to our understanding of the early language classroom.

Jeannette Borich provides an excellent description of this research process in her article, "Learning through Dialogue Journal Writing: A Cultural Thematic Unit" (2001).

National Board Certification

The National Board of Professional Teaching Standards was established in 1987, as a result of a key recommendation by the Carnegie Task Force on Teaching as a Profession in its 1986 report *A Nation Prepared: Teachers for the 21st Century.* The board issued its policy statement in 1989, *What Teachers Should Know and Be Able to Do,* which has served as a guide for schools, states, and teacher preparation institutions in establishing a vision for teacher preparation and teacher development.

This policy statement also serves as the foundation for National Board Certification, a voluntary system for certifying teachers who have met a set of advanced standards representing accomplished practice. National Board Certification is a symbol of professional teaching excellence, designed to recognize and reward the excellent teachers who are already at work in the schools. Only teachers who have had at least three years of experience at the designated age level are eligible for certification. Teachers who apply for certification go through a rigorous process; they construct a portfolio that represents an analysis of their classroom work, and then undergo testing and a variety of other activities that allow them to demonstrate their knowledge, dispositions, and professional judgment.

A number of states and individual school districts have set up reward systems for teachers who receive National Board Certification, sometimes including yearly salary increments. Some districts and some states offer to pay the costs of registration for the process for a limited number of teachers who apply. Teachers who have completed the process praise its rigor and the quality of the experience. World language teachers were participants for the first time in the 2001–2002 school year, in one of two categories: early and middle childhood or early adolescence through young adulthood.

All of the processes leading to National Board Certification are based on the five core propositions set forth in the 1989 policy statement, *What Teachers Should Know and Be Able to Do* (National Board of Professional Teaching Standards 2003a, 2):

Proposition #1:	Teachers are Committed to Students and Their Learning
Proposition #2:	Teachers Know the Subjects They Teach and How to Teach Those Subjects to Students
Proposition #3:	Teachers are Responsible for Managing and Monitoring Student Learning

Proposition #4: Teachers Think Systematically about Their Practice and Learn from Experience

Proposition #5: Teachers are Members of Learning Communities

The overview of the National Board standards for World Languages Other Than English, reprinted here (National Board of Professional Teaching Standards, 2003b, 5–6), sets a vision for the kind of teaching and thinking that are the goals of teacher development for teachers in the classroom. These standards describe the accomplished professional teacher of languages at all levels, ages three to eighteen plus. Specific interpretations of the standards for the early and middle childhood certificate give more detailed guidance.

Preparing for Student Learning

I. Knowledge of Students
Accomplished teachers of world languages other than English draw on their understanding of child and adolescent development, value their students as individuals, and actively acquire knowledge of their students' competencies and interests as individual language learners.

II. Fairness
Accomplished teachers of world languages other than English demonstrate through their practices toward all students their commitment to the principles of equity, strength through diversity, and fairness. Teachers welcome diverse learners who represent our multiracial, multilingual, and multiethnic society, and they set the highest goals for each student.

III. Knowledge of Language
Accomplished teachers of world languages other than English have the ability to function with a high degree of proficiency in the languages they teach, know how the languages work, and draw on this knowledge to set attainable and worthwhile learning goals for their students.

IV. Knowledge of Culture
As an integral part of effective instruction in world languages other than English, accomplished teachers know and understand the target cultures and target languages and know how these are intimately linked with one another.

V. Knowledge of Language Acquisition
Accomplished teachers of world languages other than English are familiar with how students acquire competence in another language, understand varied methodologies and approaches used in the teaching and learning of languages, and draw on this knowledge to design instructional strategies appropriate to their instructional goals.

Advancing Student Learning

VI. Multiple Paths to Learning
Accomplished teachers of world languages other than English actively and effectively engage their students in language learning and cultural studies; they use a variety of teaching strategies to help develop students' proficiency, increase their knowledge, strengthen their understanding, and foster their critical and creative thinking.

VII. Articulation of Curriculum and Instruction
Accomplished teachers of world languages other than English work to ensure that the experiences students have from one level to the next are sequential, long-range, and continuous, with the goal that over a period of years students will move from simple to sophisticated use of languages.

VIII. Learning Environment
Accomplished teachers of world languages other than English create an inclusive, caring, challenging, and stimulating classroom environment in which meaningful communication in the target languages occurs and in which students learn actively.

IX. Instructional Resources
Accomplished teachers of world languages other than English select, adapt, create, and use appropriate resources to help meet the instructional and linguistic needs of all their students and foster critical and creative thinking among them.

X. Assessment
Accomplished teachers of world languages other than English employ a variety of assessment strategies appropriate to the curriculum and to the learner and use assessment results to monitor student learning, to assist students in reflecting on their own progress, to report student progress, and to shape instruction.

Supporting Student Learning

XI. Reflection as Professional Growth
Accomplished teachers of world languages other than English continually analyze and evaluate the quality of their teaching in order to strengthen its effectiveness and enhance student learning.

XII. Schools, Families, and Communities
Accomplished teachers of world languages other than English work with colleagues in other disciplines, with families, with members of the school community, and with the community at large to serve the best interests of students.

XIII. Professional Community

Accomplished teachers of world languages other than English contribute to the improvement of instructional programs, to the advancement of knowledge, and to the practice of colleagues in language instruction.

XIV. Advocacy for Education in World Languages Other than English

Accomplished teachers of world languages other than English advocate both within and beyond the school for the inclusion of all students in long-range, sequential programs that also offer opportunities to study multiple languages.

Summary

The preparation and licensure of teachers for elementary school foreign language programs is of the highest priority if foreign language programs are to become an important part of the elementary and middle school curriculum. An early language teacher needs to have the qualities of both an excellent foreign language teacher and an excellent elementary or middle school teacher. As these qualities are now becoming clearly identified and defined, programs can be developed to prepare the best possible teachers for these classrooms.

Guidelines for teacher preparation are now available from ACTFL and NCATE, the most widely used independent certification organization for college and university teacher education. These guidelines describe the teacher candidate in a standards- and performance-based context. The National Board of Professional Teaching Standards (NBPTS) has described standards for the accomplished world language teacher that can guide the professional development of the career teacher. The number of states offering or requiring K–12 foreign language teacher licensure encourages the development of college and university programs to prepare teachers for the growing number of elementary and middle school programs.

As early language programs emerge to play an important role in the education of every child, the challenges of defining goals clearly and of preparing teachers effectively take on considerable significance. There is strong evidence that these challenges are being met and that early language programs will continue to develop as a secure and well-grounded part of the curriculum, unshaken by fad and respected throughout the education community.

FOR STUDY AND DISCUSSION

1. Why is it important that states develop licensure standards for teachers of foreign languages at the elementary school level?

2. What special skills and background do K–8 teachers need that might not be provided in a methods program designed primarily for secondary school teachers?

3. Download a copy of the ACTFL Program Standards for the Preparation of Foreign Language Teachers (www.actfl.org). Using the rubrics that appear in the document, evaluate your own progress toward meeting the standards and supporting standards for teachers in K–12 foreign language programs.

4. How can National Board Certification contribute to the effectiveness of K–8 foreign language teachers and to the credibility of the foreign language teaching profession?

FOR FURTHER READING

The following sources are recommended for additional information about material covered in this chapter. Chapter citations are documented in Works Cited at the end of the volume.

American Council on the Teaching of Foreign Languages. *Guidelines for Foreign Language Teacher Education Programs.* Hastings-on-Hudson, NY: ACTFL, 1988.

———. *Program Standards for the Preparation of Foreign Language Teachers.* Yonkers, NY: ACTFL, 2002. Available on-line at www.actfl.org.

Chamot, Anna Uhl. "The Teacher's Voice: Action Research in Your Classroom." *FLES News* 8, no. 1 (fall 1994): 1, 6–8.

National Board of Professional Teaching Standards (NBPTS). *Standards for World Languages Other than English.* Available on-line at www.nbpts.org/standards/stds.cfm (accessed 4/14/03).

———. *What Teachers Should Know and Be Able to Do.* Available on-line at www.nbpts.org/standards/stds.cfm (accessed 4/14/03).

ACTFL Performance Guidelines for K–12 Learners

Comprehensibility: How well are they understood?

Novice Learner Range Grade K–4 or Grade 5–8 or Grade 9–10	Intermediate Learner Grade K–8 or Grade 7–12	Pre-Advanced Learner Grade K–12
Interpersonal	**Interpersonal**	**Interpersonal**
• Rely primarily on memorized phrases and short sentences during highly predictable interactions on very familiar topics; • Are understood primarily by those very accustomed to interacting with language learners; • Imitate modeled words and phrases using intonation and pronunciation similar to that of the model; • May show evidence of false starts, prolonged and unexpectedly placed pauses, and recourse to their native language as topics expand beyond the scope of immediate needs; • Are able to meet limited practical writing needs, such as short messages and notes, by recombining learned vocabulary and structures to form simple sentences on very familiar topics.	• Express their own thoughts using sentences and strings of sentences when interacting on familiar topics in present time, are understood by those accustomed to interacting with language learners; • Use pronunciation and intonation patterns which can be understood by a native speaker accustomed to interacting with language learners; • Make false starts and pause frequently to search for words when interacting with others; • Are able to meet practical writing needs such as short letters and notes, by recombining learned vocabulary and structures demonstrating full control of other time frames.	• Narrate and describe using connected sentences and paragraphs in present and other time frames when interacting on topics of personal, school, and community interest; • Are understood by those with whom they interact, although there may still be a range of linguistic inaccuracies, and on occasion the communication partner may need to make a special effort to understand the message; • Use pronunciation and intonation patterns that are understandable to a native speaker unaccustomed to interacting with language learners; • Use language confidently and with ease, with few pauses; • Are able to meet practical writing needs such as letters and summaries by writing descriptions and narrations of paragraph length and organization, showing sustained control of basic structures and partial control of more complex structures and time frames.

Presentational

- Use short, memorized phrases and sentences in oral and written presentations;
- Are understood primarily by those who are very accustomed to interacting with language learners;
- Demonstrate some accuracy in pronunciation and intonation when presenting well-rehearsed material on familiar topics;
- May show evidence of false starts, prolonged and unexpectedly placed pauses, and recourse to their native language as topics expand beyond the scope of immediate needs;
- Show abilities in writing by reproducing familiar material;
- Rely heavily on visuals to enhance comprehensibility in both oral and written presentations.

Presentational

- Express their own thoughts, describe and narrate, using sentences and strings of sentences, in oral and written presentations on familiar topics;
- Use pronunciation and intonation patterns that can be understood by those accustomed to interacting with language learners;
- Make false starts and pause frequently to search for words when interacting with others;
- Communicate oral and written information about familiar topics with sufficient accuracy that listeners and readers understand most of what is presented.

Presentational

- Report, narrate and describe, using connected sentences, paragraph length and longer forms of discourse, in oral and written presentations on topics of personal, school, and community interest.
- Use pronunciation and intonation patterns that are understood by native users of the language, although the listener/reader may on occasion need to make a special effort to understand the message;
- Use language confidently and with ease, with few pauses;
- Communication with a fairly high degree of facility when making oral and written presentations about familiar and well-researched topics.

Comprehension: How well do they understand?

Novice Learner Range Grade K–4 or Grade 5–8 or Grade 9–10	Intermediate Learner Grade K–8 or Grade 7–12	Pre-Advanced Learner Grade K–12
Interpersonal • Comprehend general information and vocabulary when the communication partner uses objects, visuals, and gestures in speaking or writing; • Generally need contextual clues, redundancy, paraphrase or restatement in order to understand the message.	**Interpersonal** • Comprehend general concepts and messages about familiar and occasionally unfamiliar topics; • May not comprehend details when dealing with unfamiliar topics; • May have difficulty comprehending language not supported by situational context.	**Interpersonal** • Comprehend main ideas and most details on a variety of topics beyond the immediate situation; • Occasionally do not comprehend but usually are able to clarify details by asking questions; • May encounter difficulty comprehending language dealing with abstract topics.
Interpretive • Understand short, simple conversations and narratives (live or recorded material), within highly predictable and familiar contexts; • Rely on personal background experience to assist in comprehension; • Exhibit increased comprehension when constructing meaning through recognition of key words or phrases embedded in familiar contexts; • Comprehend written and spoken language better when content has been previously presented in an oral and/or visual context; • Determine meaning by recognition of cognates, prefixes, and thematic vocabulary.	**Interpretive** • Understand longer, more complex conversations and narratives as well as recorded material in unfamiliar contexts; • Use background knowledge to comprehend simple stories, personal correspondence, and other contextualized print; • Identify main ideas and some specific information on a limited number of topics found in the products of the target culture such as those presented on TV, radio, video, or live and computer-generated presentations, although comprehension may be uneven; • Determine meaning by using contextual clues; • Are aided by the use of redundancy, paraphrase, and restatement in order to understand the message.	**Interpretive** • Use knowledge acquired in other settings and from other curricular areas to comprehend both spoken and written messages; • Understand main ideas and significant details on a variety of topics found in the products of the target culture such as those presented on TV, radio, video, or live and computer-generated presentations, although comprehension may be uneven; • Develop an awareness of tone, style, and author perspective; • Demonstrate a growing independence as a reader or listener and generally comprehend what they read and hear without relying solely on formally learned vocabulary.

Language Control: How accurate is their language?

Novice Learner Range Grade K–4 or Grade 5–8 or Grade 9–10	Intermediate Learner Grade K–8 or Grade 7–12	Pre-Advanced Learner Grade K–12
Interpersonal • Comprehend messages that include predominantly familiar grammatical structures • Are most accurate when communicating about very familiar topics using memorized oral and written phrases; • Exhibit decreased accuracy when attempting to create with the language; • Write with accuracy when copying written language but may use invented spelling when writing words or producing characters on their own; • May exhibit frequent errors in capitalization and punctuation when target language differs from native language in these areas.	**Interpersonal** • Comprehend messages that include some unfamiliar grammatical structures; • Are most accurate when creating with the language about familiar topics in present time using simple sentences and/or strings of sentences; • Exhibit a decline in grammatical accuracy as creativity in language production increases; • Begin to apply familiar structures to new situations; • Evidence awareness of capitalization and/or punctuation when writing in the target language; • Recognize some of their own spelling or character production errors and make appropriate adjustments.	**Interpersonal** • Comprehend messages that include unfamiliar grammatical structures; • Are most accurate when narrating and describing in connected sentences and paragraphs in present time with decreasing accuracy in past and future times; • May continue to exhibit inaccuracies as the amount and complexity of language increases; communicate successfully by applying familiar structures to new situations; • Rarely make errors in capitalization and in punctuation; are generally accurate in spelling or production of characters.
Interpretive • Recognize structural patterns in target language narratives and derive meaning from these structures within familiar contexts; • Sometimes recognize previously learned structures when presented in new contexts.	**Interpretive** • Derive meaning by comparing target language structures with those of the native language; • Recognize parallels between new and familiar structures in the target language; • Understand high-frequency idiomatic expressions.	**Interpretive** • Deduce meaning in unfamiliar language passages by classifying words or concepts according to word order or grammatical use; • Apply rules of language to construct meaning from oral and written texts; • Understand idiomatic expressions; • Move beyond literal comprehension toward more critical reading and listening.

continued

Novice Learner Range Grade K–4 or Grade 5–8 or Grade 9–10	Intermediate Learner Grade K–8 or Grade 7–12	Pre-Advanced Learner Grade K–12
Presentational	**Presentational**	**Presentational**
• Demonstrate some accuracy in oral and written presentations when reproducing memorized words, phrases and sentences in the target language; • Formulate oral and written presentations using a limited range of simple phrases and expressions based on very familiar topics; • Show inaccuracies and/or interference from the native language when attempting to communicate information which goes beyond the memorized or pre-fabricated; • May exhibit frequent errors in capitalization and/or punctuation and/or production of characters when the writing system of the target language differs from the native language	• Formulate oral and written presentations on familiar topics, using a range of sentences and strings of sentences primarily in present time but also, with preparation, in past and future time; • May show inaccuracies as well as some interference from the native language when attempting to present less familiar material; • Exhibit fairly good accuracy in capitalization and punctuation (or production of characters) when target language differs from native language in these areas.	• Accurately formulate paragraph-length and longer oral and written presentations in present time, on topics of personal, school, community and global interest; • May show some inaccuracies and/or interference from the native language when presentations deal with multiple time frames and/or other complex structures; • Successfully communicate personal meaning by applying familiar structures to new situations and less familiar topics, and by integrating information from audio, visual, and written sources; • Exhibit awareness of need for accuracy in capitalization and/or punctuation (or production of characters) when target language differs from native language in these areas.

Vocabulary Use: How extensive and applicable is their vocabulary?

Novice Learner Range Grade K–4 or Grade 5–8 or Grade 9–10	Intermediate Learner Grade K–8 or Grade 7–12	Pre-Advanced Learner Grade K–12
Interpersonal	**Interpersonal**	**Interpersonal**
• Comprehend and produce vocabulary that is related to everyday objects and actions on a limited number of familiar topics; • Use words and phrases primarily as lexical items without awareness of grammatical structure; • Recognize and use vocabulary from a variety of topics including those related to other curricular areas; • May often rely on words and phrases from their native language when attempting to communicate beyond the word and/or gesture level.	• Use vocabulary from a variety of thematic word groups; • Recognize and use vocabulary from a variety of topics including those related to other curricular areas; • Show some understanding and use of common idiomatic expressions; • May use false cognates or resort to their native language when attempting to communicate beyond the scope of familiar topics.	• Understand and often use idiomatic and culturally authentic expressions; • Recognize and use vocabulary from a variety of topics related to other curricular areas; • Use more specialized and precise vocabulary terms within a limited number of topics.
Interpretive	**Interpretive**	**Interpretive**
• Recognize a variety of vocabulary words and expressions related to familiar topics embedded within relevant curricular areas; • Demonstrate increased comprehension of vocabulary in spoken passages when these are enhanced by pantomime, props, and/or visuals; • Demonstrate increased comprehension of written passages when accompanied by illustrations and other contextual clues.	• Comprehend an expanded range of vocabulary; • Frequently derive meaning of unknown words by using contextual clues; • Demonstrate enhanced comprehension when listening to or reading content which has a recognizable format.	• Comprehend a wide range of vocabulary in both concrete and abstract contexts; • Infer meaning of both oral and written texts by recognizing familiar words and phrases in new contexts; • Use context to deduce meaning of unfamiliar vocabulary; • Recognize and understand the cultural context of many words and phrases.

continued

Novice Learner Range Grade K–4 or Grade 5–8 or Grade 9–10	Intermediate Learner Grade K–8 or Grade 7–12	Pre-Advanced Learner Grade K–12
Presentational	**Presentational**	**Presentational**
• Use a limited number of words and phrases for common objects and actions in familiar categories;	• Demonstrate control of an expanding number of familiar words and phrases and of a limited number of idiomatic expressions;	• Demonstrate control of an extensive vocabulary, including a number of idiomatic and culturally authentic expressions, from a variety of topics;
• Supplement their basic vocabulary with expressions acquired from sources such as the teacher or picture dictionaries;	• Supplement their basic vocabulary, for both oral and written presentations, with expressions acquired from other sources such as dictionaries;	• Supplement their basic vocabulary by using resources such as textbooks and dictionaries;
• Rely on native language and phrases when expressing personal meaning in less familiar categories.	• In speech and writing, may sometimes use false cognates and incorrectly applied terms, and show only partial control of newly-acquired expressions.	• May use more specialized and precise terms when dealing with specific topics that have been researched.

Communication Strategies: How do they maintain communication?

Novice Learner Range Grade K–4 or Grade 5–8 or Grade 9–10	Intermediate Learner Grade K–8 or Grade 7–12	Pre-Advanced Learner Grade K–12
Interpersonal • Attempt to clarify meaning by repeating words and occasionally selecting substitute words to convey their message; • Primarily use facial expressions and gesture to indicate problems with comprehension.	**Interpersonal** • May use paraphrasing, question-asking, circumlocution, and other strategies to avoid a breakdown in communication; • Attempt to self-correct primarily for meaning when communication breaks down.	**Interpersonal** • Are able to sustain an interaction with a native speaker by using a variety of strategies when discussion topics relate to personal experience or immediate needs; • Show evidence of attention to mechanical errors even when these may not interfere with communication
Interpretive • Use background experience to anticipate story direction in highly predictable oral or written texts; • Rely heavily on visuals and familiar language to assist in comprehension.	**Interpretive** • Identify the main idea of a written text by using reading strategies such as gleaning information from the first and last paragraphs; • Infer meaning of many unfamiliar words that are necessary in order to understand the gist of an oral or written text; • Use contextual clues to assist in comprehension.	**Interpretive** • Use background knowledge to deduce meaning and to understand complex information in oral or written texts; • Identify the organizing principle(s) in oral or written texts; • Infer and interpret the intent of the writer.
Presentational • Make corrections by repeating or rewriting when appropriate forms are routinely modeled by the teacher; • Rely heavily on repetition, non-verbal expression (gestures, facial expressions), and visuals to communicate their message.	**Presentational** • Make occasional use of reference sources and efforts at self-correction to avoid errors likely to interfere with communication; • Use circumlocution when faced with difficult syntactic structures; • Problematic spelling, or unfamiliar vocabulary; • Make use of memory-aids (such as notes and visuals) to facilitate presentations.	**Presentational** • Demonstrate conscious efforts at correct formulation and self-correction by use of self-editing and of reference sources; • Sustain length and continuity of presentations by appropriate use of strategies such as simplification, reformation, and circumlocution; • Make use of a variety of resource materials and presentation methods to enhance presentations.

Cultural Awareness: How is their cultural understanding reflected in their communication?

Novice Learner Range Grade K–4 or Grade 5–8 or Grade 9–10	Intermediate Learner Grade K–8 or Grade 7–12	Pre-Advanced Learner Grade K–12
Interpersonal • Imitate culturally appropriate vocabulary and idiomatic expressions; • Use gestures and body language that are generally those of the student's own culture, unless they are incorporated in to memorized responses.	**Interpersonal** • Use some culturally appropriate vocabulary and idiomatic expressions; • Use some gestures and body language of the target culture.	**Interpersonal** • Use culturally appropriate vocabulary and idioms; • Use appropriate gestures and body language of the target culture.
Interpretive • Understand both oral and written language that reflects a cultural background similar to their own; • Predict a story line or event when it reflects a cultural background similar to their own.	**Interpretive** • Use knowledge of their own culture and that of the target culture(s) to interpret oral or written texts more accurately; • Recognize target culture influences in the products and practices of their own culture; • Recognize differences and similarities in the perspectives of the target culture and their own.	**Interpretive** • Apply understanding of the target culture to enhance comprehension or oral and written texts; • Recognize the reflections of practices, products, and/or perspectives of the target culture(s) in oral and written texts; • Analyze and evaluate cultural stereotypes encountered in oral and written texts.
Presentational • Imitate the use of culturally appropriate vocabulary, idiomatic expressions and non-verbal behaviors modeled by the teacher.	**Presentational** • Use some culturally appropriate vocabulary; idiomatic expressions and non-verbal behaviors; • Demonstrate some cultural knowledge in oral and written presentations.	**Presentational** • Demonstrate increased use of culturally appropriate vocabulary, idiomatic expressions and non-verbal behaviors; • Use language increasingly reflective of authentic cultural practices and perspectives.

WORKS CITED

For Further Reading at the end of each chapter lists additional reference books and articles that may be of interest for specific topics.

Some of the resources listed are identified by an ERIC (Educational Resources Information Center) document number (e.g., ED 208 653). These documents can be read on microfiche at libraries with an ERIC collection, or ordered in paper copy from the ERIC Document Reproduction Service (EDRS), DynEDRS, Inc., 7420 Fullerton Road, Suite 110, Springfield, VA 22153-2852. Toll-free phone number: (800) 443–ERIC (3742), e-mail: service@edrs.com, URL: www.edrs.com

For the location of an ERIC collection nearest you, write to ERIC Clearinghouse on Languages and Linguistics, Center for Applied Linguistics, 4646 40th Street NW, Washington, DC 20016-1859, or e-mail info@cal.org.

Academic Preparation for College: What Students Need to Know and Be Able to Do. 1983. New York: The College Board.

Alkonis, Nancy V., and Mary A. Brophy. 1961. A Survey of FLES Practices. In *Reports of Surveys and Studies in the Teaching of Modern Foreign Languages, 1959–1961.* New York: The Modern Language Association of America.

Alvis, Vicki Welch. 2002. Let's Assess in FLES: Reaching Beyond the Customary Borders of Evaluation. Paper presented at the American Council on the Teaching of Foreign Languages (ACTFL) annual meeting, November 23, Salt Lake City, Utah.

American Council on the Teaching of Foreign Languages. 1988. *ACTFL Teacher Education Guidelines.* Hastings-on-Hudson, NY: ACTFL.

———. 2003. *ACTFL Integrated Performance Assessment.* Eileen Glisan, ed. Yonkers, NY: American Council on the Teaching of Foreign Languages.

———. August 2002. *American Council on the Teaching of Foreign Languages (ACTFL) Program Standards for the Preparation of Foreign Language Teachers.* Yonkers, NY: American Council on the Teaching of Foreign Languages. Available on-line at www.actfl.org/public/articles/ncate2002.pdf Accessed April 14, 2003.

Anderson, Helena. 1980, 1982. Conversation with author, Milwaukee, WI.

Andersson, Theodore. 1969. *Foreign Languages in the Elementary School: A Struggle Against Mediocrity.* Austin, TX: University of Texas Press.

Andrade, Carolyn, and Julie Benthouse Banner. 1993. The Writing Process: From Single Words to Student-Authored Books. Paper presented at the Central States Conference on the Teaching of Foreign Languages, March 27, Des Moines, IA.

Andrade, Carolyn, Richard R. Kretschmer Jr., and Laura W. Kretschmer. 1989. Two Languages for All Children: Expanding to Low Achievers and the Handicapped. In *Languages in Elementary Schools,* edited by Kurt E. Müller, 177–187. New York: The American Forum for Global Education.

Armstrong, Penny W., and J. D. Rogers. 1997. Basic Skills Revisited: The Effects of Foreign Language Instruction on Reading, Math and Language Arts. *Learning Languages* 2, no. 3 (spring): 20–31.

Armstrong, Thomas. 1994. *Multiple Intelligences in the Classroom.* Alexandria, VA: Association for Supervision and Curriculum Development.

———. 1993. *Seven Kinds of Smart: Identifying and Developing Your Many Intelligences.* New York: Penguin Books.

Asher, James J. 2000. *Learning Another Language through Actions: The Complete Teacher's Guidebook.* 6th ed. Los Gatos, CA: Sky Oaks Publications.

Ashton-Warner, Sylvia. 1963. *Teacher.* New York: Simon and Schuster.

Bamford, K. W., and D. T. Mizokawa. 1991. Additive-Bilingual (Immersion) Education: Cognitive and Language Development. *Language Learning* 41, no. 3: 413–429.

Barnum, Nancy. 2001. E-Mail in FL Instruction. Handout for presentation *Das Bild der Anderen, ein "Kochbuch" für Email Anfänger DaF* [The Image of the "Other," a "Cookbook" for E-mail Beginners in German as a Foreign Language]. Paper presented at the ACTFL annual meeting, November 17, Washington, D.C.

Begley, Sharon. February 19, 1996. "Your Child's Brain." *Newsweek.* 55–58.

Bloom, Benjamin S. 1956. *Taxonomy of Educational Objectives: The Classification of Educational Goals, by a Committee of College and University Examiners.* New York: D. McKay Co.

Borich, Jeanette Marie Bowman. 2001. Learning through Dialogue Journal Writing: A Cultural Thematic Unit. *Learning Languages* 6, no. 3 (spring): 4–19.

Boudreaux, Ellen. 1991. Strategies of Immersion Teaching and Special Education. Handout for presentation at the Advocates for Language Learning Conference, October.

Breiner-Sanders, Karen E., Pardee Lowe Jr., John Miles, and Elvira Swender. 2000. ACTFL Proficiency Guidelines—Speaking. Revised 1999. *Foreign Language Annals* 33:13–18.

Breiner-Sanders, Karen E., Elvira Swender, and Robert M. Terry. 2002. Preliminary Proficiency Guidelines—Writing. Revised 2001. *Foreign Language Annals* 35: 9–15.

Bring, Sandra. 1986. Conversation with author, Glyndon, MN.

Brown, Christine. 1995. A Case for Foreign Languages: The Glastonbury Language Program. *Perspective, Council for Basic Education* 7, no. 2. Available on-line at: www.educ.iastate.edu/nnell/glastonb.htm

Brown, H. Douglas. TESOL at Twenty-Five: What are the Issues? *TESOL Quarterly,* 25, no. 2 (summer): 256–257.

Brown, Jeff. 1996. *Flat Stanley.* Steve Björkman, illust. New York: HarperTrophy.

Bruck, Margaret, Wallace E. Lambert, and Richard Tucker. 1974. Bilingual Schooling through the Elementary Grades: The St. Lambert Project at Grade Seven. *Language Learning* 24, no. 2:183–204.

Bruner, Jerome. 1990. *Acts of Meaning.* Cambridge, MA: Harvard University Press.

———. 1996. *The Culture of Education.* Cambridge, MA: Harvard University Press.

Caine, Renate Nummela, and Geoffrey Caine. 1991. *Making Connections: Teaching and the Human Brain.* Alexandria, VA: Association for Supervision and Curriculum Development.

———. 1997. *Education on the Edge of Possibility.* Alexandria, VA: Association for Supervision and Curriculum Development.

California Language Teachers Association, California Foreign Language Project. 2002. *Internet Activities for Foreign Language Classes.* Available on-line at: www.clta.net/lessons/evalform.html. Accessed November 2002.

Campbell, Russell N. 1984. The Immersion Approach to Foreign Language Teaching. In *Studies on Immersion Education: A Collection for United States Educators,* 114–143. Sacramento: California State Department of Education.

Campbell, Russell N., Tracy C. Gray, Nancy C. Rhodes, and Marguerite Ann Snow. 1985. Foreign Language Learning in the Elementary Schools: A Comparison of Three Language Programs. *The Modern Language Journal* 69, no. 1 (spring): 44–54.

Canadian Parents for French. 2001. *The State of French Second-Language Education in Canada 2001.* Available on-line at www.cpf.ca.

Canale, Michael, and Merrill Swain. 1979. *Communicative Approaches to Second Language Teaching and Testing.* Toronto, Canada: The Minister of Education.

Carle, Eric. 1983. *The Very Hungry Caterpillar.* New York: Philomel Books.

Carpenter, John A, and Judith V. Torney. 1974. Beyond the Melting Pot. In *Childhood and Intercultural Education: Overview and Research,* edited by Patricia Maloney Markun. Washington, DC: Association for Childhood Education International.

Center for Advanced Research on Second Language Acquisition (CARLA). Immersion Teaching Strategies Observation Checklist. University of Minnesota, Minneapolis. http://carla.acad.umn.edu/immersion/checklist.html. Accessed April 14, 2003.

Center for Applied Linguistics (CAL). 1999. *Directory of Total and Partial Immersion Language Programs in U.S. Schools.* Washington, D.C.: Center for Applied Linguistics. Available on-line at www.cal.org/ericcll/immersion/

———. 2001. *Directory of Two-Way Bilingual Immersion Programs.* Washington, D.C.: Center for Applied Linguistics. Available on-line at www.cal.org/twi/directory/

———. 2002. Rhodes, Nancy. "Using Videos in the Early Language Classroom." Presentation at Leaders'

Meeting for the National K–12 Foreign Language Resource Center, September 21, Washington, D.C.

———. "Benefits of Being Bilingual." Available on-line at: www.cal.org/earlylang/benbi.htm. Accessed April 13, 2003.

———. 1987. *Total and Partial Immersion Programs.* Washington, D.C.: Center for Applied Linguistics. Handout.

———. 1999. *Total and Partial Immersion Programs.* Washington, D.C.: Center for Applied Linguistics. Available on-line at www.cal.org. Accessed November 15, 2002.

Chamot, Anna Uhl. 1994. The Teacher's Voice: Action Research in Your Classroom. *FLES News* 8, no. 1 (fall):1, 6–8.

Chamot, Anna Uhl, and J. Michael O'Malley. 1986. *A Cognitive Academic Language Learning Approach: An ESL Content-Based Curriculum.* Rosslyn, VA: National Clearinghouse for Bilingual Education.

Christian, Donna, Christopher L. Montone, Kathryn J. Lindholm, and Isolda Carranza. 1997. *Profiles in Two-Way Immersion Education.* Washington, DC: Center for Applied Linguistics and Delta Systems Co.

Cloud, Nancy, and Fred Genesee. 1998. "Multilingualism Is Basic." *Educational Leadership* 55, no. 6 (March): 62–65.

Cloud, Nancy, Fred Genesee, and Else Hamayan. 2000. *Dual Language Instruction. A Handbook for Enriched Education.* Boston: Heinle and Heinle.

Cohen, Andrew D. 1974. The Culver City Spanish Immersion Program: The First Two Years. *The Modern Language Journal* 58, no. 3: 95–103.

College Board. 1983. *Academic Preparation for College: What Students Need to Know and Be Able to Do.* New York: College Board.

Cummins, James. 1981. The Role of Primary Language Development in Promoting Educational Success for Language Minority Students. In *Schooling and Language Minority Students: A Theoretical Framework.* Los Angeles: Evaluation, Dissemination, and Assessment Center, California State University.

———. 1990. The Academic, Intellectual, and Linguistic Benefits of Bilingualism. *So You Want Your Child to Learn French.* 2nd Rev. ed. Ottawa: Canadian Parents for French. Accessed on-line September 11, 2002, at www.cpf.ca/English/Parents/benefits-bilingualism.htm

———. 2000. *Language, Power and Pedagogy: Bilingual Children Caught in the Crossfire.* Clevedon, UK: 68.

Curtain, Helena. 1994. Immersion Education and the Teaching of Subject Content: A Qualitative Research Project. Unpublished manuscript.

Curtain, Helena, and Carol Ann Dahlberg. December 2000. *Planning for Success: Common Pitfalls in the Planning of Early Foreign Language Programs.* Washington, DC: Center for Applied Linguistics, ERIC Digest. Accessible on-line: www.cal.org/ericcll/digest/0011planning.html. Accessed April 15, 2003.

Day, Elaine M., and Stanley M. Shapson. 1987. Assessment of Oral Communicative Skills in Early French Immersion Programmes. *Journal of Multilingual and Multicultural Development,* 8, no. 3: 237–260.

Day, Elaine M., and Stanley M. Shapson. 1996. *Studies in Immersion Education.* Clevedon, UK: Multilingual Matters.

Dodge, Bernie. 1997. Some Thoughts about WebQuests. San Diego State University. Web article. Available on-line at http://edweb.sdsu.edu/courses/edtec596/about_webquests.html

Doloff, Deby. 1999. *Te Quiero, Tito*—FLES Email Project. *Learning Languages* 4, no. 3 (spring): 21–23.

Donoghue, Mildred R. 1968. *Foreign Languages and the Elementary School Child.* Dubuque, IA: William C. Brown.

Dulay, Heidi, Marina Burt, and Stephen Krashen. 1982. *Language Two.* New York: Oxford University Press.

Echevarria, Jana, and Anne Graves. 1998. *Sheltered Content Instruction: Teaching English Language Learners with Diverse Abilities.* Boston: Allyn and Bacon.

Egan, Kieran. 1979. *Educational Development.* New York: Oxford University Press.

———. 1986. *Teaching as Story Telling.* Chicago: University of Chicago Press.

———. 1988. *Primary Understanding.* New York: Routledge.

———. 1992. *Imagination in Teaching and Learning: The Middle School Years.* Chicago: University of Chicago Press.

———. 1997. *The Educated Mind: How Cognitive Tools Shape Our Understanding.* Chicago: University of Chicago Press.

Elementary School (K–8) Foreign Language Teacher Education Curriculum. 1992. A Joint Project of the North Carolina Department of Public Instruction and the Center for Applied Linguistics. Raleigh, NC: North Carolina Department of Public Instruction and Washington D.C.: Center for Applied Linguistics.

Emberley, Ed. 1992. *Go away, big green monster!* Boston: Little, Brown.

Estelle, Emelda. 1985. Conversation with author, Chicago.

Fluegelman, Andrew, ed. 1976. *The New Games Book.* Garden City, NY: Doubleday.

Fortune, Tara, and Helen Jorstad. 1996. U.S. Immersion Programs: A National Survey. *Foreign Language Annals* 29, no. 2: 163–190.

Foss, Nancy. 1994. "Foreign Language and Style: A Guide for the Application of Style Sensitive Instruction in the Foreign Language Classroom." Unpublished manuscript.

Foss, Nancy. 2002. Conversation with author, November.

Gardner, Howard. 1983. *Frames of Mind: The Theory of Multiple Intelligences.* New York: Basic Books.

———. 1993. *Multiple Intelligences: The Theory in Practice.* New York: Basic Books.

———. 1999. *Intelligence Reframed: Multiple Intelligences for the 21st Century.* New York: Basic Books.

Garfinkel, Alan, and Kenneth E. Tabor. 1991. Elementary School Foreign Languages and English Reading Achievement: A New View of the Relationship. *Foreign Language Annals* 24, no. 5 (October): 375–382.

Genesee, Fred. 1989. Second Language Learning in School Settings: Lessons from Immersion. Paper presented at the Conference on Bilingualism, Multiculturalism and Second Language Learning in Honor of Wallace Lambert, May, Esterel, Quebec, Canada.

———. 2000. Brain Research: Implications for Second Language Learning. *ERIC Digest.* December. Available on-line at www.cal.org/ericcll:digest/0012brain.html

———. 1984. "Historical and Theoretical Foundations of Immersion Education." In *Studies on Immersion Education: A Collection for United States Educators.* Sacramento: California State Department of Education.

———. 1987. *Learning through Two Languages: Studies of Immersion and Bilingual Education.* Cambridge, MA: Newbury House.

Georgia Department of Education. 1997. *Georgia Model Programs: Statements of Understanding.* One-page handout to teachers and administrators throughout Georgia.

Gilzow, Douglas F., and Lucinda E. Branaman. 2000. *Lessons Learned: Model Early Foreign Language Programs.* McHenry, IL: Center for Applied Linguistics and Delta Systems Co.

Gilzow, Douglas F., and Nancy C. Rhodes. 2000. *Establishing High-Quality Foreign Language Programs in Elementary Schools.* Northeast and Islands Regional Educational Laboratory at Brown University: Perspectives on Policy and Practice, December.

Ginott, Haim G. 1972. *Teacher and Child: A Book for Parents and Teachers.* New York: Macmillan.

Goleman, Daniel. 1995. *Emotional Intelligence.* New York: Bantam Books.

Good, Thomas, and Jere Brophy. 1994. *Looking in Classrooms.* New York: HarperCollins.

Grady, Michael P. 1984. *Teaching and Brain Research: Guidelines for the Classroom.* New York: Longman.

Gramer, Virginia. 1999. Advocacy for Early Language Education: A School Board Presentation. *Learning Languages* 4, no. 3 (spring): 4–8.

Grittner, Frank. 1977. *Teaching Foreign Languages.* New York: Harper and Row.

Hadley, Alice Omaggio. 2001. *Teaching Language in Context.* 3rd ed. Boston: Heinle and Heinle.

Hakuta, Kenji. 1986. *Cognitive Development of Bilingual Children.* Los Angeles: University of California, Center for Language Education and Research. *ERIC Digest* EDRS ED 278 260.

Hans, Patricia Ryerson. 1999. Story Telling and Children's Literature. Paper presented at Concordia College, June 30, Moorhead, MN.

———. 2002. Conversation with author. November 13.

Harley, Birgit. 1986. *Age in Second Language Acquisition.* Clevedon, UK: Multilingual Matters.

———. 1998. The Outcomes of Early and Later Language Learning. In *Critical Issues in Early Language Learning: Building for Our Children's Future,* edited by Myriam Met, 26–31. Glenview, IL: Scott Foresman–Addison Wesley.

Haxhi, Jessica Lee. 2001. Long-Term Advocacy: Keeping the Magic of a Japanese Program Alive. Paper presented at the Northeast Conference on the Teaching of Foreign Languages, March 31 New York, NY, .

Heining-Boynton, Audrey L. 1991. The FLES Program Evaluation Inventory (FPEI). *Foreign Language Annals* 24, no. 3: 193.

Holobow, Naomi, Fred Genesee, Wallace. E. Lambert, Myriam Met, and Joseph Gasright. 1987. Effectiveness of Partial French Immersion for Children from Different Social Class and Ethnic Backgrounds. *Applied Psycholinguistics* 8, no. 2 (June): 137–51.

International Society for Technology in Education (ISTE). 2000a. *National Educational Technology Standards for Students: Connecting Curriculum and Technology.* Eugene, OR: ISTE.

———. 2000b. *National Educational Technology Standards for Teachers.* Eugene, OR: ISTE.

Jackson, Claire W., ed. 1999. *A Challenge to Change: The Language Learning Continuum.* New York: College Entrance Examination Board.

Jensen, Eric. 1998. *Teaching with the Brain in Mind.* Alexandria, VA: Association for Supervision and Curriculum Development.

———. 2000. Brain-Based Learning: A Reality Check. *Educational Leadership* 57, no. 5 (April): 76–79.

Johnson, David W., Robert T. Johnson, and Edythe Johnson Holubec. 1994. *Cooperative Learning in the Classroom.* Alexandria, VA: Association for Supervision and Curriculum Development.

Johnson, David W., and Robert T. Johnson. 1987. *Learning Together and Alone.* Englewood Cliffs, NJ: Prentice-Hall.

Jonas, Sister Ruth Adelaide. 1969. The Twinned Classroom Approach to FLES. *Modern Language Journal* 53, no. 5 (May): 342–346.

Kagan, Spencer. 2002. *Cooperative Learning: Resources for Teachers.* San Juan Capistrano, CA: Resources for Teachers.

Kennedy, Dora F. and William De Lorenzo. 1985. *Complete Guide to Exploratory Foreign Language Programs.* Lincolnwood, IL: National Textbook Company.

Knop, Constance K. 1985. *A Guide to Curriculum Planning in Foreign Languages,* edited by Frank Grittner. Madison: Wisconsin Department of Public Instruction, 55.

Kohn, Alfie. 1994. The Risks of Rewards. ERIC Digest EDO PS 94 14. ERIC Clearinghouse on Elementary and Early Childhood Education, December.

Krashen, Stephen D. 1981. *Second Language Acquisition and Second Language Learning.* Oxford, UK: Pergamon Press.

Krashen, Stephen D., and Tracy Terrell. 1996. *The Natural Approach: Language Acquisition in the Classroom.* Rev. ed. Englewood Cliffs, NJ: Prentice-Hall.

Krashen, Stephen D., Robin C. Scarcella, and Michael H. Long, eds. 1982. *Child-Adult Differences in Second Language Acquisition.* Rowley, MA: Newbury House.

Kretschmer, Richard R., and Laura W. Kretschmer. 1998. "What Special Challenges Do Learners with Disabilities Bring to the Foreign Language Classroom?" In *Critical Issues in Early Second Language Learning,* edited by Myriam Met. Glenview, Illinois: Scott Foresman–Addison Wesley: 65–68.

Kuck, Pam, and Kaye Lietz. 1998. *Taming the Wild, Wild Web: WebQuests.* PowerPoint presentation. Available on-line at: www.cesa8.k12.wi.us

Lambert, Wallace E. 1984. An Overview of Issues in Immersion Education. In *Studies on Immersion Education: A Collection for United States Educators,* 8–30. Sacramento: California State Department of Education.

Lambert, Wallace E., and G. Richard Tucker. 1972. *Bilingual Education of Children: The St. Lambert Experiment.* Rowley, MA: Newbury House.

Lambert, Wallace E., and Otto Klineberg. 1967. *Children's Views of Foreign People.* New York: Appleton-Century-Crofts.

Landry, Richard G. 1973. The Enhancement of Figural Creativity through Second Language Learning at the Elementary School Level. *Foreign Language Annals* 7, no. 1 (October): 111–115.

Lange, Dale L. 1999. Planning for and Using the New National Culture Standards. In *Foreign Language Standards: Linking Research, Theories, and Practices,* edited by June K. Phillips, 57–135. The ACTFL Foreign Language Education Series. Lincolnwood, IL: National Textbook Company.

Lapkin, Sharon, Merrill Swain, and Stanley M. Shapson. 1990. French Immersion Research Agenda for the 90's. *Canadian Modern Language Review* 46: 638–674.

Lawrence, Geoff. 2002. A Touch of . . . Class! *The Canadian Modern Language Review* 58, no. 3 (March): 465–472.

"Learning Languages and the Developing Brain." *Learning Languages* 1, no. 2 (winter 1996): 17.

Linse, Caroline. 1983. *The Children's Response TPR and Beyond Toward Writing.* San Francisco, CA: Alemany Press.

Long, Michael. 1983. Native Speaker/Non-native Speaker: Conversation in the Second Language Classroom. In *On TESOL '82: Pacific Perspectives on Language Learning and Teaching,* edited by M. Clarke and J. Handscomb. Washington, DC: TESOL.

Marcos, Kathleen M. 1998. Second Language Learning: Everyone Can Benefit. *The ERIC Review: K–12 Foreign Language Education* 6, no. 1 (fall): 2–5. Available on-line at www.cal.org/ericell/ericreview.pdf

———. 1997. Why, How, and When Should My Child Learn a Foreign Language? Washington, DC: ERIC Clearinghouse on Languages and Linguistics, 2003. Available on-line at www.accesseric.org/resources/parent/languages.html

Martin, Bill Jr. 1983. *Brown Bear, Brown Bear, What Do You See?* New York: Henry Holt & Co.

Marzano, Robert J., Debra J. Pickering, and Jane E. Pollock. 2001. *Classroom Instruction that Works:*

Research-Based Strategies for Increasing Student Achievement. Alexandria, VA: Association for Supervision and Curriculum Development.

Masciantonio, Rudolph. 1977. Tangible Benefits of the Study of Latin: A Review of Research. *Foreign Language Annals* 10, no. 4 (September): 375–382.

McLaughlin, Barry. 1989. Second-Language Development in Immersion Contexts. In Lorenz, Eileen B., and Myriam Met, eds., *Second Language Acquisition.* Rockville, MD: Montgomery County Public Schools, 5–31.

Met, Myriam. 1982. Conversations with author, Cincinnati, OH.

———. 1999. Making Connections. In *Foreign Language Standards: Linking Research, Theories, and Practices,* edited by June K. Phillips, 137–164. The ACTFL Foreign Language Education Series. Lincolnwood, IL: National Textbook Company.

Met, Myriam, and Eileen Lorenz. 1991. *What It Means to Be an Immersion Teacher.* Rockville, MD: Montgomery County Public Schools.

———. 1997. Lessons from US immersion programs: Two decades of experience. In *Immersion Education: International Perspectives,* edited by R. K. Johnson and S. Merrill, 243–264. Cambridge, UK: Cambridge University Press.

———. 1988. *What It Means to Be an Immersion Teacher.* Rockville, MD: Montgomery County Public Schools.

Met, Myriam, and Eileen Lorenz, ed. 1993. *Culture Scope and Sequence Kindergarten through Grade 8.* Rockville, MD: Montgomery County Public Schools.

Met, Myriam, and Nancy Rhodes. 1990. Elementary School Foreign Language Instruction: Priorities for the 1990s. *Foreign Language Annals* 23, no. 5 (October): 433–443.

Middle School Task Force of the Wisconsin Association of Foreign Language Teachers. 1991. Foreign Languages in the Middle Level School: Guiding Principles. Unpublished manuscript handout, November 15. Madison, WI.

Milwaukee Public Schools. 1985. *Rising High with Thinking Skills.* Milwaukee, WI: Milwaukee Public Schools.

Mohan, Bernard. 1986. *Language and Content.* Reading, MA: Addison-Wesley.

Morrow, Keith. 1981. Principles of Communicative Methodology. In *Communication in the Classroom,* edited by Keith Johnson and Keith Morrow. Burnt Mill, Harlow, Essex, UK: Longman.

Nash, J. Madeleine. 1997. Fertile Minds. *Time,* February 3, 49–56.

National Advisory Board on International Education Programs. 1983. Critical Needs in International Education: Recommendations for Action. A Report to the Secretary of Education. Washington, DC: U.S. Government Printing Office.

National Board of Professional Teaching Standards (NBPTS). 2001. *Standards for World Languages Other than English.* Available on-line at: www.nbpts.org/standards/stds.cfm

———. 1989. *What Teachers Should Know and Be Able to Do.* Available on-line at www.nbpts.org/standards/stds.cfm

———. 2003a. www.nbpts.org/about/coreprops.cfm. Accessed April 14, 2003.

———. 2003b. www.nbpts.org/pdf/ecya_wloe.pdf. Accessed April 14, 2003.

National Council of State Supervisors of Foreign Languages (NCSSFL). 2002. A Rationale for Foreign Language Education. Accessed on-line September 7, at www.ncssfl.org/rationale.htm

National Commission on Excellence in Education. 1983. *A Nation at Risk: The Imperative for Educational Reform.* Washington, D.C.: U.S. Government Printing Office.

National Standards in Education Project. 1999. *Standards for Foreign Langauge Learning in the 21st Century.* Lawrence, KS: Allen Press, Inc.

Nerenz, Ann, and Constance Knop. 1982. The Effect of Group Size on Student's Opportunity to Learn in the Second Language. In *ESL and the Foreign Language Teacher,* edited by Alan Garfinkel. Skokie, IL: National Textbook Company.

News in Science. 2002. Bilingual Kids Not Slowed by Second Tongue. July 11. Accessed on-line December 30, 2002, at www.abc.net.au/science/news/stories/s720173.html

North Carolina Department of Public Instruction. 1991. *Building Bridges: A Guide to Second Languages in the Middle Grades.* Raleigh, NC: North Carolina Department of Public Instruction. ED 343 428

Office of Public Affairs, U.S. Department of Education. November 20, 2002. "Paige Outlines New International Education Priorities." Available on-line: www.ed.gov/Press/Releases/11-2002/11202002. html. Accessed December 5, 2002.

Olsen, Roger E., W. B. Olsen, and Spencer Kagan. 1992. "About Cooperative Learning." In *Cooperative Language Learning: A Teacher's Resource Book,* edited by Carolyn Kessler. Englewood Cliffs, NJ: Prentice-Hall Regents.

Pacheco, Jean L. 2001. A Successful Keypal Project Using Varied Technologies. *Learning Languages* 7, no. 1 (fall): 10–14.

Pappas, Christine C., Barbara Z. Kiefer, and Linda S. Levstik. 1990. *An Integrated Language Perspective in the Elementary School.* New York: Longman.

Penfield, Wilder, and Laram Roberts. 1959. *Speech and Brain-Mechanisms.* Princeton, NJ: Princeton University Press.

Pesola, Carol Ann. 1991. Culture in the Elementary School Foreign Language Classroom. *Foreign Language Annals* 24, no. 4 (September): 331–346.

———. 1995. Background, Design and Evaluation of a Conceptual Framework for FLES Curriculum. Ph.D. diss., University of Minnesota, Minneapolis, MN.

Peyton, Joy Kreeft. 1993. Dialogue Journals: Interactive Writing to Develop Language and Literacy. *ERIC Digest.* April. Available on-line at www.cal.org/ericcll/digest/peyton01.html

Phillips, June K. 1984. Practical Implications of Recent Research in Reading. *Foreign Language Annals* 17, no. 4: 285–296.

Piaget, Jean. 1963. *The Language and Thought of the Child.* New York: W.W. Norton and Company.

Politzer, Robert L. March 1991. Speech and handout provided at Conference on Articulation, University of Wisconsin–Milwaukee.

President's Commission on Foreign Language and International Studies. 1979. *Strength through Wisdom: A Critique of U. S. Capability.* Washington, DC: United States Government Printing Office.

Rafferty, Eileen A. 1986. *Second Language Study and Basic Skills in Louisiana,* 80–85. Baton Rouge: Louisiana Department of Education.

Ratte, E. H. 1968. Foreign Language and the Elementary School Language Arts Program. *The French Review* 42.

Redmond, Mary Lynn. 1998. ATTENTION! Are You Seeking a Position with Excellent Long-Term Benefits? Be an Advocate! *Learning Languages* 4, no. 1 (fall): 4–9.

Rhodes, Nancy C., and Lucinda E. Branaman, 1999. *Foreign Language Instruction in the United States: A National Survey of Elementary and Secondary Schools.* Washington, DC and McHenry, IL: Center for Applied Linguistics and Delta Systems.

Rhodes, Nancy, and Ingrid Pufahl. 2002. Video-Based Foreign Language Programs for Children. Presentation and handout for National K–12 Foreign Language Resource Center meeting at Center for Applied Linguistics, Washington, D.C.: September 21.

Rieken, Elizabeth, et al. 1996. Building Better Bridges: Middle School to High School Articulation in Foreign Language Programs. *Foreign Language Annals* 29, no. 4: 562–570.

Riley, Richard W. 1999. Changing the American High School to Fit Modern Times. The National Press Club, September 15. Available on-line at www.ed.gov/Speeches/09-1999/990915.html

Rivers, Wilga M. 1986. Comprehension and Production in Interactive Language Teaching. *The Modern Language Journal* 70, no. 1: 1–7.

Robb, Thomas N. 1996. E-Mail Keypals for Language Fluency. *Foreign Language Notes* (Foreign Language Educators of New Jersey) 38, no. 3 (fall): 8–10. Accessed on-line November 30, 2002 at www.kyoto-su.ac.jp/~trobb/keypals.html

Roberts, Deborah Fernald. 2002. Group Work: Practicing Language in Context. Paper presented at the ACTFL Annual Meeting, November 3, Salt Lake City, UT.

Romijn, Elizabeth, and Contee Seely. 1983. *Live Action English.* Elmsford, NY: Pergamon Press.

Rosenbusch, Marcia. 1991. Elementary School Foreign Language: The Establishment and Maintenance of Strong Programs. *Foreign Language Annals* 24, no. 4 (September): 297–314.

———. 1992a. *Colloquium on Foreign Languages in the Elementary School Curriculum. Proceedings 1991.* Munich: Goethe Institut.

———. 1992b. Is Knowledge of Cultural Diversity Enough? Global Education in the Elementary School Foreign Language Program. *Foreign Language Annals* 25, no. 2 (April): 129–136.

———. 1995. Language Learners in the Elementary School: Investing in the Future. In *Foreign Language Learning: The Journey of a Lifetime,* edited by R. Donato and R. Terry. Lincolnwood, IL: National Textbook Co.

Samples, Alisha Dawn. 2002. Conversation with author, December 12.

Sandrock, Paul. 1993. Presentation at Wisconsin FLES Fest, Milwaukee, WI, March.

———. 2002 . Conversation with author, November 4.

Saunders, Carol M. 1998. The Effect of the Study of a Foreign Language in the Elementary School on Scores on the Iowa Test of Basic Skills and an Analysis of Student-Participant Attitudes and Abilities. Ph.D. diss., University of Georgia, Atlanta, GA.

Savignon, Sandra J. 1997. *Communicative Competence. Theory and Classroom Practice: Texts and Contexts in Second Language Learning.* 2nd ed. New York: McGraw-Hill.

Schank, Roger C. 1995. *Tell Me a Story: Narrative and Intelligence.* Evanston, IL: Northwestern University Press.

Schinke-Llano, Linda. 1985. *Foreign Language in the Elementary School: State of the Art.* Washington, DC: Center for Applied Linguistics.

Schnitzler, Wolfgang. 1986. Conversation with author, New York.

Seelye, H. Ned. 1993. *Teaching Culture*. Strategies for Intercultural Communication. 3rd ed. Lincolnwood, IL: National Textbook Company.

Segal, Berty. n.d. *Teaching English through Actions*. Brea, CA: Berty Segal, Inc. Available from Berty Segal, Inc., 1749 Eucalyptus St., Brea, CA, 92621.

Short, Deborah J. 1991. *How to Integrate Language and Content Instruction: A Training Manual*. Washington, DC: Center for Applied Linguistics.

Simon, Paul. 1980. *The Tongue-Tied American: Confronting the Foreign Language Crisis*. New York: Continuum Publishing.

Singleton, David M. 1995. A Critical Look at the Critical Period Hypothesis on Second Language Acquisition Research. In *The Age Factor in Second Language Acquisition*, edited by David Singleton and Zoltan Lengyl. Clevedon, UK: Multilingual Matters.

Smith, Frank. 1988. *Joining the Literacy Club: Further Essays into Education*. Portsmouth, NH: Heineman.

———. 1994. Paper presented at the California Association of Bilingual Education (CABE), San José, CA, February 2.

———. 1997. *Reading without Nonsense*. 3rd ed. New York: Teachers College Press.

Snow, Marguerite Ann. 1987. *Immersion Teacher Handbook*. Los Angeles: UCLA, Center for Language Education and Research (CLEAR).

Snow, Marguerite Ann, Myriam Met, and Fred Genesee. 1989. A Conceptual Framework for the Integration of Language and Content in Second/Foreign Language Instruction. *TESOL Quarterly* 23, no. 2: 201–217.

Sprenger, Marilee. 1999. *Learning & Memory: The Brain in Action*. Alexandria, VA: Association for Supervision and Curriculum Development.

Standards for Foreign Language Learning in the 21st Century. 1999. Yonkers, NY: National Standards in Foreign Language Education Project.

Strength through Wisdom: A Critique of U.S. Capability. 1979. Washington, DC: U.S. Government Printing Office.

Swain, Merrill. 1979. What Does Research Say About Immersion Education? In *So You Want Your Child to Learn French*, edited by Beth Mlacak and Elaine Isabelle. Ottawa, Canada: Canadian Parents for French.

———. 1984. A Review of Immersion Education in Canada: Research and Evaluation Studies. In *Studies on Immersion: A Collection for United States Educators*, 87–112. Sacramento, CA: California State Department of Education.

———. 1985. Communicative Competence: Some roles of comprehensible input and comprehensible output in its development. In *Input in Second Language Acquisition*, edited by Susan M. Gass and Carolyn G. Madden, 235–253. Series in Second Language Research. Rowley, MA: Newbury House.

———. 1988. Manipulating and Complementing Content Teaching to Maximize Second Language Learning. *TESL Canada Journal* 6: 68–83.

Swain, Merrill, and Sharon Lapkin. 1986. Immersion French in Secondary Schools: "The Goods and the Bads." *Contact* 5, no. 3: 2–9.

Swender, Elvira, and Greg Duncan. 1998. ACTFL Performance Guidelines for K–12 Learners. *Foreign Language Annals* 31, no. 4 (winter): 479–491.

Sylwester, Robert. 1995. *A Celebration of Neurons: An Educator's Guide to the Human Brain*. Alexandria, VA: Association for Supervision and Curriculum Development.

Tammy's Technology Tips for Teachers. 2002. Web site for Educational Services and Staff Development Association of Central Kansas. Available on-line at www.essdack.org/tips/. Accessed November 2002.

Tardif, Claudette, and Sandra Weber. 1987. French Immersion Research: A Call for New Perspectives. *Canadian Modern Language Review* 44, no. 1: 67–77.

Teacher Partnership Institute. 1994. *Relevant and Essential Background for the K–6 Foreign Language Teacher*. Ames, IA: Iowa State University National K–12 Foreign Language Resource Center.

Total and Partial Immersion Programs. 1987, 1999. Washington, DC: Center for Applied Linguistics. Available on-line at www.cal.org.

Tucker, G. Richard, and Richard Donato. 1999. "Designing and Implementing an Innovative Foreign Language Program: Reflections from a School District–University Partnership." *Learning Languages* 4, no. 2 (winter 1999): 4–12.

U.S. House of Representatives. Goals 2000: Educate America Act. H.R. 1804. Available on-line at www.ed.gov/legislation/GOALS2000/TheACT/

Van Ek, Jan Ate. 1977. *The Threshold Level for Modern Language Learning in Schools*. The Council of Europe. London, UK: Longman.

Vygotsky, Lev. 1986. *Thought and Language*. Cambridge, MA: MIT Press.

Waynryb, Ruth. 1986. Story-telling and Language Learning. *Babel* 21, no. 2 (August): 17–24.

Weatherford, H. Jarold 1986. Personal Benefits of Foreign Language Study. Washington, DC: Eric Clearinghouse on Languages and Linguistics. *ERIC Digest*, EDRS 276 305.

Webb, Elizabeth. 2001. "Summary of Research on Early Foreign Language Learning." Unpublished document prepared as a handout. Atlanta: Georgia Department of Education.

Wiggins, Grant. 1992. Creating Tests Worth Taking. *Educational Leadership* 49, no. 8 (May): 26–33.

Wiggins, Grant, and Jay McTighe. 1998. *Understanding by Design.* Alexandria, VA: Association for Supervision and Curriculum Development.

Wolfe, Patricia. 2001. *Brain Matters. Translating Research into Classroom Practice.* Alexandria, VA: Association for Supervision and Curriculum Development.

Wong, Harry K., and Rosemary T. Wong. 1998. *The First Days of School: How to be an Effective Teacher.* Mountain View, CA: Harry K. Wong Publications, Inc.

Wong-Fillmore, Lily. 1983. The Language Learner as an Individual: Implications of Research on Individual Differences for the ESL Teacher. In *On TESOL '82: Pacific Perspectives on Language Learning and Teaching,* edited by M.A. Clark and J. Handscombe. Washington, DC: TESOL.

———. 1985. When Does Teacher Talk Work as Input? In *Input in Second Language Acquisition,* edited by Susan M. Gass and Carolyn G. Madden. Rowley, MA: Newbury House, 17–50.

Zeydel, Edwin H. 1961. The Teaching of German in the United States from Colonial Times to the Present. *Reports of Surveys and Studies in the Teaching of Modern Foreign Languages, 1959–1961.* New York: The Modern Language Association of America.

Index